THE STORY OF MAN

The Story of Man

A History of the Great Spiritual Traditions

HUGH JAMES

Contributing Writer
C.A. Schmidt

APOLLO UNIVERSITY

PRESS

OREGON HOUSE, CA

2019

Apollo University Press, PO Box 1037, Oregon House, CA 95962

Published in the United States by Apollo University Press
www.apollouniversity.org

Hugh James and C.A. Schmidt
The Story of Man, A History of the Great Spiritual Traditions

Book design: William Bentley

First Edition

ISBN 978-1-7335653-0-1

Printed in the United States of America

To Robert Earl Burton, who – on several different levels – made it all possible.

TABLE OF CONTENTS

    The theme of the Story – Our relation to the Sphere of Sentient Being – The two phases of Man's creation – A community is needed to sustain the link to higher levels of creation – The community of Man and the community of the Gods – The plan for the development of humanity – The context of the work of the Spiritual Traditions

    Definitions: the Universe, the Absolute, God, Creation, the World – The nature of the Absolute – Cosmos – The Universe as Macrocosm – The Microcosmos Man – Man's special gift – Society

    Distinction of the internal and external work of the Traditions – Establishing consistent terminology – The lower centers and the illusion of 'I' – The context for thinking about higher centers – The higher emotional center – The higher intellectual center – The different levels of Man – Distinction of the internal and external work of the Traditions – Two different levels of internal work – The Heart – The fatal conflict between the White Queen and the Black Queen – The Work of the Steward – The Concentration of the Steward – The link with essence – The Teaching of the Steward and the Great Work – Some definitions

AUTHOR'S ILLUSTRATIONS

ACKNOWLEDGMENTS

Thanks To:

Dr. Kenneth Dorter for the initial encouragement to write, and to the Apollo University for its unwavering support.

My wife Tamara for her patience and her support through the long years of writing.

I would like particularly to acknowledge the book's contributing writer, C.A. Schmidt, without whose guidance and collaboration over a period of more than nine years this book could not have been written.

My deepest thanks to Robert George and Robert MacIsaac for reviewing and criticizing the manuscript from its inception, encouraging me to add material where substance was wanting, while always pressing for greater conciseness and clarity. Both gave generously from time they did not have. I have also benefited greatly from James Poe's long years of experience and study in the Far East, and Luis Lombo's perceptive and empathetic understanding of the Mesoamerican civilizations. And many thanks to Susan Luccini for her professional editing of the final manuscript.

Special thanks go to Dorothy Victor, Lucas Cambridge, Robert George, Sandra Steinwehe, Robert MacIsaac, John Craig, Pauline Stuart, Uriel Giveon, Hugh Lusted, Emily Browning, and Tamara James for accepting the role of 'first readers' – living with the book for many weeks in their already busy lives, and providing detailed and insightful feedback in the form of written comments, suggestions, corrections, and reactions.

To tell the Story of Man as it deserves to be told – even with the historical legacy that has come down to us from the great Spiritual Traditions of the past – would be an impossible task. Yet, knowing our own limitations, and taking full responsibility for the inevitable flaws, inaccuracies, and misunderstandings that will occur, we still feel that this is not sufficient reason to refrain from attempting to tell the story, as that is possible for us at this time in history.

Hugh James
April 2019

THE STORY OF MAN

PREFACE

What are the Spiritual Traditions?

The Story of the Spiritual Traditions traces, from the midst of the last ice age up to the present day, the history of a small segment of humanity, which – working at different times and in different places, sometimes separately and sometimes in concert – has sought to comprehend the cosmic meaning and context of human existence. The people of whom we speak were not naïve; they knew the meaning of human existence could not be found by propitiating natural forces, by delving ever more deeply into their own subjective worlds, or by creating wish-fulfilling myths. What defines the peoples of the Spiritual Traditions is that they were, from the very beginning, connected to an objective source of revealed truth on which they could base their lives and through which they could affect the lives of others.

Here we speak of the ancient seers of our pre-history, of the great Rishis who were the source of the Vedas, of the priest-caste that ruled early Dynastic Egypt, of the Prophets – Abraham, Zoroaster, Moses, Buddha, Jesus, and Muhammad – who directly perceived higher reality and taught from that perception. We speak of the Taoist masters of Ancient China, of the lineages of Lamas who – for eight centuries – ruled the mountain kingdom of Tibet, of the great monastic traditions that developed out of Catholic and Orthodox Christianity, and of the many Sufi Orders of Islam. It is through these people that Mankind has received the truths that are encoded in the mythologies, the sacred texts, and the seminal works of art and architecture that have given richness and depth to the human experience. They have, in their different ways, provided us with a cosmic measure without which we would be immeasurably less.

At any point in our history the Spiritual Traditions have represented only a small part of the human race, yet this small part has existed at almost every point along the line of time. While the Spiritual Traditions represent only a tiny portion of humanity, they are integral to it, and at the same time they are integrally connected to one other. They are connected in the line of time, where, historically, they have profoundly influenced one another. More importantly, they are connected through a common relation to a higher level of creation and through being bound to the universal truths that inhere in that level. In studying these connections, we see the dim adumbrations of a single great plan that unites them, and we shall do our best to bring this plan into relief in the telling of our story.

For almost all of human history, Mankind has existed within a context created by the Great Spiritual Traditions. At the highest points of man's existence the inner teachings of the Traditions informed and gave life to the Great Religions and the Civilizational Orders with which they were connected. In these 'formative' moments Mankind was more aware of its place and purpose in a living universe. We shall, in the pages to follow, clearly distinguish the Spiritual Traditions from the Great Religions – with which they are often confused – while carefully relating them to each of the major Civilizations known to history. While the context created by the Traditions has now disappeared, the traces of it still remain – and we are fortunate in being able to draw on these traces to assemble the elements of our story.

But what, then, became of the Spiritual Traditions? Somewhere in the midst of the 19th century, in the heat of the first industrial revolution, the importance and centrality of the Great Religions was usurped by the combination of accelerated economic life, international power politics, the emergent sciences, and the manifold effects of a rapidly expanding mass media. While the Spiritual Traditions are distinct from the Great Religions, they too were profoundly impacted by this social convulsion. The upheavals of that age – both social and ideological – disrupted the inner work of the Traditions while relegating the myths and legends that formed the unspoken backdrop of their work to the less frequented back-chambers of the human mind.

This 'original ground' of primeval myth, which had developed out of the teachings of the Traditions, had been universal before the coming of the modern age. It took different forms amongst the different cultures of the world, but whatever form it took, it presented a vision of the universe as a living whole. The first industrial revolution radically undermined this vision and at the same time greatly accelerated the process by which the 'men of the enlightenment' proceeded to externalize, objectify, and quantify their experience of this whole.

While this process began in the West, it soon spread the world over. In a series of almost imperceptible shifts, the traditional myths and legends lost their centrality. While the images and stories connected with these myths and legends lived on, the context that had given them deeper meaning was irretrievably lost.

From this time forward Western man began to take his present aspirations – whatever these might be – as the 'end' of history. Each generation became a kind of *enfant terrible* that took itself to be the reference point for everything else, and the vision of each generation was rapidly displaced by that of the generation to follow. The 'isms' followed quickly, one upon the next, from laissez-faire liberalism to millenarian socialism, to utilitarianism, to anarchism, to communism, to fascism, to postwar social-democratism, and finally to post-modernism. Each of these 'isms' has slipped, in its turn, from being the signal of the new age to being one grey ideology in a litany of grey ideologies. It does not seem likely that Mankind will achieve its optimal state by simply keeping on in this way, until some future generation happens upon the truth.

And so, today, like so many atoms floating in a 'social soup' of divergent ideologies, we are left to our own devices. When our children ask what kind of a world they have come into, we must scrape together whatever makeshift explanation we can.

As a result we are now starved for a sense of meaning that previous generations took for granted. This explains the extraordinary popularity of J.R.R. Tolkien's legendarium *The Lord of the Rings*, Clive Staples Lewis' *Chronicles of Narnia*, and J.K. Rowling's Harry Potter stories. Each of these authors has provided a mythical setting in which the lives of their characters become meaningful. Millions of people have read and enjoyed these works, as an escape from the banality of our own age – but the point is that we are actually in the midst of such a story! And the very fact that we are collectively unaware of it is part of the story itself.

Of course to digest and interpret the immense body of information necessary to making an authoritative presentation of the history of the Spiritual Traditions is an impossible task. But while it may be impossible to 'get the story right,' it may still be possible to 'get something of the story.' While the Spiritual Traditions themselves have appeared and disappeared over a vast span of time, amongst highly diverse cultures, separated by great geographical distances, they nonetheless all shared and taught the same objective truth. As we become familiar with this truth, we begin to see the influence of the Traditions in history; we see them as a part of our history. And in this light we see that, while the history of our species contains a great deal that is intrinsically meaningless, and a great deal more that is not of particular credit to the human race, it is not "a tale told by an idiot, full of sound and fury, signifying nothing." It is a story that has a theme, and it is a story we can hope to understand. It is the challenge of this book to demonstrate – by showing the extent to which the aims of the Spiritual Traditions were actually realized in history – that this is indeed our story.

Structure of the Book

Before presenting the 'story' of the Spiritual Traditions, as that unfolds over the centuries and millennia, we must describe in greater depth the context within which the Traditions originated and developed. We must be able to answer the question of who these men and women actually were. What was their ultimate purpose, and how did they fulfill that purpose?

These are, indeed, questions that the Traditions asked of themselves – and to the best of their ability they provided answers, some provisional and others quite definite. We shall attempt to consolidate and share these answers in Book I to follow. The four Chapters of Book I will serve as the foundation for the story itself – which will begin in Book II.

In Chapter 1 we shall speak generally of the place of mankind within the Macrocosm of creation, and of the particular role of the Spiritual Traditions in relation to that. In describing this 'place' we shall describe the special context that gave the Spiritual Traditions their purpose and spiritual direction.

In Chapter 2 we present the more specific cosmology of the Spiritual Traditions. Cosmologies refer to a primary reality, which is the 'original ground' of the human experience. Many of the Traditions have described this primary reality as a hierarchy of states of consciousness existing in relation to a primordial 'First Cause,' which pervades and gives form to the whole. But just what this primordial First Cause is can never be adequately expressed in words: it beggars all description. Therefore the men and women who have had first-hand experience of it, and who have tried to communicate something about it, have emphasized different aspects to different people at different points in time. What we shall present in Chapter 2 is a 'generalized view' that draws from the recorded cosmologies of all the Great Traditions, which – despite the many differences in emphasis and detail – all point to the same thing.

In Chapter 3 we shall describe the disciplines that define the internal work of the Spiritual Traditions. It is the precision, simplicity, and depth of their spiritual work that distinguishes the Traditions from the religions, the systems of folk-ritual, the mystery cults, and the occult teachings that are so often found in their proximity. It is these same disciplines that the Traditions used to secure their own connection to a higher level. We shall also explore the composition and the internal workings of the Traditions, as those derive from the basic functions they perform.

In Chapter 4 we will examine how mature Spiritual Traditions, capable of sustaining a direct connection to a higher level, form a working relationship to the societies in which they exist. A Tradition must have a right relationship to its 'host' society in order for it to carry out its external tasks in relation to the Great Religions and the Civilizational Orders which are its medium of existence.

Having laid the foundation for understanding the nature and function of the Spiritual Traditions, we shall then tell their story, beginning from the mists of pre-history, in Book II, and continuing through Books III, IV, V, and VI to the present day. In Book VII we will present an overview and conclusion.

THE STORY OF MAN

BOOK I

The Spiritual Traditions' View of Man in History

The Story of Man is an attempt to tell the spiritual story of Mankind, as that unfolds along the line of time. Our point of departure is not metaphysics or theology, but a certain understanding of the potentials contained within human nature. Here, then, at the very beginning, we must address the most difficult task of the book: to represent this understanding of human potential, and so to recreate the context in which the Spiritual Traditions functioned. For only on this basis can we understand the role of the Spiritual Traditions in history. Book I is devoted to this problem, developing its implications at length, so that they can be properly applied to the outline of history that follows.

CHAPTER 1

Mankind's Most Precious Gift

The Theme of the Story of Man

What, then, are the potentials contained in human nature? We must begin from direct experience, not from theory, for all of the work of the Spiritual Traditions is grounded in experience.

Many men and women have had – under duress, as the result of prolonged effort, or simply as an unexpected momentary opening – an experience of BEING without limit or boundary in any direction: an experience of pure, unqualified existence. The normal feeling of 'I' dissolves, opening out into a vast space resonant with consciousness and higher life. We describe this space as sentient – because it is the only word in the English language that suggests a synthetic unity of consciousness, conscience, and will. When one's identity shifts into this unboundaried domain, one sees the objects that comprise the world we know as part of a perpetually unfolding pattern. These objects do not appear as separate from the primordial state of BEING but reveal themselves as its various signatures in the line of time. Such an experience transcends the created world and yet contains it. We are beyond our normal sense of space and time. Having entered the Sphere of Sentient Being we are 'off the wheel of life,' looking back on the world of man like a 'stranger in a strange land.'

Such an experience is not the perfection of our human faculties but the momentary acquisition of new and higher faculties. Many men and women have had such an experience, but few have been able to remember and integrate it in such a way as to give permanent direction to their lives. What we call the Sphere of Sentient Being – known by the Spiritual Traditions of history by many different names – is a doorway. It is a sphere that opens into greater spheres. Humanity, taken as a whole, has been unable to go through this doorway, and so has been unable to relate the 'expanded' experience of the Sphere of Sentient Being to its everywhere more limited and more culturally determinate experience of life.

This cosmic potential has been 'built into' us, for we could never have built it into ourselves. It is literally a gift. We do not know the circumstances under which the gift was given, or the intentions of the powers that gave it, but we can know – in the moment when the experience comes – something of its implications for our lives. Once we have entered the unboundaried domain of BEING, it becomes clear why other men and women have attempted, through history, to make this experience central to their own lives and more central to the life of Mankind itself. Such an experience represents a partial realization of Man's original potential and a partial knowledge of the measure of human history. It was a gift given by the powers that created us. It is through this lens, then, that we can view the successes and failures of the generations that have preceded us.

In taking our initial bearings we must ask – more specifically – from whom we received this gift, and to what end? No amount of intellectual speculation will answer these two questions. Rather we must look to the answers left us by those who – through the millennia of our history – have penetrated the Sphere of Sentient Being, have understood themselves in relation to it, and have then left significant traces of what they understood. We are speaking here of the adepts of the Spiritual Traditions – the men and women who have always known that Mankind's existence was grounded in this sphere.

While those who did the initial, difficult work of putting experience into words remain – for the most part – anonymous, many of their teachings, in the form that they were transmitted forward by the Spiritual Traditions, still survive. And thus these nameless adepts became known to us as the Rishis of Vedic India, the 'desert fathers' of Early Christianity, the sheikhs of the Sufi Orders of Islam, the 'Toltecs' of ancient Mesoamerica, and the Vajrayana Masters of India and Tibet, to name just a few of those whose remarkable stories we shall attempt to tell.

In trying to understand the 'answers' they left us, we must first understand something of the context in which they were given – and the most important aspect of this is to understand the function that the Traditions fulfill.

THE FUNCTION OF THE SPIRITUAL TRADITIONS

As we noted in the Preface, the Spiritual Traditions represent that part of humanity which has dedicated its life to receiving influences from the level above its own and to deepening the connection between Mankind and the Sphere of Sentient Being. When this connection is secure it is reciprocal: it is a connection both from the bottom up and from the top down. When the relationship between a higher level and a lower level is reciprocal in this way, the working condition of that relationship is that the lower level be held accountable to the higher. This is necessary because – in a 'working' connection – either the lower level conforms to the standards of the higher or there is a gradual dispersion of the energies of the higher level. This principle is illustrated by the analogy to a grade-school classroom, which – though mundane – is quite descriptive. To the extent that a grade-school teacher becomes like the children he instructs, he becomes unable to teach the children the self-discipline and mental focus needed to solve problems in the way that an adult would. The teacher must establish a right distance in relation to his pupils and retain that, or the pupils will not move from the more relaxed and disorderly state in which they feel at home. In other words the pupils must 'be like' the teacher in order to address the problems properly.

Thus – to generalize – the higher level always makes a demand on the lower level to become like it. With respect to the Traditions, in relation to the level that is immediately above their own, this demand is a benediction. Why so? Because the lower level is quite incapable of making such a demand upon itself. It is only capable of imagining its own development in the terms already familiar to it. For the lower level to become more than what it presently is requires actual, direct exposure to the higher level and the consequent ability to value what it represents. The Traditions are this point of contact for humanity; they accept the demands that the higher level makes upon them, and they, in their turn, make the same kind of exacting demands on the men and women who come to them seeking instruction.

Fulfilling the requirements of the reciprocal connection is the role of the Spiritual Traditions, and they perform this role on behalf of humanity as a whole. When this connection exists, all of humanity is – knowingly or unknowingly – affected by it. In some inexplicable way the whole of humanity is lifted and leavened. Indeed, this connection is the most precious thing that humanity possesses. It represents the only relation humanity has to something higher in the universe that asks it – objectively and impartially – to become more than what it presently is. And we all need someone or something to ask this of us.

With the reciprocal connection open, the 'answers' that the Spiritual Traditions came to with respect to Man's gift of spiritual potential and the purposes for which it was given *came directly out of the Higher Level itself.* In other words, they came directly out of the Sphere of Sentient Being. But, because the principal requirement of the reciprocal connection was that man develop his latent higher faculties, these answers were not initially received in conceptual form. Rather, they came as the direct insights of man's emergent higher faculties, as developed under conditions of the most careful supervision and control. This kind of insight is exceedingly difficult to translate into words. The labor of translation is the particular task of the men and women who are the vehicles for these insights.

The members of the Spiritual Traditions strove, then, to make bridges from their moments of deepest insight to the discursive forms of thought common amongst men. This posed significant problems, because the 'answers,' as immediately experienced, would be inevitably reduced in their translation to discursive form, and this reduction would lay them open to many different kinds of misunderstanding. The tendency of the lower level is always to reduce higher understanding to its own terms, and this is the ultimate source of the historical conflicts and misunderstandings between the Great Religions.

Nevertheless the Men of the Traditions[1] felt that, because the 'answers' gave deeper meaning and significance to human existence, they represented a value of which humanity should not be deprived. In other words the value to be gained more than compensated for the misunderstanding that would inevitably be created – and so the Traditions made the attempt. The result has been the precious legacy of the Vedas, the Upanishads, the Bhagavad Gita, the Zoroastrian Avestas, the Dhammapada, the dialogues of Plato, the Torah, the Gospels, the Koran, and the Kabbalah – amongst others. In examining these texts we see that each Spiritual Tradition has represented to us, in its own terms, a remarkably similar hierarchy of levels that reaches from the first moments of a man's self-realization to the primordial sentience that is at the heart of the Universe.

These same texts give us deeper insight into the reciprocal connection itself, for this connection – which we must understand in order to understand the Traditions – is not

---

1. With this term, we use 'Men' in the sense of humankind, which includes both men and women, and 'Tradition' in the sense of 'all Traditions.'

THE STORY OF MAN

straightforward. Man cannot simply serve the First Principle of the Universe, because direct communication between Man and the First Principle is not possible. The gap in understanding would be greater than the gap between an individual man and a one-celled animal. How, then, are the necessary requirements to be made on the lower level? And how are these requirements to be received and integrated by that level? How are they enforced or implemented? In short, how is the door to the higher level held open for man, and under what conditions? In considering these questions there is another element that must be taken into account.

All of the Spiritual Traditions acknowledge that the Sphere of Sentient Being is the abode of beings whose identity is rooted, not in organs and cells, but in consciousness itself. We shall generalize these 'other forms of being' by calling them the Gods. In right order the Gods are the interlocutors between Mankind and the Primordial Sentience of the Universe.[2]

Let us return, then, to our two questions: from whom have we received the gift of this higher potential, and to what end? The teaching of the Spiritual Traditions is that this potential was given us by the Gods – with a view to what we might achieve by realizing it, as an element of our common life though history. And this is the true beginning of our story.

Having said this much, we can state our theme more clearly: this book is the story of the relation of the Gods to Mankind through history. It is, at the same time, the story of the Great Spiritual Traditions, which were, at different times and in different places, the vehicle for this relationship. More concisely, then, it is the history of Mankind's relationship to the Gods, through the Great Spiritual Traditions.

But in saying this, we have gotten ahead of ourselves. Who are the Gods, and why the relation of the Gods to Man through history? And what about God himself?

To consider these matters in greater depth we must be more specific. What we have called the Sphere of Sentient Being could be likened to a space that is itself comprehended in other spaces of a higher order. The Universe itself could be characterized as the progressive integration of these 'higher spaces,' each upward shift in the series representing a transcendence of the preceding phase. And each phase is inhabited by beings that are – in some way – concentrations of the state of consciousness that inheres in that level. These are the beings that we have called the Gods. At the center of the Universe is an all-encompassing sentience which both contains and transcends the series: the

---

2. See the Glossary for the terms 'Sphere of Sentient Being' and 'Gods.'

inscrutable First Principle. Every stage of the series, in its own way, reflects the inner nature of the first principle; nothing exists independently of it.

St. Theresa of Avila, in her work *The Interior Castle*, represented this 'order of higher spaces' as a luminous globe in the shape of a castle. The castle itself contains seven mansions, each mansion representing a stage of the inner journey. The passage through the seven mansions – one opening into the next – culminates in a union with God that both transcends and contains the stages of consciousness that lead to it. Because the union with God occurs only in the disembodied state, it is the 'angels' who inhabit the higher mansions of the castle who act as the intercessors for Man.

To understand the involvement of the Gods with Mankind, we must consider more closely the difficulties that attend the reciprocal connection. The Spiritual Traditions are in the position of having to act as a link between different levels of consciousness in the hierarchy of creation, yet – as we noted – the gap in consciousness between even the most advanced adepts of the Spiritual Traditions and the First Principle of the Universe is too great to allow any certain or reliable communication. In a reciprocal or 'working' connection the Traditions are held accountable to the levels above their own. They are tasked with truly and objectively serving both the level above themselves and the 'greater humanity' of which they are a part. The Traditions are thus faced with 1) the difficulty of interpreting the requirements of the higher level, 2) the considerable difficulty of having to internalize and 'live' those requirements, and 3) the additional difficulty of sharing the understandings that come from the reciprocal connection with the rest of humanity – many of whom will be actively resistant.

From the beginning it was clear that the Men of the Tradition would not themselves be competent to fulfill these obligations, for it is only the Gods – who inhabit the levels above our own – who are competent to complete the connection. The Gods are competent, in a chain relation, to interpret the intentions of the First Cause to Man, and it is they who enable the interface between mankind and the cosmic center.

Having established that the Gods act as mentors and guides to the Spiritual Traditions, we may then ask what the Tradition's responsibilities with respect to the Gods are? Firstly, to accept their leadership with respect to the actions needed to make the connection between Mankind and the Sphere of Sentient Being secure. Secondly, to represent to Mankind the levels above its own, in the manner that the Gods deem suitable. This does not mean directly representing the Gods to Mankind as a 'step-down' authority from the cosmic center and creating a religion around them. In relation to humanity at large the Traditions have more frequently been asked to make a representation of the Living Universe, showing man's place in the cosmic drama and showing something of what was wanted of Man himself. The place of the Gods might or might not be represented in this picture, but when it is included it must always be presented in such a way that can be received by the people of a particular place and time. And thus the 'Gods' appear in the revealed truth of the Traditions as the angels and archangels of Judaism, Christianity, and Islam; the 'Buddha Manifestations,' *tathagatas*, and *bodhisattvas* of India, China, and Tibet; and the *amesha spentas* and *yazatas* of Zoroastrian Persia.

Our telling of the Spiritual Story of Man differs from the earlier and more partial tellings in giving the Gods their proper place.

Before going further, however, we need to re-examine the initial theme – the relation of the Gods to Mankind through history – in relation to what we have said concerning the Sphere of Sentient Being.

Our Relation to the Sphere of Sentient Being

The existence of a Sphere of Being that contains and transcends material creation implies a sentient universe: a universe both conscious and alive. Indeed, if one takes *one step* beyond the level that Mankind normally inhabits, the universe is perceived as a living unity. The person who takes this step will still be far from comprehending the Whole, but what he does see will be seen as a unity.

Many people believe that their first experience of the Sphere of Sentient Being is an experience of 'God,' but it is only the first step on a very long path that leads to God. This brings us directly to the question of who or what 'God' is. The universe does have a central or directing sentience. And any person who has penetrated the Sphere of Sentient Being knows that human sentience is only the beginning of sentient life in the universe. For this very reason it can only be the beginning of the knowledge of God. We can – even the best of us – say very little about God himself! Nevertheless, very many people have said a very great deal about God, and, as a result, the term has acquired many quite contradictory connotations. For this reason the Spiritual Traditions have often used a more abstract term, such as 'the Absolute,' to refer to the directing sentience.[3] We have selected this term for our own use, as being the closest general English

---

3. See the Glossary entry for 'Absolute.'

approximation of the many terms used. But we must consider this idea a little more closely before proceeding.

Let us begin by reflecting on the physical embodiment of the Absolute, as that is known to 21st century humanity.

The physical universe has an estimated diameter of 93 billion light years. It is comprised of somewhere between 200 billion and two trillion galaxies, each harboring between 10 million and one trillion stars. The surface temperature of a single galactic core can reach 20,000 degrees Kelvin. The currently accepted theory describing the visible universe hypothesizes an originating Big Bang about 13.7 billion years ago, where energy began its transformation into different forms of matter. Before the Big Bang there existed a primary condition which is utterly beyond the capacity of modern physics to describe. The concentrations of heat and energy in the originating moments of the universe were so great that atoms could not form. Such concentrations are entirely inconceivable to Man. Following the Big Bang, energy transformed into outwardly-expanding matter, in a correspondingly expanding context of time and space. It congealed – stage by stage – into atoms, stars, planets, and galaxies.

Let us now, in our mind's eye, remove the temporal filter which acts as a brake on human perception. What if all of this exists now: the unknown state that pre-existed creation, the Big Bang, and the expansion of matter into space – which over the millennia congealed into stars, planets, and galaxies? What if a single omnipresent sentience comprehends both creation and the uncreate – past, present, and future? If this is true, these inconceivable magnitudes can be taken as indices of the embodiment of Absolute Spirit. It is clear that Absolute Spirit utterly transcends the scale of an individual human psychology. We could not know its intentions and purposes. And here we are considering only the quantitative indices given by science, which are conceived in three dimensions of space and one dimension of time. There are more than four dimensions. Scientists may speculate concerning the fifth or sixth dimensions, but they cannot conceive these dimensions in terms of how they might be experienced, because they can only be fully experienced by faculties higher than the human intellect. And the human intellect is the only tool that science has. Thus, while individual scientists may reflect on the possibility of higher dimensions, this is quite different from actually seeing the world in terms of them. The difference – to perception and cognition – of the addition of a single dimension is absolute. Each higher dimension opens to us a world that is both unified and purposeful in a way that we cannot presently comprehend. These shifts in

THE STORY OF MAN

dimensional awareness move us quickly from the quantitative indices of science to the qualitative indices of absolute compassion, absolute will, and absolute value.

All of these considerations heighten our sense of the vast distance that exists between Man, as the most developed organic life form on the planet earth, and the Absolute, straddling Creation and the Uncreate in Eternity. These reflections on the cosmic scale also shed light on our relation to the Gods. Considering all that has been said above, it would be the most extraordinary vanity – and would show the most remarkable want of imaginative power – to believe that no other form of sentient being exists between ourselves and Absolute Spirit. But where are these other forms of sentient being? Why does the contemporary world have no awareness of them? Why do they not appear before us, like the Jedi Knights of the *Star Wars* trilogy?

While we do not have direct or open contact with any species higher than our own – in the way that science fiction would depict it – this should not surprise us. The state of being unable to perceive the next highest level appears to be shared by every level in the hierarchy below us. Each level sees the levels above it in its own terms. In other words it cannot see the higher levels as they are in and for themselves, but only in relation to itself.

The cell, the bacteria, the polyp, the ant, or the lizard know nothing of intelligence above their own. Other levels, further up the scale of organic life, may have an awareness that there is something more powerful or intelligent than themselves, but they see that power or intelligence as an extension of the powers they already possess. They do not see the next highest level as being higher or more developed: in fact they are unable to conceive of what something higher is!

There are exceptions to this rule, but they are the exceptions that prove the rule. The dog, the horse, and the monkey may begin to see a more developed being in Man. But this is true exactly to the extent that the function of emotion – something 'more than just the animal' – becomes active within them. It is, for them, a higher function. The relation of the higher animals to Man is, in this regard, exactly analogous to the relation of Man to the Gods that are above him. In other words, to the extent that we begin to possess faculties that are 'more than human' we can begin to relate to the beings who possess those faculties in more developed form. From this point of view it is not 'we' who can recognize something higher than ourselves, but something latent within us that perceives its own like in more developed beings. And this 'latent something' is buried to a depth from which it cannot easily be retrieved. Because most men and women do not acknowledge the possession of these higher faculties, they are unable to recognize anything higher than themselves – or worse, they imagine 'something higher' in terms of the qualities which they already possess and the motivations which are their own.

The Spiritual Traditions have made the claim that the Gods are responsible for monitoring the development of the human race. But in stating this they acknowledge that the aims and purposes that move the Gods – who are in a direct, working connection with the levels above their own – are utterly beyond the comprehension of Man. And this would include even the most advanced members of the Spiritual Traditions. A man whose higher faculties are developed can interface with the Gods, but he cannot understand them as they understand themselves. Thus to serve the Gods involves a profound surrender, for one is serving something one cannot fully understand. Here trust is essential; indeed it is the necessary condition of a working relation between a lower level to a higher level under any circumstances. The single measure of truth that we have in relation to the Gods is that something latent within us can perceive its own like in them and that they show themselves quite expert at nurturing this part in us.

The Spiritual Traditions that serve as the vehicle for Man's relationship to these Gods have taught that there are different levels of them and different kinds of them. Some of the Gods were created in the early phases of the universe, preceding the creation of the galaxies. Some emerged at a much later point in time, arising out of the medium of organic life as that developed on certain of the planets. Indeed, the more recent generations of the Gods were once organic beings like ourselves. Under the guidance of the earlier and more ancient Gods they were able to penetrate the Sphere of Sentient Being and to sustain themselves within it. In so doing they came into contact with the celestial hierarchy of beings which pre-existed them. With the help of the older Gods the younger Gods learned to stabilize themselves in this new medium. They were taught to function independently of their cellular bodies and they were trained in conscious service to the Absolute. And here another qualification: when embodied beings such as ourselves – still in the process of emerging from the medium of planetary life – become conscious of their connection to the Sphere of Sentient Being and begin to successfully sustain themselves in relation to it, they are both humans and fledgling Gods. We shall call the men and women who find themselves in this position conscious beings.

Almost certainly the Absolute communicates directly with those Gods who are closest to him and who can understand him best, for these are the ones best able to assist him in his projects of world creation and world maintenance. These Gods have been called the Archangels. The communications that Mankind receives from levels above its own almost always come – not from the Absolute or his Archangels – but from the Gods who are closest to us. These are the Gods who had their origin in the medium of organic life, and who once were human beings.

The Two Phases of Man's Creation

We are now in a position to look at the problem of the creation of Man. At what point did the complex system of terrestrial life forms, which developed out of a medium of heat, scoriac rock, and water, produce a being that had the potential to connect through to a conscious level of the universe, which pre-existed even the planet itself? The problem is really that of relating the origin of the human physiology (which can be traced directly back to the primates) to the origin of the link between Man and the Sphere of Sentient Being, which is absent in all other primate forms. One must understand from the very beginning that these are two different things.

It was the Gods who developed the human physiology out of the complex and hierarchical system of organic life forms. As a result of their celestial engineering *Homo sapiens sapiens* appeared as the 'crown' of that hierarchy. This was an organic being possessed of both intellect and discriminating emotion. At a certain point, then, the Gods engineered the special link which connected their creation to the unbounderied space of Being which they themselves inhabit. To make an analogy to the world of cells, we could say that the Gods' new creation was like a sex-cell, endowed with a special genetic coding, which enabled it – not simply to replicate itself – but to actually transcend itself. In Man a number of component elements were brought into a very special alignment, which would enable a cellular being, whose organs of perception had been developed within the time-space manifold, to experience what is beyond that domain.

Man was 'inseminated' with these special potentials at the time of the development of the pre-frontal cortex, which distinguishes *Homo sapiens sapiens* from the other homonid forms. The Gods selected one particular homonid form and seeded it with a divine potential, so making it Man with all of the tensions and contradictions and possibilities that this entails.

Thus it is through the Gods that we have our relation to the Sphere of Sentient Being and to the Absolute who stands behind it. It is to these Gods, rather than to the uncaring cycle of organic life, that we owe our allegiance.

This brings us to another important aspect of our story: the development of Man's highest potentials cannot be realized by the individual working in isolation.

An individual man is no more capable of activating the link that connects him to the Sphere of Sentient Being than a child is capable of teaching itself how to speak. With respect to speech, the child has the capacity but needs the context to develop that capacity – and so it is with our transition to this transcendent space. The Gods, having invested so much in their self-transcending 'organic' being, had to ensure that its potentials could actually be realized. Not only did they need to ensure that the internal 'engineering' was correct, they needed to ensure that there would be a situation within the human community where development could occur.

A Community is Needed to Sustain the Link

The help that the individual needs to penetrate the Sphere of Sentient Being may come from either the Gods themselves or from other men and women who have already penetrated that sphere and achieved competence there. However, for a man whose potentials are still only latent, to be placed in continuous contact with the Gods would be extremely challenging. It would be like taking a person who had just learned how to swim and suddenly dropping him into the trial competition for the Olympic 100-meter freestyle event. This would be a waste of time for both the swimmer and for those responsible for the event! Thus, the direct and continuous intervention of the Gods in an individual human life is rare, for most of us would be unable to endure it. Just as our connection to the Absolute is mediated through the Gods, our connection to the Gods is usually mediated through other men and women, particularly those that we have called conscious beings.

In sum, in order for us to acknowledge our allegiance to the Gods, a certain number of our species – a certain determinate proportion of it – must be able to work together with the explicit aim of developing the potentials we have been given. This is the first task of the Great Spiritual Traditions. On the scale of humanity, the Traditions are the link between our species and the Sphere of Sentient Being from which our species was created. More explicitly, the Traditions are the working link connecting humanity to the realm of the Gods. The Gods themselves understand the purposes behind our creation. The Traditions are the medium through which those purposes can be realized in the line of time. These purposes include **1**) the awakening of individual human beings, **2**) the creation of a social environment in which human beings can awaken, and **3**) the specific external tasks which the Gods may assign Mankind in the course of history.

A Spiritual Tradition is, then, the special community required to transmit the teaching which enables Man to enter the Sphere of Sentient Being and to sustain himself there. This teaching has been transmitted, in one form or another, through most of the long life of humanity. Examples of Living Traditions – in their golden hour – would include the Vedic Tradition of India from the tenth century BC to the sixth century AD, the Toltec Tradition of Mesoamerica in the first through the seventh centuries AD, the Tradition of Orthodox Monasticism in the third through the fourteenth centuries AD, the Traditions of Western or Catholic Monasticism in the sixth through the twelfth centuries, the Traditions of Sufi Orders of Islam in the eighth through the sixteenth centuries, the Vedantic Tradition of India in the ninth through the fourteenth centuries, and the Traditions of Tibetan Buddhism in the twelfth through the eighteenth centuries. These Traditions, each in a very significant way, gave life to the civilizations of which they were a part and transmitted higher influence to the individuals who comprised them. Indeed true civilization requires the influence of the Great Spiritual Traditions.

Having said all of this, we must emphasize that it is a great challenge for the Spiritual Traditions to sustain and develop their work from one generation to the next. It is very difficult to be aware of, and to be held responsible for, Mankind's so tenuous connection to a Higher Level. One is constantly reminded that everything that is most important stands in the balance. And, in terms of the life of everyday, there is little material security; one must always be ready to sacrifice whatever one has. Moreover, it is very difficult to sustain the level of internal effort necessary to enable higher consciousness within oneself. Last but not least, the very closeness to a higher level produces unrelieved tension; it is glorious but at the same time extremely demanding. Despite all of these difficulties, or perhaps because of them, the work of the Traditions is the greatest adventure that can be imagined.

Sometimes the work of a single Spiritual Tradition is consecutive over many centuries or even millennia. At other times the thread of the work is broken; it may be recovered, or the dying Tradition may find itself able to transmit the seeds of understanding to a fledgling successor. The work of the Spiritual Traditions is anything but a triumphal march; it is always a struggle, and it has always been a question mark – for it is a work that is easily corrupted. Those who are deeply involved in this work are continuously being tested in different ways by the level one above – and they are often persecuted by humanity on the level immediately below. Finally, whatever success a Tradition has, its survival remains a moment-by-moment matter, for it is the survival of a certain state of consciousness, and nothing is more easily lost than this.

Thus we have introduced the ideas of the Gods and of the Spiritual Traditions. The latter cannot be understood without reference to the former. The Spiritual Traditions, in their general influence on humanity, we take to be the central theme in the Story of Man. And if the Spiritual Traditions are indeed the link to a higher level of Creation, this is the 'real' story of the human race. To understand what the 'centrality' of the Traditions implies we must understand more of what is necessary to support the link connecting Man to the Sphere of Sentient Being.

We noted that the development of the individual requires a certain development of the community. Just as there exists a pattern or coding enabling the individual to transcend himself, so there exists an 'ideal form' for the human community which enables the optimal realization of human potential. There exists an archetypal pattern of human relations in which the greed, fear, hatred, violence, and selfishness of Man's animal nature, which has dogged humanity through its history, is in a degree neutralized – so that the higher forms of activity, related to higher functions and faculties, can emerge.

The study of history shows clearly that our animal inheritance, genetically encoded in our physiology, has not been left behind; our specifically 'human' capacities have simply been added on to it. Each of us – as individuals – carry within ourselves the psychological inheritance of the animal world. And, in the same way, the human community carries within itself the inheritance of the herd or the pack. From this point of view our 'development' is not a matter of evolving naturally from the animal to the human, but a painful, protracted, and uncertain struggle to affirm the human component of our nature over the animal component.

From the perspective of our animal nature, any form of human organization is simply an extension of our individual self-interest. This self-interest is extended into the self-interest of our kinship bloodline and its related tribal groupings. To the extent that those who hold responsible positions within the human community place their own interest first, the social order of which they are a part will be forever under the shadow of a system of client relationships – and so under the animal will to power. A social order of this kind does not transcend the individual self-interest of its members. But there is a vision of the social order that does transcend the individual. In this vision we work in concert to create a network of human relationships that will allow us to become more than what we presently are. In this vision we work not only for the present but for the future, and the first result of our labor must always be a more universal, more developed, and more conscious humanity.

Certainly one approach to the realization of human potential is simply to leave the 'human' part behind and move directly to the cosmic. This is the path of the fakir, the ascetic, or the renunciant. The risks involved are great and the casualty rate is very high. But in a larger view you can bring the cosmic into the human, and here we have the real basis for human civilization.

But, we may ask, how can there be continuity between the human and the cosmic? The Sphere of Sentient Being is so distant from the patterns and preoccupations of everyday life, how could a human community ever serve as the training ground for it? This is possible because – as we shall later see – society itself is capable of producing forms of individuality which have the qualities of the universal.

In the highest phases of social life we transcend the negative, or purely animal side of individuality; we see ourselves in and through other people. We become more transparent to ourselves, and others become more transparent to us. We might call this experience the emergence of 'true' individuality, an individuality which enables us to see ourselves as part of a living whole. In the highest social functions – in philosophy, in the arts, in education, in the more developed forms of civil administration – the individual centers of experience which comprise society are brought into deeper harmony with the whole. We are made more aware of the needs of the whole, and, at the same time, our personal prejudices and private fears are brought more into the light of day. In this more open environment deficiencies of character can be compensated for, and individual qualities reinforced, by the qualities that we see in others. Aristotle taught that simple acts of social duty gradually open us to a wide horizon, which can, over time, connect with the wide horizon emergent in others to form a single visual field – a kind of shared vanishing point – towards which we all progress. In such an environment the end of society, which is implied in its whole structure, becomes the true end and aim of each individual member. This is a movement towards universality which is, at the same time, a movement in the direction of the Sphere of Sentient Being.

We have come to one of the main chords of our theme: the ideal community is an embodiment of the relation between true individuality and collective life. This community is not a simple collectivity. It is a social order which is responsible for its individual members and whose government is accountable to them, but – at the same time – it is not held in check by that function. The ideal community can, at any time, be raised and re-formed by the highest understandings that exist within it – without having to validate those understandings before a 'collectivity' that is unable to understand them. In other words it is not limited to the understanding of its own lowest common denominator. This becomes all the more clear when we remember that, in the most developed form of human community, Mankind is serving aims given from the Gods who created it, and the ability to understand those aims is not universal – but related exactly to the degree to which an individual is able to separate himself from his animal nature.

Here we are describing an 'archetypal' community, which has never been fully realized. It cannot be realized as a radical democracy, because it must recognize a real hierarchy of ability and moral worth. It cannot be realized as a pure aristocracy, because it requires complete accountability, complete transparency, and genuinely representative forums. There are different paths to it, both aristocratic and democratic, but the archetypal signature is beyond these two. Consider that real hierarchy and complete transparency are not principles that can be defined by the letter of the law; they can only be achieved by men and women working together in a certain spirit. Perhaps, indeed, the spirit of 'true individuality' – in its pure form – is found only in the community of the Gods.

In the archives of our literature we have images of the archetypal community. One of the most vivid of these images is found in Dante's *Paradiso*.

After Dante has passed through the *Inferno* and the *Purgatorio*, Virgil brings him into view of the community of the Gods. When he first looks up to heaven, he sees a series of concentric rings, vast and luminous. Suddenly …

> The rings blazed with sparks,
> as iron glints and sparkles when it boils …
> and every spark turns in a fiery ring,
> and the sparks were so many that they ran
> to the thousands, more than man can calculate.
> I heard Hosanna sung, from choir to choir,
> to that fixed point which holds them all in place
> and will always hold them so …
> Thus swiftly they pursue their rounded paths
> in order that they may become as like
> the point as possible, and this they can
> in measure as their vision is sublime …

Dante enters a state of awe, and then the complete image of the Celestial Hierarchy unfolds before him. He sees a series of concentric rings, each connected to the others through its internal motions so that together they form a vast spiral vortex.

> The two highest rings – the Principalities
> and the Archangels – are turning …
> and in the last the Angels realize themselves in joyous dance.
> Each of the heavenly orders revere what is above them
> and draw reverence from what is below them
> so that all draw and all are drawn into God.[4]

Dante is here describing true freedom: the freedom of the members of the Angelic Orders to see and to enter into the life of the Order one above, to the extent of their capacity. But for the members of each Order there is equally a relation to the Order one below. Part of their freedom, then, is to emulate the Absolute in serving the emergent life on the level below their own and so to promote the life of the whole.

In this image Dante portrays the ideal relation between True Individuality and Collective Life. He shows us something of the way in which the part can embody the life of the whole. It is, at the same time, an image of self-realization in service. The Early Christian writer Dionysius the Areopagite describes this relationship more explicitly. Having represented the Celestial Hierarchy much as Dante did, he writes:

[HJ: The Gods exhibit] an unbounded elevation to that which is above, freedom from any earthly tendencies and freedom from any inclination to the bondage of discord. They are entirely without tyrannical impulse, and are at the same time exempt from any trace of servility: for they are untouched by inconsistency. They are true Lords, providentially fashioning themselves and those below them, as far as possible, into the likeness of true lordship. They do not turn towards vain shadows, but wholly give themselves to True Authority.

The most venerable Order of the Celestial Intelligences, which is closest to God, is consecrated by his first and highest Ray [HJ: of irradiations], and as that Order uplifts itself directly to that Ray, it is purified, illuminated, and perfected in the Light of the Godhead, as though transparent. And by this again the second [HJ: Order of the Gods] in its own degree, and by the second the third.

The highest Orders possess in fullest measure the sacred characteristics of the lower, but the lowest do not possess the pre-eminent unitive principles of those more

---

4. From the *Paradisio*, Canto 28, translated by Luigi Baccetti.

venerable than themselves, because the First Radiance is imparted to them through the First Orders, according to their capacity to receive it.

Each Order, by moulding itself to the likeness of the one above will, as far as possible, be assimilated to it, receiving its form from it, and being uplifted by it to the transcendent source of the entire Hierarchy.

Thus, throughout the Celestial Hierarchy there is a lift, level on level, which begins with the Absolute and carries through, in its nethermost reaches, to the world of Man, whose spiritual potentials are only latent. But once this impulse makes the downward transition into the more unstable medium of cellular life its effects are not uniform.

… the heat of fire imparts itself more readily to that which is more adapted to receive it, being yielding and conducive to its likeness; but upon substances of opposite nature which are resistant to it, either no effect at all or only a slight trace.[5]

To the extent the Celestial Archetype imparts itself to those "more adapted to receive it," it is internalized and given form in the life of the Great Spiritual Traditions. To the extent the Traditions are able to assimilate this influence, it can in turn be assimilated – in the manner that is possible for it – by the wider human community. In our history we have the visible traces of this, for wherever it occurs we have the greatest civilizations known to Man. While the human social order, as the inheritance of the pack or the herd, is nothing to be admired, the faint traces of the archetypal form, as we glimpse those in the fabric of history, are worthy of our reverence.

Each of the great civilizations known to history has given us, in different ways, a taste of the celestial archetype, but each – to this point – has been a partial statement, and each has eventually descended into a system of conflicting interest and compromise. The ideals which inspired a civilization in its golden hour become, over the centuries, abstract principles which are then used to mediate conflict or suppress dissent.

One sees traces of the archetype, in its different aspects, in the Greek *polis*, in the *covenant* of ancient Israel, in the *cursus honorum* of Imperial Rome, in the enlightened rule of the Yarlung Kings of Tibet, in the societal order engendered by the Islamic *sunnah*, in the 'fledgling America' of Lincoln's Gettysburg Address, and in the ideal of the International Civil Servant articulated so beautifully in the speeches of Dag

---

5. These passages are taken from an anonymous early 20th century translation of the *Celestial Hierarchy*, published by the *Shrine of Wisdom*. Selections have been grouped and slightly modified with reference to more recent translations. The five passages can be found, respectively, in Ch. VIII, para 2; Ch. X, para 1; Ch. XI, last paragraph; Ch. VIII, last paragraph; Ch. XIII, para 3.

THE STORY OF MAN

Hammarskjold. Yet despite the traces that we see, a higher level of civilization has yet to be achieved.

An approximation of the celestial archetype has been achieved – albeit on a more limited scale – within the Great Spiritual Traditions. Here the archetypal form was mirrored, not for a generation, but often for centuries consecutively. It was the task of the Spiritual Traditions to ensure that the link between Man and the Sphere of Sentient Being was perpetuated from one generation to the next. And this task has very specific requirements. It involves Men of the Traditions working on different levels, engaged in different but related tasks, whose roles interlock harmoniously. The Traditions themselves are under fewer but more demanding laws than the Civilizational Orders that are their immediate context. The leaders of the Spiritual Traditions are directly answerable to the Gods, and within the community that they define the development of human potential is understood objectively. This 'objective' understanding includes an understanding of the requirements for entering and sustaining oneself in the Sphere of Sentient Being. The Traditions are directly and essentially connected to this Sphere. To work within a Tradition is to strive to achieve a community where men treat one another as beings in the common presence of God. It is a community that adopts the standards of the level one above: where each member is permanently committed to disengaging himself from his animal nature – his aggression, his territoriality, his greed, his fear, his selfishness, his vanity, his inertia, and his sloth.

We can summarize all of this by saying that the quality of the relationship between Mankind and the Gods is directly related to the quality of the relationship between men in the human community, whether this is the 'community' of a Tradition or the 'community' of the Civilization which is its context. For when, within a Tradition, the quality of the relationship between men reaches a high-water mark, this has consequences for the Civilization that sustains it. Indeed, the work of the Spiritual Traditions is behind every true civilization.

We have spoken of the existence of different archetypes for Traditions and Civilizations. From one point of view these are variations of the relation between true individuality and collective life. Perhaps there is a single archetype, such as that depicted by Dante, and on this model various archetypal forms have been created by the Gods, like so many variations on a musical theme: some for Civilizations, some for Traditions, some which have been actualized in history, some which have not. Perhaps there is a library of archetypal forms stored up in eternity, like so many different DNA polymers, one for each of the variant forms of the cosmos of man.

As the work of the Traditions has so many different aspects, it must be approached from different points of view. From the perspective of how this work unfolds along the line of time, the archetype is realized in particular patterns of human lives. Within any given Tradition these patterns are usually revealed in the lives of the first few generations. They could be likened to the scripts for plays: the Life of the Buddha and his disciples, the Life of Jesus and the apostles, the Life of Muhammad and his Companions. There are actually different kinds of scripts which can be actualized in different degrees in different historical circumstances.

To pursue the analogy of a play: Shakespeare created an enormous potential for the theater in writing the script for *The Tempest*. It is a play that can create a very special state in both the actors and the audience. This potential has been realized in greater or lesser degree by different directors and different actors in different theater companies over the last four hundred years. In just the same way, the 'drama' of each of the great Traditions realizes, in greater or lesser degree, the potential contained in the archetypal master script stored in the cosmic library. The Traditions, where they have succeeded in invoking higher life in their participants, have been able to give something of the universality of the cosmic archetype to the Civilizations that have been connected with them.

Thus we can say that Man was created with the potential to achieve an archetypal form both as an individual and as a community. But the potentials given Man may or may not be realized in the line of time. Man can use the faculties he has been given to become a dangerously intelligent animal, or he may use these same faculties to transcend animality. We can relate our experience of life to the Gods and to the Sphere of Sentient Being, or we can use the sacred vessel we have been given for the purposes of self-gratification. Everything has been given – the responsibility lies with us, in our choice.

With respect to realizing the potential that is contained in the archetypes there are two important qualifications.

1) There will be no utopia.
This first qualification derives from teachings given by the old alchemical schools, reaching back to the teachings of the Egyptians and the Sumerians. The alchemical

teachings saw the created universe as a hierarchy, comprised of different vibrational levels. In the higher levels the density and frequency of vibrations was greater, and in the lower levels the density and frequency was less. We could say (using more contemporary terms) that the created universe was perceived as a hierarchy of vibrational 'bandwidths.' The frequencies of each bandwidth defined the experiences and the activities proper to it, from the mineral level, through the vegetable, and on up through the angelic hierarchies. The different bandwidths are not exclusive of one another. They overlap, and the processes that are proper to each one link it to the bandwidth one above and the bandwidth one below. The human bandwidth, at least in its highest range, touches the angelic, but – at the same time – it has deep roots in the animal, vegetable, and even mineral levels. This means that the organic and mineral 'sediment' attaching to the human bandwidth will never change; it is a 'given' of the cosmic place we occupy. Thus, while the individual may transcend the human bandwidth entirely, shedding the physical body and functioning independently of it, and while our social order may embrace higher functions than those it presently performs, we will never be free – as a species – from the vibrational frequencies of the animal, the vegetable, and the mineral realms. For this reason neither embodied individuals nor the human social order will ever be free from flaw. All of this is to say that a utopia was neither intended nor possible for Mankind. We shall never be without the kinds of difficulties and challenges that we have known through history.

2) It will not happen by itself.

The realization of our spiritual potentials – individual and collective – is not part of a fixed agenda for the future, and there is no certainty connected with it. Potentials exist in the present as something which may or may not be realized in the future. This view of human potential is opposed to the 'progressivist' view of Man, which emerged in the nineteenth century and which has become part of the invisible 'background tone' of our own age. In the progressivist view we are improving as we go along, simply by doing more of what we are presently doing. The present offers an endless field for experimentation where all of the good things that we do and discover will gradually sum to change the human condition. In the nineteenth century this view was linked to the achievement of material well-being, the control of disease, the prolongation of human life, and the creation of equal economic and educational opportunity for all. In the twentieth century we added to this list the ideas of the biosphere and of a better integration with the order of nature. In the 1960s the progressivist view was linked to a naïve – or psychedelic – idea of Man's spiritual potentials, and the result was what is called 'New Age' thinking. In this view 'our time is coming,' as a natural expression of the development of the universe. In the 70s and 80s this kind of thinking easily and naturally linked with the effort to deconstruct the past, so as to clear the ground for whatever the New Age might bring. This impulse to critical or 'deconstructive' thinking then combined with a kind of cynicism, which first appeared in the popular culture of the 60s. The result was a general attitude that criticism is good in itself and will always produce a good result. But criticism, unless it serves a higher purpose, can easily destroy, and the criticism that we speak of certainly did not serve a higher purpose. The progressivist impulse – in both its constructive and its deconstructive phases – is rooted in a naïve belief about what is possible on the human bandwidth. There can be no real development, individual or social, without an acknowledgement of our real limitations, and a commitment to actual internal change. We refer here to the kind of change described by Dante and Dionysius the Areopagite, in their description of the assimilation of the lower Angelic Orders to the Higher. This is a labor attended – on both sides – by purposive, directed effort of the most concentrated kind. In short, nothing of real value 'happens by itself,' and it is certain that nothing of real or substantial value will be engendered by simple criticism.

Given these caveats, the approximation of the archetype of true individuality and collective life is our birthright and our destined task.

It is clear that the view presented here is at odds with certain views that are prevalent in our own time. From the standpoint of the Traditions the true measure of Man was known from the beginning. Man was asked to transform his animal nature and realize the spiritual potentials that were given with it – and each of the Great Traditions has re-stated this task in the terms appropriate to its own place and time. We have already been given all that can be given.

When we view history in this light we see evidence of many different attempts to realize the archetypal social order. But to recognize these attempts for what they are requires a discerning eye, for our animal nature is always with us, and it is always the minority who have worked with this vision in mind. It is also true that the noblest men and the highest polities are often found side by side with the most destructive and the most debased. At whatever point Man begins to rise there is resistance, both internal and external, for – following the precepts of the old alchemical teaching – we actually need such resistance to develop. More specifically, we need external pressure to spur the internal separation of the coarser matter from the fine.

The Plan for the Development of Humanity

We have some knowledge of the special potentials that were given in the beginning, but we have only the fragments of the original plan that lay behind them. The visible dispensation of the Gods to humanity includes the major Prophets, the Great Spiritual Traditions, and the Eternal Teachings, as those have been embodied in sacred texts, myths, and symbols. But in the original plan there was more than this, and the Prophets, the Traditions, and the teachings are only the traces of that 'something more.'

The plan that we are speaking of was not a blueprint to be actualized, step by step, along the line of time. Because this plan was formulated on a higher level than our own, any view we may have of it is bound to be partial. Additionally, there is a marked element of uncertainty given in the plan itself, for only where there is real uncertainty can real potentials be developed. Thus the plan may fail, or it may be realized in greater or lesser degree.

One of the first problems in presenting our Story is that the initial chapters, and the revealed truth that was given in them, have been lost to history. This truth may have been transmitted orally for several millennia, and traces of it may even have survived into ancient times, but the fragments that remain no longer have the force of the original teaching that was behind them. Relevant symbols and myths may still be with us, but we have lost the context that once gave them meaning.

Thus, over the span of recorded history, each man has enacted his part in the 'drama of humanity' knowing little or nothing of the original script. Prophets may have seen sections of it and created a working theater around themselves. But knowledge of the larger design was lost in our pre-history. However, although we have lost the original plan, we do have the 'measure,' and this is enough to reconstruct much of the story line. Additionally we know that the Spiritual Traditions were the vehicle for any plan coming to Mankind from the Celestial Hierarchy, and we have abundant evidence of their work to study.

The Context of the Spiritual Traditions

To this point we have related the Work of the Traditions to the realization of Man's potentials through history. To create a broad backcloth for our story we need to sketch in a few other elements. To begin with, there are two links which connect the Work of the Traditions to humanity at large – Living Religion and True Civilization.

Living Religion is religion that acknowledges, and does not suppress, the work of the Tradition connected with it. When Living Religion receives conscious life from a Tradition, it is in turn able to give life to the Civilizational Order of which it is a part. Dead religion is only a system of belief, ungrounded in first-hand experience. The light of higher worlds cannot reach humanity through such a resistant medium.

True Civilization is the human community given life by the thread of a connection through to the Order of the Gods. This may come through a Tradition acting upon a Living Religion, as Benedictine Monasticism influenced Medieval Europe through the Christian Religion. Or it may come from the direct action of a Tradition, as the 'School of Athens' directly influenced the City-State of Athens in the 5th century BC.

Whenever the links between Spiritual Tradition, Living Religion, and True Civilization are in place, all of Mankind benefits from the Work of the Traditions, but this has occurred only intermittently through recorded history.

This brings us to another condition for the successful presentation of the Story of Man. Our Story must acknowledge the mass and the significance of the different chapters of history that have preceded our own. It must be able to appreciate the very considerable achievements of past Civilizations, because, for the most part, these achievements have not been cumulative. Many of them remain only as 'traces' which have not carried forward as active or formative elements of human society. The historical present enormously overrates itself in this regard. Our own civilization rates other civilizations by its own measure, but this measure is itself a simple product of politics, technology, and historical circumstance. It is without objective value.

Today there is no architecture to match that of the Ancient Egyptians, the Classical Greeks, or the Gothic Freemasons; no theater to match that of Aeschylus, Sophocles, or Shakespeare; no painting to match that of Leonardo, Titian, or Rembrandt; no music to match that of Bach, Handel, or Mozart; and – above all – no faith to match that of the disciples of the Buddha, the apostles of Jesus Christ, or the ten companions of Muhammad. These achievements were not simply the inspired works of gifted individuals; they were – at the same time – the expressions of the state of a civilization, and in some way completed that civilization.

If we understand the achievements of past civilizations, we can in no way support the view that history is a necessary progression. This is not to deny that development has taken place, and that modernity has its own achievements. But the achievements of the modern age relate principally to the conditions of material well-being, in all its different aspects. They are not achievements that relate Mankind to its true place in the living universe.

With the first industrial revolution, the rise of the free-market economy, and the emergence of the world socialist movement, human development became increasingly equated with changes in the material conditions of life. These changes were seen as the fulfillment of 'basic human rights.' While a decent standard of living for all men and women is a goal to be striven for in any age, both the liberal and the socialist thinkers of the nineteenth century began to equate change in the material conditions of life with change in the quality of life itself. These are two quite different things. Longevity, good health, and nutrition have little to do with changes in Man's essential nature or in his understanding of his higher potentials.

Additionally, if we view humanity in the twenty-first century as a global community, we see that it still has all the problems it ever had: poverty, disease, malnutrition, and war. Let us consider the century prior to the time of writing, that is, from about 1910. While medicine has undoubtedly progressed and modern antibiotics have neutralized the effects of viral epidemics, smallpox, and tuberculosis, people now live a few years longer before dying of heart disease or cancer. And the extra ten or fifteen years they gain are not the years in which a person makes an essential contribution to society. War has been more prominent than in any preceding century, at least since the tenth century AD. The First World War cost 18 million lives, principally those of the combatants. The Second World War saw the indiscriminant slaughter of over 60 million people from all walks of life. The struggle of the Nationalist and the Communist Chinese, which began in 1927 and continued until 1950, cost – at the very least – another 25 million lives. Major regional conflicts have continued through to the present, almost without interruption. And we seem, as a species, not to have learned the lessons from the two great wars. Weapons of mass destruction were devised at the end of the Second World War, and there has been a rapid proliferation of those weapons – particularly in the past few decades. At the time of writing two nuclear powers are actively threatening to make use of these weapons on their neighbors. We all know that a Third World War, if it did not bring an immediate end to the species, would cause a collapse of the global economic system on which we all depend and so, inevitably, trigger further conflicts. Even without a Third World War the global economic system is tenuous, and, at the same time, the problem of human overpopulation now eclipses anything known to history. Under these circumstances a global depression would probably cost us tens of millions of lives and might well trigger the nuclear conflict we all fear. Finally, if we consider a bottom-line measure of sheer human barbarity, the last century has seen genocide on a scale never previously known. This began, in 1915, with the Ottoman slaughter of 1.5 million Armenians. It was followed by the Stalinist slaughter of 14 million assorted 'enemies of the state,' the Nazi liquidation of 9-11 million Jews and Poles, the Khymer Rouge massacre of 1.5 million Cambodians, and the general extermination of 25-40 million Chinese during the cultural revolution. (Even the records were destroyed.) This grisly impulse continues to find expression in the more recent 'ethnic cleansings' in Bosnia, Herzegovnia, and Rwanda. While we may balk at stories of the Roman Colosseum, the television and the internet now happily provide us with the same kind of entertainment, fulfilling the same needs and generating the same violent impulses. For most of us these facts look worse on paper than we remember them to have been in the course of our own lives – but the peoples of recorded history would all have said the same, for history brings the exceptional and grotesque into relief while blurring the life of everyday. In fact the past is much less different from the present than we imagine, and for long periods – in different times and places – human life was probably on balance happier, because it contained the essential values needed to give it meaning.

When we acknowledge both the achievements of the past and the uncertainties of the present, we see that our story contains a tragic aspect. This is not necessarily a bad thing. We can understand the tragic aspect of humanity by looking at the tragic aspect in the life of an individual. In the life of any man or woman, the potentials given in the beginning are always only partly realized. At any point in the life the 'actual' will be at variance with the 'potential' that was given at the beginning. Nevertheless, if the protagonist continues to develop his potentials through each of the major trials that come to him, then his final achievement will transcend the elements that were given in the beginning. Not all of his potentials will be realized, and significant potentials for happiness and personal fulfillment may remain unfulfilled, but he will become more than what he was at the beginning. Such a life will be tragedy with transcendence. In this regard it will be similar to Sophocles' *Oedipal* cycle of tragedies. If, on the other hand, the protagonist fails in the principle trials of life, the pathos of his failure stands only as a stern reminder to the rest of us. In this case you have tragedy without transcendence, along the lines of Shakespeare's *Macbeth*.

Both the life of the individual and the life of Mankind will always have a tragic aspect, for – given our place in the alchemical hierarchy of bandwidths – the uncertainty of tragedy is necessary in order to force real development. But because the uncertainty is real, the outcome may equally be the disaster of *Macbeth* or the triumph of *Oedipus at Colonus*. All of this was given in the Absolute's initial plan to nurse consciousness out of the matter of creation.

Our challenge is to look at the 'play' of humanity from the standpoint of the historical present, not knowing whether – on the scale of the play as a whole – we are Oedipus or Macbeth. Even if our story is, in the end, as clearly transcendent as Euripides' *Iphigenia in Tauris*, the relation of potential to actual in any particular historical circumstance will be complex and difficult – and it will need a discerning eye to bring main themes into relief.

The metaphor of tragedy is particularly applicable to the life of the Great Spiritual Traditions. We recall that the potentials of the Traditions are very great; their vision – more than that of any other aspect of humanity – is transcendent. Yet such a vision can never be fully realized along the line of time, and – in such a resistant medium – there is always the imminent possibility that the project will fail entirely. This is the tragic necessity of the Traditions, for without this necessity there is not the dramatic tension required to produce actual transcendence. There is not the tension that drives the high drama of Aeschylus, Dante, or Shakespeare.

Understanding this we see that the element of tragedy will always deeply permeate the work of the Traditions. Yet the struggle with tragic uncertainty reveals shades and nuances of the greatest beauty, not detailed in the archetypal master-plan. At the end of the story the transcendent truth of the archetype merges with all of the beauty and nobility created in the long and bitter struggle with the tragic flaw – and time yields something to eternity.

In summary, in this chapter we have considerably developed the context for the Story of Man, having introduced:

1. The theme of the realization (or non-realization) of the objective potentials that were given us at the time of our creation,

2. The ideas of the Gods, the Great Spiritual Traditions, Living Religion, and True Civilization,

3. The idea of a plan for humanity, involving at least a partial actualization of the archetypes for Tradition and Civilization.

Thus we have a theater, the principal actors, and a script of all recorded history, but we do not yet have a play. What is needed to drive it all forward is the active relationship between these parts. For this we need four more things: **1**) a more complete conception of the Absolute, **2**) an understanding of the idea of Cosmos, which allows us to think of Creation as a living whole, **3**) a more direct look at the inner life of the Traditions and the essential teachings that guide that inner life, and **4**) an understanding of the external work of the Traditions.

We shall deal with **1**) and **2**) in Chapter 2, **3**) in Chapter 3, and **4**) in Chapter 4.

Finally, in Book II, we shall begin to examine the Story of Man as this unfolds along the line of time.

CHAPTER 2

Man and the Absolute

Some Definitions

Each of the Spiritual Traditions has represented the relation of Man to the first principle in the universe differently, but the substance of their teachings is the same. The reason for the different presentations is that the first principle is incomprehensible, and therefore indescribable, to beings such as ourselves. The Traditions can represent this side of it or that side of it, but not the whole of it. Nevertheless, for people attempting to evolve, it is useful to have some idea of the overall context of their evolution, and for this reason each of the Traditions has attempted to make a representation appropriate to its place and time.

We begin by noting that the first principle is an unconditioned reality that entirely transcends the world of time, space, and matter. While it is the context of our day-to-day existence, it is – at the same time – invisible, inaccessible, and utterly remote. The Spiritual Traditions have often referred to this primary reality using impersonal terms, like 'the Absolute,' because terms such as 'God,' 'Ahura Mazda,' 'Zeus,' or 'Jehovah' lend themselves to anthropomorphic associations. In other words, they can be used to support the belief in a purely external deity who is capable of responding personally to humanity's prayers and petitions. Whenever the first principle is viewed in this way, it is invariably conceived as a kind of expanded mirror-image of Man. This is the sphere of Religion, and this kind of faith is far removed from the work of the Traditions.

From the standpoint of the Traditions the Absolute is both internal and external. It is internal in the sense that our consciousness is a by-product of its first-given sentience; we would not exist but for this extraordinary parentage. In this regard it is quite unlike the external 'things' that we see around ourselves. It is external in the sense that it utterly transcends human subjectivity, both in the scale of its existence and because it is the original source of everything we know. It is possessed of an authority that we cannot even imagine, and that authority is 'external' to us.

And thus the enigma: we would be utterly incapable of 'internalizing' the Absolute, yet, at the same time, it is not 'external' to us. Having made this point, we must add that it is possible for individual men and women, who have made the appropriate preparations, to approach a direct or first-hand experience of the Absolute. Yet it is impossible to choose to have such an experience, precisely because – when the experience comes – it is the Absolute itself revealing itself to the person in question, in a form that person can bear. We see this expressed in the sacred Hindu text, *The Bhagavad Gita*, where Krishna reveals himself to Arjuna as *Brahma*. He cannot do so directly, but does so through a succession of different forms that Arjuna can perceive and assimilate.

While a Prophet or an Avatar can know something of the Absolute, what they know is always related to their particular individuality, and thus it is always a particular window on the Absolute. No man or woman can ever know the Absolute as it is in and for itself. Yet, the 'particular windows' are always the windows that the Absolute has chosen, for – as we noted – it is the Absolute that reveals itself to man. While these windows are partial they are quite real; they have been 'intended' by the Absolute itself, and have been so intended that Mankind should make use of them. For example, at one time the Absolute may have revealed himself as the 'Creator' and at another as being 'beyond Creation.' Both are true. And so the Spiritual Traditions – who have these 'windows' as part of their legacy – attempted to preserve the understandings connected with them in different ways. Certain Traditions have conveyed these understandings through abstract concepts: the Vedantic *Para Brahman*, the Buddhist *Adi-Buddha*, or the Hebrew *Ein Sof*. Other Traditions have presented them in the form of myth: the Egyptian *Ra*, the Zoroastrian *Ahura Mazda*, or the Greek *Zeus*. Sometimes a single Tradition does both. Myth is often more intuitively satisfying and can convey certain things that simple conceptual abstraction cannot. Yet myth carries with it a greater danger of subjective interpretation; it excites the all-too-human tendency to revere God as a purely external Divinity. And here we must note that the Traditions are never divided, for they know the states of consciousness behind the myths and representations. The Religions, by contrast, are often deeply divided – and so the endless disputes over Monism vs. Dualism, Atman vs. Anatman, Creation vs. Eternity, and so on.

In this chapter we shall begin by embracing these dichotomies, and then try to present the Absolute in the way that the Spiritual Traditions did: both as something 'internal' to ourselves and as something 'external' and prior to human existence; both as an abstract, unknowable reality and in the context of a formative myth.

Thus, what follows is an attempt to abstract the recorded cosmologies of the Spiritual Traditions into a single, unified model. This will assist us later, when we examine the cosmologies of the individual Traditions in greater detail. Hopefully our model will be open enough to allow us to also specify the differences between the cosmologies of the Traditions, which relate to the different contexts in which they taught.

Each Tradition represented what was most useful to the people of its own place and time, and each one was selective, with the aim of creating the optimum circumstances for the people involved with it. The presentation that follows, while attempting to represent the substance of what all Traditions taught, is also selective – and for just the same reasons.

In order to proceed we must first clarify our use of a few general terms.

The Universe   The Universe is the whole, viewed from the standpoint of man, given the limitations of human perception. It is the natural standpoint of science. It implies nothing about the content of that whole, that is, whether it is sentient or insentient.

The Absolute   The term Absolute, or "Absolute Spirit," implies a view of the universe which acknowledges that the whole is sentient: that is, a synthetic unity of consciousness, feeling, and intelligent will. This sentience is not dispersed or generalized but concentrated and centralized in graded levels, with greater sentience at the higher levels. While sentience pervades the whole, it has a 'point of convergence' that is endowed with ultimate and unquestionable authority. This is the Absolute. While a man – using the tools of the Traditions – can deepen his understanding of the Absolute, he can never know the Absolute as it is, in and for itself.

God   God is a term that has been used by the religions of history to refer to the creator and ruler of the universe. It has sometimes been used in exactly the same way that we have used the term the Absolute above. But more frequently it has been used to portray a Supreme Being whom we might know and be known by, and with whom we might have a personal relationship. This usage implies that God's subjectivity is in some way analogous to human subjectivity. God becomes, then, a kind of supreme subjectivity or 'superhuman subject.' In the most debased usage of the term, God becomes – almost literally – 'an old man in the sky.'

The Traditions never conceive of God in this way. While they may work in conjunction with a Religion that supports such a view, the Spiritual Traditions themselves use the term God to refer to either **1**) the Absolute or **2**) the latent Higher Self that exists within each one of us. The Vedantic Tradition – for example – is quite explicit in this regard:

- In speaking of the 'first cause' it speaks not of 'God' but of the trinity of *Brahmā* (creator), *Vishnu* (sustainer), and *Shiva* (destroyer). The term for this triad, taken altogether, is *Ishvara*. In other words the triad of Brahmā, Vishnu, and Shiva, viewed from the standpoint of humanity, is known as *Ishvara*. This, then, represents the 'personal face' of the trinity, and corresponds to the 'God' of the popular religion.

- But, at the same time, the Vedantic teaching refers to a level beyond the triad of Brahmā, Vishnu, and Shiva that corresponds exactly to what we have called the Absolute. This is Brahma (without the *ā*). It is the unknowable face of God that cannot be seen or even conceived of by an embodied human being.

- Finally, the Vedantic Tradition refers to the latent Higher Self of the individual – that is the 'God' within us – as the *Atman*.

Given that the Traditions never use the term God to refer to a 'supreme subjectivity,' it is in a way appropriate that many of them should use it to refer to the Higher Self within.[1] This is because the Higher Self represents the actual presence of a higher level in us and is – at the same time – the doorway to those levels of Creation that work in the direct light of the Absolute. When the Self comes, it so far transcends any external teaching – any theology or philosophy – that it is appropriate to use a term that is reserved for what is most sacred.

In the gospels of the New Testament (which are the direct work of a Spiritual Tradition), the word God is used both in its meaning as

---

1. The 'Higher Self' is a more general term that refers to the two 'Higher Centers.' See Glossary.

'Absolute' and in its meaning as 'Higher Self,' according to the context. This is done in such a way that the Religion connected with the Tradition may safely take both usages to refer to a Supreme Being.

Thus, in the terminology of the Traditions you can know 'God' from within, but you cannot know the Absolute in the same way. While the Absolute is indeed the ultimate source of all individual sentient beings, and while our presence is indeed derivative of its own, it is comprised of a fineness and intensity and concentration of energy that is utterly inaccessible to us.

Creation   Creation is a term used in relation to the Absolute; in other words it refers to what the Absolute created. In some ways it is an awkward term, because 'creation' is an act that takes place in the line of time, and the Absolute exists outside of time – at least as we can understand time. In the pages that follow we have called the physical universe 'Creation' because the Absolute is responsible for determining its form and for sustaining that form through time. We will examine the 'determining and sustaining' aspect more closely in the next section, "The Absolute." Within the parameters established there, 'Creation' proves a meaningful term for the telling of our story. But from a different point of view we could just as easily say that Creation is the 'manifest dimension' of the Absolute – the aspect that manifests itself to us, the face of the Absolute we can 'see.'

While the Absolute itself is unknowable, Creation is a structured whole which can be known – although only a very small part of it can be known through the conceptualizations of science or the doctrines of philosophy. Creation, we will recall, includes the several realms of the Gods. From the standpoint of the Gods our knowledge of Creation, in each one of its many levels, will always be woefully inadequate.

The World   The World refers to everything within the scope of our experience – both the events of our personal life and everything that is external to us. This takes into account the fact that our experience may include things not accessible to the senses. Thus, 'the World' does not refer to the planet 'earth,' because we know this only through our general conception of it, not through our direct experience. What we take to be our 'World' changes profoundly with our state of consciousness, and for this reason we can say that a man literally experiences different 'Worlds.'

We shall begin with a representation of the Absolute and of Man's relation to him. Then, to clarify this relationship, we shall examine the principle of cosmos, as that has come down to us from the Spiritual Traditions of the Ancient World. This principle will be used to interpret the structure of Creation as that proceeds from the Absolute. Once these terms have been defined, it will be possible to examine the relation of Macrocosm to microcosm, which describes the link between the different levels of Creation. This will allow us, finally, to define the place and evolutionary potentials of the microcosmos Man.

All of this allows us to present the Story of Man from the standpoint of the first principle, in so far as the Great Traditions themselves have ventured to undertake such a presentation. In other words all of this allows us to take THE ABSOLUTE as the real beginning of our story, making it a 'top-down' story – which is the kind of story modernity is least able to understand. But we must take this risk, because it allows us to think about the place of Man in the Universe in the way that the Spiritual Traditions did for the millennia preceding modernity.

The Absolute

Many of the Traditions of the Ancient World – including the Egyptian, the Vedic, the Hermetic, the Platonic, and the Zoroastrian – viewed the Absolute as a three-fold process existing outside of time and space. This three-foldness was represented in a range of different philosophic and mythic terms, which we shall generalize (and anglicize) as a triad of 'Being,' 'Not-Being,' and 'Beyond-Being.'[2]

This three-fold presentation emphasizes the transcendent aspect of the Absolute, the 'Beyond-Being' dimension. Admittedly not all of the Traditions used this particular emphasis, but whenever they did not make use of it, they carefully avoided any direct association of the Absolute with a supreme subjectivity. The great advantage of the triadic presentation is that – as we shall soon see – it enables us to relate the characteristics of an utterly transcendent entity to the more palpable level of Man in history. And this, of course, fits with the task we have in hand. In the paragraphs that follow we shall isolate the transcendent aspect of the Absolute, distinguishing it from both 'Being' and

---

2. See the Glossary entries for these terms for their historical origin and usage in the Greek Tradition.

'Not-Being.' Once having done this, we will depart from the usual impersonal forms of reference, and refer to it as 'him.' The reason for doing so is that the pronoun 'it' is less than personal, while the Absolute himself is, on a scale quite transcending the personal, "our Father who art in heaven."

When we speak of the Absolute, we imply something that exists more fully than anything else. We imply a more completed Being. This 'more completed Being' is not simply something that contains everything else. Nor is it something so void of quality that it cannot be distinguished from Not-Being. It is 'more complete' precisely because it embodies a greater depth of value.

We can better understand what is implied in this statement by examining the relation between Being and Not-Being. However we think of Being, and on whatever scale we conceive it, it must have some kind of substance which distinguishes it from what it is not. If you think of God, you must think of him in relation to what is Not-God. But the Absolute is the Whole, and so, in some sense, the Being of the Absolute is both God and Not-God, Being and Not-Being, 'I' and 'Not-I.' We are not, then, speaking of a theistic monism, where God is a 'subject' – single and unified – apart from everything that is outside of him, and with an unlimited authority over it. Nor are we speaking of a dualistic view of Being and Not-Being, where there is a perpetual struggle between darkness and light which never reaches the moment of transcendence. The Absolute, as a Being without predicates of any kind, cannot be opposed to something that is outside of himself (for example, a principle of Not-Being). We do not inhabit a universe where a 'spiritual' deity is confronted with a non-spiritual 'other': a mindless void or a universe of anti-matter. There is always a context or larger 'container' for the opposition of two forces, and the being of the Absolute must somehow include that context.

In the Absolute, then, we have a Being which is of an entirely different order than any created being. We could say that Absolute Spirit is beyond both God and Not-God, Being and Not-Being, 'I' and 'Not-I.'

Alternatively we could say that the Absolute is a kind of Being capable of containing its own 'Not-Being' and so being at one with it. In other words, it actually contains its own opposite as a part of itself. But here we must ask, what – exactly – contains what? Indeed, it is impossible to conceive of this relationship in only two terms. This is why the Traditions have generally represented it in three terms, or as a triad. Absolute Spirit, then, is not a simple unity, but a dynamic unity of three forces in one. We might say a 'dramatic unity' of three forces in one: a trinity. How, then, can we conceive of this?

The first response to this question is ... "Very Imperfectly!" But at the same time, because the people of the Traditions viewed this relationship as the context of their daily lives, there must be some way in which we can represent it to ourselves. Because the task is a challenging one, let us approach it in the spirit of play. Let us play at making a myth, remembering that our game is not frivolous – for, in drawing on the teachings of the Spiritual Traditions, we are drawing on the attempts of other, much more advanced players.

In the paragraphs to follow we shall present a drama that exists outside of time as we know it, as though it occurred within time and as though it occurred to an entity who was in some way similar to ourselves. Having said this, we do accept the ancient Hermetic teaching that time exists in different modalities at all levels of the Universe, and so our temporal metaphor is not completely illegitimate.

We begin by emphasizing that the Absolute is a very special kind of Being: not just a Being capable of 'containing' its own opposite, but a Being that is capable of willing its own opposite, and so becoming at one with it. And here we call attention to that aspect of willing which implies acceptance. The Absolute's will is based on a total acceptance of – and so complete internalization of – everything that he is not. This acceptance is not something abstract.

To illustrate the point, we must set forth the myth proper. We must imagine that, prior to Creation, there existed a dimension, or a sphere of existence, in which the Absolute was less than what he presently is: in which the Absolute was a Divine Being that was somehow less than universal. He was less than universal in the sense that he experienced something that was 'over and against' himself. In the beginning this sense of an 'external other' was not specific; we might characterize it as 'meaningless void,' 'dead space,' or 'inert vacuum.' But as the Absolute became more aware of this shadowy presence (or absence), he began to understand its implications. He saw that it was in fact his own opposite – his own Not-Being – and that, as such, it threatened all that was of value to him. As the significance of this situation came ever-clearer to him, his 'external other' came into full relief as a negative infinity, a destructive entropy, or a debilitating void. The Absolute saw that, by opening his awareness to fully include his own

THE STORY OF MAN

opposite – by looking directly into what had been, up to this point, his own shadow side – he would have to accept it as it was, in itself. In so doing he would, inevitably, make it internal to himself. This consequence follows naturally from the fact that the universe has no external boundaries; if internal boundaries existing on a universal scale are eliminated, the result is a cumulative One.

The Absolute knew that, in taking this dangerous step, he was placing at risk everything that he knew and valued. He was, in fact, making the supreme sacrifice of actually willing his own negation.

We might ask what benefit such an acceptance, and such a dangerous internalization, might bring?

FIRSTLY, the Absolute had come to realize that his 'Being' was in some way undermined by the immediate proximity of his 'externalized' Not-Being. By internalizing his own Not-Being, the Absolute might hope to neutralize its debilitating effects.

SECONDLY, and more importantly, the acceptance and internalization of this Not-Being would allow the Absolute, for the first time, to truly represent the Whole: to literally 'be everything' and so be completely real.

Thus, in some unknown drama that occurred prior to Creation, the Absolute took this incredible step and made this incredible sacrifice. He understood that the negative infinity he was about to embrace might destroy all that was of value in his own being. In contemplating and in actually taking this step, he underwent the most profound suffering.

Because it is impossible for us to represent an infinitely meaningless and potentially destructive Void to ourselves, we cannot imagine what the Absolute went through. Nor can we imagine the ultimate values that he hoped to preserve, for these would be qualities that were – at least potentially – Beyond-Being: beyond the state of Being that the Absolute originally existed in.

When the Absolute made the decision to encompass the Whole by internalizing his own opposite, he trusted that he would somehow be able to sustain what was of value within that Whole. In other words he trusted that, as a result of his deed, the Whole would not collapse into meaningless indeterminacy. One of the reasons the Absolute made this decision was that – even before his dangerous act of internalization – he had begun to perceive that a range of different energies existed, both within himself and in relation to the sphere of Not-Being. The energies that comprised this range were of different qualities: there were higher or more refined energies and there were energies that were comparatively coarse or degraded. The Absolute saw that if the Whole that was to result from his act of internalization was to be comprised of an indeterminate mixture of all of these energies, the higher energies would be gradually dispersed. As a result the level of the Whole would gradually descend. He saw that, in order to preserve what was of value in the Whole, the higher energies would have to be placed over the lower energies, in such a way that they could manage and orchestrate them. The Absolute must have seen this necessity as a pressing one, in that he was about to ingest a range of energies that were lower than any that existed within his Being.

Thus the Absolute faced, not just a single act of sacrifice, but the ultimate trial of will. And in fact, as this trial unfolded, his will deepened in stages. In such an ordeal there is a moment when Acceptance and Will become one. In the moment the Absolute embraced the abyss, he saw clearly, and for the first time, everything that was at stake. His success became a matter of life or death, not only for himself, but for all of the un-realized potentials in the Universe. At the point of greatest uncertainty, when the full range of energies became visible to him, his will was suddenly galvanized into action.

With greater will and greater insight came a greater capacity to determine. Having seen the different levels of energy that now comprised his being, the Absolute exercised his now fully-awakened will to determine the relationships between these levels, such that the higher energies would always manage and organize the lower energies. This was the seed-plan of Creation. At the same time, and more importantly, the spiritual qualities that had been latent within the Absolute became fully active and self-aware. The Absolute transcended himself; he became consciously, and at the same time, both Being and Beyond-Being. What is Beyond-Being is Ultimate Value. This is what Plato, in certain passages of the *Timaeus*, refers to as the indescribable Demiurge (δημιουργός / *Demiourgos*), and what the ancient Vedantic teachers called the *Para-Brahma*.

We are finally in a position to clarify the three elements in the triad of Absolute Spirit that loom so large in the cosmologies of the ancient Spiritual Traditions.

1. The Absolute as God, or **Being**,

2. The negative infinity that was his opposite, or **Not-Being**,

3. The Absolute as he was, after having integrated and transcended his own opposite, or **Beyond-Being**.

The Absolute as 'Being' and the Absolute as 'Beyond-Being' were not separate before the Absolute's act of self-sacrifice, but with this act they did become separate. They are now separate! When, on having examined this drama, we draw back from it, we see only the result: a Universe centered by an utterly transcendent Absolute. The threat of Not-Being, and the struggle to neutralize its effects, disappears from our view. There is a single unknowable Demiurge, the Crown of all Creation. For in the moment of the Absolute's self-transcendence he became the very incarnation of Value – entire and complete. He made ultimate Value real and explicit throughout the Universe. His will embraced the Whole, without let or limit: incredibly strong, totally self-transparent, totally grounded, totally transcendent. Absolutely inconceivable.

In the terms of our myth, then, the Absolute is a Being capable of willing his own negation. As such he is capable of transcending himself completely while existing as himself completely. He is three forces in one, united in a timeless act of will. Because he contains his own opposite, he has no limit; he is a 'true' or transcendent infinity.

The 'true' infinity that is Absolute Spirit can be better understood by distinguishing it from a simple infinity of endless quantity. The infinity of endless quantity implies an infinite reproduction of 'limit.' It is always more than 'this last limit,' but in fact it is simply an endless reproduction of limit. It is therefore a 'false' infinity. It is only an idea and not an experience. True infinity is an experience which transcends limit. It is absolute, unqualified identity. On this basis we can say that the Absolute is the only real individual in the universe: he is complete, comprehensive, and wholly self-determinate. He is infinite in the highest sense; he has willed his own negation and so owns himself completely. His existence is without predicates of any kind. By contrast all finite beings are only partly individual, partly self-existent, partly real.

In distinguishing the three forces that comprise the Absolute, we have emphasized that his will and his identity are one. We are obliged to think of the Absolute's self-creation as a drama of three forces unfolding along the line of time only because of the limitations of the human intellect. But – at the same time – the Spiritual Traditions teach that the three forces are real, that the drama did occur, and that it is the defining factor of our life-situation. The risk, the sacrifice, and the suffering were all real, and they are all still essential to what the Absolute is. They simply occurred in a dimension that is beyond time as we can conceive it.

It is from the perspective of the drama of the three forces, as taught by the Spiritual Traditions, that we can best understand their view of the structure of Creation. When the Absolute, in his moment of acceptance, willed a separation of the different levels of energy that now comprised his being, he simultaneously willed a living whole, willing other beings – like himself – into existence. Not only did he give them life, but – in an act of unparalleled compassion – he created them in his own likeness. He made them each signatures of himself, with the potential to transcend themselves, just as he had transcended himself. Thus, in the same crucial moment that the Absolute affirmed ultimate Value in himself, he instilled Value in Creation. Creation is, then, the embodiment of the Absolute, and it has the Value that it does precisely because of his compassionate act.

All of the dynamic and positive qualities of Being that we see within Creation derive from the Absolute's initial act of Will. It is the element of Will that gives Created Being real Value. In the Absolute's initial exercise of the Will there was – and here we borrow from the Greeks:

Divine Love (ἀγάπη/*agape*) – the love of the higher for what is potentially 'like itself' in the lower. It is like the mother's love for her child in that it evokes unconditional self-sacrifice. It is reflected more purely, within creation, by the actions of the Gods, who – recognizing their own like in our latent spiritual potential – have worked selflessly for us through the millennia.

Sublime Beauty (τον κάλλον/*ton kallon*) – the beauty that is an expression of a fundamental nobility of nature.

Transcendent Vision (εἶδος/*eidos*) – the transparency of self-knowledge. The clarity that came originally from the Absolute's internalization of his own Not-Being and that can be realized – at least in a degree – by any being within Creation in the moment that it sees the living unity behind the multiple forms.

These three qualities resonate through all Creation.

While Creation has the intrinsic positive value that the Absolute gave it, it was – at the same time – a mechanism for neutralizing the effects of the negative infinity which had threatened him in the beginning. Even after the act of Creation, the principle of

Not-Being was to remain part of the essential triad of forces, and it continued to exercise significant effect within the fabric of Creation. This fact gives us an important key to understanding the role of Man.

Because Creation was originally an affirmation of Being, as intrinsic value, over Not-Being, as meaningless void, all created things displayed a greater or lesser degree of substantial being. But at the same time – within Creation – whatever has 'being' at one point does not have it at another. This universal coming-into-being and passing away is a result of the passage of time. The 'voiding' effect of time is evidence of the principle of Not-Being as that manifests within the different descending levels of Creation.

Because every level of Creation is, in its own way, subject to time, we could say that every level contains its own negation, in the form that is appropriate to it. On our own level this negation includes actual physical death. Negation – at whatever level – is painful to the beings who are subject to it, but at the same time it always has the effect of forcing development. By challenging us so directly and so deeply, it pressures us to ever-greater self-knowledge, and, at the same time, makes transcendence a real possibility. The fact that Not-Being is part of Creation shows that the Absolute gave Creation the highest degree of reality that he could: something in it mirrors his own realization of his highest potential. Indeed, it is the 'relative reality' of Creation that enables the beings that are part of it to participate in the drama of the Absolute and – more importantly – to actually serve him.

To understand more about Man's place in Creation we must understand something more about the form of Creation. That is, we must understand the form as a mechanism designed to neutralize the effects of Not-Being. In trying to understand this area we draw on the understandings of the Greek and the Greek/Hermetic Traditions. They described Creation as a Macrocosm.[3]

A *Macrocosm* is a hierarchy of cosmoses in which the lower cosmoses are created out of and contained within the higher cosmoses. From the standpoint of each higher cosmos the cosmos below it is a *microcosm*, and from the standpoint of each lower cosmos the cosmos that contains it is a Macrocosm. Usually, however, the term Macrocosm is used to refer to the entire interlocking system. Within this system any microcosm is both a microcosm of the cosmos one above and, at the same time, a microcosm of the Whole. Such was the genius of the Creator! In order to understand all that is implied in this we must give the terms 'cosmos,' 'Macrocosm,' and 'microcosm' a little more

---

3. We have chosen to use initial capitals for Macrocosm throughout this book, as we have Absolute, Logos, and Agathon, because they refer to universals.

substance. We shall do this in "Cosmos" and "The Universe as Macrocosm" below. Then, in the remaining sections we shall complete Book II by defining the place of the microcosmos Man, with a view to understanding his potentials. This will give the clarity that we need with respect to the theme of our story.

Cosmos

A cosmos is a system with its own internal coherence, which is capable – at least potentially – of self-development and ultimately of self-transcendence. We can find an example of this that is within the realm of our experience, the human organism, which is a true cosmos on a very small scale.

The human cosmos is distinguished from a simple a-cosmic organism by the fact that it can coordinate its functions in relation to an aim, beyond the mere will to survival or the impulse to self-gratification. We could say that a cosmos is an organism with a spiritual dimension.

In an organism which does not have a spiritual dimension, the different internal functions (physical and psychological) each work separately, in response to different external stimuli. Each function responds in its own way to the threats, the challenges, and the opportunities that everyday life presents – and then reacts upon the other functions. The sum of these involuntary reactions is what we call the organism's behavior. The different functions are coordinated only to the extent that consistency is required to support the life process.

In order to ensure that the functions of the organism work together to support its overall life process, they must be coordinated by a function of self-maintenance. In plants, animals, and human beings, this is what we call the basic instinct for survival – which is taken in all its ramifications, including the reproduction of the species.

A cosmos, by contrast, is a being whose internal functions are capable of working together in service of an aim higher than simple, instinctive self-maintenance. A cosmos has a germinal awareness of its place in the universe; it can know that there are levels above it and that it has the potential to realize itself in relation to those levels. From this awareness comes the drive to self-perfection. When an organism begins to function as a cosmos, it is organizing itself in relation to a higher level. We could say that its spirit is linked to life on a higher level; it is linked to something outside of itself that is higher than itself, and this gives a different quality to its life. Thus, in an evolving human being, there is something in the life of the whole that is greater than the sum of its parts.

　　　　　　　　　　　　　　　　　　　　　　　　THE STORY OF MAN

This brings us to a point important for our history: not only is an individual man a cosmos, the human community is also 'a body whose internal functions are capable of working together in service of a higher aim.' Like the individual human being, the human community may or may not realize this potential. However, the analogy between the individual man and the human community, as cosmoses, is not exact. The human community was brought into being to serve both the level above itself (the Gods) and the level below itself (Nature). When it realizes itself in relation to both the Gods and to Nature, it becomes 'the Cosmos of Man.' The idea of a Cosmos of Man – which we shall explore in greater depth in Chapter 4 – does not imply that every human being should become enlightened, but rather that the human community should begin to internalize the standards of the higher cosmos which it serves. As it does so, it becomes more and more able to respond to the demands that the Gods, who inhabit that cosmos, make upon it. To the degree that it does so it becomes more and more a part of a Living Whole, inclusive of the cosmos one above. In the completed cosmos of Man there is, then, open communication between the community of Men and the community of the Gods, such that the former can begin to internalize the standards and values of the latter. All men and women do not become conscious, but a series of men and women are continuously in the process of achieving consciousness. Such a community is, if you will, a means of generating consciousness. And this is exactly what the Absolute's intention was, at the very beginning of things.

Having defined Man as a microcosmos, we can now elaborate the idea of the created universe as a Macrocosm.

The Universe as Macrocosm

We shall begin by re-stating our vision of the Created Universe as a whole, in its relation to the Absolute.

The universe is a hierarchy of cosmoses, each contained within the next, where the lift from level to level is ultimately an expression of the activity of Absolute Spirit. It is a hierarchical universe of Spirit, which overreaches all Being and comprehends within itself all Value. While the hierarchy of the Created Universe is the Macrocosm, the Absolute himself is beyond Creation and includes within himself both Not-Being and Beyond-Being.

In the section on "The Absolute" we presented Creation as an expression of Absolute Spirit willing its own negation. This view of the universe is very old. It can be found, in different forms, in the Egyptian, Zoroastrian, Vedantic, and Greek/Hermetic Traditions. More recently it has been given expression in those passages of Hegel's *Phenomenology* which deal with the theory of negation and in the writings of the influential twentieth century spiritual teacher George Gurdjieff. It is an attractive view, in that it takes us past a narrow monism or a radical dualism. It allows us to understand the chaotic and violent conditions that we often see around ourselves as being in some way 'natural,' and part of a whole that is infused with real spiritual value.

But how, then, do we see the hierarchy of cosmoses as an expression of the ongoing activity of Absolute Spirit? What are the links between the different levels that cause them to work together? And what is the place of Man in all of this?

These questions were dealt with explicitly by George Gurdjieff, and it is possible to relate what he presented to what has already been presented here, because we have developed our myth in the full knowledge of what he wrote.

At the beginning of Book I we described the triad of Absolute Spirit, beginning with the opposition of Being and Not-Being. George Gurdjieff described this same initial opposition in slightly different terms. In place of Not-Being or Void he emphasized the unconditioned infinite, which he equated – in a general way – with time. He saw the passage of time as a signal of the ultimate impermanence and transience of existence. At the highest level time is a kind of remorseless entropy, which brings a gradual and irreversible diminution of Absolute Spirit.

Thus Gurdjieff emphasized the unconditioned infinite as an intrinsic threat to the Absolute in the period prior to Creation. This made it clear why the Absolute was forced to act in order to 'internalize' this negative and debilitating force. But Gurdjieff takes the story one step further. The Absolute, having completed this incredible deed, was now faced with an 'internalized' crisis of entropy. He found himself subject to the same gradual dissipation of vital energies that he had been subject to prior to the internalization of the unconditioned infinite. But precisely because this crisis was now internal, he was able to neutralize its effects by creating a kind of master-form or energy-container, which Gurdjieff called – following the Greek/Hermetic Tradition – the Macrocosm. The creation of the Macrocosm enabled two important things: 1) a second and more complex internalization of time and 2) the creation of the physical universe in the form that we know it.

Gurdjieff then stated that the step of creating the Macrocosm was only made possible by the coming-into-being of a universal law that registered the limiting effect of time in the structure of Creation. This law, which he called the Law of the Merciless

Heropass, is inscribed in all the processes of Creation. It was the pre-condition of Creation; it allowed Creation to stabilize in an environment where the de-stabilizing influence of Not-Being continued to have its effect. On each level of the Created Universe the Law of the Merciless Heropass had the effect of a deadline, either forcing development or cutting it short, but always ultimately coming into play. But the most important part of this structuring and stabilization was that it allowed the whole to generate new conscious energy, to correct the initial condition of entropy.

The physical universe is, then, a Macrocosm – under the limiting Law of the Merciless Heropass – which enables the generation of spirit out of matter and so neutralizes the effect of the unconditioned infinite. Gurdjieff was clear that the generation of spirit out of matter takes the form of the creation of new conscious energy, in the form of new conscious beings – who are ultimately capable of transcending the limitations of the physical universe. But what does it mean that the Macrocosm must generate 'new' conscious beings? What is the difference between a 'newly generated' conscious being and an 'old' conscious being?

We begin with Gurdjieff's statement that Creation was the means by which the Absolute neutralized the destructive entropy of time. Even those Beings dwelling in the cosmoses closest to the moment of Creation are affected by the passage of time, but they are nevertheless capable of regenerating themselves in relation to it. In other words they have a degree of self-identity, which enables them to neutralize the effects of time and to maintain themselves as conscious citizens of the Eternal City. They are within the sphere of the Absolute's will, and they live eternally, as he does. These Beings are the Absolute's agents and accomplices in his great struggle to maintain the necessary equilibriums of the Macrocosm. They maintain the machinery of Creation in such a way that consciousness may emerge from its workings on a more or less continuous basis. They live in the eternal moment of NOW, as he does.

As we descend through the different levels of Creation, each successive level comes increasingly under the influence of the laws of time, space, and matter. The beings that exist on the lower levels are almost completely subject to the laws which govern coming-into-being and passing away (the Law of the Merciless Heropass, as that applies on their scale of creation). Below a certain point, which Gurdjieff designated as World 12, all life forms exist through organic bodies, and the death of these organic bodies erases all memory of previous experience. We call the beings subject to these tragic laws 'mortal.'

Within the sphere of the Absolute's will there is harmony, as an expression of the fundamental cosmic balance which defines that sphere. As we proceed downwards, the experience of life becomes increasingly discontinuous, and the patterns of events that comprise an individual life become increasingly arbitrary. Nevertheless, even at the low level of creation we inhabit, we find organic beings who have been created in the form of microcosmoses. Although they are born of matter, they are capable of coming under the laws which define conscious life.

Thus, from the thin film of organic life which covers the planet earth, there has arisen the microcosmos Man, who is capable – with guidance and instruction – of generating enough conscious energy to re-generate himself as a conscious being. When a man achieves immortality, his self-transcendence brings something new to the higher orders of creation, and at the same time he defies the fundamental condition of entropy that physical creation was intended to correct. Thus, in realizing his potentials Man supports the Absolute, neutralizes the effects of the unconditioned infinite, and makes the universe a better place than it was before.

But it is not quite as simple as this. In fact it is rather difficult, because the Law of the Merciless Heropass, which is inscribed in all the processes of Creation, is a universal law: it applies not only to Creation but to the Absolute himself. It limits the extent to which the Absolute can intervene in the processes of Creation, and – particularly – it restricts him from intervening directly to help Mankind achieve consciousness.

If the ultimate purpose of Creation is to generate consciousness out of matter, and the condition of that happening is the stabilization of Not-Being within Creation under the Law of the Merciless Heropass, then the game must be played according to the established rules. As George Gurdjieff put it, "Even the Lord himself cannot beat the ace of trumps with the ordinary deuce." This explains both the perilous position of Man and the great responsibility that falls upon him. It also highlights the necessary role of the Gods in Man's development, which we briefly outlined in Chapter 1.

There is another important point to be made before proceeding further. If the microcosmos man was created from a higher level and was designed with the potential to serve the purposes of that level – as the Traditions tell us that it was – then the realization of this potential is the true measure of Man. This measure is not, like Rousseau's social contract, a measure invented by Man to apply to himself, but something given in the very moment of his creation. Thus the theory of the cosmoses shows that, despite the vast difference in scale, there is a relationship between the Absolute and the microcosmos Man.

THE STORY OF MAN

When we stand back and look at the life of the Macrocosm as something which exists within the Being of the Absolute, we see that there is a continuous transmutation and rearrangement of all its elements. The life experience of each of its different members is constantly adjusted and readjusted in relation to the life experience of the Whole. Those elements which show themselves capable of further development are included in an ever more complete whole of experience. Those elements which show themselves incapable of further development are shifted one step down. This movement of cause and effect is what the Vedic and Buddhist Traditions call the law of karma. The Macrocosm is a system in which all things are arranged and understood in their multiple relations to one another. This process of arrangement and rearrangement is REASON (διάνοια/ *dianoia*) in the Platonic Sense; it is the movement towards coherence and clarity in a living whole. It is the integration of the lower into the higher, the part into the whole, and the less conscious into the more conscious. Complete coherence is found only in the Absolute, involving, as it does, the systematization and completion of all finite minds. The Absolute himself is, then, the ultimate experience and the ultimate reality. He is not something separate from or over-and-above finite things, but the totality or full realization of all of them. In the thinking of the ancient Greeks he is *telos* (τέλος): truth or completion. From this point of view the Absolute is immanent in each finite individual, just as the life of an organism is immanent in each of its component cells.

In describing the hierarchy of cosmoses that comprises Creation we have used the terms 'higher' and 'lower.' We note that this metaphor is avoided by those Traditions which have defined their teaching as a rejection of monistic theism (God as a supreme subjectivity), and so we must qualify our use of it. To be 'higher,' in this context, means to be possessed of deeper life, and – at the same time – to function at a higher vibrational frequency. The Absolute, at the top of this hierarchy, is the deepest and the most concentrated being that exists. He functions at the highest vibrational frequency. He is 'internal' to everything else, and everything else is, consequently, external to him.

As we extend outwards from the Absolute into the Created Universe, we reach levels of being or 'worlds' that function on progressively coarser frequencies. They are possessed of correspondingly lesser degrees of will, transparency, harmony, and unity. At every stage in the series the higher is both more refined and more concentrated than the lower. For this reason it can exist independently of the forms required to sustain existence on the level immediately below it. Each higher cosmos in the series of cosmoses is simpler, deeper, and under fewer laws than the cosmos immediately below it. At the same time, being closer to the Absolute, the fewer laws that it is under make proportionately greater demands upon it.

Our own level of Creation is certainly 'less real' than the cosmoses that are above it. Every cosmos above our own is, in some way, aware of its relation to the Absolute. Ours is not. But the reality that we experience on our own level is not 'illusion' – in the sense of being an arbitrary dream without meaning or direction. It has been designed, with the greatest degree of intention, to allow the microcosmos Man to realize his highest potential and thus to open him to the levels that are above him.

The Microcosmos Man

Let us now try to clarify the place of Man in all of this. As we noted, Man is a microcsosmos: a part in whom the Whole is immanent. As part of the overall cosmic design, he is under a subtle but unrelenting pressure to realize the potentials that are immanent within him.

This pressure arises from a fundamental tension or contradiction, which is the basis of all human life.

On the one hand Man is bound within the limited sphere of his immediate needs and perceptions. He understands himself in terms of the system of reference points which constitute his life-world. Under these conditions he is able to concentrate within himself only a limited range of external impressions. Functioning from within this sphere he believes himself to be an independent self-contained individual. This belief is strongly reinforced, at every point, by the effects of what we have called the *function of self-maintenance*. The function of self-maintenance represents Man's will to survive and to assert himself in his immediate environment. Indeed, it is not even specifically human, for it has been 'given with' the physiology that we inherited from the animals. To the extent Man develops this function, he inevitably reinforces his sense of being a self-contained individual. In effect, he makes a false claim to absoluteness and then reinforces this claim in all his deeds.

On the other hand every man carries within himself the subliminal awareness of the whole: of the Sphere of Sentient Being that contains him. Beyond this, he carries a germinal awareness of his own divine potentials and a corresponding impulse to nurture and develop those potentials. He was born part of a living universe, and he retains a germinal awareness of this.

To the extent that a man remains divided between **1**) a false claim to absolute individuality and **2**) the latent sense of a connection to a higher level, he will not develop further. Indeed, in most people, the sense of a latent connection to a higher level atrophies. But for those in whom the contradiction is acute, their development is spurred by the fact that the World will never support their claim to absolute individuality. It is filled with loss, destruction, disease, death, and all the vagaries of fortune to which Mankind is subject. It is life under the Law of the Merciless Heropass, which makes us acutely aware of our many limitations. Man is never able to solve his problems in a complete or final way, and at the same time, he retains a subliminal awareness of the higher life that is within him, which makes him always expect or hope for something more.[4]

We could say that Man's strivings are driven by the contradictions of finite life. But he can only resolve these contradictions by passing beyond the limiting context of a finite 'self' that struggles to sustain itself in the line of time. He must ultimately let go of his accustomed feeling of 'I' and the sense of a past and a future that goes with it. He can only do this by allowing his identity to shift into the very moment of NOW, for the point-instant of NOW is the key to the secret entrance to the Sphere of Sentient Being so closely guarded by the Merciless Heropass.

A man can be taught to center his being in the point-instant of NOW by prolonging self-awareness, or prolonging presence. This is the science of the Spiritual Traditions. What does not fit into the nanosecond of NOW is the subjective sense of 'I' and all of the complex reaction patterns that are required to support it. To disengage from this invisible network of 'I'-centered reaction patterns requires specialized technique, and this technique is the practical teaching of the Traditions, which we shall describe in greater detail in Chapter 3.

With the basic information that we have, we are now able to see the way in which Man resembles the Absolute and the way in which he may imitate the Absolute. We have described the Absolute's Not-Being as chaos, void, and mindless entropy. Man's Not-Being is the illusion of a unified subjective self, which includes the extensive network of reaction patterns that is needed to support it. This is – under its surface appearance

---

4. This contradiction is what Bernard Bosanquet called, in a slightly different context, the 'contradiction of the finite self.' See his work *The Principle of Individuality and Value* (Gifford Lectures for 1911, Lecture VI).

of unity – chaos, void, and mindless entropy. Subject to such a crippling deformation, our will is neither simple enough nor strong enough to penetrate the Sphere of Sentient Being. It is always skewed by a false sense of 'I'. We could say that the subjective 'I'-network is the 'anti-Self,' the Void, the meaningless Not-Being, of which Mankind is, as a species, unaware.

Put differently, Man has lost the awareness of his latent Higher Self because of the particular way in which the illusion of 'I' has been superimposed on his psychology. For Man to become aware of the subjective 'I'-network as his own Not-Being, he must first accept it, just as – in the prelude to Creation – the Absolute accepted the Void. Each one of us must acknowledge our own chaotic inner landscape and commit ourselves to working within those limitations. In releasing the illusion of 'I', Man is not trading identity for meaningless void, but trading illusory identity for the beginning of real identity. By entering into a state of prolonged presence, Man realizes himself as a microcosm of Absolute Spirit.

This hidden potential for self-transcendence is a gift, and it is a gift in two senses: **1**) it is the Absolute's gift to Man, and **2**) it is Man's potential to make his own gift to the Universe at large, by accepting this work of self-transformation and bringing new consciousness into the Universe. Man thus rises to correct the fundamental condition of entropy that exists in the whole and so fulfill the role the Absolute had originally intended for him. This is Man's special gift; this and this alone gives dignity to the human race.

The Nature of Man's Gift

Presence, or the awareness of one's Real Self in the moment of now, is the link between the limited experience of the part and the unlimited experience of the whole. When identity shifts into the very moment of now, one transcends the subjective 'I' network, there is no contradiction between one's actuality and one's unrealized potentials. And the immediacy of now never changes. All of external reality changes: our body changes, our thoughts and feelings change, the seasons change, the patterns of external life change – but NOW never changes.

Unfortunately the nanosecond of NOW is not a stable state from which we can view the unfolding of our lives in the line of time. A moment of presence can come to any one of us and can disappear without leaving a trace. It is only when presence is prolonged through time that it can reach a point of concentration where it suddenly recognizes itself for what it is. Then there is *presence fully self-aware*.

When presence is sustained through time it can – in the most miraculous way – learn to exist independently of the thoughts, feelings, sensations, and motor-responses that continually cycle through our being. It can learn to sustain itself. It is only in this space of prolonged presence that the latent potentials given Man by the Absolute can be realized. Thus, what at first seems a momentary realization of 'nothingness' proves to be a state capable of almost unlimited development. It is only when the awareness of presence can be sustained through time that we see the theater of outer life unfolding before us as a moving display, from which our true identity is entirely independent. This is identity on a much deeper level than the everyday sense of self. When we are able to look back on the created world from this vantage point, we have transcended the 'merely human.' Instead of being hypnotized by the colors, forms, and images that continually appear before us in the present, we have stabilized in presence itself.

Having shown the significance of presence fully self-aware, we are in a position to understand the role of society in a new light. The social environment can work both for and against the creation of this state, and to understand the work of the Traditions we must understand how this is so.[5]

The Work of Man:
The Completion of the Cosmos of Man

What contains the human individual and what effectively constitutes his life world is society. All of the demands that are made on a man, and all of the contradictions that he faces, come to him through society. If a man's social order is not of a certain level – if he cannot find within it certain basic values and certain kinds of influence – he will lack the foundation needed to develop past a certain point. So Man and Society are intimately connected.

As we noted above, human society is linked both to the level immediately above (the Sphere of Sentient Being) and the level immediately below (the medium of Nature). Both levels make firm demands on it. Our species must labor ceaselessly to sustain its life-process in relation to Nature, and – with respect to the cosmos immediately above – there is the requirement that a certain number of men and women achieve conscious-ness and so affirm the purposes originally given from the Absolute. The demands made

---

5. See 'Prolonged Presence' and 'Presence Aware of Itself' in the Glossary.

on society – both from above and from below – are reflected in the demands that society makes on each of its individual members. Society makes these demands through its different social organs or 'institutions': the families, the schools, the social-service organizations, the churches, the various organs of government, and – in more developed societies – the Spiritual Traditions.

In order for a society to function as a Civilization the individuals who comprise it must be able to respond fully to the demands that society makes upon them. Each generation – as it comes to maturity – must be able to enter into the social functions that comprise the Civilization that it belongs to and the particular institutions that embody those functions. Its members must be able to 'find themselves' in these institutions, make them their own, and then transform them into something more than what they originally were. As each social institution is in some way an expression of the whole, its members can experience the life of that whole through it. This requires, of course, that they function as a team. In situations where there is real teamwork – the extension of the individual into the group – the individual acquires something of the flavor of the other members, with their distinctive gifts and qualities, and something of the flavor of the whole itself. The individual, less narrowly focused on himself, becomes more interesting and reflects, in ever greater degree, the qualities of the whole.

In this context what we have called 'the will to self-maintenance' can be neutralized, for an individual cannot serve the interests of society without correcting and adjusting his will so that it is in harmony with the real needs of others and the real needs of the Civilizational Order. A fully coherent will is able to take into account both the potentials that exist in other men and women and the potentials that exist in the Civilization itself. It is very different from a will that has not undergone this process.

Thus, while society can bind Man to finite life by strengthening the function of self-maintenance, it can also serve as a training ground for the development of true individuality. In fact Man could not evolve without this aspect of social life.

In the movement from the animal will to survival, to the will that has been adjusted to the needs of others, to the will tempered in service to a higher level, there is a continuous shedding of one form of individuality and the acquisition of another. The higher forms of individuality have greater objective value, but they are not free from conflict and contradiction.

Movement towards the infinite, towards an individuality that does not exclude any other form of individuality, is freedom. It is the only real freedom that Man can know. The true infinite is not limited by anything outside of itself, for its will is one with the will of the whole. We know that Absolute Spirit willed the total context of its own existence. A man is like the Absolute in those moments when he feels at one with what is outside of himself. You see your Self in the World around you. Your will is engaged in that world and engaged in the service of universal principles which you have affirmed as your own.

Man develops from a purely animal individuality through the affirmation of a particular way of life. Social Man is then educated to affirm the principles which define a Civilization. Beyond the principles that define civilizational order are the principles that define the invisible Self. These are truly universal; they are independent of time and space. Only this final affirmation completes what Aristotle called the *ergon anthropawn* (ἔργον ἀνθρόπων): *the Work of Man*. Not only is an individual incomplete without having realized his immortal self through prolonged presence, human civilization is incomplete without the linked hierarchy of labors which unite it in service to the cosmos one above. These labors include the service of nature, the service of one's fellow man, and the service of civilizational order. But these three are only summed and completed in the fourth and greater labor of realizing Mankind's spiritual potentials in service of the Gods. This, then, is the work of the Great Spiritual Traditions, and it was this labor, in centuries past, which – at least in certain times and places – made Mankind into a living cosmos.

CHAPTER 3

The Great Spiritual Traditions

The Two Different Levels of Internal Work

Now we must look, more directly and more practically, at what the inner work of the Spiritual Traditions entails. There is a preparatory work, which, once completed, enables a work of deeper inward penetration. As the former is the precondition of the latter, we could call them the **First Work** and the **Second Work**. (The successful fruition of the First Work in the Second Work allows for the 'external' work of the Traditions.) To distinguish clearly between the First and the Second Work we must introduce two new terms: consciousness and functions.

Consciousness

Consciousness is *concentrated presence*, taken independently of whatever external phenomenon (or phenomena) one happens to be present to. Consciousness has many different degrees, and the degree of consciousness is quite independent of what one is conscious of.

Functions

The functions are the many different forms of awareness, or 'modes of perception,' or 'mechanisms of stimulus and response' that connect us to the external world. These would include the five senses, the capacity for thought, the capacity for emotion, and the capacity for movement. While these are, after some fashion, 'forms of awareness,' they are not in themselves conscious. While consciousness may be added to them, it is not given in them. Additionally to being 'forms of awareness,' the functions are the means by which these forms of awareness are translated into action. Taken together, the bundle of functions is what constitutes a normal human psychology. In the Buddhist teaching of the *Abhidharma* these functions are described, exactly, as the many *dharmas* connected with embodiment.

The preparatory work of the Traditions (*the First Work*) is to distinguish between consciousness and functions. This is very difficult because the aspirant has almost no 'consciousness' to begin with. He or she may experience momentary concentrations of conscious energy, but they are almost immediately dispersed by the normal activity of the functions. To recognize and to retain consciousness is an art, and to learn this art requires the guidance of a person in whom the principle of consciousness has become permanent and stable.

As conscious energy concentrates within spiritual aspirants, they begin to observe their functions from the standpoint of consciousness. When this happens, the aspirants begin to see themselves impartially as a bundle of functions operating all at once. As observation becomes more accurate, an aspirant becomes increasingly competent at implementing the techniques utilized by the Traditions to create presence.

As the work proceeds the aspirant creates a kind of 'center' within that can recognize and respond to consciousness. Through this concentration of fine molecular energy the aspirant develops the capacity to **1**) distinguish consciousness from functions and **2**) initiate the kinds of efforts that spark consciousness internally.

The specialized or characteristic work of the Traditions (*the Second Work*) is the development of this 'point of concentration' to a pitch or a degree where it can continuously serve the emergent principle of consciousness. In the Second Work the special knowledge of the functions that comes from observing them impartially is used to separate consciousness from functions and to guide efforts to sustain consciousness independently of the functions. Thus the 'point of concentration' that develops in the First Work matures to a degree where it can directly enable consciousness. Where the First Work distinguishes consciousness from functions, the Second Work enables direct work on consciousness. Within the Spiritual Traditions the First Work has been variously referred to as the work of the *rassaphore* (Orthodox Monasticism), the work of the *salik* (Sufism), and the work of the *hinyana* path (Tibetan Buddhism). The Second Work has been referred to as the work of the 'grand schema' monk (Orthodox Monasticism), the work of the *murid* (Sufism), and the work of the *vajrayana* path (Tibetan Buddhism). To summarize, then –

The First Work, while it brings the experience of consciousness, is principally a matter of changing one's relation to the functions. From this point of view it is a study of "what I am not." While it may produce a more positive person, it is principally a 'negative' work. The Vedantic Tradition characterizes this work as a cumulative series of discriminating moments: "I am not this, I am not that, I am not the other," etc., etc. (*neti, neti*). Buddhism pursues this as the separation of one's identity from the lower *skandhas*. In Sufism it is called the study of the *nafs*, while in Christian monasticism it is the study of the virtues and the vices. Whatever form this study takes it is the necessary preliminary to disengaging an identity based on consciousness from an identity based on functions.

The Second Work is, by contrast, a 'positive work.' It is the recognition that I am the emergent consciousness; it is – ultimately – the transference of identity from functions to consciousness. This is the Vedic 'I am Atman,' the Buddhist identification with the 'Buddha-nature,' or the Hermetic identification with 'the Self.' It is the Benedictine monk who – after long years of apprenticeship – has finally learnt 'to abide in God.' A mature student of the Second Work begins to know himself as consciousness, over and against the functions.

The 'point of concentration' that develops from the First to the Second Work is what we shall call **the Steward**. We shall, from this point forward, refer to the Second Work as **the Work of the Steward**. As the First Work has many different aspects and develops differently in different circumstances, we shall retain the more generic name – understanding that it is involved with the lengthy work of developing the Steward. Despite its varied forms the First Work is – in all circumstances – the necessary preliminary. Interestingly, its result or fruition, the Work of the Steward, is much more uniform. This is partly true – as we shall later see – because *the form of the Work of the Steward is directly related to how man was originally constituted or designed*. The Work of the Steward was given Man, from the level from which the microcosmos of Man was originally created, to help individual men and women activate latent higher functions, connected with consciousness, that were designed into that microcosmos.

We have distinguished the two levels of work in principle, but to describe the actual practice of the First Work and the Work of the Steward, and to clarify the differences between the two, we will have to introduce the 'psychology' of the Spiritual Traditions. This is the breakdown of human psychology into 1) the study of the functions connected to the working of the organism (sensation, thought, emotion, movement) and **2**) the two higher functions which are only latent in us. It is these two higher functions that the Second Work is designed to activate. We noted that the higher functions are 'conscious'; that is, they function by conscious energy. When they are activated they each generate conscious energetic bodies, additional to our physical body, which connect man to the cosmoses above the human. You cannot identify yourself as 'consciousness' (the Second Work) until you have entirely changed your relation to the functions (the First Work).

The functions are often called 'centers' because they exist independently of one another, each having its own needs and desires. In effect they are centers of psychic activity.

The representation of the two Higher Centers is important to the development of the theme of our story. It will allow us to represent the 'different levels' of man, which is essential to defining the Spiritual Traditions and to distinguishing them from the Religions and from the different forms of esoteric work which are preliminary to the Second Work.

Additionally, to create the context necessary to understand the Higher Centers – both in relation to the lower centers and in relation to humanity as a whole – we must introduce the idea of different 'Worlds.'

The presentation of this body of material varies greatly by Tradition. Indeed it constitutes an entire discipline of study about which many books could be written. However, it is not necessary to have a comprehensive understanding of this discipline in order to awaken, and, indeed, the preoccupation with the study of 'functions' or 'esoteric psychology' can sideline the work to awaken the latent Higher Centers. For this reason most Traditions represent only those aspects of the discipline that are relevant to their own time and place and to the techniques of work in which they are most specialized. Most have done this in mythical form. Because our story embraces the work of so many different Traditions, we cannot rely on a simplifying analogical myth. We must attempt to provide an overview. For this purpose we shall use a schematic presented by George Gurdjieff in the early years of the twentieth century. The study of the 'centers,' the study of the different levels of man as that is based on the study of the centers, and the study of the different Worlds that are the context for both the higher and the lower centers, is presented in the terms used by Gurdjieff. Given our choice of the Gurdjieffian 'shorthand' a few words about the man himself are appropriate.

GEORGE GURDJIEFF

George Gurdjieff (1866-1949) was a Cappadocian Greek, born in the Russian Caucasus in the mid-nineteenth century. He was at the very juncture of East and West at a time when the West was achieving global hegemony and expanding into the East. By 1860 the modern world had emerged complete: the sciences were developing by leaps and bounds, mathematics was finding many new applications, and the triumphs of the first industrial revolution were generally transforming the world. But all of this was taking place in a context where there was still a reverence for traditional society and the values, culture, and religious teachings which inhered in it. In other words, a 'sense of the sacred' still existed. We must remember that it was only after the First World War that the general discrediting of *ancien regime* Europe (as rigid and artificial) and the 'traditional societies' of Asia and the Middle East (as primitive and backward) took place.

Many aspects of the traditional cultures and civilizations that are now obscure to the modern world were still quite accessible in the late nineteenth century. At that time it was still possible to contact living Spiritual Traditions. In the late nineteenth century it seemed, at least to some, that this traditional heritage could be re-possessed for the modern world – and the prospect was intoxicating. There was the feeling that, by combining the two, something greater than either might emerge. This was, indeed, part of the *zeitgeist* of that age. The list of those who pursued this goal would include such figures as Max Müller (1823-1900), Helena Petrovna Blavatsky (1831-1891), Paul Deussen (1845-1919), Vladimir Solovyev (1853-1900), Rudolf Steiner (1861-1925), and René Guénon (1886-1951). All of these people – on the basis of their research – espoused the universality and common source of the Great Religions. Yet George Gurdjieff was better equipped than any of them by geography, by ethnicity, and above all by the fact that he had been given to experience states of consciousness which made clear to him the nature and scope of the potentials that had been given to Man.

From his native Russia Gurdjieff acquired the inheritance of 'modernity': the 'hard' sciences, mathematics, engineering, the possibility of extensive travel, and the feeling that anything was possible. As a boy raised in the Eastern Orthodox Church, he was directly exposed to living religion. His childhood confessor, with whom he remained in touch well into his adult life, studied both at the monasteries of Mount Athos and with a branch of the Essene Brotherhood in Israel. As a resident of the Caucasus, Gurdjieff had easy access – by railway – to all points between Istanbul in the West and Tashkent in the East (even to the borders of Tibet). As a Turkish language speaker he could communicate easily with people throughout this vast region. Under these propitious conditions Gurdjieff developed a deep connection to several of the principal Sufi Orders. He accessed a profound formulation of the Zoroastrian teaching, and he was able to make a careful study of Egyptian myth, art, and architecture – thus forming a relationship, albeit at a distance, with the Spiritual Tradition of ancient Egypt. Finally, somewhere in Eastern Central Asia, Gurdjieff came into contact with a teaching that had synthesized the understandings of the ancient Greek, dynastic Egyptian, and ancient Mesopotamian Hermetic Traditions.

Gurdjieff not only studied material from these different sources, he met people who either represented Living Traditions or who had connections with Traditions that had only recently expired. In this context he sought tirelessly for the inner teachings of those Traditions and took upon himself (or was given) the task of bringing the 'wisdom of the East' to the emergent industrial West. To achieve this goal, however, he had to re-state the traditional teachings independently of the myths and the religious teachings that were their context. A Hermetic presentation was most suitable to this task. On the basis of the Hermetic doctrine he had discovered in Central Asia, he took similar ideas from each of the Spiritual Traditions that he knew and created universal or abstract models that applied to all.

While Gurdjieff's detailed portrayal of the functions of human psychology uses a peculiarly Western terminology, it covers exactly the same ground as the Egyptian teachings of the Tarot and – in a different way – the Buddhist teachings of the *Abhidharma*. The *Abhidharma* is a more dynamic presentation, showing the functions as they reconstitute themselves in action. Gurdjieff's study of the centers is more static and more strictly systematic, but it has the advantage of focusing more directly on the qualitative distinction between the levels of consciousness and functions. In that regard it is less subject to misinterpretation. The emphasis on different levels proved valuable for Gurdjieff (as a Western spiritual teacher) in that it acted as a corrective to the subjectivist psychologies (Freudian and Jungian) that became popular in Europe and America in the first half of the twentieth century.

The Psychology of the Spiritual Traditions

In order to create the context needed to describe the First and the Second Work, we shall now present the concepts of the four lower centers, the two higher centers, the different levels of man, and the different 'Worlds.' As we noted, it is in the First Work that an aspirant learns to distinguish between consciousness and functions. Competence in this area usually develops over a long period of time, during which the aspirant's observations of the different centers are validated repeatedly under the guidance of a Master. The aspirant must learn the system of division of centers that is particular to his Tradition and become able to objectively identify the mechanical provenance of each emotion, thought, or sensation that presents itself in the moment. Gurdjieff's detailed presentation gives us a flavor of the moment-to-moment internal work that is required to develop the part of the Steward that can view the functions objectively.

The Lower Centers and the Illusion of 'I'

The key to understanding the study of the centers – as the Spiritual Traditions understand them – is to first understand that *there is no center that regulates the other centers.* Put bluntly, the individual man or woman has different chakras or centers but no unified identity welding them together. They have the illusion of possessing such an identity, but this is a much different thing. The teaching of the Traditions emphasizes that we lack the first thing that we normally claim for ourselves, a single unified 'I.' The psychology of an individual could thus be likened to a complex mechanism driven by external impacts and the internal reaction to those impacts. Under the force of external stimulus, different thoughts, emotions, and sensations are continuously evoked in us, and the sense of a unified identity that builds out of this process comes only 'after the fact.' Thus, Man's behavior is the resultant of the many different 'I's that succeed each other in the line of time. The illusion of a single permanent 'I' comes from the name that we have been given and the way in which we have been taught to respond to it. An infant is not born under the illusion of 'I'; it is something acquired in the process of socialization. We are each under considerable pressure, from our earliest years, to be responsible for our actions and to present ourselves as having a unified identity. Schizophrenics sometimes lose this ability, and while they are indeed subject to a crippling disorder, they see many things that normal people do not.

The understanding of man's lack of unity only becomes practical when we are able to understand that we do not possess one brain, but that our behavior is the result of the working of a number of different brains or centers. In Gurdjieff's model there are seven. These seven centers do not work together in a harmonious way; rather they continuously pre-empt one another, causing us to feel differently and to behave differently at different points in time. As we noted, they are divided into five lower centers and two latent higher centers. The five lower centers are the intellectual center, the emotional center, the moving center, the instinctive center, and the sex center. As the sex center functions differently from the other four centers, and impacts their working in a different way, it is generally studied as it manifests through the other four. Indeed some Traditions treat sex energy as an energy generated by the organism which is not localized in a center but which profoundly affects the workings of the other four centers. We shall follow this convention here, and speak of the four lower centers as intellect, emotion, movement, and instinct. These are what comprise a normal human psychology. The teachings of ancient times uniformly refer to the four lower centers by their characteristic energies: air, fire, water, and earth.

Although the four lower centers do not work together harmoniously, they are integrally connected. Within each center there are subdivisions based on a combination of the energy of that center with the energies of the other three. For example, within the emotional center, there is an intellectual part, an emotional part, a moving part, and an instinctive part. Each of these parts is again divided into parts of parts. Further, each center and each part of a center is divided into positive and negative halves, which communicate the positive and negative experiences of that center. For the emotional center this would be positive and negative emotions; for the instinctive center, physical sensations of pain and pleasure; for the moving center, the experience of motion and of stillness; and for the intellectual center, the experience of affirmative as opposed to critical thought (or intellectual negation).

The Tarot deck – which comes to us from the Egyptian Spiritual Tradition – provides a complete breakdown of both the lower and the higher centers, showing both the divisions and the divisions within divisions. Surprisingly, the normal deck of playing cards still carries the imprint of this knowledge. To that extent it can be used as a teaching tool for the study of the centers. We will bring out the correspondence with the normal deck of playing cards, and – throughout this book – use the names of the common playing cards to refer to the different divisions of centers, because this gives us an easily recognizable terminology.

The suits of hearts, diamonds, spades, and clubs can be used to represent emotion, intellect, motor function, and instinct. It is interesting that the two Higher Centers are represented by the two jokers, which are usually the first cards lost!

The breakdown of the four suits into face cards and number cards can be used to represent the breakdown of the centers into their component parts. In each one of the

THE STORY OF MAN

Figure 1. **Face cards of the common playing deck (jack, queen, king of hearts)**

four lower centers there are intellectual, emotional, and instinctive/moving parts. It is convenient to group the instinctive/moving parts as one because, in certain respects, they actually function together. (We note that in the original Tarot deck, there are four face-card divisions, and the instinctive and moving parts are kept separate.)

The three face-card divisions of the common deck of playing cards are, respectively, **the kings**, which can be used to represent the intellectual divisions of centers; **the queens**, which can be used to represent the emotional divisions; and **the jacks**, which can be used to represent the instinctive/moving divisions. Each of these face-card divisions is again broken into intellectual, emotional and moving parts, respectively. The divisions of the king (the intellectual part of the center) are the 10, 9, and 8; the divisions of the queen (the emotional part) are the 7, 6, and 5; and the divisions of the jack (the instinctive/moving part) are the 4, 3, and 2.

The cards shown in Figure 1 (all hearts) represent the primary divisions of the emotional center: the king (the intellectual part), the queen (the emotional part), and the jack (the instinctive/moving part).

In these cards we see illustrated the idea that each center (and each part of a center) has positive and negative halves. Each of the face cards can be reversed, rightside up or upside down, according to whether the perception is positive or negative.

The suits of hearts and diamonds (emotional and intellectual centers) are red, as they represent the centers that are specifically human, while the clubs and spades (instinctive and moving centers) are black, as they are shared with the animals.

Within certain Traditions, particularly those associated with healing, there has been a specialized study of the centers, parts of centers, and even parts of parts of centers. Most Traditions, however, study the centers only inasmuch as they are relevant to awakening. To the extent one is able to observe the centers impartially one is able to understand – in quite a practical way – that there is not one 'I' but many 'I's and that these 'I's change according to circumstance. In the First Work one acquires the ability to see these changes, as they occur, without completely losing one's attention on each change.

Each of the four lower centers spontaneously communicates its needs, its desires, its hopes, and its fears, and so we live in an ongoing stream of thoughts, images, sensations, and motor impulses. Each one of these impulses is a distinct 'I,' unconnected to the others, yet we somehow take all of these – without any sense of contradiction – as being 'ourself.' This is because, superimposed on the unruly chorus of 'I's, is the sense of a unified identity, which – though illusory – is the mark of our membership in human society.

In infants the four lower centers live close to the immediate stimuli that surround them in the present moment. The world is vivid and alive. As we grow older our 'internal life' becomes increasingly complex and increasingly divorced from the immediate experience of the present. The life of an adult is riven with hopes, fears, anxieties, and ambitions of many different kinds. The impulses of the four lower centers are no longer signals which express their immediate experience of the present, but voices that exist in relation to a complex and tortured identity created and re-created along the line of time. With the development of our sense of 'I' – through childhood, adolescence, and maturity – the activity of the four lower centers becomes increasingly reflexive. In other words it increasingly 'refers back' to an ever-more-developed 'I,' which carries an ever-greater burden of past experience. And thus the impulses of the lower centers become ever-more connected to the hopes, the fears, the desires, and the ambitions of the imaginary identity that has built up around them. All of this activity concentrates into an ongoing, involuntary stream of images, emotions, and discursive thought, which the Tradition of Orthodox Monasticism called *phantasia* (φαντασία) or 'imagination.'

Having understood the inner structure of the centers, we must now understand the imagination that they generate. We provide two very precise descriptions, one from the late fourteenth century, and one from the mid-twentieth century. They are striking in

THE STORY OF MAN

that they describe exactly the same thing in exactly the same way. The reality that they describe is continuous.

We quote from the fourteenth century author known as the Anonymous English Monk:

> Imagination is a faculty by which we form images of all absent and present things; and both it and the matter on which it works are contained [HJ: or should be contained] by consciousness. Before humanity sinned, imagination was so obedient to reason [the Higher Centers] – to which it is, as it were, a servant – that it never supplied it with any disordered image of a bodily object or any delusion of a spiritual object; but now it is not so. Unless it [imagination] is controlled by the light of grace in the reason, it will never cease, asleep or awake, to form alien and disordered images of bodily objects, or else some delusion or other, which is nothing but a bodily conception of something spiritual or a spiritual conception of something bodily. This is always deceptive and false, and always associated with error.[1]

From the twentieth-century author, Rodney Collin:

> [HJ: The process of imagination] is a continuous production of waste images, the by-product of past perceptions, which flow through and out of the brain in a meaningless and unbroken stream. Just as eating is intermittent, so is the excretion of faeces: but since the inflow of perceptions is continuous, so also is this off-scouring of imagination continuous. When the direct impact of the outside world is quieted by sleep, it even becomes visible to us as dreaming. In fact, dreaming goes on night and day, without a break, as anyone who has acquired the power of arresting the more active thinking process of the mind for a few moments, can readily establish. … It is as though all the waste clippings of a great cinema-studio were stuck together at random and the result run continuously day and night through some forgotten projector in a back-room.[2]

This process of imagination is involuntary and it is universal. It determines the very course of our lives. Taking one's sense of identity from this imagination is a major barrier to awakening, and thus learning to recognize it – and learning not to place one's identity in it – is a primary focus of the First Work.

It is our imagination that gives false substance to the 'reflexive' (or 'I'-centered) activity of the four lower centers. It creates the necessary context for all of our negative

---

1. The Anonymous English Monk, from *The Cloud of Unknowing And Other Works*, trans. A.C. Spearing, Penguin 2001, p. 90 (written second half of the fourteenth century)
2. Rodney Collin, *Theory of Celestial Influence*, Watkins, London, 1980, p. 182 (written 1947-8, published 1954)

emotions, as any negative emotion that is sustained and repeated must be supported by negative imagination.

As a result of this imagination the four lower centers cease to function as simple organs of perception. In other words they cease to connect us in an immediate way to what is in the present moment. Our internal life becomes a complex pattern of self-reflexive activity which actually veils reality, and as a result we interact with one another through the covering veils of imagination. The process of socialization becomes, then, a matter of acquiring the appropriate veils, so that all adult members of the community are able to participate in a shared state of imagination. As a result every single adult human being maintains an imaginary internal discourse which places him at one remove from reality. To be able to bring the intellectual, moving, emotional, and instinctive centers back into the present, free of the illusion of 'I,' would be a great achievement for any man. It would be to return to the primal world known to infants in the first months of life. But even the primal experience of the infant – the clear and direct perception of the four lower centers – falls far short of the experience of presence given from the Higher Centers.

We have now introduced enough material to suggest the extent to which the lower centers are capable of holding in check the development of the latent Higher Centers. As we noted, the recognition and acknowledgment of the state of the lower centers is part of the First Work. It is this work that gives the vantage point for an altered view of the functions. In the life of a normal person the Higher Centers are occasionally stimulated, but their brief moments of existence either **1**) pass unnoticed, **2**) are quickly forgotten, or **3**) are remembered as something separate from the normal pattern of events. The Higher Centers are, then, the direct object of the Second Work – the Work of the Steward.

The Higher Centers must be seen in the context of the different 'Worlds' because, once beyond the lower centers, we expand into the hierarchy of states of consciousness that, in its turn, opens into the sphere of the Absolute. When we pass beyond the lower centers, many different 'worlds of experience' begin to open up at once – the higher containing and permeating the lower. Once this context has been specified we can relate the Higher Centers to the particular Worlds that are their source. But while the Higher Centers do each correspond to a particular World, the Worlds that they correspond to exist independently of the Higher Centers of any individual human being; they are part of the universal order, and they fulfill particular functions within that order. In other words the Worlds are not limited to the experience of Higher Centers in individual human beings. The work of the Traditions, in bridging the gap between humanity and the higher levels of Creation, involves an understanding of this universal level. For example, a 'conscious' work of art or architecture, generated from a Spiritual Tradition with the aim of elevating a particular Civilization, may objectively and intentionally reflect the energy of specific Worlds above the human – although it is not itself possessed of Higher Centers. The higher the level of a Civilization, the higher the Worlds that may be 'imaged' into it.

The Context for Thinking about Higher Centers: Different Worlds

The four lower centers all exist – more or less – on the same plane. The Higher Centers, by contrast, function in relation to very different planes. Using the alchemical reference we introduced in Chapter 1, we could say that the four lower centers all function on a set of closely overlapping vibrational bandwidths. The Higher Centers function on different bandwidths, giving access to other worlds than our own. They represent a connection to the bandwidths on which the Gods normally function. To develop this alchemical system of reference, we shall present the Hermetic teaching that relates different vibrational bandwidths to different Worlds of experience.

The Hermetic teachings (which we shall discuss in greater depth in Book III) originated in Egypt in the third century AD as a composite of Greek, Egyptian, and assorted alchemical teachings. What unites these teachings is a concern with the different levels of energy in the universe and how the relation between these different levels is determined by universal cosmic laws. The theory of the cosmoses, mentioned above, was first elaborated here. While most of the records that we have of the early Hermetic teachings appear syncretic, there were almost certainly more developed Hermetic teachers – now lost to history – who produced formulations of great integrity. The Hermetic formulation we use here is more or less that of Gurdjieff's.[3]

---

3. George Gurdjieff received a unique set of Hermetic teachings in the late nineteenth century and recast it in a form appropriate to the twentieth. In these teachings the Greek side of Hermeticism (cosmoses and the macrocosm under a transcendent Absolute) and the Egyptian/Sumerian side of Hermeticism (interlocking vibrational levels/Worlds under different orders of laws/triadic Absolute) are seamlessly integrated with material found in Pythagoras (the theory of octaves and intervals). The theory of

THE HERMETIC TEACHING OF THE DIFFERENT WORLDS

Each being within the Macrocosm of Creation has a range of bandwidths which are its 'home.' Some of these bandwidths are central to its experience of life and to the main activities which it performs, while others are more peripheral.

A single vibrational bandwidth does not provide a complete life experience; a related set of bandwidths is necessary to support the complete and rounded experience of a life. Certain bandwidth ranges support a number of complementary functions, which have the potential to congeal into a centered life experience – yielding a coherent sense of who or what one is in the universe. In any created being – on whatever level it might exist – the higher frequency bandwidths will be more 'internal' (psychological) and the lower frequency bandwidths will be more 'external' (purely functional or physical). These sets of 'centered' bandwidth ranges are different for Gods, for men, for animals, for vegetables, and for minerals.

The 'centered' bandwidth-ranges can be called **Worlds**, because they are literally different worlds of experience under different orders of laws. *Each world is given its defining character by its central bandwidth.* In other words, for an entity established in a particular World, the experience of life will revolve around the central bandwidth of that World, even though the peripheral bandwidths remain part of that experience. Because each World is comprised of multiple bandwidths, the different Worlds can overlap. Thus we, as human beings, share directly and deeply in experiences that correspond to the animal and vegetable levels of existence, such as sex, sleep, and the digestion of food. We also, at least potentially, share in experiences that are part of the angelic range.

George Gurdjieff's Hermetic presentation very carefully defined the set of Worlds relevant to the human experience. He did so by using a numeric reference for the vibrational frequency of the 'central' (or determining) bandwidth of each world. This numeric reference was based on the number of 'laws' which act in that World. The 'number of laws acting' and the 'defining bandwidth frequency' are two different ways

---

octaves and intervals probably originated in much more ancient Sumerian/Chaldean teachings, which Pythagoras accessed in his travels. The perfect integration of these different sides of Hermeticism is symbolized in the figure of the enneagram. These elements were probably synthesized in classical (or early medieval) times, but the system as a whole continued to develop by integrating material from many sources. By the time Gurdjieff received it, it reflected careful study and analysis of a wide range of Sufi, Buddhist, and Vedantic teachings. It is now impossible to determine what Gurdjieff received and what he himself developed. Whatever the case he was able to master the material, understand its significance, and present it in a Western context – which represents a very considerable achievement.

of saying the same thing, but it is easier to connect a numeric reference to the former than to the latter. The reasoning is as follows:

- The Absolute, the first World, is under no laws. It cannot be, for the Absolute has willed its own opposite and so owns itself completely. World 1 represents unqualified unity and unqualified transcendence. It exists in the realm of the uncreate. The Absolute, as World 1, is the creator of all the other Worlds; he is unlike all of the other Worlds in that he is himself beyond creation.[4]

- The first World created from the Absolute is World 3. This is what the Hermetic teachings call the Created Macrocosm. It is external to what the Absolute is in and for itself.[5] At the level of World 3 we are at the level of the *unity* of the Created Macrocosm, which is under only three laws. One of those three laws is the will (or the direct influence) of the Absolute. World 3 is the only World that is subject to the direct influence of the Absolute in this way.

- The number of laws acting in the World immediately below the unity of the Created Macrocosm is 6, and in the World below that 12, and so forth down the line.

The greater the number of laws acting in a World, the lower the vibrational frequency. Thus, the greater number of laws acting in the lower Worlds represents – for each – its characteristic limitation, and so determines the nature of the psychological dramas that will be enacted within it.

In the Hermetic view there is nothing that has no vibrational frequency. Everything is, in some degree, animate or alive. This classification of matter by average vibrational frequency (and so by the World it inhabits) is a way of qualifying matter by its degree

---

4. And here there is an important technicality to note. The first triad in the series embraces the primordial tension of Being and Not-Being and its transcendence in Beyond-Being. This triad exists *within* the Absolute; it is internal to the first World. We could say that this first triad is the 'form' of the moment of transcendence. It shows us that the Absolute is not just a central all-powerful being, but contains within itself the transcendence of everything that stands outside of it. It contains a dimension that the whole rest of the Ray of Creation lacks. This dimension exists at the place of the third force in the internal triad. In all of the Absolute's actions, and in the execution of its many functions, everything aligns with this transcendent aspect, but the transcendent aspect itself just "is." It is untainted by anything that transpires outside of it. Terms for the transcendent aspect of the Absolute, given from the Traditions, include: the Vedantic *Para-Brahman;* the Tibetan Buddhist *Dharmakaya Buddha;* the South East Asian Buddhist *Adi-Buddha;* the Zoroastrian *Ahura Mazda;* the *Ein Sof* of the Kabbalah; and the *Absolute Spirit* of Western philosophy.

5. See P.D. Ouspensky's reports of George Gurdjieff's discourse in, *In Search of the Miraculous: Fragments of an Unknown Teaching,* Routledge & Kegan Paul, London and Henly, 1969, pages 79-80.

of animation. Every animate (or sentient or self-conscious) entity in the universe tends to gravitate towards a bandwidth that is central or 'defining' for a particular World so that it can function effectively within that World. While each being is centered in one bandwidth (and so in the World that contains it), the higher the level of the being, the greater the number of Worlds that will be concentrated in its life experience. For example, man, at the top of the hierarchy of organic life, includes within himself many functions that were originally developed in the animal and vegetable Worlds. We could say that he has both an 'animal' and a 'vegetable' inside of himself! What is specifically human is superimposed on the animal and vegetable levels, and what is potential in the human goes well beyond the central or 'defining' range.

Gurdjieff stated that the Worlds relevant to the human experience begin from the mineral (under 384 laws), and extend to include the plant (under 192 laws), the invertebrate (under 96 laws), the vertebrate (under 48 laws), the specifically human (under 24 laws), and finally – at least potentially – through to the Worlds beyond the human (under 12, 6, and 3 laws, respectively). All of these different realms or Worlds correspond to different aspects of our experience. We note that the classification of the 'human' as World 24 refers to what is specifically human. But in its present state of imagination (which sustains a wide array of negative emotions) humanity tends to function principally from Worlds 48 and 96. In fact World 24 is a relatively high experience for a normal human being and comprises a relatively small part of our lives. Indeed, there are many people who function only from the vertebrate and invertebrate levels within themselves; in other words, what is 'human' in them (such as, language and the power to form concepts) consistently serves impulses that arise from the animal and vegetable Worlds (Worlds 96 and 192). There are even human beings who are so hardened that they function principally from the mineral level (World 384). Individuals of this kind show a complete disregard for human life. This class of human being would include corrupt dictators and their henchmen, professional criminals, and a certain class of occult practitioner. The surprising picture that results is that some politicians and professional criminals are centered in a bandwidth lower than that of domestic animals, while the great Prophets and Avatars are centered in a bandwidth that corresponds to the angelic. This is something that, in a higher state of consciousness, one can actually see.

Thus, in Gurdjieff's nomenclature, the normal range of the human experience covers Worlds 96, 48, and 24, the subnormal range Worlds 182, 384 (and under remarkable circumstances 768), and the supernormal range Worlds 12, 6 (and under remarkable circumstances 3). Just as one's 'center of experience' shifts entirely in the passage from sleep

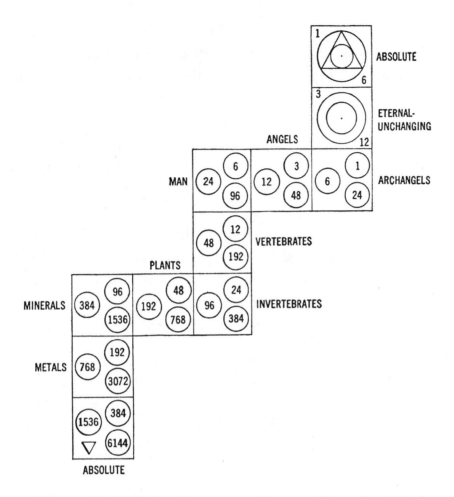

Figure 2. **Gurdjieff's Step Diagram, or 'Diagram of Everything Living'**

to the normal waking state, so one's center of experience shifts in the transition from one of these Worlds to another. The awareness of these shifts and transitions comes with the practice of the First Work.

The kind of 'I' that a human being is capable of supporting fades out at both World 3 and World 728 – the former into a transcendent experience that has little relation to what happens on the planetary surface and the latter into the lowest of imaginable hells.

We return to the point, then, that Man is born with two latent Higher Centers. These exist within him in undeveloped form. The Higher Emotional Center functions naturally at a level of World 12 and the Higher Intellectual Center functions naturally at a level of World 6. Man is not born with a center that corresponds to World 3, but if the Higher Emotional and Higher Intellectual Centers have become active, if they link correctly, and if the processes and functions normally connected with them are being realized, then access to World 3 becomes a possibility. We might say that man can form a center for World 3. From this place World 1 – The Absolute – can reach him. To be explicit, the Absolute may directly contact a being in whom both Higher Centers are active, and the connection between them has developed to a point which allows access to World 3. But this takes us beyond the normal human range of experience into the sphere of celestial alchemy.

In this frame of reference what we have called the Sphere of Sentient Being is a deep World 12, viewed as the gateway to Worlds 6 and 3. It represents – more or less – the cosmos above the cosmos of man: the level one-above humanity in the celestial hierarchy.

There is a relation, of course, between 'World' and the term 'cosmos' which we introduced earlier. Just as Gurdjieff grouped sets of vibrational bandwidths to describe the range of different 'Worlds,' it is possible to group sets of bandwidths to describe the functions and activities proper to the different cosmoses which comprise the Macro-cosm of Creation – but this takes us beyond the scope of the Story of Man.

In Figure 2 we have provided one of George Gurdjieff's teaching diagrams, the Diagram of Everything Living, representing this scale of bandwidths.[6] It is a simplified scale, designed to bring out underlying principles, the most important of which is that the diagram itself is intended as a 'moving' image. In other words it represents a process of continuous motion. Each different 'step' in the hierarchy has three vibrational numbers associated with it. Gurdjieff stated that the number shown on the center-left of each step (in the two top steps it is displayed in the upper left corner) is 'what it is,' the number on the top right is 'what eats it,' and the number on the bottom right is 'what it eats.' This gives the key to linking the different steps and seeing in what way the diagram is a 'moving diagram,' but, at the same time, it is an almost impossible simplification. The range of 'what it eats' and 'what eats it' actually extends well into the steps above and below the center number given, and the variations of these relationships by species can be used to distinguish the species within a *genus*.[7] But beyond this, and more importantly, the relationships to the level one above and the level one below are actually two-sided. The 'what eats it' is also, and at the same time, the highest level it can receive influences from. The 'what it eats' is also, and at the same time, the level that it can communicate its own influence to – in such a way as to raise or elevate it. The 'what it is' (center-left)

_____

6. Taken from Peter Damien Ouspensky's *In Search of the Miraculous: Fragments of an Unknown Teaching*, Routledge & Kegan Paul, London and Henly, 1969, p. 323.
7. See *In Search of the Miraculous*, pp. 327-328.

Figure 3. **Medieval Step Diagram**

number represents the number of the World that corresponds to the combination of processes that naturally take place at that step.

Naturally, the strongest influences on each World (the number on the left side of each square) are the Worlds immediately preceding and succeeding it. When we look, for example, at the horizontal tier labeled 'Man,' 'Angels,' and 'Archangels,' we see that the Angels, centered in World 12, receive influences from the Archangels on the level one above (World 6), and communicate influences to Man on the level one below (World 24).

Figure 3 shows a medieval diagram[8] of exactly the same thing, from about 1300. Man appears both as a species within the fabric of organic life (the tiny man on the

---

8. A woodcut by Ramon Lull (1232-1325), first published in *Liber de ascenscu et decensu intellectus*, Valencia, 1512.

right pointing to the stair labeled 'homo' or 'man') and as a microcosm of the whole (the larger man on the left, holding a symbolic representation of man's possibilities fully realized).

While emphasizing the universality of the principles behind this teaching, we shall – in the remainder of this book – follow George Gurdjieff's particular numeric designation of Worlds in our representation of the two Higher Centers – the Higher Emotional Center and the Higher Intellectual Center – and of what he called World 3, the 'Crown of Creation.'

The Higher Emotional Center

When the Higher Emotional Center becomes active in us there is a different sense of self, no longer based on the illusory feeling of 'I.' There is a sense of identity which is rooted, not in thought, feeling, sensation, or movement – but in presence itself, presence without reference point or qualification of any kind. Presence aware of itself as such. From this place the world around us may appear quite differently than it normally does. Often the novice will confuse a movement of the Higher Emotional Center with sudden perceptions of 'energy fields,' 'astral bodies,' or the animate qualities of apparently inanimate objects. In fact these perceptions derive from the shift in the feeling of 'I' (which is easy for the novice to overlook). They are what the lower centers begin to perceive when they function independently of the illusion of 'I.' It takes a great deal of time and experience to distinguish the changed sense of 'I' from the changed perceptions of the lower centers which it enables. Indeed, these altered perceptions may or may not come with the change in the feeling of 'I,' and they are relatively unimportant in relation to it. One could have a complete experience of the Higher Emotional Center without an altered perception of one's surroundings. What is important is that the Higher Emotional Center recognize itself as an awareness separate from the functions and learn to sustain this self-recognition through time. This is what is meant by 'presence aware of itself.' Gurdjieff referred to this sphere of experience as a World under twelve orders of laws, or World 12. It is the sentience of this World that the practitioner of the First Work must learn to distinguish from the stream of impulses that continuously arises from the four lower centers – each one claiming to be 'I.'

In World 12 one is relieved of the many restrictions on thought, feeling, and action which are in place when the lower centers are subject to imagination. The false reference point of imaginary 'I' ties us to all of the feelings of guilt, fear, regret, recrimination, and aggression that are the unspoken backdrop of life on the human level. Presence is centered in itself, and knows itself independently of all the complexes of thought, feeling, and sensation that make up our personal psychology and to which we are normally enslaved. Indeed, it is hard for us to imagine a world completely free of this 'all-too-human' shadow. And so it is with each of the Worlds beyond World 12.

The Higher Intellectual Center

Where the Higher Emotional Center brings a profound change in our experience, the Higher Intellectual Center transcends experience itself. It transcends the duality of the one who has the experience and the content of his or her experience. It is a state of unity that is impossible for a normal human being to comprehend. Here the very idea of 'I' begins to lose its meaning. From this place we can begin to understand cosmic laws. We can begin to see, in the unfolding pattern of the world around us, the expression of the laws that govern a higher level of creation. Indeed, it is as though the universal laws begin to know themselves through us. Words, concepts, and language are utterly inadequate to describe this level of perception. Gurdjieff referred to this as World 6. When a man is stationed or centered in World 6, he feels his own planetary 'vehicle' (including this thoughts, feelings, and sensations) as something external to himself. When an unprepared man has a deep World 6 experience, he feels himself near to the death of his body. Even in the highest spiritual teachers experiences of World 6 are not sustained over long periods of time.

The Crown of Creation

Beyond World 6 is a World that does not correspond to a 'center' – latent or active – in the energy field of a human being. To make any sense of it one must have both Higher Centers developed. Gurdjieff called this level of experience World 3, and it is a sphere to which humanity has only the most distant relation. World 3 is near to the transcendent life of the Absolute, which surpasses both Creation and the Uncreate. It is the level at which the Absolute is three forces in one: a will that wills its own negation and so transcends itself. This is a miracle, which, in its completeness, is quite beyond the comprehension of any embodied being. In its depth it is beyond even the understanding of the Gods. Mankind has a relationship to World 3 through those rare individuals in whom both Worlds 12 and 6 are developed, and who have been tasked – from the level of World 3 – in relation to the human race. To the extent that humanity is able to make these tasks its own, it has a relation to World 3. Thus, while World 3 is beyond the imagination of men, mankind does have a relationship to it, and this relationship is important to its destiny. We shall explore this area more deeply in studying the lives of the Prophets.

Having outlined the theory of the seven centers, we are now in a position to distinguish the different levels of human development. Here again we shall make use of the neutral terminology of George Gurdjieff, who abstracted from the more colorful nomenclature used by certain of the Spiritual Traditions. It is not our aim here to emphasize the wonders of the different states and stations of existence but to make accurate distinctions.

The Different Levels of Man

When a man has subordinated the activity of his four lower centers to the pursuit of the Higher Centers, we speak of him as a **Man Number Four**. A man at this level has – through struggle – reduced imagination to a point where the Higher Emotional Center can periodically appear, and the moments of more concentrated presence that it enables guide and center his work. He may even have glimpses of the Higher Intellectual Center.

When the Higher Emotional Center becomes permanently active in a man, he has made the transition through to the level of **Man Number Five**. This level comprises many different degrees of development. In the beginning stages a Man Number Five can easily lose everything that he has acquired. A complete Man Number Five is capable of functioning independently of his cellular body and of withstanding the shock of death. He has achieved a kind of immortality. Such a person would have more frequent experiences of the Higher Intellectual Center and would be able to interpret and integrate those experiences in a way that a Man Number Four cannot.

While the appearance of the Higher Emotional Center requires a certain development (refinement and cleansing) of the four lower centers, the development of the Higher Intellectual Center does not follow naturally from a certain development of the Higher Emotional Center. In other words we do not graduate, in stages, from the development of the four lower centers, to the development of the Higher Emotional Center, to the development of the Higher Intellectual Center. In the course of our evolution the two Higher Centers develop, at first independently, and then, increasingly, in unison, to bring ever deeper perceptions of our being within the being of the universe.

When the two Higher Centers finally reach a point where they work continuously in unison we speak of a **Man Number Six**. At a certain point the two Higher Centers recognize their profound kinship … and 'lock.' This fusion is the most definite moment in the path of a man's spiritual development. Gurdjieff termed it the 'crystallization' of the Higher Centers. It is irreversible, and defines forever the course of evolution for the person who undergoes it. The union of the two Higher Centers makes a clear and permanent link to the cosmos above the cosmos of man. While a Man Number Five can lose everything that he has, a Man Number Six cannot.

We could say that while a Man Number Five becomes transparent to himself, a man number six actually becomes translucent, such that the light of a higher level shines through him. While the existence of Men Number Five is significant for humanity, it is the level of Man Number Six that is important for the Spiritual Traditions – for it is from this level that a working relation with the Gods can be established.

A Man Number Six is capable of creating a very dynamic teaching environment. He, and he alone, is competent to create the situation in which a Man Number Four – who has made all the necessary preparations – can make the transition through to Man Number Five. At the same time he is capable of stabilizing and correcting a mature Man Number Five in relation to World 6.

What, then, lies beyond the level of Man Number Six? The range of development of the fused Higher Centers is so great that it makes little sense to speak of all men and women in whom they have crystallized as belonging to the same level. Indeed it has been said that the range of development from Man Number Six on is greater than the range that begins from the spiritual novice and ends in a freshly-crystallized Man Number Six. For this reason the Spiritual Traditions have spoken of levels beyond Six. Gurdjieff spoke of **Men Number Seven**, and once referred to Jesus, Buddha, and Moses as being **Men Number Eight**. Fortunately we do not need to understand these further divisions in order to tell the Story of Man. We just need to remember that they exist.

All of this is necessary for understanding how a Spiritual Tradition works. But to understand this practically we need to elaborate the relationships between the different levels of man in greater detail.

For a Man Number Four to attempt – without guidance – the level of effort required to become a Man Number Five would be a severe test of his or her mental balance, for one sees many things that are not normally seen or acknowledged. The difficulties and demands of this work are daunting, and it is very easy to develop a negative view of oneself and one's possibilities. Also, the example of success, the presence of a Man Number Five, is important. To have the guidance of a single Man Number Five would be an immeasurable benefit, but even this is not a sufficient condition. A Man Number Five understands his own awakening, but he does not understand the general context of awakening in a way that would allow him to understand – with surety – all of the different paths that lead to it. And different people, with different characters and dispositions, must necessarily follow different paths. Also, a Man Number Five cannot clearly understand and interpret the symbolic dimension of the events which unfold around him, and this means that he cannot reliably interpret communications from the Gods.

A Man Number Six, by contrast, is 'beyond' the created world. He has crossed the great divide and from that standpoint understands the different pathways that lead to the destination he has reached. Because he has definitively emerged from the mass of humanity, he must preserve his independence in order to teach what he understands. He cannot make too many concessions to his students, or his teachings will be interpreted on a level lower than the level on which they were given, and his effort will be wasted. Yet if a Man Number Six were to teach unprepared men directly from his locked Higher Centers, they would think him mad. Even if he were to speak directly to prepared Men Number Four, they would understand him only imperfectly. Given this, it is the responsibility of a Spiritual Tradition to create the conditions in which a Man Number Six can teach from himself. This means that he must be supported by a number of Men Number Five, who can act as his translators and interpreters. This 'step-down' situation gives a considerable breadth to the teachings of the Men Number Five who are capable of performing this function. They are able to perform much better as teachers in the presence of someone higher than themselves. The emergence of such a 'hierarchy of being' allows a much larger number of Men Number Four to respond fully to the teaching, each from the level that he or she is on.

When a mature Man Number Four is placed in the company of several Men Number Five, themselves working under the guidance of a Man Number Six or Seven, he is suddenly in a position to understand much more about his situation – because there is a much higher level of shared understanding in the teaching community. To move a spiritual novice into such an environment would be like moving a child, with a special gift for dance, from classes held at the local high school to the beginner's class at the Mariinsky School of Ballet. The child itself is not changed by the change of circumstances, but the forces and influences acting on that child change very greatly – so that what was impossible in the one context becomes quite possible in the other.

For all of these reasons a tradition is able to offer its students a situation especially conducive to awakening.

So a Spiritual Tradition needs, minimally, a Man Number Six. His presence creates a situation where Men Number Four can become Men Number Five, and where Men Number Five can work to become Men Number Six. In short, he creates an environment where many obstacles to human evolution can be minimized. Men Number Seven (and beyond) make the link to the cosmos above the cosmos of man all the more secure, and in so doing they make it more possible for the Gods to make their impress on humanity at large.

We have defined a Spiritual Tradition as a School which practices the Second Work under the guidance of Higher School. We are now in a position to provide **a second, working definition of a Spiritual Tradition**:

> The Great Spiritual Traditions are each able to provide an environment in which a very high Teacher guides the work of several Men Number Five, themselves working to become Men Number Six. Below this there is a much larger number of Men Number Four, actively working to become Men Number Five. Below this there is an even greater number of Men Number Four who are stable in their line of effort at that level. And below this there is the largest segment of all: spiritual novices aspiring to the level of Man Number Four.

Each of these levels serves the level one above and lifts the level one below. Such an extended Tradition, lifting level on level, is capable of giving life, not only to its members but to the Religion and to the Civilizational Order of which it is a part. In this regard it mirrors the image of the concentric circles of the Gods, represented in the quotations from Dante and Dionysius the Areopagite presented in Chapter 1.

Once the hierarchy of being which defines a Spiritual Tradition has been achieved, you have an atmosphere of the miraculous – of awe, of wonder, and of the renewal of life. There is a sense of the sacred. Understanding this makes it possible to understand an important aspect of the work of the Traditions; in such an atmosphere the creation of great art is possible. Not every Tradition is specialized in producing great art, but it is a natural form of expression for the Traditions. The art of the Traditions has been called 'objective art,' as it knows the effects that it creates in those who experience it. It gives man a certain awareness of his place and possibilities in the universe, without manipulating his feelings or playing upon his imagination. What we can call, by contrast, 'subjective art' simply creates different effects, whether pleasant or unpleasant, upon the four lower centers.

Art that is objectively great lifts humanity. The Sphinx, the Parthenon, the Hagia Sophia, and the Gothic Cathedrals have made humanity more than it would otherwise have been. Objective art gives a civilization something matchless; it gives its people something to live for. Historically, the Traditions have produced visual art, architecture, poetry, drama, literature, music, and dance that have changed the human race. Reflecting on these subjects leads us to the topic of the External Work of Spiritual Traditions, which we shall take up in Chapter 4.

Having described the different levels of man, and having used these descriptions to represent a second aspect of the work of the Spiritual Traditions, we must return to the realm of psychology to describe the internal work that the Traditions must accomplish.

The Internal Work of the Spiritual Traditions

To describe the Second Work, which is the *sine qua non* of the Traditions, we must be able to accurately distinguish it from the First Work. As we noted, the First Work is the work of the purification of the lower centers. We have established that the lower centers must be relatively free from imagination before the Higher Centers can become active. This means that the lower centers must literally be brought out of imagination into the state of direct perception that is known to infants in the first months of life. This is a 'presence' that is short of the presence of the Higher Centers, but which is, nevertheless,

82   THE STORY OF MAN

the necessary point of departure for the Great Work. The difference between the presence of the lower centers and the presence of Higher Centers – more than anything else – marks the chasm between the First Work and the Second Work.

Different Kinds of Presence and Different Kinds of Work

The lower centers can be present to what is before them in the moment, but they cannot know presence itself, independently of thought, emotion, sensation, and movement. Indeed, a profound moment of wordless presence is a 'break' in the life of the four lower centers. It is an entirely different quality of experience. There is presence, and there is something that knows itself to be present … moment after moment after moment. The life of the Higher Centers begins in these gaps between the 'I's and culminates in the transcendent, universal life of a God.

The aim of the Traditions is the realization of a presence independent of the life of the four lower centers. But, as we cannot begin from the Higher Centers, how are the lower centers to 'make' something higher than themselves happen? How is it possible to link time and eternity? The answer to this question is not easy.

To begin, we must distinguish three phases of work:

1. To **develop** the lower centers (which is part of the normal growth and education of every man and woman, and prior to the First Work),

2. To **purify** the lower centers of imagination and negative emotions (which is the specialty of the First Work), and

3. To **enable** the Higher Centers (which is the specialty of the Second Work).

The development of the lower centers is in itself unrelated to their purification or to the realization of the Higher Centers. It is right that the lower centers should be developed and that their particular capacities and potentials be realized. But the development of the lower centers does not, in itself, lead to Higher Centers. A child with undeveloped lower centers normally has more glimpses of the Higher Centers than a fully mature adult.

Having made this point, it is nevertheless true that a certain specialized development of the lower centers is necessary, both to the process of purification and to the process of enabling the Higher Centers. While the lower centers are normally developed to serve the imaginary 'I,' they can also be developed, in a very different way, in service of Higher Centers.

This alternative path of development is centered on the special capacities of a single division of the emotional center, one that can be trained to recognize and to remember the experience of consciousness, as distinct from the range of experiences given from the four lower centers. This is an inner division of the emotional center, permeated with the energies of the intellect. Technically it is **the intellectual division of the emotional center**, or in the nomenclature of the playing cards, the King of Hearts. We could say that it is intelligent emotion. The intense and refined energies that reside in this part of a center allow for a memory of peak emotional experiences, such as a pledge of love, a vow to change one's life, or a glimpse of the Higher Centers. This capacity for the recognition of Higher Centers is most concentrated in the emotional part of the King of Hearts, or in the nomenclature of the playing cards, **the Nine of Hearts**.

While not all Traditions engaged in a specialized study of the centers and divisions of centers, all acknowledged this special function of the emotional center, although, of course, they referred to it by different names. A term that acquired general usage – in whatever language – was 'the Heart.'

The Heart

The Heart is essential to the Work of the Steward because it is the only center that has been given to Man which can be trained to recognize, remember, and value consciousness. For this reason, the Heart is the only thing in the 'bundle of functions' that can serve as a direct link to Higher Centers.

In the Egyptian Tradition the function of the heart was most often represented by the Goddess Isis. The Sufi Orders of Islam taught that the remembrance or recollection of God is in the heart, and that the Work of the Steward (for them, the practice of the silent *zhikr*) occurs in the heart and purifies it. Orthodox monasticism called its meditative technique the 'prayer of the heart,' and spoke of the transition to the Work of the Steward as the 'dropping of the mind into the heart.' In the Vedantic Tradition of Bhakti yoga the surrender of the level of the functions to the invisible Self (Atman) is clearly centered in the heart. The Buddhist 'heart sutra' describes the connection of the lower functions to higher consciousness in terms of the heart, represented as the goddess Avelokitesvara.

Thus, in the work of the Traditions, the 'concentration of consciousness' (or the development of the Steward) has its locus in this particular part of the emotional center. This division or part was designed into Man with the explicit purpose of enabling his awakening. It is the necessary counterpart of the latent Higher Centers. The fact that it is seldom used for this purpose, and may indeed be used to serve other purposes, does not in the least change the reason it was originally given us – to recognize and to enable the Higher Centers.

We could say that the Heart 'comes with' the bundle of functions that defines Man. It is a given. The Steward does not come with this bundle of functions; it is created in the work of the Spiritual Traditions. Thus, enigmatically, the Heart – which is a given – is only developed in its true function by the application of a teaching that is learned. Yet this teaching is as old as humanity itself. While this teaching was not given in our biology, it has been given as part of our destiny. It is the work – of course – of the Spiritual Traditions, which developed out of the direct involvement of the Gods with the first generations of men. We shall proceed, then, to examine how this particular division of the emotional center is used, in the context of a developing Steward, to discover and to sustain one's invisible Self.

It is the special capacities of the Nine of Hearts that give us our real chance at awakening, for when Higher Centers can be recognized and remembered, the experiences we have of them can be assimilated. Only when these experiences have been assimilated can they give direction to our lives. And the emotional part of the king of hearts – the nine – can do more than recognize and remember. This subdivision can act for the Higher Centers on the level of the lower centers by summoning and directing individual 'I's that promote internal work. It is the presence of this quality of energy in the field of the cellular body, with its direct affinity to the energies of the Higher Centers, that makes man – at least potentially – a self-evolving being.

The Fatal Conflict between the White Queen and the Black Queen

While the Nine of Hearts has clearly been designed into us to enable the connection to Higher Centers, there are thirty-five other divisions of centers, and there is very little in these other thirty-five divisions that has any interest in the Higher Centers. Indeed the instinctive center, taken as a whole, *actively resists the Higher Centers*. Why should this be so?

The natural 'home' of the instinctive center is the earth, and its principal concerns are food, shelter, mate, and children. The Higher Centers represent for it a foreign and ultimately threatening experience. They are not part of the world of its basic needs and, at the same time, their presence somehow changes everything. They imply a different set of priorities. For this reason the Higher Centers are perceived by the instinctive center as a threat. It is the intellectual division of the instinctive center that defends the life of the organism against external and internal threats. It is behind both the working of the immune system and the sudden access of energy and awareness that comes to us in times of danger. This primitive 'will-to-life' that is the control center of the physical organism is the foundation for the instinctive sense of unity on which the imaginary 'I' is based. As a result the intellectual division of the instinctive center will react to and oppose any threat to the imaginary 'I' and any sustained attempt to enable the Higher Centers. The instinctive center, in the shorthand of the playing cards, is the suit of clubs. The inner division of the instinctive center which coordinates the resistance to the Higher Centers is the **nine of clubs**, or – technically – the emotional part of the intellectual part of the instinctive center. This is the seat of the will to self-maintenance that we share with the animals, and, unless – over the course of our lives – we are able to develop something stronger, it remains the strongest thing in us.

We see a 'profound' contradiction in the respective roles of the Nine of Hearts and the nine of clubs, and this brings us to the fatal conflict that can – under certain circumstances – take place between them.

The conflict of the Nine of Hearts and the nine of clubs is well represented by the game of chess, which – like the Tarot deck – comes down to us from the ancient Egyptian Spiritual Tradition. The original game was called *skeet*, and, just like the Tarot, it was imbued with esoteric meaning. As the game developed it came to revolve around the two most powerful pieces on the board: the white queen and the black queen. These can be seen to represent what we have called the Nine of Hearts and the nine of clubs, so that the game of chess itself can be used to represent the struggle to awaken. To develop this analogy, it is the **Black Queen** (the nine of clubs) who tries to arrange the other chess pieces (divisions of centers) so that the **White Queen** (the Nine of Hearts) will be unable to preserve the **White King** (Higher Centers). The alignment of the majority of the pieces on the board on the side of the Black Queen is collectively called the **Lower Self**.

The term Lower Self (which originates from the Sufi Traditions) is more suitable than 'ego' for referring to the part of our being which is resistant to awakening, because what resists awakening is not a 'thing' but a complicated process. The process that sustains the ego through time does not originate from the ego itself but from the hidden control-center, existing just below the level of our normal awareness, that we have labeled the Black Queen.

The term Lower Self is also more appropriate than the term 'false personality' – that was used by George Gurdjieff to describe the outer personality (or combination of personalities) that is generated on the basis of the imaginary 'I.' The 'false personality' is a cosmetic front that constantly adjusts one's behavior to other people and to external circumstances. It is something that forms within us, independently of our own choice or decision, as part of our adjustment to society, and the first person to be deceived is oneself. But to understand the deception itself we must go deeper.

The sense of a unique and unchangeable 'I,' adjusting easily to every change of circumstance through a rounded personality, develops ultimately out of the Black Queen. The imaginary 'I,' once formed, has the effect of locking our personality (or personalities) to the strongest force in us: the instinctive will to self-maintenance. This working combination, under the ultimate control of the Black Queen, is the Lower Self. It is not all of what we are, but all of what we are is held in subjection to it. This situation is represented perfectly in the story *The Sleeping Beauty*, in which the Wicked Queen holds the Princess Aurora (the latent higher centers) in an enchanted sleep.

Once the artificial 'I' is in place the Black Queen does have control, directly or indirectly, over the great majority of pieces on the chessboard. But here there is an important point to note: she is not a sinister master-mind. In other words she does not exercise her control in a 'Machiavellian' way, but as an instinctive reflex, so that from one point of view she is blind and unknowing and from another extremely quick, quite vigilant, and completely relentless. One can only combat the Black Queen by seeing her for what she is: an ancient, autonomous, animal function, necessary to the process of organic life, but impassable to Higher Worlds. Our price of entry to those Worlds is the disengagement from her spell.

From the moment a Man recognizes this fact he lives in a divided house; his being becomes a field of war between the two opposing forces. In order for the White Queen to win the game, she must be able to organize and deploy those pieces on the chessboard capable of serving her and neutralize those that cannot. This, then, is the Master Game.

Reviewing this situation we can see that the White Queen faces very long odds – and in this way the Master Game differs from the game of chess. In the Master Game there are, even from the beginning of play, more pieces in service to the Black Queen than the White. According to the teaching of the Spiritual Traditions this imbalance has been designed into us, because the pressure of intense inner struggle is needed to develop the quality of will necessary to penetrate the Sphere of Sentient Being.

We note that this is the same archetypal pattern of struggle that we saw in the Absolute's confrontation with his own Not-Being, and it is reflected on all levels of the Macrocosm of Creation. It is a struggle that the Spiritual Traditions have represented in different ways in their cosmologies and mythologies; but, beyond this, it is a struggle that the Gods themselves have inscribed in the psychology of the microcosmos man – as the pattern for his own transcendence.

The nature of this archetypal struggle is perfectly illustrated in the chess game that is portrayed in Ingmar Bergman's film *The Seventh Seal*. The white side is represented by a Knight who is engaged in a contest with Death, who of course represents the black side. The game that takes place between the two of them is acted out in the medium of everyday life. The white side's different moves are the Knight's decisions and actions in relation to the unfolding pattern of his own life. The Knight has the advantage of the first move, but the difficult challenge for him is that he must always remember that he is playing the game. Whenever the Knight is caught up in the drama of his outer life and takes actions without respect to the Master Game that is being played behind the scenes, Death is able to make a decisive move … because Death never forgets. Every time Death takes a white piece off the board he appears before the Knight, holding the chessboard, and demonstrates to him the move that has just occurred: "Black bishop moves to QR1 to take white rook." Death smiles, and the game then continues. The analogy here is exact; once we have entered the Master Game we can never forget we are in it.

Having established the context and distinguished between the 'organic' presence of the lower centers and the divine presence of the Higher Centers, we can make a preliminary sketch of the internal Work of the Traditions.

The Work of the Steward

We have emphasized that the work of the Spiritual Traditions is to directly open and enable the Higher Centers. It is this work that distinguishes the Spiritual Traditions from the Esoteric Groups and the Living Religions, which have been – for most of our history – their cultural and social context. We have called the work of the Esoteric Groups and the Living Religions the First Work. It is focused on the purification of the lower centers, and it involves direct struggle with the many forms of negative imagination and negative emotion: false hopes, ungrounded fears, and extreme desires. The First Work results in **1**) an 'opening out' of the four lower centers to what is immediately before them in the present, **2**) the correction of certain personal weaknesses, **3**) the development of compassion for other human beings, and **4**) the capacity to distinguish consciousness from functions. This work makes a person more transparent to himself and so prepares the ground for direct work on consciousness. But the First Work cannot directly bring into question the sense of 'I,' which is both the barrier and the gateway to Higher Centers. To question the illusory sense of 'I' consistently you must have something more real to put in its place, and that requires a greater discipline than the disciplines of the First Work.

Having made this point we must emphasize that the work to open and develop the Higher Centers is not independent of the work to purify the lower centers. The latter is the precondition of the former. Unless we can bring some presence to the lower centers, the Higher Centers will not emerge. Where the Traditions work in harmony with Living Religion there is a natural division of labor between the two. Where the Traditions work separately from Living Religion, they must accomplish both the preparatory and final stages of the work by themselves.

Each of the Great Spiritual Traditions is clear about the distinction between these two kinds of work. The First Work is the work of the spiritual novice, the *salik* or the hinyana monk, while the Second Work is the work of the *starets*, the *murid*, or the vajrayana practitioner.

We noted that, until the First Work has been mastered, the second phase of the work is all but impossible. But, at the same time – and from another perspective – there is a danger that the First Work – taken as an end in itself – will actually create an obstacle to the work on Higher Centers. The First Work produces a 'good' Christian, a 'good' Muslim, or a 'good' Buddhist, who can say "I am present!" But unless the sense of 'I' itself can be displaced, the First Work will produce a 'good' man, but a man still driven by external impacts and influences. The illusion of unity, on the level of the lower centers, will remain secure – and this means that the Black Queen is still, ultimately, in control. Until the Black Queen loses her hold on Man's sense of 'I' you do not have Higher Centers aware of their own existence. You do not have the sustained presence of the Higher Centers existing independently of the scattered and intermittent 'presence' of the lower centers. The presence known to Higher Centers is utterly independent of being a 'good' Christian, a 'good' Muslim, or a 'good' Buddhist.

It is only at the level of the Higher Centers that you have true universality. This was achieved by both the Christian monastic orders and the Sufi orders of Islam during what we call the Middle Ages. While Islam and Christendom fought to the death, there were many circumstances in which the Sufis and the Christian monks communicated easily about many things. The stained glass windows of the Gothic cathedrals were created through techniques learned from Sufi craftsmen. Muhammad himself was first recognized as a prophet, not by an Arab, but by a Syrian Christian Orthodox monk.

The universality of the Work of the Traditions comes from the fact that it transcends the individual's work on himself. It represents a link to a level which is quite independent of the individual's personal problems and concerns, including those connected with self-preservation, sex, ethnicity, and avowed faith.

We are now in a position to understand the core ideas of this Second Work – as 'direct work on consciousness,' that is, the work of the individual to realize his or her own Higher Centers. It revolves around what we shall call the Work of the Steward – the preparation of a part within us that can, under the guidance of the White Queen, confront the imaginary 'I' and so confront the Lower Self. While it is referred to quite differently in each of the Traditions, it is clearly marked in each one. We can best understand it by looking at the characteristic limitation of the First Work.

In the First Work we are trained to make the efforts required to bring presence to each of the four lower centers – and it does require both sustained effort and strong desire to arrest the uncontrolled flow of imagination that proceeds from each one. The problem is that *all the efforts we can make are initiated from the lower centers themselves.* While the Higher Centers may periodically flash into being, they are, at this stage, incapable of initiating a line of effort on their own. The problem is, then, that the intense and concentrated effort required of the lower centers actually takes the space the fledgling Higher Centers need to breathe.

Thus, in the First Work a medium of uninterrupted imagination is replaced by a medium of active struggle, in which the Higher Centers may intermittently appear. But, from the standpoint of the Higher Centers, all of the efforts we can make are just part of the chorus of 'I's that continuously arises from the lower centers. The Higher Centers may make more frequent appearances in this context, but they cannot come into their own in a field that is dominated by active struggle. Thus, having mastered the methods of the First Work, we are left in the midst of a stalemated struggle punctuated by moments of Higher Centers. This can go on forever. A permanent transition through to Worlds 6 and 12 requires something more.

The Work of the Steward takes us past the sticking point of the First Work by creating an internal space which is between the world of the four lower centers and the world of the Higher Centers – and within this space a different kind of effort becomes possible. This can be achieved because – as we have noted – there is a division of the lower centers that can recognize and respond directly to the Higher Centers: the Nine of Hearts. The special space for making efforts is, then, created around the Nine of Hearts, under certain controlled conditions. To understand just how the Steward functions in this space we must look a little more closely at 'the Heart' – the emotional division of the intellectual division of the emotional center.

THE NINE OF HEARTS

When the king of hearts has been developed in the First Work and is repeatedly exposed to Higher Centers, the Nine of Hearts becomes able to make – with accuracy – two different kinds of perception:

1. Negative perceptions of what it means to live under the control of the Lower Self.

2. Positive perceptions of the independent presence of the Higher Centers.

These perceptions are, respectively, the perceptions of the negative and positive halves of the White Queen. The two halves can be trained to work together, in the constantly changing circumstances of external life, to produce a continuity of effort. But there is an additional quality in the White Queen which makes it possible – in certain moments – to transcend effort and so to create the 'special space' between the lower centers and the Higher Centers. This quality is based on its capacity for memory. The Nine of Hearts can connect with what is called 'objective memory.' What is this?

OBJECTIVE MEMORY

Moments of presence self-aware create memory in the Nine of Hearts that is of an entirely different quality than the memory created in the other divisions of centers. This is not the kind of memory that is conjured up in the mind's eye when one is asked about things that happened long ago. Objective memory is the direct imprint of what actually happened, like the image on a photographic plate. It is, if you will, a memory of the present. It is free of the distortions imposed by the subjective sense of self; it is not a memory of "what happened to me" but a memory of 'presence' itself and what presence was present to. It is an accurate memory, not only of the contents of the moment, but of the Higher Centers that appeared within it.

Moments of objective memory are often created in infancy and early childhood, when the imaginary sense of 'I' has not completed its development. They are normally forgotten – or rather 'buried' – as our adult identity begins to form. But should we acquire the special ability to re-access these moments we would find them still there, in all their purity, and we would find that they still influence our life. There is a certain potential embedded in each one of them, for these are the moments when our latent Higher Centers remembered to remember themselves, and the more they remember themselves, the more they can remember themselves.

The Nine of Hearts, once trained, can access this special kind of memory. It is all the more able to do so after it becomes involved in making the very efforts that create such memory. As the Heart becomes able to remember presence itself, independent of the external circumstances of the moment, *objective memory becomes cumulative*. Thus, whenever we add fresh moments of memory we are creating 'flash points,' which will – over time – sum to give the Nine of Hearts a permanent orientation towards the Sphere of Sentient Being.

Once this process is under way, the Heart can become continuously emotional about the Higher Centers. The emergence of this constant emotion signals a new level of development for the White Queen, who then begins to experience new kinds of emotion – related to the emergence of a presence that is fully aware of itself. Thus, as the Nine of Hearts disentangles herself from the interests and concerns of the lower centers, she begins to re-member the Real Self, and becomes ever more inspired to make the efforts that will bring it into being. Every moment that we return to presence our 'objective memory' is strengthened, and the ability of the White Queen to use special-ized Work 'I's to sustain presence is correspondingly enhanced. These specialized Work 'I's form the core of the Steward, allowing the White Queen to deftly pursue her work in the chaotic stimulus-response environment of the lower centers. The texts of the Orthodox Monastic Tradition are very clear about this transition; they say that when it occurs "the mind drops into the heart."

Having described the development that allows the Nine of Hearts to create a 'special center of effort,' we must now describe what must be 'created around' it in order to complete the Steward.

Because this emergent 'center of effort' is not connected to our usual sense of 'I' but – ultimately – to the memory of our Higher Centers, the White Queen becomes unusually adept at gathering useful Work 'I's, putting them into practice, and perfecting the use of each one. We could say that the 'I's belonging to the entourage of the White Queen are 'precision-engineered,' in the sense that they are activated in silence, in accordance with the Queen's changing perception of the needs of the moment. They are not the occasional 'spin-offs' of an ongoing internal discourse about the work. The Steward is, then, the combination of a specially-developed White Queen – the 'Heart' – with the small retinue of Work 'I's which are at her immediate command.

Before continuing, let us clarify what we mean by precision-engineered Work 'I's.

Through constant practice over the entire period of the First Work, the aspirant develops a core of Work 'I's that cover – more or less – the different situations that he or she encounters in the course of a day. In each of these different areas, three aspects of his or her work cumulate:

1. The understanding of what it means to be fully awake in that circumstance,

2. The desire to maintain the awakened state at any cost,

3. The many (and inevitable) observations of the failure to sustain presence.

On the basis of this a body of understanding develops in each different area of work that can be condensed into a single Work 'I' which sums it all up. When there is enough objective memory behind this Work 'I,' it can sometimes be reduced to a point-syllable – a single syllable which simplifies, and so heightens, its effect. While this phrase or syllable may have little meaning in itself, the understanding and objective memory behind it gives it special impact. In this way a whole world of understanding can be concentrated into a single phrase or even a single syllable.

We provide an example of three 'precision-engineered' Work 'I's, taken from a set of eight introduced by the twelfth-century Sufi Teacher, Abd al-Khaliq Ghujdawani.

Watchfulness (nigah dasht)	MEANING: Do not be carried away by your emotional reaction to other people or situations. Do not allow your emotions to connect with thoughts unrelated to awakening. Struggle immediately with all emotional impulses unrelated to the realization of your Higher Self.

COMMENT: Such an 'I' would be appropriate in times of emotional stress or when one feels oneself entering a state of self-preoccupation. It could be reduced to a single syllable by replacing 'watchfulness' with 'drop it,' and then reducing that to 'drop.' Or there could be a sequential use of 'watch' and 'drop.'

Watch your step!
(*nazar bar qadem*)

MEANING: Keep your intention before you at every step. Remember where you came from and where you are going. Do not become fascinated with the external activities with which you are involved.

COMMENT: This could be used when you are shopping, or when you are walking through a downtown area, or when you are performing chores. It could be reduced to the single syllable of 'aim.'

Journey Homeward
(*safar dar watan*)

MEANING: Travel constantly from the world of appearances to the world of unity and transcendent reality.

COMMENT: This would be useful in the natural break or pause between activities. It could be reduced to 'Self' or 'BE.'

The great advantage of the precision-engineered Work 'I's is that they are not discursive and so escape the context of 'me thinking about myself.' They are just 'punched in' in service of presence, according to the Nine of Heart's assessment of the situation. Should one Work 'I' fail, the next is ready at hand.

Having sketched the nature of the White Queen and her retinue of Work 'I's, we are in the position to make an important point. While the perfected Work 'I's serve the emergent presence of the Higher Centers, the White Queen stands ever-poised to give ground, and to disengage from these Work 'I's the moment that the Higher Centers emerge. She can sense when something higher than herself has emerged and immediately bow to that. She can also sense when this special presence has disappeared and knows the exact moment to re-initiate efforts to displace the Lower Self. The trick is not just in knowing how to sustain a line of effort, but – at the same time – knowing how to yield to the Higher Centers in the moment they arrive. It is the development of this

Figure 4. **Six Angels Bowing**

capacity in the Steward that creates the 'space' in which the White Queen can hope to win the Master Game.

The Concentration of the Steward

We have, then, opened the door to the mysteries of the Steward. This term comes to us from George Gurdjieff, who drew it from ancient teachings of Central Asia and the Middle East. The analogy to the 'good steward' illustrates well the principles of the Great Work and is worth exploring in depth.

This analogy is based on the respective roles of Steward and Master as they existed in the homes of the traditional nobility, where many servants were employed. The role of the Steward was to manage the running of the house for the Master. In the Master's absence he maintained the house and managed the staff as they would have been maintained and managed in the Master's presence. In other words the Steward attempts to do all the things the Master would do if he were there. When the Master returns, the Steward hands over the control of the house to him. But the Master's rule is different from the Steward's. His aim is not simply to maintain the house, but to use it for his own purposes: to entertain, to host gatherings, to make political and family alliances. The Steward must step back, then, and allow the Master's greater vision to hold sway. But when he does so he does not cease to serve. He continues to ensure that all the detail work is correctly done and that all the deadlines are met – so that the concerns of maintaining the house do not take up the Master's time. The good Steward is adept at alternating between the active and the passive modes of service.

Developing this analogy, the condition of our 'house' is that the Master has gone on indeterminate leave. It is not that the house does not have a Master, but that he will not return until such time as the house has been properly prepared – because he will not be able to do what he needs to do unless the house is ready. To make matters worse, we begin without a Steward. We have only the general staff and the knowledge that a Steward is needed. So we must somehow 'train up' a Steward to manage the house until such time as the Master returns. Additionally – unlike the noble household – we must train the Steward to recognize the Master when he comes so that he can change the kind of work he does the moment the Master arrives. Our Steward must become adept at working in both the active and the passive modes. Very specifically, the Steward must be trained to **1)** control and monitor the level below himself and **2)** allow himself to be used by a higher level.

This understanding of the role of the Steward allows us to better understand the under-lying conflict between the Black Queen (the nine of clubs) and the White Queen (the Nine of Hearts).

The Black Queen is active day and night, guarding against anything that might in-terfere with the animal process of instinctive self-maintenance. In the beginning of the Work the retinue of the White Queen has nothing like the Black Queen's vigilance or consistency. There are only moments of presence in a day, and only a very small part of us understands the implication of these moments. Even when we experience prolonged presence, a host of thoughts, feelings, and motor-impulses quickly re-engages us in the life of the four lower centers. Once we begin to acquire proficiency in the work, the situation becomes even more difficult. Moments of consciousness begin to show as unidentified 'incursions' on the radar-scan of the Black Queen, and – just as she knows how to release different antibodies to counter different toxins and bacteria – she releases the thoughts, feelings, and motor-impulses that will deflect our work. The potential ruses of the Black Queen are almost unlimited.

Our situation does indeed seem grim. But the White Queen has one advantage: her memory can connect with moments of presence that have occurred in the past. And the more of this 'objective memory' we have, the more the White Queen can 'remember' the reality of Higher Centers when we are in the grip of the Lower Self. Objective memory gives strength, hope, and purpose. With access to this memory, the White Queen can know her aim, know what she is doing, and so learn to persist in that. The Black Queen, on the other hand, just 'does what she does,' trying to perpetuate things the way they are, without knowing what – exactly – that condition is or what the work of the White Queen entails. Thus, while the game begins on the Black Queen's ground, she herself is unaware of the larger context or of what is ultimately at stake. While she is supremely vigilant within her sphere and possessed of almost unlimited tactics, she has no underlying strategy.

The White Queen, understanding something of the context of this struggle, is able to gather about herself a circle of tried and tested Work 'I's – her Steward. But she will not be able to achieve victory by simply adding to this retinue until her forces outnumber those of the Black Queen. *If her retinue becomes too large she will be defeated*, because the will of the Steward will be split into many little wills, which are easily deflected by the many devices of the Black Queen. Additionally, if the group of work 'I's in service to the White Queen is too large and too loosely organized, the sense of immediacy required to penetrate the moment of NOW will be weakened. Once a small disciplined core of 'I's has been fined and honed in her service, it will be much harder for the Black Queen to take possession of them.

When the White Queen has established her small but effective retinue, she can guide or coordinate all of the less focused work-related 'I's that were developed in the course of the First Work. If, for example, we are trying to sustain a World 12 'presence' while driving a car, the White Queen can make use of the 'I's from the lower functions that know how to drive a car well and make them serve that higher 'presence.' She will not allow herself to become dispersed in the car-driving 'I's because she does not take them at their own valuation. By maintaining an awareness of these 'I's as being separate from herself, she is able to use them rather than be used by them. The moment we stop driving the car they drop back into storage, and we give our energies entirely to the challenge of the next moment.

And so we come to the principle of **the concentration of the Steward**. The more developed the Steward, the smaller and more concentrated it is. It is this very concentration that enables it to make intentional use of more and more of the pieces on the chessboard. Each time the Steward becomes smaller we experience a kind of death. We leave behind an older, more 'casually-expansive' self. Indeed the process of awakening can be viewed as the series of 'deaths' that occur as the circle of 'I's around the Steward becomes smaller and more concentrated – and so more deft and precise in their work to enable the Higher Centers. After each phase of concentration the 'I's that were cast out can return, but not as part of the Steward itself. They simply re-enter the larger retinue of 'I's that exists in the Steward's immediate vicinity. After decades of work our identity becomes concentrated into a single point-instant that can see all of the 'I's that exist outside of it and use or counter them as necessary. This point-instant can then command the whole of the person that we are while at the same time existing independently of it.

To enable this process the Spiritual Traditions often employ a mantra, or prayer, or *zhikr* – a short sequence of spoken or unspoken words. These can run over many hours consecutively, as in the Orthodox 'prayer of the heart' (which is considered to be the 'Unceasing Prayer' that the Apostle Paul advocated in the New Testament) or in a particular pattern of alternating mantra and wordless presence prescribed by the Tradition. The sustained use of this 'sequence' acts as a forcing house, educating and concentrating the Steward.

Of course it is possible that the process of concentration could occur without the use of a special technique, but it would then need direct and almost continuous guidance from a conscious source. The aspirant would have to somehow be brought to a continuous, impartial awareness of the internal resistance to awakening (the Lower Self). The 'center' of that resistance – the Black Queen – would then have to be evoked with a certain frequency so that the aspirant would be forced to separate his or her identity from it. Without this repeated exposure the aspirant would never struggle hard enough.

The 'repeated' exposure could be engineered in different ways. An aspirant uninstructed in the 'science of centers' could be given a special duty by the Gods and then shown repeatedly that he was unable to fulfill that duty. In this way he could be made aware that there was something inside of him that was working directly against the aims given him by the Gods. In reaction to this disturbing insight he might then attempt to find out what this resistance was and begin a concentrated struggle to disengage from it. For this method to succeed, just enough pressure would have to be applied in just the right way – not enough to defeat or destroy – but enough to significantly motivate. And this critical balance would have to be maintained over an extended period of time.

As human beings are utterly incapable of arranging these circumstances for themselves, the 'direct method' would in fact require the direct involvement of the Gods. Historically, this kind of involvement occurs when a conscious role is necessary to a Civilization, such as the role of Socrates to Classical Greece, or the role of Queen

THE STORY OF MAN

Elizabeth I to England, or the role of Abraham Lincoln to fledgling America. It is wonderful when it happens, but it happens only to a few. Therefore the Spiritual Traditions, in order to succeed, must perfect different methods.

There is a final point to be made: the Steward is not a 'thing.' There is a danger in thinking of the Steward as a something 'I' possess. This kind of thinking allows the illusion of 'I' to persist. The Steward only exists as a living exercise of the will, one effort after the next, alternating with the intentional and timed cessation of effort. Continuity is given by the connection to objective memory that resides in the Nine of Hearts and the unique valuation for the awakened state that arises from that. The Steward could thus be likened to a concentrated field of energy, which must further concentrate itself or be dispersed. In the moment we imagine we have a Steward, independently of making the effort which that moment requires, the Black Queen can insert herself – claiming a sense of identity as the 'developed Steward,' the 'virtuous monk,' or the 'devoted yogi.' And thus the teaching of the Steward brings us to the sustained tension of the Master Game.

From the Steward to Higher Centers

Having defined the Work of the Steward, we can examine the relation of the Steward to the level that is immediately above it: Higher Centers. This is – at the same time – looking at what happens when the teaching of the Steward is applied.

We will begin by clarifying the distinction between the Work of the Steward and the First Work, or the work that is initiated from the four lower centers. *The First Work* is reactive. Sensations, thoughts, and feelings continually arise in us. We recognize them for what they are, and we bring the appropriate Work 'I' to counter them. With some training we are able to consistently counter the 'I's of the Lower Self, and at this point a real struggle begins – but *it is a struggle that takes place on the terrain of the Lower Self.* Both the 'I's generated from the Lower Self and the Work 'I's that counter them arise from the level of the functions, and on this level the Lower Self holds sway. Thus the Lower Self always has the initiative, imagination is always already there, and we achieve only occasional moments of freedom from it. To succeed we need to move away from a 'reactive' work to a kind of work where the White Queen is able to take the initiative.

We noted that, in the Work of the Steward, the aspirant is trained to use a mantra, or short sequence of words, to increase the frequency of effort. This sequence provides, at the same time, *a timed space of non-effort* in which the fledgling Higher Centers can realize themselves. The timed gap is usually measured by a set number of wordless inhalations and exhalations of the breath. In this way the sequence incorporates the principle of non-effort and allows for the cumulative deepening of what we have called 'objective memory.'

With the help of such a technique *the Steward is able to take the initiative from the Lower Self and to pre-empt it*. With practice, the Steward can anticipate the Lower Self's interruptions to the mantra and counter them before the interfering 'I' is able to occupy the space. Thus, where the lesser work is reactive, and battles on the terrain of the Lower Self, the greater work engages the Lower Self by attempting to occupy all the space of our being. This more continuous initiative brings to light the subtle and continuous ploys of the Black Queen, and we become yet more adept at predicting and preempting these ploys.

But, at the same time the Steward takes the initiative from the Lower Self, it must learn to become increasingly sensitive to the emergent Higher Centers and yield space to them in the moment they appear. This is – for the Steward – an acceptance of death. In 'kneeling' to Higher Centers the Steward must ultimately and unconditionally 'give way.' **The Death of the Steward** is, in fact, a learned discipline, requiring great rigor. All Traditions highlight this moment in one way or another: in the Sanskrit of the Vedas it is the surrender of *ahamkara* ('I'-related mental activity); in the Pali canon of the Buddha's teachings it is *anatta* (not 'I-making'); in the Sufi teaching it is *fana* (the annihilation of self in God); in Christian monastic practice it is the transition from active contemplation (πραξις, praxis) to infused contemplation (θεωρία, theoria). The Death of the Steward is the final moment of the transition through to the new level; if the Steward does not yield the new level will not come.

Thus, a fully developed Steward works in the continuous awareness of three different levels: **1)** that of the Lower Self, **2)** that of its own internal dynamic, and **3)** that of the Higher Centers. It must know to respond immediately to developments on each level, and it must know when and how to cease its own activity. Thus the chosen technique – sequence, mantra, or other – creates a kind of provisional form which, on the one hand, places strict limitations on the Lower Self, and, on the other hand, creates a space in which Higher Centers can emerge.

The transition we have just described represents a fundamental change in the way the Master Game is played, and there is an analogy that illustrates this difference. Under the pressures of competition a champion billiard player, a world-class tennis player, or a chess master may achieve a complete concentration of attention – for ten or fifteen minutes at a time. This is called 'being in the zone.' Being in this state is actually becoming one with the game itself, so that one's personal hopes, fears, and enmities simply go up in smoke. One becomes the living incarnation of billiards, or tennis, or chess. In the Work of the Steward 'being at one with the game' is working directly in the light of Higher Centers. Imagination is no longer an obstacle – the lower centers are both completely engaged and completely transcended.

These moments of transcendence, when one's energy is not entirely absorbed in the cut and thrust of struggle, directly create objective memory. One knows that one knows that one knows. When moments such as these become more frequent, the Work of the Steward becomes cumulative in a way that the First Work could never be. The context of one's work begins to shift from the field of the four lower centers (Worlds 96, 48, 24) to the plane of the Higher Centers (Worlds 12 and 6). To return to the analogy of sport, where, in the First Work, the combatant retires exhausted at the end of every round, and when the bell sounds for the next round the opponent is already in center ring, in the Second Work one is always already there, and the Lower Self is always on the defensive.

When we accumulate conscious energy in this way, the invisible screen of awareness, which is the forgotten backdrop of our existence, begins to shimmer into life. Higher Centers begin to become aware of themselves. Thus we initiate a line of effort, not just in reaction to the 'I's generated by the Lower Self, but in the attempt to sustain the mirror-like awareness of Higher Centers. One lets go of the future and the past, allowing the short sequence to occupy the center-space of one's being. At this stage each breath, each word of the sequence or mantra, becomes a world of its own as we prepare ourselves to go through the 'eye of the needle.' Our entire being is concentrated into the point-instant of 'now.' It is like Aladdin learning to rub the magic lamp in just the right way to make the genie appear.

When the Steward achieves this level of concentration, it can attempt to sustain the same level of work even when the chosen sequence or mantra is not in use. But whether a sequence is used or not, this is the intensity required to make an 'active link' to Higher Centers. One sees both the threat of the Lower Self and the potential for Higher Centers all of the time.

At this point it becomes much easier to adjust one's line of effort to the periodic experiences of Higher Centers that do occur. In moments of Higher Centers we see, in much greater depth than we normally do, the difference between consciousness and functions; we see how to observe and counter the many 'I's without engaging them;

we see how to fine-tune the timing of our efforts; we see which efforts are suitable to which circumstances; we may even see new places to make efforts from. Thus, when the experience of Higher Centers comes, it does not pass away as though it had never been but leaves traces that educate and refine our line of effort. All of this can be achieved because *a space has been created in which the Nine of Hearts can receive communication from Higher Centers.* The Higher Centers can teach the White Queen to value transcendent reality for what it is, and the White Queen can, in her turn, adjust the different parts of centers and the particular Work 'I's that are incorporated into the Steward to make an optimal line of effort.

In order to complete our understanding of the difference between the First Work and the Work of the Steward, we must look more closely at a particular aspect of the latter: *the Work of the Steward both requires effort and transcends effort.*

We will recall that the goal of the First Work was to bring the four lower centers into an open and receptive state. This is a goal to be achieved in the line of time, and progress towards it can be benchmarked in different ways. A person becomes less selfish, more open, more receptive, and more compassionate. However, this attitude of 'gradual improvement' does not apply to the Work of the Steward. The goal to achieve prolonged presence cannot be seen as something which is achieved in the line of time, at least not in the way that the First Work understands it.

Here is the problem in a nutshell. Given that Higher Centers represent the highest value known to man, it is impossible not to experience ambition in relation to them, and effort driven by ambition is a direct obstacle to their realization. Ambition exists in the line of time, and it is essentially selfish. True presence exists outside of time. It exists before we make our effort, while we are making it, and after the effort is complete. And it is completely unselfish.

The Work of the Steward must, then, finally transcend the goal-seeking attitude that is part of life in the line of time. In the First Work we make efforts in the anticipation of a result. In the Work of the Steward we must continue making efforts, and even make more efforts than we made before, but we must separate ourselves from any expectation of a result. This is a fundamental truth taught by all the Spiritual Traditions, and beautifully expressed in the Bhagavad Gita. Krishna, representing the level of World 6, instructs Arjuna, representing the Steward:

> When all a man's emprises
> Have neither motive nor desire for fruit
> His works consumed in wisdom's fire –

Then wise men call him learned.
Content to take whatever chance may bring his way,
Surmounting all dualities, knowing no envy,
The same in failure and success,
Though working still, he is not bound.[9]

In this way we separate our sense of identity from the efforts that we make. When we become adept at disengaging from our efforts, we begin to master the art of sustaining presence and making effort at the same time. This is not an art that can be mastered through the lower centers alone. To achieve mastery both the developed Steward and the emergent Higher Centers must be active at the same time. When a right balance is achieved between these two, the Higher Centers may, in certain moments, take control and begin to work for themselves.

This explains why, although the aim of the Traditions is to awaken Higher Centers, the focal point of their teaching is the Work of the Steward – for the Steward is not only the means to enable Higher Centers, *it can become the means by which Higher Centers sustain themselves.* Whatever level the Higher Centers of a man or a woman may reach, the Steward is their necessary vehicle, as long as that person is embodied. And when an embodied being develops a level of consciousness that survives its own physical death, enabling a purely molecular embodiment, the functions of the Steward persist, although in an entirely different form. This qualifies what we have said about the death of the Steward. But, when the Higher Centers are themselves able to manage the functions of the Steward, we have gone beyond the work of the Schools of Men on earth. We must speak, then, of Schools that exist in the Realm of the Gods. Indeed the development of Higher Centers only begins in the work of the highest Saints and Avatars. The work that is initiated by the Spiritual Traditions is pursued and completed in other Higher Schools.

And at this point we are in a position to clarify what we mean by *Higher Schools*, and what it means that the Spiritual Traditions are linked to them.

Rodney Collin, whom we quoted above on the subject of imagination, stated that any real school of human development (any Spiritual Tradition) is connected to a Higher School: "a school on a higher level than the one being created … where the regeneration of higher beings than ordinary man is being conducted."[10] The Teacher of such a

---

9. Verses IV19 and IV22 of the Bhagavad Gita translated by R.C. Zaehner, from *Hindu Scriptures*, ed. Dominic Goodall, Phoenix, London, 1996, p. 227.
10. Rodney Collin, *Theory of Celestial Influence*, p. 328.

Tradition would be, at the same time, a beginning student in the Higher School that was connected to it. This fact strongly links the two levels of school. One thing this linkage implies is that when a man becomes fully conscious and succeeds in disengaging his identity from his cellular body, he continues to evolve – in a molecular body – under the guidance of yet higher beings.

There are several levels of Higher School. We recall Dante's description of the concentric rings of Gods, who 'pursue their rounded paths' in order that they may become as like the Absolute as they can. In so doing each of the Gods actively aspires to enter into the ring that is immediately above his own and to lift the Gods who are in the ring immediately below it. Dante's image represents what Rodney Collin called the different levels of Higher School. The Gods on each ring aspire to enter the ring above and promote the evolution of those on the ring one below.

These concentric rings are not simply means for the Gods to ascend. Each ring has its necessary function within Creation. A single ring cannot be vacated. Thus, in their ascent from ring to ring, the Gods need to replace themselves. When they succeed in doing this, the rings, or 'coils,' remain intact while the individual Gods move upwards through them. What we have called the Great Spiritual Traditions are the lowest level in this hierarchy, but they are equally subject to the law of 'replacement.' The Traditions are unique in that, in the process of replacement, they must draw from a level of sentient being (i.e., humanity) in which the Higher Centers are only latent. And thus the necessary progression of the First Work and the Work of the Steward.

The Link with Essence

Having outlined the Work of the Steward, we can return to the problem broached in the section "Different Kinds of Presence and Different Kinds of Work." How is it possible that there can be any continuity between the experience of the lower centers and the experience of the Higher Centers? How is it possible to link time and eternity? To state the problem in its most extreme form: if a man were to achieve a transcendent presence that was entirely independent of his four lower centers, this would represent a definitive break in his experience of life. In other words, there would be no continuity between the new identity, based on the Higher Centers, and the old identity, rooted in the lower centers. Awakening would then, from the human point of view, be death and nothing more.

We have already qualified the idea of such a radical break by showing how the lower centers can serve the Higher Centers and how the Nine of Hearts can connect with the 'memory' of Higher Centers. These links are formed through the agency of the Steward. But this does not alter the fact that, at some point, the Steward itself must permanently and finally yield to Higher Centers. There will come the moment when a complete molecular body has been developed, and the Higher Centers have matured to a point where they can directly face the challenges that are before them – and at this point the Steward (at least the Steward as developed out of the lower centers) falls away.

We are now in a position to outline a second line of continuity between the life of the lower centers and the life of the Higher Centers that is literally 'from here to eternity.' To understand this we must understand **the idea of essence**. The practical teaching of each of the Traditions includes the cultivation of an aspect of our being that has been called 'essence.' While this term sounds philosophical, it refers to something quite simple and personal that can only be understood on the basis of first hand experience. In other words you learn to determine when you are 'in essence' in the same way you learn to determine whether or not you are coming down with the flu, or whether or not a strong romantic attraction is actually the basis for marriage, or whether a certain kind of job or career is the one 'for you' – by direct and careful observation.

Briefly stated, essence is 'who you are' at the level of the four lower centers, without artifice or deception of any kind. This is the natural condition of an infant. In certain moments we have all seen infants in a completely open state, at one with whatever is around them yet at the same time existent in themselves. They are who they are, in a very open and receptive frame of mind, and there is a fluid, spontaneous joyfulness connected with this.

While this state affects each of the four lower centers, it is based in the emotional center; it is, from one point of view, a certain quality of emotional life. Normally, as we grow older and the emergent 'false' personality grows, creating a coarse carapace of negative emotions around the emotional center, essence recedes. This is how it is able to survive. The process accelerates particularly during the years of adolescence. Indeed essence often becomes completely dormant in adults, yet it does have its place in the normal adult life: in the period when young parents play with their children, in the deepest moments of love, and in the presence of great beauty. Having a healthy essence is a condition for entering the work, in that the work must be based on what is most real in us. The seed must be planted in good earth.

Thus, it is the responsibility of the Spiritual Traditions, particularly during the period of the First Work, to ensure the development of essence – for a human being cannot form a right connection to Higher Centers except from this place. This situation exactly parallels that of human learning in other fields. A great ballet principal must dance from her essence, a great violinist must play from her essence, a great actor must act from his essence – or their performances will not be art. And this is most true of the greatest art of all: the work to enable Higher Centers. The deepest challenge that essence can face, beyond love and beyond art, is the direct experience of Higher Centers.

One reason we must begin from essence is that, in essence, the barriers of artificial individuality are not strong. When you fall in love, you can feel at one with the other person. When you hear a great concert performance, you feel at one with the music. And in the same way, when you enter deeply into the work, you must be able to feel at one with it. This does not just happen. Essence must be healed and nurtured in many ways before this can occur. With patience, over time, essence can be trained to higher things – firstly, things compatible with the work, and then the work itself. Essence is the foundation in the human for a result that transcends the human.

This is one reason why the Traditions have so consistently used art. Just as essence can be trained to respond to art, it can be trained to respond to presence itself, and even to take presence as its highest value. The objective art of the Traditions is the perfect bridge between the two. We recall the 'atmosphere' of the miraculous in which the Traditions work: awe, wonder, and the renewal of life. In such an environment essence can be instilled with a sense of the sacred. One thinks of the experience of a child on a clear summer night, looking deep into the starry heavens.

At a certain point in the development of the Steward, essence begins to evolve in relation to it. The process of 'coming into being' attracts essence in just the same way that falling in love with another person attracts essence. It is the destiny of essence to love the emergent Higher Centers, a destiny that far transcends the highest mortal love. Thus, as the action of the Nine of Hearts concentrates the Steward, essence becomes more and more integrated into its workings. Our essence is then in the process of awakening. But where the rational structure of the Steward must yield to Higher Centers, essence can fuse with them to produce something entirely new. They will become one. Specifically, the fine molecular energies of essence actually unite with the molecular and

THE STORY OF MAN

electronic energies of the emergent Higher Centers to produce a new kind of being in the Universe.[11]

Thus, there is something in essence that can ultimately survive the death of the Steward. It is through this fusion of essence with Higher Centers that man brings something original and unique into the higher levels of creation.

The Teaching of the Steward and the Great Work

With the direct work on Higher Centers and the heightening of the conflict between the Black Queen and the White Queen, we enter the sphere of the Great Work. Through the development of the Steward, we have created the space in which the Nine of Hearts can communicate with the fledgling Higher Centers, and – at the same time – we are faced with the moment-to-moment resistance of the Lower Self. We live in the immediate memory of Higher Centers and in the moment-to-moment awareness of the initiatives of the Black Queen. From this point onward there is no turning back; you must now play the game until the clock runs out. At least this is how it looks from the level of the Steward. But in moments of 'prolonged presence,' when the Higher Centers come into their own, we are already beyond this.[12] We have transcended the battle while the enemy is still engaged. We are both on and off the chessboard.

From one point of view this is the Story of Man: that men enter into this space and live from it, and that through this Higher Centers become part of the human experience. To the extent that this is possible, Higher Centers can guide or influence human affairs, and the link between this world and higher worlds is opened. Mankind can then re-enter its original state, where there was a direct and open communication with the Gods.

And, as we have already noted, human evolution ultimately goes beyond the Work of the Steward. While the education of the Steward is the art of the Traditions, it is so

---

11. Franklin Merrell-Wolff describes this mystical fusion in his own terms in *Pathways through to Space* (Julian Press, NY, 1973 – first written 1936). When, in the passage to follow, he uses the term 'microcosm,' he refers to the inner life of the four lower centers, as given form by our personality. When he refers to a 'fluidic vortex of force,' he refers to essence, in the state that makes its transition from the environment of the four lower centers to the environment of the Higher Centers. On page 202 he writes: "The microcosm is melted, as it were, so that it is no longer crystallized but remains as a fluidic vortex of force, continuous with the Universal Force, yet, in a sense, distinguishable as a vortex. This is the Path that leads to the highest Destiny of Man."

12. See the Glossary entry for 'Prolonged Presence.'

because it is the means of bringing Higher Centers into existence. What the Work of the Traditions enables goes infinitely beyond our initial, halting experiences of presence.

Rainer Maria Rilke puts this well:

> Center of all centers, core of cores,
> almond self-enclosed and growing sweet –
> all this universe, to the furthest stars
> and beyond them, is your flesh, your fruit.
> Now you feel how nothing clings to you;
> your vast shell reaches into endless space,
> and there the rich, thick fluids rise and flow.
> Illuminated in your infinite peace,
> a billion stars go spinning through the night,
> blazing high above your head.
> But in you is the presence that
> will be, when all the stars are dead.[13]

In such a state of presence the connection between men and Gods comes alive. Having said this, we can say something more about the connection itself, which is the very basis of the Great Work.

Because the difference between Men and Gods is not a difference of quantity but a difference of quality, the relation between the two can never be casual. Even within the highest Spiritual Traditions, there would only be a few capable of communicating directly with the Gods and that under enormous pressure. For those communications to have any impact on humanity at large, the circle surrounding these individuals would also have to be working at a high level. The link between levels, once established, is the relation between Life and Higher Life. It is like an open vein that enters deep into the heart of Man. Once this channel has been opened, the Gods want those closest to its source to change, to open themselves to communication on ever deeper levels. This is difficult because the obstacles to communication lie at the very roots of human nature. And, in the environment of the Gods, the demand to 'move from the place that you are' – to open, to yield, to surrender one's passions and life-illusions – is unrelenting. For this reason the atmosphere of the Traditions is never even; it is an atmosphere of crisis and transcendence, for it is only when we are deeply challenged that we are at our

---

13. 'Buddha in Glory,' from *Ahead of All Parting: The Selected Poetry and Prose of Rainer Maria Rilke*, (ed. and trans. Stephen Mitchell), Random House, Inc., New York, 1995.

best. In a situation where everyone is confident, happy and outwardly fulfilled … there the Gods are not.

Opening communication with the Gods enables man to render conscious service to them. It is this capacity to serve that ensures that the connection is more than casual or arbitrary. Service to the Gods means accepting their initiatives with respect to Higher Centers, but it also includes carrying out specific tasks in relation to the external world. The Great Work is completed, then, by the external tasks given the Traditions by the Gods. These tasks allow the Traditions to serve humanity at large and in so doing to complete themselves as the last concentric ring of the Celestial Hierarchy.

We are now in a position to complete our definition of a Spiritual Tradition:

1. A Spiritual Tradition engages directly in work to open and enable the Higher Centers. It teaches and transmits the Work of the Steward.

2. A Spiritual Tradition is connected to Higher School, and its most developed members are held directly accountable to the Gods. When this condition holds, a Tradition is competent to practice The Great Work.

3. A Spiritual Tradition is a school with different operative levels which are closely connected. It provides an environment in which a very high Teacher monitors the work of several Men Number Five. Below this there is a much larger group of Men Number Four, working to become Men Number Five. Below this there is an even larger number of Men Number Four who are stable in their line of effort at that level. Below this there is the largest level of all – spiritual novices aspiring to the level of Man Number Four. Each of these levels serves the level one above and lifts the level one below.

Some Definitions

We have, over the preceding pages, introduced a set of related terms which are not in common usage and not easy to understand. As the meanings of these terms are interdependent, it is useful to review them all at once. Some of the terms listed below have already been defined, some have been introduced but defined only provisionally, and a few appear for the first time. Presenting them together, in direct relation to one another, will allow us to consolidate what we have understood, before proceeding to Chapter 4.

Higher School

A school in which the regeneration of higher beings than ordinary man is conducted. Generally this term is used to refer to the level of school that is immediately above the schools of men, although it is sometimes used as a shorthand reference for 'all levels of school' above the human. The Gods who are students in Higher School are attempting to:

1. Help the most developed members of the human race enter the Sphere of Sentient Being, and

2. Achieve the level of work that defines the next 'concentric ring' of the Celestial Hierarchy.

As the Gods need to 'put someone in their place' in order to ascend, so they need to draw into their company the men and women in whom Higher Centers have begun to become active. They do this principally through the Spiritual Traditions. Because the Gods are reliant on the Spiritual Traditions for their 'replacements,' they must ensure that both the Traditions themselves and the different Civilizations that support them are in a condition to provide candidates.

Spiritual Tradition

A Spiritual Tradition is a vehicle for the Great Work and so must exist in a direct relation to Higher School. Indeed the defining point of a Tradition is that *it originates in the work of Higher School.* This relationship is secured in the line of time by the work of conscious beings who are members both of the Spiritual Tradition and of the Higher School with which it is connected. This link being secured, the Tradition is both responsible to and representative of Higher School. The first task of a Tradition is to sustain the Work of the Steward in such a way as to enable Higher Centers within its members. If it can succeed with this task – and only if it can succeed with this task – it will have the hope of succeeding with the various external tasks given it from Higher School.

Presence

The standard English language usage of the word 'presence' does not allow us to tell the story of the Spiritual Traditions, because this usage refers to the presence of the four lower centers. In these pages we also use this term to refer to the presence of the two Higher Centers, always keeping the distinction between the two clear.

The lower centers can be present to what is before them in the moment, but they cannot know presence itself, independently of thought, emotion, sensation, and movement. Indeed, a profound moment of wordless presence is a 'break' in the life of the four lower centers. It is an entirely different quality of experience. There is presence, and there is something that knows itself to be present … moment after moment after moment. The life of the Higher Centers begins in these gaps between the 'I's and culminates in the transcendent, universal life of a God.

Prolonged Presence

Prolonged Presence is a state of presence that is sustained through time. Only when presence is sustained through time can it know itself for what it is and become fully self-aware.[14] With special work, moments of presence self-aware can turn into *presence self-sustaining*. This is not the presence of the lower centers sustained by effort but the newly-awakened Higher Centers learning to sustain themselves. This 'special work' is the culmination of the work of the Spiritual Traditions. When presence is able to sustain itself through time, we have the beginning of an entirely new kind of identity, the completion of which is sometimes called the Self, or Soul.[15]

14. See the Glossary for 'Presence Aware of Itself.'
15. See the Glossary for a more detailed definition of 'Prolonged Presence.'

The Work of the Steward	The specific line of inner work taught by the Traditions. This work is designed to enable the transition through to the Sphere of Sentient Being. For the practitioners of this work everything becomes irrelevant but the present, or – put differently – everything becomes a means to presence. The ultimate fruition of the Work of the Steward is a state of Prolonged Presence, in which the presence of the Higher Centers becomes fully self-sustaining.
The First Work	A work preparatory to the Work of the Steward. It prepares the four lower centers for the direct work on Higher Centers that takes place within the Traditions. In the European Middle Ages it was called the 'Work on the Virtues.'

Both the First Work and the Work of the Steward are focused on presence, but this focus takes different forms. The difference in focus between the First Work and the Work of the Steward is given by the condition of the four lower centers. The First Work is for someone who is still striving to win freedom from certain personal problems and certain kinds of negative emotion. The Work of the Steward is for someone whose lower centers are already in an open and receptive state and who has – in some degree – transcended his or her personal longings. At this stage awakening is no longer something that 'I' want for 'myself.'

The First Work is a main point of focus for the Living Religions and also for the esoteric 'Groups' (which we shall define in Chapter 4). The First Work is also practiced by the Spiritual Traditions, but only as a means of enabling the Work of the Steward.

If an aspirant has not completed the First Work, the Work of the Steward will very likely produce wrong results.

The Great Work	Higher School has a clear understanding of the plan for each Spiritual Tradition, and for humanity itself. The plan for humanity is quite unlike the plans that humanity invents for itself. It is much more along the lines of a gardener's plan

for breeding new varieties of rose. The gardener makes tests and watches carefully for the results. He then takes new initiatives on the basis of these results. Where the gardener works in light of an ideal of beauty, Higher School works in light of the archetype of true individuality and collective life. Thus, while the plan for humanity allows for experiment, it is a plan designed to produce definite results. These results were given in the higher potentials which Mankind was inseminated with at the time of its creation.

Higher School's plan for humanity translates, in the actual circumstances of history, into the many particular plans implemented by many different Traditions. Higher School executes its plans through the Traditions. The specific tasks that are produced from these plans may include the creation of new civilizations, the regeneration of existing civilizations, the development of new social institutions, and the creation of great art, monumental sculpture, and enduring architectural works. Thus, when the Traditions execute these plans, they are serving both the level one above and the level one below, while being held accountable to both levels.

The necessary condition of all of these plans is that the members of the Traditions place a first priority on awakening, and thus the Work of the Steward is always the first dimension of the Great Work.

Death of the Steward The intentional cessation of the activity of the Steward in the moment that Higher Centers make their appearance. The Steward must learn to immediately and unconditionally yield to the Higher Centers in the moment they appear, or it will impede their coming. The Death of the Steward is a learned discipline, requiring great rigor. It is the final moment of the transition through to the new level; if the Steward does not yield, the new level will not come. As the

Steward evolves and concentrates, it dies to itself repeatedly, like a snake shedding successive skins.

Teacher

With respect to entering a state of prolonged presence and penetrating the Sphere of Sentient Being, men need to be taught. This is much more like being taught how to swim than being taught philosophy or theology. The people who teach swimming must themselves know how to swim and so reassure their students that it is possible. It is a very practical matter. We have chosen the term 'Teacher' over terms like 'guru,' 'master,' or 'saint,' because of the romantic and subjective overtones the latter have acquired.

Prophet

A world-historical Teacher sent from Higher School. The Prophet is tasked from Higher School not only with respect to the Spiritual Traditions that develop from his work, but with respect to the Civilizational Order that supports these Traditions, and with respect to Humanity at large. The Prophet is at a level where he can understand all paths to awakening and can see all men as images of himself. The Prophet is the foremost vehicle of the Great Work.

Prophetic Tradition

A Spiritual Tradition that takes form under the influence of a Prophet. It arises out of the life of the community that develops around the Prophet when he begins to teach. In the intensity of the first years of Prophetic teaching, the distinctions between Tradition, Living Religion, and Civilization are blurred – usually achieving stable external form only after the Prophet's death. Within the Prophet's community, during his lifetime, we could say that the Tradition is the 'inner form' and the Religion is the 'outer form.' A minority of Traditions are Prophetic Traditions, but most Traditions do refer themselves to one Prophet or another – signifying that they came into being in the environment that a particular Prophet helped to create.

Living Religion   A Religion which acknowledges and receives life from a Tradition. Such a Religion has some ability to recognize 'consciousness' in the senior members of the Tradition to which it is connected. A Living Religion sustains the First Work and may itself support certain conscious roles.

Living Religion shows openness and compassion; it is the 'charity' of the European Middle Ages or the spirit of the bodhisattva vow in ancient India. There is not a judgment of the world outside of religion, but understanding and a genuine acceptance of the human condition.

Unfortunately, in the fabric of history, Living Religion usually coexists with Dead Religion and can – as if by magic – disappear into the latter at any time.

Dead Religion   A Religion which is not connected to a Tradition and which does not acknowledge conscious influence. Its worship is based on prescribed forms and procedures and on previously recorded knowledge rather than on the direct experience of Higher Centers. Dead Religion can descend to become the opposite of Living Religion, actually persecuting the Spiritual Traditions and pursuing its own material interests through warfare and barbaric practices.

Religion   We have sometimes used this term in the descriptive, generic sense to refer to the great religions of history, such as the Hindu, the Buddhist, the Judaic, the Christian, and the Islamic. These Religions may be at one time living and at another time dead.

Civilization   A Civilization is a human community connected, in an essential or formative way, to a Spiritual Tradition. All true Civilizations originate in the work of a Tradition, tasked by Higher School with the founding of such an order. The Tradition may or may not act through the intermediary of a Living Religion. The legacy of the Tradition to the Civilization is a coherent set of values, with a defining art and culture. A true Civilization shows some semblance of a cosmos, as the process of regeneration (the Great Work) is alive within it.

Without the connection to a Tradition there is only simple human community, which is little more than the life of its individual members. In such a community the sense of 'cosmos' atrophies.

School Civilization

A School Civilization is a Civilization *actually governed* by a Spiritual Tradition, and, through this Tradition, it is connected directly to Higher School. It does not simply have the semblance of a cosmos; it is a cosmos. In a School Civilization, Mankind is governed by the principles of the Great Work and so enters into service to the Absolute. The events that befall it are not accidental but part of a preordained destiny.

We shall now introduce three new terms which were used by the Hermetic/Alchemical Traditions to define three different levels of energy that are processed by the human organism and that form the context of human development. In the pages to follow we shall use these terms (amongst others) to distinguish Tradition, Religion, and Civilization. Different words have been used to label these energies over the centuries. The labels we have selected are 'cellular,' 'molecular,' and 'electronic.' In the Vedic Tradition they were called gross, subtle, and mental; in the ancient Hermetic Traditions etheric, astral, and causal. We have chosen the terms cellular, molecular, and electronic because they are closer to those of modern science and will probably be more intuitive to a modern reader. Each of these energies has a 'body' which corresponds to it. Our cellular body exists fully formed, while the molecular and electronic bodies are only potential in us. Having said this much, we must add a fourth term to the list: 'mineral energy.' While we do not have a 'mineral body,' we have a definite component of mineral energy, and it enters deeply into our experience of life – and thus the term is needed to complete the set. While these four terms overlap with those used in modern science, they are not here used as scientific concepts. Our usage is closer to the usage of the 'compound substance' classification in the earlier Hermetic sciences.

Mineral Energy   Simply put, the crystalline mineral compounds are viewed as energy, or as matter having a certain vibrational frequency – and so as being, at least in some degree, 'animate.' Mineral energy is an essential component of the human organism. It is certainly not what defines us as human, but mineral salts are essential to the composition of both our blood and our bones. It could be said that we are 'mineral' by our bone structure. Because mineral energy is part of our composition, we can experience – psychologically – the extraordinary limitations of the mineral world. In the Hermetic classification, the 'average' bandwidth range of the mineral world is that of World 384 (although it extends – through its metallic elements – down into World 768). Thus, as Electronic Energy (Worlds 6 and 3) is at the top of the range of human possibilities (opening into an experience of transparent luminosity, radiance, and cosmic love), Mineral Energy is at the bottom of that range (opening into the claustrophobic and painful experiences of Worlds 384 and 768). The experience of the mineral world corresponds to the terrific density, pressure, and crystallized immobility of the earth's barysphere. It is, for one born human, a state of utter hopelessness and despair, bringing with it the sense of an ultimate evil from which there is no escape.

Cellular Energy   Cellular energies are the energies of physical life. They constitute the 'matter' of our body and its organs. An abundance of cellular energy ensures physical strength, good health, and the ability to efficiently process the different matters that pass through the body. We associate cellular bodies with defined surfaces, physical substance, and a definite weight. Cellular energy is not in itself a sufficient condition for life. For any organism to have 'life,' its field of cellular energies must be completed by at least some molecular energy, for example, that connected with the central nervous system. When the organism dies, its cellular form and the field connected with that form disintegrate entirely.

Molecular Energy

Molecular energy is 'finer' than cellular energy, vibrating at a much higher frequency. It is the energy internal to each of the four lower centers, and, as such, is the 'substance' of our thoughts and feelings. It has much greater powers of penetration and diffusion than cellular energy. Sometimes, for example, we can know the thoughts and feelings of another person, although we are separate from them in space. What we call phantoms or spirits are formations of this energy, existing independently of a cellular body.

It is the molecular range of energies that defines our character, or 'who we are.' In the normal course of life the energies of thought, feeling, and sensation combine into habitual states of anger, fear, envy, love, hope, and joy. As our personality takes form, these habitual 'molecular' states combine in a particular way, in response to the external impacts and pressures of our lives, to form a kind of *ad hoc* molecular body.

This haphazard molecular body (sometimes called the 'desire' body) can survive the death of the 'host' cellular body for a period of time – but not indefinitely. It needs the 'anchoring' of the five senses to relate it to the external world, or it will eventually disperse. A molecular form that is permanently independent of the cellular body can be created by making an intentional use of the 'higher range' of molecular energies, in other words, those that correspond to Worlds 24 and 12. These higher energies are normally mixed in with the 'habitual molecular states' in such a way that they heighten those states and make them seem more real. It is the higher energies normally associated with World 12 – for example – that can mix with emotions of fear, desire, and hatred, giving them an extreme edge. These finer energies must be disengaged from the constricted condition of the 'habitual states' in order to be used for higher purposes.

When the molecular body begins to exist independently of the cellular body, it can itself be 'centered' by electronic energy. When this occurs, a man has acquired a conscious soul.

To say the same thing in a different way, the right use of our molecular energy is to form a Steward in service to the emerging Higher Centers. The Steward can be diverted from this function by **1**) a reassertion of the 'habitual states' or **2**) the fascination of molecular energy with itself, that is, by spiritualism and by different occult practices.

Electronic Energy   An energy much finer than molecular energy, vibrating at a proportionately higher frequency. The electronic energies are not part of the pattern of a normal human life, for the cellular body is not normally able to register the electronic range. In other words, the electronic energies are 'realized' in states so far removed from the experience of everyday that we would not normally be able to remember them. We may momentarily experience electronic energies in crisis moments of our lives or in near-death experiences. Each man and woman experiences electronic energy directly at the time of birth and at the time of death, and this is part of what draws the veil of memory between lifetimes.

Matter in the electronic state produces energy that illuminates everything with which it comes in contact, just as X-rays illuminate the interior of solid objects or ultraviolet rays can cause substances to glow or fluoresce. A body comprised of such energies would be its own illuminant, and a community of such bodies would live in a state of complete transparency to one another. A completed electronic body would give free access to World 6 and, under certain conditions, to World 3.

While electronic energy has little relation to an individual human life, it remains important to humanity – in the sense that it gives Mankind its relation to the Absolute. This relationship is established through those great Teachers and Prophets who possess completed electronic bodies. Those who possess completed electronic bodies influence those who possess completed molecular bodies, who in turn influence the rest of humanity. These influences are exercised through Tradition, Living Religion, and Civilization, each of which contains or concentrates these energies in a certain way.

Having made these distinctions, we can now address the transformation of the human social order into a living cosmos.

CHAPTER 4

The External Work of the Spiritual Traditions

The Cosmos of Man:
The External Dimension of the Great Work

Given the understanding of the Work of the Steward that we have outlined in the previous chapter, Man remains in the longer-term position of doing his best and hoping that grace will come. There is no way of directly invoking Higher Centers, and – at the same time – there is no way of making a truly conscious effort unless Higher Centers are actually present. We cannot change this situation, and for every individual who enters the Great Work it is a periodic source of despair. But there is a way of neutralizing the preoccupation with it and at the same time building a permanent reminding factor. This method is to connect the activities of a School to something outside of itself, through service to the Gods on the level one above and service to humanity on the level one below. Such a double-edged commitment helps to neutralize the inherent, instinctive selfishness which – in every circumstance and in every individual – holds Mankind back from its true line of development. Additionally, it gives something of the universality of the state we hope to achieve. It helps to create a space where something higher than the Steward can emerge, and at the same time it helps to complete the Cosmos of Man. This, then, is the external dimension of the Great Work. Concrete examples of this work would include the construction of the pyramids, the reconstruction of European Civilization after the fall of Rome, and the reconstruction of Islamic civilization in the wake of the Mongol Invasion.

Thus, the men and women who have mastered the Great Work are not all ascetics bound in permanent retreat; they are Peter and Paul, Abu Bakr and Ali, Rabia, Shakespeare, Elizabeth I, and Rembrandt. They are men and women – known and unknown – whose Higher Centers have influenced history. From another point of view we could say that Higher Centers have acted through these men and women to change the world on all levels, for in the world all levels are connected.

At first we noted that the Work of the Traditions, in its external dimension, helps to reconnect humanity to the plan originally created for it. Just as the lower centers of a man can reconnect with his latent Higher Centers, so the different elements of humanity can rediscover the plan or pattern that was given in the beginning. This plan almost certainly included the transformation of humanity into a living cosmos, into a whole whose parts are capable of working together in service of a higher aim. We are now in a position to be more explicit about just what this is, and can address the transformation of the human social order into a living cosmos.

Symbol of the Cosmos of Man:
The Pyramid

The Traditions have used several different symbols to represent the cosmos of man: the Pyramid (Hermetic), the Chain (Orthodox Christian & Sufi), the City (Classical), and the Ladder (Orthodox Christian and Catholic Christian). We will use the symbol of the Pyramid here, because it is the most appropriate for specifying the different levels of human society.

We could visualize a Pyramid with its rarest and most significant elements concentrated near the apex and its least significant and most common elements (those most closely related to the processes of organic life) forming the base.

Because the Pyramid describes a chain of conscious influence, we have not included Dead Religion in the diagram. While we have included Living Religion, it is not a necessary stage of the Pyramid. The functions of Living Religion can be completely fulfilled by a Civilizational Order which is directly connected to a Tradition. This version of the Pyramid, then, has five levels:

1. The Gods or Higher School, existing above Mankind, who recruit from (and regenerate)…

2. Tradition at the top of the human pyramid, which recruits from (and regenerates)…

3. Living Religion, which recruits from (and regenerates)…

4. Civilization, which recruits from (and regenerates)…

5. The general human community.

These elements can exist quite independently of each other, but the optimal situation for humanity is that they should be linked together in the manner shown in Figure 5. This rarely happens. A strong indication of the 'completeness' of the Pyramid – in an actual society – is a working relation between Tradition, Religion, and Civilizational Order. When the Pyramid is complete, there is a living, conscious link between the individual members of a Civilization, the Civilizational Order itself, the Living Religion that it contains, the Tradition that supports the Living Religion, and – through the Tradition – the Gods themselves. Under such circumstances the Civilizational Order

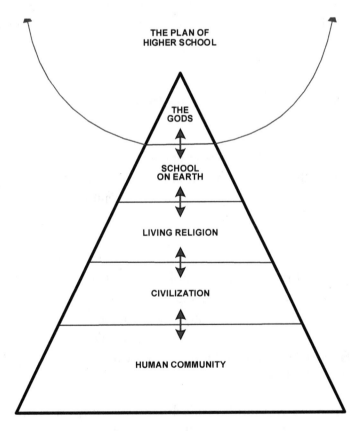

Figure 5. **Diagram of the Pyramid of Man**

exercises a 'draw' or upward lift on the general mass of humanity. Examples of a completed Pyramid might include early dynastic Egypt, Vedic India, the apostolic phase of Early Christianity, the first few generations of 'Muhammad's community,' and Tibet in the fourteenth through sixteenth centuries.

When the Pyramid of Man has been established, there is a continuous upward movement of men and women from the lower levels to the higher levels, and indeed this upward movement is the condition of the involvement of the Gods. When a person moves from one level to another, that person makes it easier for people on the level immediately below to move up into their place. As this applies on every level, it creates a vertical 'lift on lift' effect. On this basis there develops a linked system of 'replacements' which is, in effect, an alchemical process – a process which ascends through a scale of progressively finer vibrational frequencies. (See "The Absolute" on page 36, with reference to the Absolute's internal distinction of energy levels.)

The top two levels of the Pyramid are not immediately visible to the general human community, for what gives them substance is the life of the Higher Centers that exist within them – and Higher Centers are invisible to the untrained eye. We provide three representations of the top two levels of the Pyramid. The first is taken from the Orthodox Monastic Tradition, the second from the Sufi Tradition, and the third from the Tradition of Tibetan Buddhism.

1. St. Simeon the New Theologian, from the **Russian Philokalia** (written shortly after 1000 AD):

> As the immaterial hierarchies of heavenly powers are illumined by God in just sequence, so that the Divine light penetrates from the first hierarchy to the second, from the second to the third and so to them all; so the saints, illumined by holy angels, are linked together and united by the bond of the Holy Spirit and thus become akin to them and of equal rank. Moreover, the saints – those who appear from generation to generation, from time to time, following the saints who preceded them – become linked with their predecessors through obedience to Divine commandments and, endowed with Divine grace, become filled with the same light. In such a sequence all of them together form a kind of golden chain, each saint being a separate link in this chain, joined to the first by faith, right actions and love; a chain which has its strength in God and can hardly be broken.

2. In about 1350 AD Shah Bahauddin Naqshband described a comparable vision of the 'golden chain' (*silsilah*) of the Khwajagan masters, in which he was the

final link. This occurred to him while he was still a youth. As a young boy he had been – much to his surprise – presented with a dervish headpiece that had been worn by the great Sufi Master Azizan Ali Ramatani. He stated: "As soon as I placed this cap on my head, my state was completely transformed. My heart was filled with the love of God, and I have carried this love with me ever since." From this time forward the young Bahauddin was subject to periodic states of ecstasy, in which he wished to escape all human contact. Consequently, during this period, he developed the habit of going at night to visit the tombs of the great saints in the cemetery of Bukhara. One evening he went to visit the tomb of Khwaja Faghnawi and found oil lamps lit all around it. Two armed riders were positioned on either side, with a third horse tethered – apparently for himself. The riders gave him a summons and together the three rode to the mausoleum of Mezdakhan.

> We arrived at the mausoleum of Mezdakhan at night's end. There I saw the lamps lit, as before. I knelt down facing the tomb and was taken by such ecstasy that I could see right through the world. I saw the wall round the tomb dissolving and a great throne became visible. On it a noble personage was seated, but there was a green veil that prevented me from seeing who he was.... A multitude of people was ranged round the throne. Among others, I saw Khwaja Muhammad Samasi. I said to myself: 'I wonder who is seated on that throne.' One of the people of the company said to me: 'The man seated on the throne is Khwaja Abd al-Khaliq Ghujduwani and those around are his successors and followers.' I saw a whole company of Khwajas: Ahmad Salik, Awiliya-i Kilan, Arif Riwgarawi, Mahmud Faghnawi, and Azizan Ali Ramatani. Baba Samasi (Shah Naqshband's teacher) has brought you into the lives of these masters. You must recognize them, for it is they who gave you the dervish headpiece.[1]

The young Bahauddin Naqshband presents a vision of his *silsilah* extending back for more than 200 years. He sees it 'all at once' outside of time and space, which is where each of the Great Spiritual Traditions have their origin.

3. In Tibetan Buddhism the idea of a linked chain of awakened beings existing outside of time and space is carefully elaborated.

    The Buddha is 'the completely awakened one' and the name of the Buddha is often used synonymously with our usage of the Absolute. In the Buddhist teaching a bodhisattva is a 'becoming buddha,' who has succeeded in transcending his

---

1. J.G. Bennett, *Masters of Wisdom*, p. 123/124, source not given.

Figure 6. **Buddhist thangka, Buddha and bodhisattvas**

personal desires and so transcending the need to reincarnate in a physical body. Yet the bodhisattva may choose – through his great compassion – to return and to inhabit successive human bodies in order to teach successive generations of men.

Tibetan Buddhism encourages the spiritual aspirant, at a certain stage of his development, to take the bodhisattva oath: to continue to work for the benefit of all sentient beings until such time as all sentient beings have awakened. This attitude neutralizes any selfish or self-centered impulse that may be linked to the desire to awaken. A developed bodhisattva inhabiting the body of a new-born child makes that child a *tulku*. The Tibetan orders were, historically, able to recognize *tulkus* and treated them, from their infancy, as spiritually mature beings. At a very early age they were reintroduced into the Order in which their previous incarnation had died. Thus each Tibetan lineage carried its greatest teachers within itself.

Tibetan *thangkas* (silk wall hangings) often represent the Buddha as a central figure with retinues of bodhisattvas hovering around him. (See Figure 6.) Some of these bodhissatvas are embodied and some have reached a level of permanent disembodiment. The three tiers – **1**) Buddha, **2**) disembodied bodhisattva, and **3**) embodied bodhisattva – represent the first two levels of our pyramid. Indeed they are often represented artistically in pyramidal form. The *thangkas* of each Tibetan Order show the great Teachers of that lineage as a recognizable part of the Buddha's retinue. The resulting images are strikingly similar to the vision of Shah Naqshband. There are many Tibetan monks who began the teaching phase of their lives with such a vision, thus becoming more aware of the Tradition that stands behind them and of which they are a part.

Given these representations of the first two levels of the Pyramid – the Gods and the Traditions – we must now consider the entire structure, including Living Religion, Civilization, and the wider human community. As we mentioned, a true Civilization is a cosmos, where the parts work together to serve the life of the whole. For most of history human society has been an a-cosmic body, where the parts do not work together in service to the whole. Either the interests of a single group prevail, or there has been a system of compromise between competing interest groups.

And here we must note a distinction that will become important, beginning in Chapter 5 to follow. While the Pyramid of Man always has the form of a cosmos, it is not necessarily a 'completed' or self-perfecting cosmos. The Cosmos of Man in its completed form is a Civilization governed and managed by a ruling Spiritual Tradition. Such a Civilization is directly connected to the cosmos immediately above it, and – as such – can be directly tasked by the Gods.

Both Monarchies and Theocracies can take the general form of a cosmos without the Tradition actually ruling the other levels. In other words all the different levels of the Pyramid of Man can be 'in place' without the higher levels governing the lower levels in light of the special understandings they possess. In a Monarchy, for example, there may be a conscious monarch, a Tradition existing in the proximity of the monarch, a Living Religion, and a highly developed social order. But all of this does not imply that the Tradition rules. The Pyramid of Man has come into being at many different points in history, but a completed Cosmos of Man may never have been achieved. Indeed, it is likely that not all Civilizations have this as a potential.

Prophets, Traditions, Religions, Civilizations

The most influential Spiritual Traditions have been initiated through the work of the Prophets. All of the Traditions that have left us with a written legacy refer to the Prophets. When we consider the line of Prophets sent to humanity, we see that each one established both a World Religion and a Spiritual Tradition. Often, in the second and third generations after the death of the Prophet, multiple Traditions develop from the single teaching. The Prophetic Traditions usually begin in a close relation with the Prophetic Religion, which continues until such point as that Religion descends.

At the time of the death of the Prophet, both the Religion and the Tradition are present in germinal form, without having undergone their final 'casting.' In the first generations after the death of the Prophet, the Religion usually contains and supports the Tradition, which in turn regenerates it. It is then, in the highest sense, a Living Religion. In other words, those of the 'clergy' who are performing the First Work understand that what the practitioners of the Great Work are doing is quite relevant to them. It is the Tradition which receives the truths of Worlds 6 and 12 and gives them practical expression in sacred texts, epics, monuments, objective works of art, or direct oral teaching. In this way the Tradition gives life to the Religion and then to the Civilization itself. Ultimately, this allows Mankind to remain in some way connected with the purposes given in the moment of its creation.

Thus, the Religion that we see in the third level of the Pyramid is not 'formal' religion but a channel for life. Both Living Religion and Living Civilization are 'cosmic' in the sense that they help to form the Cosmos of Man. Religion divorced from Tradition rapidly descends into ideological conflict and the sectarian pursuit of power. Humanity entirely divorced from the Traditions and from Living Religion is a unity of peoples without core values. Humanity needs core values to relate its existence to the potentials that were given it at the beginning. The late Roman Empire actually realized this about itself and tried to enforce the core values of the Republican era – but without the Stoic teachers who had given those values substance. It did not work, and a fledgling Christian Civilization rose out of the chaos of the late Roman Empire.

To the extent that Religion loses contact with Tradition and society becomes a field of conflicting interest groups, the Traditions must find ways of maintaining themselves independently of both Church and State. They must cleave to their primary aims while finding their own channels of recruitment and their own sources of material support. The Tradition of the Tarot, for example, appears to have existed independently of the religions of its time.

The original Prophetic Traditions are what we might call the mainstream Traditions, formative for the family of human civilizations. The Traditions deriving from the work of a Prophet create an environment for humanity in which the 'Pyramid' can emerge.

The non-Prophetic Traditions may have the role of regenerating already existing civilizations or of leaving particular esoteric legacies for the future. These Traditions face the challenge of creating an institutional form in which they can exist, support their members, and recruit new members as, before the late eighteenth century, there was no neutral 'civil society' in which a Tradition could both sustain itself and conceal itself.

The Prophetic Traditions are partial 're-statements' of the original design created by the Gods for humanity. The Prophet actualizes himself in a role created by the Gods. Almost every person on the planet has heard the names of Moses, Gautama Buddha, Jesus Christ, and Muhammad, although the most recent of these figures died 1,400 years ago. This kind of impact is not something that can be engineered by human intelligence or arranged 'after the fact' by followers and adherents. It is given in the very fabric of history. Even the enemies of these men testify to their greatness. It is as though the whole of history conspires to produce the role of the Prophet. The prophetic teaching is revealed truth, which is given form by the Traditions in the art and religion of the prophetic time. When this work is done well, both the Religion and the Civilization bear the prophet's signature.

We noted that the Prophetic Traditions begin in a dynamic relation with the Prophet's Religion. The tiny cell of individuals at the core of the Tradition, who are opening the link to Higher Worlds, create an atmosphere of the miraculous that affects both the Tradition and the Religion which contains it. The Religion, in its turn, connects this legacy of Worlds 6 and 12 to the Civilizational Order. This dynamic balance cannot, however, be taken for granted. It can be lost in a single generation. When a right balance exists, humanity stands in a certain relation to the Gods, and the Great Work becomes accessible to a much wider range of its members. When there is not a right balance, the work of the Traditions fragments, Religion becomes institutionalized, and Civilization becomes 'general society.'

The Civilization inseminated by a Prophetic Tradition is not without its problems. It begins in the work of the Prophet himself, who has seen something of the plan for his own life and something of the plan that Higher School has for the Civilization. The process by which the Prophet initiates the Civilizational Order occurs under the tremendous pressures created by the Gods. While the Prophet has an awareness of the original plan, the actualization may not be identical with the plan itself, and the Prophet's vision – while great – is still partial. As a consequence there are many points at which the Prophet must act on faith. Many times, in the heat of action, he must guess. He must do something rather than nothing, and the consequences of his deed may be far-reaching and unintended.

This element of uncertainty, this possibility of imperfection, is even more pronounced in the generation to follow. The Prophet gives direction during his own lifetime and, the Tradition works at its best in the generations to follow, but the element of uncertainty remains ... and the element of human weakness remains. So the Prophetic vision is always realized in a degree only. The extent to which it is realized is given by the quality of the material at hand. This would include the level of the disciples that the Prophet attracts and the general cultural level of the Civilizational Order that supports the Prophet's role.

In reflecting on the different degrees of perfection that exist, we can make an analogy to the creation of a perfect diamond. Diamonds are crystals of carbon, which have had the impurities removed. Tremendous heat and pressure are needed to create a flawless diamond. The greater the heat and the pressure, the fewer the chemical impurities, the more perfect the alignment of the carbon atoms, and the more perfectly formed the crystal. Where a rough diamond, formed at lower temperatures, is opaque and cannot be used to make a jewel, a diamond formed at high temperatures, under tremendous pressure, is translucent, casting deep spears of light into the surrounding world. It looks, indeed, like something that came to us from the stars.

The heat and pressure needed to form a perfect diamond are like the heat and pressure needed to fuse the Higher Centers of the Prophet and to align the work of his inner circle. When the Prophet becomes translucent, reflecting directly the light of higher worlds, then his inner circle comes under enormous pressure to clear their own impurities and to align themselves rightly, both with each other and with the Prophet himself. They are like the individual atoms of carbon in the diamond-in-the-making; when a correct alignment is achieved, the stone itself becomes translucent. When the members of the Tradition are able to bear rightly the pressure of the Prophet's role, the Tradition itself is raised to translucence, and the light of higher worlds is reflected in all the different activities of the prophetic civilization.

THE STORY OF MAN

With every Prophet, and with every great Spiritual Teacher, the quality and level of the Higher Centers is different, the capacity of the disciples to respond is different, and the culture of the host-civilization is different. To pursue our analogy, the quality of the material available to form the diamond is different, and for this reason the amount of heat and pressure that can be administered varies. Therefore, when the Prophet's teaching is complete and the diamond finally cut and faceted, the degree of light which enters the life of man will vary. Only very rarely in the Story of Man do we find a flawless diamond.

We have been emphasizing the importance of the integration of the different levels of the Pyramid, but the defining point of a Spiritual Tradition is that it originates in the work of Higher School. All of the rest derives from this. It is through the work of the Traditions that the light of Higher Worlds enters humanity. The Traditions are the form that embodies that light, enables it to replicate itself, and so allows it to radiate through to the different levels of the human race.

When a Tradition emerges from the life of a Prophetic Community, we could say that the Tradition is the inner form of that life, while the Religion is its outer form. The life of the Religion comes from the side facing the Tradition. In every age Living Religion supports a dynamic balance between its inward-facing and outward-facing aspects. When the dynamic balance between Tradition and Religion is upset, the Religion is absorbed by its outward-facing aspect. It gradually atrophies and humanity enters a period where its possibilities are more limited. Divorced from the Traditions, the major Religions exist as dead shells, driven this way and that by purely external forces. Indeed the conflicts between the major Religions, as we know them through history, have often fallen to the level of simple barbarism.

In the mature phase of a Tradition, a break with Religion disrupts the natural relation between the First Work and the Work of the Steward. Temporary breaks of this kind are not uncommon, and they can act as shocks that re-animate a decadent or partially decadent Tradition. A temporary break of this kind occurred in the relation of the Sufi Traditions to the Islamic Religion at the time of the Mongol conquest of Islam. The Tradition – and the Muslim civilization itself – were then rejuvenated through the work of the Khwajagan Masters in the thirteenth and fourteenth centuries. A similar break occurred between the Tibetan Buddhist Traditions and the Tibetan Religion with the violent repression of Buddhism in the ninth century AD. The regeneration of the Tibetan Traditions, and the consequent re-integration of the Buddhist Religion, was effected by the work of the men like Tsongkhapa, Gampopa, and Sakya Pandita. In India, in the eighth century AD, a break occurred between the work of the Vedantic Traditions and the Brahmanic Religion, with the general rigidification of the caste system and the consequent formalization of Religion. The work of the Vedantic Tradition was regenerated, at the beginning of the ninth century, through the work of Adi Shankara and his associates, and the work of the Religion in the generation following.

The Traditions must keep themselves alive, and the Men of the Tradition must do what they can to give life to the First Work, as that exists within the Religions. Religion itself is subject to the same law that governs all organic life: the self-maintenance and self-perpetuation of its instinctive existence. The Black Queen thus has a natural place within it. The will to self-maintenance easily connects with the idea of being an elite or 'chosen people,' with the sense of ethnic identity, or with the wielding of temporal power – and it often connects with all three at once! Any stimulation of the Black Queen produces an immediate constriction of the First Work; the Religion justifies itself not to Tradition but to its own officials – who are concerned to influence and control client-factions in the Civilizational Order of which they are a part. It is a problem, then, if the Religion begins to directly manage the affairs of civil society, for this strengthens the influence of the Black Queen within the Religion itself and further attenuates the delicate lifeline between Tradition and Civilization. Each of these three levels should have its own independent efficacy.

Interestingly, when there is a live relation between the three levels (Tradition, Religion, and Civilization), there are often key players who are active on several levels at the same time. The role of the Prophet is the best example of this, for the same man is formative with respect to Tradition, Religion, and Civilization. However, this phenomenon is not restricted to the 'Prophetic' environment. There are other circumstances in which key players can be active on several levels at once. An example of this would be Bernard of Clairvaux, who was 1) a man of the Traditions, 2) a policy maker within the Church, and 3) a respected arbiter of secular disputes. Other examples would include the Abbot Hugh of Cluny, King Songsten Gampo of Tibet, and the Sufi prince Khalil Ata.

Thus a sign of health in human society and an indication of the existence of the Pyramid is a working relation between Tradition, Religion, and Civilization. Muhammad showed direct concern with this in the last decade of his life, when he strove to create the groundwork for the *sunnah*, the *sharia*, and the *fiqh* (as we shall see in Chapter 32, "The Life of Muhammad"). The great plans and projects of a society, which have a span of many generations, can only be carried out in good spirit when there is a cooperation between these three levels – for only then can real priorities be remembered. Talent is drawn from civil society and brought into an arena where the influence of the Traditions can be felt. This vivifies the entire Civilizational Order, allowing enlightened principles to penetrate public life. The 'right relation' is achieved when each level truly serves the level one below.

Many of the Traditions have directly served the Civilizational Order of which they are a part. This service can take the form of charity, of healing, or of the presentation of art in the form of dance or drama. In extending themselves to society in this way, they are giving it something of real value, demonstrating good will, and at the same time providing guidance and inspiration. This opens an avenue by which people can see the spirit at work behind the external form of a Tradition and choose to become a part of that work.

The service to the level one below neutralizes the tendency of the Traditions to self-preoccupation, relaxes the hold of the Black Queen on the Religions, and allows a general flowering of the First Work. At the same time it creates an environment where the Civilization as a whole can recognize and respond to influences coming from a higher level.

Before going further we must note that there is not a one-to-one relationship between Prophet, Tradition, and Civilization – each Civilization having one Prophet and one Prophetic Tradition connected to it. There are clearly related 'families' of Civilizations, and there are main and subordinate Traditions in relation to these families. If you take, for example, the Renaissance phase of Christian Civilization in Western Europe, you have the English Civilization, the French Civilization, and the Spanish Civilization. A single Prophet is the reference point for this entire family, and a multiplicity of Traditions are at work within this context. Such a pattern of 'civilizational families' could be likened to an 'organic development,' where strict rules do not apply. These 'families' can only be understood by actual historical study – and in this expanded context, the archetypal forms are realized in different ways.

All Traditions are One Tradition

In considering the original plan of the Gods for Mankind, we suggested that, although the different Traditions emerge at different points in space and time, they are all the products of a Single Source which exists outside of the time/space manifold. In light of the original plan, then, all Traditions are One Tradition and all revealed truth is One Truth. Taken in the strong sense, this means that all the Traditions are developing at once and all are immediately affected by one other's achievements. Viewed from this perspective, they are all entering the moment of the eternal NOW, each inching closer and closer to the Absolute's timeless act of will.

Yet historically, the prophetic statements are not uniform, and the work of the different Traditions has varied widely. How are we to explain this?

The particular prophetic statements vary according to the time, place, and circumstances of the people who are to receive them. Understood on the highest level, there is a complete oneness of intent, purpose, and method. All teachings refer to the same point-instant of NOW, existing outside of time and space. But the individual prophetic statements cannot be complete, for the lower centers – that is, humanity as we know it – cannot assimilate them as complete. We could say that they are 'partially complete' in different ways.

The teachings of the different Traditions are also, in some degree, complementary; they have different points of emphasis in order to balance their serial effects in the line of time. The Vedic and Buddhist Traditions emphasized yogic and meditational technique; the Zoroastrian Tradition emphasized service to the level one above; the Christian Tradition, service to the level one below.

Whatever the case, at the core of each Tradition are teachings which are primordial. They are always the same and always refer to the same experience of Higher Centers. While the inner teachings of the Great Religions are close, their outer forms may be distinct and even contradictory.

We noted the tragic fact that the 'dead shells' of Religions may become the source of social strife, taking men below the level of the animals. This too is part of a cosmic pattern, in the sense that both destruction and crime are natural processes within a cosmos. Without destruction, at certain points, there can be no renewal. However, when these processes of destruction are not contained or neutralized, a cosmos descends rapidly into chaos. Here the Traditions are at a distinct disadvantage, as they cannot fight crime with crime, and they are not equipped to counter coercion and violence with greater coercion and violence.

Phases in the Life of the Spiritual Traditions

There exists an ancient teaching concerning the life of Prophetic Traditions in the line of time. This is **the myth of the four ages of man**. It is found in the Vedic teachings (the Laws of Manu), the Zoroastrian teachings (the Avesta), the Old Testament (the dream of Nebuchadnezzar), the Greek myths (of both Hesiod and Plato), the Roman myths (Ovid), the Christian teachings (Saint Jerome), and the Aztec texts of the Tradition of the Five Suns. Certain of these myths do not refer to a 'prophetic teaching' but to periods of 'direct communication between men and Gods' – which amounts to the same thing. The Vedic, Greek, and Roman myths all equate the four ages of man with different metals: gold, silver, copper, and iron. Using this nomenclature, we shall provide a very general synthesis and overview:

The Golden Age is the first phase of the prophetic teaching. The Prophet is surrounded by his community, the people of his own generation who help him to realize his historical task. It is a time of undifferentiated intensity. The highest teachings of the Prophet are alive, and at the same time his teaching is understood on many different levels simultaneously. The life of the Prophetic community is like an archetypal 'play' that culminates in the death of the Prophet himself. This period is, at the same time, a crisis and a test for his closest followers.

The Silver Age follows the death of the Prophet. Gradually the white heat of his teaching cools, congealing into Tradition (red hot), Religion (hot), and Civilization (warm). This defines the prophetic 'sphere of influence.' Traditions often arise from the period of great uncertainty that immediately follows the death of the Prophet. Those of the Prophet's disciples who have awakened articulate and develop his teaching, and it may acquire a more definite form than it had during his lifetime. In this period there is a particularly dynamic relation between Tradition and Religion – which translates through to the Civilizational Order.

The Copper Age sees a further cooling. As institutionalized Religion develops, it becomes increasingly connected to material interests and to political life. There is an exactly proportionate increase in theological dispute, which begins to acquire an ideological flavor. At the same time a network of mutual dependencies develops between church and state. The original connection between Tradition and Religion is gradually undermined, and a definitive break between the two becomes ever more likely. Relative to the Gold and Silver ages it is a time of decadence. Yet there may still be long periods, and even centuries, very favorable to the Work of the Traditions. When the crises of the Copper Age come to Tradition and to Religion, they may still be followed by marked phases of renewal.

The Iron Age sees the final break between Tradition and Religion, which tends to reduce the work of the Traditions to more eclectic forms of group work. Generally speaking, there is a movement from living teaching to dead ideology, from states to words, from direct experience to belief. All of this fatally undermines the conditions required for continuity in the Great Work. The Pyramid linking humanity to the Gods is broken at all points. Muhammad called this the *al-Jahiliyyah* or age of ignorance. The Buddhist Tradition calls it 'the end of the middle period' or the age of the Setting Sun. In the Hindu tradition it is called the *Kali Yuga* or age of vice.

The myth of the Four Ages is usually interpreted as a record of universal stages in the life of Man. Actually it represents – very clearly – the four states of civilizational order that exist in any Civilization that develops out of a Prophetic Tradition. These 'Four Ages' will then repeat themselves with the coming of a new Prophet. Having said this, it remains true that there is probably a great 'cycle of cycles' that will bring our present humanity to the end of its time on the planet earth.

The crisis of the Traditions, which begins in the Copper Age, is often connected to the relation between Church and State, the gradual absorption of the Church into the State, and – more generally – to the corruptive influence that power has on men. When a Religion begins to have a real influence on Civilizational Order, it becomes dependent on patronage of different kinds, engaged in the struggle for temporal power, and involved in both theological and ideological dispute. The Tradition is inevitably exposed to these influences. And here temptation enters. Even in the inner circle of the Traditions, every man has his weakness; every single member is subject to temptation of different kinds. There arise conflicting allegiances, and there are – always and everywhere – people who imagine themselves to be what they are not. It happens easily that authority based on spiritual level is displaced by authority based on place and position. The crises that arise from such a situation may press the inner circle of a Tradition to a higher level of work, but equally the work of the Tradition itself may break under pressure. And here we find some of the greatest tragedies of Mankind. A tragedy, we may remember, is not a simple conflict of good and evil, but the story of good mixed with evil – in which the protagonist fails to accurately differentiate the different elements within himself and so fails in a determining trial.

The Condition of Humanity in the Age of Iron: Groups and Cults

We noted that in the Age of Iron – with the break of Tradition and Religion – the Traditions themselves may splinter into more eclectic forms of group work. The groups, once they begin to operate independently, can easily descend to the level of 'cults' without conscious leaders. Under these conditions the Religion is no longer able to give life to the Civilization of which it is a part, and consequently the Civilization descends to the level of simple society.

In the period immediately preceding the Dark Age, and then, more markedly, during the Dark Age itself, the work of the Groups and the Cults becomes prominent. It is appropriate, then, to clarify what we mean by these terms.

The Groups are conscious teachings which have become dissociated from the Great Spiritual Traditions, and usually – but not always – from the Religions connected with them. The Groups are generally able to sustain themselves in the medium of civil society and tend to work independently of one another. They are at a disadvantage in that they are unable to draw screened candidates from the First Work of the Religions. Within the Group you do not have a defined order in which students work simultaneously on different levels, each lifting the level one below. Nor does the Group have the ability to bring students through to the Great Work according to their individual abilities and merits.

The Group has a conscious Teacher and may even have a very high conscious Teacher, but – relative to the Traditions – it has a weak inner circle. This is true by definition, in that the inner circle of a Tradition includes mature Men Number Five, but it is also true in a different way. For a conscious teaching to achieve all that can be achieved, there must be a deep mutual commitment between Student and Teacher – for in the work to achieve Higher Centers all the weaknesses of human nature will be exposed and brought into the light. This means that these weaknesses must be understood and accepted, for it is impossible to simply 'change' something that is central to one's nature. The inner circle, understanding this, must be for one another. They must understand each other and wish each other well. This is a deep level of intimacy, comparable to the intimacy of a family which is prepared to support a deeply troubled member. Not every Teacher is willing to extend himself in this way, and most students are unable to make this level of sacrifice. In Groups the quality of the bond uniting the inner circle is weaker. Yet we affirm that Group work has seen all the finest things of which human beings are capable.

When the Teacher of a Group dies, he is seldom succeeded by another conscious Teacher within the same Group, because the lower level of the Group makes the recognition and acceptance of a new Teacher more difficult. Thus there is not a continuity of Teachers, one following the next, nor is there an environment where several Teachers can work together, in harmony, within the same organization. When a Teacher dies, his successor, if there is one, is often forced to begin again on his own. There is not, therefore, the passing on of a cumulative teaching experience, from one generation to the next.

Additionally, the Groups are often either too conciliatory or too harsh. The Teacher may focus on seeking out potential candidates for teaching roles so that he himself can teach on a higher level. As a result he may put a great deal of pressure on the entire group, many of whom are not ready for it. Alternatively, he may give his attention to the few while giving the majority a general teaching that allows them to rise only marginally above the level of Religion.

In short, the culture of the Groups lacks the universality of the Great Work. At the same time the Gods do monitor the work of the Teacher, who is conscious and who must do the best he can under the circumstances. As we have noted, a Group can have a very high Teacher. This may relate to the contribution that a particular Teacher has to make in creating the ground for a Tradition in the generations to follow. On the other hand the limitation of a high Teacher to group work may simply be the result of imperfections in the 'lattice structure' of the diamond (or social body) that reflects the Teacher's light. Perhaps the potential was there in the Teacher but not in the society of which he was a part.

The Pseudo-teachings and the Cults appear when a conscious Teacher dies and his teaching is carried on by students who are not themselves conscious. They can also begin from a 'rogue' student who leaves a conscious teaching and begins to teach on his own. The Cults make use of the materials and techniques left by the Traditions, but they do so in an idiosyncratic or fragmented way. They are unpracticed, and thus the occult and pseudo-esoteric teachings have an anarchic nature. In the cults there is no contact with the Gods or the general plan for humanity.

While the Cults tend to be introverted, there also arise self-proclaimed and un-enlightened 'teachers,' who function in a more public milieu. The appearance of these unenlightened teachers is, in a way, quite natural. We can understand this phenomenon with reference to the different 'bandwidths' of human experience. Only one step beyond the normal bandwidth-range of the four lower centers – and very far short of the experience of the Higher Centers – everything begins to look quite different. While this 'one step beyond' is a long way from the experience of a mature Man Number Five, it is very much different from the 'veiled' experience that is shared by most of the human race.

Under these conditions the illusion of enlightenment can be compelling, par-ticularly when there is no one there to correct it. Uninstructed people find them-selves in this situation and then begin to teach the traditional teachings, add new teachings to the old, and mix in things that were never there before. Thus you have the self-appointed hierophants of Hellenistic Egypt, the wealthy Epicurean 'Teach-ers' of Imperial Rome, and the love-and-light 'Sufi Masters' of the 1960s and early 1970s. In our own time, inspired but unenlightened teachers often suggest that spiritual experiences will come effortlessly to many people, as part of the spon-taneous emergence of a 'New Age.' They publish books, they speak at inter-faith conferences, they appear at New Age seminars, and they get carried away with the response that they evoke. But this has nothing to do with the work of the Great Spiritual Traditions. In fact the Teachers of the Traditions are careful to eliminate any vestige of satisfaction in the 'little bit beyond.' They are committed to bringing their students through to a full experience of Worlds 6 and 12, and they understand that nothing of enduring value comes easily.

Having distinguished the Traditions and the Groups from each other, we must be clear that their world is very different from that of the pseudo-teachings and the Cults. Every conscious being has, in a terrible struggle, gone through the eye of the needle into the Eternal Now. To teach truly, and to preserve himself in the state that he has entered, a conscious being must carefully mark his distance from the 'consensus reality' of his own time. He must hold to his own standard. He must make the right kinds of demands on himself and he must make the right kinds of demands on his students. He can never allow himself to imitate an image, generated out of the popular culture, of what an enlightened Teacher ought to be.

More generally, if a Teacher becomes a public figure, he is not free to teach what he knows to properly prepared people. If a real Teacher were in the position to teach prepared people, he would spend all his time doing that. He would not be making public appearances. There are exceptions to this rule – most notably the Prophets – and these exceptions relate to the particular historical tasks given the Traditions by the Gods. Conscious roles with a 'legitimate' public dimension occur more frequently in the Gold and Silver ages, when the public is at a higher level, than during the Copper and Iron ages.

Every Teacher who has reached the level of Man Number Five is 'accountable,' both to the Gods and to his own Higher Centers. He does not, therefore, play to his audience or allow his Lower Self to be fed by recognition. It is simply in the nature of things that a Teacher cannot teach by trying to meet the expectations of the students: it is the students who must respond to the truth presented by the Teacher. If the Teacher is a Man Number Six, he is like a great mirror, open to higher worlds, directly reflecting their light. He acts out of necessity in relation to the level that is above him; he does not guess, and he does not do what he wants. He does what he must. Both the Tradition and the Group are distinct from the Cult Teachings in that they do not cater to the popular culture of their own time. The Tradition is unlike both the Cult and the Group in that it liberates the Great Teachers to teach.

Shadows of the Master Plan: A Summary of Man's Potentials

On the basis of the material we have assembled so far, we can make a provisional reconstruction of the master-plan for humanity.

The potential of the individual human being is to nurse consciousness out of functions, to awaken the Higher Emotional and Higher Intellectual Centers, to bring the two Higher Centers to the point of fusion, and so to join the order of the Gods. To realize this potential is, at the same time, to fulfill the original plan of the Absolute by generating conscious life out of material creation.

The potential of a Spiritual Tradition is to sustain the Work of the Steward and so to sustain prolonged presence within a select community. The realization of this potential makes it possible to connect the world of Higher Centers to the general experience of humanity. But to secure this link the Tradition must **1)** sustain a working link with the Gods and **2)** truly serve the level immediately below it.

The potential of a Civilization is to form the Cosmos of Man. While the Traditions potentiate this, it must be the work of the entire social order. In other words the social order must have brought itself to a point where it can acknowledge conscious leadership. Failing this very high goal, the potential of Civilization is to maintain the semblance of a cosmos (not to become a-cosmic) and so to keep the level of the social order at a point at which it can continue to experience the influence of the Gods through the Traditions. The potentials of a Civilizational Order are represented beautifully in Plato's *Republic*, which is the one image that we have of a Civilization ruled by a Tradition. It is based on a vision of the integration of the Great Work with developed forms of civic life.

When all three of these potentials are realized, at least in a degree, humanity has a living connection to World 3. It then reflects the archetypal relation of True Individuality to Collective Life; it serves the Gods above and the world of nature below.

The Traditions Create a Sacred World

When Man lives in light of the Spiritual Traditions, he is connected to the purposes that were given at the time of his creation. When men are together, as families or communities, they should be able to feel themselves as equivalent beings in the presence of God. It is not that we should indoctrinate our children with this idea, but that we should realize it in our lives so that our children are not deprived of this experience. We might say that every man has this as his birthright but that most men, at most times in history, have been deprived of it by the general level of society.

But to realize our potentials we need more than just the work of the Traditions; we need the completed Pyramid of Man, for the influences that come from the apex of the Pyramid can only have their full effect when the structure is complete. And when the Pyramid is complete Higher School is not limited to set lines of transmission but can make its influence felt in many ways, which resonate through the entire fabric of the Civilizational Order.

This brings us to another aspect of the Pyramid of Man, which has – through most of history – been a significant part of the human experience.

One of the most direct connections that humanity has to the forces at the apex of the Pyramid is the Love of Beauty. Here we do not speak of the idea of beauty that is prevalent in our own time, but of an older and more essential idea. The term the ancient Greeks used for beauty is *ton kallon* (τον κάλλον). This is a beauty that is never separate from nobility of nature, a beauty that creates openness, awe, and wonder in those who see it. Plato equated *ton kallon* with the recognition of what is higher. It gives us our sense of the sacred. When the qualities of Beauty and Truth merge in this way, there is the Love of what is higher. When one recognizes what is higher, one cannot but love it, for in the moment of recognition one becomes like what one sees.

The love of beauty has – historically – been developed to its highest point where the Cosmos of Man has been formed (or approximated) through the development of civic life. Here we think of the remarkable capacity of the Greeks for embodying their ideals in public art and architecture and of the Roman genius for modeling civic space. In Archaic and Classical Greece there was intelligent patronage of the arts, with a constant concern to achieve high culture and to raise the level of the popular culture. The Greeks understood the formative power of art and its potential for molding the essence of Man. When a child learns to love great art, that art changes the child's nature.

Art opens us to beauty, but the highest beauty a man can know is the beauty of the Self, existing independently from all the created universe. The beauty which follows most closely on this is the beauty that the Self sees in creation, understanding that it has been created from a Higher Level. It is able to see the relation that exists between the original archetypes of things and the individual specimens that exist in the line of time. The Self then perceives Harmony or the divine pattern of things. As Shakespeare put it in *The Merchant of Venice:*

> Look, how the floor of heaven
> Is thick inlaid with patines of bright gold;
> There's not the smallest orb, which though behold'st,
> But in his motion like an angel sings,
> Still quiring to the young ey'd cherubins:
> Such harmony is in immortal souls …

Art reveals harmony and the beauty which comes from harmony. Beauty reveals the splendor of Truth. Great art inspires the Love of Beauty, displacing the lower self by creating states of openness, awe, and wonder.

When you have Beauty, Truth, and the Love of what is Higher in close alignment, you have what Plato called the *agathon* (ἀγαθόν) or the Good, the aim of all human endeavor. When you have this, you have a sense of Value which applies to all that a Man can do or know. To the extent that a Man has Value, he must will the Good.

With these understandings Mankind can create a Sacred World. This can only be done when Man is connected to the Gods and when he is aware of the tasks the Gods have given him. When Man realizes that he has been asked by the Gods to be more than what he presently is, he transcends the merely personal. He experiences a sacred necessity and enters a World infused with Value, for he realizes that Higher Forces have extended to him the possibility of becoming like them.

The Great Traditions, each in their golden hour, have lived in and created a Sacred World.

BOOK II

The Beginning of Things – Our Forgotten Prehistory

In Book I we created the context for the Story of Man; we used the surviving texts and records of the Spiritual Traditions to describe their origin, aim, and purpose. Now we must do our best to sketch in the story line, which begins somewhere in the middle of the last ice age, some 35 to 40 thousand years ago. But, before going back to the fourth interstadial period of the last ice age, we must consider the enigma of Man's creation, for this – after all – is the real beginning of our story. We shall first relate the creation of Mankind to the Absolute's original act of creation. We shall then describe the involvement of the Gods – acting as the Absolute's agents – in:

1. Creating the template for the human form, and

2. Helping man, once created, to get started on his journey.

And thus, in the course of Book II, we shall introduce the speculative material needed to give continuity to our story: to link the concepts of Book I to recorded history as we know it. This presentation is not intended as a finished theory. It is an approximation which allows the story to go forward. If it is not true, then something even more wonderful is – and hopefully future researchers will be able to bring this into relief.

CHAPTER 5

The Absolute's Creative Act

In Chapter 2 we emphasized that the creation of the universe was the result of a cosmic drama in which the Absolute – in his primordial state – became aware of a fatal condition of entropy that existed in relation to what was 'outside of' his own Being. What was outside of his Being was, from one point of view, his own Not-Being. In this chapter we shall substitute the term 'Not-Being' with George Gurdjieff's term 'the unconditioned infinite,' in order to represent the chaotic and disintegrative effects that 'Not-Being' has within Creation.

In the beginning the Absolute saw that the unconditioned infinite was gradually but relentlessly undermining his own sentience. In an act that is unimaginable to us, he willed his own negation, internalizing the unconditioned infinite and then, in a second master-stroke, generating the Macrocosm of Creation. In this act the Absolute:

1. Transcended himself, so confirming his existence as beyond both Being and Not-Being;

2. Placed himself in a position to neutralize the fundamental condition of entropy – or Not-Being – that now existed both in himself and throughout Creation.

Because the Absolute now contained the condition that he hoped to neutralize, he was in a position to deal with it directly. He determined that the energy required to correct the condition of entropy was that of consciousness, viewed in its physical aspect as conscious energy. The Absolute's plan was to create a system that would generate consciousness not already given in his own consciousness. This, then, was the first requirement of Creation.

Let us examine this first requirement more closely.

In the moment the Absolute internalized his own opposite many different things occurred. He suddenly found within himself an extended scale of energies that he had not previously been aware of. Not all of these energies were benign. The energies connected to (or derivative of) the 'unconditioned infinite' exerted a deleterious and disintegrative effect on the whole. Having realized that the energies now internal to him were of different objective value, the Absolute willed the hierarchical structure of Creation. In so doing he did not simply propagate the entire range of energies in an unsorted mix; he placed the higher energies over the lower energies, in such a way that the former might govern and regulate the latter. He thus willed a living whole, or a Macrocosm. In the same action he willed into existence a multitude of beings, as the multiple components of that whole. Not only did he will them into existence, he created them in his own likeness, with the same capacity for self-transcendence that he possessed.

The Absolute created new Celestial Beings both in the moment that he willed Creation and, indirectly, as one of the anticipated results of Creation. These beings were of several different kinds. For the purposes of our story we need distinguish only two:

1. There were those beings who preceded or developed in parallel with Creation as we know it. In other words, these Celestial Beings were complete before Creation was complete. Their consciousness was directly derivative of the consciousness of the Absolute, and they never were embodied, at least as we understand embodiment. In the complete unfolding of Creation that was to follow – the spawning of tier upon tier, world upon world, microcosm within macrocosm – these first-born beings were the Absolute's principal agents and executors. And they are still his principal agents and executors in the Great Works that he undertakes now.

2. There were conscious beings who were generated at a later stage in the life of the universe. These beings emerged out of the lower tiers of Creation, only after the medium of organic life had been established on certain of the planets. This 'second generation' of conscious beings began their existence as organic life forms, without self-consciousness, and developed full self-consciousness only in slow degrees. The second generation conscious beings were an important part of the original plan, because in them the 'image' of the maker was more exact. These beings were like the Absolute in that they could only achieve consciousness by confronting and transcending their own not-being. What they confronted as

THE STORY OF MAN

their own 'not-being,' at the level of organic life, was the force that we have called the Black Queen: the controlling 'organismic' intelligence that instinctively resists being displaced by any higher form of intelligence. By coming-into-being in face of such resistance, the second generation conscious beings fulfilled – and do now fulfill – the foremost requirement placed on Creation. They generate 'new' consciousness out of created matter and so neutralize the condition of entropy that Creation was designed to counteract. Effectively they are 'twice-born' – once as organic life forms and a second time as fully conscious beings.

It appears, then, that the first-created conscious beings are less strategically important to the Absolute's plan than the 'second generation,' because the consciousness of the latter – being directly derivative of the Absolute's own – does not counteract the fundamental condition of entropy. Here a clarification is necessary. While the consciousness of these primordial beings is a form of consciousness that has not yet transcended itself, it is like the consciousness of the Absolute (who has transcended himself) in that it anticipates transcendence. But it will only achieve this transcendence with the Absolute himself (for him for the second time) in a context which is utterly unimaginable to us. Thus, the consciousness of these first citizens of the universe is immeasurably greater than that of the Gods to follow. The self-transcendence that they labor for is on the scale of the life of the universe itself. They have intimate knowledge of the aims of the Absolute as Beyond-Being, and their existence is as essential to him as it is to us. They are at the point of transition to a dimension that is utterly beyond our conception. To create a metaphor based on the material given in Chapter 3, these first-created beings are like the work 'I's in the Steward of the Absolute. Having said this, even these primordial entities are in a complete and permanent state of awe with respect to the Absolute himself.

Following the Judaic, Christian, and Islamic Traditions we shall call the beings who paralleled or pre-existed Creation the Archangels. We shall call the conscious entities generated out of the fabric of Creation the Gods. Amazingly, it is our own species – Man – along with like species on other planets, who are the microcosmoses from which the Gods develop.

In order to follow the relation of Man, Gods, and Archangels through the labyrinth of recorded history, we need to be more specific about what we have called 'self-transcending'

consciousness. We understand that the Absolute's initial project required the generation of consciousness not directly derivative of his own, and that this consciousness had to be somehow generated out of the Created Universe. In the scheme of Creation, self-transcending consciousness can only be produced from the thin film of Organic Life that appears on certain of the planets, for it is here that the downward movement from macrocosm to microcosm finally comes to an end. At every level above the level of Organic Life there is a degree of consciousness 'given from' the Absolute, but at the level of Organic Life there are only traces of conscious energy, in the unconcentrated form that is necessary to the life-process. These unconcentrated traces can – under certain conditions – produce flashes of presence, but these flashes of presence are connected to neither the 'generalized' consciousness of the higher levels nor to a consciously present 'Self.'

The highest organic life forms – those possessed of both intellect and emotion – have been given the capacity to process these 'traces' internally to produce permanent self-consciousness. This possibility (our possibility) is the result of two independent yet closely connected aspects of our being:

1. We have been so designed that the 'traces' of conscious energy that enter our system do so at very precisely determined points. (While we cannot define these points here, they are derivative of the points of intake of food, air, and sensory impressions, described in detail by many of the Traditions.) From each point of entry there are a series of knock-on effects, which can, under certain artificially-created conditions, coalesce to produce consecutive 'flashes' of presence.

2. We each carry within ourselves two latent Higher Centers (which are entirely unnecessary to our life as organic beings).

The connection between these two aspects is that the former (the process of generating 'flashes' of presence) is the means of activating the latter (the latent Higher Centers). The result is a presence – sustained through time – which knows itself as such. Learning the art of managing and concentrating this conscious energy could be compared, more poetically, to Aladdin learning to rub the magic lamp – in just such a way that the genie will appear.

This entire set of delicately orchestrated linkages that gives us the possibility of activating the Higher Centers was mapped out in detail by George Gurdjieff, in what he called the 'food diagram.'[1]

Clearly, this set of linkages was designed with the development of the Steward in mind, for only the action of a developed Steward can process the conscious energy from the different points of input to spark the Higher Centers. The special design of the linkages is, then, our 'cosmic signature.' This signature is impressed in the being of every man and woman, given in our very genetic code. It is this and this alone that makes it possible for members of the human race – with special guidance and special effort – to develop higher levels of consciousness and to penetrate the Sphere of Sentient Being. It is literally true that this 'conscious seal' was the gift of the Absolute and his Archangels. It is the gift of a potential only, but a potential whose value is so great that it cannot be measured or assessed.

The medium of Organic Life is, then, the only place within the Macrocosm from which new consciousness can be generated. For this reason it is the first step in the great reversal. Man, at the top of the hierarchy of organic life forms, is the agent intended to effect this reversal and to correct the fundamental condition of entropy that exists throughout the created universe.

Given the physical scale of the Macrocosm it seems hard to believe that beings like ourselves – even existing at multiple locations throughout the universe – could play this role. But the difficulty that we may have in believing this is due only to our false perception of 'matter.' Viewed objectively, the energy of higher consciousness is immeasureably more real than what we perceive to be matter. To the uninstructed man or woman higher consciousness is a dream and matter is a hard reality. The Spiritual Traditions hold the opposite view.

Thus our cosmic signature is a divine inheritance, but it is not without its difficult ramifications. When we become aware of this hidden potential, we feel impelled to realize it, yet the environment in which we find ourselves seems unconducive to doing so. In fact it is an extremely difficult environment, and was intended to be so, because 'self-developing' consciousness needs constant resistance, just as the gifted athlete needs ever-greater resistance to realize his potential. The medium of Organic Life provides this resistance, in the form of the organically-sourced Black Queen – the powerful instinctive intelligence that has been built into Man's four lower centers (as well as into the

---

1. This has been recorded, with Gurdjieff's commentary, in Chapter IX of Peter Ouspensky's *In Search of the Miraculous*.

lower centers of all the animals) for the purposes of self-preservation. The Black Queen functions exclusively in a 'self-versus-other' mode – whether aggressive or possessive – and actively resists any attempt to unlock attention or energy from that constricted state. But this is just one aspect of our situation. With the Black Queen came the external conditions in which – in the downward thrust of Creation – we finally arrive at a level where no consciousness at all is 'given from above.' Thus, with respect to what we have called 'consciousness,' the sentient beings who inhabit this level are literally 'working in the dark'! The combination of these two circumstances creates a situation in which *we need help to fulfill our own destiny*. And here the plot thickens.

The very fact that the medium of Organic Life is the critical 'turning point' for the generation of new consciousness creates a problem for the Absolute. It is difficult for us to evolve and, at the same time, *it is impossible for him to help us*. To understand why this is so we must review the Law of the Merciless Heropass, as described by George Gurdjieff.

THE LAW OF THE MERCILESS HEROPASS

The Law of the Merciless Heropass is what contains or limits the effects of the 'unconditioned infinite' that the Absolute internalized at the time of Creation. It was only the Absolute's acceptance of the limitations given by the Merciless Heropass that enabled him – at the very beginning of things – to place the higher energies over the lower energies in such a way that the Macrocosm of Creation could stabilize in a hierarchical order. But this created an environment in which the deleterious effects of Not-Being were felt directly and continuously at each level of the hierarchy.

Under these conditions, the Not-Being that had, in the Absolute's act of internalization, become an inseparable part of Creation inevitably entered – or insidiously penetrated – the will of all the beings that were generated out of it. One of the most important functions of the Merciless Heropass, then, is to sharply circumscribe the effects of such an aberrant will. Thus, the beings that are generated out of this level are subject to a cyclical form of existence punctuated by the corrective 'return to unity' which we call death.

In this way the Law of the Merciless Heropass ensures the integrity of the Macrocosm as a 'generator of consciousness,' despite the continued existence of the unconditioned infinite. On each level of the Macrocosm it has the effect of a deadline, either forcing development or cutting it short, but always ultimately coming into play. The

Macrocosm of Creation can only hope to neutralize the effects of the unconditioned infinite by defining itself as a self-sustaining energy system that both limits and enables development. And it does so by obeying the limiting law which is the very condition of its existence.

Unfortunately the same law that allows the Macrocosm of Creation to sustain itself, limits the extent to which the Absolute can intervene in its processes. We remember that the Absolute labors on the far side of the Merciless Heropass, at a level where cosmic laws are determined rather than at a level where they have already been determined. Once the system of Creation has been established, the Absolute cannot intervene in it directly without undermining its integrity as a (potentially) self-sustaining system.

Thus the Absolute *cannot directly intervene in the hierarchy of worlds he has created* nor can he directly aid the internal work of the beings who inhabit them. And it is just at this point that random elements – that are ultimately the effect of the unconditioned infinite – enter in. The lower the World, the more the will of its inhabitants will carry the imprint of the Absolute's Not-Being and the more severe the corrective effects of the Law of the Merciless Heropass will have to be.

For all of these reasons, the laws governing each World determine the forms of Time and Death that are appropriate to it. With respect to the beings who inhabit the lowest Worlds there is much that is accidental and imperfect in their will, and the actions of the Heropass are proportionately more severe. As a consequence their lives are more deeply disrupted by time and death. At the end of the chain of Creation you get beings who live very short lives, with very little opportunity to make any sense out of what is happening in them, and this is us!

This shows clearly why *the Absolute needs the assistance of the Gods in managing Creation* – both the Archangels and the 'twice-born' Gods that emerge from the medium of organic life. The Archangels, who are close to the Absolute, are capable of moving freely from the higher to the lower levels of Creation, and the twice-born Gods – under the authority of the Archangels – are capable of representing his will, insofar as that can be represented, within the more limited sphere they inhabit. The Archangels have a much deeper understanding of the intention of the Absolute. The twice-born Gods are more adept at communicating directly with human beings. But both these levels of Gods are greatly pressured to do the will of the Absolute without distorting it in the manner that is characteristic of their own level. This challenge is – for each of them – their own trial and their own reward in the over-arching drama of the Great Work.

We now see why the Absolute created the Archangels and the twice-born Gods and why any kind of direct involvement with human beings has been delegated to them. Understanding this we can see how, and in what way, the limitation of the Law of the Merciless Heropass defines – with precision – the place of Man in relation to the Archangels and the twice-born Gods and so describes the theater in which the Story of Man will be enacted.

Clearly the Absolute's plan has worked up to this point in time. The medium of Organic Life, on this planet and on others, has generated a sufficient number of twice-born conscious beings to counteract the effect of the unconditioned infinite. But the Story of Man is far from over, and the ultimate outcome still hangs in the balance. Indeed, it is one of the most important aspects of the *Story of Man* that the story of the Absolute and his Creation is itself incomplete. A common theme of both these stories is that more consciousness is required of Creation, and how much more, and over what period of time, we do not know.

The relationships described above – between the Absolute, the Archangels, the twice-born Gods, and Man – bring out the significance of the human race. We are members of a species that has been generated right at the critical turning point in the downward thrust of Creation. We are important precisely because we have been generated out of the medium of Organic Life, where there is no more consciousness 'given from above.' We shall begin our story, then, with a brief reflection on this medium; it had to be there so that we could be there, and it remains the permanent medium of our development. Additionally – as we shall see – it is not a passive medium, but a unified sentient whole.

THE STORY OF MAN

CHAPTER 6
The Unity of Organic Life

Organic Life is the interconnected system of life forms which has arisen on the planet earth. All of our cells, tissues, and bodily organs are by-products of this system. They were developed and perfected in other organic life forms, before being combined – in a certain way – in our own. We occupy a particular place in this predefined order, and we are entirely dependent on it and on the other organic life forms that exist in our proximity.

Every single organic life form has a world of its own and an experience of its own. Every organism is deftly and completely fitted into its 'life world' through its organs and its perceptual apparatus. Additionally, every individual organism exists as part of a species, for all organic beings perpetuate themselves as species. Thus each organism, as well as having its own life experience, is the 'member' of a species-mind: there is a collective experience behind each individual experience. But *there is also a species-mind of species-minds*, and this we shall call *the Unity of Organic Life*. Here we are following the biology – although not the exact terminology – of Aristotle, Leibniz, and Goethe.

In this view the medium of Organic Life is not just the physical aggregate of its many life forms, *it is the living unity of their experience*. The Unity of Organic Life has an intelligence independent of, while at the same time embracing, the many different species which comprise it. It can thus develop and perfect its manifold functions through the complex hierarchy of life forms which are its extended body. While it is itself an organic being it is not restricted by the effects of time and death in the same way that the species which comprise it are. It has a primitive fourth-dimensional intelligence, which enables the multiplication of species and which perfects adaptations of different kinds. It knows something of the future and something of the past and so has, within its limits, a most remarkable accuracy. Traces of this fourth-dimensional intelligence are etched in its three-dimensional time-space body by invisible, almost hidden, movements. Many of its actions redefine the relation between the different species and the 'unity of the species' through the manipulation of genes. A recent example of this occurred in the wake of the 1986 Chernobyl meltdown, when nuclear waste-eating flora appeared in the surrounding radioactive area. Another example occurred following the 2010 BP oil spill, when oil-eating bacteria proliferated in the area, in a degree sufficient to mitigate the effects of the disaster.

Because the fourth-dimensional intelligence of Organic Life is One, any particular function, once perfected, can be reintroduced in another organismic life form at another place and time. Thus the Unity of Organic Life Forms is a constantly developing field of experimentation with an intelligence behind it. From this point of view the theory of the 'survival of the fittest' contains an element of truth, but it is a truth situated in the context of an experimenting intelligence rather than a context of random adaptation.

While the Unity of Organic Life is an organismic intelligence that centers a vast field of experience, it is not, like an individual man, capable of self-transcendence. Rather it is firmly and exclusively dedicated to its own survival. As long as Man has a physical body and as long as he is part of this living unity, he will be strongly influenced by it – and a part of him will always remain just as firmly and exclusively dedicated to his own survival!

One common ground between the Unity of Organic Life and the Microcosmos Man is that neither could have created themselves. While the Unity of Organic Life is capable of developing its own projects and conducting its own experiments, it could not possibly have manufactured itself. We take a step back, then, and reflect. The Absolute's original purpose in creating the Macrocosm had been – as we know – to provide a medium for the development of conscious life, and the Unity of Organic Life was a key part of this strategy. The conditions for its emergence had to be created. But, as the Absolute himself was incapable of intervening in the processes occurring on the planetary surface, he entrusted this task to his first-born children, the Archangels. Being independent of Him they were not subject to the Law of the Heropass in the same way that He was. They could traverse the Celestial Hierarchy to fulfill His will. The price they paid for this freedom was the real possibility of failure in their appointed task and the consequent pressure to develop themselves in such a way that they might further His aims. While the Archangels did have a degree of independence from the Absolute, their close proximity to Him enabled them to understand the Unity of His Vision for Creation, and – at the same time – the greater degree of freedom that corresponded to their station allowed them to move easily amongst its different levels. And so, behind the Unity of Organic Life lies the careful engineering of the Archangels. But, once the Unity of Organic Life has been established on a particular planet and shown itself to be self-sustaining, the Archangels need not remain continuously active behind it. Given that these six-dimensional Celestial Beings retain a full awareness of all their experiments, they can return at any time they wish to make adjustments.

We can imagine, then, the four-dimensional shape of the Unity of Organic Life becoming translucent at the points where the six-dimensional Celestial Beings are engaged in their work of re-engineering. The involvement of these Celestial Beings makes possible many things that would be otherwise impossible, for they hold in their consciousness a range of energies that the Unity of Organic Life cannot comprehend, specifically the molecular and electronic energies of Worlds 12 and 6. Knowing what is outside of it as well as what is inside of it, and what is above it as well as what is below it, they can – with some certainty – modify it to its own advantage.

We can look for the influence of the Archangels wherever a more integrated or developed form emerges that could not have been 'anticipated' by a series of survival-oriented genetic modifications. Almost surely Archangelic intervention occurred at the time the first one-celled animals appeared on the planet and, later, at the point when slight traces of conscious energy were assimilated into the reproductive pattern of organic life forms. We might expect the involvement of six-dimensional beings during the extraordinary transition that resulted in independently mobile creatures living on dry land; so many factors had to converge to bring about this result. We would expect the same kind of intervention behind the emergence and development of the family of mammalia, which appears to have been enabled through a series of natural disasters. The supreme example of Archangelic intervention, however, would be the series of genetic manipulations required to enable conscious energies to concentrate in a cellular being to produce a state of prolonged presence. The appearance of the prefrontal cortex in Man would have been the immediate precursor of this development. While it is very difficult to explain the emergence of the prefrontal cortex as a series of genetic adaptations, it is utterly impossible to explain, in this way, the emergence of the complex internal network enabling the concentration of conscious energies into sustained presence. The Unity of Organic Life could never have engineered man's latent Higher Centers, because it could never have anticipated the purpose that they serve. To presume that an organic being – on whatever scale – could design a working link to the electronic world would be like presuming a cat could invent an electric light!

We attribute this unparalled feat of celestial engineering to the Archangels. But the Archangels, like the Absolute, cannot do whatever they want. While they succeeded in creating an organism with a set of internal linkages which enable it to sustain consciousness, they could not create the consciousness that vehicle was designed to sustain.

Let us reconsider the Microcosmos Man in this expanded context:

- **From the point of view of Organic Life** the human organism – with its highly developed nervous system – is the culmination of the hierarchy of organic life forms.

- **From the point of view of the Archangels** humanity is the site of a very carefully engineered experiment to generate consciousness out of organic life.

- **From the point of view of Mankind** our capacity to transcend the medium from which we were created is related to our capacity to achieve a certain kind of individuality and self-consciousness.

Thus Man, at the top of the hierarchy of organic life forms, is the embodiment of a profound contradiction. He stands between two worlds, the organic and the celestial. In this situation he can experience fully the tension between his own finite individuality and the infinite living whole that contains it. This tends to make him neurotic. The 'crisis of human individuality' has remained a deep source of anxiety for the species, pushing its members alternately towards the false security of collective life, or the perilous attempt to achieve true individuality.

True individuality – individuality based on BEING without limit or boundary in any direction – is a sword that cuts with two edges. In order to acquire it a man must first acquire the individuality that is normal to his species. But in the course of acquiring this 'normal' individuality a man can very easily cut himself off from the intuitive awareness of Organic Life that all the other animals share. Beyond this, he will almost certainly cut himself off from the awareness of other men and women as his own exact equivalents – or as different versions of himself. In fact human beings almost never achieve 'normal' individuality without losing both of these forms of awareness.

To acquire true individuality a man must press past the self-reflexive activity of the four lower centers – capped, as it is, by the imaginary 'I' – to achieve a more universal form. This is the most difficult task that any man or woman can attempt. To expect that a person accomplish this without the guidance of beings who have already gone through the process would be like throwing a newborn child into the water and expecting the child to swim.

Thus, just as the Gods labored to create the human vessel out of the medium of Organic Life and to complete it with the divine seal of Higher Centers, so they must labor to nurture the spark of consciousness in embodied men and women. And here we mark an important distinction. While the Celestial Beings that we have called the Archangels created Organic Life and engineered the archetypal man, they do not usually undertake the second labor of helping individual men and women to awaken. This task is normally allocated to the twice-born Gods who themselves developed out of the medium of Organic Life and for that very reason have a first-hand understanding of the process.

What we have called the 'crisis of human individuality' was probably less pronounced in the first-created men, as their connection with the Order of Nature was more intact. In other words the hardships of existence in Paleolithic times were mitigated by the fact that man himself was probably more balanced; he took life more as it came to him and was less subject to imaginary fears. Additionally the ancient Shamen – the conscious cells in the Paleolithic social body – had a developed awareness of the Unity of Organic Life and so could give guidance to their people in the vast and mysterious world where mankind was not yet the dominant species. And of course behind the Shamen were the Celestial Beings who had selected our species from the several other varieties of early man as the vehicle for Higher Centers. It was these Beings who stood directly behind the early shamanic lines of transmission.

In this context the hardships of prehistoric existence were offset by an incredible richness of perception, a profound understanding of symbol and ritual, and a certain understanding of the working of fate in an individual human life. These understandings gave early man the ability to accept pain, loss, and death. So, while prehistoric man had a shorter life span than we do, and faced greater physical hardship, he was at least as human as we are, and in some ways may have been more so.

CHAPTER 7
The Origin of Man

We have taken, as our definition of Man, a homonid in whom the Celestial Beings have established a hidden potential for awakening in the form of the two Higher Centers.

Because the link between man's cellular body and his latent Higher Centers does not leave direct traces in the skeletal system, we have no way of determining when it was established. But the engineering of this link almost certainly corresponded to physiological changes that occurred in the particular variant of *homo sapiens* destined to become modern man. We surmise that this occurred at the time early man underwent an enlargement of the prefrontal cortex, a region of the brain which is associated with planning, the determination of the future consequences of present actions, and the ability to work towards a defined goal. The prefrontal cortex also acts to control irrational impulses coming from those parts of centers that we share with the animals, such as pain, pleasure, rage, panic, and basic sexual responses. The skull of a primate in whom the prefrontal cortex is developed displays a prominent forehead, which sits in a 'forward' position, more or less above the dental arch.

The variant of *homo sapiens* in whom the emergence of the prefrontal cortex was destined to take place was already distinct from the other forms of early man, such as Neanderthal Man or Peking Man, that existed in the period immediately before the last Ice Age. Because this new variant of *homo sapiens* was to become the central species of the genus *homo*, scientists gave him – on the basis of hindsight – the name *homo sapiens sapiens*. The skull of *homo sapiens sapiens* was larger than that of his contemporaries and his posture was more erect. This enlargement of the skull case was well underway in skulls found in Ethiopia dating back 160,000 years and in skulls found in China dating back at least 70,000 years. Both display a skull of comparable size to that of modern man, but both retain the prominent brow ridges and receding forehead of the archaic *homo sapiens*. The prominent brow ridges are protective and at the same time anchor heavy muscles connecting to the lower jaw, which enable the mastication of roughage of different kinds.

Much later, 35,000 to 45,000 years ago, a very definite change came over *homo sapiens sapiens:* the heavy ridge of the brow receded and the forehead became more prominent – in a way that indicates the development of the prefrontal cortex. At the same time the teeth became smaller and more refined, the front of the dental arch shifted back to a point just below the brow, the base of the skull enlarged, and the connection between the skull and the spinal column shifted down to a point directly beneath the skull – corresponding to a fully upright stance. Man had taken the upright position and learned to use his hands to prepare and to cook his food. We shall call the first phase of *homo sapiens sapiens* with a fully erect posture **Early Modern Man** and the second phase, defined particularly by the development of the prefrontal cortex, **Modern Man**.

The earliest skulls of Modern Man that we have discovered date from about 35,000 years ago, somewhere in the midst of the last Ice Age. It is remarkable that, while the different races which comprise Modern Man vary considerably, none of them can be traced further back than this time, and all of them completed the same morphological changes in exactly the same way.

When you look at the skull of Modern Man and compare it with the skulls of the other homonids, you immediately sense an invisible force field of energy. You feel that this skull was the locus of a certain kind of psychological life; you sense that an intelligence dwelt therein. This is the tortured, erratic, yet brilliant intelligence of a microcosm endowed with a subliminal awareness of the infinite living whole. We know that the Higher Centers, when they come, bring an enormous pressure and a remarkable refinement. They allow for a complete and unbroken control of the attention in all four of the lower centers. The creature whose fate it is to bear latent Higher Centers, and to take responsibility for forming a permanent relation with them, must display some corresponding characteristics. If a homonid form is to become the vehicle for Higher Centers, it must be able to take instruction and guidance from the flashes of Higher Centers that precede their full awakening. It must have at its disposal refined and highly sensitive equipment.

When you look at a chimpanzee you see openness, spontaneity, and charm – but you do not see the capacity for sustained concentration or the extreme refinement that we associate with all of human art and science. This simply does not lie within the animal's range. When you enter the caves at Lascaux, created by early Modern Man 35,000 years ago, you immediately sense a human ambience; there is a refinement, an intelligence, and – above all – a feeling of the sacred.

It is surely not an accident that the physical changes we have described occurred 35,000 to 45,000 years ago – concurrently with this remarkable cultural development. Man began to produce art. In the cave paintings at Lascaux, La Marche, Chauvet, and Altamira (Figure 7 to Figure 11), there is draftsmanship at a very high level, showing a developed sense of line and form. But beyond this there is a profound spiritual symbolism which we may never completely understand. Many quite refined and developed images appear in recessed and almost inaccessible passages, hidden from the light of day – and we cannot know the reason why. Additionally scholars have been unable to explain how the geographically isolated and dispersed groups of early Modern Men could have created images that are so similar at the same time, as they could not have been in direct communication with one another. When you walk into these caves you immediately feel the sensitivity and intelligence of the people who once dwelt there. These are men and women like ourselves, who do not know some of the things we now know but who knew other things that we have long forgotten.

The combination of these factors suggests that this second stage in the development of *homo sapiens sapiens* signaled the decisive intervention of the Gods in the

Figure 7. **Chauvet – four horses**

Figure 8. **Altamira – bison, herd animals**

Figure 9. **Altamira – bison**

Figure 10. **Chauvet – lions**

Figure 11. **Lascaux – stags crossing river**

creation of Man. This, then, is the 'Man' who is the protagonist of our story.

And here we must pause to question the image of early man that has been created for us by a social order that sees man as having developed out of the level *below* the level he is on.

In re-thinking this image we must remember that from the very beginning Modern Man had three qualities: **1)** he was very much less in imagination than contemporary human beings are, **2)** he had a direct and working contact with the Gods, and **3)** he had a deep intuitive connection to the Unity of Organic Life. Personality as we know it was almost undeveloped, and essence much more prominent. Modern Man came into existence as a totally vulnerable being. At the level of his four lower centers he lived moment by moment because he had to. His fears were not negative imaginings but real fears, calling for real responses. In trying to reconstruct his situation we may ask: How or in what form did the Gods reveal themselves to him? How did he see himself in relation to other created beings? When we make the effort to place ourselves in his position, he appears to have been more awake than we are now; indeed he must have felt himself to be in the midst of a living universe. Our forgotten ancestor has a very distinguished position in history. As a result of his capacity to respond to the instruction of the Gods he generated the first 'twice-born' conscious beings in our solar system and constituted

THE STORY OF MAN

the first Spiritual Tradition. Indeed, these remain the principal achievements of the human race to this date.

In looking back at the prehistoric period, there is a point to emphasize. Prehistoric man did not distinguish between his inner world and the world outside of himself in the way that we do today. For him there was only life itself: only the process of sustaining himself in a continuous unfolding of internal and external events. Everything that existed in the external world was animate and took part in the life of the experiencing subject. The psychic forces that existed within his being were seen as continuous with psychic forces existing outside of himself, and the external objects that appeared in his immediate surroundings were accepted as elements of his internal world. Prehistoric man was thus surrounded by unknown powers, and even the simplest things could appear as enigmas.

In short, prehistoric man was without the artificial boundaries that are created by a conceptual language system. It may have seemed to him, in certain moments, that he extended deeply into the universe; that the universe itself was an enlargement of his experience. To give an illustration: a small child on a windy spring morning, where there has been both rain and sunshine, may be riveted by the impression of the moving cloud formations. They exist at a great distance above, in the limitless blue dome of the heavens, but – at the same time – they change with a moment to moment immediacy that impinges powerfully on the child's experience. The cloud formations appear at one moment threatening, dark, and sinister. In the next moment the sun breaks through, and the vista is transformed into a radiant crescendo of light. And then the vast, convoluted shapes begin to move again, bringing darkness and a sudden chill. It appears to the child as a Wagnerian spectacle. The disadvantage of such unconditional openness is the almost paralyzing intensity of experience, but the advantage is an extreme sensitivity to a range of forces and energies that are no longer directly accessible to man.

From the standpoint of simple self-preservation, it was necessary for prehistoric man to define and distinguish this tide of incoming impressions, and to direct behavior according to certain guidelines or principles. Discovering the appropriate guidelines and applying them in everyday life was almost certainly part of the work of the first Spiritual Traditions. We do not know what guidelines were used, or how the Traditions chose to distinguish external from internal, but we know that they must have provided an orientation that allowed man to function in a balanced way.

Given prehistoric man's state of unconditional openness, the use of magic came naturally to him; it was one of the available tools in an otherwise very limited toolkit.

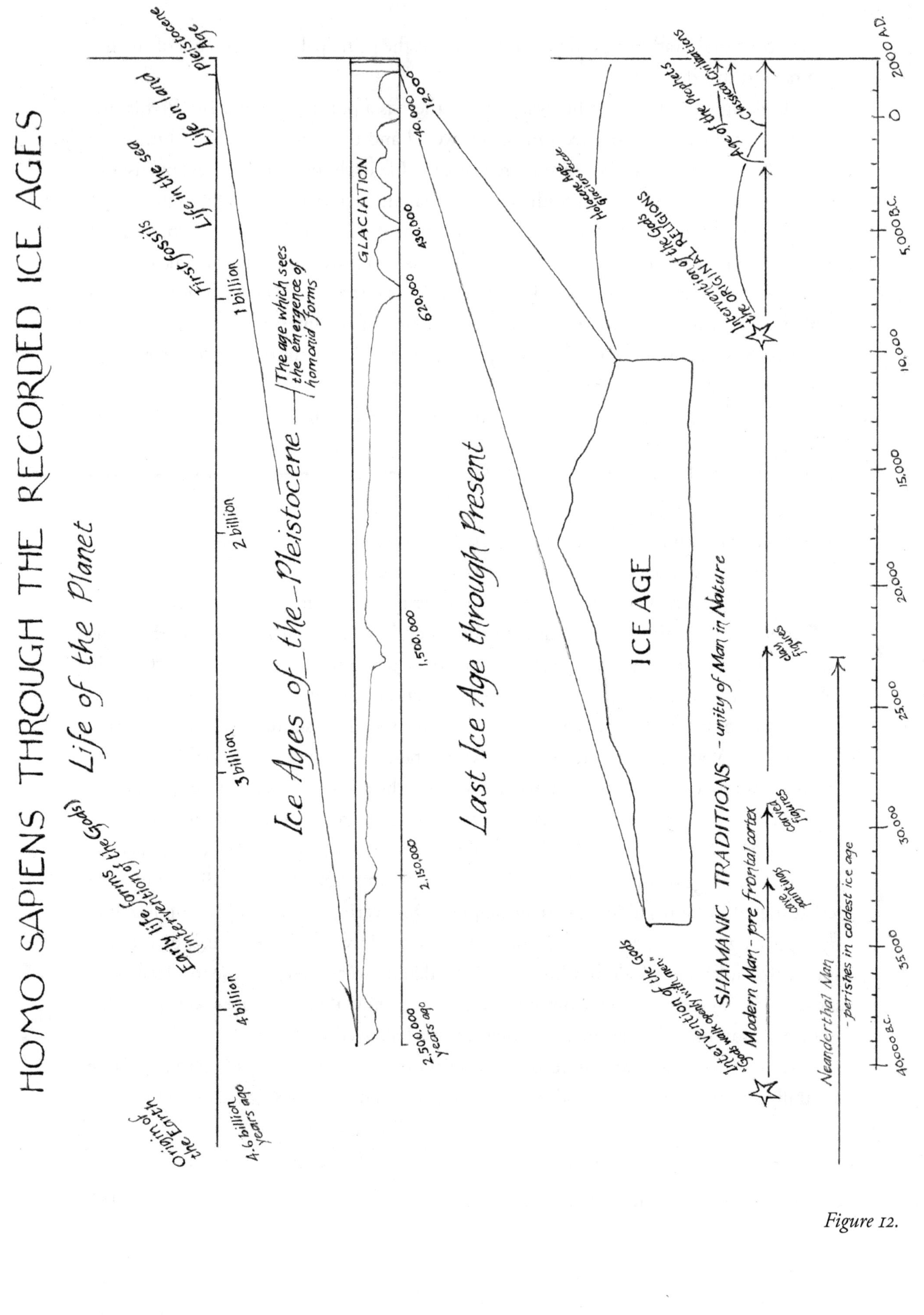
HOMO SAPIENS THROUGH THE RECORDED ICE AGES
Life of the Planet
Origin of the Earth
4.6 billion years ago
4 billion
3 billion
2 billion
1 billion
Early life forms (intervention of the Gods)
First fossils
Life in the sea
Life on land
Pleistocene Age
Ice Ages of the Pleistocene
The age which sees the emergence of hominid forms
GLACIATION
2,500,000 years ago
2,150,000
1,500,000
620,000
430,000
40,000
12,000
Last Ice Age through Present
ICE AGE
Holocene Age glaciers recede
Intervention of the Gods "Gods walk openly with men."
Modern Man - pre frontal cortex
SHAMANIC TRADITIONS - unity of Man in Nature
cave paintings
carved figures
clay figures
Intervention of the Gods
the ORIGINAL RELIGIONS
Age of the Prophets
Classical Civilizations
Neanderthal Man
- perishes in coldest ice age
40,000 B.C.
35,000
30,000
25,000
20,000
15,000
10,000
5,000 B.C.
0
2000 A.D.

Figure 12.

And thus he attempted to establish control over the overwhelming play of forces and counter-forces that comprised his experience. He devised rites and mantras to evoke certain forces and to dispel others.

We know from the study of historical shamanism that shamanic practices develop in a relation to what we have called the Unity of Organic Life. Nature, as the sum of all its organic life forms – from organelle, to amoeba, to vegetable, to invertebrate animal, to vertebrate, to mammal, to human – has a vague and titanic self-awareness, in which man himself can participate. Prehistoric man almost certainly did so participate, and particularly in the person of the shaman. This link then gave the prehistoric community some direction and control in a world that constantly threatened to overwhelm it. The participation in Great Nature was probably the point of departure for the work of the Traditions. In other words, the training for what we have called the first and second work was built on this foundation. The initiate was first brought into contact with Great Nature and then instructed in how to go beyond it. Contact with what transcends Nature would have been represented in myths and symbols that are now lost to us. The interpretation of the surviving artifacts must remain speculative, as these myths and symbols could only have been understood in living contact with a being who had transcended the natural order in this context. From one point of view prehistoric man had many advantages, but from another point of view he faced a particular disadvantage; the unity of nature has a fascination that is hard to surmount. It is also the natural domain of the Black Queen. Thus our ancestors had to pass a particular trial to enter the Great Work, different but not more difficult than the trials that we face today

The Preliminary Period

The precursor to Modern Man, *homo sapiens*, existed for at least four million years. Indeed six major Ice Ages have come and gone since man's biological ancestors first appeared. Neanderthal man, advanced by homonid standards, came into existence relatively recently, only 350,000 to 400,000 years ago. He had rudimentary language and was able to use primitive tools and implements. Neanderthal and Peking man both pre-existed *homo sapiens sapiens* by hundreds of thousands of years and shared the planet with him through the first hundred thousand years of his own existence. By the end of the last Ice Age, however, all non-*homo sapiens sapiens* had become extinct in some unknown drama that cleared the stage for the development of Modern Man in the age to follow.

Let us look at timeline drawings which show the different species of the man-like beings who are the precursors of Modern Man (showing several Ice Ages) and then the timeline of the mankind of which we are still a part (showing the end of the last Ice Age).

We can make a brief outline of the geographical spread of *homo sapiens sapiens* in order to more clearly mark the transition to Modern Man towards the end of the last Ice Age. Here we follow the standard paleontological researches.

THE APPEARANCE OF EARLY MODERN MAN:
THE FIRST STAGE OF HOMO SAPIENS SAPIENS

It seems likely that Early Modern Man had made his appearance in Ethiopia 160,000 years ago, although some argue that other men reached this stage of development independently in Asia. By 85,000 years ago Early Modern Man had appeared in India, Southeast Asia, and China.

About 70,000 years ago the eruption of Mt. Toba in Sumatra probably killed the majority of the human race – firstly through ash and secondly by initiating a dangerously 'cold' millennium.

Beginning from 65,000 years ago Early Modern Man began to move north. This movement corresponded to the peak period of the last Ice Age. The concentration of water at the ice caps may have produced droughts in regions closer to the equator, forcing the northward migrations.

Between 65,000 and 52,000 years ago he moved into the Levant: Mesopotamia, Turkey, Syria, Lebanon, Palestine, and Israel.

Between 52,000 and 45,000 years ago he entered south/central Europe – from Bulgaria, across to Austria, France, and Spain. Here he joined Neanderthal man, who had been living there for several hundred thousand years.

From 45,000 to 40,000 years ago he went from Iran and Pakistan into Central Asia and from Indochina (Burma, Thailand, Cambodia, Laos) into China, populating for the first time the Yellow River Basin. There is also, at the same time, a movement from Central Asia into South Siberia.

At the same time he went west from the Levant into Mediterranean North Africa and Egypt.

It is from this point onward that we see the emergence of Modern Man from Early Modern Man, and our story becomes more interesting.

MIGRATIONS of EARLY MAN

Figures show thousands of years before the present
Small circles (o) mark 'hubs' or radial points

Man reaches anatomical maturity 200,000 years ago, and begins his migrations from the general area of what is now the Sudan about 160,000 years ago. Man reaches psychological maturity, becoming what we have called 'Modern Man' – with **latent** Higher Centers – about 40,000 to 45,000 years ago.

Figure 13.

THE APPEARANCE OF MODERN MAN:
THE SECOND STAGE OF HOMO SAPIENS SAPIENS

From 45,000 to 25,000 years ago men populated northeastern Europe and moved up to what is now the Arctic Circle in Eastern Europe and Asia. It is somewhere in the middle of this period that Modern Man emerged to produce the great cave paintings of Lascaux, La Marche, Chauvet, Altamira, and Cosquer. Thus it is probably at this point that we have the first great intervention of the Gods and the establishment of the link to Higher Centers.

About 14,000 years ago he crossed the ancient land bridge over the Bering Strait to enter North America.

From 12,000 to 8,000 years ago he entered and populated South America.

In the time of Early Modern Man there were only a few million people on the planet, and they could not, by any means, be considered the dominant species. Early Modern Man led a precarious existence, driven largely by necessity, and many of his migrations may have been forced.

However, from the time of the emergence of Modern Man we see clear evidence of the development of culture and of tools. While this process may have begun as early as 45,000 years ago, most of our evidence dates from 35,000 to 30,000 years ago. The same stage-change may have occurred simultaneously in Central Asia, India, and China, although here the evidence is more fragmentary. Indeed, while modern science has done a great deal of work in tracing early homonid species and the various lines of genetic descent, it has been completely unable to trace the origin of what we have called Modern Man, that is, man with a developed prefrontal cortex, such as all races presently display.

We note in passing that Modern Man emerged only after Early Modern Man had settled in Asia, the Levant, and Europe. And it was only Modern Man who experienced a cultural renaissance during the last Ice Age, and then, as the ice receded, multiplied to become the dominant species on the planet. *Once Modern Man appears the suitable vehicle for Higher Centers has been finally determined and the other homonids vanish.*

Modern Man came into existence in widely variant forms: Oriental, Negroid, Arabic, Indian, and Caucasian. These forms vary almost as much as some of the earlier species of *homo sapiens*, yet each of these show the basic change in morphology we have spoken of. Do these ethnic variations stem from a common parent form, or did a number of different pre-modern men transition through to the modern phase independently? Did the early forms of Modern Man interbreed with various pre-modern men to produce the racial differences that we see today? Modern science has only preliminary theories in this area.

Whatever the case, from about 35,000 years ago there were men as we know them: men capable of remembering the past and anticipating the future, with the power to initiate new kinds of activities. They were capable of cooperating in shared projects and supporting one another in communal forms of life. These men leave us with evidence of developed language, religion, and art. Beyond this they leave us with religious symbols imbued with great depth of meaning. It appears, then, that the previous homonid forms were only experimental men and that the Gods selected the line of *homo sapiens sapiens* for a new phase of development. This 'second phase' would have involved not only the more advanced morphology of the skull, the fully upright posture, and the development of the prefrontal cortex, but all of the delicate inner mechanisms for the transformation of energy that are required to secure the connection to the Sphere of Sentient Being. Once this divine seal had been set, Man was established as a living microcosm of the Absolute.

From the point of view of the initial requirements made on Creation, Modern Man appears, to quote Gurdjieff, as a kind of 'chemical factory,' designed for the transformation of a range of intense and unstable energies into concentrated consciousness. His inner transformative mechanisms are poised to connect to the Sphere of Sentient Being. He stands as a clear example of an evolutionary development where the end defines the process. We could say, using the language of Aristotle, that Higher Centers were the *final cause* of Modern Man.

CHAPTER 8
The Prehistoric Spiritual Traditions

Now, to recapitulate, and at the same time to establish the scale of the human experiment, let us briefly review the potentials that were given in the beginning.

1. The first, and far the most important, is the awakening of Higher Centers. This refers not only to man's capacity to experience Higher Centers, but to his ability to modify his life and inner being so that they may become permanently awake in him. The full realization of Higher Centers – the most difficult task for an individual man – has, in fact, been achieved by many men in many different times and places. Indeed, there have probably been conscious beings continuously on the planet for the last 35,000 to 40,000 years.

2. The second potential is to form a Spiritual Tradition. This Man has achieved, at least intermittently, over the last forty millennia.

3. The third potential is to form a community under the leadership of a Spiritual Tradition; in other words, a School Civilization, or completed Cosmos of Man. This, and this alone, would allow mankind to act in unison to **a)** improve its psychological and spiritual condition and so secure its link to the cosmos one above and **b)** monitor its relation to the other species of organic life. While there is clear evidence that mankind has, at different points, attempted to realize this potential, we have not yet had any enduring success.

   We note that the third potential is not the potential for a utopia. Mankind's permanent link to the Worlds below – 96, 192, 384, and 768 – disallows this. In other words, our place within Creation makes it more or less impossible. But the tensions and contradictions of the place we occupy do still enable the transcendence we were designed to effect. Thus, what is possible for a man (to be governed by his own Higher Centers) is possible for a Civilization (to be governed by its conscious aspects). This in no way implies that a School Civilization would be free of strife, confusion, and suffering – but that it would be able to sustain its core values in face of these, as civilizations have in fact done for centuries at a time.

4. In addition to this, in reviewing the works of modern science, we note that the physiology of Modern Man contains all of the most developed systems produced by organic life over the previous three billion years. Modern Man is, in a very special way, the 'crown of nature.' Through the intellectual part of the instinctive center, in its connection to the emotional center, he is capable of reading the patterns of nature and of perceiving the molecular energy fields of organic beings. When you combine this with the capacity to communicate directly with the Gods who created both himself and the Medium of Organic Life, you see that Modern Man is uniquely equipped to complete and to manage the system of life forms which comprises it. He has the capacity to understand the needs of Organic Life and to help it to come to completion. He is therefore, at least potentially, capable of raising its level, and so raising the level of the planet itself. It seems very likely that this is one of the 'ends' for which Man was created. In the book of Genesis, God says, "Let us make man in our image, after our likeness: and let them have dominion over the fish of the sea, and over the fowl of the air, and over the cattle, and over all the earth, and over every creeping thing that creepeth upon the earth." In the original Zoroastrian teaching this function is actually detailed. While there is a record of this kind of thinking in history, there is little evidence of its implementation. Indeed, from the time Modern Man emerged he has caused the extinction of one species after another, and in the last two hundred years the entire web of organic life has suffered heavily from the extraordinary over-population of *homo sapiens sapiens*.

While the potentials to create a Spiritual Tradition and to achieve School Civilization were given in the beginning, it is unlikely that a complete vision of all that was involved was given at the same time. It would have been difficult for the first Modern Men to understand the idea of a 'School Civilization' when the human community was comprised of groupings of extended families. Probably Modern Man was initially given **1)** a direct vision of the level from which he was created and to which he must return, **2)** a vision of the ideal relation between self and others, and **3)** a corresponding vision of the Great Work. The other elements were given at later stages in human history, and we shall attempt to mark the different points at which we see evidence of them.

From the moment that mankind was given this set of potentials, **there is a measure in human history**. As we noted, Mankind could not realize these potentials unaided. We can be sure that the Gods would not have labored for countless millennia to endow man with such a legacy without ensuring that the conditions existed in which it could be realized. We have emphasized Man's need of help in penetrating the Sphere of Sentient Being. We shall now emphasize Man's need of help in establishing and stabilizing a Spiritual Tradition and a Civilization informed by that Tradition – so endowing him with the means to create **a Sacred World**.

Man needs a way of communicating about his experience of Higher Centers, and he needs the means of receiving communication from the Gods. He needs at least a rudimentary language and he needs a means of representing experiences that transcend language. Given that man had only a rudimentary language in Paleolithic times, these means may have been – in the beginning – symbolic. In other words man's first representations of a sacred world, and of a corresponding path of development, were probably symbolic. We see remarkable evidence of this in the cave paintings made during the last Ice Age. Once the essential teachings had been secured through a set of relevant keys and symbols, shamanic practices would have been able to produce the required results.

For all of these reasons we surmise that, after the link to Higher Centers had been engineered, there was a long period of open communication between Men and Gods. Indeed almost all ancient mythologies refer to a Golden Age before the fall of man when Men and Gods walked together. Perhaps we can make an analogy between the life of Mankind and the life of an individual human being. The infant arrives in the world without a personality; it is almost entirely essence. It has an innocence and purity which only a very few will recover again in the mature phase of their lives, and that only through great suffering. Modern Man would have been like this. But he, unlike ourselves, would have been close to essence and close to the Gods at the same time. The

Gods would have encouraged his essence and interacted directly with it. The insemination of essence by the Gods is unspeakably rare; it is to be formed by the level one above in the present. These early men had an unthinking, childlike closeness to the Gods which our contemporary culture has entirely lost.

In this regard it is clear that the material and technical accomplishments that our own civilization values so highly have little direct relation to realizing the highest possibilities that exist in man. They are incidental to what is more real, and they are not necessary to achieving it.

The Prehistoric Spiritual Tradition, in its many different branches and in the many communities which supported it, was probably centered around the person of the Shaman. As we noted above, a great Shaman would have the capacity to see into the Unity of Organic Life and so would have been capable of providing guidance and hope for his small community in a threatening world. The Shamen, we surmise, were often conscious beings; but there would have been many Shamen in whom only the powers of sorcery were developed. A great, or conscious, Shaman would have had the additional responsibility of trying to raise the 'mere sorcerers' from their preoccupation with things not central to the plan of the Gods for Mankind.

After the passage of the initial phase of intimate contact with the Gods, the now-established Shamanic Traditions probably preserved something of the direct revelations of the Golden Age. In other words, they probably retained some understanding of the real purpose of human existence, as it was originally given. We must also consider that men may have been close to the Gods and shared their understandings for quite a long period of time. There is an analogy here to the 'time' of a human life. In the first weeks and months, time passes very slowly. The day of a newborn infant is weeks or months in the life of an adult. The immensely long span of the prehistoric era could be likened to the disproportionately long span of the first years of a human life.

In the prehistoric period the Shaman was not only a source of teaching, but of healing, of religion, and of government. He was at the center of a cluster of extended families. The inner teaching would thus have existed in unity with the shamanic religion, as part of a communal way of life. This 'casual' relation of a conscious being to an extended family line (as distinct from the relationship he would have to his circle of initiates) continued – in traditional societies – into modern times. An example would be the nineteenth century Sufi *tekkes* of Central Asia.

Where the ancient Shaman was fully conscious, the essential teaching needed to actualize Higher Centers would have been transmitted as it had been given in the beginning. Where the leader of the community had shamanic powers but was not conscious, the essential teaching would have been taken more in its outer meaning. The original shamanic communities, working in blood-related lines, may have developed a deep understanding of what Hinduism calls 'the transmigration of souls' and of what was possible for each soul in a given lifetime.

The immeasurably long infancy of man was filled with dramas that we can only now surmise: the movement into the Russian steppes at the end of the last Ice Age, the concentrations of population in Central Asia around an ancient 'core' Tradition, and the amazing migrations through the Bering Strait land bridge to the New World.

Could the myth of the 'fall of man' be related to a great drama that occurred when the Gods withdrew from direct and open contact? When did they withdraw, and after how many millennia? Was their purpose to enable man to achieve certain potentials that he could not achieve within the original community? Had early Modern Man developed a dependency on the Gods? Had he come to take them for granted in the wrong way? Was he therefore sent out to learn to 'be' on his own? Or was there an ancient struggle between white and black sorcerers, the former in service of man's Higher Centers and the latter in service of the occult powers connected with the Black Queen? Was there an initial fall from grace due to the influence of the black sorcerers, which was then followed by a long period in which the white sorcerers struggled to recover what had been lost? Was this state of grace recovered and then lost again? Scenarios of this kind would create the uncertainty which is needed to foster the work of the Spiritual Traditions.

Whatever happened in our prehistory, a pattern of development unfolded, one millennium after the next, through the immensely long span of the last Ice Age. There may have been unique opportunities in this period, just as there are unique opportunities in the first years of a human life. But – just as with the passage from childhood to adolescence – more was to be required. The critical changes, which brought the new requirements, came at the end of the last Ice Age, 12,000 years ago.

CHAPTER 9

The Prehistoric Expansion

Beginning from the end of the Ice Age, there was a rapid population increase in the only remaining species of *homo sapiens*. We have noted that, from before the end of the Ice Age (12,000 years ago), there were communities of men in Ethiopia, the Levant, Egypt and North Africa, India, China, Southeast Asia, Central and Western Europe, and Mesoamerica. Beginning from 10,000 BC these communities grew rapidly.

There was, from about 12,000 BC, an important migration into the fertile plains of Central Europe and the Russian Steppes, as these were freed up by the retreating glaciers. Huge concentrations of herd animals appeared in these regions, and tribes of nomadic hunters followed them. In the millennia that followed a major prehistorical cultural development occurred in this region to parallel the developments that occurred in Southern France, Egypt, India, and China.

CHAPTER 10

The Development of Material Culture

It is hard to establish accurate dates in this area, and new discoveries bring almost continuous revisions of our understanding. We do know that Modern Man, the carrier of the original teaching of the Gods, continued for tens of thousands of years as a nomadic hunter and gatherer. Then, shortly after the end of the last Ice Age, he began to domesticate sheep, cattle, and pigs and at the same time started to plant and harvest grains. Man became both a herdsman and a farmer. These different practices began amongst different groups in different locales and gradually spread to the population as a whole.

We have evidence of the domestication of animals from somewhere between 9000 and 7000 BC.

There is evidence of wheat production in Syria from 11,000 BC, and we see the beginnings of agriculture in Turkey and Israel from 9000 BC. Wheat and barley were domesticated in the Middle East in the eighth millennium BC. Squash was raised in Mexico by 8000 BC. Millet and rice were domesticated in China and Southeast Asia by 5500 BC. Vegetables were grown in Thessaly and Macedonia from 6000 BC. We know that there was agriculture on the Russian Steppes and in Central Asia from a very early period of time. Both the Tigris-Euphrates river basin and the Nile river basin were the source of extensive agricultural activity by 6000 BC.

The ability to irrigate land is critical to the development of agriculture. Long before irrigation systems were developed, agriculture was pursued in the hills of Anatolia, where there was regular rainfall. Agriculture came to full maturity in the four great riverine civilizations which developed around the Tigris-Euphrates river basin, the Nile river basin, the Indus river basin, and the Yellow River basin in China – for at these four sites the waters of the rivers could be diverted for purposes of irrigation.

With agriculture comes village life. In farming communities the 'homes' of extended families grouped into little villages, surrounded by fields. The production of surplus crops led to trade and to further population expansion, which again encouraged the development of village life. This was a turning point in the development of civilization.

Jericho in Israel, Catalhoyuk in Turkey, and Mehrgahn in the Indus river valley emerged as large agricultural villages as early as 9000 BC. By 5000 BC the valleys surrounding the Tigris-Euphrates rivers were filled with villages and townships.

With the irrigation systems that developed around the Tigris and Euphrates, the Nile, the Indus, and the Yellow River in China, a greater social surplus was produced. This freed certain members of society from spending all their time securing the immediate necessities of life and enabled a greater continuity of cultural development from one generation to the next. From this, and from the attendant development of trade, large urban centers began to develop.

True cities had made their appearance by 3000 BC: the city of Uruk in Mesopotamia; the cities of Memphis and Thebes in dynastic Egypt; the cities of Mohenjo-daro and Harappa in the Indus valley. Of these the Mesopotamian and the Egyptian cities display monumental art and architecture, connected with the religions of those peoples. The remains of ancient cities have also been discovered in Central Asia.

We may note that simultaneously with the development of cities, a very high level of culture was achieved in the village civilization of the Russian Steppes.

From these indications we see that a major phase in human development had been completed in the period before recorded history. We shall now try to reconstruct what was at the center of this change and consider how man's experience of his own existence was changed – but before doing so we must make a brief note on the recurrent legend of a lost civilization which existed in the millennium or two after the retreat of the glaciers.

THE LEGEND OF ATLANTIS

All of the interest in a possible Atlantean civilization originates from material found in Plato's *Critias* and *Timaeus* dialogues. The *Critias* references Solon's researches in Egypt, and Plato himself lived in Egypt for several years. We have no firm evidence of a second source, although a student of Plato's student Xenocrates, by the name of Crantor, claimed to have found columns in Egypt with the history of Atlantis written in hieroglyphic characters. Crantor's works have been lost, and we know of this only by the report of the ancient historian

Proclus. So, while we acknowledge that Plato's remarkable vision of Atlantis has left a deep imprint, the historical references to its actual existence are little above the level of rumor.

Contemporary interest in the legend of Atlantis originates from the work of three psychics inspired by Plato's vision: Helena Petrovna Blavatsky, Rudolf Steiner, and Edgar Cayce. All three agree on dating the fall of Atlantis in the millennium or two following the retreat of the glaciers (9000-7500 BC). On the basis of their closely-related visions many researchers have attempted to gather information to support the hypothesis of a historical Atlantis. While there is much debate on this subject, there is still little hard evidence in support of the theory.

Psychic inspiration aside, it seems strange to propose a technical society at this time in our prehistory, particularly when we consider that technological development equates with neither the objective level of the civilizational order – as approximating the Cosmos of Man – nor the higher consciousness of the Spiritual Traditions. The civilizations of the eighth and ninth millennia BC may not have been 'technical,' but they were developing in different – and ultimately more important – ways.

CHAPTER 11

The Birth of Religion

With the development of agriculture the scale of human society began to change, and this brought with it both possibilities and dangers.

We do know that in the period immediately after the Ice Age there was a population explosion, a technological revolution, and a marked development of language skills. There was a change of focus in relation to the external world as man became the dominant species on the planet, and this brought a greater sense of security to the developing social order. There was an ever-greater emphasis on an ever-greater number of activities taking place in relation to the external world. There was, then, the strong likelihood that the original revealed teaching of the Gods, which had been transmitted so carefully from one generation to the next, would be distorted or mixed with other things. At the same time, the increase in population and the emergence of Man as the dominant species would naturally require a new vision. Could the inner teaching be carried forward within this new vision?

It is almost certain that the first great Religions made their appearance at just this time. They were not – in their first years – Religions as we know them today, but Living Religions, backed by Spiritual Traditions in actual communication with the Gods. These Religions were to displace Shamanism as the principal vehicle for the Traditions, and they were to give life to emergent civilizations in Mesopotamia, Egypt, and India. While they were not the Religions as we know them today, they provided the backdrop for the religions known to history; we might call them the **Original Religions**.[1] The form of these Religions was in many ways incompatible with the practices of Shamanism, certainly with the outer forms of the old Shamanic religion.

---

1. See the Subject Bibliography under the heading 'The Original Religions' and the author Eliade, Mircea. Our characterization of the Original Religions owes much to his pathbreaking work.

The Original Religions, when they came, broke the immediacy of the union of Man with Nature, claiming that there is a reality above the Order of Nature to which Man owes his allegiance. They emphasized a single God, or a single sentience transcending Nature, and they provided a corresponding myth of the Origin of Things. This foundation myth describes the sequence of creative acts which brought the Universe into being and so made cosmos out of chaos. This series of divine acts represented, at the same time, the essential processes through which the Microcosmos Man creates and re-creates his own World. In describing the original events that gave form to both Man and Nature, the Great Myths described the basic functions man must fulfill in order to sustain the social order. All of the essential human roles – the Great Warrior, the Great Builder, the Great Father, the Great Mother – are interpreted as the re-creations of archetypal acts existing outside of time and space. The myths of the Original Religion also encompass the role changes that take place in an individual human life: from infancy to childhood, from childhood to maturity, and from maturity to old age – but above all, those role changes connected with the mysteries of birth and death. Each of these archetypal acts was represented as ritual, which was intended to renew and to sustain the original moment of creation.

In the Original Religions the sequence of archetypal acts – the ideal forms existing outside of time and space – described all that was essential to maintaining human existence within the stream of time. However, the actual patterns of events which spun out from the archetypes might deviate from the ideal forms. To the extent a man deviates from the archetype, or becomes estranged from it, he enters the realm of the inessential and the meaningless. The purpose of the Original Religion was, then, to help Man live in the archetype and so retain his sense of the meaning of life.

In the Original Religions everything was seen to have a divine origin, outside of time and space as we know it. There is, then, existence continuous with this divine origin, and there is also the possibility of falling away from the divine origin. Loss of connection with the origin of things brings with it a loss of meaning, a loss of integrity, and a loss of essential force. This 'falling away' from the divine origin is – at the same time – a 'falling into' the stream of time. In the Original Religions the wearing and debilitating effects of time are seen as a departure from the purity of the original acts of creation.

The gradual falling away from the divine archetype through time and the return to the purity of the original moment is seen as a cycle. The Original Religions thus presented the Universe as a system of cycles: the cycle of day and night, the cycle of the seasons, and the cycle of life and death. The latter cycle was in turn broken into the cycles of infancy, childhood, maturity, old age, and death. The cycle of human life itself was renewed in re-birth.

The debilitating effects of time were, then, abolished by a return to the divine archetype. The Original Religions enabled this by rituals which re-created the critical deeds and moments of a human life. There were – at the same time – rituals of sacrifice, which represented mankind's relation to the order of the Gods. An act of sacrifice reproduces the initial sacrifice revealed by the Creator God at the beginning of time, when he willed his own negation. Not only does Man's act of sacrifice reproduce the act of the God, it is understood to occur in the same mythical instant of beginning. Thus, through the imitation of the archetypes man re-enters the mythical epoch in which the archetypes were first revealed.

Here we have the division of what Mircea Eliade called *the Sacred and the Profane*.[2] The 'sacred' is the mythical time of origins, the primal intensity and simplicity of existence outside of time. The zone of the sacred is at the center of a living Universe. The 'profane' is the departure from original purity; it is a descent into meaningless complexity, confusion, fear, and greed. It is the region where man has no pattern and where he loses his very 'self.' The Original Religions gave man tremendous strength, for even great suffering can be linked to the archetype of the Suffering God. In this way participation in the archetypes enabled man to endure even the moments of birth and death.

In this relation of the sacred and the profane, there is the possibility of an ultimate falling away from the 'sacred center,' a permanent dissociation from the renewal of cyclical time. By losing his sense of the sacred a man enters the irreversible forward flow of historical time where everything changes all the time and nothing comes back to its beginning. Mircea Eliade referred to this loss as 'the terror of history.' It is the movement into a world where life is devoid of inherent value. The irreversible forward flow of historical time introduces an unknowable 'future,' whereas the cyclical time characteristic of the Original Religions offers the security of repetition, redemption, and renewal.

Thus, while the Myths of the Original Religion enable man to bear even the harshest suffering, they do not enable him to bear irreversible time. The Original Religions enabled him to return to the zone of the sacred; the rituals of those Original Religions restored the mythical time of the origin of all things.

In speaking of the content of the Original Religions we are speaking of Living Religion, not of the Great Work itself, for this is ever the same. Nevertheless the Original

---

2. See the Subject Bibliography under the heading 'The Original Religions,' and the author Eliade, Mircea.

Religions, as Living Religions, enabled man to pass through the preparatory stages of the First Work, and we can easily see the connective points to the Great Work. The work of the Spiritual Traditions is the renewal of presence in the point-instant of NOW. Presence is prolonged independently of the four lower centers and so independently of every act and change of life that Man can experience in the line of time. Thus in the transition to the Great Work there is movement from the renewal of the life of the four lower centers to the renewal of one's Invisible Self, which exists outside of time. The Traditions enable man to escape from the debilitating effects of time by entering into and becoming one with the eternal present rather than by securing attitudes which help him to 'endure the blows.'

This chapter in the Story of Man sees a new vision of the human community combined with an enormous change in its physical scale. This vision revealed the potential for a School Civilization through the myth-based social order. It may also have brought an awareness of Man's potential to consciously complete the process of organic life. Whatever the case, a strong link between Civilization, Religion, and Tradition existed within the Original Religions, as these elements could not exist peripherally to society – because there was no 'outside' of society to exist in!

The Original Religions were almost certainly launched from Spiritual Traditions, whether Shamanic Traditions given a new mission or new Traditions initiated by the Gods through chosen men. In either case, the outer shell of the Original Religion would have allowed the initiates of the Tradition to maintain all of the practices of the Great Work in the midst of a larger community.

We may surmise that there was, in some cases, a crisis or collision between the Shamanic Traditions and the proponents of the Original Religions. In other cases there may have been relative continuity. Where there was continuity, the Religion would have intentionally added an outer layer of Religious myth to the work of the Shamanic initiates, who – at the same time – preserved the original teachings. Thus the dispersion of the original 'inner' teachings that would naturally follow from a population explosion was anticipated by creating a division of an inner teaching and an outer teaching. The development of the outer teachings would at the same time be the development of the pattern for a complete and coherent culture. With hindsight we can see a second point of continuity. The Original Religions, while having placed the Gods above Nature, did preserve something of the Shamanic vision of the unity of man in nature – but they adjusted this vision to the experience of agricultural life. And thus Shamanism and the

Original Religions show the same ritual acknowledgment of all the cycles to which organic life forms are subject.

In those regions where there was not a continuity of shamanic practice with the emergent Religions, the shamanic practices were eventually pushed to the fringe of the social order. There may have been a period of struggle between the Original Religions and Shamanism, just as, in historical times, there were struggles between the Original Religions and the Religions of the Prophets. While tensions and struggles of this kind are never sought by Spiritual Traditions, they often create the conditions which allow for an intensification of inner work. Living Traditions are vivified in hard trials while the 'dead' Traditions, which easily fall into the role of the 'opponent,' are ultimately sloughed off.

Having attempted to represent the Original Religions in their inner principle, we have one more task before we can continue the Story of Man. The most enduring contribution of this 'second age' of Modern Man, was developed language forms. They are, indeed, the taken-for-granted basis of our social life today. We shall lay the foundation for our study of the 'historical' period by examining the enigmatic link between these new language forms and the Original Religions.

CHAPTER 12

Language and Bennett's Hypothesis of Four Original Religions

We know that somewhere between 10,000 and 8,000 BC man acquired a more developed language structure. This is the same period in which a much enlarged population acquired a more complex religion and mythology. Thus a number of basic language types and a number of basic mythologies appear at the same time.

We speculate that these changes were connected with a second major intervention of the Gods in human history, the first being related to the development of the prefrontal cortex which occurred somewhere in the midst of the last Ice Age. Mankind would almost certainly have had some simple form of language from the time of the first intervention, but there were not then the circumstances to foster the development of the more advanced language types we know today.

A NOTE ON LANGUAGE

Just as the skull shape which corresponds to the existence of the prefrontal cortex is common to all surviving races of men, so is this more developed language usage. We have, of course, no way of dating the use of developed grammatical forms, but linguists agree that amongst all the races that comprise contemporary humanity, there are no primitive languages. While languages differ in the extent of their vocabulary and while their lexicons spread to cover different subject areas, all possess the grammar and syntax required to say the things that can be said in the other languages.

The commonality of linguistic forms suggests a predisposition to language in that form of *homo sapiens sapiens* which is Modern Man. There is a strong argument in contemporary linguistics that man, as we know him, possesses innate language structures. In this view babies are born with a capacity for forming grammatical structures and need only learn the particular features of the first language they are exposed to. They do not learn a language by learning its grammatical rules but by hearing it used, and by responding to it intuitively through the innate language structures.

Another remarkable discovery of linguistics is that the syntax and grammar of many ancient languages, such as Old Sanskrit, Ancient Hebrew, or Ancient Greek, are more developed than those of modern languages, just as the syntax and grammar of Latin are more developed than those of the modern Romance languages – French, Italian, Spanish, and Romanian – that derive from it. The ancient languages frequently showed a rigorous syntax while at the same time being heavily nuanced and inflected. Additionally, it has been shown that the most primitive language forms that exist today are not the survivals of a more primitive age but are languages that have descended from more developed proto-languages! We surmise that the languages given Man by the Gods at the end of the last Ice Age were more developed in their capacity to refer to the realm of the sacred than the languages of the present day. Reflecting on the 'dead' languages of which we still have records, both Old Sanskrit and Ancient Greek have a greater capacity to represent metaphysical reality than any of the languages spoken today.

The philologist J.R.R. Tolkien made a very insightful remark in this regard: "Legends depend on the language to which they belong; but a living language depends equally on the 'legends' which it conveys … Esperanto, Ida, and Novial are dead, far deader than ancient unused languages, because their authors never invented legends."[1] The age of myth and legend has passed, and in our own time languages develop in relation to the functional requirements that are made upon them. They are not more, but less adapted to poetry, to metaphysics, and to myth.

J.G. Bennett, in his work *The Masters of Wisdom*, suggested that, in the period following the last Ice Age, the Gods simultaneously initiated a number of Great Schools. Each of these schools inculcated a more developed language and a correspondingly more developed vision of the place of man in the universe. Each new vision then served as the foundation for a post-Shamanic Religion, suited to the genius and inner inclination of the people who were to become its bearers. While the elements of deep-language structure existed in man before the coming of the Great Schools of the tenth millennium BC, it is with the coming of these Schools that they are developed – for in this historical phase are the external requirements to call them forth and the enlarged human community

---

1. *The Letters of J.R.R. Tolkien*, ed. Humphrey Carpenter, Houghton Miflin Company, Boston, 1981, p. 231.

to support them. With the more developed use of language came an agricultural/technological revolution, which allowed the human social order to generate a social surplus, freeing man from the extremes of scarcity and allowing for the greater development of culture: cities, monumental art, mathematics, astronomy, and astrology. We would, of course, understand Bennett's 'Great Schools' to be the Spiritual Traditions.

Thus, at the time of the post-Ice Age population explosion a generation of Spiritual Traditions appeared to help humanity through the remarkable transition which it then faced. The earlier Shamanic Traditions, whose context had been the extended family, were taxed with the larger and more extensive communities that were developing at that time; their lines of esoteric transmission were becoming diluted and weakened. Thus the emergence of agricultural systems and villages in the tenth millennium BC undermined both the cohesiveness of the old order and the integrity of its teachings. The initial task of the new Spiritual Traditions was to draw groups of men apart, at a set number of predetermined points on the planet, and instill proficiency in a set of more complex language forms. **At the same time they presented a new vision of Man in the Universe.** Hence the more specific representations of the relation between Man and God provided by the Original Religions and by the Religions known to history that followed from them.

The nineteenth-century scholar Max Müller, who first translated the Vedic and Vedantic literature into the European languages under the tutelage of Ramakrishna Paramhansa, suggested three primordial 'unities' of language and religion: **1)** Aryan/Indo-European, **2)** Semitic, and **3)** 'Turanian' – which included Finnish, Tartar, Siberian, and Mongolian. J.G. Bennett, taking up on Müller's work, accepted the idea of three basic language types but suggested that there was a fourth Original Religion – peculiar to Asia Minor and the Levant. This Religion did not have a corresponding language type, as it did not need a more developed language to convey its essential teachings.[2] Bennett, working in light of a further eighty years of linguistic research, formulated the three primordial language types as **1)** the family of Hamito-Semitic languages, originating in what is now Egypt, Mesopotamia, and Israel/Judea, **2)** the inflected Indo-European languages, originating in Central Europe west of the Urals, and **3)** the 'polysynthetic and agglutinative languages' of Central Asia and the Far East.

We will accept Bennett's basic breakdown of the three language types and the four Original Religions as a working hypothesis, in order to proceed with our story. We do not know if his correspondences of language type and Religion are exact, but we are

---

2. See Bennett, J.G., *The Masters of Wisdom*, pp. 31-32.

prepared to accept that there is something behind his general approach.[3] Certainly, there is a relation between language and the capacity to represent different aspects of transcendent reality. While language itself is inadequate to represent the higher dimensions of the human experience, it can suggest them, and particular languages suggest them in different ways according to their peculiar capacities. For this reason the Greek of Homer's *Iliad* or the Sanskrit of the Vedantic *Upanishads* can never be translated with the force and clarity of the original.

The four Original Religions that Bennett hypothesized were **1)** Great Spirit, **2)** Great Mother, **3)** Creator God, and **4)** Savior God. While we employ Bennett's general categories, the history and the interpretation of the peoples, Traditions, Religions, and Civilizations which 'fill in' these categories – which begins with Book III, "The Original Religions" – has been guided by other historical research than Bennett's, as referenced in the text and bibliography.

1) **The Great Spirit or Shamanic-Taoist culture, originally native to Central Asia**
This culture extended, originally, from the eastern coast of the Caspian Sea to what is now the Chinese border. Its language grouping would include the Turkish, Chinese, Mongolian, Siberian, and Malay languages. This ancient Central Asian culture recognized a universal source of life: Sky, Heaven, or **Great Spirit**. Thus the shamanic awareness of the Unity of Nature was completed by a vision which integrates Sky or Heaven into what we have called the Sphere of Sentient Being and so integrates the Sphere of Sentient Being with the *living whole of the world that we know*. The Teachers of this Tradition probably cultivated a sense of the life of the Earth itself.

Here the tension between the earlier Shamanic Traditions and the New Religions would have been minimal. In other words, the Religion connected with the new Tradition probably did not develop in a rupture with the prehistoric Shamanic Teachings. Taoism – for example – is a religion compatible with Shamanism and so we have characterized this Original Religion as **Shamanic-Taoist**. Under these circumstances we can imagine the ancient Shamanic practitioners being directly tasked by the Gods to initiate the New Religion, which brought out and developed the 'Great Spirit' dimension of the older Shamanic teachings.

---

3. In his writings Bennett does not make it clear to what extent his correlations were based on a study of language types (i.e., languages distinguished by the system of the arrangement of morphemes, the smallest units in their grammatical structure) and to what extent they were based on a study of proto-languages (i.e., on the study of the origin and development of languages).

We find the remnants of the ancient Shamanic-Taoist practices buried in the Taoism known to history. We find them also in the Vedantic schools, in Tantric Buddhism, in Turkish Sufism, and generally in the Oriental martial arts. But there is also evidence of another kind. Both the Hindu *Rigveda* and the Iranian *Avesta* give reports of a Great Civilization existing prior to their own in Central Asia, and this corresponds to many recent archaeological finds in Afghanistan and Iran. According to both the Hindu and the Avestan myths, this ancient civilization was pushed out of Central Asia by the Aryan peoples migrating south. Although it was displaced, the Shamanic-Taoist culture retained its spiritual vitality and the Tradition that was behind it established branches in China, Mongolia, Tibet, and Siberia. Probably both the Mongolian and Tibetan peoples are descendants of this older civilization.

2) The Great Mother religion of remote antiquity

This Religion developed in those places where agriculture, the domestic arts, and animal husbandry originated: the Middle East, the eastern Mediterranean, and Asia Minor. Nature itself is seen as the Great Mother: the Cybele of the Phrygians, the Rhea of the Minoans, the ancient gods of the Cycladic civilization. We trace again a close link to the Shamanic unity with nature. It is a myth of creation that is based on an analogy with natural creation. And we know that these peoples retained many shamanic practices. The Minoans, for example, were quite adept at sorcery. We have no definitive record of the Great Mother religion, only speculation based on the analysis of common elements found in later religions in the same geographical area.

3) Creator God of the Mesopotamians, the Egyptians, and Hamito-Semitic peoples

This would include the pattern of creator worship, ruler worship, and sun worship, which finds expression in the religions of the peoples of the Hamito-Semitic languages. This language group includes ancient Egyptian, Coptic, Akkadian (or Assyro-Babylonian), Aramaic, Phoenician, Hebrew, and Arabic. The religion of the Creator God is conducive to a strong link between religion and law, which most of these cultures display. The most prominent of the Creator God Religions, in the period before 1000 BC, were the Egyptian and Sumerian/Babylonian. The Judaic religion arises on this same linguistic base; indeed it seems likely that there is a family relation between the Sumerian, the Egyptian, and the Judaic.

4) The Savior God of the Vedic and Avestan Traditions

This religion began its existence in the Russian Steppes east of the Urals and just to the north of the ancient Central Asian civilization mentioned above. This was the region where prehistoric hunters had gathered to pursue the herd animals which became so prolific at the end of the last Ice Age. The Russian Steppes were the original home of **the ancient Aryan/Indo European peoples**. These peoples had an overwhelming sense of human impotence in face of the forces of nature. As Man has need of the Gods, so God himself needs man to evolve and develop according to his plan. In this culture the notions of good and evil are pronounced. There is the idea of man's almost hopeless condition, of sin, and of the need for help and divine mercy in achieving self-transcendence. More generally, the ideas of devotion and of service are well marked.

In about 1600 BC the Aryan/Indo-European peoples begin to migrate south into India and southwest into Iran. Both the Hindu *Vedas* and the Zoroastrian *Avestas* derive from the older Indo-European language. This was the source, then, for both the Iranian Avestan and the Indian Sanskrit.

From the time of the second intervention of the Gods in our history we begin to see the dynamic of Spiritual Tradition, Living Religion, and Civilizational Order, which was to continue into the nineteenth century after the birth of Christ. We suggest that this same great intervention may have brought the vision of a School Civilization (Civilization ruled by Tradition) and the image of man as the 'gardener' of Organic Life. It is from this point that we can begin to delineate the Spiritual Traditions known to history through their relation to the Original Religions.

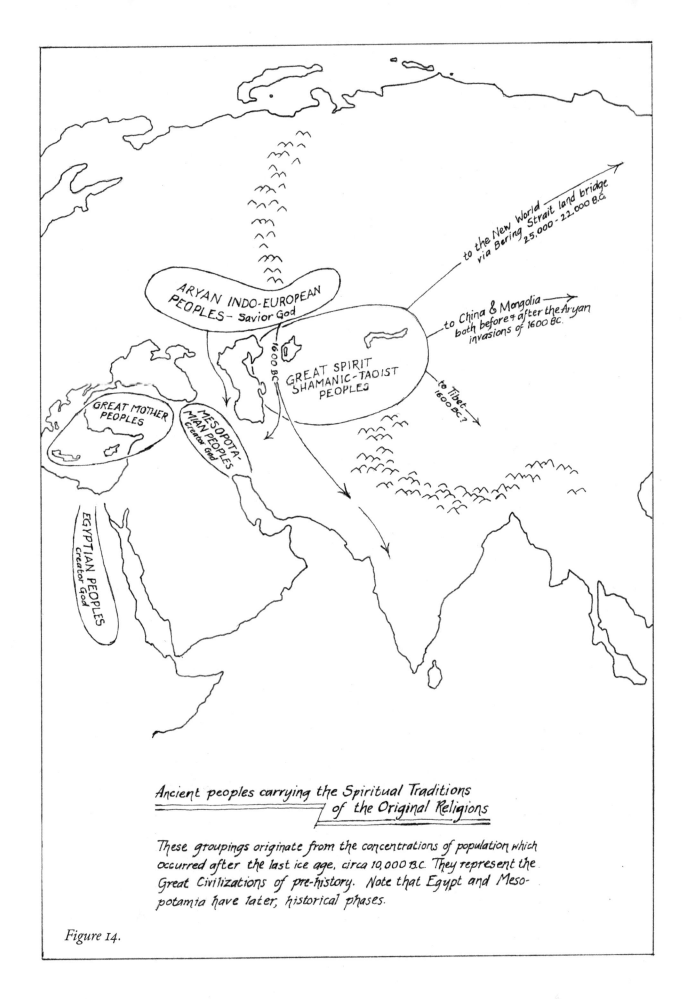

to the New World
via Bering Strait land bridge
25,000 - 22,000 B.C.

ARYAN INDO-EUROPEAN
PEOPLES - Savior God

to China & Mongolia
both before & after the Aryan
invasions of 1600 BC.

1600 BC

GREAT SPIRIT
SHAMANIC-TAOIST
PEOPLES

to Tibet
1600 BC?

GREAT MOTHER
PEOPLES

MESOPOTA-
MIAN PEOPLES
Creator God

EGYPTIAN PEOPLES
Creator God

Ancient peoples carrying the Spiritual Traditions
of the Original Religions

These groupings originate from the concentrations of population which
occurred after the last ice age, circa 10,000 B.C. They represent the
Great Civilizations of pre-history. Note that Egypt and Mesopotamia have later, historical phases.

Figure 14.

BOOK III

The Original Religions

We will now take the four hypothesized Original Religions – Great Mother, Creator God, Great Spirit, and Savior God – and relate them to the Spiritual Traditions that we know from history. The aim here is to paint a general picture, and to this end we range freely back and forth along the line of time; from inevitably speculative beginnings, to endings that come well within the span of our historical memory. With Mesopotamia, Egypt, and the New World Civilizations, we are well within the ambit of recorded history, running parallel to the Prophetic Religions, and to Classical Civilization itself. This historical overlap is evidence of the substantial and enduring influence that the Original Religions have had on the world that we know.

CHAPTER 13

The Great Mother Religion

Modern research of a Great Mother Religion began in the early twentieth century with the work of James Frazer, Robert Graves, and Sir Arthur Evans. These men hypothesized that the images of the 'mother goddesses' that we see in many ancient civilizations were interchangeable and that a Great Mother Religion was universal to humanity in the Paleolithic Period, that is, before recorded history. This hypothesis – a product of the Freudian atmosphere of its time – has since been criticized. Later research has shown that the images Frazer, Graves, and Evans referred to were neither interchangeable in the way that they suggested nor did they imply a 'universal' Paleolithic religion. Nevertheless, there was almost certainly something behind the ideas that these men put forward – in the form of an Original Religion that was alive in the places where agriculture first began. Unfortunately we have no original texts nor any record of religious practices.

We can, however, generalize from the archetype of a 'mother goddess' that we find in the religions of ancient times. The goddess is a nurturing, vivifying source of life, and Man's worship of her is the return to the life-giving source. The other side of the Great Mother is the love of the goddess for her children, which encourages a love given in return. In the Spiritual Tradition behind the Great Mother Religion, this 'love given in return' would have referred to the love of the Nine of Hearts for the Sphere of Sentient Being. The archetype of the Great Mother also relates the range of human activities to the principle of serving life, particularly appropriate to an agriculturally-based civilization.

Frazer, Graves, and Evans were probably also right to suggest that much of this prehistoric religion was sublimated and carried forward in the religions of the ancient world. Our earliest historical records reveal a common pool of myths and stories in the Eastern Mediterranean, Anatolia, and the Near East. Some of these stories may have arisen spontaneously; some were components of prehistoric mythologies; some were fragments divorced from a now unknown source. Each new religious mythology, as it came into being, integrated these older stories. Thus, just as the Great Mother Religion had easily integrated the older Shamanic practices, the formative myths of the Great Mother Religion were easily integrated into the Religions which were to follow. Thus a prehistoric Great Mother Goddess may have been reborn in the Syrian Astarte, the Phrygian Cybele, the Sumerian Ninhursag, the Babylonian Ninsun, the Canaanite Asherah, and the Minoan Potnia Theron and Rhea. The Greeks, who inherited and revised the Minoan religion, took Potnia Theron as their Artemis and Rhea as the pre-Olympian Titan of that same name. In the Olympian generation of the Greek Gods, the goddesses reflecting their Great Mother origin would include Demeter, Hera, Artemis, Athena, and Aphrodite. The Romans – in their version of this same religion – developed a gestural reference to 'Magna Dea,' the 'Great Goddess' who anticipates pantheistic or monotheistic worship. Considering the religions of classical times, Rome has more of the heritage of the Mother Goddess than Greece, in the sense that the Roman civilization had a profound sense of nature, of natural beauty, and of the cycles of nature. Again, we emphasize that neither the Greek nor the Roman mythology is a Great Mother mythology, the firm paternal figures of Kronos, Zeus, and Jupiter clearly marking the great divide.

The Great Mother Religion, as one of the Original Religions given mankind in the centuries following the last Ice Age, probably emerged out of the Shamanic Religion in a relatively easy transition, with the development of agriculture and herding. Worship of the shamanic spirits was transmuted into the worship of spirits infusing each of the cycles of agricultural life and the activities of the family. In every sphere, the emergence of life and the sounding of the formative notes in the development of life are related to a single original source, and there is a perpetual renewal of life through birth. This can be sharply contrasted to the figure of the firm creator-god, generating systems of law and bringing order out of chaos. We note a marked tendency in the historical religions that followed, especially the Roman and Judaic, to return, in their phases of civilizational disorder, to the comfort and reassurance of the 'old' Great Mother.

While the Great Mother Religion originated from the work of the Spiritual Traditions, it fades from our view at the dawn of recorded history. While the Great Spirit,

Creator God, and Savior God Religions were each a defining influence on the Prophetic Religions to follow, the Great Mother Religion was not. Nevertheless the religious tradition of the Great Mother remained as the general background of the Prophetic Religions, and it retained a tremendous appeal through classical times. It is certainly behind many of the popular Latin cults of the Madonna. But it was rejected by each of the Prophets in turn and so was not fated to survive the classical period. Indeed the 'atmosphere' of the old Great Mother religion is a key to understanding the atmosphere of classical times as distinct from our own.

CHAPTER 14

The Creator God of Mesopotamia and Egypt

It is likely that the Original Religions of Mesopotamia and Egypt are related in their origins, although they developed independently from one another. We will here treat the Mesopotamian and Egyptian Civilizations as two late re-castings of the original Creator-God Religion. They are the closest windows that we have on that lost world, which is the parent of our own.

We note that, before 4000 BC, modern historical chronology becomes tenuous, and history itself tends to become speculative. The beginnings of agriculture, of village life, and of the creation of towns takes us back to 10,000 BC, leaving a full 6000 years open to speculation. It is likely that an entire cycle of Original Religion Civilizations existed, between the end of the last Ice Age and the rise of ancient Sumeria and Dynastic Egypt. A prehistoric Central Asian Civilization, for example, is a strong likelihood.[1] Such a Civilization is spoken of in the Vedic literature and in various Eastern and Central Asian myths – and there are extensive unexcavated remains in that area. The connection to such a Civilization would explain the level of art, architecture, engineering, and ceramics that we find, from the very beginning, in both Sumeria and Egypt. It might also explain the remarkable durability of both the Sumerian and the Egyptian religions.

---

1. What the major centers of human population were, in the six millennia between the end of the last Ice Age and the beginnings of Sumeria and Egypt, is very much a matter of speculation. That a 'Hamito-Semitic/Mesopotamian/Egyptian' grouping of language-type and religion may have existed does not imply that the originating School was located in the Tigris-Euphrates or Nile river basins.

CHAPTER 15

The Mesopotamian Civilizations

The Tigris-Euphrates river basin, named by the Greeks 'Mesopotamia' (or 'between the two rivers'), has often been called the cradle of civilization. For nearly five millennia, from 5300 BC until the Persian conquest of 539 BC, a related family of peoples formed a stable context for Civilizational Order. This Civilizational Order permanently influenced the Egyptian, the Judaic, and the Persian Civilizations and was generally formative for the social order that exists on the planet today. Written language, the epic form of poetry, mathematics, law, astronomy, engineering, administration, irrigation systems, and road systems all began here. Yet the history of Mesopotamia is, for us, a prehistory – in the sense that all of the different peoples who comprised that Civilizational Order have now disappeared from the face of the earth. Indeed, most of the original Mesopotamian peoples had dispersed, or integrated with other populations, by the time of the *Pax Romana*. Thus the reconstruction of the early phases of Mesopotamian history is now the work of archaeologists and linguists. We can be certain that the Mesopotamian family of Civilizations, seminal for so many of the civilizations to follow, was a result of the work of the Great Spiritual Traditions in conjunction with Higher School. And we know that the Mesopotamian Tradition was able to transmit its understanding to the Egyptian, the Judaic, and the Persian-Zoroastrian Traditions, and – through the Persian-Zoroastrian Tradition – to the Sufi Orders of Islam.

The Principal Players

In order to present an overview of this complex and only partly known history, we must first be able to distinguish the major players.[1]

---

1. Many nationalities, other than the ones mentioned below, came and went in the Tigris-Euphrates river basin. In this brief overview we can only sketch those that were formative to the Mesopotamian

The Sumerians were the first of the Mesopotamian peoples to enter the Tigris-Euphrates river basin, sometime before 5500 BC. They settled the vast flood plain, at the river system's lower reaches, which opens into the Persian Gulf. The Sumerian peoples probably originated from a yet more ancient Civilization which existed either in Central Asia or in what is now known as Iran. They trace their origins to peoples that pre-existed the flood described in the Old Testament.[2] Whatever the case, the Sumerians are the only Civilization in the Mesopotamian family to carry the clear imprint of a preceding Civilizational Order – and they transmitted this imprint to all the Civilizations that were to follow in their line.

The Akkadians entered and settled the central section of the Tigris-Euphrates river basin in a time before our historical records. We have evidence of their presence from 2500 BC.

The Assyrians entered and settled the northern section of the Tigris-Euphrates river basin at approximately the same time that the Akkadians entered the central section. Both the Akkadians and the Assyrians may have been driven from the East by drought or changing climactic conditions.

Of these three peoples, it was the Akkadians who first rose to material empire, establishing control over the entirety of the Tigris-Euphrates river basin. Under Sargon of Akkad (2334-2279 BC) they conquered both the Assyrians to the north and the Sumerians to the south.

When the Akkadians conquered the much older Sumerian Civilization, they were themselves conquered by its more developed culture. The fusion of the Akkadian and the Sumerian cultures served as a foundation for all the Mesopotamian Civilizations to follow. The Akkadians were able to contribute their organizational, military, and administrative capacities to a rich and already ancient cultural base. The languages of the Akkadians and Sumerians interpenetrated, with a Sumerian form of Akkadian becoming the spoken language while the Sumerian language was preserved as the sacred language of myth and religious ritual. This, then, became the dual language base for all of the Mesopotamian Civilizations to follow. The original set of Sumerian myths – the *Epic of Gilgamesh*, the *Enuma Elis* (creation myth), and the *Atrahasis* (creation and

---

Civilizational Order.

2. Lambert, G. and Millard A.R., *Atrahasis: The Babylonian Story of the Flood*, Oxford, 1969. While the Atrahasis myth exists in a Babylonian presentation, it is of Sumerian origin.

history before the flood) – were to form a permanent cultural context for the entire civilizational family.[3]

The Assyrians, on being conquered by the Akkadians, were integrated into the Akkadian empire and – over time – absorbed both the religion and the language forms that were shared by the Akkadians and Sumerians. The Assyrians, however, retained their own Aramaic language in a heavily Akkadianized form and were thus bilingual at the level of popular culture and trilingual at the level of high culture. When the Akkadian Empire finally came apart in 2154 BC, it left – after a chaotic century – an Assyrian nation in the north and an alliance of Sumerians and Akkadians in the south. From this point we shall refer to the southern composite as the Sumero-Akkadians, because the Akkadians were no longer the dominant element in the alliance. Into this Sumero-Akkadian base, over the next 1300 years, came three succeeding peoples: **the Kassites, the Amorites**, and **the Chaldeans**. Each of these peoples migrated into the south/central region of the river basin, and each of them, in the centuries in which they became established there, were integrated into the Sumero-Akkadian culture, language, and religion. Yet each of these peoples was to play, in their own time, a leading role. The Amorites, in their imperial phase, founded the city of Babylon, and the cultural synthesis that was realized in that city permanently changed the complexion of the Sumero-Akkadian South. From that point forward the peoples of the south tended to be known collectively as **the Babylonians**. Thus, from about 1800 BC, the political configuration of Mesopotamia devolved into a balance of power between the Assyrians in the north and the Babylonians in the south.

And so a world was created, with a context of meaning that was to sustain some of the greatest Civilizations known to man. This family of Civilizations is unique in that a single Civilizational Order absorbed a series of ethnic identities, each of whom, in their turn, shed their ethnic allegiance and realized their potentials through the new order that they had embraced. This could only have occurred through the agency of a

---

3. We have these, in their most complete form, in the Babylonian versions. The translation of the Gilgamesh epic we favor is *The Epic of Gilgamesh*, by Andrew R. George (translator and editor), Penguin Books, 1999. The translation of the *Enuma Elis* we have used is found in *The Seven Tablets of Creation, the Babylonian Legends of Creation*, by E. A. Wallis Budge, 1921, at sacred-texts.com. The translation of the *Atrahasis* we have used is *Atrahasis: The Babylonian Story of the Flood*, by G. Lambert and A.R. Millard, Oxford, 1969. There exists a version of the flood story in the Sumerian cuneiform, from approximately the same period, named *Eridu Genesis*, translated by Thorkild Jacobsen in *The Harps that Once … Sumerian Poetry in Translation*, Yale University Press, 1987. Throughout this text we will refer to the better-known Atrahasis. These are the principal myths that survive, and doubtless there were others that have been lost.

Spiritual Tradition. This now forgotten Tradition represented – to a nucleus of initiates in each successive people – the objective connection to a higher level of creation.

For the greater part of its final millennium (1600-600 BC) the Mesopotamian family of Civilizations was under the leadership of the Assyrians, who – like the Akkadians and the Babylonians before them – rose to a phase of empire. But the geographic extent of the second, or 'Neo-Assyrian,' Empire makes them appear to history as a latecoming *enfant terrible*. We are reminded of Lord Byron's lines from the *Destruction of Sennacherib*, "The Assyrian came down like the wolf on the fold, and his cohorts were gleaming in purple and gold." The Neo-Assyrian Empire included all of Mesopotamia, all of the Levant, all of Egypt, much of Turkey, the northern Arabian peninsula, and western Iran. In considering this Empire we must keep in mind that the Assyrian culture had been formed more than a millennium before, in the pre-Kassite, pre-Amorite, pre-Chaldean phase of the Mesopotamian Civilization. Thus, to some extent, Assyrian leadership was a reintegration of the Sumero-Akkadian past. Even at the maximum point of expansion of the Assyrian Second Empire, it is still fair to say that Assyria represented the Mesopotamian family of Civilizations. Internal cleavages and divisions certainly remained, but to understand the world of ancient Mesopotamia we must always keep in mind its fundamental unity. While the Sumerians, Akkadians, Assyrians, and Chaldeans are distinct, they cannot (except in the first phase of Sumerian Civilization) be understood independently of one another. They are the variant expressions of a single cultural template that was formed sometime in the sixth millennium BC.

In the seventh century BC there was a final resurgence of the Babylonian Empire, and, once again, the Assyrian and Babylonian Empires competed actively. The late sixth century, however, saw the decline of both the Babylonian and the Assyrian Empires. The Mesopotamian template for Civilizational Order had exhausted its capacity to generate new forms; its potentialities had been actualized in the line of time, and it was the time for a new order to follow.

The Sumerians as Founders

Having laid out the ground plan, we can now 'tell the story' from the standpoint of the Spiritual Traditions.

Spiritually, and in terms of core values, the **Sumerians** were the founders of the entire line of Mesopotamian Civilizations. Their language continued as the 'sacred' language for the duration of the cycle. Their mythology was a foundational mythology.

The first evidence that we have of the Sumerians, from 5500 BC, shows a superior level of agricultural development, of engineering, of architecture, and of ceramic art. They had the most sophisticated irrigation system in the world and a developed Chalcolithic technology two full millennia before the coming of the Bronze Age. It is Sumeria that provides us with the earliest evidence of written language on the planet. The Sumerians had a developed mathematics, with a combined base-ten/base-sixty number system. They had a profound knowledge of astronomy and astrology, and they were the first people that we know of to map the constellations. The universal conventions of 24 hours to the day, 60 minutes to the hour, and 360 degrees to a circle are inherited directly from the Sumerians.

We know of the Sumerians only from archaeological excavations, from the impact that they had on the civilizations to follow, and from a few surviving myths. The first Sumerian city of Eridu arose from a composite of villages near the mouth of the Euphrates river around 5500 BC. It is estimated that the initial population was about 4,000. In the centuries to follow thirty-two such settlements arose in the broad delta complex at the mouth of the Tigris and Euphrates rivers.[4] The better known of these include Ur, Nippur, Eshunna, Shuruppak, Marad, Isin, Adab, and Kullah. These cities were governed by priest-kings who together comprised a ruling priest caste. From about 2100 BC there is a 'king list' defining a single point of governance. On or about 3700 BC Eridu (after 1,800 years of continuous existence) was supplanted, as the civilizational center of ancient Sumeria, by the city of Uruk, which was an urban center on a different scale. It reached a population of 80,000 in the 33rd century BC. From 3600-3200 BC there is evidence of what archaeologists call an 'Uruk expansion'.[5]

In the second century after Uruk's ascendency settlements of 10,000 to 20,000 people, clearly based on the model of Uruk, began to appear throughout the Tigris-Euphrates

---

4. While thirty-two settlements are known from excavations there may have been more.

5. See Algaze, G., *The Uruk World System: The Dynamics of Expansion of Early Mesopotamian Civilization*, The University of Chicago Press, Chicago, 1993. We do not, in these pages, isolate an 'Uruk world system' (as a byproduct of Immanuel Wallerstein's world systems theory) from the Sumerian civilizational order. Uruk was a product of the Sumerian culture and embraced the existing body of Sumerian myth, which provided a common horizon of meaning, describing the place of men in relation to gods and in relation to what we have called the Absolute. Additionally, Algaze claims Uruk as the world's first city, based on a definition of city that corresponds (amongst other things) to a certain level of trading activity. In the view presented here stone age villages, such as have existed since 10,000 BC, can be very significant cultural centers affecting a much larger population in their surrounding region. In other words it is theoretically possible that Eridu (in the 54th century BC) might have been culturally more significant than Uruk (in the 33rd century BC.)

river basin, in lands occupied by the adjoining peoples. These settlements were created with the apparent agreement and acceptance of the peoples of those lands. Part of their function was to serve as trading stations. Twenty-nine such sites have been excavated throughout the Tigris-Euphrates river basin. A northernmost cluster is found in Turkey, where the Karasu and Murat Rivers meet to form the Euphrates. Scattered settlements are then found along the Euphrates through to the river's mouth on the Persian Gulf. Similar settlements exist along the length of the Tigris River. This system of settlements or towns, as a working connection to the peoples in the adjoining lands, continued to function for about four hundred years. Each settlement had monumental public buildings, and carefully planned residential and administrative sectors. The remains of Sumerian ceramics are found at each site. The populations of these settlements were a mixture of colonists and peoples native to the region; more settlers than needed for trading, but not enough for occupation or control. And so it is clear that the Sumerian culture impacted the entire Tigris-Euphrates river basin in the fourth millennium BC.

More specifically, how do we understand this system of settlements, all made on the Sumerian pattern? With the ascendency of Uruk, the Sumerians knew they had made the transition to a new level of civilizational order, and wished to establish trading relations with the peoples outside of their sphere. Sumeria needed hardwoods, copper, wool, obsidian tools, and marble. While the Sumerian civilization was agriculturally based, it could not preserve, and so could not export, its own agricultural surplus. It was able to export only processed goods: ceramics, metalwork, decorated fabrics, jewelry, ornaments, and wine. Thus the Sumerians knew that, in order to initiate an ongoing exchange, they would have to create the need for a more advanced level of culture in their trading partners. These facts give the parameters of the trading system that has been called the 'Uruk expansion.' But – from a less utilitarian point of view – it is clear that Sumeria was not just trying to raise its import quota; it was exporting its civilization, its way of life, and its formative mythology. The Sumerians brought not only a developed Chalcolithic technology, written language, mathematics, and a pattern of urban life, but a significant and powerful body of myth that gave meaning to these elements in relation to a higher level. They may indeed have appeared to their trading partners as a race of magicians: magicians willing to share their magic. We note here that the connection to Higher School, even in the earliest times, was experienced by the Traditions as something universal to humanity, although a single people might be its vehicle over a particular period of time.[6]

This is what we can make of the Sumerians based on the archaeological evidence; but what, in the clay tablets that survive, do the Sumerians say of themselves? The Sumerian creation myths (the *Atrahasis* and *Enuma Elis*) present a transcendent, unknowable Absolute, existing before Creation and containing the entire Universe. These myths give us a taste of what the teachings behind the Original Religions might have been, and they dispel the idea – derived from Judaic, Christian, and Muslim theology – that the pre-Judaic religions were polytheistic. Beyond this, the *Atrahasis* myth speaks of a time "when gods were in the ways of men." This may refer either to **1)** the initial phase of human development – after the connection to Higher Centers had been established – when the Gods worked directly with men to make them aware of their new possibilities or **2)** the direct intervention of the Gods that occurred at the end of the last Ice Age, when the Original Religions were first introduced. Or it may refer to both of these. The *Enuma Elis* gives the purpose for which Mankind was created as service to the Gods. The surviving Sumerian myths, including the *Epic of Gilgamesh*, show not only an understanding of Man's place in relation to the Gods but also an understanding of the relation of the human Civilizational Order to the Divine Order. In all of these myths there is the definition of a space, or a set of conditions, in which Men and Gods may interact. And all of these myths, and the symbolic rituals which were associated with them, were permanent for the life of the Mesopotamian family of Civilizations. Every other people who came into contact with these myths and teachings, down to the time of the Persian invasion in 539 BC, accepted them – and this very strength and resilience suggests that there was something behind them. It is possible that a single Spiritual Tradition, comprised of individuals who were stable in the experience of higher consciousness, sustained itself in the Tigris-Euphrates river basin for more than 5000 years.[7]

There is a final point to be made about the original Sumerian Civilization. Ancient Sumeria was a system of relatively independent city-states ruled by a priest caste. The

---

6. We shall see this ecumenic quality clearly expressed by the Buddhist, Judaic, Christian, Confucian, and Islamic Traditions in Chapters 28 through 32.

7. The present writer is unable to determine if there was a single Mesopotamian Tradition or several related Traditions. There was certainly an original Sumerian Tradition, which may have branched into a second Assyrian Tradition, at the time of the Assyrian First Empire. There was a significant renewal of the Sumerian Tradition in the generation of Hammurabi, which may – or may not – have constituted a new 'Babylonian' Tradition. Whatever the case, these Traditions, or these different branches of the same Tradition, worked to neutralize the conflicts that occurred at the level of religion and national polity.

Figure 15. **Remains of the Sumerian Ziggurat of Ur**

Sumerians did not have a centralized warrior caste, and so were vulnerable to conquest. It appears, however, that destiny gave the Sumerians an initial halcyon-age of 3,000 years, free from any external threat. This is extraordinary, in the sense that Neolithic, Chalcolithic, and even Bronze Age agricultural civilizations are typically vulnerable to recurrent nomadic conquest. Thus it is possible that this first 3,000 years – through circumstances unknown to us – was one of the rare spans of human history where a Spiritual Tradition was able to rule directly. The External Religion connected with the Spiritual Tradition then became the means by which the general population could exist in some relation to the transcendent world which the Men of the Tradition knew at first-hand.

As the Sumerians were absorbed into other, larger national units – firstly by the Akkadians, then by the Amorites, and finally by the Assyrians – the outer forms of the External Religion adjusted to the consequent changes in polity and language usage. But underneath these surface adjustments, the inner teaching, and the essential myths, remained unchanged. The Sumerian study of mathematics and astronomy – which complemented the inner work of the Spiritual Tradition – was taken up and developed by the entire line of Mesopotamian Civilizations to follow, most devotedly by the Chaldeans in its final phase. What were, then, the 'essential myths?'

Let us now review the mythology more closely.

The Mesopotamian Myths

The principal source for the Mesopotamian myths is the excavated remains of Ashurbanipal's library at Nineveh.[8] This library was razed and burned in 612 BC. The clay tablets that comprised the library were so hardened by fire that fragments were retrieved intact when archaeologists excavated the site in 1849. Ashurbanipal himself was an Assyrian king, late in the cycle of the Mesopotamian Civilizations (668-627 BC). While the scribes of that time were required to master the Sumerian language, the surviving texts are principally in Akkadian cuneiform, and the presentation of the mythology is Babylonian (i.e., dating from after 790 BC). Nevertheless, all of the myths sourced from this library – the *Epic of Gilgamesh*, the *Atrahasis*, and the *Enuma Elis* – are Sumerian in their origin.[9]

The Babylonian myths present an infinite and unlimited Absolute – Ad – who is never named in religious ritual and is utterly unknowable to Man. Ad represents a state of unity that is beyond Being and Not-Being.[10] Below Ad is the Godhead – which we have presented as the principle of Being – and this is termed Anu. Anu is the highest entity that can be worshipped by humanity. Below Anu is Bel, the creator of the physical universe, or the dimension of the Godhead facing Creation. Bel is not an entity that created the universe at some point in the past. He represents the ongoing process of Creation, the ceaseless labor of the primeval demiurge.[11] The active principles of Anu and Bel are tempered by the passive principle of Ea. It was Ea who created humans out of clay to do the work of the Gods; his name is associated with wisdom, magic, incantations, and the full spectrum of the arts and crafts.[12] From the standpoint of the Universe as a whole, Ad represents the transcendence of a triadic relation between Anu,

---

8. Ninevah was the capital of the Neo-Assyrian Empire.

9. Earlier fragments of the *Atrahasis* and *Enuma Elis* have been discovered in Iraq, at sites in Ashur, Kish, and Sultantepe. Some of these date back to the seventeenth century BC. As the nomenclature of these fragments is not consistent, we will here use the names of the gods used in the tablets retrieved from the library at Ashurbanipal. These were the names of the Babylonian period. In the passage immediately below we have referred to Ad, Anu, Bel, and Ea. The Sumerian equivalent of Ad (as the Absolute) is An, when it is distinguished from and prior to Anu. The name of Anu is the same in the Sumerian and the Babylonian texts.

10. The Sumerian equivalent is An, as prior to and distinguished from the god Anu. The Chaldeans later used the term Ilu in the same way.

11. In the Sumerian, Bel is Enlil.

12. In the Sumerian, Ea is Enki.

Bel, and Ea. From the standpoint of humanity, the triad of Anu, Bel, and Ea occurs on the original ground of Ad. Real human understanding, as that is possible in this context, arises from the individual spiritual aspirant's struggle to engage the wisdom of Ea to escape the illusion of his or her personal 'I,' and so transform the apparent negation of death.

Having introduced the primary deities, we shall sketch their relation to the human social order. Bel's act of creation created the context for human existence, but it was Ea who actually created men. The *Enuma Elis* makes it clear that men were created to be the servants of the Gods, and the myth of *Gilgamesh* makes it equally clear that a Sumerian king was held accountable to the Gods. But Ea did not just create a race of men ruled by a series of tenuously accountable kings, he created the full spectrum of activities that defines civilizational order. In so doing he connected men to the intents and purposes of the Gods in a practical way, for it is through this spectrum of activities that Man has the possibility of creating cosmos out of chaos, and so relating the human order to the divine. The individual activities that comprise this magical spectrum were known as the *mes*. The teaching of the *mes* comes to us from an ancient myth that signaled the transfer of the Sumerian civilizational center from the city of Eridu to the city of Uruk, which occurred in or around 3900 BC. The myth is appropriately named *Inanna and Enki: The Transfer of the Arts of Civilization from Eridu to Uruk*. Inanna, the patron goddess of Uruk, receives the elements of civilizational order from Ea at the already ancient city of Eridu. It is likely that the original myth listed more than one hundred *mes*, although the fragmentary tablets that remain to us list only sixty-four.[13] We provide the complete list, as compiled by Samuel Noah Kramer, with the caveat that the English translations are quite inadequate to convey the force of the ancient mantric invocations. Additionally we must emphasize that the symbolic dimension of these terms is now impossible to accurately reconstruct. In the order given in the tablets, Kramer lists:

> 1) *EN*ship, 2) Godship, 3) The exalted and enduring crown, 4) The throne of kingship, 5) The exalted scepter, 6) The royal insignia, 7) The exalted shrine, 8) Shepherdship, 9) Kingship, 10) Lasting ladyship, 11) "Divine lady" (a priestly office), 12) *Ishib* (a priestly office), 13) *Lumah* (a priestly office), 14) *Guda* (a priestly office), 15) Truth, 16) Descent into the nether world, 17) Ascent from the

---

13. Kramer, Samuel Noah, *The Sumerians: Their History, Culture, and Character*, The University of Chicago Press, Chicago, 1963, page 116.

nether world, 18) *Kurgarra* (a eunuch, androgyne or transsexual), 19) *Girbadara* (a eunuch), 20) *Sagursag* (a eunuch, entertainers related to the cult of Inanna), 21) The battle-standard, 22) The flood, 23) Weapons, 24) Sexual intercourse, 25) Prostitution, 26) Law, 27) Libel, 28) Art, 29) The cult chamber, 30) "Hierodule of heaven" [HJ: "Hierodule" is a Greek term for a slave freed from slavery to be dedicated to a god, perhaps: "the slave of heaven"], 31) Guslim (a musical instrument), 32) Music, 33) Eldership, 34) Heroship, 35) Power, 36) Enmity, 37) Straightforwardness, 38) The destruction of cities, 39) Lamentation, 40) Rejoicing of the heart, 41) Falsehood, 42) Art of metalworking, 43) Scribeship, 44) Craft of the smith, 45) Craft of the leatherworker, 46) Craft of the builder, 47) Craft of the basket weaver, 48) Wisdom, 49) Attention, 50) Holy purification, 51) Fear, 52) Terror, 53) Strife, 54) Peace, 55) Weariness, 56) Victory, 57) Counsel, 58) The troubled heart, 59) Judgment, 60) Decision, 61) *Lilis* (a musical instrument), 62) *Ub* (a musical instrument), 63) *Mesi* (a musical instrument), 64) *Ala* (a musical instrument)

The list of *mes*, as a complete presentation of "the arts of civilization," represents a bridge between the shamanic world of direct perception and the Hermetic principle of cosmos: a living unity in which the whole is greater than the sum of its parts. Interestingly the first *me* given is *EN*ship, which signifies the combined power of priest and king (or ruler). *EN*ship defines the point at which the cosmos of man – as distinct from the individual human being – can receive direction from the Gods. *EN*ship refers not to the priest in himself or to the king in himself, but to the combined function of the two. As a result of this combined function, the patterns of human life can be adjusted to conform to the laws that govern a higher level. The second *me* is Godship, without which *EN*ship is stillborn. The third through fourteenth *mes* represent the sacred and ruling functions that direct the other functions necessary to sustaining civilizational order. The *mes* themselves cover the complete range of human activities, including sex, reverent silence, the making of fire, and the making of law. Nothing is left out. The complete list is thus a signature of civilizational order: a vision of its unity. This represents not just the order of the city of Eridu or the order of the city of Uruk, but Civilizational Order itself, in any context. The Sumerians were thus able to share this divine signature with the Akkadians, the Assyrians, and – through the syncretic Spiritual Tradition that developed – the Kassites, the Amorites and the Chaldeans.

Here we must step back for a moment and reflect. The *mes* are presented in the myth of *The Transfer of the Arts of Civilization from Eridu to Uruk*. After nearly two millennia the Sumerians had achieved a new societal order, fully realized in the city of Uruk, and this order is celebrated with a complete presentation of the *mes*. The Sumerians had either reached a new phase of their already ancient civilization, or they had reached a phase in which they could give a more complete expression to core values. The myth of the transfer of the *mes* to Uruk may have signaled the completion of the *mes*, in the final image of a cosmos. On the other hand, it may be that the Sumerians received a complete system of the *mes* from their parent civilization. With the development of the city of Uruk they found themselves able to articulate the *mes* in a form appropriate to an urban center of 80,000 people with a highly developed division of labor. We noted that, with the Uruk expansion, there appeared settlements throughout the Tigris-Euphrates basin bearing the imprint (the general layout and planning) of the city of Uruk. Perhaps this external similarity was based on a more essential similarity? Perhaps each settlement had been designed to bear the imprint of the *mes*, and the Sumerian colonists had been intended to communicate the teaching of the *mes* to the other peoples of the Tigris-Euphrates River basin? That might explain why, in the centuries after the conquest of the Sumerians by the Akkadians, so many of the peoples of the region readily accepted Sumerian myth and culture.

Having looked at the myths that describe the relation of the Gods to Civilizational Order, we can now look at the myths that define Mankind's place in the Universal Order, and so represent Man's fate and destiny.

The most substantial of the surviving myths is the *Epic of Gilgamesh*. It is the first epic, and indeed the first 'literature,' known to history.[14] Even in the fragmentary manuscript that we have, it is clear that the *Epic of Gilgamesh* represents an account of the place of man in a living universe, where the lower levels are derivative of the higher levels and where Man has the potential to enter into communion with the Gods.

The hero, Gilgamesh, is the king of the city of Uruk. While he is a powerful and charismatic figure, great in war, he is an arrogant and oppressive ruler. To correct this 'will to power' the gods send Gilgamesh a permanent companion, Enkidu, who will give him the inner balance that he needs to function in a more compassionate way.

---

14. Scholars date the epic from the third dynasty of Ur, which existed from the twenty-first to the twentieth centuries BC. This was the last Sumerian dynasty, which briefly flourished after the decline of the Akkadian Empire. It was during this time that Gilgamesh, who was the King of Uruk, reigned. It is almost certain, however, that the stories which comprise the epic pre-date King Gilgamesh and that the *Epic of Gilgamesh* is a re-telling of earlier (i.e., pre-Akkadian) Sumerian myths.

Enkidu comes from the wilds. He is representative of essence and – more generally – the intuitive side of human nature. An immediate bond forms between the two men, and Gilgamesh is able to see in Enkidu his 'other self.' Enkidu, like Gilgamesh, is powerful, but he is without Gilgamesh's arrogance.

Once Enkidu has had a moderating effect on Gilgamesh's will to power, and so on his rule over the city, Gilgamesh proposes that he and Enkidu win honor for themselves by undertaking a difficult task that will benefit all the peoples of Mesopotamia. They are to seek out the monstrous ogre-guardian of a cedar forest at the north of the Tigris-Euphrates river basin and slay him. This monster, named Humbaba, creates paralyzing fear in all those who encounter him. In the myth Humbaba represents a manifestation of the Lower Self. Gilgamesh and Enkidu journey north to the cedar forest and confront the monster. Conquering their fear, they are able to physically overcome him, but he retains a psychological hold over the two men. It is only with an ultimate effort of internal separation that Gilgamesh and Enkidu are able to free themselves from Humbaba's influence and to slay him. But this victory is only the beginning of Gilgamesh and Enkidu's journey into the unknown. Having successfully confronted the Lower Self in one of its manifestations, they have unleashed the manifold forces that it has at its disposal. In one of their later trials Gilgamesh and Enkidu succeed in vanquishing the 'Bull of Heaven,' but in the moment of victory Enkidu shows a marked disrespect for the gods. This he pays for with his life. Gilgamesh is filled with grief at the loss of his companion, but at the same time the loss of Enkidu focuses Gilgamesh on a quest for the secret teaching that will allow Man to join the Gods in eternity.

The keeper of this secret teaching is a man called Utnapishtim (also known as Atrahasis) who holds a special place in the Mesopotamian mythology. He is the one mortal man who is known to have actually entered the circle of the Gods in eternity. He became immortal only after having served the Gods in the completion of a great task. Utnapishtim was born into the Civilization which preceded the Sumerian, in its final decadent phase. At a certain point in his life Utnapishtim was asked by the god Ea to abandon his worldly possessions and to create an ark. We have noted that Ea is associated with the underworld; he is the god of wisdom and the teacher of men. The ark that Ea asked Utnapishtin to create was to be called the 'preserver of life.' It was intended to enable a small circle of men and women to survive a great flood, which the Gods were preparing to expunge a decadent humanity. This ark was the seed of the Sumerian Civilization. Utnapishtim (or Atrahasis) is thus a background figure in all Sumerian mythology.

It is stated that, prior to the flood, Utnapishtim was in communication with Ea. The Atrahasis myth states that his "ear was open to his god … and his god would speak to him." Both the *Atrahasis* and the *Gilgamesh* myths emphasize that Utnapishtin did not gain immortality for himself; he was given immortality by the Gods. He did practice the teaching that Ea gave him, and he did serve the Gods faithfully in his external task – but that was not enough. Immortality can only, ultimately, be given from a level above the level of the Steward. The functions of the lower centers can only enable, but not ensure, conscious identity. Consciousness must somehow be born of itself, and that birth needs the stabilizing influence of the higher level. A cosmic birth requires a cosmic midwife.

When, after innumerable hardships and trials, Gilgamesh locates Utnapishtim, he immediately asks him for the secret teaching. After emphasizing that immortality is something that can only be given, Utnapishtim proceeds to test Gilgamesh by tasking him with a vigil of six days and six nights, saying, "Prevail against sleep and you will prevail against death." Gilgamesh fails in this trial – as Utnapishtim knew he would – and fails in a way that clearly demonstrates his unpreparedness. It is apparent that Gilgamesh's desire for immortality, and his efforts to achieve it, are still very much grounded in the four lower centers. Until Gilgamesh has been humbled to a point where he can understand his helplessness (until he has experienced and understood the failure of the Steward), he cannot take the teaching into himself in the right way. In other words, until he has been rightly prepared, he cannot practice the teaching from a place within himself that will actually enable Higher Centers. His practice will be driven by a 'personal' ambition to awaken.

Utnapishtim's verdict of failure seems harsh, but he remains firmly behind it. However, when the chastened Gilgamesh is ready to leave, Utnapishtim's wife gives him a gift: a sacred plant that will bring eternal youth and worldly happiness. This gift is in fact another test, but Gilgamesh, not knowing this, feels somewhat consoled for his failure. He does not immediately consume the plant. He decides to bring it back to Uruk, with the hope of testing it and possibly sharing its benefits. Here we see a motivation of service. However, on the long journey home, the magical plant is stolen from him, and this loss brings him to the very depths of despair. He has now lost everything, and he sees that the loss of happiness and youth are nothing compared to the loss of a possible connection to the Gods. He is powerless. He has lost all he had, *but the opportunity to serve his city.* Service, we note, is both 1) the function of the Steward and 2) what the Gods require of Men. In fact, Gilgamesh has reached the point where he is ready for the teaching … but the conclusion of the epic is missing from the connected set of tablets (I-XI) that were excavated from the Library of Ashurbanipal.

However, two fragments survive, from earlier tellings of the myth, which describe aspects of the epic's completion.[15]

In the first of these tablets (known as Tablet XII) Gilgamesh's companion and 'other self' Enkidu (who has somehow reappeared) agrees to enter (or re-enter) the underworld. Enkidu will be able to return from the underworld only if he follows a special set of instructions given by Gilgamesh. It is clear that Gilgamesh has received a kind of knowledge that he did not have in the earlier sections of the epic. Enkidu does descend into the underworld but fails to follow Gilgamesh's instructions, just as Gilgamesh had earlier failed to follow Utnapishtim's instructions. However, at the very point of Enkidu's failure, Ea intervenes to assist him, and he is able to return to the world of the living. We see that Enkidu had to experience the same ultimate failure that Gilgamesh did, in order to win Ea's assistance. Having returned to the world of the living, Enkidu can now complement the teaching Gilgamesh has given him with the knowledge that he has gained from his own experience. There is thus an integration of death and life and a further integration of the nature of Gilgamesh with that of his mirror-image, Enkidu.

The second tablet, a fragment from an old Sumerian poem, describes Gilgamesh's death and burial, followed by his consecration as a God, reigning over and giving judgment upon the dead.

Both of these fragments indicate Gilgamesh's ultimate success. In sum, Gilgamesh had the courage to directly confront the Lower Self, and in so doing unleashed the forces by which it defends itself. In combating these forces Gilgamesh applied the teaching of the Steward, and – in great pain and labor – ultimately witnessed the surrender of the Steward to Higher Centers. Finally, he received the benediction of the Gods. Having realized the secret teaching and having achieved full self-knowledge, Gilgamesh will be able to both serve the Gods and justly rule his people.

We note that neither the *Epic of Gilgamesh*, the *Atrahasis*, nor the *Enuma Elis* give the ancient teaching directly; they give its symbolic frame of reference. They give the context without which the teaching cannot succeed. It is clear that, within the Mesopotamian Tradition, the teaching itself was given – as it should be – only to those who had made the necessary preparations.

---

15. These fragments were also excavated at the Library of Ashurbanipal, but they come from earlier sources.

Thus, from the broken tablets retrieved from the Library of Ashurbanipal at Nineveh and from the sites at Ashur, Kish, and Sultantepe, we have evidence of a teaching that probably reaches back to the core teachings of the Original Religions – as they were given in the second direct intervention of the Gods in human history, at the end of the last Ice Age. These myths, formative for the Mesopotamian family of Civilizations, were also formative for the mythic structure of the great religions to follow. Tablet XI from the Library of Ashurbanipal, which tells the story of the flood, is clearly the model for the story of the Genesis flood narrative. Gary Rendsburg points out that the account of the flood in Genesis follows the *Gilgamesh* account "point by point in the same order, even when the story permits other alternatives."[16] Additionally, the parallel between the seduction of Enkidu by the priestess Shamhat (which occurs prior to his meeting with Gilgamesh) and Eve's temptation of Adam is unmistakable. The 'two faces' of Shamhat presented in the text of the myth correspond to the 'two Eves' in Zoroastrianism and Judaism: the first being the evil Lilith and the second a positive representation of the eternal feminine. The later, Christian Eve is presented – initially – only in her negative face.

Having provided a brief overview of Mesopotamian mythology, we shall continue our historical narrative.

The Mesopotamian Line of Civilizations

As we noted above, the **Akkadians** and the **Assyrians** had established themselves in the Tigris-Euphrates river basin by 2500 BC. In about 2300 BC the Akkadians conquered both the Sumerians to the south and the Assyrians to the north, establishing the first Mesopotamian empire. After about 180 years the Akkadian empire crumbled, and from that time the balance of power in the region shifted back and forth between the Assyrians in the north and the Sumero-Akkadians in the south.

In 1900 BC the **Amorites**, nomadic herdsmen inhabiting the lands west of the Euphrates, migrated into the central/south region of the Tigris-Euphrates basin. They were allowed to settle by the Sumero-Akkadians, who extracted a nominal rent-tribute. The Amorites adopted both the Sumerian religion and the Sumero-Akkadian language base. Over time they developed their own system of city-states, one of which was the city of Babylon. In about 2000 BC they were able to usurp the line of Sumero-Akkadian

---

16. Rendsburg, Gary, "The Biblical flood story in the light of the *Gilgamesh* flood account," in *Gilgamesh and the World of Assyria*, eds Azize, J. and Weeks, N., Peters, 2007, p. 117.

rulers and establish an Amorite dynasty. The Amorite city of Babylon then became the capital of the entire southern river basin, and it was from this time that southern Mesopotamia became known as **Babylonia**.

The sixth Amorite king, Hammurabi (1810-1750 BC), brought Babylon to its first imperial phase. He extended the city's control over the entire Tigris-Euphrates river basin by successfully defending its territories against neighboring kingdoms, turning one region after another into a Babylonian protectorate. In this way the whole of the Tigris-Euphrates basin came under his rule, less the northern reach of the Tigris – where the Assyrian population was concentrated. He then implemented a centralized system of government with a coherent system of taxation, which enabled the great building projects and public works that characterized his reign. It was from this time that the city of Babylon became the site of monumental architectural works, and it was in this context that Hammurabi formulated one of the first codes of law in human history.[17]

Hammurabi encouraged the worship of the Sumero-Akkadian gods, and the older Sumerian myths and epic tales were scrupulously copied, translated, or adapted with only minor alterations. The Sumerian language was again retained as the sacred language. At the level of the popular religion, the Babylonian regional deity Marduk was introduced as a central God of worship. But the Babylonian 'first principle' was Anu, which is continuous with the earlier Sumerian myth.

After Hammurabi's death his empire disintegrated, and the city of Babylon itself was eventually sacked by the Hittites. In the chaotic period that followed, the Amorite peoples were completely integrated into the Sumero-Akkadian base. At the same time the Assyrians to the north, who had been able to resist the Hittite invasion, become proportionately more powerful. From this time forward the dynamic of Mesopotamian politics begins to revolve around a Babylonian south in rivalry with an Assyrian north.

In the early sixteenth century BC the **Kassites** migrated into the southern Tigris-Euphrates basin and – over time – showed themselves able to represent the 'Babylonian' south against the continuing incursion of the Assyrians and the Hittites. The city of Babylon regained its full independence under the leadership of a Kassite dynasty, which ruled for more than half a millennium (from 1595 to 1019 BC). It was under the Kassites that the lands of Babylonia experienced their period of greatest peace and internal

---

17. The Code of Ur-Nammu is the oldest code of law known, written during the reign of the Sumerian King Ur-Nammu (r. 2112-2095 BC) in Ur about 300 years before the code of Hammurabi. The Code of Ur-Nammu is marked by its leniency – it provides compensation rather than punishment for most offenses. The Code of Hammurabi is among the earliest to introduce the idea of "innocent until proven guilty" and to allow the accused as well as the accuser to present evidence.

stability. While the Kassite kingdom was not a theocratic state, there was a powerful priesthood, capable – in times of uncertainty – of determining succession, and in that kingdom religion was considered central to life. Babylon was considered one of the holy cities of the world.

The phase of Kassite rule ended when Babylon was conquered by the **Elamites**. The Elamite kingdom was to the immediate south of the Tigris-Euphrates river basin, on the eastern side of the Persian Gulf. Within a few years of the Elamite conquest, the native Sumero-Akkadians retook the city and established the Second Dynasty of Isin (1155-1206 BC). The most distinguished leader of that time was Nebuchadnezzar I (1124-1103 BC), who defeated the Elamites, drove them from Babylonian territory, invaded Elam, and sacked the Elamite capital of Susa – while establishing an entente with the Assyrians to the north. Nebuchadnezzar was able to extend the Babylonian Empire to its traditional boundaries, which defined its borders until what is called the 'Bronze Age Collapse,' which occurred in the mid-tenth century.

In the historical scenario of the Bronze Age Collapse, a people originating in western Anatolia acquired iron-age technology and – with their superior weapons – ravaged the eastern Mediterranean basin from 1055-936 BC. These nameless invaders were known to the Egyptians as the 'Sea Peoples,' and this is how they have become known to history. During this dark century every significant city in the eastern Mediterranean was sacked, looted, and destroyed. The existing pattern of Civilizational Order was completely disrupted. The peoples of the eastern Mediterranean were forced – by the sheer necessity of self-preservation – to adopt iron-age technology. Only the Assyrian Empire was able to survive this period intact, and so, as the Sea Peoples began to return to their original place in the working of things, Assyria became a controlling force in the Tigris-Euphrates basin. By 911 BC Assyria ruled all of what had been the Babylonian Empire.

This was the beginning of the second or 'Neo-Assyrian' Empire (911-612 BC), which was the greatest imperial expansion that occurred in the cycle of the Mesopotamian Civilizations. Assyria gained control, not only of the entirety of the Tigris-Euphrates basin, but the entirety of Egypt, the entirety of the Levant, and large parts of the Arabian peninsula, Turkey, and Iran.

During this period the Assyrian language, Aramaic, became a popular language, alongside the Akkadian that was spoken throughout the region. At the same time, the Assyrians preserved Sumerian as a sacred language and continued to faithfully copy the

Epic of Gilgamesh, the *Enuma Elis*, and the *Atrahasis*. Indeed it is through the Assyrian copies that we know these myths.

We note that, for a full three centuries, the Neo-Assyrian Empire included Egypt, and during the period of occupation many Egyptians entered Mesopotamia and settled there. Increasingly the educated classes of society became a cultural composite, and it is certain that the Mesopotamian and Egyptian Traditions were in direct contact at this time.

The Mesopotamian cycle closes with a resurgence of the Babylonian Empire in the late seventh century BC. The Neo-Babylonian Empire was to run parallel with a reduced Assyrian Empire until the end of the cycle. The resurgence of Babylon occurred under the leadership of the Chaldean peoples.

The **Chaldeans** entered the southern Tigris-Euphrates river basin in the eleventh to tenth centuries BC, at the time when it was under the control of the Assyrian Second Empire. Through the Second Empire, whenever Assyria had trouble in maintaining its control over the south, the peoples of the Babylonian composite would attempt to throw them off. From about 900 BC it was the Chaldeans who provided the most active and organized resistance to the Assyrians.

In 620 BC Nabopolassar (658-605 BC), a Chaldean chieftain who was able to unite the Babylonian peoples under his leadership, seized the city of Babylon from its Assyrian rulers.

Like the Amorites and Kassites before them, the Chaldeans came into a leadership role only after having completely absorbed the Mesopotamian culture. But they went further than either the Amorites or the Kassites in developing a self-sustaining priest caste with a very considerable say in the succession of the Kings.

The Chaldean priest caste was able to transcend the regional and ethnic divisions of the area and absorb the Mesopotamian heritage – back to its earliest Sumerian origins. While they were predominantly Chaldean, they preserved a continuity with the existing Sumero-Akkadian priest caste who had trained and educated them. The Chaldeans interbred with the Sumero-Akkadians, and the original ethnic grouping was absorbed into the general mix of the Babylonian south. The term 'Chaldean' came to refer only to the priest caste. The Chaldean priests became renowned for their understanding of astrology, astronomy, and mathematics and were acknowledged throughout the ancient world as masters of incantation, augury, sorcery, and the magical arts. They were specialists in reading omens and in prophecy. Beyond this, they actively integrated the Egyptian teachings, the Zoroastrian teachings, and the Vedic teachings.

Figure 16. **Ruins of Bablyon**

After having taken the city of Babylon, Nabopolassar was able to establish rule over the entirety of the Babylonian south in addition to former Assyrian possessions in what is now Syria, Lebanon, the Levant, and the northern part of Arabia. He was succeeded by his son, Nebuchadnezzar II, who took his name from the Sumero-Akkadian king Nebuchadnezzar I, so affirming continuity with the earlier Sumero-Akkadian phase.

We note that the Assyrian records of this period show that the majority of the Egyptians resident in the Assyrian-controlled areas of the north remained in place after Egypt itself regained its independence. It is likely that many of the Egyptians who had settled in the south during this time also remained.

Nebuchadnezzar II rebuilt all of the cities of Babylonia on a spectacular scale. The rebuilding of Babylon itself transformed it into the city of legend that it has since become. The reconstructed city was contained by a system of moats and a double circuit of walls with the Euphrates flowing through its center. At the very center of the city was the great ziggurat Etemenanki – literally 'House of the Frontier between Earth and Heaven.' The expert irrigation and landscaping skills of the residents were employed to produce the 'hanging gardens of Babylon,' which became one of the Seven Wonders of the ancient world. The three square miles of the city would have been beautifully landscaped with long avenues of palm trees.

THE STORY OF MAN

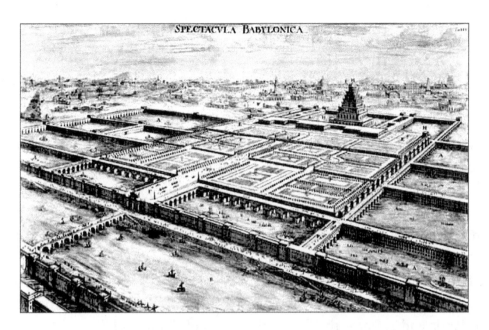

Figure 17. **Reconstructed view of Babylon**

While Babylon was being rebuilt, Nebuchadnezzar II conducted a series of successful military campaigns, securing the great Phoenician cities of Sidon and Tyre and the Aramean capital of Damascus. He captured Jerusalem in 597 BC and deported thousands of Jews to Babylon to man his great construction projects. This is the famed period of the 'Babylonian Exile,' which we shall document in Chapter 28 of Book IV, "The Age of the Prophets." We note that the Judaic presence in Babylon corresponded to the presence of **1)** a highly concentrated Chaldean priest caste and **2)** a resident population of Egyptians. Whatever the Israelites suffered under the Babylonians, they were allowed to continue their religious practices, and the prophets Ezekiel and Daniel remained active through the period. It is almost certain that the Judaic Tradition had open contact with the Chaldean Tradition during this time, for this is the period in which the *Song of Solomon* was written – which are unique amongst the Hebrew scriptures. The *Song of Solomon* makes no reference to law, covenant, or Yahweh, but apply – at the level of great art – the imagery of sexual love to the love of Man for God.[18] The more formal Judaic teachings were also re-caste during the Babylonian captivity, undergoing a significant concentration. Indeed, the most authoritative version of the Torah was authored by the Babylonian Jews, and, to a very large degree, the Babylonian Jews directed activity in Israel through to the time of the Hasmonean and Herodian dynasties. They

18. The *Song of Solomon* has been dated to this period by its Aramaic, Persian, and Greek vocabulary.

did not remain in Babylon through laxity of spirit, but because they were situated in a great center of spiritual life.

In 568 BC Nebuchadnezzar II inflicted a series of defeats on the Egyptians and briefly invaded Egypt itself.

All of these movements, perturbations, and resettlements were the after-effects of a program of imperial conquest, yet, as a result of this, there emerged a class of people with a broader view – independent of national polity and of the belief systems of the particular religions. There emerged a small stratum of people who had a distinct feeling for the collective inheritance of Mankind in a sentient universe. The existence of this stratum is reflected in the Greek literature of the time, which shows a marked respect for, and a positive interest in, contemporary doings at Babylon, Memphis, Thebes, Sais, Persepolis, and Susa – even when the Greeks were at war with these peoples. The immediate cultural sphere of Mesopotamia would have included – beyond the great cities of Persia and Egypt – the Phoenician cities of Sidon and Tyre, the Assyrian cities of Nineveh and Assur, the Median capital of Ecbatana, and the Aramaean capital of Damascus. Additionally, there was a direct connection to the great centers of Vedic India: Aror, Bairat, Sravasti, Sagala, Chunar, and Madurai. Ancient Mesopotamia was central, in a way that it is hard for us now to imagine. It was also cosmopolitan, in a much younger world than the world of today: in a world that had a more immediate sense of its source in a higher level. There were men alive within that world who were able to understand the monotheistic, dualistic, and triadic versions of creation as the variant thematic expressions of a single underlying truth – and understand this truth in its relation to the nature of consciousness itself. These would have been the Men of the Traditions – the Mesopotamian, the Egyptian, the Zoroastrian, the Judaic, the Vedic, and the Greek – which flourished together in that time as never since.

Having said this, the Babylonian Second Empire was short-lived. Nebuchadnezzar II's successor Amel-Marduk was degenerate and alienated the Chaldean priest caste. He was murdered by his successor Neriglissar, who reigned from 560-556 BC, and of whom we know little. Neriglissar's successor was a boy, Labashi-Marduk, who, after nine months, was murdered in a conspiracy engineered by one Nabonidus, who replaced him as king. Persian and Greek sources cite Nabonidus as being mad or deviant. Whatever the case, he directly opposed the Chaldean priest caste and worshipped other Gods than theirs. In 539 BC Babylon was conquered by Cyrus II of Persia, who viewed himself as a liberator. The Persian account claims that the gates of Babylon were opened to him.

It is probable that the Chaldean priest caste foresaw the Persian conquest, sensed the end of the Mesopotamian cycle of Civilizations, and prepared themselves for the transition that was to follow.

The Legacy of Mesopotamia

The Mesopotamian Order, in its heyday, ran parallel with the Dynastic Egyptian and – once it arrived on the scene – the Judaic. These three Civilizational Orders profoundly influenced one another, and the Mesopotamian Order was the eldest brother of the family. There are indisputable lines of influence running from Mesopotamia to Egypt. Sumerian influence is revealed in the art and architecture of old Upper Egypt and can be seen particularly in seal impressions, temple façades, florette motifs, and paneled-façade architecture. Mesopotamia conquered Egypt twice, first under the Assyrians and then under the Chaldeans. During the three centuries of the Assyrian rule of Egypt, there was a significant settlement of Egyptians in Mesopotamia. At several points there were profound, formative interactions between these two Civilizations. With respect to the Judaic Civilization, the Old Testament story of Exodus describes the connection between the Judaic and the Egyptian Civilizations, while the story of the Babylonian Captivity describes the link to the Mesopotamian Civilization. Mesopotamia is an essential part of the context of Judaism, as that is presented in the Torah. But where Egypt impacted all of posterity through its monumental architecture and through its formative influence on the Classical World, the Mesopotamian Civilization did not leave the same kind of imprint on the Civilizations to follow. The life of the Egyptian Civilization significantly overlapped that of the Classical Civilizations, which reflected it in many ways. The Old Mesopotamian Order, by contrast, did not overlap the Classical Civilizations and so did not have a direct influence on the many Civilizations that were spawned from them.

We note that, when the Persian conquest of Mesopotamia came, the Zoroastrian Magi tolerantly accepted the Chaldean priest caste and allowed it to continue in its religious practices. The Magi had almost certainly made a connection with the Chaldeans in the centuries preceding the Persian invasion, and by the time of Cyrus's invasion there was a significant ongoing exchange between the two Traditions. This dialogue would have contributed to changes that occurred in both Traditions through the sixth and fifth centuries BC.

In the Zoroastrian Teaching there was a refinement of the original Zoroastrian dualism, which clarified the place of a transcendent Absolute. We have evidence, from the early fourth century BC, of the doctrine of Zurvan, which parallels much more closely the Chaldean and Vedic conceptions of the Absolute. The seeds for this doctrine would have been sown in the century preceding.

In the Chaldean Teaching there was a deepening understanding of the process of negation, which must be based on a clear understanding of the function of (what we have called) the Black Queen. The Zoroastrians understood negation, on a cosmic level, as the over-arching presence of Angra Mainyu – who is the 'other face' of the divinity (Ahura Mazda). Angra Mainyu is understood to be present, both in Creation and in each individual. The presence of Angra Mainyu in the individual is understood exactly as we have described the role of the Black Queen in Chapter 3.[19] Beginning from the sixth century BC this understanding is more directly reflected in the Chaldean teachings.

Beyond these doctrinal changes, there was an exchange of method and technique related to divination, mathematics, and astrology, which both parties practiced actively. Indeed many Greek and Roman sources of the period actually fail to distinguish the Magi from the Chaldeans, as both were understood – in the Greek Koine and in Latin – to be the equivalent of the Modern English word 'magician.'

In retrospect the Chaldean priest caste – the distilled extract of ancient Mesopotamian culture – had only 80 years of independent activity before Cyrus the Great's conquest. The Persian occupation, when it came, was not the end of the priest caste, or of Babylon as a religious center. It is a signal of Achaemenid tolerance, and of the ecumenic spirit of the Persian Empire, that neither the Babylonians nor the Assyrians were forced to convert to the Zoroastrian religion. The city of Babylon remained intact, and the traditional Mesopotamian religion continued to be practiced actively. The Chaldean priest caste developed an identity that had become independent of its civilizational base, and was recognized throughout the Mediterranean basin and the Near East as a carrier of the 'inner teachings' and prophetic understanding of the Mesopotamian Tradition.

Having been absorbed into the Achaemenid Empire, Mesopotamia was then conquered by Alexander in 331 BC. Two full centuries after the Persian conquest Alexander was so impressed with the city of Babylon that he decided to make it the capital of

---

19. For a full presentation of the Zoroastrian position see Chapter 27 of Book IV, "The Age of the Prophets."

his new world empire. After his death, and the division of his conquests amongst his successors, Mesopotamia was integrated into the Seleucid Empire. The Seleucids then ruled Mesopotamia for 180 years, until it was conquered by the Parthians, who, like the Seleucids, were religiously heterogeneous. Trajan then conquered all of Mesopotamia in 116-117 AD, but on his death his successor Hadrian relinquished all Roman conquests east of the Euphrates. Mesopotamia was then divided between the Romans and the Parthians, until it was reconquered by Septimus Severus in 198 AD. It was then ruled by the Romans continuously from 198 AD to 637 AD, when it was finally conquered by the armies of Islam.

While neither the Babylonian nor the Assyrian populations converted to Zoroastrianism, they both did convert to Christianity when it came, more than 600 years later (in the period of Parthian/Roman rule). It was the conversion of the majority of the Babylonian and Assyrian peoples to Christianity in the first century AD that signaled the definitive end of the ancient Mesopotamian culture.

In the second century AD, while the Romans and Parthians vied for control of the northern Tigris-Euphrates basin, a number of independent Neo-Assyrian states arose, and of these the fledgling kingdom of Osroene became the first state to adopt Christianity as its official religion. It is often forgotten now that Osroene preceded Rome as the first Christian government. A profound Syriac Christian culture developed in Osroene, which produced the "Church of the East," later known as the Nestorian Church. The Nestorian Church spread Christianity deep into the Far East and became, in the twelfth and thirteenth centuries, the largest Christian Church in the world. Syriac Christianity remained a major center of Christian influence until, in the fourteenth century, Tamarlane waged his campaign of annihilation. Thus, as Christians, the Assyrians were persecuted, first by the Persians, then by the Arabs, and finally and most dramatically by the Mongols. Interestingly, Egypt was also a foundation for Early Christianity, the School of Alexandria providing its first theology, and the Egyptian Desert Fathers providing its first monastic practice. We see, in the case of both Mesopotamia and Egypt, the peoples of a Great Ancient Civilization, having exhausted their vision in the line of time, able to recognize the greatness they had lost in Early Christianity.

While the Sumerian, Babylonian, and the Assyrian civilizations faded into the pages of history, something of ancient Mesopotamia still survived. There was a Hermetic teaching and a mythology that had begun from Sumeria, developed through the periods of Akkadian, Babylonian, Assyrian, and Chaldean rule, and finally outlived the Civilizational Order which had been its base. In the writings of the fifth century Neoplatonists

(Iamblichus and Proclus), we find clear references to a known and respected Chaldean priest caste, which had survived the conquest of Babylon *by more than 800 years*. With the seventh century Islamic invasion this priest caste finally disappeared, but there is evidence that the Mesopotamian teachings themselves survived. Mesopotamian Hermeticism was based on a unique sensitivity to energies – both densities of energy and qualities of energy – extending from the mineral through to the cosmic. In its Chaldean phase it integrated elements of the Neoplatonic, Vedantic, and Zoroastrian cosmologies. In the late nineteenth century George Gurdjieff discovered a School, carrying just such a teaching, in the depths of Central Asia – claiming direct descent from Amorite Babylon.[20] The organization that Gurdjieff discovered disappeared from view in the upheavals that followed the Russian Revolution.

---

20. George Gurdjieff's references to this School can be found in conjunction with his remarks on the Sarmoung Brotherhood in *Meetings with Remarkable Men* (p. 147 to 164) and in conjunction with his remarks on Babylon in *Beelzebub's Tales* (p. 472-479). For a record of the content of this teaching see Peter Ouspensky's *In Search of the Miraculous*.

CHAPTER 16
The Egyptian Civilization

Figure 18. **Great Sphinx of Giza**

The Egyptian Civilization endured for more than three millennia, and it had a seminal impact on every civilization that it came into contact with. The Spiritual Tradition behind the Egyptian Civilization was a parent Tradition to the Judaic, the Greek, and the Christian – yet we cannot know the Egyptian Tradition as we can know its offspring. When we look at the Judaic, Greek, or Christian Traditions, there are many available sources which state, in one way or another, "This is how it was for us." For Egypt this is not the case; the direct lines of transmission from the original Spiritual Tradition have long since been obliterated. And so we are reduced – as with Mesopotamia – to archaeology and linguistics, and to the reports that have come to us from the civilizations contemporary with it. Additionally, much of what we now know of Egypt we know from the last 300 years of its decadent old age, when it began to merge into the then dominant milieu of Classical Civilization.

This is unfortunate, because the Egyptian Tradition was one of the greatest Spiritual Traditions of human history. It was able to unite myth, ritual, monumental sculpture, architecture, and the decorative arts into a single unique statement in a way that no other Civilization has done.

Egyptian Religion and the Creator-God

The Egyptian Religion is, like the Mesopotamian, a Creator-God Religion. The mythical presentation of the act of creation is important, for it tells us much about the proximity of Spiritual Tradition to Civilizational Order. There are three possibilities for the 'creation' myth: **1)** to slip into a rigid theism, **2)** to veer towards a 'looser' polytheism, or **3)** to open us – in a very special way – to dimensional differences that are beyond the perceptual and cognitive capacities of man. The Egyptian myths clearly fall into the third category. In no case does the Absolute – as Ra – act as an originating subject, initiating creation in an act which takes place at the 'beginning' of our time. Creation always relates to a level that is outside of time and space as we know it.

And here we emphasize that, despite the speculations of many of the original Western researchers, the Egyptian Religion was monotheistic and had been clearly monotheistic from its inception. The sense of the Absolute permeates all. Yet, at the same time, the Egyptians recognized a hierarchy of Gods who managed the different levels of Creation. It is this sense of diversity in a context of underlying unity – the sense of cosmos – that provides the foundation for the Egyptian culture. The 'monumentality' of Egyptian Art is not a result of man 'pushing himself up' to new heights, but of man recognizing and acknowledging a scale above his own. Egyptian monumental art always brings the sense of unity on a cosmic scale.

We are here treating the Egyptian Religion as the last of the 'Original Religions,' and because of the amount of available material, we will be able to examine the Egyptian pantheon of Gods in greater depth than we did the Mesopotamian. In order to understand the Egyptian conception of the Absolute (Ra) in its relation to the pantheon of the Gods, we must first take our bearings in relation to the Original Religions.

THE EGYPTIAN RELIGION AND
THE MONOTHEISM OF THE ORIGINAL RELIGIONS

The Traditions behind the Original Religions were the first to place emphasis on a central and preeminent God, relevant to every sphere of human activity. Under this primary deity there would be a pantheon of lesser Gods. The original God usually had many manifestations and might appear in different aspects in different circumstances. The Gods of the pantheon are then used to express these multiple manifestations. Thus we find the worship of a single God, with many names, many different forms of expression, and many images used to represent it.

In the Egyptian example, Ra, the sun-god and creator, is most frequently spoken of through other gods of the pantheon, for example, the face of Ra that is Atum, the face of Ra that is Horus, the face of Ra that is Amun, and so on. This use of multiple manifestation-expressions can be quite subtle and deep. The different 'aspects' of Ra may represent how he is seen in different dimensions. The Absolute is so many things that it only makes sense for us to speak of him in a dimension that is relevant to our own experience, and even that changes according to time and circumstance. By being able to specify his multiplicity in this way, we preserve his oneness. His 'unity' is not abstract but vibrantly present in everything.

And so, despite the nearly 700 gods of the Egyptian Religion and the innumerable cults that spawned from them, the sense of the Absolute permeating all was never lost. For three thousand years the Egyptian Civilization revealed this in all of its art, its architecture, and its myth. The preservation of the 'sense of the Absolute' was the sacred intent of the Men of the Tradition, hard at work behind the 'official' Religion. In an extraordinary effort, sustained over three millennia, they represented the identity and the principal characteristics of one immanent Absolute, no matter what pressures were brought to bear by the Religion or the Civilizational Order.

The confusions with respect to Egyptian 'polytheism' came originally from the reaction of the Early Christian Church to the plethora of Egyptian cults that existed in its time. Additionally the Egyptian Religion, as one of the Original

Religions, included cults with still-visible roots in the older Shamanic rituals and practices. In Egypt all of these elements united in a seamless whole, which included the 'official' state Religion and the Spiritual Tradition that was (at least sometimes) behind it. The Christian Religion, as a Prophetic Religion, originated in a definite break from the form of the Original Religions. Thus, while the Christian and the Egyptian Spiritual Traditions certainly knew and respected one another, the two Religions were incompatible and hence the labeling of the older religion as 'occultism' and polytheism. This confusion was magnified by the Western researchers of the nineteenth and twentieth centuries, who had no 'keys' with which to interpret the Egyptian artifacts, no first-hand experience of Higher Centers, and no Spiritual Tradition to guide them. They naïvely took the art, the architecture, and the fragments of myth that they found to be evidence of polytheism – and this fitted with the 'progressivist' *zeitgeist* of their own age, which viewed cultures in the past as necessarily 'less developed' than their own. Having classified the Egyptian Religion as an Original Religion, we note that the Egyptians took their myths and symbols further than any Religion that preceded them. It was, perhaps, the 'last and the greatest' of its kind. The Egyptian Religion sometimes seems like something between an Original Religion and a Prophetic Religion; indeed, in many ways, the Egyptian figure of Osiris anticipates the Prophets.

Part of the genius of the Egyptian myths is their flexibility. They are immediately relevant to both Religion and Tradition, and it is precisely this sustained double meaning that reveals the formative role of the Tradition. While the myths present a vision of the universe of great scale and subtlety – relevant to the level of Religion – they each contain an immediate invocation to presence that is relevant to the Tradition. That they fulfill both of these requirements completely and simultaneously is evidence of considerable inspiration.

The principal meaning of the myths for the Religion is the representation of Ra, as the Absolute, in a living interconnected whole that gives man a definite place and purpose. Particularly, this allows man to prepare for his death and to see the significance of 'death' for his life. In other words, the myths provide a unified view of the different aspects of the human experience. The depictions of the Absolute as Ra are never purely speculative; they are always grounded – if sometimes at several removes – on real insight. The attempts to represent Ra as Creator show him in a dimension that transcends both Creation and the Uncreate. Ra's Created Universe is represented as being in a continual state of flux, but not of chaos, for the myths themselves reveal the laws that govern that flux. Thus they create a sense of awe in relation to the Uncreated Ra and a sense of security with respect to his orderly governance of his Creation.

The principal meaning of the myths for the Spiritual Tradition is, by contrast, internal: the representation of the Work of the Steward in its many forms and phases. The Egyptian myths acknowledge that – while awakening is simple – the resistance to it is massive, varied, and ever-changing. One simple effort repeated through time will not bring victory; a variety of different tools, applied under different circumstances, is necessary.

Given these differences the Gods of the Egyptian pantheon are interpreted in one way by the Religion and in another by the Tradition. For the Religion the Gods are usually 'step-down' deities, who will hear supplication and prayer. They may also be the patron-Gods of certain cities. For the Egyptian Tradition the Gods are, at different times: **1)** 'markers' for the nameless disembodied celestial beings who serve the human race, **2)** representations of cosmic forces operative at different levels of the universe, and **3)** representations of different aspects of the internal Work of the Steward.[1]

Let us move on, then, to a brief review of the mythology itself and the key figures of the pantheon.

After the unification of Egypt the priests at Heliopolis presented a unified view of the principal gods: Ra and the first few generations of his children. Such a view is known as a *pesedjet*, and this was known as the *pesedjet* of Heliopolis. We shall present this short myth and then provide a more extensive description of the Gods. To show the whole in action, we shall then tell the story of Isis and Osiris and examine its relation to the Work of the Steward. Finally we will complete the picture with a brief look at the two great funerary documents known as *The Amduat* and *Journey Forth by Day* (more familiar to us, mistranslated, as *The Egyptian Book of the Dead*). Finally, on this foundation, we shall examine again the Egyptian view of the Absolute.

---

1. We are particularly indebted to ongoing research by the School of Robert Earl Burton for our understanding of the esoteric 'keys' used in the Egyptian Spiritual Tradition. Note that these keys were introduced in earlier chapters and are applied throughout the book to assist in understanding the foundational myths and cosmogonies of all the Spiritual Traditions. See also Burton in the Bibliography.

The Pesedjet of Heliopolis

In the early dynastic period the priests of Ra established the city of Annu (now known as Heliopolis) as the religious capital of the country and presented a central myth, to which the local Gods of the different regions could be assimilated. This myth achieved its finished form in the third to fifth dynasties (2780-2300 BC). It remained the most important grouping of the Egyptian mythology and was called the *Great Pesedjet*. The nine deities of the *pesedjet* are in four generations: the Sun God himself (Ra/Atum), his children Shu and Tefnut, their children Geb and Nut, and their children Osiris, Isis, Seth, and Nephthys. In this short presentation Ra wears the 'face' of Atum – the creator or the 'completed one.'

The first of the Gods evolved out of chaos and darkness and brought order into the universe. In the beginning were only the primeval waters, which were unconscious and incapable of focused action. Ra raised himself, on a hill, out of the waters and created himself. Thus Ra is a self-created deity, the first being to emerge from the dark and endless watery abyss that existed before creation. He was born alone. Alone, he raised himself out of the darkness. Emerging from the primeval darkness he saw, for the first time, his own shadow. And then – in a single, critical, formative act – he embraced it. *Only after he had embraced his own shadow* did it become possible for him to generate both divine and human beings. First he produced Shu, the god of air, and Tefnut, the goddess of moisture or water. From one God there were suddenly three Gods. This act immediately resulted in the existence of light and the dispersal of chaos. After creating himself and his two children, Ra wept, and his tears became mortal men and women. Thus humanity is conceived at a very early stage of the process and has an important place in the working of things. Shu (air) and Tefnut (water) then joined as man and wife and from their union came Geb, the god of the earth, and Nut, the goddess of the sky. Nut and Geb, locked in an endless embrace, then provided the universe with the gods and goddesses who completed the *Great Pesedjet:* Osiris, Isis, Seth, and Nephthys. But there was an additional god, central to the myths of Heliopolis, who was Horus. He existed in two forms, which represent his existence on two different levels: Horus the God, as the fifth child of Geb and Nut, and Horus the Steward who enables the God within, as the son of Isis and Osiris. Of the ten Gods of this *pesedjet*, Osiris and his son Horus are used to represent the link between Men and Gods, in all its implications.

The Egyptian Gods

Now we shall present our own more extended *pesedjet* of eleven (of the more than 700) Egyptian Gods.

RA, the Sun God, moves across the sky during the hours of the day and through the underworld during the hours of the night. His life parallels our own in that, in the underworld, he dies and is reborn, returning again and again to the light of day. His circular journey is made in two solar boats: the Mandjet (morning boat) which carries him through the sky and the Mesektet (evening boat) which carries him through the underworld. As a God he is particularly associated with the hours of morning and midday when the Sun is so brilliant that you cannot look at it. Ra, as the Creator, called into existence all forms of life by speaking their secret names.

In the Old Kingdom (at least from the fifth dynasty) Ra was identified with the sun god Atum. In the Middle Kingdom Ra was merged with Horus, the falcon. In the eighteenth dynasty of the New Kingdom he was briefly displaced by Aten. Finally he was associated increasingly with Amun and known as Amun-Ra. We note that, in these several accretions of Ra with other Gods, the Men of the Tradition always preserved the 'Absolute' nature of the newly-named face of Ra.

ATUM: While Ra was associated with the morning and high-noon sun, Atum was associated with the evening sun, and so he 'looks back' on Creation. In the slanting rays of the evening sun Mankind can more naturally 'look up' to him. Ra himself, in his brilliant intensity, transcends Creation. The name Atum means to complete or finish. He is the 'completed one' and the finisher of the world. As the Creator he was seen to be the underlying substance of the world. He is the BEING, which by 'being' generates beings. Both Gods and men are the expressions of his being.

OSIRIS: Osiris' origins are pre-dynastic and prehistoric, linking him perhaps with an even more ancient Spiritual Tradition that is now lost to us. He is one of the most important gods in the Egyptian pantheon. Osiris was originally a ruler of men. Does he then hearken back to the 'Golden Age' when Gods walked

Figure 19. **Ra**   *Figure 20.* **Atum**   *Figure 21.* **Osiris**

with men? Certainly his existence as a God-Man predates the dynastic period. In Egyptian myth he was killed by his jealous brother Seth and so became the only God of the pantheon who experienced and passed through death. In this respect he is the God most like men and the God who can teach men to face the trial of their death.

The *Great Pesedjet* tells that the tragic death of Osiris caused the Gods to consider how death itself could be overcome, thus initiating a subject that was to dominate Egyptian society on all levels. In the central Osiris myth, Seth – having killed Osiris – cut his body into pieces and cast the pieces into the Nile. Osiris' wife Isis, after a long and arduous search, was able to collect the pieces and reassemble the body. Thoth and Anubis then wrapped it in a mummy's bandages and restored it to its original shape. Osiris was indeed 'dead' to the world of men but in some way also 'preserved.' He had, in effect, become an 'intermediary' being. Through Thoth's magic the 'preserved' Osiris was able to sire Horus on Isis, and Horus was to replace him as 'Pharoah' in the world of men. From this point forward Osiris became the God of the underworld and master of the mysteries of birth and death.

In the reconstructing of Osiris, Isis and Thoth developed a method of 're-membering' that actually induced a renewal of life. This method was to become the ritual of salvation for all Egyptians and the means of self-transcendence for

THE STORY OF MAN

Figure 22. **Horus**   *Figure 23.* **Apophis**   *Figure 24.* **Seth**

those of the Spiritual Tradition. For the Men of the Tradition the re-membering of Osiris is a regeneration that takes place in the world of living men and women – and it is meant to occur before the moment of physical death.

Despite the regenerative process that brought Horus into being, Osiris did remain dead to the world of the living. The 'life' created was the life of Horus. Osiris voluntarily remained in the underworld and used his special understanding of the 'night side of life' to help mankind with the difficult transitions that occur there – for it is here that we most completely lose memory and continuity of being. Thus Osiris willingly stayed in the underworld to help Mankind, allowing his son to fulfill his public role in the world of the living. He is thus both the savior and the servant of mankind; he is a God-become-Man through his knowledge of mortality, and he is – at the same time – a king amongst men who is actually a God. In his original form he was a conscious Pharaoh, completing the Cosmos of Man on earth.

In the underworld it is Osiris who has the deciding role in the judgment of the dead. While, in the moment of judgment, it is Anubis who weighs the human heart on the scales, it is Osiris who has the decisive say in determining the fate of the individual. He does so with what is, ultimately, compassion. He helps those who can be helped, both in life and in death. He is the God that councils and advises us through the most difficult moments of our waking life, so that we lose ourselves neither in life nor in death. He is thus a special link between men and the Gods, and represents the possibility of defeating death, not only for the Pharaohs but for all Egyptians.

Osiris symbolizes the 'great labor' of transformation that turns death into a re-birth, preserving all that is worthy of being carried forward. He does this both in death itself and in the many deaths that come to us in the course of life. For the Tradition he is the laboring Steward who, through 'dying daily,' preserves and prolongs presence until presence can sustain itself.

HORUS is the son of Isis and Osiris, who, like Osiris, originated in pre-dynastic times. He is forever linked with the image of the Falcon and the person of the Pharaoh. The inner nature of the Pharaoh is somehow given in the combination of Horus and Osiris: Pharaoh-as-Horus in life and Pharaoh-as-Osiris in death. More generally, he is associated with the sky (the unbounded space that contains creation), with war (the struggle against the Lower Self), and with the ability to protect (to guard and nurture the emerging Higher Centers).

We noted that Horus is directly linked to Osiris, as his son. He is the replacement for Osiris and the avenger of his father's death. It is Horus who defeats Seth and in so doing becomes the 'true' Pharaoh that his father was. It is natural that Horus be the protector of the Pharaonic line. It is through association with Horus (or the Horus within himself) that the Pharaoh gains divinity. Horus is then, potentially, the completion of the Cosmos of Man.

More specifically, in the teaching of the Tradition, Horus is the 'transcendent' Steward, directly supporting Ra. This is the Steward in its passive, or 'executant' mode, regulating the functions while the Higher Centers steer their course.

APOPHIS is directly the foe of Ra; he is 'Not-Being,' void, and meaninglessness. As Seth was the foe of Osiris and Horus in the world of the living, so Apophis is the foe of the sun god himself in the underworld. He is chaos and evil in dimensions beyond our imagining. He is represented as a gigantic snake who encircles the earth. Despite his vast size he is very hard to see, almost unidentifiable. From another point of view he is what Ra – as the universe – does not see about himself. He stands always there as an agent for the return to chaos. While Ra's rule cannot be challenged during the light of day, Apophis can attack him in the difficult transitions he must undergo each night. Every single night Apophis encounters Ra at a particular hour, and Ra must withstand his assault.

Apophis thus represents the 'other face' of Ra, the a-cosmic chaos that must be neutralized in the workings of the Living Whole. In the funerary texts he is also used to represent the a-cosmic chaos (i.e., uncontrolled imagination) that exists in every individual human psychology.

SETH: One of the children of Geb and Nut. Like Osiris and Horus he is a God of pre-dynastic origin, but he represents an aspect of the pre-dynastic religion that has been lost to us. In dynastic times he was shown principally in his negative aspect, representing the forces of the Lower Self – the part of us that is resistant to awakening. He is strong, violent, cunning, and uncontrollable. He is the instigator of confusion and chaos. He is a deserter, a drunkard, and a brawler.

Seth was the murderer of Osiris and the enemy and combatant of his son Horus. As an enemy he is – like Apophis – hard to find. In all the chaos and tumult that he creates, he is himself hidden. This is an exact depiction of the Black Queen – the intelligence behind the Lower Self. If, after many years of work, you begin to glimpse her directly you must then confront and defeat her, or the victory will be hers. It is only Horus (the Steward) who – after numerous mistakes and with remarkable persistence – finds and defeats Seth (the Lower Self).

The defeated Seth takes his place as a servant of Ra. He is foremost in the night bark and uses his strength, determination, and unceasing alertness to detect Apophis in the darkest hours of the night. This reflects the transformation of a profoundly negative energy into its positive aspect. It is an example of the complete transfiguration of all the elements that exists in Egyptian mythology.

ISIS: After Ra, Isis, the wife of Osiris, is the most powerful of all the Gods. She is the God closest to Ra, and she knows his secret name. In other words she knows the 'Ra' that is beyond Being and Not-Being. Isis never revealed Ra's secret name and never used its power for her own sake, but only to increase the power of her son Horus – in his role as Steward to Higher Centers. For the Egyptian Tradition, Isis is that part of the emotional center which is directly in service to the level one above: what we called in Chapter 3 the Nine of Hearts or the White Queen. We note that it is Isis (the White Queen), rather than Horus (the infant Steward), who can appeal directly to Ra (Higher Centers).

It is because Seth cannot kill the powerful Isis that he attempts to destroy first Osiris and then the youthful Horus. While Isis is unable to reverse Seth's destruction and bring Osiris back to life, she is able to protect the infant Horus.

Figure 25. **Isis**   *Figure 26.* **Nephthys**   *Figure 27.* **Khepri**

She works in league with him, as the Nine of Hearts in an 'active' Steward, seeking to regenerate the 'matter' of human psychology. But it is the developed Horus who must actually confront Seth. Seth is extremely hard to find, intelligent, and eternally vigilant. He deceives even Isis at certain points. But as Horus becomes practiced in his role his own vigilance becomes unceasing, and with the guidance of his mother he is able to defeat Seth.

NEPHTHYS is the daughter of Nut (Sky) and Geb (Earth). She is paired with her sister Isis in funerary rites, because of their role as protectors of the mummy of the god Osiris. She assists Isis to reassemble the body of Osiris, and she becomes the primary nursing-mother of Horus; she is the watchful guardian to the infant king. She is known to have a fiery breath and is capable of incinerating the enemies of Ra. She is a very dangerous God.

While some say Nephthys was married to Seth, there is little linking her to Seth in the early Egyptian sources. Nor was Nephthys' marriage to Seth any part of the myth of the murder and resurrection of Osiris. We conclude that Nephthys was not paired with Seth the villain, but with Seth's positive aspect, the guide of Ra's night barque and the ever-vigilant enemy of Apophis. Their roles in the underworld as protectors of Ra are complementary.

Figure 28. **Ptah**   *Figure 29.* **Thoth**

KHEPRI: This is the most graphic image of the transcendent Steward in all of Egyptian mythology. He is an aspect of Ra, the magic scarab beetle who rolls up the sun in the mornings and is sometimes seen as his 'morning manifestation.' He is the god of creation and re-birth. He represents the strength of Ra's regenerative power, which is the power of the Steward to transform any circumstance – internal or external – into prolonged presence.

The image of the scarab is well chosen. In nature the scarab beetle lays its eggs in dung and then rolls them into a tiny dung ball. She continues to roll the ball until it becomes much larger than she, capable of supporting and protecting the larvae in their first weeks of life. The rolling of the ball is a long and strenuous job. The labor of the little scarab is the act of serving and enabling new life.

To understand the poignance of this image you need only watch the little scarab beetle at work. The dung ball, in the very shape of the sun-disk Ra, soon becomes much larger than the beetle herself. You cannot believe the little beetle can continue to push the ball, yet it remains unremittingly focused on its task, undeflected by any obstacle, and persistent in the most amazing resourcefulness. Everything in the little beetle moves the ball! It holds nothing back; there is no doubt, no hesitation, just action in service of emergent life. The phrase Men-Kheper-Ra is translated 'strong-transforming Ra,' or 'Ra's steadfastness of transformations.'

In the funerary text of the *Mes*, Khepri symbolizes Ra's difficult transformation in the sixth hour of the night. Through Khepri new light is kindled after the two darkest hours of the night journey.

PTAH is a deification of the primordial mound in the *Great Pesedjet* of Heliopolis. The primordial mound is the 'hill' upon which Ra raised himself out of chaos. We could say that the 'mound' represents the intermediary moment between cosmos and chaos. As Ra emerged from chaos his Ptah-face came forward. From that moment Ptah became the 'dimension' of Ra facing from chaos towards Creation. In fact Ptah is the Creator himself. He called the World into being by first 'dreaming' it, and then 'speaking' it forth. The name Ptah means literally 'opener' or 'the opener of the mouth.' As the Creator himself, the very 'fashioner of the earth,' Ptah is the artisan of artisans and their patron god.

His image is that of a man wearing a blue skull cap, in wrappings, like a mummy. His scepter is made of three symbols: **1)** the long pole of the scepter itself (representing strength), **2)** the ankh (representing life), and **3)** the *djed* pillar (representing stability). As the Creator he is associated with Maat, the goddess of justice and cosmic balance.

THOTH appears either as a strange ibis-headed creature or as a baboon. He is sometimes represented as the mind and tongue of Ra, his executant in creation, his will translated into speech. He was the arbiter of godly disputes, he was intimately involved with the judgment of the dead, and he was the god of magic. Within the Microcosmos Man, Thoth represents 'the heart,' the center of spiritual intelligence. Like Osiris and Seth he was pre-dynastic in his origins.

In later times Thoth was more generally a god of wisdom: of science, of medicine, of writing, of mathematics, and of astronomy. Thoth used his knowledge of mathematics to measure the seasons and regulate time. He surveyed the heavens and planned the shape of the earth. His will kept the earth, and everything in it, in a state of equilibrium. The 'Book of Thoth' was said to contain magical formulae for controlling nature and for controlling the world of the dead.

We shall now bring the elements of Egyptian mythology together, by presenting the one complete story that survives – through Plutarch's telling of it.

The Myth of Isis and Osiris

Osiris was the Pharaoh and Isis was his queen. Seth was the Pharaoh's jealous brother, who continually plotted to seize the throne. Horus was the son of Osiris and Isis and so the true heir to the throne. The outer meaning of the myth is an affirmation of Pharaonic rule. Its inner meaning can be keyed by the follow interpretation of the characters:

Osiris represents the Steward in active form.

Isis represents the White Queen within the Steward, aligning its elements and giving it an unwavering direction in relation to the level that is one above.

Seth represents either the Lower Self or the intelligence behind the Lower Self – the Black Queen.

Horus represents the Steward in its 'transcendent' form, in direct and knowing service to Higher Centers.

It is only after Isis and Osiris have successfully disengaged themselves from the Lower Self that they are able to produce Horus, who – once he has emerged – shows himself capable of more focused, more continuous, and more deftly targeted effort.

Our story begins when Seth kills Osiris, places his body in a casket, and throws the casket into the Nile, where the current carries it away. Isis, overcome with grief, searches all over Egypt to find the casket containing Osiris' body, with the hope of somehow bringing him back to life.

After many adventures Isis is able to recover Osiris' coffin, which had come into the hands of the Queen of Byblos in Lebanon. On seeing Osiris' coffin in the Queen's palace, Isis immediately takes steps to enter her service. After having served the Queen in different ways, she asks for and receives the coffin as a reward. On having received it she promptly sets out for Egypt. On the first night of her journey, believing herself to be alone, she opens the coffin and gazes upon Osiris, who seems still to be alive. She embraces him and works to bring him back to full awareness.

But the ever-vigilant Seth, constantly scanning his realm, sees Isis with the coffin, and recognizes what is occurring. While Isis sleeps he breaks into the coffin, removes Osiris' body, tears it to pieces, and spreads the pieces out all over the world.

When Isis sees the empty casket, her cry of anguish pierces earth and heaven. This represents the moment of the overthrow of the Steward by the Black Queen. Note that Seth must wait until Isis sleeps before he can make his move. Seth's action of destruction, splitting Osiris into many unconnected pieces, is a representation of the Black Queen's splitting up of the White Queen's retinue of work 'I's. The Black Queen achieves this effect by releasing powerful groups of 'I's within the four lower centers, unrelated to the aims of the White Queen. These engage and overwhelm the working group of 'I's that comprise the Steward and so break the link between the White Queen and her working body. In the end there are only unconnected 'I's; the memory of what had once united them has vanished into thin air.

Isis' piercing cry is the Nine of Hearts awakening to the overthrow of the Steward and understanding the implications of what has occurred. Without hesitation and without recrimination, she resumes the role of tireless seeker, recovering and reassembling the parts. Her cry is like the steam whistle that announces the departure of the train. Isis never forgets; she is the embodiment of ceaseless devotion to the Self. She sets out on an almost impossible task with perfect resolution, when, only moments previously, she had been on the verge of being reunited with Osiris.

But the Nine of Hearts cannot work alone. She needs the support of her working group in order to monitor the four lower centers; she must re-create the body of the Steward in order to accomplish her aim.

Isis first calls to her sister Nephthys for help. The two of them set out together to search the world for the pieces of Osiris, and they search for many long years. In this part of the myth Isis becomes the 'face' of the Nine of Hearts directed towards re-assembling the Steward while Nephthys is the 'face' that is receptive to influences coming from a higher level. Because of her role Nephthys is capable – without hesitation – of incinerating the enemies of Osiris. She doesn't enter into argument with imaginary fears, longings, and recriminations; she vaporizes them on the spot.

Over many years Isis and Nephthys are able to recover all of the parts, except the part that is directly involved with regeneration, the phallus. This had been eaten by a fish. Isis takes the other parts and begins to make them into the first mummy. This is an attempt to re-create the Steward with the aim to preserve presence. But Isis is again attempting the impossible, for she does not actually have the regenerative part. The impotence of Osiris acknowledges the fact that the only presence of which the Steward is capable is that of the four lower centers – which can never be presence itself, fully self-aware. The Steward can never be the Higher Centers it supports.

THE STORY OF MAN

Both Isis and Osiris must somehow rise above this impossible situation. They must stop seeking a solution on the same level as the problem, transcend their spatio-temporal environment, and effect the transformation of consciousness that is the aim of their existence. At just this point Thoth (the intellectual part of the Steward) comes to the aid of Isis. He gives her the magical words (the special mantra to prolong presence) that can be used to resurrect Osiris so that she herself can be impregnated and give birth to Horus. Through Thoth's magic Isis fashions a phallus of gold and then breathes new life into Osiris using Thoth's special incantation. She is then able to conceive the child Horus. By making use of the special mantra Isis has simulated the action of the regenerative part and so invoked the higher consciousness necessary to complete the transformation. And thus Horus is born.

Isis' actions following the dismemberment of Osiris represent the two stages of the Work of the Steward. Firstly the reunion of the Nine of Hearts with the working body of the Steward and secondly the re-creation of the Steward on a higher level where its role is that of passive executant to Higher Centers. The former is **the Osiris-fate** of the Steward and the latter is **the Horus-fate** of the Steward.

- *The Osiris-fate of the Steward* is realized in the turbulent depths of the underworld (or in the turbulent depths of a human psychology). It is to steadily knit itself back together, until the Nine of Hearts bonds permanently with the set of Work 'I's that can function as the Steward. This bonding is achieved by the use of special techniques. It is necessary to prepare Osiris for the challenges he will face in the darkest hour of the night.

- *The Horus-fate of the Steward* is realized in the light of the world of the living. It is to recognize the existence of Higher Centers and to serve them. In other words it is the Steward in a living relationship with Higher Centers. In this regard Horus can – in Egyptian mythology – represent the presence of the God. In the myth, Horus takes up the fight against Seth, wins his father's throne, and becomes the King of Egypt. This represents the Steward's mastery of the four lower centers, but at the same time it represents – quite literally – the conscious Pharaoh. The template of the 'Egyptian Pharaoh' was seen as a form of Horus, because, as Horus, he is fully qualified to rule. He is the falcon that flies between the earth and the sun. He symbolizes the connection with the cosmos above the Cosmos of Man, made complete.

And thus the myth of Isis and Osiris ends in an image of the perpetuation of Spiritual Tradition, Living Religion, and Civilizational Order. It is both the Steward enabling the Higher Centers (the ritual path of Osiris by which each Egyptian can safely pass through death) and the conscious ruler completing the Cosmos of Man.

The Funerary Texts: The Amduat and Journey Forth by Day

The Egyptians saw life and death as a unity. The process of death is the 'other' side of life. It is, at the same time, a test determining what possibilities will be open to us when we re-enter the 'life-side' of existence. The funerary texts prepare the aspirant for what is coming in the period between the end of the earthly life and the completion of the 'night journey.' This is the primary meaning for the Religion, as practiced by most ancient Egyptians. But the primary meaning for the Spiritual Tradition is to apply the teachings NOW – in this present moment and in every moment throughout the life-journey – knowing that severe trials and obstacles will be put forward, on an almost continuous basis, by the Lower Self. In this view the demons encountered in the underworld are the demons resident in our own nature; demons that appear clearly before us whenever the Black Queen tries to distract the Steward from its work to promote prolonged presence.

To understand the funerary texts more fully we must understand the distinction between the Egyptian terms *ba* and *ka*. They are very close to our terms 'spirit' and 'matter,' but they apply on many different levels. The created universe, for example, is *ka* in relation to the *ba* of the Absolute.

In a normal man the *ka* is the life-force of the physical body. *Ba*, then, is the 'heart'; it is the most sensitive energies of intellect and emotion, combined with traces of 'objective memory,' out of which a conscious soul will eventually be formed. In a more developed man the *ba* will be the Steward itself.

In a fully conscious man the *ba* will be the Higher Centers enabled by the Steward. In this case the *ba* is able to subsist independently of the *ka* of the physical body.

In death most men and women will experience acute confusion, forget everything that went before, and end in repeating their experience of life in a new body – either on a higher or on a lower level than the life they had completed. A conscious being, by contrast, will connect his *ba* (his now-independent consciousness) to the *ba* and the *ka* of a higher level and sustain himself there.

Before proceeding, a word about funerary texts themselves. Both the *Amduat* and *Journey Forth by Day* are products of the New Kingdom, but they have a long history.

The first funerary texts we know of, the **Pyramid Texts**, come from the time of the Old Kingdom (c. 2400 BC). They are known only from pyramid inscriptions and appear to have been used only by the Pharaonic circle. They record a series of spells or incantations that are focused on **1)** the preservation of the Pharaoh's being, **2)** his reanimation after death, and **3)** his ascent into the company of the Gods.

The **Coffin Texts** begin to appear in the First Intermediate Period (2181-2055 BC). This was a period of strife, in which it was not possible to construct pyramids. These texts were written on coffins – not only on the coffins of the Pharaonic circle but on the coffins of anyone who could afford one. Whereas in the Pyramid Texts the balance of the material concerns the celestial realms, the Coffin Texts focus more on the journey through the underworld and on the judgment that must be faced in the presence of Osiris.

The *Amduat*[2] and *Journey Forth by Day*, which are based on the material of the older texts, appeared much later, in the time of the New Kingdom.

The **Amduat** is translated as "That Which Is In the Afterworld" and would normally have been inscribed on the inside of the Pharaoh's tomb. The first example that we have appears on the tomb of Tuthmosis I (1506-1493 BC), and from that time it appears on a number of the tombs in the Valley of the Kings. The *Amduat* was strictly reserved for the Pharaonic circle, at least until the beginning of the Third Intermediate Period (1077-943 BC).

The text of **Journey Forth** was first formulated by the priests in Thebes and came into use during the Second Intermediate Period (c. 1700 BC). By the time of the beginning of the New Kingdom (1550 BC) its use had become widespread. During the Third Intermediate Period the *Journey Forth by Day* papyri were updated, revised,

---

2. Useful sources on the ancient text include Abt, Theodor and Hornung, Erik, *Knowledge for the Afterlife: The Egyptian Amduat – A Quest for Immortality*, Living Human Heritage Publications, Zurich, 2003, and Erman, Adolf, *The Ancient Egyptians: A Sourcebook of their Writings* (translated by Aylward M. Blackman), Peter Smith, Gloucester MA, 1978.

and standardized. The rituals were practiced generally until around 50 BC. There is no single canonical version of *Journey Forth by Day*, and there is a great deal of variation in the existing versions.

While the examples that we have of the *Pyramid Texts* and the *Amduat* are limited to the Pharaonic circle, the *Coffin Texts* and the papyri of *Journey Forth by Day* were used much more widely. Because the content of these texts is directly related, it is certain that the beliefs behind them were general. They informed rituals that were practiced at all levels of society. There were funerary practices, of one kind or another, for all Egyptians, and there were ceremonies marking the important transitions of life: birth, naming, and death. Naming, for example, was taken to be an important part of every person's destiny.

The great temples at Philae, Luxor, Karnak, and Abu Simbel were used by all, although certain activities were closed to lay people. There were innumerable smaller local chapels, and individual households had their own small shrines. More generally there was a wide variety of practices, for people in different walks of life, to discern the will of the gods and to determine right action in relation to it. These included both dream interpretation and the consultation of oracles.

The Amduat

The *Amduat*, or "That Which Is In the Afterworld," is one of the earliest and most detailed descriptions that we have of a Spiritual Tradition's representation of Mankind's habitual state of imagination or 'waking sleep.' It further describes the process of Man's emergence from this state into a state of 'consciousness' through the work of the Steward (Osiris) and the resultant appearance of the Higher Centers (Ra).

This highly-ordered set of pyramid inscriptions first appeared in the tombs of the Pharaohs. They detail the Sun God Ra's cyclical journey through the 'underworld,' which begins from the time when the sun sets in the west and ends when it rises again in the east. For the Sun God, day and night are two sides of the experience of existence – consciousness and unconsciousness. As Ra enters the underworld, he will be overwhelmed by the state of imagination, or unconsciousness, that is the habitual state of Mankind. With the help of the Steward (Osiris) and the Nine of Hearts (Isis), he will pass through this perilous state, be reborn within its darkness, and then emerge again into the daylight of full consciousness.

This eternal journey from 'waking' to 'death' to 'waking' again is an archetypal image representing the Egyptian Pyramid of Man on three distinct levels: **1)** for the Tradition, the journey represents the Steward's moment-to-moment struggle to emerge and re-emerge from imagination into the prolonged presence of Higher Centers, **2)** for the Living Religion, Ra's cyclical journey from light through darkness to light again represents the Absolute's capacity for perpetual self-renewal, and **3)** for the Pharaoh, ruler of the Civilizational Order, it is his sacred role upon death to take the journey of his father Ra on behalf of his people; in this he fulfills the wish of all humanity to attain immortality.

Yet the successful journey through the underworld is by no means guaranteed. The *Amduat* makes the dangers of the journey clear.

The underworld is carefully divided into the twelve hours of the night, each hour presenting the different allies and enemies that the Pharaoh/Sun-God must encounter. The *Amduat* gives the special names of each of these entities. When the spirit of the Pharaoh knows the names of his allies and his enemies, he can call the allies for help or use the names of his enemies to defeat them. This 'naming' refers to two things:

1. The ability to produce and to implement the Work 'I' most appropriate to one's immediate circumstances;

2. The ability to quickly and correctly identify the 'I's in service to the Black Queen and separate one's identity from them. (In the *Amduat* Apophis represents the Black Queen.)

In the first hour of his journey the Sun God descends below the western horizon and enters night. In the second and third hours he travels through watery worlds, where it is important for him to find balance. In the third hour there is an inundation of water and the night-barque becomes four boats, in which we find deficient or mutilated forms. At this point things are beginning to come apart; the illusion of a unified identity is dissolving and the dying person is exposed to a disorderly riot of 'I's emerging from each of the four lower centers. In the fourth hour the Sun God reaches land, entering the realm of Sokar, where he traverses zig-zag pathways and where his progress is repeatedly blocked. It is as though he has entered a cavern, and in this hour the light is finally extinguished; there is only sound, intuition, and uncertain images. The solar eye is here threatened by the powers of evil, but Sokar is there to assist and allows Ra to continue his journey. For the Egyptians the *ba* of Ra rests in his divine eyes, representing the two

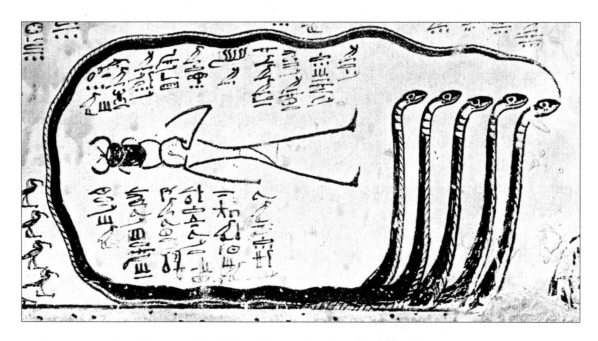

Figure 30. Amduat: **Sixth Hour, detail**

Higher Centers, and at this point his eyes are significantly weakened and he is helpless. The dying person has only what presence he can muster and must go forward in trust. In the fifth hour he comes to the tomb of Osiris, where he encounters Isis and Nephthys in the form of two kites. From this point forward he is more directly in touch with protective forces, but he will be in sore need of these in the hours to follow.

The sixth hour (Figure 30) is the most significant.

The *ba* of the Sun God, in the form of the solar-beetle Khepri, unites with the *ka* of Osiris within a circle defined by a black serpent. At the very moment the *ba* of the Sun God unites with the *ka* – making an integrated Steward – the divine eye, which had been obscured in the fourth hour, appears regenerate as a pair of eyes in germinal barely-visible form. These represent the two Higher Centers in their latent state, very much in need of service and support! It is a moment of great significance and also of great danger, for in the seventh hour Ra's opponent, the Apophis-serpent, will make his assault. The serpent can only be subdued with the help of the magic of Isis and the strength and vigilance of Seth. A process of accelerated regeneration begins; the two tiny eyes somehow penetrate the gloom, and the now-stabilized *ba* is able to rally Isis and Seth – who are well-prepared to perform their functions. Once the attack of Apophis has been deflected the doors of the tomb of darkness open, and in hour eight, Ra leaves Sokar, returning, in hour nine, to the watery worlds.

Figure 31. Amduat: **Tenth Hour, detail**

The tenth hour (Figure 31) begins with a re-birth from Khepri, representing the mature strength of Ra's regeneration. This is the acme of human achievement – a regenerate Steward in service of Higher Centers.

As a result the eyes of the Sun God are fully restored. One eye is re-born out of a double snake; the other emerges out of a hieroglyph for 'God.' Thoth (penetrating wisdom) and Sekhmet (in this instance healing), in hour 11, unite to restore the smaller of the two eyes.

In Figure 32 on page 256, we see the eyes restored and sense the unified being that is behind them.

In hour twelve, shown in Figure 33 on page 257, the *ba* of the Sun God, in the form of the solar-beetle Khepri, now lays aside the *ka* of Osiris. This act is shown in the bottom register. The discarded *ka* is leaning on the curved wall at the right – the pale empty image of Osiris. This pale figure represents the 'Death of the Steward' in archetypal form. As the *ka* of the Sun God, Osiris represents the 'active' Steward: the form of the Steward that must actively fight the forces of the Lower Self until Ra (Higher Centers) appears and grows into full self-awareness. In the image we see that the active Steward, Osiris, has now been discarded – his task complete. He lies at the very edge of the underworld, looking backward into the dark realm of which he is the ever-vigilant ruler – the eternal fighter of the forces of imagination and unconsciousness.

Figure 32. **Amduat: Eleventh Hour, detail**

Above him, in the middle register, we see the transcendent form of the Steward, Khepri, who is intimately connected with the rebirth and regeneration of Ra. Khepri is actively serving the latent, as yet unmanifest, Higher Centers. His forelimbs reach out towards Ra, in his final efforts to prolong presence. He has now gone as far as he can go – up to, but not fully absorbed into, the mature Ra. As Ra emerges from the underworld – as the solar disk grows strong enough to sustain itself in the day – Khepri will fall back and 'die,' his task complete. This fate is, then, pre-figured in the pale image of Osiris lying against the wall below.

Looking back up to the middle register, we see the final effort of the transcendent Steward, Khepri, pushing Ra out of the underworld into the daylight. Yet it is only the sun disk that is *actually emerging* from the underworld. Ra alone will emerge into the light. Ra alone will 'journey forth by day.' In the upper register, the praying figures are saying "Born is he who is born, who has emerged, has emerged (the Higher Self, Ra)."

The Khepri-Steward, however, must remain eternally in the underworld. Khepri represents the re-birth of consciousness in the underworld, the state of unconsciousness. His 'death' is only one moment of a repeating cycle. He will repeatedly unite with,

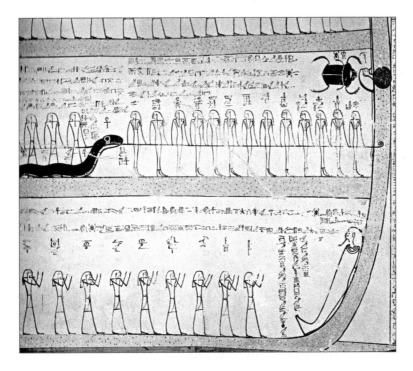

Figure 33. Amduat: **Twelfth Hour, detail**

give assistance to, be transformed by, and ultimately be cast off by his Higher Self. Ra alone can exist fully and naturally in the immortal worlds above the human.

What is represented in this image has been referred to, in many Traditions, as 'dying to oneself.' This is the Steward's willing sacrifice of itself, as an active participant in enabling consciousness, once the Higher Self has appeared. After the Steward has prepared the way for the arrival of Ra, it must now move out of the way: lay itself aside and 'die' to itself. Yet, at the same time, it remains ready, in a passive state, to sustain the presence of the Higher Self as needed. Ultimately, the Self that is fully aware will need no assistance and, like Ra, journey forth by day into eternal presence.

Journey Forth by Day

Journey Forth by Day is less 'exclusive' than the *Amduat*, integrating material from the popular Religion, from the 'First Work,' and from the Work of the Steward. It develops the themes originally introduced in the *Pyramid Texts*, the *Coffin Texts*, and the *Amduat* – but in one respect it goes beyond them. The priests at Thebes who originally produced this text succeeded in integrating the 'inner' and 'outer' meanings of the preceding texts by centering them around the moment of judgment as a literal reality that we all must face. This trial can be related to both the First Work (which may lead to continuance of human existence, but on a higher level) and the Work of the Steward (which may lead to a complete transcendence of the human condition). As in the *Amduat* or the *Pyramid Texts*, success in this process is not taken for granted. Each must do all that is possible and hope.

In *Journey Forth by Day* death is more clearly the disintegration of the various *kheperu* or 'modes of existence' that comprised earthly life. This would be the different sets of 'I's connected with the four lower centers and their divisions, each with their relevant blocks of memory. The funerary rituals were intended to integrate the different aspects of a person's being in such a way that the aspirant might face the moment of judgment at his or her best. The *ka*, or life force of the dead person, remains in the tomb with the body, while the *ba* or heart begins to move independently of it. The *ba* may:

1. Move to its destruction, divorced forever from its *ka*,

2. Link with a new *ka*, or

3. Realize its destiny, merging with Ra and joining the company of the Gods.

The *ba* of the dead are first taken to the place of the god Osiris, where they will be judged. The path to judgment, like the passage through the hours of the *Mes*, is a perilous one. It is a path choked with the dense imagination continuously generated by the Lower Self. The deceased must proceed through a series of gates guarded by demonic beings, which represent the characteristic fears and life-illusions of the deceased – the negatively-charged 'I's that the man had been unable to separate his identity from in the course of the preceding life. If the *ba* is not confused or deflected, it will eventually be lead by Anubis into the presence of Osiris. In the presence of the God the heart of the deceased will be weighed on a set of scales against the feather of Maat. Maat, we will recall, is the goddess of justice. The feather of Maat represents *the potential for development that was given at the beginning of the life*. If the side of the scale holding the feather does not drop, this will indicate that the deceased has done what he or she could to realize the potential originally given. Thoth stands adjacent, displaying a blueprint of the completed life, as it appears when viewed outside of space and time. The scales will reveal – exactly – the gap between the 'actuality' of the life as lived and the potential that was given at the beginning. As there is always a gap the process of the weighing is

Figure 34. **The judgment of the soul against the feather of truth**

always a difficult experience. Only for the prophets and the avatars do the scales stand stable; for most of us they teeter, and for many of us they drop. If the *ba* is shown to be ascending (if the feather does not drop), Anubis will take the deceased into the presence of Osiris who will then find him his place in the afterlife, becoming *maa-kheru*, meaning "vindicated" or "true of voice." If the actuality of the life as lived shows a disregard for the potential that was given, the *ba* will be cast into the jaws of Ammit the devourer, who sits waiting.

If the soul passes judgment, fully realizing its potentials, it will join the Company of the Gods and enter the Fields of Eternity. But even here challenges await it. While these are indeed the fields of paradise, they demand great labor. The fledgling soul is significantly challenged to find its way and to take its place in the company of the mighty entities who have preceded it. To assist the soul in the start of its labors, the priests would place a number of tiny statuettes called *ushabti* within the coffin. These 'symbolized' spirits are capable of great industry and will help the soul to find its footing in a new world. It is clear from this that the dead do not just go to a place where the gods live, *but become gods themselves* and undertake the labors appropriate to their station.

Thus the identity of the earthly man is finally left behind. In this difficult passage the *ba* first takes the identity of the Steward (Osiris), and, through the purification process enabled by the mantra or sequence,[3] finally achieves its Ra-identity in the Fields of Eternity.[4]

The Egyptian Gods in Relation to the Three Creation Myths

With this mythology behind us we can return to the Egyptian conception of the Absolute. We shall study this through studying three different foundation myths depicting the act of Creation. These three variations reflect different points of emphasis and different modes of expression, corresponding to the changing needs of both Religion and Civilization:

> An *Atum*-based creation myth originated from Heliopolis at the beginning of the Old Kingdom (third to fifth dynasties – c. 2800 BC).

> A *Ptah*-based creation myth originated from Memphis in the time of the sixth dynasty (2345-2181 BC) when that city became central to 'Greater Egypt.'

> A *Thoth*-based creation myth originated from Heliopolis in the Late Period (747-332 BC), just before the coming of the Ptolemies.

All three myths reveal the anterior presence of Ra through different 'faces,' like so many different windows on Creation. Ra's initial movement, from the state which pre-existed Creation to the Created Universe, involves a dimensional change which is quite beyond our power to conceive and which – for that very reason – lends itself well to mythic interpretation. Indeed, the three creation myths could be viewed as three different ways of registering the dimensional difference between the 'Beyond-Being' of Ra and the 'Created Being' of the Universe. The mythological necessity of presenting Ra's 'Creator-face' – whether as Atum, Ptah, or Thoth – is given by this 'great divide.' Because the transcendent Ra cannot intervene directly in the system of Creation, the Gods are prominently placed, and we, beneath them, are completely subject to the strict laws governing the macrocosm.

---

3. See Chapter 3.
4. See too the discussion of the role of mantra or sequence in "The Concentration of the Steward" in Chapter 3, "The Great Spiritual Traditions."

RA-ATUM

This 'Creation' is the one represented in the *Pesedjet* of Heliopolis. The Creator-face is Atum, known as 'the complete one' or the 'finisher of the world.' Of the three myths, the Atum-myth takes most pains to avoid emphasizing the dimensional difference between the Creator and his Creation. Simply 'it is done.' The Atum myth emphasizes what is 'like' in **1)** the Creator, **2)** the macrocosm of Creation, and **3)** the Microcosmos Man. Atum is most frequently depicted as a man holding an *ankh* (the key to higher life) and a *was* (the scepter of power and dominion). He was considered the first God; he created himself, and then he created the World out of his own substance. Thus, in the phase prior to the creation of the World, his substance was both in an 'integrated' and 'disintegrated' state: Atum (the more integrated substance) created out of indeterminate chaos (the less integrated or disintegrated substance). It is just here that the Ra-Atum myth touches the triadic nature of the Absolute, for Atum did this only after he had embraced his own shadow. In other words, using the terminology of Chapter 2, he performed the act of creation only after he had willed (fully accepted and embraced) his own Not-Being.

What the Heliopolis myth emphasizes is that Ra-Atum is both complete and self-created, and here there is a direct analogy to the Steward. Through the development of the Steward we are self-created in a way that no other kind of conscious entity can be, and in this regard we are similar to the Absolute.

RA-PTAH

Ra-Ptah was originally a deification of the primordial mound described in the Atum-creation: very simply 'risen land' or 'head finally above the water.' It is somehow 'prior to' Atum. This developed into the most evolved Egyptian concept of the Creator. Ptah is most frequently depicted as a mummified man, wearing a blue skull cap. Like Atum he holds an *ankh* and a *was*, but additionally he holds a *djed*, the pillar of stability and permanence.

Having first embraced his shadow (in the dimension that is 'prior to' Creation) Ptah 'dreamt' Creation in his heart. He then called his dream into being by speaking it out. He uttered the 'secret names' of all things and so brought them fully into being. Thus there are three levels to Ptah-creation, which we can interpret in light of the categories of Chapter 2:

STAGE 1: Ra-Ptah (as Being) embraces his shadow, or internalizes his own opposite (Not-Being). In so doing he effects the transformation that allows him to fully realize the dimension of himself that is 'Beyond-Being.'

STAGE 2: Having internalized his own opposite and understood the threat that it represents (the threat of the ever-present Apophis), he 'dreams' the pattern of Creation; he generates images of the over-arching pattern of the 'secret names.' In other words he conceives the macrocosm, with its unity of the archetypes. It is clear, then, that Ptah knows the unity of the spirit-realm before uttering the 'dimension' of its material embodiment. He knows, from the first moment of Creation, the true measure and purpose of Man.

STAGE 3: In 'speaking out' the secret names Ptah brings fully into being all levels of the macrocosm. He gives definite form to material Creation and so brings the entire time/space manifold into being. Here we have a great 'opening out,' from the level of the archetypes into the multiplicity of individual entities which comprise Creation as we know it. Ra-Ptah was thus known to the Egyptians as 'the opener.'

RA-THOTH

Ra-Thoth is most frequently depicted as an ibis-headed man. He is considered, in relation to the Microcosmos Man, as 'the heart' or seat of real spiritual intelligence. On a universal scale he is represented as the 'tongue of Ra,' the means by which Ra's will was translated into speech. In giving utterance to the will of Ra, he is the Creator of the visible universe. He is *the god of utterance.* As the Creator he knows the mind of God and bridges a gap between dimensions which is impassable to the mind of Man. He knows the order of the spirit-world which preceded the physical world.

Thoth is the reflection of the Creator *insofar as that can exist within creation.* This conception of Thoth is an almost exact representation of what the Zoroastrians called Ameysha Spenta and what the early Christian thinkers called the Holy Spirit or Holy Ghost.

Thus, on the scale of an individual human life, Thoth understands the 'measure' of human existence in relation to what we have called the law of the Merciless Heropass. He understands the necessary place of the Black Queen in forcing human evolution and so transcends the appearances of 'good' and 'evil.' In this regard he is rather frightening, and for this reason he is the one who can accurately read the human heart and assist with the judgment of the dead. Additionally Thoth is seen as the source of inspiration for all real works of science, religion, philosophy, and magic. Relative to the Atum and Ptah creation myths, he is the Creator seen *in relation to Man*.

Of the three versions of Creation, the Ptah myth provides the purest expression of the dimensional difference between Being and Beyond-Being. It places the Absolute at a greater distance from Man than either the Thoth or the Atum versions. Indeed, in this version, Ptah creates Atum to rule over and maintain Creation.

Additionally – and more importantly for the Traditions to follow – the Ptah myth gives a complete presentation of the doctrine of 'cosmic utterance' (which is also clearly present, although in less developed form, in the Thoth myth). The substance of this doctrine is found in **1)** Ptah's creation of the archetypes and **2)** the 'opening-out' of the created archetypes. This, then, is the original form of the doctrine of the *Logos*, which became so important to the Classical World. In this doctrine we have evidence of a direct continuity from the teachings of the Egyptian priest caste to classical Greek philosophy and Christian theology. It is worth exploring this link in some detail for the light it throws on both the Classical and Christian Traditions, which will soon appear in the chapters to follow.

THE DOCTRINE OF THE LOGOS

The word Logos originates in the Greek Λόγος (*Logos*). We first hear of the doctrine of the Logos from Pythagoras and Heraclitus and then – more explicitly – from Plato. Both Pythagoras and Plato *had lived in Egypt* and there made contact with the Egyptian Spiritual Tradition. They did not simply study the 'fragments' and hieroglyphs that are available to us today; they *had discourse with the priests at Saïs;* they had contact with members of the Egyptian Tradition who had profound experiences of Worlds 6 and 12.

In Classical times the Greek word Logos (Λόγος) was used in at least three different ways, which we interpret as follows:

1. *First usage*: The Mind of God in its perpetual act of articulating and giving form to the Universe. This is what we might call Logos with a capital L: the unfolding cosmic pattern. The term was used consistently in this way by the pre-Socratic philosophers and later by Stoic philosophers. This usage was generally understood in Classical times.

2. *Second usage*: Man's attempt to use all of his faculties, including his Higher Centers, to understand his relation to the 'Mind of God' and the unfolding cosmic pattern. This is human reason in its highest form; we could say that it is Reason with a capital R.

3. *Third usage*: The discursive activity of the human intellect. This sometimes occurs in support of the 'second' logos (described above) but normally occurs independently of it. The 'independent' use of the intellect would include the conceptual work of science. It is human reason in its most pedestrian form, limited to the sphere of conceptual activity.

Plato brought the first usage to the level of 'high art' in the *Timaeus* dialogue. In the *Sophist* he addressed the second usage, but he also emphasized what was common to the first and second usages. He made it clear that the first and the second logos each have a necessary connection to BEING. The 'Being' to which Plato refers is the unboundaried sentient space that contains and sustains Creation. It is, if you will, the Being of God that is 'in' Creation, abstracted from the dimension of his 'Beyond-Being.'

In the *Sophist*, Plato presents the first logos as the self-revealing of BEING, in and through Creation. The second logos, then, is the process by which Man himself (in imitation of the Absolute) comes into BEING and so rises to perceive the first logos.

Thus, in the discourse of the *Sophist* the second logos implies every possible variation of 'opening': the opening that is the 'self-revelation' of God; the opening of Man to God; and the opening of Man to the conscious aspects of Creation. We can understand this better when we understand that Plato's BEING is not separate from the many 'beings' that continuously emerge within it. There is a unified pattern of beings 'being' in BEING. Plato sometimes referred to this as the doctrine of 'the many and the one,' because the many are also the one. To the extent we enter into the second logos, we see the macrocosm 'from the inside,' and what we see is a totally transparent 'resonating' unity of beings 'being' within BEING. To use the Egyptian terminology, we become the students of Thoth, who was the link between the 'cosmic utterance' and the human practices of science, religion, philosophy, and magic.

To summarize, from the standpoint of God the Logos is 'cosmic utterance.' From the standpoint of Man the awareness of God's Logos is given by his ability to enter into the state of BEING and so to perceive the particular dimension of things that reveals their inner relation to BEING. One aspect of the second logos is Man's ability to give expression to this insight. Plato emphasizes that for a man to express this truly (to be a true philosopher) he must sustain – and not for one moment lose – his connection to BEING. This is what we referred to in Chapter 3 as the state of 'prolonged presence' and it is possible only with the development of Man's Higher Centers.

Plato's mature philosophy was influenced by, but not derived from, Egyptian mythology. Plato's theory of the Ideas, as developed in his later dialogues (the *Parmenides*, the *Theaetetus*, the *Sophist*, and the *Statesman*) is unique, and is based on his own direct insight. Yet his presentation of the first logos in the *Timaeus* is continuous with the Egyptian presentation of the 'opening' of Ptah. Put differently, the 'first logos' – taken as that aspect of the Living Universe which is an unfolding hierarchy of unity in diversity – is given lucid expression in philosophy by Plato, and an equally vivid expression in myth by the Egyptians. While the medium of expression is different, the underlying images and forms given expression are almost exactly the same! [5]

Having outlined the Greek logos in its relation to the Ptah-myth we can now move to the Christian conception of logos, which derives not from the teachings of Jesus but from the opening words of the Gospel of John: "In the beginning was the *Logos*, and the *Logos* was with God, and the *Logos* was God." This passage is not stating that the Logos is identical to God; it is there 'with' God. But at the same time it 'is' God; it is his direct expression. This statement was a direct product of the Christian Tradition in the formative years of the Early Church. It was, in other words, the product of an environment in which both the Platonic Logos and the Ptah-myth were well understood. (We shall explore this environment in greater depth in "The First Three Centuries of the Church" in Chapter 31 of Book IV, "The Age of the Prophets.") It is clear that the word *logos* in the Gospel of John should be translated as 'cosmic utterance' rather than its tertiary meaning as 'word' or discursive activity.

And now we are in a position to take the 'Egyptian connection' a step further. The Logos-aspect of the Ptah-myth provides a context in which the much-confused Christian conception of 'Holy Spirit' makes sense. It is a term that Jesus used, but neither Jesus nor the apostles left us any clear definition of what it meant to them. If the Holy Spirit is not God and not Man, what is it? For the 'second generation' of the Christian Church (the generation after the apostles) the concept of 'Holy Spirit' was somehow 'in' Creation, but somehow also 'above' the cause-and-effect influences that impact us in the line of time. It was not God but it reflected the influence of God. It was certainly

---

5. An excellent exposition of the Egyptian creation-myths, which brings out these commonalities, is found in Pritchard, James B. (ed), *Ancient Near Eastern Texts Relating to the Old Testament*, Princeton University Press, Princeton, 1969.

a 'higher influence' but, for the most part, the Early Christians were not sure what it meant. It was often thought of as a 'state' that might come over Christians assembled in a group. Theologians of modern times usually present the term as a category linking a theistic subject-diety with three-dimensional material creation. But the first real Christian theologian, Origen Adamantius (185-254 AD), presented the 'Holy Spirit' as God's utterance in a spiritual dimension that preceded and made possible the final physical expression of Creation. Here we have *exactly* the Ptah-myth of Creation, with which Origen was familiar. He was, after all, an Egyptian!

Origen – as the head of the Catechetical School in Alexandria – was responsible for presenting the Christian teachings in an environment where both Greek philosophy and Egyptian myth were well understood. He was thus in the position of having to respond to many challenging questions, and it became necessary for him to develop a clear and consistent way of thinking about what Jesus called the *pneuma*, or Holy Spirit. As we noted, Origen's teaching was based on the 'distant' view of the Absolute that is given in the Ptah-myth. Thus Origen viewed the macrocosm of Creation as existing relatively independently of the 'Beyond-Being' of the Absolute. Creation had, to some degree, been left to 'run on its own steam.' The term the Holy Spirit was, in some way, a bridge term connecting God to Creation.

In order to understand Origen's usage more precisely we need to understand a little more of the context in which he taught. The teaching of the Early Christian Church was based on a feeling of the immediacy of God's statement to Mankind through the 'person' of Jesus Christ. This sense of immediacy would be weakened by endless philosophical argument, or by the presence of a host of intermediary dieties. Origen's audience took 'Creation' as the world of time, space, and matter that was the immediate context of their daily lives. They had to relate the Christian teaching to this. But in fact 'this world' is only the thin outer layer of the 'created' macrocosm. The archetypes 'informing' material creation exist within the macrocosm and continuously exercise their influence in order to sustain Creation. Additionally to this there are the Archangels, inhabiting the higher tiers of Creation, whose understanding partially bridges the dimensional gap to the 'Beyond-Being' of the Absolute. The understanding of the Archangels exists both within and beyond Creation and can be communicated, in different ways, from the higher levels to the lower levels, according to the level of the one who receives these communications. In short, there is an abundance of influences acting on Mankind from the levels above it, of which Origen was aware – although he probably would not have used the terms we have used here to describe them. The prospective

Christians of the Classical World had many questions about these 'higher' influences, so the reality of the different levels had to be stated in a way compatible with the simple, forceful teaching of the Early Church.

Origen's 'Holy Spirit' includes, in a very general way, both **1)** the influence of the 'spiritual' dimensions of Creation on the world that we know and **2)** the knowledge of these influences by men, which is a different thing. The knowledge of these influences by men is a passive knowledge, for to 'know' the spiritual order is to be formatively influenced by it. If we use the term God as BEING (rather than Beyond-Being) we could say that the Holy Spirit is the 'opening' of God to Men and the passive opening of Men to God. This 'passive opening' includes the awakening of Man's Higher Centers. Thus you can say there is a Holy Spirit both within us and without us. Like the Egyptian doctrine (and unlike the Platonic) Origen's presentation of the Holy Spirit includes 'miracles' of different kinds (the laws of a higher level manifesting on a lower level) and the Early Christian notion of 'presence' descending on a group of assembled Christians.

And so the Egyptian idea of Creation as opening entered **1)** the Greek, **2)** the Roman, and **3)** the Early Christian worlds. We emphasize in passing that the Greeks, so wonderfully adept with concepts, certainly knew the Egyptian teaching, and knew it directly from its original source. They would have learned it by contact with Egyptian conscious beings, who could communicate the state that was behind the Egyptian myths and symbols. The Greeks would then have faced the considerable challenge of expressing this in conceptual terms. Thus Pythagoras, Plato, and the unknown 'Hermetic' Greek teachers of the late second and third centuries AD struggled to translate and to re-present things known to the Egyptians in their own conceptual language. This general field of activity was the background-environment of Christian theology, when it began to take form at the beginning of the third century.

Of course, in reconstructing each of the three Egyptian creation-myths, we build on fragments. We cannot hope to reconstruct the force and directness these myths would have had when presented orally by the Old Kingdom Masters of the Egyptian Tradition.

When we study the Egyptian creation myths we see that Egyptian mythology acknowledges an utterly transcendent diety. The creator (Ptah/Atum/Thoth) is the original opening, beyond which we cannot see. The so-called 'monotheism' of eighteenth dynasty Pharaoh Akhenaten, which lasted only for a generation, is actually a lesser faith, closer to the God of popular Christianity.

The Historical Unfolding

Having provided this context, we are ready to return to the 'story' of Egypt itself. Acknowledging the difficulties of interpretation, and with little more to go on than the content of tombs, we must nonetheless attempt to give the premiere historical Spiritual Tradition its proper place.

THE BEGINNINGS AND THE GENERAL CONTEXT

By 5500 BC small tribes had inhabited the Nile valley: the Badari, the Amratian, the Berzina, and the Naqada. These tribes developed into a series of related cultures. The Naqada culture had begun to expand along the Nile by about 4000 BC, establishing centers at Hierakonpolis and later at Abydos. Dynastic Egypt, known to history, begins in about 3,150 BC with the first pharaoh – Menes – who was able to unite Upper and Lower Egypt and to establish a center of rule at Memphis.

Some early texts suggest that Dynastic Egypt was the creation of a ruling race, which entered Egypt from the northeast at the end of the fourth millennium BC. Whether this theory is true or not, it is clear that a strong Sumerian influence entered Egypt at this time. There is a striking similarity between the decorative elements and artistic motifs that occur in both cultures: a bark approaching a paneled or niched building, intertwined serpents, paired monsters with intertwined necks, cylinder seals, and niched brick architecture. Additionally the development of Egyptian hieroglyphic writing was very likely spurred by contact with Sumerian scribes, for at the beginning of the Egyptian dynastic period Sumerian writing was still hieroglyphic. What particularly points to a link between the two civilizations is that they both display a level of technical and cultural development for which, in the late fourth millennium BC, there was no parallel on the planet earth.

With the theory of the 'Dynastic race' coming from the east, we have suggested a relationship between the Egyptian Dynastic Tradition and the already-ancient Sumerian Tradition. Even if the Dynastic race theory is true, it is likely that Pre-dynastic Egypt had a Spiritual Tradition of its own. This earlier Tradition may have fused with the incoming 'Sumerian-related' Tradition, as Egypt achieved unity. On the other hand, it is possible that the Pre-dynastic Egyptian Tradition evolved directly into the Dynastic

Tradition and, during this transition, drew on its contact with the Sumerian Tradition. (It is also possible that both the Sumerian and Egyptian Traditions were influenced by an older Tradition which has been lost to history.) Whatever the case, the kinship of the Sumerian and Egyptian Traditions is likely, given that both had a firm vision of the Cosmos of Man. The point to be made here is that both Dynastic Egypt and Sumeria have a past which is unknown to us and which is probably, in some sense, a shared past.

Whatever its origin, the Dynastic Egyptian Civilization developed rapidly to make its own unique statement, which has had a permanent and irreversible influence on humanity. The Egyptians proved a more practical people than the Sumerians. While they were less gifted in mathematics and astronomy, they had a more advanced knowledge of engineering and surveying and were capable of undertaking huge construction and irrigation projects. They were also adept at quarrying and metallurgy. They were masters at glassmaking, faience (earthenware and colorful glazes), textile manufacture, and dyes. As with the Sumerians, they excelled in medicine and the healing arts.

While Egypt is within the 'historical' period, there is not enough available material to reliably interpret the relation of the Egyptian Spiritual Tradition to the different phases of dynastic rule. But it is possible to see something of the social 'space' in which this Tradition existed. Here we must keep in mind that the Egyptians did not have something we often take for granted, an autonomous 'civil society' – an open, unstructured sphere of social life – outside of 'the state' with its many agencies, the strictures of the official religion, and the bonds of the individual family. Without there being a civil society a Tradition needs a social niche in which it can exist. It needs either **1)** an established relation to a Living Religion, **2)** a 'place' in a secure stratum of society, such as that of the scribes or artisans, or **3)** some form of direct patronage. We have noted that there was, in Dynastic Egypt, the direct link between Religion and Civilization that was characteristic of the Original Religions, and certainly for much of the time, even into the Ptolemaic period, the Egyptian religion was a Living Religion. So we see the potential for the 'social niche' to exist in relation to the Living Religion. But when we study Egyptian history we see that what became the official 'State Religion' almost certainly did not have a direct or one-to-one relation with the Egyptian Tradition over the entire dynastic period. It is a relationship that must have taken different forms at different times.

Before proceeding we must address one further general misconception – that of the Pharaoh being viewed as a God-King or an embodied diety. The term *pharaoh* actually means 'great house' and was not used to describe the ruler himself until the New Kingdom period. In the beginning the person of the Pharaoh was a symbol of the whole; it was the inner principle of pharaonic rule – not the man who happened to be the Pharaoh – that was considered divine. The principle of the pharaoh as 'Great House' was represented by the goddess Maat, the consort of the Thoth-Creator. She is the symbol of universal order, justice, and balance. Maat was instrumental in making order out of chaos at the time of Creation, and she is, at the same time, the goddess who weighs the souls of the dead. The Pharaohs were often depicted with her symbol, the ostrich feather, to emphasize their role in upholding the laws of the Creator. Thus the function of the Pharaoh, as an embodiment of Maat, was to ensure right order, peace, harmony, and prosperity. The other symbol of the Pharaoh (as 'Great House') was Horus, representing the Steward. Horus, then, represents the Pharaoh's impossibly difficult task of evoking and sustaining Higher Centers in the service of Creation. He does this **1) directly** in himself, so that he can receive the influence and direction of Higher School and **2) indirectly** in the external social order, by enabling and support-ing the Great Work in the Egyptian Tradition. Thus the Pharaoh is nothing 'in himself' but everything in the successful fulfillment of his role – linking the different levels of the Pyramid of Man.

The Pharaoh was nominally the 'high priest' of every temple for every god through-out Egypt. In practice, however, different high priests were appointed in each of the temples to function on his behalf – and this selection was usually made by the priest caste itself. It was only in the time of the New Kingdom that certain dynasties con-nected the idea of divinity of the Pharaoh with the legitimation of pharaonic rule.

THE TRADITION

When we examine Egyptian history it becomes apparent that the Egyptian Spiritual Tradition must have faced many crises sustaining its 'niche' in society, and for this rea-son it would have been forced to become quite adept at covering its tracks. For exactly the same reason it is very difficult for us to trace.

In the beginning the Tradition was probably directly connected with the Pharaonic line, and may have included a number of the first Pharaohs. But this could not have been a stable relationship, as the corruptive influence of temporal power on human beings, in every place and time, is very great. This effect would have been amplified in

Egypt by the unitary state Religion, in which the Pharaoh held such a special place. From the standpoint of the Great Work temporal power is particularly difficult for two reasons: 1) whatever you imagine or desire is very easily realized in the external, and 2) in this position other people's weaknesses are particularly visible to you, and so it is very hard to retain a fundamental respect for human dignity.

Thus, at one point the Egyptian Tradition may have been associated with the Pharaoh and his retinue, at another with the priests, at another with the scribes, and at yet another with the artisans. Indeed, the level of refinement of the Egyptian arts and crafts suggests a close proximity. And so, by its very nature, the Tradition is hard to track, yet it leaves the most remarkable evidence in every century; it metamorphasizes itself to reassert itself time and again. What we can say is that its principal manner of expression was symbolic and that it excelled at the art of creating symbols.

The Egyptian Tradition, walking a constant tightrope, developed a double-edged skill: it excelled at making itself invisible, and at the same time it excelled in expression and communication. An unusual combination! It could effectively conceal itself within the forms of the popular religion, while transmitting its message in a way that would affect anyone capable of receiving its influence.

Having qualified ourselves by distancing the Tradition from both the Egyptian Religion and the Pharaonic order, we may now emphasize that its influence was very great. It probably brought as many Egyptians to the Great Work as was possible over a period of more than three thousand years. It had such a profound influence on the Egyptian society that there were historical 'convergences,' similar to those that occurred in Tang and Ming Dynasty China, in the Golden Age of Greece, and in the birth-phase of Augustan Rome. In 'convergent' historical moments everything within the social fabric resonates with the influence of the Tradition: art, architecture, and the great public projects of the time. There is enough regeneration within the social body that the whole is suddenly penetrated, in a certain way, with the unity of its own archetype. Thus in Egypt we see, time and again, the shadow of the Cosmos of Man.

Even today, when you look at the pyramids at Giza and the Sphinx you think immediately of the scale above the human. You cannot, perhaps, represent to yourself why this is so; it just is. They somehow succeeded! Never did a civilization spend so much of its social surplus paying tribute to the Gods, and never did a civilization produce such enduring results. And it is impossible to produce such results without the people involved feeling themselves fulfilled in it. This is a signal of the Cosmos of Man. In this regard the great monumental sculptures of Egypt are like the Parthenon or the Hagia

Sophia. They were more than the genius of any one man; they are general historical 'convergences' that draw on whatever genius is in their proximity. Further to this, the people involved in this work are depicted – in their own art – as open and relaxed, with lustrous wide-open eyes, smiling quietly back at us. It is this closeness to the invisible measure of Man that gives the permanence and the enduring appeal of Ancient Egypt.

In the Hermetic Tradition there is a statement (attributed to the Greek god Asclepius) which is indicative of how certain of the Greeks saw Egypt in the time of its own golden age: "Egypt is an image of heaven, or, to speak more exactly, in Egypt all operations and all powers which operate above have been transferred below." In other words it is a society which aspires to be a completed cosmos or self-transcending whole.

With this in mind, we can review the thirty dynasties of Egyptian history, from 3100 BC through to 332 BC. These three millennia were not – from the standpoint of the Egyptian Tradition – an eternity of sunny stability, but a series of challenging situations which offered every kind of test and trial. Having said this it was certainly true for the Civilization as a whole that there were centuries of peace and stability such as we have not known in modern times. Viewed over its three millennia, there were long spans of unbroken dynastic succession interrupted by periods of relative instability, known as the 'intermediate periods.'

DYNASTIC EGYPT

What follows is not a history of Dynastic Egypt or of the Egyptian Tradition in Dynastic times. It is an outline that attempts to sketch the 'social space' of the Tradition, show the impacts which must have affected it, and register the influences that came from it at different times.

THE EARLY DYNASTIC PERIOD (3100-2686): Dynastic Egypt begins when Menes was able to unite Upper and Lower Egypt, establishing an administrative center at Memphis. This created what we would now call 'regional economies of scale,' from which both Upper and Lower Egypt derived marked benefit. On this basis the first Pharaohs were then able to actively develop the agricultural potentials of the fertile Nile delta region, while opening up critical trade routes into the Levant (Mesopotamia, Turkey, Syria, Lebanon, Palestine, and Israel).

THE OLD KINGDOM (2686-2181): As the civil administration became more centralized the resources of the nation were marshaled towards great irrigation and construction projects. This led to better economic planning, increased agricultural activity, and a further expansion of trade. At the same time there were the most extraordinary advances in architecture, art, and technology. Monumental works of art appear on a level never achieved before or since. The pyramids built by Djoser, Khufu, Khafre, and their descendants represent some of the most memorable symbols of civilization in any age. The *Pyramid Texts* began to emerge around 2350 BC – possibly the oldest known religious texts in the world. The extraordinary development of Old Kingdom art suggests that the Tradition – wherever based – had direct links with the artisans. The Old Kingdom diorite portrait of the pharaoh Khafre (2558-2532) shows a transcendent refinement, reminiscent of the greatest works of Leonardo da Vinci. The face shows both tremendous compassion and a cosmic scale, and yet – as human – it is inconspicuous and unassuming. When you see the figure frontally, you do not see the falcon, but as you turn, you see, in a breathtaking moment, the god immediately behind him, guiding him – for Horus can signify not only the developed Steward but the presence of the God that the Steward invokes. This image reminds us of the *unthinking closeness to the Gods* that was the hallmark of the 'Golden Age' of early Modern Man. With respect to the pharaoh himself, there seems to be no personality, only essence and Higher Centers. It is the very embodiment of the Old Kingdom conception of the pharaoh as GREAT HOUSE, or universal order.

The art of the Old Kingdom achieved a level never quite matched in the art of the Middle or New Kingdoms.

With the growth of the central administration there came a rising class of scribes and officials. More and more frequently the Pharaohs made land grants to regional cults and to local temples, in order to ensure that they would have the resources to sustain the temples over time. However, five centuries of this practice slowly eroded the economic power of the Pharaoh himself. By the end of the Old Kingdom the regional powers began to assert themselves, and this, coupled with the severe droughts that occurred between 2200 and 2150 BC, caused the country to enter a 140-year period of famine and strife known as the First Intermediate Period.

THE FIRST INTERMEDIATE PERIOD (2181-2055): Egypt's central government gradually came apart, and many of the regional governors were able to assert complete independence. This brought civil strife, as local leaders competed for territorial control. But the Egyptian culture itself continued to develop through the period. The first *Coffin Texts* began to appear. How, then, we may ask, did the Tradition – which was surely

Figure 35. **Old Kingdom diorite portrait of the pharaoh Khafre**

connected with the Pharaonic order in the Early Dynastic Period and through much of the Old Kingdom – adjust to this change of circumstances?

THE MIDDLE KINGDOM (2055-1650): Order was re-established under Mentuhotep II, and his eleventh Dynasty successors established a center of rule in Thebes, which was to continue, more or less, for the life of dynastic Egypt. But from this point onwards the pharaohs maintained a significant standing army. The Middle Kingdom also saw far-sighted land reclamation and irrigation schemes.

THE SECOND INTERMEDIATE PERIOD (1650-1550): In 1650 BC Asiatic immigrants called the Hyksos seized control of the northern half of the Nile Delta and established their capital at Avaris. For the first time in its history, after more than a thousand years of continuous self-rule, a large part of Egypt was ruled by foreigners. The Hyksos kings imitated the Egyptian model of government and presented themselves as pharaohs. The Egyptian pharaonic line – the 'Theban Kings' – then found themselves trapped between the Hyksos to the north and the Kushites to the south. We envisage the Tradition centered, with the pharaonic order, in Thebes. After a century (in 1555 BC) the Theban forces gathered strength to challenge the Hyksos. Ahmose I waged a series of successful campaigns and finally drove the Hyksos out of Egypt. In the New Kingdom period that followed, the military became central to the kingdom itself.

THE NEW KINGDOM (1550-1069): The New Kingdom pharaohs initiated a period of prosperity by securing their borders and strengthening diplomatic ties with their neighbors. They launched a large-scale building program to promote the god Amun, whose growing cult was based in Karnak. However, this direction was soon to change. Around 1350 BC Amenhotep IV ascended the throne, renaming himself Akhenaten.

Akhenaten instituted a series of radical reforms, making the previously obscure sun god, Aten, the supreme deity and suppressing the worship of other deities. Akhenaten's radical monotheism excluded reference to the older gods, and he initiated a wide-scale erasure of their names, especially the name of Amun. The rituals centered on these gods were part of the very fabric of Egyptian life, and had been for more than a millennium. It is hard for us to imagine the level of anxiety and concern this would have created. Akhenaten's isolation of Aten and suppression of the other deities seriously challenged the power of the existing priest caste at its base in Thebes and in the many cults that developed throughout Egypt. He was, in many ways, an inspired figure, but he was strangely self-centered. His identification of himself with Aten was bizarre, in that previously the Pharaoh had been represented by Horus, the Steward serving Ra, rather than by Ra himself. It would have been outrageous to present oneself as a direct embodiment of Ra.

Was Akhenaten with the Tradition, splitting Tradition from Religion and so forcing the Religion itself into a phase of regeneration? Or was he the deviant product of a 'true' Tradition that remained based in Thebes?

On vacating Thebes Akhenaten had the city of Akhetaten built (at Amarna) in honour of the 'new' Aten. Akhenaten centered his court at the new city and focused on a re-casting of the Egyptian religion, to the detriment of foreign policy or of a coherent plan of national development. In Akhetaten he commissioned a great quantity of monumental art in an entirely new style. The official images of him show a bizarre, elongated face: in a strange way 'personalized.' Generally the figures excavated from Akhetaten are presented with elongated heads, heavy hips, and thin arms and legs. The 'archetypal' aspect of the portrait of Khafre entirely disappears.

In the midst of the construction of the new city a pandemic broke out, seriously depleting its population and quickly spreading throughout the Middle East. This must have accentuated the almost unbearable internal tensions of the time, and it must have been taken by the priest caste as an unfavorable omen of the desertion of the traditional gods.

Akhenaten was married to Nefertiti, as his principal wife. He sired six daughters by her, and a single son – his male successor Tutankhamun – by a secondary wife. It appears that Nefertiti became co-regent with Akhenaten during the latter years of his reign, and some feel that she survived him, strongly influencing the young Tutankhamun. Akhenaten died after seventeen full years of rule, when Tutankhamun was only a baby. There was a period of regency before the boy ascended the throne, at the age of nine, and this regency must have continued until his death at the age of nineteen.

From the moment of Akhenaten's death things changed. The Pharaoh's memory was obliterated in the decade after his death, and it is only modern excavators who have recovered him for us. At the same time his wife and co-regent, Nefertiti, became a timeless icon of Egypt. Did she play a key role in the Regency period when everything changed?

Let us review what is known. When Akhenaten was succeeded by his son, the boy immediately changed his given name Tutankhaten ('living image of Aten') to Tutankhamun ('living image of Amun'). He vacated the city of Akhetaten in the second year of his reign (1332 BC), shifting the pharaonic center back to Thebes. When he came of age he married his half-sister, the daughter of Akhenhaten and Nefertiti. The city of Akhetataten itself fell into ruin and subsequent pharaohs erased all mention of Akhenaten's 'heresy.' In Tutankhamun's reign there was a reassertion of consistent foreign policy, a reanimation of the traditional cults and temples, and a recreation of the traditional forms of Egyptian society.

Needless to say this change of direction was not the work of a nine-year-old boy. It is possible that Nefertiti, the co-ruler surviving Akhenaten, guided the ship of state through this most perilous period. She had been at the very heart of Akhenaten's regime and the new religion he initiated, so she was in a position to see clearly into many things.

Was Akhenaten a conscious being, perhaps Man Number Five, who had begun on the basis of great vision and who crystallized wrongly under the influence of the temporal power that he wielded? Was Nefertiti also conscious, insightful into all that was occurring and capable of correcting Akhenaten's error? Did the gods work directly with her? We can only imagine how it was for her in the terrible years between the beginning of Akhenaten's deviation and his death. And how did the Egyptian Tradition handle these extraordinary developments? Were the members of the Tradition originally aligned with the Theban priest caste? Or did they follow Akhenaten's lead? Or did they split, some remaining in Thebes and some moving to the new city? If a group went

THE STORY OF MAN

Figure 36. **Akhenaten**   *Figure 37.* **Nefertiti**

with Akhenaten, were they then part of the corrective transition managed by Nefertiti, and did they then re-connect with the priest caste at Thebes? At one point Nefertiti's official image, as co-regent, is simply the female stamp of Akhenaten's. At another her portraits come into their own, to the unique beauty that we know. And then, in a third phase, she suddenly becomes more invisible, distancing herself from the developments that she saw around her. We can but imagine how it was for her to see the plague ravaging Akhetaten.

When Tutankhamun died in 1323 his line continued in relative prosperity. Within fifty years, however, the Hittites, the Libyans, and the Sea Peoples began to encroach on the Egyptian borders. Around 1279 Ramses II (the Great) defeated the Hittites at the battle of Kadesh and successfully held the Libyans and the Sea Peoples at bay. At the same time he initiated huge building projects and vast works of monumental art, representing a high point for Egyptian Civilization that was never again attained. Was the basis for this achievement the terrible trial of Nefertiti and the split in the Tradition that ultimately generated new understanding? The late Middle Period brought the ever-increasing power of the priests of Amun and at the same time saw an increase of external threats. Towards the end of the New Kingdom period Egypt lost both Syria and Palestine.

THE THIRD INTERMEDIATE PERIOD (1069-747): After the death of Ramses XI in 1078 BC, Smendes assumed authority over the northern part of Egypt, while the south came under the control of the High Priests of Amun at Thebes. There was a definite split at this time between the pharaonic order and the priest caste. Which way did the Tradition go? Do the High Priests at Thebes represent a combination of Living Religion and Tradition, or do they represent Religion only? Or did the Tradition become entirely separate from the priest caste, shifting into the artisanal class or the class of scribes? With the north and the south divided in this way, the neighbouring Libyans were able to settle the western delta and gradually took control of it. At the same time Kushites threatened from the south. Between 671 and 667 BC the Assyrians began their attack on Egypt. Ultimately they pushed the Kushites back into Nubia, occupied Memphis, and sacked the temples at Thebes.

THE LATE PERIOD (747-332): With no permanent plans for conquest, the Assyrians left the control of Egypt to a series of vassals who became known as the Saite kings (the twenty-sixth dynasty). By 653 BC the Saite king Psamtik I was able to oust the Assyrians with the help of Greek mercenaries, who were recruited to form Egypt's first navy. In 525 BC the Persians, led by Cambyses II, began their conquest of Egypt. Cambyses assumed the title of Pharaoh but ruled Egypt from his home of Susa, leaving Egypt under the control of a satrapy. While there were recurrent nationally-based revolts, the Egyptians were never able to permanently overthrow the Persians, and Egypt was joined with Cyprus and Phoenicia as part of the sixth satrapy of the Achaemenid Persian Empire. The period of Persian rule is known as the twenty-seventh dynasty, which ended in 402 BC. From 380-343 BC the thirtieth dynasty ruled as the last native royal house of dynastic Egypt. A brief restoration of Persian rule, sometimes known as the thirty-first dynasty, began in 343 BC, but within a decade the world-historical figure, Alexander the Great, appeared on the scene and conquered the entire territory of the Persian Empire. In 332 BC, the Persian ruler Mazaces handed Egypt over to Alexander without a fight.

THE PTOLEMAIC DYNASTY (332-30): Alexander was welcomed by the Egyptians as a great deliverer. It is hard for us now to understand the influence that Alexander had in his own time, for there has been no comparable world-historical figure since. Time places the Caesars, Charlemagne, and Napoleon a little closer to us, and so they appear in a comparable light, but they were not of the same order. People felt in Alexander, and through him, an entirely new future. The administration established by

Alexander's successors in Egypt, the Ptolemies, was based on the traditional Egyptian model and centered in the new capital city of Alexandria. This city then became a great center of learning and a bridge from Egypt to the rest of the world.

Alexandria was, on the one hand, an astounding demonstration of Hellenistic culture and on the other, the means through which the traditional Egyptian culture penetrated the Hellenistic World. Alexander himself chose a site twenty miles west of the Nile Delta so that the silt carried by the river would not block the harbor. He then had a canal constructed to link to the Nile, and created two harbours for the city, one for Nile river traffic and one for Mediterranean shipping. After his death Alexander was succeeded in Egypt by Ptolemy Soter, one of the famous *diadochi* (successors) to Alexander. This second generation of Macedonian leaders became the pillars of the Hellenistic world. Ptolemy Soter began the Ptolemaic line of pharaohs. He directly continued Alexander's work, beginning the construction of the 600-foot lighthouse on the Island of Pharos. The lighthouse of Alexandria lit the way for an unceasing stream of ships which kept trade flowing through the city, as the Ptolemies made commerce and revenue-generating enterprises their top priority. This lighthouse became the seventh wonder of the world and stood for 1,600 years.

But more importantly, Ptolemy Soter initiated the great Library of Alexandria, which was initially managed by Demetrius of Phaleron, a student of Aristotle. It became a meeting place for men of knowledge, such as had never existed before, and this had major implications for the Story of Man. Over the next two centuries it became a point of assimilation of, and a melting pot for, the Egyptian, Hellenistic, and Judaic cultures. From the third century AD it became one of the principle receptacles of Christianity and was one of the original sources of Christian monasticism.

But to return to Hellenistic Egypt, within the country itself, Hellenism did not supplant the native culture. Alexander himself had been fascinated with Egyptian culture and supported it in a way that the Persians had not. The Egyptians thus continued to build new temples in the established style and maintained their traditional cults, while the Ptolomies styled themselves as pharaohs. Cultural traditions merged, and Greek and Egyptian gods were sometimes syncretized into composite deities, such as Serapis.

Thus as Hellenistic culture penetrated inward, Egyptian culture expanded outward. Hypothetically we ask: how did the Egyptian Tradition deal with this 'expansive' phase? Did it leave Egypt to the Pharaonic Religion and move out to the frontiers? Did it become connected to the Hermetic teachings of classical times and to the figure of Hermes Trismegistus?

Throughout the Ptolemaic period, there were continued national revolts and bitter internecine dynastic rivalries. In the meantime Rome began to displace the Hellenistic Empires as the dominant power of the Mediterranean basin. As Rome came to rely more and more on imports of grain from Egypt, she took greater and greater interest in the internal politics of the country. When the situation in Egypt destabilized, Rome sent forces to secure the country as a province of its empire – and so the tragic drama of Mark Antony and Cleopatra, which ends with Cleopatra placing the asp to her breast and consigning her spirit to the sun.

With the coming of Rome, Egypt became a province of the Empire and was administered as such. This was the end of the Egyptian Civilizational Order which had begun with the First Dynasty 3,000 years before.

The Egyptian Legacy: Judaic, Christian, Hermetic

From this outline we can see that the Egyptian Spiritual Tradition, practiced in the art of survival, endured many changes. It surely metamorphosized itself in the Ptolemaic and Roman periods, and one result was that Egyptian culture and influence became pervasive. It is often now forgotten that Egyptian culture was part of the general atmosphere of what we call the Classical World.

The Egyptian Tradition was extraordinarily successful in deftly encoding its myths and cosmologies in its art and architecture, accurately splicing symbols of the living universe with symbolic 'keys' to the esoteric practices that would open that universe to Man. These keys and these mythical images reappear, time and again, in the Traditions which succeeded the Egyptian in the Mediterranean basin, including the Graeco-Roman, the Christian, and the Islamic.

The Egyptian Religion left an indelible impression, first on the Greek-speaking peoples and then on the Romans. In Hellenistic times Egyptian temples and sanctuaries were established within the Greek city-states, nestling in with the older classical temples. In Roman times the Egyptian cult-temples were found both within Rome and throughout the cities of the Empire. They coexisted; they did not compete. The Emperor Hadrian, a passionate philhellenist and a serious student of Greek philosophy, made use of the Egyptian cults without any sense of contradiction.

Looking further back, it is certain that the Egyptian Tradition had formative contacts with both the Judaic and Christian Traditions. We can summarize the legacy of Egypt.

Influence on the Judaic Tradition: The Egyptian Tradition almost certainly transmitted its teaching directly to the Hebrews in the centuries before the Exodus. The relation of the Judaic people to the Egyptians during their sojourn in Egypt was dual. During the period that the Hebrews were a client population to the Egyptians, there were many tensions at the level of government and administration, but there was also a very high quality of communication between esoteric initiates.

Influence on the Christian Tradition: The Egyptian Tradition had a formative influence on Christianity, not so much in the generation of Jesus Christ as in three generations following. This we shall explore in the chapters on the Christian Tradition.

The School of the Tarot: The teaching connected with the tarot deck came originally from Egypt and was able to perpetuate itself in the Classical World, the Medieval World, and the World of the Renaissance. While the Tarot is now associated with fortune telling, it contains, in quite sophisticated form, all of the esoteric material presented in Book I.

The Hermetic Teachings: What are called the Hermetic teachings emerged in Alexandria in the early third century AD. They represent – amongst other things – the final attempt of the Egyptian Spiritual Tradition to pass on its inner teachings to a possible successor. Unfortunately it is now difficult to reconstruct what the Hermetic teachings were; all of the texts that survive are at many removes from the original teaching. The original Hermetic teaching proliferated rapidly into a host of occult pseudo-teachings of the kind that were common in Egypt at that time. Hermeticism now appears to us as a syncretic bundle of Pythagorean, Neoplatonist, Judaic/Sethian, Zoroastrian, Chaldean, and alchemical teachings, sheathed in ancient Egyptian lore and presented under the name of Hermes Trismegistus. In the 'hot-house' environment of the third and fourth centuries Hermetic pseudo-teachings, the most amazing myths, were invented, drawing principally from the earlier Egyptian material. But behind the smokescreen of bizarre myths and occult practices was a substantial teaching. An inner Tradition of Hermeticism sustained itself, probably in secret, for many centuries. We have evidence of a great integrity of Hermetic work in **1)** the Medieval-Christian Tradition, **2)** the Islamic Tradition, and **3)** the teachings that George Gurdjieff attributed to the Sarmoun Brotherhood.

The serious work done under the name of Hermeticism sought to preserve the triadic (non-theistic) conception of the Absolute that is found in the ancient Egyptian creation myths. It also preserved and elaborated the Greek concepts of cosmos, macrocosm, and microcosm, and in this regard there was a serious development of the work already done by Pythagoras and Plato. Hermeticism also integrated the different forms of 'proto-chemistry' that existed in Greece and Egypt and that went under the general name of alchemy. In the post-Classical period the efforts to create a coherent all-embracing cosmology were guided and inspired by the integration of the much earlier Sumerian/Chaldean material.

Like the Tarot, the Hermetic teachings survived Egypt. They were discredited and suppressed by the Early Christians in the late-Classical period, but when Islam conquered Egypt in 640 AD it found these teachings still intact in Alexandria. The Muslims then appropriated Hermeticism, particularly its 'alchemical' aspect, and this provided stimulus for the emergent Islamic sciences. In the twelfth century AD – with the penetration of Christian Europeans into the Islamic regions of Spain – these same teachings re-entered Europe, and there was a marked revival of Hermeticism, which reached its full flowering during the Italian Renaissance. Unfortunately the same occult proliferation that had occurred in third century Alexandria occurred again in fourteenth century Europe. The Renaissance scholars who recovered the 'Hermetic' texts believed that they pre-dated Moses and on this basis invented legends that surpassed even those of the third century. However, just as there was serious work done in the ancient Hermetic Schools, there was serious work done during the Renaissance. There was further development of the principles of macrocosm and microcosm, and, on the 'alchemical' side, there was a very complete reappropriation and digestion of Classical science. Indeed Renaissance Hermeticism became the basis for modern Western science.

In closing we emphasize that, while the Hermetic is directly derivative of the Egyptian, it is not the Egyptian. The vastness, force, and simplicity of the ancient Egyptian teachings could not be carried forward into a civilizatonal order that had not wholeheartedly embraced its own myths. Like the teaching of the

Tarot, Hermeticism was a seed-case to carry forward what had been known in the past, but it did not contain the genetic code for a new Civilization, based on the pattern of the Egyptian Civilization.

In a given moment the Egyptian Tradition – perhaps the greatest of the ancient Spiritual Traditions – disappeared, leaving a few tantalizing myths and a magnificent legacy of monumental art. It is unique amongst Traditions in the universality of its statement and in its amazing longevity. Having delivered its truth for nearly three millennia, it vanished – leaving Egypt a fertile receptical for whatever was to come after. As we noted, in the third century AD it became the original source of Christian monasticism. In the seventh century it became one of the most receptive vessels for Islam, eventually producing such prominent orders as the Shadhiliyya and Badawiyya, and becoming – in the period of the Mongol occupation – the very seat of the Islamic Caliphate.

The Egyptian Tradition was a bridge between the Spiritual Traditions of the Original Religion and the Prophetic Traditions to follow. In this regard it is similar to the Vedic/Vedantic Tradition which was the seeding ground for both Buddhism and Indian Sufism. But while the Vedic/Vedantic Tradition lived on, changing into something quite different from what it had originally been, the Egyptian Tradition – so central, so ancient, and so profound – disappeared behind a veil and now looks inscrutably back at us through the eyes of the Sphinx.

CHAPTER 17

The Great Spirit of the Ancient Shamanic-Taoist Religion

People first settled in the region we call Central Asia some 45,000 years ago. Central Asia is the vast expanse of land between the Caspian Sea and China, bordered on the north by Russia and on the south by Iran and Afghanistan. The original settlers migrated north from India and Pakistan and east from the Levant: Lebanon, Syria, Jordan, and Israel/Palestine. At that time, before the great deserts of Central Asia – the Taklamakan, the Kizil-kum, and the Gobi – had come into being, the area was comprised of pasturelands and plains, which supported herds of animals, which in their turn were capable of supporting nomadic tribes.

We note that the settlement of Central Asia occurred just before **the first direct intervention of the Gods** which resulted in 'Modern Man'; in other words, before a varietal of *homo sapiens* was given the 'divine signature' linking him directly to the Sphere of Sentient Being. Because prehistoric Central Asia became such a great source for both Spiritual Tradition and Civilizational Order, we hypothesize that it was one of the 'places' where the first direct intervention was made. Perhaps the domestication of herd animals was one of the first achievements that followed this intervention of the Gods in Central Asia.

In the **second direct intervention of the Gods**, in the immediate aftermath of the last Ice Age, Mankind received both universal Religion and a more developed linguistic structure. At this time the Central Asian peoples developed a linguistic system based on syllabic tonality, which now includes the Turkish and Chinese languages.

As recently as the nineteenth century there were still many tales and legends told of this region that mentioned a brotherhood of wise men, versed in all the techniques of the transformation of human energies, which had existed for untold millennia. The earliest historical records of both the Iranians and the Hindus mention settlements of people in the oases of Central Asia possessed of a culture more developed than their own. We recall, too, that the mythical kingdom of *Shambhala*, mentioned in the Buddhist sutras, was located in Central Asia. However, the Central Asian Civilization that was behind these stories is now known to us only through its influence on the more recent Civilizations.

John Bennett felt that the original peoples of Central Asia were not exclusively nomadic but that groups settled in the valleys of the Hindu Kush and Altyn mountains. Richard Frye, in *The Heritage of Central Asia*, points out that there were no cities in ancient Central Asia similar to the great cities of Mesopotamia or the Indus River Valley. Large cities require a development of agriculture sufficient to support a tripartite division of **1)** priests, **2)** warriors, and **3)** farmers and artisans – and our Central Asians were pastoral herdsmen. Yet, in the period after the domestication of animals, pastoral peoples were able to exist in both settled and migratory states. Archaeological work done in Central Asia has revealed innumerable prehistoric settlements, which unite adjoining villages in relation to a 'center' or temple complex.

But, to return to the emergence of Modern Man in Central Asia, the original Shamanic culture, established perhaps 40,000 years ago, remained in its Central Asian 'garden of Eden' for more than 20,000 years. Slowly the climate changed, and fertile pastureland turned to desert. Periodic shortages of food and pasturage forced 'settled' Central Asian pastoralists to move deep into the steppes and thus to become true nomads. And so began the great Central Asian migrations into Siberia and northern China. Before the end of the last Ice Age (and so before the coming of the Original Religions) Central Asians actually crossed the Bering Land Bridge and – over several millennia – continued a southward migration to populate North and South America.

While the emigrations out of Central Asia continued over ten thousand years, the base population remained stable. Then, in about 1700-1600 BC, the Aryan peoples of the Russian Steppes, just to the north, began a southward migration, driving out all who stood before them. By this time the Central Asian Civilization was already old; its cultural ideals and its Spiritual Tradition were still alive but its social order vulnerable and weak. The Aryan invasion sparked a final and permanent wave of emigration. The peoples at the old civilizational 'center' began to spread east to other parts of Asia and to China and Tibet. In China the Spiritual Tradition carried by these Central Asian immigrants was almost certainly the source of the way that was later called the *Tao*. In Tibet

THE STORY OF MAN

the ancient Central Asian Spiritual Tradition became one of the formative influences on the ancient Bon religion, which pre-dated the arrival of Buddhism.

The Original Religion of Central Asia was probably continuous with the **prehistoric Shamanic Religion** that was universal at the end of the last Ice Age. To emphasize this continuity we shall call it the **Ancient Shamanic-Taoist Religion**. In the Spiritual Tradition connected with this Religion the secrets of the spirit world were understood as they never have been – before or since – and all the techniques of spirit-possession were skillfully employed. It was almost certainly the source of the yogic and tantric methods which re-surfaced over the centuries in Vedantism, in Chinese Taoism, in Indian and Tibetan Buddhism, and in Turkish Sufism. And here we must clarify our use of the term *yoga*.

YOGA

By this we mean a body of specific practices and techniques which utilize the instinctive and moving centers to heighten awareness. In the Hermetic terminology we have introduced, they bring certain of the energies of World 12 to the perception of the four lower centers. These techniques include breath control and the various methods used to develop an awareness of the energy channels and energy centers connected with the human body. These practices may include the use of stimulants and the sexual act. When they involve stimulants they are often connected to the Shamanic techniques of spirit possession. These techniques may be quite dangerous, requiring guidance for their exercise, or they may be very simple and directly conducive to health. We have taken the Indian term *yoga*, derived from the ancient Sanksrit, as it was used in both the Vedantic and Buddhist Spiritual Traditions. We acknowledge that, within the Vedantic Tradition, the term was often used in a more universal way to refer to all meditative practices – including those of the highest level – but we are limiting ourselves here to the narrow usage in order to characterize practices that were common throughout Asia.

We hypothesize that the most advanced yogic techniques originated in the prehistoric Shamanic Spiritual Tradition. When prehistoric Shamanism passed into history, these techniques were preserved and developed in the ancient Shamanic-Taoist Tradition of Central Asia. These techniques appear not only in Vedantic India and Buddhist Tibet; they are equally manifest in the Chinese Taoist *chi gung* and *ni gung* practices. Indeed, before the twentieth century, and extending back through recorded history, there was a 'general culture' of these techniques in Asia and Central Asia. Many people would devote their entire lives to mastering a few of them, pursuing what George Gurdjieff later called 'the way of the fakir.' Techniques of this kind have often, historically, been used for the limited aim of achieving occult powers. They are not necessarily, or even usually, associated with the Great Work. But the Spiritual Traditions have often made use of them and sustained connections with the small communities of those proficient in them. Individual Traditions may have made certain techniques their own for a time or sent individual students to practice – for a set period – with a person who had mastered them.

Thus – of the four Original Religions – the Ancient Shamanic-Taoist 'Great Spirit' Religion probably emerged from its prehistoric 'shamanic' antecedent in the smoothest and most seamless transition. While this Tradition, and the culture connected with it, pre-dates our own historical memory, it has been a formative influence on the world we know. It remained a significant backdrop for many of the civilizations of the historical period. When the Central Asian Civilization was dispersed by the Aryan migration, the eastward moving Central Asians became the basis of the Tibetan, Mongol, and Manchurian cultures. And, as we noted, the Ancient Shamanic-Taoist Tradition became the basis for the Taoist Spiritual Tradition in China.

At this point we can think back to the earlier emigrations from Central Asia, before the end of the last Ice Age, which led to the first settlement of Northern China, Mongolia, and Siberia. The furthest reach of these migrations was the perilous crossing of the Bering Land Bridge, which seeded the Pre-Columbian New World Civilizations. Thus there is a 'family' relation between the New World Spiritual Traditions and the Ancient Shamanic-Taoist Tradition. Both were expert in the techniques of yoga, but the New World Civilizations were probably closer to the yogas practiced by the predecessor to the Ancient Shamanic-Taoist Tradition, in the times before the end of the last Ice Age. Thus the techniques of spirit-possession – as they were applied to the spirits of plants, animals, and 'other molecular beings' – passed from the Central Asian prehistoric Spiritual Tradition to **1)** the Ancient Shamanic-Taoist Tradition and **2)** the Traditions of the Pre-Columbian Civilizations. In the Mediterranean World this same transition did not occur. There we see clear evidence of these techniques, as preserved and practiced by the Egyptians, but they did not carry forward into the Classical World – for they conformed neither to the spirit of the Classical Age nor to the Prophetic Religions that emerged within it.

Thus the prehistoric Central Asians appear as the Proto-Mongolians, the Proto-Tibetans, the Proto-Manchus, the Proto-Turks, the Proto-North American Indians, and the Proto-Mesoamericans. Eventually, the civilizations deriving from the prehistoric Central Asian Spiritual Tradition were to cover half of Asia and most of the Americas. Their mark on humanity was indelible; we would not be the same without them. The prehistoric source culture was re-focused and re-centered by the Ancient Shamanic-Taoist 'Great Spirit' religion when it emerged after the last Ice Age. The second (Aryan inspired) dispersion – which included the Ancient Shamanic-Taoists – had a profound and formative impact on the cultures of Central Asia and of Asia itself.

We shall now pursue the Mongol and the New World Civilizations, as carriers of Shamanic-Taoist Spiritual Tradition.

CHAPTER 18
The Mongol Civilization

The Mongol Civilization was based on the prehistoric immigrations of Central Asians into what is now Kyrgyzstan, Tajikistan, northwestern China, and Inner and Outer Mongolia.

The Mongol tribes were migratory herdsmen, following the movement of their herds throughout the year. The development of the stirrup and the complete adaptation of the horse to the human rider occurred sometime after 500 AD. The Mongols mastered this new medium and in so doing became the first true nomads, perpetually on the move. They were also probably the greatest horsemen known to history, for they virtually lived on horseback.

The typical Mongol tribe managed herds of horses, cattle, camels, and sheep. Each herd required distinctive forms of care, and each subsisted on different sorts of grazing land. Because of the varied needs of the different herds, their annual migrations demanded an exact knowledge of many different terrains and of how these terrains changed in the different seasons of the year. The management of the herds thus made strict demands on the Mongol tribe: the highest degree of collective discipline, a very tight command center, and efficient task management at every level. The movements of the Mongol tribes required a complete coordination of the community, and in this lay the greatness of the Mongol peoples.

It was the Mongols who first perfected mounted archery, enabling their cavalry to shoot swiftly and accurately while in motion. The Mongol cavalry was able to cover great distances at high speed, with a degree of coordination and communication between remote cavalry units that was unmatched. Because it was part of the pattern of their daily life, the Mongols were always able to mobilize at a moment's notice. Their almost complete lack of identification with fixed points made them unpredictable, expert at recognizing opportunities, and capable of assessing risks. They could move, as a group, with the suddenness, speed, and devastation of a force of nature.

And this was not all. From their Shamanic heritage the Mongols had a remarkable sensitivity to different molecular energy fields and an ability to sense their concentration in people and in places. They were also great adepts at reading the patterns of nature. They saw everything as an unfolding and interconnected pattern, and for them the open sky, not the fixed earth, was the focal point of this pattern. The Mongol Shamen had a profound understanding of Nature as a living unity and were expert at interpreting the symbols generated out of the Great Pattern.

At the beginning of the thirteenth century the Mongols were poised, under the leadership of Genghis Khan (1162-1227 AD), to embark on a project of world conquest. They had a supreme self-confidence and a world historical vision, although it is difficult for us now to reconstruct exactly what this vision was – as it was not recorded. As we noted the Mongol Shamen were adept at predicting the patterns of Nature. They also understood mankind as an aspect of Great Nature; they could see and predict the patterns of human life and the cycles of social order – and give counsel on this basis. Whatever beliefs lay behind the Mongol expansion, it is certain that Genghis Khan had the conviction that he was leading a 'chosen people' – but we suggest this conviction was based on a kind of instinctive certainty and was not the result of an explicit 'revelation.'

While the Mongols often showed a casual disregard for human life, they were tolerant of, and receptive to, the holy men of the three world religions that they encountered: Buddhism, Christianity, and Islam. It is a paradox that the Mongol peoples began their world conquest with complete self-conviction, yet were – at the same time – quite ripe for contact with the World Religions of their time. And here we must consider the variable of the Spiritual Traditions that were connected with these Religions. There were doubtless conscious Mongol shamen, leaders amongst their people, who discouraged interest in the different Religions of the lands that the Mongols conquered. But here we are speaking of Dead Religions only. Living Religion is an entirely different thing; it is connected to a Spiritual Tradition that is in full communication with the cosmos above the Cosmos of Man. It seems likely that the Mongol Shamen and the Khans were able to recognize Living Religion and the work of Tradition that lay behind it. Whatever the reason, the great Khans made no attempt to convert the many peoples that they subjugated to the Mongol form of Shamanism, and they were themselves prepared to convert to the religions that they encountered – always on the condition that the representatives of that religion had a genuine level of spiritual attainment. This brings us

THE STORY OF MAN

to the greatest paradox of the Mongols: they showed an almost utter disregard for the individual human life, yet they were able to perceive higher life and to foster it in the places where they found it.

We shall not pursue the history of the Mongols further, for, from this point, they are not so much themselves a civilization as a catalyst for change of civilizational order in the cultures that they conquered. In other words, while the early Mongol culture was a civilization unto itself, the Mongol Empire was not. But while we do not follow the line of their history, we shall encounter them time and again; they will reappear in the stories of the Confucian, the Indian Buddhist, the Tibetan Buddhist, and the Islamic Spiritual Traditions.

CHAPTER 19

The New World Civilizations

To pursue the history of the New World Civilizations we must go back again to Central Asia in the period immediately before the coming of the Original Religions, for our history begins with Central Asian migrants moving eastward across the Bering Land Bridge about 15,000 years ago. The Bering Land Bridge links Asia with North America only in those periods when the planet's northern ice cap is at its maximum and when the sea level drops to expose a strip of dry land linking the two continents.

We know that the Bering Land Bridge closed before the coming of the Original Religions, so what these migrants brought was a Shamanic Spiritual Tradition, and probably a Shamanic Spiritual Tradition of very high order. Recent genetic research has demonstrated that a small group of seventy people passed its DNA signature to all the pre-Columbian New World Peoples. This represents a single crossing of the Bering Land Bridge.[1]

More recent studies have shown that it is likely that this first crossing (which imprinted all the New World peoples) was followed by two later migrations over the same land bridge. The later migrations were not more than a few hundred people each. It is speculated that all three of these populations were contained by glaciation in the Alaska/Yukon region, probably for more than a millennium. This speculation is based on both the study of glaciation and on the evidence of extensive interbreeding between the three groups. When the glaciers eventually began to recede, it was the people of the first migration who proceeded south, through what is now western Canada and the western United States into Mesoamerica and South America. The genetic traces of a second migration were detected in populations speaking the Eskimo-Aleut languages, which are

1. In this regard, see Wang, Sijia; Lewis, C. M. Jr.; Jakobsson, M.; Ramachandran, S.; Ray, N.; *et al.* (2007) *Genetic Variation and Population Structure in Native Americans*, PloS Genetics 3 (11). Also Tamm, Erika; et al. (2007) *Beringian Standstill and Spread of Native American Founders.*

found in Alaska, northern Canada, and Greenland. These people must have migrated east from Alaska, remaining above the 60th parallel. Traces of a third migration were detected in a Canadian Chipewyan group. The third migration must have travelled southwest, across the North American continent, remaining above the 42nd parallel.

When we go back in our mind's eye to the end of the twelfth millennium BC – 15,000 years ago – and imagine these tiny tribal groupings – containing the seeds of all the New World civilizations – making their perilous crossing of the soon-to-close land bridge, we feel the hand of Higher School.

For thousands of years after their crossing these peoples sustained the Shamanic Spiritual Tradition that had brought them to the new continent. The Eskimos and the North American Indians directly continued this teaching, and the Shamanic Religion connected with it, into modern times. But in what is now Mexico and Central America a transition from the prehistoric Shamanic Religion to the Original Religion occurred. This happened shortly after the first millennium BC, in the Olmec Civilization. The Olmecs went through all the social and cultural transformations that the transition to Original Religion implies. Their religion and their social order then became the formula for the other Mesoamerican peoples, who made the same transition – at different points – in the centuries to follow.

MESOAMERICA

This term refers to the indigenous cultures that existed in the area extending from Central Mexico through Central America. It would include the civilizations of the Olmecs, the Zapotecs, the Maya, the civilization of Teotihuachan, the Toltecs, and the Aztecs. Each of these civilizations had **1)** developed agriculture, **2)** an advanced division of labor, **3)** large urban centers, and **4)** monumental art and architecture. Beyond this they had a related mythology, related mathematical and writing systems, an extremely accurate Long Count calendar, and a characteristically intense 'ball game' which was both a sport and a religious ritual.

The Mesoamerican transition parallels exactly the tenth millennium BC transition – from the prehistoric Shamanic Civilization of Central Asia to the Ancient Shamanic-Taoist Civilization. The New World transition resulted in the Mesoamerican family of Civilizations and, indirectly, the great South American Civilization of the Incas.

In the Mesoamerican Civilizations there remained a strong continuity with the ancient Shamanic teachings, but a new influence – of unknown origin – entered at the point of transition to Original Religion. This influence may have come through conscious beings within the existing culture who were the recipients of and conduits for influences coming from the Gods. The new influence may also have come from a contemporary Original Religion, in a transfer of culture from east or west that is lost to history – though subject to continuing archaeological speculation. For example, the beginning of the pre-classical period of the Mesoamerican Civilizations (circa 1,500 BC) corresponds to the beginning of the Egyptian New Kingdom (Eighteenth Dynasty) and to the Civilization of Hsia Dynasty in China. The Mesoamerican transition to Original Religion may also have come from a combination of indigenous creation and external influence. In any case – in and about 1500 BC – the riverine Olmec peoples first developed an agricultural system and an advanced division of labor, which allowed for the development of cities and for the creation of monumental art and architecture. The Olmec ruins in San Lorenzo date from this time.

By the time the Maya developed urban centers and monumental art (about 250 AD) the Egyptians had been under Roman rule for nearly three centuries. The creation of indigenous monumental art had ceased long ago. Any contact with Mesoamerica that occurred during the third century AD would have been immediately known through-out the Classical World. The Aztec and Inca Empires rose long after the collapse of the Egyptian Civilization, and so we see these later developments as entirely indigenous to Mesoamerica. At the same time the Maya and the Aztec are, in a degree, derivative of the Olmec, and thus Egyptian or Oriental influence could have been transmitted through the Olmec to the later Mesoamerican Civilizations.

Scholars break the history of this family of civilizations into three general phases.

A Pre-Classical Period, from about 1500 BC to 200 AD. In this time the kinds of changes which heralded the Original Religions in the Old World took place. There was population growth based on the development of agriculture, the formation of villages and towns, and a certain social stratification.

A Classical Period from 200 AD to 900 AD which sees the development of great cities with monumental art and architecture: Monte Albán in Oaxaca, Teoti-huacan in Central Mexico, and the Mayan cities of Tikal, Palenque, and Copan.

We note that the Olmecs achieved their 'classical' civilization in what scholars call the 'pre-classical' period. The ruins at San Lorenzo date from 1,500 BC, and the great Olmec city whose site is at La Venta was inhabited from about 900 BC to 400 BC. Yet these developments involved a very small portion of the Mesoamerican population. They were only to have their full effect on the other Mesoamerican cultures in the classical period. The classical and the post-classical periods were general developments, affecting all Mesoamerican peoples. The influential Mayan city of El Mirador, for example, dates from 500 BC and was deserted 500 years later.

The Post-Classical Period, from 900 AD until the arrival of the Spanish conquistadores in the early sixteenth century. In this period the 'great cities' evolved into imperial systems of city-states. This period was summed and completed in the Aztec civilization.

To characterize the New World civilizations we shall review only four: the Olmec, the Maya, the civilization of Teotihuacan, and the Aztec. Related to this family of civilizations, but separate from it, is the Inca Civilization of South America, which we shall touch on briefly.

Having said this, we must acknowledge the North American Indian and Eskimo cultures, which sustained – often at a very high level – the original Shamanic Spiritual Tradition which the Central Asian migrants brought across the Bering Land Bridge. The existence of these cultures represents a rich and wonderful world of experience. We affirm that the North American Shamanic Traditions may have been spiritually equivalent to the great Mesoamerican Spiritual Traditions, perpetuating distinguished teaching lineages which pre-date the last Ice Age.

The Olmec Civilization

The 'classical' Olmecs (or those of whom we presently have record) were based in the tropical lowlands of what is now southeastern Mexico, bordering on the Gulf of Mexico. They were a coastal, riverine civilization. While they may or may not have been the first Mesoamericans to undergo the social and cultural transformations that attend the transition to Original Religion, they were certainly the first to produce large urban centers and monumental art. They invented the writing system that was to become the basis of all Mesoamerican writing systems, and they devised the cosmological reference – the Long Count calendar – that became common to all the Mesoamerican civilizations.

Figure 38. **Pyramid at La Venta**

The earliest Olmec ruins discovered to date are from 1500 BC. The earliest Olmec center that had been excavated at the time of this writing is in what is now San Lo-renzo. It was destroyed, either through civil war or invasion. The second, at what is now La Venta, was inhabited from about 900 BC until about 400 BC, at which time it was abandoned. The Great Pyramid of La Venta was the largest Mesoamerican structure of its time, rising thirty-four meters above the surrounding landscape.

The Olmec Civilization was clearly the beginning, for it is here that we see, for the first time, the image of the 'feathered serpent' – Quetzalcoatl – who is the central deity of all Mesoamerican religions. While we have no Olmec manuscripts that detail the mythology depicted in Olmec art, we know from the later Mesoamerican Civilizations that Quetzalcoatl represents the power of self-transcendence. He is like certain of the Vedantic presentations of the principle of 'Brahma,' in that he can represent – at the same time – both a self-transcended human being and the Absolute.

We noted that the earliest Olmec culture we know of, in 1500 BC, would have been contemporary with the first phases of New Kingdom Egypt. We hypothesize that the original, complete pattern of a Mesoamerican civilization was created amongst the Olmec peoples. Whatever influences may have been at work in its formation, it was a unique statement, suggesting a very great indigenous Spiritual Tradition. It was a new beginning, for the vision of the Olmecs became the vision of Mesoamerica.[2] The Maya and the people of Teotihuacan elaborated on and developed this vision in many different ways, introducing original themes which are repeated in all the Mesoamerican civilizations.

Olmec artworks are amongst the most striking and beautiful of ancient Mesoamerica. The Olmecs produced sculptural works in jade, clay, basalt, and greenstone. Some are quite naturalistic while others show fantastic anthropomorphic creatures of symbolic significance. Their art shows a range of animal spirits as 'transformational' agents, hearkening back to ancient Central Asian beliefs. The Olmec masks have a peculiar intensity and focus. The appearance of Olmec art and artifacts far outside the traditional Olmec territory suggests long-range trade and a merchant class.

We do not know the cause of Olmec decline. There was a considerable depopulation beginning from 400 BC, and historians speculate earthquakes, plague, drought, or a silting up of the rivers needed for irrigation. Individual Olmec cities and settlements long survived the general depopulation, and Olmec influence continued to radiate outward to the other Mesoamerican peoples for at least half a millennium, so that we can safely say that the Olmec were a direct formative influence on the Maya.

The Maya Civilization

The Maya produced the longest-lived of the Mesoamerican civilizations. Individual Mayan sites (prehistoric and certainly pre-classical) have been carbon-dated from 2600 BC. The Mayan calendar, the most developed and exact of all the Mesoamerican Long Count calendars, begins on a date equivalent to 11 August 3114 BC – although, of course, this may pre-date the existence of the Maya as a people.

The first clearly defined Mayan settlements that have been excavated date from about 1800 BC, and from this time we find many settlements in southwest Mexico, southeast Mexico, the Yucatán Peninsula, and the northwestern Central American region. This constitutes a vast and varied landscape, from the mountainous regions of the Sierra Madre to the semi-arid plains of northern Yucatán.

The transition to a developed agricultural system capable of supporting large urban centers came much later, in about 250 AD, paralleling the decline of the Olmecs. This

---

2. Here we follow the teachings and writings of Laurette Sejourne. See the entry under that name in the subject bibliography, under the heading 'New World Civilizations.'

Figure 39. **City at El Mirador**

corresponds to the beginning of what scholars call the 'classical' Mesoamerican period (250-900 AD).

The Maya civilization had a ruling dynasty, a noble class, and an elaborate court life. This hierarchical structure was seen to reflect the structure of the universe itself. The Mayan cities could thus be seen as replications of the cosmic order; they were self-proclaimed centers of moral, cultural, and artistic value. In the great Mayan cities the aesthetic of 'high civilization' was achieved.

Thus we see, in the Maya Civilization, an agriculturally developed, city-centered empire, comprised of many different city-states. Each of the Mayan cities sustained long-distance trade with the other Mesoamerican cultures, so that there was generally – in the Mayan period – a high degree of cultural diffusion throughout the Mesoamerican region.

RELIGION

The Maya had the same understanding of time as the cyclical re-creation of an archetype that characterizes all Original Religions. All Mayan rituals and ceremonies were associated with either celestial or terrestrial cycles. The Maya believed that knowing the past meant knowing the cyclical influences that create the present, and that by knowing the influences active in the present one could see the patterns of the future.

The Maya saw the universe as three intersecting planes: the earth, the underworld, and the heavens – the whole governed by the heavens. The night sky openly revealed the workings of the universe and made these workings intelligible to the mind of Man, who existed at the intersection of the three planes. The Mayan gods, like the Egyptian, play different roles at different times and have many different aspects. The Maya understood the universe as a living process, with constantly changing relations between the different levels of things.

We know that the Maya practiced human sacrifice, which must have been in some way connected to the ritual regeneration envisaged by most Original Religions. But the Mayan sacrifice was ritual, not the politically motivated mass sacrifices that Cortez found in decadent late-Aztec culture.

ACHIEVEMENTS: LANGUAGE, ART, AND ARCHITECTURE

The first written inscriptions that we have date from about 250 BC, and we find these in areas that had once been under Olmec control. Indeed the Mayan hieroglyphs are quite similar to the ancient Olmec glyphs. The Maya developed the Olmec glyphs into the only pre-Columbian writing system that was capable of directly representing the spoken language of its community.

With respect to mathematics the Maya developed a base-20/base-5 system, which included the concept of zero. They also developed the Mesoamerican Long Count calendar to its highest point. They had many observatories and a developed astronomical science.

Mayan art is the most sophisticated and beautiful of the 'ancient' New World. In their sculpture we see an accurate observation of the human form, and they provide us with the most fantastic and complex relief carvings. Both their ceramic work and their murals show a beautiful turquoise blue color, which is known to modernity as 'Maya Blue.'

With respect to architecture, the Maya replicated the Olmec stepped pyramids, developing them on an even grander scale. The Mayan cities varied in form, each adapted to the topography of its region. Classical Mayan urban design centered on the layout of great monuments, causeways, plazas, and public gathering places. A city was begun on a single axis, established in a cardinal direction. As it expanded and as more structures were added, the existing structures were continually re-created and remodeled. As a result the great Mayan cities developed in rather a higgledy-piggledy fashion. Within each city, however, great care was given to constructing temples and observatories in accordance with the Mayan interpretation of the orbits of the heavenly bodies.

DECLINE

In 900 AD a social decline began. Historians have speculated its cause to be epidemic, overpopulation, peasant revolt, or the attack of a rival civilization. As with the Olmec collapse we have no real understanding of what occurred. While the decline of civilizational order – and the rise of the succeeding Aztecs – long predates Spanish colonization, many Mayan cities still existed at the time of the Spanish conquest. Thus, as the empire collapsed, many of the individual city-states were able to continue independently. When the Spanish finally came, they found it much more difficult to subjugate the individual Mayan cities than they did the Aztec Empire, the Spanish conquest of the Maya Yucatán taking 170 years. This fierce resistance reflects the strength of the core values of the ancient Mayan culture.

While the particular achievements that we associate with the Maya, such as writing, symbolic religious art, and the Long Count calendar, did not originate with them, it was the Maya civilization which brought them to their full development. We could say that the Maya developed and centered the Mesoamerican culture, which the Civilization of Teotihuacan was to take to its highest point.

The Civilization of Teotihuacan

About thirty miles north of Mexico City are the remains of what was perhaps the greatest Mesoamerican city, Teotihuacan (Figure 40 on page 304). Construction began in about 200 BC, and continued until the fall of the city in about 750 AD. In the third to fifth centuries AD the population of the inner-city rose to about 200,000, with a greater area population of close to one million.

This was not just a city, it was a civilizational center for all of Mesoamerica. Influence radiated outward from this point to all other points on the Mesoamerican horizon. While scholars have been unable to determine the Mesoamerican people who built

Figure 40. **Ruins of Teotihuacan**

the city, they are able to determine Totonac, Zapotec, Mixtec, and Maya 'quarters' within the greater area. The 'Teotihuacanos' – if we can call them such – had a particularly close relationship to the Olmecs. Does this relation imply a close relation to the original Spiritual Tradition which first produced the religion and foundation myth of Quetzalcoatl?

Whether the Teotihuacanos were in direct contact with the Olmec Spiritual Tradition or not, the 'central' myth of Quetzalcoatl finds its most perfect visual expression in the art of Teotihuacan (Figure 41). We recall that Quetzalcoatl is a diety of self-transcendence on both the individual and the universal scale; Man is seen as a microcosm of the universe. Rodney Collin, in his pamphlet *Pyramid of Fire*, interpreted the images of the 'plumed serpent' at Teotihuacan to represent spiritual transformation. Quetzalcoatl begins as the lowly snake who travels the earth on his belly. He is close to the ground and he carries the 'poison' of his own negativity within himself. By transforming this poison internally (and not simply expelling it into the outer world), he is able to sprout feathers (Higher Centers) and ultimately to fly into the sun (World 12). Here we see again the universal triad of transformation described in Chapter 2 – Being absorbing Not-Being to engender Beyond-Being. It is as true for the Absolute as it is for his image, Man. The central figure of Quetzalcoatl is also associated, in the later Aztec presentation, with the 'dark face' of Tezcatlipoca – representing the forces of chaos, aggression, and disorder.

Figure 41. **Quetzalcoatl, the plumed serpent**

Thus there is a dualistic aspect to the religion of Quetzalcoatl, which was interpreted in different ways at different points in Mesoamerican history, sometimes slipping down – at the level of Popular Religion – into crude opposition. But wherever transformation is understood on the human level and wherever duality resolves into transcendence, we know that behind it is the Work of the Traditions.

While the influence of the peoples of Teotihuacan is universally acknowledged, they remain unknown to us. We are only able to reconstruct a view of their civilization through the evidence of the site itself and through the legends of the Aztecs, who saw them as their predecessors and mentors.

The site, which long predates the Aztec Empire, transcends the Mayan and the Olmec cities in its vast, spacious, and completely integrated layout. The architectural complex, like the ancient complex of the Great Pyramids and the Sphinx, immediately produces the sense of a living cosmos. It links the earth and the sky. The arrangement of the elements does not 'contain' a space but 'opens' space, and so connects Man to the level one above his own. Teotihuacan integrates the Maya and Olmec achievements, while taking them to a new level.

It was the Aztecs who created the name 'Teotihuacan' for the city they thought was the place of the legendary Toltecs. The name means literally "city where men became gods" or "place of those who have the road of gods." Teotihuacan is also linked to the

Aztec myth of the 'sacred city of Tollan': a universal city, which was the origin of Mesoamerican culture. And it is through the Aztecs that we must link our mysterious city 'where men became gods' and the Spiritual Tradition connected with it to the more general history of Mesoamerica. Here we shall follow the general lines of the interpretation given by Laurette Sejourne in *El Universo de Quetzalcoatl, America Latina: Antiquas Culturas Precoluminos* and *Teotihuacan: Capital de los Toltecs*.

As so often is the case with the interpretation of ancient history, to clarify the past we must first run ahead in time.

The Aztec Empire, when it came, was the project of Nahuatl-speaking peoples who emigrated into Central Mexico from the north, possibly from what is now the southern United States. It is likely that they emigrated under duress, seeking better fortunes in a world that was new to them. They were nomadic peoples who entered the world of the Mesoamerican Civilizations when it was in its prime. In the difficult centuries of adjustment they found a 'mentor' people whom they revered and to whom their myths constantly refer. It appears that the mentors of the Nahua were the descendants of the people of the Civilization of Teotihuacan. They must have been descendents, and not the original Teotihuacanos, because the city had fallen 200 years before the first Nahua emigrations. It seems highly likely, then, that the mentor-people were not a Civilization but a Spiritual Tradition, extending directly from the Tradition of Teotihuacan. The active role of a Spiritual Tradition – rather than a Civilization – in integrating the Nahua into Mesoamerica seems likely for a second reason. A Tradition is capable, as a Civilization is not, of accurately separating the essential from the inessential, and so of communicating its inner truths to people who are outside of it. In other words it does not force upon them the ideology and the ethnicity of the 'carrier' civilizational order. The new people can then 'own' the vision in just the same way that the original people did. The Spiritual Tradition, certain in its core teaching, can even help the new people to re-caste the Religion in a form more appropriate to their situation – should that be necessary – making it a Living Religion. We hypothesize, then, that the Spiritual Tradition of Teotihuacan survived the parent city and was able to directly infuse the Nahua peoples with the ancient core teachings that came down from Olmec times. (We shall detail this linkage further in our presentation of the Aztec Civilization.)

What happened to the Civilization of Teotihuacan itself we can only speculate. The ruins give evidence of violence: of fire and of the destruction of monumental art. Internal strife is likely. Perhaps this is the repeating story of the corruption of the Men of the Tradition by temporal power. This, we will remember, was the greatest threat to the Egyptian Tradition over its three millennia, and hearkens back to the struggle of the Black and the White magicians which occurred in the twilight of the prehistoric Shamanic Religions. How might this story have worked out in Teotihuacan? Perhaps those of the Tradition of Teotihuacan who were directly associated with the Imperial House developed sorcery as a means of wielding power and were corrupted by the very tool they used, so becoming a 'dead' – but very active – Tradition. The faction of the Tradition that was able to preserve the true teaching then shifted its social niche, distancing itself from the Imperial House, and managing to re-establish itself amongst the priests, the artisans, or the craftsmen. Eventually the corruption of the Imperial House was reflected in tensions which developed throughout the society, connecting to every social stratum. At the same time the 'white' Tradition made its own network of connections, and civil war followed. This internal struggle might then have extended into a system of alliances with other Mesoamerican peoples, and the victory of one side was followed by the invasion of its supporters.

However the fall of Teotihuacan occurred, some of the survivors migrated to the northwest, connecting with the Toltecs in Tula, some fifty miles to the north. We hypothesize that the Tradition of the 'white sorcerers' (the cult of Quetzalcoatl) survived the fall of the Civilization in this way. The 'white' Tradition, well-adapted to artisanal existence, may have been able to perpetuate itself within a Toltec 'container.' It is also possible that the people of Tula took their 'Toltec' name from the immigrants and that 'Toltec' was the real name of the people of Teotihuacan. The first possibility is the more likely, for the evidence of Tula civilization shows it to be rough and militaristic, falling far short of the achievement of Teotihuacan. It does not reflect the same level of leadership that the Civilization of Teotihuacan knew, in its years of greatness.

The civilization centered in Tula, Hidalgo, which we hypothesize as the 'carrier' of the Tradition of Teotihuacan, is dated by archaeologists from 800 to 1000 AD. As Teotihuacan came to its end in about 750 AD, there is sufficient overlap to explain a significant transfer of cultural influence. The first Nahuatl came south in 550 AD and thus they have a long overlap with the Toltecs of Tula.

However it happened, the Men of the Tradition were somehow able to survive and to preserve the memory of the values and the inner teachings of the great civilization that had gone before. In time they were able to communicate their vision to the more humble – and so more receptive – Nahuatl speakers. Thus, what was not fully realized with the more warlike Toltecs of Tula had the promise of full realization with the incoming Nahua peoples.

These Nahuatl-speaking nomads were the ancestors of the Aztecs. They accepted the myths and the teachings of the ancient parent Tradition, and they accepted its people as mentors and guides. They idealized the civilizational order that they encountered in its final phase. On the other side, the members of the 'Teotihuacano' Spiritual Tradition must have seen real potential in the proto-Aztecs and seen them as the possible inheritors of their teaching.

The current of influence from the civilization of Teotihuacan (ending in 750 AD) to the 'proto-Aztec' Nahuatl peoples confounds many modern historians. But we know that the Spiritual Traditions are expert at preserving and transmitting core understandings, as they sustain themselves by preserving and transmitting a state of consciousness that transcends those understandings. If the higher state of consciousness is preserved, its external expressions in civilizational order can much more easily be preserved, for they are seen in relation to that which they refer. And, of course, beyond this, there is the connection to the cosmos above the Cosmos of Man.

The Aztec Civilization

This leads us naturally into the story of the Aztecs. We noted that the proto-Aztecs were Nahuatl-speaking peoples who emigrated south into Central Mexico, beginning from about 550 AD. For 550 years (until 1100 AD) they sustained themselves as nomadic hunters, becoming widespread only in the fourteenth and fifteenth centuries. Each different Nahua tribe, on settling in the Mexico valley, became the client-population of an existing city-state, and in this way it absorbed the Mesoamerican Culture and ultimately the teachings of the Mesoamerican Spiritual Tradition. Finally, in the fifteenth century they began to assert themselves.

In its maturity the Aztec civilization was centered at Tenochtitlan, now the site of Mexico City. It was the last of the great Mesoamerican Civilizations, and in its Imperial phase it became the 'melting pot' of all its predecessors.

Aztec is the Nahuatl word for 'people from Aztlan,' a mythological place for the Nahuatl-speaking culture of prehistoric times. The myth of the sacred city of Aztlan transferred – under the influence of their Mentor-Tradition – to the historical city of Teotihuacan (the ruins of which the Nahuatl knew well). The Nahuatl people (rightly or wrongly) identified Teotihuacan with the name 'Toltec,' and (rightly) with the cult of Quetzalcoatl. Thus Teotihuacan became, for the Nahuatl, the mythical Toltec city of Tollan, and the several Nahuatl-speaking tribes took the name 'Aztec' for themselves.

Figure 42. **Aztec temple at Chichenitza**

While there is some disagreement amongst scholars on this subject, the majority (including such scholars as Laurette Sejourne) use the term 'Toltec' to refer to the people of the civilization of Teotihuacan.

Thus the Nahuatl-speaking tribes who took the name of 'Aztec' for themselves inherited all of the hallmarks of Mesoamerican culture: the pantheon of Mesoamerican Gods, the cult of the Plumed Serpent, the 'Long Count' calendric system, written language, mathematics, and astronomy. They excelled particularly at the art of poetry. They constructed the traditional step-pyramids and were ardent players of the Mesoamerican ritual ball game. They also adopted the Mayan custom of human sacrifice.

The Aztecs had several complementary creation myths, which can be summed up as follows.

THE AZTEC MYTH OF CREATION

Four Great Ages preceded our present age. Each of these ages ended in catastrophe and was followed by new creation. Our age, the fifth age, is thus the fifth creation. It has escaped catastrophe to this point only due to the sacrifice of a god, Nanahuatl, who was transformed into the Sun. The myth of the near-catastrophe of the fifth age was associated with the city of Teotihuacan, which, as we noted, had already been destroyed when the Nahuatl peoples came into the Valley of Mexico.

The creation of the World, in all of its ages, was the work of the twin gods Quetzalcoatl and Tezcatlipoca. Quetzalcoatl represents what we have called 'consciousness' and the values that inform civilization. He is the God of the rising sun and the master of healing, regeneration, art, poetry, wisdom, and crafts. Tezcatlipoca is his opposite; he is the God of night and war. He is also – unhappily – the ruler of the earth's surface. Quetzalcoatl and Tezcatlipoca represent the lighter and the darker sides of human nature, respectively.

In the Aztec myth, at some point near the beginning of the present age, Quetzalcoatl was banished from the surface of the earth by Tezcatlipoca, and as a result war came to dominate human affairs. It was Tezcatlipoca, in the age after Teotihuacan, who had demanded blood sacrifice as his tribute.

Aztec scholars predicted the return of Quetzalcoatl, the Plumed Serpent, in the year 1519. This was to herald the beginning of a new age in which Mankind would return to the way of life that was known in the sacred city of Tollan. Some said that Quetzalcoatl would return in the company of 'white Gods'; and this was at least part of the basis for the tragic Aztec surrender to Cortez.

Considering our hypothesis of a struggle between a living Spiritual Tradition of white sorcery and a 'dead' Tradition of black sorcery, this presentation of the Aztec myth is clearly a 'white sorcerer' view. Yet the black Tradition persisted and would have presented the same story in quite a different light. While the White Tradition, which makes the figure of Quetzalcoatl central, rejected blood sacrifice, the Black Tradition, centered in the Lower Self's will to self-preservation, saw human sacrifice as a necessity. Both Traditions agreed that when the God Nanahuatl sacrificed himself to preserve the world, he was transformed into the Sun. But for the Black Tradition this did not finish the matter. In order for the sun to move continuously through the heavens and for humanity to preserve itself from a fifth catastrophe, Nanahutal's act of sacrifice had to be perpetuated through time. Human sacrifice was thus necessary to keep the sun moving through the heavens.

Almost certainly the form that the human sacrifice took, the cutting-out of the heart, was a distortion of the esoteric idea that one must sacrifice one's heart to the emergent God that is one's Higher Self. In other words, one must sacrifice the gamut of normal human emotion to the disciplined and unceasing longing for the Higher Self.

But to return to history, as the centuries passed the Nahua ceased to be simply a client-population. By the fourteenth century the Valley of Mexico contained several city-states of Nahua-speaking people. From about this time no city-state in the valley was able to decisively dominate the others, yet there were definite spheres of influence. All of the Nahua peoples affirmed their 'Toltec' heritage, and it appears that the original Spiritual Tradition was quite alive amongst them, for the Aztec chronicles refer to this time as a 'golden age' when people still learned directly from the Toltecs.

We know of one historical personage said to be an incarnation of the golden age: *Nezahualcoyotl* (1402-1472 AD).

Nezahualcoyotl was the prince of Texcoco, and perhaps the greatest of the Nahua poets. He had a profound experience of the "unknown, unknowable Lord of Everywhere" to whom he dedicated a temple which was left entirely empty. This represents a state of consciousness, taught by all Spiritual Traditions, in which Higher Centers can emerge and begin to function independently.

While Nezahualcoyotl was still in his childhood, the neighboring Tepaqnecs conquered Texcoco. As Nezahualcoyotl was heir to the throne, he went directly into exile. On reaching maturity he was able to arrange an alliance with the leading Nahua cities of the time, to defeat the Tepaqnecs. He proved to be both a natural leader and a great general. The Nahua alliance was the basis of the 'Triple Alliance' by which the Aztecs later established their sovereignty over the Mesoamerican World. On succeeding to the throne Nezahualcoyotl actualized the values of the Tradition of Teotihuacan to bring about Texcoco's Golden Age. He established a code of law, created an extensive library, and established an academy of music. He was himself an architect and town planner, and created a system of aqueducts and gardens in the city. As a poet he used conscious art to communicate the teachings of the Tradition of Teotihuacan.

Yet it was not Nezahualcoyotl of Texcoco who finally brought unity to the Nahua. Strangely, it was the last-coming of the Nahuatl peoples, the **Mexicas**, who were to be the leaders. The Mexicas were, perhaps, the most warlike of the Nahautl, and initially hired themselves out as mercenaries in the wars between the city-states, breaking the natural balance of power that existed between them.

The Mexicas had migrated south into the Valley of Mexico in the thirteenth century. They had a difficult time establishing their place and were forced to spend time in the empty barrens of Tizapan. There they became a tributary of the Azcapotzalco, a strong regional power of that time. At the same time they absorbed the Teotihuacano culture just as their Nahua predecessors had done.

In 1323 the Mexicas, on the site of what is now Mexico City, were shown a vision of an eagle perched on a prickly pear cactus, eating a snake. This vision indicated that the site was to be their permanent home. It was then under the control of the Mexicas' tributary rulers, the Azcapotzalco. The Mexicas nevertheless determined to found the town of Tenochtitlan on that site. To that end they formed an alliance with the Texcoco and the Tlacopan – known as the 'Triple Alliance' – which was able to defeat the Azcapotzalco. This alliance, which was completed in 1427, became the basis of the Aztec Empire. Indeed, the general use of the term 'Aztec' really only begins with the Empire, when the need for a generic term for the three allies was first felt.

Over the next 100 years the Triple Alliance came to dominate the Valley of Mexico, extending its power to the Gulf of Mexico on the east and the Pacific Ocean on the west. The people of Tenochtitlan became the unquestioned leaders of this Alliance.

The Empire itself developed as a system of tribute rather than as a system of monolithic rule. Indeed the idea of an 'Aztec' Civilization is best understood as a particular horizon of the more general – and much older – Mesoamerican Civilization.

Generally, once a city-state was conquered, the local rulers were restored to their positions and the Aztecs refrained from interfering in local affairs as long as tribute was paid. On the positive side, membership in the Empire gave access to its markets and its trading system, which created regional economies of scale. An extensive system of communications developed, linking the many cities of the Empire. Within the Empire there was mandatory, universal education for juveniles, from the age of fourteen. There were two types of schools, one for practical and military studies and one for advanced learning in writing, astronomy, statesmanship, and theology. An important aspect of education was learning the collections of sayings that embodied Aztec civilizational ideals, as these had been received from their parent-Tradition.

Probably the most developed expression of the Aztec phase of Mesoamerican Civilization was song and poetry. These were highly regarded and always performed at the great festivals of the Aztec year. At these festivals there were also dramatic and acrobatic presentations.

However, civilizational order did not develop continuously out of the Nahua 'Golden Age.' The Black Tradition – the Servants of Tezcatlipoca – somehow came to the fore, bringing a forced revision of the 'official religion' and a program of war and of human sacrifice.

In 1440 the two half-brothers Tlacaelel (1397-1487) and Montezuma (1398-1469) became the leaders of the Alliance. The latter, as Montezuma I, became the official emperor, but his older brother Tlacaelel was the power behind the throne. Tlacaelel rewrote the history of the Aztec people, emphasizing the black sorcerer Texcatlipoca over the white sorcerer Quetzalcoatl and placing the old Nahua tribal gods on the same level as these two. He transformed the structure of the Aztec government to conform to the new beliefs and burnt the great bulk of Aztec manuscripts so that nothing would contradict his re-presentation of history and religion. Tlacaelel taught the necessity of repeated human sacrifice and emphasized ritual warfare as a way of having a constant supply of trained warriors. He linked the two by making defeat in ritual war a possible condition for sacrifice. At this time there was a marked increase in the use of human sacrifice, which was institutionalized in 1484 under Tlacaelel's guidance. From this point forward human beings were sacrificed on each of eighteen annual festivals – an estimated annual total of between 6,000 and 12,000 victims. Aztec chronicles report clearly that 84,400 human sacrifices were offered over a period of four days on the occasion of the dedication of the main temple of Tenochtitlan in 1487. Contemporary scholarship sees this figure as purposefully exaggerated, and a more moderate estimate is 10,000.

Here we may note that sacrifice – which is not a part of contemporary Western culture – is an act of great power. In societies where it was practiced and understood, it was often used as a political tool, to control and influence a population. Aristotle criticized this use of the mass sacrifice of animals in the *Nicomachean Ethics*. His critique was based on a recognition of the very real power that was in this act, which he had witnessed at first hand. It unifies the spectators in a certain way while releasing the molecular energy of the organisms being sacrificed. Needless to say, the sacrifice of human beings releases a much greater molecular energy and affects the audience even more deeply. This use of 'organismic' molecular energy is aligned with sorcery, and not with the work of the Spiritual Traditions.

Having said all of this, the impact of mass human sacrifice on the Aztec population would have been extraordinary. In an atmosphere steeped in admiration for the culture of Teotihuacan and in the cult of Quetzalcoatl – which forbids human sacrifice – this would have created a crisis. Despite the destruction of the existing manuscripts, the nobility would certainly have been aware that the religion created by Tlacaelel was a forgery. All of this disposed the Aztec Civilization to an internal split in the decades immediately preceding the coming of Cortez. Cortez's arrival in 1521 brought the split into the open, as many of the Aztecs allied themselves with the conquistadores. We note that Cortez came only thirty-seven years after the institutionalization of sacrifice, and only two years after the prophesied return of the Plumed Serpent.

Thus, when Cortez came, he quickly divided the Aztecs and so conquered them. He allied first with the Tlaxcala and Texcoco, who had already begun to resist Aztec rule. In this context, he was seen by many as an incarnation of Quetzalcoatl. At one point, feeling threatened by thousands of Aztec warriors, Cortez brought forth the Aztec Emperor (Montezuma II, the descendent of Tlacaelel's brother), whom he held as hostage, in order to pacify the crowd. But the Aztecs, unhappy with Montezuma, stoned him to death. This shows the depth of division of the Aztec culture in its final hours.

On having defeated the government of Montezuma and razed the city of Tenochtitlan to the ground, the Spanish founded a new settlement on the site of the ruined Aztec capital, which became Mexico City. In the years immediately after the conquest the Spaniards treated the Aztec nobles as noblemen, but later there began a systematic suppression of Aztec culture. The destruction of the traditional culture was facilitated by disease and depopulation. The indigenous population of the Valley of Mexico is estimated to have declined by more than 80 percent in the course of the next sixty years.

We can only regret the destruction of this great civilization and culture, yet the causes of the destruction of a civilization are never entirely external. Tlacaelel sounded a criminal note, so different from the note sounded by Nezahualcoyotl only a few generations before, and from this came the corruption of both Spiritual Tradition and Living Religion. And so the play of Teotihuacan was replicated: the pursuit of temporal power and the consequent corruption of the Tradition displacing the Great Work in the life of Civilization.

The Incan Civilization

The Empire of the Incas, at its height, ran down most of the Western seaboard of the South American continent, from Ecuador in the north to central Chile in the south. The relation of this civilization to the Mesoamerican family of civilizations was not direct, but its achievement was certainly related to their achievements.

Figure 43. **Ruins at Machu Picchu**

The Incas do not follow the 'classical' Mesoamerican formula, which includes step-pyramids, the Long Count calendar, and the Mesoamerican ball game. The Incan writing and number systems were only germinal, and their art was significantly different from Mesoamerican art. Yet they did achieve the same transition to the phase that we have called Original Religion; they did have a highly developed agricultural system, and they did have monumental art and architecture. They produced truly magnificent temples and the most extensive and well-maintained road system in the New World. They also had the most developed metallurgy of the New World peoples, and their craftsmanship in gold and silver ornament was unmatched.

All of the Andean civilizations, on which the Inca civilization was based, had developed agricultural systems. The Andean environment forced a mountainous step-system of agriculture, which required a high-maintenance irrigation system involving the whole community. The carefully terraced slopes were used to grow staples of maize, potatoes, and quinoa, and a host of supporting crops – including cotton, which became the basis for the most beautiful textile work.

The Incan civilization began as a tribal society in what is now Peru, where the first *Sapa Inca* (paramount leader), Manco Capac, founded the Kingdom of Cuzco in about 1200 AD. According to the Incan legend he carried a golden staff, given him by the Gods. The Gods had instructed him to travel the world, beginning from his hometown of Pacaritambo, until he found a spot where the staff sank into the earth and at that point to create a Temple to the Sun. After a journey of many years, which included a tour of the underworld, he arrived at Cuzco, where the staff sank into the ground – and the Inca people promptly built their temple to the sun.

Under the leadership of Manco Capac's descendants the Incas began to absorb other Andean communities, and by 1438 AD most of modern-day Peru had been integrated into the Incan system. Cuzco was rebuilt as an imperial city; it was the center of a vast cultural, administrative, and trading network. In 1442 a *Sapa Inca* by the name of Patchacuti began an even more far-reaching program of expansion. Patchacuti's agents researched the different Andean communities which he wished to include in the empire. Emissaries were then sent out to these communities to represent the specific benefits they would gain from joining the Empire. The emissaries presented the vision of the civilizational order the client community would be a part of, and the many advantages of trade within it. Most of the peoples approached accepted this offer, and if they did not accept, they were subdued by force.

As the empire expanded, both north and south, a carefully designed system of provincial governments formed around the central administration in Cuzco. While the Incas tolerated or even incorporated elements of the religions of other Andean peoples, they presented their own mythology as central. The Incan empire was a theocracy in which the Inca king, *Sapa Inca*, was seen as the descendant of Inti, the sun god.

The entire system was specifically adapted to the social system of *ayllu* agriculture, which had been practiced by all the Andean communities since before the time of Manco Capac. The ayllus were communities, based on blood ties, which operated as economic and social units. Within the community there was collective ownership of land, of any herd animals, and of water resources. The success and cohesiveness of the Andean ayllus were related to their communal dependence on the remarkable step-system of agriculture. Indeed, the Incan Empire could be characterized as a family of Andean ayllus controlled from an administrative center.

One aspect of becoming part of the Empire was that the children of any regional ruler would be brought to Cuzco to receive special instruction in both the Incan religion and the Incan system of administration. On their return these children would implement this system in their own native lands. The centralization of education brought the children of the regional nobilities into contact with the Incan nobility during their formative years and created an environment that encouraged intermarriage. This had the longer-term effect of creating an integrated imperial nobility.

Sixteenth-century Spanish observers noted that the Incan imperial system incorporated levels of tolerance and practices of official clemency unheard of in the European kingdoms of their time.

Was there a Spiritual Tradition active behind the Inca Religion and system of rule? The remarkable degree of social cohesiveness, and the relative lack of corruption, suggests this, for a connection through to the Gods produces a 'lift upon lift' effect, connecting all levels of society. And at the level of the everyday, it gives a set of shared ideals. Indeed the ethos of the Incan civil service was remarkably similar to that of the Roman civil service in Augustan times.

By 1500 the Incan Empire extended from Ecuador and Colombia in the north through Peru, Bolivia and Chile, and south to parts of Argentina. In the mature imperial phase every male capable of military service was subject to draft, for either a single campaign or for permanent service. There was an educational or 'formative' aspect to this service, as the army was envisaged as a force which labored in the interest of the whole. It was not seen as a means of extracting tribute, as certain of the Mesoamerican armies were, and the strictest discipline was maintained with regards to any abuse of civilians.

To give free movement to the army and to facilitate the system of trade that linked the ayllus, the Incans constructed the most remarkable system of roads. It was based on two main roads which ran the length of the country: the Royal Road that ran through the Andean highlands for a distance of 3,250 miles and the Coastal Road which followed the seacoast for 2,520 miles.

The chief achievement of the Incas, however, was their architecture, and particularly their temples. Architecture was seen as the most important of the Incan arts. In the world of the Incas architecture represented the zone of the sacred. The beautiful decorative designs that we see in their ceramics and textiles – birds, waves, felines, and geometric patterns – all reflect motifs first developed in architecture. The Incas were able to construct their huge stone temples without the use of mortar, fitting irregular stones so tightly that you could not drive a knife edge between them. The main examples of Incan architecture are the remains that exist at Cuzco and the remarkable site at Machu Picchu.

While the Incas had no iron or steel, they had developed an alloy of bronze that was superior to the bronze alloys of their Mesoamerican contemporaries. We know that they excelled in working gold and silver, but we have lost the best examples of their art, as all their greatest treasures were melted down by the conquistadores.

How, then, did it all come to an end? In the early sixteenth century the empire was split by a dynastic civil war, and at the same time an epidemic of smallpox spread from Central America and greatly weakened the country. In 1533 the Spanish conquistadores, led by Francisco Pizarro, took advantage of this situation and conquered the Incas, eventually consolidating power over the whole Andean region.

Thus the Incas were identical to the Aztecs in one unfortunate regard – their phase of expansion preceded the Spanish conquest by only a century. From the phase of expansion initiated by Patchacuti in 1442 to Pizarro's conquest in 1533 is a span of only ninety-one years.

Considering the civilization as a whole we could say that the communal spirit fostered by the system of ayllus made the rule by Spiritual Tradition possible, and it was the genius of the Incas and the leadership given by the Tradition that brought it to the level of high civilization. We have one European impression of this social order in its prime. Don Mancio Serra de Leguisamo, the last survivor of the original conquistadores, wrote, in 1589, after his return to Spain:

> We found these kingdoms in such good order, and the said Incas governed them in such wise manner that throughout them there was not a thief, nor a vicious man, nor an adulteress, nor was a bad woman admitted among them, nor were there immoral people. … each one knew his property without any other person seizing it ... the motive which obliges me to make this statement is the discharge of my conscience, as I find myself guilty. For we have destroyed by our evil example, the people who had such a government as was enjoyed by these natives.[3]

In contemplating the Mesoamerican civilizations in the pre-Columbian period, we are amazed at the spectacle of the rise and fall of highly developed social orders, leaving traces in small communities which may or may not carry forward to successor civilizations. While these 'civilizational collapses' can be explained in terms of natural disaster, pandemic, the rebellion of a suppressed peasantry, or destruction by a rival civilization, there is also – certainly – a more universal principle at work. In the Absolute's Creation a living being, or a living civilizational order, does not come to its end purely through 'external' factors. Some inner life principle is no longer able to develop in this particular form. There is the element of tragedy, then, for the end of life can come when there are

3. Markham, Clements, *The Incas of Peru*, E.P. Dutton and Company, New York, 1910.

still many elements of real value within a Civilizational Order. Could a given Civilization not have been given a second chance? Or – failing that – could the Gods not have intervened so that its achievements might be perpetuated in another context? There are two considerations to be kept in mind:

1. *Exhaustion*: As in the case of the Egyptian Tradition in Ptolemaic times, a particular context may simply have played out all its possibilities in the line of time. Better to re-start and allow the 'bleed-through' of selected aspects to the civilizational orders to follow.

2. *The emergence of a deviant or malefic force*: A power developed, on the level we inhabit, by men who are not conscious, yet who achieve a significant concentration of molecular energy: in other words, occult power of great magnitude. Such an influence, in concentrated form, might impinge on the cosmos above the microcosmos of Man – and this the Gods will not tolerate.

We have seen, in the last century, that even the most technically and culturally developed civilizations may enter a sinister or malefic phase. It is the Black Queen threatened, asserting control of a culture, *and it happens easily*, for it is simply the uncontrolled development of her right function. In the great wars of aggression, ethnic cleansings, and political purges of the twentieth century, we can safely say that no Spiritual Tradition was involved or implicated, except negatively. The Spiritual Traditions had long since been 'flushed' from the centers of temporal power. But in the Mesoamerican Civilizations we have seen state religion similar to that of Ancient Egypt, and the Traditions – through the Religions – close to the centers of power. The deviant tendency may have taken the form of a sudden ascent of sorcery, leading to a re-enactment of the prehistoric struggle of the Black and the White sorcerers.

But to proceed with our story, we must turn the clock back again to the great turning point in the history of Man when the last great Ice Age came to an end, and *homo sapiens sapiens* became the dominant species on the planet.

CHAPTER 20

The Aryan/Avestan Savior God

As the glaciers receded and the fertile plains of the Russian Steppe were exposed to direct sunlight, the largest species of herd animal – bison, wild cattle, caribou, antelope, and gazelle – began to concentrate there. Hunting and gathering peoples from Eastern Europe, the Levant, and Central Asia followed the herds into this area. The steppes soon became a flash-point for humanity, a place where scarcity did not exist. Over the centuries agriculture and animal husbandry came to supplement hunting, and – in the period before the first cities – a great civilization developed here. The histories of both the Iranian and the Hindu races affirm the existence of high civilization in the steppes in prehistoric times. The religion of this civilization was polytheistic, at least in its outer presentation. Both the Hindus and the Iranians called these peoples the *Aryan* race, and both trace their origins to it.

Somewhere in and about 1600 BC the Aryans migrated south from the Russian steppes in two separate streams:

1. *The Proto-Iranians* who moved southwest into Persia, and

2. *The Proto-Hindus* who moved directly south into India, conquering the Dravidian peoples who inhabited the Indus Valley. The Dravidians were then pushed into the south of India, where they were later to make their own contribution to world history. The word 'Hindu' is in fact Dravidian, meaning literally 'coming from the other side of the Indus River.'

In the beginning these groups shared the same mythology and spoke a common language. What is remarkable is that each Aryan stream arrived at its destination with a revealed religion that was to influence all history to follow.

- The Proto-Iranians, just as they began their movement south, were sent one of the first great Prophets, Zoroaster. They accepted him and they accepted the revealed truth that he presented them with.

- The Proto-Hindus received a comparable body of revealed truth in the form of the Vedas, which were delivered by great Teachers whom the Proto-Hindus called *Rishis*. Some of the Vedas were delivered before the southward migration of the Proto-Hindus, some during the migration itself, and some after their arrival in India. In order to express their valuation for the teaching of the *Rishis*, as it unfolded during this time, the Proto-Hindus made a rigorous distinction between revealed truth and truth that was merely inspired. Where other sages might falter, the *Rishi* always spoke the truth because he spoke directly from a Higher World in which he was permanently established. Of the seventeen *Rishis* of whom we have record, seven were of the prehistoric 'mythical' period, three came after the Proto-Hindus were well established in India, and – according to the *Mahabharata* – seven were of the post-Vedic or Vedantic period. As a culture, the Proto-Hindus had a remarkable focus on penetrating the Sphere of Sentient Being and a unique genius for metaphysics.

We shall explore the Zoroastrian teaching of the Proto-Iranians in "Zoroaster" in Chapter 27 of Book IV, The Age of the Prophets, as Zoroaster was one of the first prophets. But the Vedic teaching, which was continuous with the original Aryan religion, we shall treat in the present Book. It was perpetuated and developed by the *Rishis* for many centuries, and in its pattern of development there remained deep continuity with ancient teachings and techniques.

We note that, in this same time period (in the centuries immediately following 1600 BC) Greek-speaking peoples migrated south from the Western Steppes (the place of origin of both the Proto-Hindus and Proto-Iranians) into what is now northern Greece and Asia Minor. If they had an ancient religion we do not know it, and it did not stop them, on their arrival, from adopting the religion of the Minoans. What we do know is that they gave the Minoan religion a definite Aryan caste, lifting it out of its Minoan 'Great Mother' context. Where the greatest metaphysical speculations of the East originated from the Vedic Rishis, the greatest metaphysical speculations of the West (both Classical and Christian) originated from the Greeks.

CHAPTER 21

The Vedic Tradition

When the Aryans-to-become-Hindus began their southward migration, they had already accumulated a treasury of spiritual laws. These laws eventually gave form to the Hindu social order, which developed, in a composite relation with the existing Harrapan and Dravidian peoples, as a system of castes under a ruling priest caste. It was, almost certainly, originally based on an understanding of the principle of the cosmos of man.

By the tenth century BC the principle of 'revealed truth' – so important to the Hindus – was made more explicit in the concept of an 'Avatar': a being who had deliberately descended from a higher level to teach on earth. Both Rama and Krishna were designated as Avatars, and both contributed to the growing body of revealed truth.

The first of the Hindu Vedas, the *Rigveda*, which dates from before the migration south, was polytheistic in its outward form. However, this polytheistic presentation came from the *Rishis'* use of the older Aryan mythology, not from the inner teaching itself. Through its first few centuries the Vedic Tradition retained this polytheistic form, but over time its metaphysic became monotheistic, and the correspondence between the God within (the Atman) and the One which encompasses All (Brahma) was perhaps more strongly marked than in any other Tradition.

The radical emphasis on nonduality corresponded to a relative emphasis on the external or visible world as being unreal. The focus of the Vedic teachings was not on the multiple forms of creation, but on the sentience that is prior to creation. Indeed, in this context, the term 'creation' is the wrong word. What the Western Traditions called creation, the Hindu Tradition called manifestation. In the Hindu view, the world that we know, and the many civilizations of men who have populated it, are all manifestations of Brahma. These manifestations are cyclical, and each particular manifestation returns in the end to unity. This process of manifestation itself is without beginning and without end. There was, in this Tradition, a deep understanding of the principal of karma, or the patterns of cause and effect in human life and through human lives. There was also a profound acceptance of the principle of reincarnation.

In the ninth century BC the teaching of the Hindu Spiritual Tradition developed through a series of commentaries on the Vedas. These commentaries were known as the *Upanishads* and the teaching of the *Upanishads* became known as the *Vedanta*. In Sanskrit 'veda' means knowledge (as a combination of seeing and knowing), while 'vedanta' is the end or final goal of knowledge.

The Vedas and the Upanishads describe an entire way of life, a complete vision of Man in the universe. The rituals and ceremonies outlined in the early Vedas describe the major transitions of life, and give the guidelines for living. They are based on an analogy between the individual human body and the body of Mankind, complete in its different functions. In other words they are rooted in an understanding of human society as a cosmos. To understand the implications of the Vedas and the Upanishads we must understand two things:

1. That they were the core literature of the ancient Hindus, and that no other comparable literature existed;

2. That all of this literature bows to a transcendent sentience.

Nowhere in the Vedas or the Upanishads does the human intellect attempt to definitively 'encapsulate' or pin down what is above it. The Brahmanic teachings are not a theology. Rather we see a transcendent sentience giving indications of itself and of its purposes, through different human vehicles, over many generations. Thus the viewpoint of Vedism/Vedantism is very much 'from the top down.' The Vedic/Vedantic body of doctrine was developed generation after generation, not by scholars, but by men penetrating into and functioning from the Sphere of Sentient Being. The variations that do exist in the Vedantic teachings are not the work of divergent sects, but simply the development of a single doctrine, according to different points of view.

The great Vedic/Vedantic Teachers presented a view of the Absolute as the unity of three forces, which is very similar to the view presented in Chapter 2. But, given the monotheistic emphasis of that time, they presented it in a special way. It is interesting to review the detail of this.

The term the Vedic Teachers used for the Absolute was Brahma. The Absolute (Brahma) is a transcendent unity of Being and Not-Being, which is, in itself, *Beyond-Being*. According to the Vedic teaching, the transcendent aspect of this unity has two determinations. These determinations are according to how it is viewed, not according to what it is in itself. Firstly, there is an impersonal and therefore absolutely objective and universal principle, which is *Brahma*. Secondly there is what we could call the 'personal' face of this transcendent unity, showing a lesser degree of universality, which is *Ishvara*. This second principle is what the Western Religions know as 'God.'

Brahma is beyond all qualification, and from one point of view nothing can be said about it. *Ishvara* is conceived as a triad, or a 'triple manifestation.' The elements of this triad are *Brahmā* (with an added accent on the last 'a'), *Vishnu*, and *Shiva*.

- **Brahmā** is Ishvara considered as the generative principle of manifested beings. He is so named because he is considered to be the direct reflection of Brahma (without the accent) in the realm of manifestation (creation). The Brahma which is 'Beyond-Being' is a neutral term, and so more universal. The accent on the second 'a' of *Brahmā* makes that term a more substantive 'masculine.'

- **Vishnu** is Ishvara considered as the animating and preserving principle of all the beings which exist within the sphere of manifestation.

- **Shiva** (Figure 44 on page 326) is Ishavara considered as the principle of negation, or the transformative principle. It has sometimes been called the principle of destruction.

Having said this much, we can now be more precise. What we have called 'Beyond-Being' is Brahma (without the accent), which is sometimes referred to by the Vedantic teachers as *Para Brahma* to distinguish it from the dimension of Ishvara that is *Brahmā*. What we have called 'Being' is – more or less – Ishvara, although Ishvara does include an aspect of Not-Being. The Being-aspect of Ishvara splits into Brahmā and Vishnu. (We might put forward Brahmā as representing the Being-aspect of the Absolute, but what we called 'Being' in Chapter 2 does include the sustaining Vishnu.) Strictly speaking, what we have called 'Not-Being' is the third component of Ishvara: Shiva. (The original, primordial dimension of Not-Being that was described in Chapter 2 does not have its correspondence in the Vedantic presentation.)

Figure 44. **Shiva**

The monistic emphasis of the Hindus highlights the Unity of the Absolute, or Brahma. The transcendence of Absolute Spirit is preserved by being viewed independently of its triadic manifestation. We could say that in this view Not-Being (Shiva) is demoted, and so the moment of transcendence itself is given less emphasis. In the view presented in Chapter 2 'transcendence' exists only moment-by-moment, within the triadic relationship. It is an act that begins and never ends. Thus negation (Shiva) is part of this act and is directly reflected in every level of creation/manifestation. This view brings out both the great uncertainty and the great potential of our situation. In sum, the presentation of Chapter 2 emphasizes the moment of transcendence itself rather than what is transcendent. It is a perspective that emphasizes the life or will of the Absolute, as opposed to the 'principle' of what he is. Again, the reality is utterly beyond our conception, and the different ways that Spiritual Traditions choose to look at it are each appropriate for their own place and time.

The Vedic/Vedantic teachers viewed the 'Self' (*purusha* in relation to Brahmā or *atman* in relation to Brahma) as the transcendent principle behind creation (or manifestation). The Hindu conception of Self is very, very close to the Objective-Universal, and it is very carefully placed in relation to Brahma, Ishvara, and Brahmā. All manifested beings, including human beings, are only the transient and contingent manifestations of this transcendent Self. The Vedic/Vedantic conception of the 'Self' is unique, in that it is a top-down view. Yet in the Work of the Tradition this concept of Self was pursued, level by level, through all its various states of manifestation, down to the state of pure potentiality (the dormant state) as that exists in each individual human being.

The various Hindu terms for 'Self' – *purusha, jivatman, atman, paramatman* – cover, in their different modalities, what we have called essence, the steward, the Higher Emotional Center, the Higher Intellectual Center, and the various degrees of union of the two higher centers ... up to a point where the locked Higher Centers lead to a direct knowledge of the Absolute. The difference with the Hindu categories is that they look from Brahma downwards, taking up and elaborating slightly different points of view as the descent proceeds. They cover the material presented in Chapter 3, and can be used to detail certain aspects of it with greater precision than we have been able to do. Indeed, in certain aspects, they go quite beyond it – for this multi-dimensional top-down presentation allows for a particular representation of what happens to men's different bodies (cellular, molecular, and electronic) after death and a description of the transition from one embodiment to another that is unmatched in esoteric literature.

As the different Hindu Teachers developed and modified these ideas in different ways a truly magnificent edifice emerged. At the same time no one Teacher would use all of these terms in the same way, and it became increasingly difficult for the novice to make any sense of the Vedantic legacy, taken as a whole. Certain Vedantic Teachers conflated (rather than related) the Atman with Brahma, thus reducing the level of what we have called the Absolute. The more sensitive formulation is that Atman – in its most objective-universal form – "is of the same nature" as Brahma. It is not equivalent to what Brahma is in and for himself! The crude reduction of Atman to Brahma probably occurred in circumstances where intellectual speculation had become rife, and Vedantic teachers were attempting to focus intellectually confused students on a simple path of meditative effort. Certain of the Vedantic teachings come close to suggesting the subjective unreality of Creation/Manifestation. In other words they presented a paradigm where the subject absorbs the object, rather than transcending itself. This was not the original teaching of the Vedic Tradition, and the range of variations that began to appear within the Vedantic literature made it very difficult for the novice to find his way. Indeed, because the Vedic/Vedantic conception of the Self does not begin from the discrete individual, it is almost impossible to understand without guidance. When viewed 'from the bottom up' the Vedantic teaching becomes a highly specialist terminology which is easily misunderstood. And the view from the 'top down,' beginning from the experience of the Atman in its relation to Brahma, is something that only a few men and women in each generation would be qualified to present. When this view was presented (or re-presented) in an authoritative way, it was invariably given with further variations and additions. Eventually the cumulative complexity became itself a problem, for the inner teachings of the Traditions must always be simple. Just as the desire of an athlete to win an Olympic gold medal must be simple, so the desire to realize the Self must be simple, so simple that it is never – for one moment – forgotten.

For these various reasons the Brahmanic social order, which was based on a correct understanding of these principles, had to be sustained by beings of the level of the Great Rishis of the second millennium BC. The moment this spirit was extinguished the entire edifice of Vedantism would 'flatten out' into an elaborate theology, supported by a system of canon law. And, at the same time, every spiritual novice would begin to use the word Atman to describe his or her first glimpses of Higher Centers. Thus – and we emphasize – the essence of such a teaching can be lost in a single generation. The Brahmanic Order both requires and presumes a continuum of very high teachers. While it seems hard for us to believe now, this condition was met in the first generations, and for many centuries to follow. Thus, behind the Brahmanism that we know was a high and ancient Brahmanic order of an entirely different kind. What gradually rigidified into the caste system was originally something quite different. In the Vedas and the Upanishads we see the shadow of an ancient community that represents one of humanity's greatest achievements.

While the castes of the ancient Brahmanic society would have been related to groupings of family lines, they were not hereditary, for this would have contradicted the substance of the original teaching. The Vedic teachings proposed a range of different potentialities in the larger body of man. Society, as the physical form of this larger body, provided the framework for the realization of this range of potentialities. To give a person with a genius for craft work a position as a merchant, when he has no feeling for commerce, is to no one's benefit. Some can grow through service, others through roles of leadership and administration. But a man cannot grow through activities that are not in accordance with his nature, and to impose a fixed hereditary system on what had been originally intended as a supervised delegation of labor by caste is to ignore both the needs of the individual and the needs of the social body that contains him.

This principle is nowhere more important than in the Great Work. There are only a few men and women in any generation who have the capacity to achieve open and locked Higher Centers. A society which aspires to sustain itself as a 'Cosmos of Man' cannot afford to fail these men and women. Here, more than anywhere, instruction must be apportioned in accordance with the real capacities of individuals. For this reason the Brahmanic teaching had to be accessible, in its entirety, to all those capable of deriving real advantage from it.

Having said this, the tendency to perpetuate and to favor one's own blood line is – historically – one of the strongest instincts of the human race. The degeneration of the Brahmanic social order into a hereditary caste system must have been seen from the beginning as a strong likelihood, and a real danger.

In summing up, we note that the legacy of the Vedic Rishis, as realized in the mature Vedantic Tradition, is very similar to the legacy of the Prophets known to history. In both cases there is a clear indication of the aim to form the completed Pyramid of Man – the union of Spiritual Tradition, Living Religion, and Civilizational Order. It is significant that both the Vedic and the Vedantic teachings are presented in a direct manner, never once speaking in veiled terms. This shows that there was no need, at that time, to take measures to avoid persecution by the uninitiated. This very openness is a demonstration of the living link that originally existed between Tradition, Religion, and Civilization. It seems to us that the teaching of the Vedas, and the way in which that teaching was realized in the Vedic community, is somewhere between that of the Original Religions and the Prophetic Religions.

The Great Traditions in India

This brief background allows us to describe the confluence of different Spiritual Traditions that occurred in India, and to show how the original Vedic/Vedantic Tradition affected the religious environment in the millennia to follow. For a moment, then, let us run ahead of our story and paint a picture of the very special environment which was to be the background for so many important developments in the Story of Man.

VEDIC TRADITION

The Vedic Tradition takes its name from the original *Vedas* that were given by the great Rishis and Avatars, beginning from about 1,600 BC. The *Vedas* were taken to be the utterances of Higher Mind and were preserved letter-perfect by a Tradition that was the priest caste for Vedic society. The Vedas themselves were related to rituals establishing the form of society as a cosmos, inasmuch as that was possible under the circumstances.

VEDANTIC TRADITION

The Vedantic teachings begin with the *Upanishads*, which first appeared in about 850 BC. These were commentaries on the *Vedas*, elaborating and expanding upon their highly compact and aphoristic verses. The *Upanishads* correspond to a more complex social order than the *Vedas*, no longer 'Aryan' but properly Hindu. The Vedic tribes had evolved into composite kingdoms, with complex systems of checks and balances on the sovereign's power. By the ninth century BC agriculture had advanced to embrace developed animal husbandry and sophisticated systems of irrigation. In the more developed division of labor of Vedantic society there was an established place for craftsmen, artists, poets, and men of letters. While the *Upanishads* began from the mid-ninth century, they were elaborated – through the work of generations of conscious beings – over many centuries. Different conscious beings developed statements, each appropriate to their own place and time; they did not strive for consistency, but simply elaborated the heritage that had come down to them on the basis of their insight.

It is in the Vedantic period that the great epics of the Indian Civilization began to take form: the *Mahabharata* (from about 750 BC) and the *Ramayana* (from about 400 BC). These reach the level of revealed truth in the *Bhagavad Gita*, which was introduced as a 700 verse scriptural insert to the *Mahabharata* in about 350 BC. These epics are conscious works, yet they are a development of the work of many – now anonymous – authors over more than five centuries. That an artistic statement of this kind could occur, as the defining cultural statement of a civilization, is a reflection of the level of Vedantic India. We may consider, by comparison, the content and substance of the most influential 'media statements' of our own time.

From the *Upanishads*, and from the great epics of the Vedantic period, came a cultural legacy of unmatched profundity, covering metaphysics, cosmology, psychology, and civilizational epic.

Here we must emphasize that, by the time of the *Upanishads*, Brahmanism – as a social order – was already ancient. The teachings of Vedantism began as a reform or regeneration of that order. Within the original Vedic teachings there had always been a tension or contradiction between the striving for absolute liberation, or *moksha*, and Man's obligation to do what is right within this world, or *dharma*. This was reflected in a secondary contradiction between the two different types of *dharma*: the *sanatana dharma* referring to the absolute moral order which cannot be completely expressed in words, and the written *dharma* of caste and canon law. These contradictions became

THE STORY OF MAN

more acute as the caste system developed and as religious practices merged with an increasingly complex social and political life. All of these contradictions were explored, and ultimately transcended, in the great Vedantic epic, the *Mahabharata*. This great work sums up every shade and nuance of classical Hinduism: its orthodox formulations, the reaction to those formulations, and the level of understanding that transcends them both.

Vedantic Civilization achieved a final Golden Age in the time of the Gupta Empire (320 AD to 650 AD). This was a Civilizational Order that acknowledged the work of a Spiritual Tradition that was internal to it. The Gupta dynasty accomplished an effective centralization of power in northern India and, by a system of alliances, through most of the Indian subcontinent. This brought both economic prosperity and social peace. The administration of the Gupta kings was efficient and mild, and the entire Brahmanic civilization was rejuvenated through its discriminating patronage. The arts flourished in all their different forms, and the magnificent Hindu temples that we know today made their first appearance. In the words of A.L. Basham (*The Wonder That Was India*), "In the best days of the Gupta Empire, Indian culture reached a perfection which it was never again to attain."

With the decline of the Gupta kings temporal power in India decentralized, devolving into several large kingdoms, each surrounded by a host of vassal states. This decentralization launched the period that is known as Late Classical Hinduism (650 AD to 1100 AD). The very fact of decentralization, and the system of regional allegiances that resulted from it, emphasized the need for doctrinal clarity. As a result, in this period, the great – yet often contradictory – teachings of Vedism and Vedantism were finally systematized. This was more than just a task of scholarly recapitulation; it reached the level of revealed truth from which the Vedas were first given. The principal figure behind this great integration was Adi Shankara, whom we shall come to after our discussion of the Mauryan Empire and the rise of Buddhism in India.

In summary, the Vedic and Vedantic teachings created a strong foundation for everything that was to follow in India. Their legacy enabled the regeneration and reformulation of the original teachings of the Rishis, and at the same time they created an environment that allowed new teachings to emerge at a high level. And of course both the Hindu Religion and the caste system did rigidify over time. But – at the same time – a Living Tradition and a Living Religion were able to perpetuate themselves within the shell of Brahmanic society for more than two millennia.

BUDDHIST TRADITION

The Buddhist Tradition which suddenly appeared in northern India in about 520 BC can be viewed as a reform of the Vedic teaching.

We noted above that the Vedic/Vedantic 'view from above,' with its very high conception of the Self, would be difficult to sustain. Without the presence and spiritual authority of the Great Rishis, the ability of the higher to lift the lower could be easily checked by the impulse of the lower to reduce the higher to its own level. By the sixth century BC the popular religion, and the values which were a part of it, may have become a barrier to any Teacher actually attempting to communicate prolonged presence.

It is small wonder, then, that the Buddhist teaching began from an opposition to the Vedantic conception of the Self. It started again from the bottom, in practical fashion, with the immediate life experience of the individual. At the same time, Buddhism took much of Vedantism into itself, both at the time of the Buddha and in the centuries to follow. Buddhism retained the integration of linear to cyclical time and the teachings of karma and reincarnation. And, at the same time, the influence of Buddhism was certainly felt within the Brahmanic world. In the centuries that followed the Buddha's death, many orthodox Hindus simply accepted the Buddha as the ninth Avatar, following Krishna. They viewed him, then, as a development of the Vedantic teaching, similar to the earlier 'determinate developments' of Shaivism and Vaishnavism, each specifying alternative Vedantic 'ways.' Such was the openness of ancient India.

JAIN TRADITION

At the very time that the Buddha introduced his criticism of decadent Brahmanism, Mahavir introduced the Jain religion as an alternative reform. Both teachings developed actively within the framework of the Brahmanic civilization and seem not to have come into conflict with each other.

RULING BUDDHIST TRADITION

In about 260 BC the Mauryan King Ashoka converted to Buddhism, which then became the state religion of India. Within a generation it was displaced by a resurgent Brahmanism, but it continued to be a very strong teaching tradition and established deep roots in northern India.

LATER VEDANTIC TRADITIONS

In about 150 BC came **Patanjali**, a significant figure in the Vedantic tradition who regenerated the teaching in southern India. He brought clarity to a host of heterodox beliefs and inspired a long line of teachers. He taught 'yoga' as the path to prolonged presence (using the term differently than we have used it here) but at the same time he effectively 'placed' the traditional yogic practices (making use of organic/molecular internal energies) in relation to it. It was one of the great strengths of the Hindu Tradition that it was able to link healing with internal development, and Patanjali made a considerable contribution to Ayurvedic medicine, based on his understanding of 'internal' energies.

By the eighth century, in the general decentralization of power that followed the decline of the Gupta Empire, many competing schools of the Vedanta developed, and the struggles between them became related to all the regional and ethnic differences that existed in the Indian subcontinent. The legacy of the earlier Vedic/Vedantic period – viewed from a purely scholarly standpoint – was vast, mixed, and often contradictory. While the principle of revealed truth was central to this legacy, at the level of discursive presentation there was inconsistency, which the many competing Vedantic schools exploited in their sectarian disputes. At the turn of the eighth century the great teacher **Adi Shankara** (788-820) appeared to resolve these confusions and in so doing completely regenerated the Vedantic teaching in India. In the Hindu world he is known as the author of the 'Classic Vedanta.' As we noted, the doctrines of the Vedanta were based on the *Upanishads*, and gave logical coherence and organized form to the many profound insights that are embedded in them. Shankara was able to reduce all the apparently self-contradictory passages of the *Upanishads* to a consistent system, setting an intellectual standard which affected all the Vedantic schools to follow – whether they agreed with Shankara's teaching or not. Shankara's teaching eclipses any conception of substantive BEING (Ishvara/Brahmā), highlighting and making central the principle of BEYOND-BEING (Brahma/Para Brahma). We shall not try to relate his terminology to the terminology presented in Chapter 2, because Shankara's concepts are closer to those of logic and metaphysics. The presentation of Chapter 2 – while it takes its philosophical, scientific, and hermetic 'bearings' – is based in myth, because this is the vehicle that allows us to bring out those aspects of the Absolute's original act of sacrifice that are relevant to our story line. While both approaches refer to the same underlying reality, the mythical presentation is the more appropriate foundation for the Story of Man.

What enabled Shankara to unite so many heterodox variants of the Vedanta was that, as an orthodox Brahman, he began by treating the existing Vedic and Vedantic literature as sacred. As we have noted, this literature is an accumulation of the work of many conscious beings who taught at different times and in different places. As the insight of Higher Centers cannot be perfectly expressed in concepts, there are many apparent inconsistencies. In order to treat these inconsistencies Shankara developed what we might call a 'double standard of truth.' On one level he accepted that the world was produced by Brahmā and went through an evolutionary process which resulted in its present physical form. This presentation acknowledges the integrity of the Macrocosm, and it is basically the doctrine taught by the Sankhya school of Vedantism. But on another level – looking from the top down – Shankara viewed the whole phenomenal universe as unreal. For from this scale – from the scale of Beyond-Being (Brahma) – even the Macrocosm appears and disappears. And on this scale the world is indeed *maya*, an illusion, a mirage. Thus Shankara integrated the 'top-down' view characteristic of Vedantism with the acknowledgment of some kind of cosmic structure.

As a spiritual teacher Shankara strongly emphasized the benefit of monastic life, and it is from him that the different lineages of Vedantic monasticism developed. Shankara initiated four great monastic lineages – one in the north, one in the south, one in the east, and one in the west of India. These were to regenerate the Hindu Religion. All four lineages taught what is known as the Advaita Vedanta (the 'non-dual' or 'unified' Vedanta), and their teaching established a standard that remains to this day.

ZOROASTRIAN/PARSEE TRADITIONS

Beginning from about 800 AD there was an emigration of Zoroastrians south into India. They were trying to escape the persecution of the Arab Muslims who had conquered their native Persia. They became known as the Parsees, and made their contribution to this increasingly colorful tapestry.

SUFI TRADITIONS

In 1200 AD the Muslim invasion of northern India destroyed Buddhism in its own core area, but failed to displace Brahmanism as the dominant faith of the Indian subcontinent. The Dravidian peoples of southern India had embraced Brahmanism with such zeal that Islam was never able to penetrate this region.

Following the Islamic conquest in 1200 AD a series of Sufi teachers entered India, and Sufism put down real roots, to the extent that, in some areas of northern India,

Brahmanism and Sufism became mixed traditions. An example of this fusion would be the teachings of Lala, in what is now Kashmir. Both Indian Sufism and Hinduism, as esoteric traditions, developed a remarkable open-endedness in northern India. Indeed, the idea of Sufism existing independently of Islam comes from early twentieth century Indian Sufis.

SIKH TRADITION

In the sixteenth century the Sikh religion – the teaching of Guru Nanak – emerged in northern India as an alternative to both Hinduism and Islam. It was to a degree syncretic, a fusion of these two teachings. It emphasized the way of devotion (*bhakti*) and was given poetic representation by Kabir.

India thus became a fertile receptacle of many religious traditions. When, in the early nineteenth century, the British displaced the ruling Mughal Emperors (direct descendents of Genghis Khan who had adopted Islam) an almost completely open-ended situation developed. The Islamic repression of the Vedantic teachings in the north came to an end, and the Vedantic teachers were once again able to teach openly. At the same time the extreme rigidification of the caste system in the south began to thaw.

By the nineteenth century the caste system, which was still the dominant social order of India, had become a restriction and nothing more. By the mid-nineteenth century it became necessary for India to throw off the social order of Brahmanism, just as, in the early twentieth century, it became necessary for Turkey to throw off the social order of Sufism.

Thus, in the 1820s the great reformer Ram Mohan Roy initiated a 'social movement' to suppress the extreme forms that had rigidified in a decadent Brahmanic society, such as widow sacrifice and the almost complete social barriers between castes. Mohan Roy became the advocate of an ecumenic, monotheistic religion, and was quite happy to work with Christian missionaries to achieve his social reforms. In this context both Christianity and nineteenth century European 'socialism' became means to social reform in India. At the same time Mohan Roy upheld the traditional Vedantic literature as representing the greatest spiritual revelation given to Man. In this environment there was a final efflorescence of Vedantism, which produced such teachers as Ramakrishna

Paramahamsa, Sri Yukteswar Giri, Narayana Guru, Swami Vivekenanda, Sri Aurobindo Ghose, Candrasekhara Bharati, and Sacchidanandendra Saraswati.

However, these later teachers appear to have worked largely independently of one another. The world of the 'Vedic/Vedantic Civilization,' which had openly supported some of the highest Spiritual Traditions known to history, had long since disappeared. Probably survivors of these ancient Traditions were still alive in the nineteenth century and may even – like the Sufi Traditions – have extended their life into the early decades of the twentieth. But they were largely hidden. In other words, the greatest teachers of the nineteenth and early twentieth centuries were probably not the names that we hear of today, but men and women who are now unknown to us. At the same time it is likely that some of the Teachers who developed a public profile in the nineteenth and twentieth centuries had contact with them.

CHAPTER 22

A Common Source?

There is the possibility of an ancient, guiding 'Tradition behind the Traditions,' running back into prehistory and surviving into Classical and even post-Classical times. We find this idea in George Gurdjieff's references to an ancient Sarmoun Brotherhood. The existence of such a 'Master-Tradition' might explain – for example – similarities between the Mesopotamian and Egyptian Civilizations that extend back into prehistory.

The idea of a Tradition behind the Traditions is suggested, in quite a different way, by Robert Earl Burton's doctrine that *All Schools are One School*. In his early book *Self-Remembering*, Robert Burton[1] clarifies Rodney Collin's concept of 'Higher School' – developing it in such a way that it becomes the foundation for his own later doctrine that 'All Schools are One School.' In Burton's view the Higher School that monitors all of the Great Traditions exists and operates outside of time and space as we know it. From that perspective all of the Great Spiritual Traditions are connected experiments that are being actualized simultaneously.

We mentioned in Book I that – ultimately – the teaching of all Spiritual Traditions must exist in the same point-instant. There is only the one NOW. To remain in the point-instant is to enter a current of higher life, which 'looks back' on everything that comprises the created world. One is then no longer a part of that world but the spectator of a constantly changing 'readout' which includes the person that one thought one was. All of the teachers of the Great Work exist in the same point-instant, and, in some way that we cannot clearly understand, **their source is one**. This single source – Higher School – relates simultaneously to the many different teachings at many different points in time. The different representations of the Gods, the Deities, the Archangels, and the

---

1. See Bibliography.

Bodhisattvas that have been generated by the Spiritual Traditions are different representations of the citizens of one and the same Celestial City.

The teachings of George Gurdjieff and Robert Burton are both, in different ways, reminiscent of the theosophical doctrine of the 'hidden masters,' but we shall here emphasize their difference from that doctrine. The hidden masters of theosophy are like more developed men, or 'super-men,' existing in a kind of 'pantheistic' void. They address men as like beings. But the authors of the drama of School on Earth are not like men. They are beings from Higher School and their existence is independent of the time/space manifold. They do not think in words and concepts, and – unlike the Theosophical Masters – they are directly answerable to a source of authority that is immeasurably higher than themselves. Our fondest hopes for a 'theodicy of Man' do not enter the outer court of their deliberations. It is not that "there is no such thing," but that they see the human experiment in an entirely different way from anything we could imagine. From this perspective the elaborate speculations of theosophy are a kind of wishful thinking that makes the Gods into something we can understand. There is an immeasurable gap between even the highest teachers of embodied humanity and the novice 'twice-born' conscious beings of Higher School – for the latter work as the functioning elements of a transparent Celestial Hierarchy that reaches up to the Absolute.

CHAPTER 23

The Original Religions Lay the Ground for the Prophetic Traditions

The Original Religions created both the atmosphere and the environment for the Prophetic world religions that were to follow. In the Late Classical period, when the Prophetic Religions were at their apogee, there were still four great 'bleed-throughs' to the earlier order of Spiritual Tradition that had established itself in the wake of the last Ice Age. In other words, there were four open channels conducting influence from the previous period: Egypt, Mesopotamia, Central Asia, and India. We note in passing that the Mesoamerican Religion did not provide such a channel through to Prophetic Religion. The Christian Religion, when it came to the Americas, already existed in its developed form, and while it was sometimes adapted to local beliefs, it remained itself unchanged by this. The Mesoamerican Tradition almost certainly went underground at the time of the Spanish conquest. How long it was able to persist before breaking into different forms of Group work is now impossible to determine.

Egypt ceased to have its 'open-channel' role in late classical times, due to the corruptive effect of the Ptolemies and the Roman rulers who followed them. The Egyptian Spiritual Tradition was extinguished under Roman rule, and the Judeo-Christian Tradition became its inheritor. The Death of such a great Tradition is a tragedy, but it is a fact that Spiritual Traditions die all too easily, for – as we noted – they require the leadership of a Man Number Six or Seven supported by the teaching of a number of Men Number Five. The conditions under which such an arrangement can be tolerated in a host Civilization are always tenuous. Having said this, we acknowledge that the School of the Tarot may have been a direct survival of the ancient Egyptian teaching. We also know that the Sufi schools and the Cathedral Builders had access to the Egyptian esoteric keys and symbols, which they probably acquired from the School of the Tarot and from the other hermetic 'survivals' of the Egyptian teaching that existed in their time.

Mesopotamia The Tigris-Euphrates river basin accumulated a body of ancient teachings – Sumerian, Chaldean, and Magian – that were later transferred to the Sufis. As with Egypt, many seeds were sown, but after the Classical Period the Mesopotamian influence was indirect.

Central Asia The Ancient Shamanic-Taoist Traditions preserved a continuity with the prehistoric Shamanic practices. These Traditions were active in both Central and Eastern Asia. They eventually broke into different forms of Group Work but maintained a very high level of yogic technique. These techniques easily combined with and fertilized other forms of esoteric work.

India remained a fertile ground for esoteric work through to modern times, where one layer after another of religious teaching was laid down. The original Vedic/Vedantic Tradition, which was continuous with the prehistoric Aryan Tradition, persevered from one millennium to the next, and remained an active source and reference point for other Traditions to follow.

The Egyptian, the Vedic, and the Mesopotamian Spiritual Traditions probably all preserved something of the original understanding of the Cosmos of Man. These Ancient Faiths had an enormous effect on the Prophetic Religions of the historical period – Abrahamic, Zoroastrian, Mosaic, Buddhist, Christian, and Muslim. But, at the same time, we must emphasize that each of the Prophetic statements represented an original re-casting of the relation of Man to God.

❧ BOOK IV ❧

The Age of the Prophets

There is a veil drawn over the time of transition from the Age of the Original Religions to the Age of the Prophets. Many sources speak of a Great Flood or of God expunging a decadent humanity. This is not the place to speculate on the Flood, for which a range of theories have been advanced. It is quite possible, however, that the practice of the Original Religions had, over the centuries, gradually descended, and that – as a consequence – a rupture occurred between the Work of the Traditions and the practice of the Religions. As a result of this rupture Dead Religion displaced Living Religion, and humanity itself became an intractable medium to the Gods. It was no longer capable of sustaining the vital link to the cosmos one above or of generating the consciousness required to stabilize Creation.

We will recall that the Original Religions inherited the vision of the Unity of Organic Life from Shamanism, in a form adjusted to an agricultural society. In each case there is the same ritual acknowledgment of all the cycles to which organic life forms are subject. In the Original Religions this developed to include the worship of a host of fertility deities, and in the popular form of the religion people made contractual relations with these individual deities. This they did through sacrifices intended to ensure good harvest, good marriage, good progeny, and so on. These practices can easily develop to the point where they obscure the One God, who transcends both Man and Nature. In this way Man's efforts to replenish his communal life through the propitiation of Nature can gradually obscure the renewal of his spiritual being in the Eternal Present. Once this process has begun there is a very strong tendency for Man to fall back on the simple unity with Nature that he had known in the past – and in this context the ancient heritage of Shamanism, particularly in the form of the practice of magic, would come alive.

We speculate that, as the Religions became increasingly a means of securing basic human needs, the Work of the Traditions became increasingly separate from them. The major themes of the Story of Man were increasingly forgotten, and the hour of the Great Prophets came ever closer.

CHAPTER 24
The Veil Lifts

Each of the Prophets – Abraham, Zoroaster, Moses, Gautama Buddha, Confucius, Jesus Christ, and Muhammad – made their appearance on the stage of history in a radical break from the religious life of their time. The Prophets are more than enlightened beings, they are the direct servants of Higher School, which is itself in direct service to the Absolute. The great prophetic statements are the most definite record we have of the intervention of Higher School in history. The lives of the Prophets are each, as it were, a signature: a permanent impress on the life of humanity. We will begin, then, with the life of each of the Prophets. These lives provide the context for the great prophetic statements, which have had such a formative influence on mankind. The Prophets are unique amongst religious teachers, in that their message is directed to all levels of society, as each level is able to understand that. At the highest level there is the unbroken depth of presence that spawns Spiritual Traditions, and even multiple Spiritual Traditions. At the lowest level there are religious rituals, restrictions on diet, and specific rules related to marriage and family life. The Prophet's message produces contradictions at every level on which it is received, and it creates even more acute contradictions in the relations between the different levels. The firm moral injunctions that are given to a community in need of guidance will contradict the direct demand on initiates to free themselves from bondage to conventional morality. Jesus ruthlessly attacked the Pharisees for a faith grounded in the adherence to Judaic law, but within a generation the apostles were working out a set of moral rules for the Christian community, which would inevitably be taken as a measure of faith. The Buddha – more than any other Prophet – taught unqualified openness, but within a generation many of his follows were attempting to define their spiritual identity in terms of a specific set of ascetic measures. And any rule that is given a community will cease to be relevant in the same way over an extended period of time.

All of these contradictions are unavoidable, because – ultimately – the level of the Absolute is an enigma to Man. But to have a humanity connected to that level, by however fine a thread, is worth any amount of confusion that might be created in the process. The contradictions inherent in this relationship cannot be resolved by the unqualified acceptance of rules, but by some understanding of the relationship between the form of the Prophetic message and its invisible essence. Where there is even the trace of such an understanding, there is a humanity that stands in some working relationship to its original source.

The field of tension that we have described is the medium of the Prophet, who, working in the light of the Divinity, is tasked with accomplishing the impossible in a very limited period of time. Having outlined the life of each of the major Prophets, we will outline their teachings, and finally examine the Prophetic Traditions that emerged from these teachings.

CHAPTER 25

The Prophetic Religions

A Prophet is the direct representative of Higher School on earth. He is a Messenger sent to humanity, who has been asked to relinquish all of his personal interests and concerns and to give himself to communicating the prophetic word. He is not simply a man compassionately trying to educate his fellow men; he is a man with very specific demands made upon him, who in turn makes demands on all the men and women who are able to respond to his teaching. It is in these circumstances that the Prophet re-states the lost measure of Man.

The Prophet is an enigma; he *is* a man but he is a different *kind* of man from the rest of humanity. He is an individual who realizes and manifests the 'all possibilities' of the human race. He is stationed in World 6, in a relation to World 3. He is on the boundary of creation and the uncreate, at the very origin of things. In having realized the 'all possibilities' of Man, he has become – to a degree – an incarnation of the archetypal Man originally created from Higher School.[1] He is thus a universal prototype for all men and women, who is capable of understanding all different types of men and women as variant expressions of himself.

An important dimension of the Prophet's role is that of renewal; he is capable of renewing Mankind's relation to a Higher Level, and so changing its relationship to all that went before. In that regard he is usually a reformer. The Prophet identifies false teachings and false beliefs and re-states – for the people of his own time – the true relation of God to Man. Abraham, Zoroaster, and Moses all spoke against polytheism, the problem not being polytheism itself but the 'externality' of polytheistic religious practices. The Buddha spoke directly against Dead Religion and the rigidified social forms that were part and parcel of it. Jesus spoke against Dead Religion, so emphatically that

---

1. See Glossary entry for 'Higher School.'

he was crucified for it. Muhammad spoke against both polytheism and Dead Religion, in such a way that he brought persecution to his followers. In every case the Prophet re-states original truths which have been distorted and forgotten in the course of time.

But the most important aspect of the Prophet's role is that he is a man who has achieved a level of development that allows the Gods to make direct demands on him. He is capable of serving the Gods, and the Gods are hard masters. A Prophet can only be understood, therefore, by understanding the level that he serves. Logical mind, the guiding light of our own age, is almost entirely wanting in this capacity, and thus the thinkers of our own age have a very weak understanding of prophetic truth.

The prophetic statements were the third of the three great dispensations given from the Gods to Mankind: the first dispensation was the great Prehistoric Spiritual Traditions of the 'Golden Age,' when communication between Man and Gods was open; and the second dispensation was the teaching of the Original Religions that came with the development of agriculture. It is likely that, to a larger degree than we can know, the Traditions – under the guidance of Higher School – carefully created the context for the role of each Prophet. With the coming of a Prophet there is, then, a realignment of the Spiritual Traditions and a realignment of the relation between Spiritual Tradition, Living Religion, and true Civilizational Order – toward the completed form of the Pyramid of Man.

Indeed, the figure of the Prophet affects humanity on many different levels. Each of the Prophets launched a Spiritual Tradition and a World-Religion at the same time, one encased within the other. Additionally, each of the Prophets either launched a new civilization or transformed the civilization which was to be the carrier of the prophetic religion.

We can make these generalizations about the role of the Prophet:

1. He restates the inner teaching at its highest level.

2. He re-casts the outer teaching to conform with the inner teaching.

3. He may give general directions of life, appropriate to a particular people at a particular place and time. These 'rules' or prescriptions generally correct established

customs which contradict the outer teachings of the new Religion, such as human sacrifice, the use of narcotics, or slavery.

4. He may be the agent of a particular historical task, and make requirements on his followers in relation to that task, as Moses asked the Israelites to leave Egypt and settle in Canaan. These tasks are often the means of transforming the inner life of the people connected to the Prophet.

5. He may bring out and emphasize one or another of the potentials of Man mentioned at the beginning of this book, as Zoroaster emphasized Man's potential to 'complete' Nature or as Muhammad sketched out the plan for a civil society compatible with the Great Work.

What makes the role of a Prophet unique is that all the circumstances of history conspire to amplify his teaching and his influence. The prophets are indeed archetypal men. We consider these three names: Jesus, Buddha, and Muhammad. Each one of these men has been dead for more than a thousand years, yet every person on the planet knows them. With the exception of those men and women who, for a few decades, loom large in the public eye, there are no comparable figures. This level of impact is not something that one man, or even a community of men, can choose to create. In other words, the influence of these men is not the result of brilliant marketing programs conceived in ancient times or of successful conspiratorial attempts to re-write history. *The pattern of history itself conspires to bring these men into relief*, and here we have the link to the plan of Higher School. The Prophets are, in some way, important or central to humanity.

At the same time, each Prophet is limited in what he can achieve. He can only succeed to the degree that the civilization which is the context for his work provides him with fertile ground. Adult life is short, and the Prophet has only a few decades in which to make his statement. No matter how gifted or how powerful a figure he is, he will be able to achieve little in a resistant medium, and so the civilization which receives him must be ripe. The Prophet's priority must be to communicate the mass of his message to those closest to him, and then to guide, inspire, and elevate the people of his immediate community. His first mission can never be to state abstract-universal truths, but to state those truths that can be told his own people in his own time. In other words, while the states of consciousness that the Prophet transmits are universal, and the teachings designed to enable those states are close to universal, the religious teachings and the general context that the Prophet creates cannot be universal in the same way. His teachings and his actions must be understandable to the people of his own place and time. To this extent he is the servant of history, and to the degree that he becomes purely abstract and universal, he will fail in the more important aspects of his mission. The limitation given by historical context means that the Prophet's teaching will have its limit in the line of time. Eventually the Prophetic Religion will become encased in the religious and political ideologies that grow around it, and a break will occur with the Spiritual Tradition that is internal to it. The result of this – in almost every circumstance – will be a Dead Religion, and a Civilization without cultural ideals. At a given moment the legacy of the Prophet will then turn into its own opposite, and the Prophet's very name can be used against the principles that he stood for in his life. The Prophet is the best and greatest that we have, but for the reasons given above, no one Prophet can tell the Story of Man.

There is another aspect of the Prophetic teachings which we must mark. There is a relation between the teachings of the Prophets and the process of History, which marks a profound break with the teachings of the Original Religions. The Prophetic Religion departs from both the mythic unity of Man and Nature and the cyclical vision of time that was characteristic of the Original Religions. In accepting the teachings of the Prophet, Mankind leaves the comfort of a 'golden age' of perpetual renewal and enters the terrifying line of irreversible time. The Prophet thus makes requirements on Man – both psychological and social – and at the same time gives him a measure by which to gauge his performance. History begins. And prophetic time is not without its own meaning. We remember that the Prophet has been tasked by the Gods to task Mankind. Prophetic time is thus imbued with the promise that Mankind may, in fulfilling these tasks, form a new relationship to the Higher Cosmos that contains it. In some respects the teaching of the Buddha is an exception to this. The Buddha did not teach irreversible time, but his teaching does emphatically break with the mythical time of the ancient religions which preceded it. The radical egalitarianism of Buddhism broke sharply with the 'eternal patterns' of Vedic society. The shock of the Buddha's teaching was – in its own time – the same or greater than that of Abraham, or Zoroaster, or Jesus, or Muhammad. Additionally, while the Buddha did not task his followers with as many 'external' requirements, he tasked them with a teaching which affected all aspects of life and which promised a new level of life for Mankind. While we cannot go into a more detailed analysis here, there can be no doubt that the Buddha is *the same kind of phenomenon* as the other prophets.

We have emphasized the break between Prophetic and pre-Prophetic Religion. But with respect to any particular Prophetic Religion there will be a degree of continuity with the pre-Prophetic period, just as there was continuity between Shamanism and the Original Religions. The 'ritual of renewal' that is found in all Original Religions (such as, the 'rite of passage' rituals surrounding birth, puberty, and death) is preserved in relation to the acts of the Prophet and the symbolism connected with those acts. Examples of rituals of renewal in Prophetic Religion would be the Catholic *Eucharist* or the Orthodox *Synaxis*. But the rituals of the Prophetic Religions clearly go beyond the simple inclination to propitiate fertility deities, to make sacrifices intended to produce particular results, or – on the lowest level – to broker deals with the Gods. The rituals of the Prophetic Religions were not intended to propitiate or to secure a safe future, but to represent the eternal principles governing human behavior, and to represent them as being internal to what we are. In the Orthodox *Synaxis* members of the church receive consecrated bread and wine, understood to be the body and the blood of Christ. This is a renewal of the moment in which Christ asked his disciples to share his body and his blood at the Last Supper, just a few days before his crucifixion. His 'body' and his 'blood' are Worlds 12 and 6, and he shares them in a moment when his teaching reached the level of World 3, so linking the 'body' of the Church to an utterly transcendent reality. In the 'renewal' of the prophetic rituals our external actions are related to an eternal measure, and we are held accountable to that measure. For the inner circle of a Prophetic Tradition, however, the return to the "zone of the sacred" can only be the entry and re-entry into the state of prolonged presence.

There are also parallels of a different kind. Just as the Original Religion had the tendency to fall back into a kind of expanded 'agricultural' Shamanism, so the Prophetic Religion had a tendency to fall back into the 'shamanic' forms of the Original Religion. An example of this would be the religion of Baal, which Moses spoke against time and again. The religious impulse to propitiate the deity, to 'broker deals with nature,' to bring to an end droughts, famines, and plagues, reappears time and again. After the passing of the Classical Age and the all-pervasive backdrop of the Original Religions, the same impulse recurs in the tendency to create a hagiography of saints, one for every occasion and one for every aspect of human life – who can then be propitiated for special favors. Such rituals relieve Man of the pressure of finding the 'measure' within himself; in other words, of awakening the latent Higher Self.

In the Prophetic teaching God calls upon a people to rise to a new level within themselves and, at the same time, to achieve particular external goals or to accept

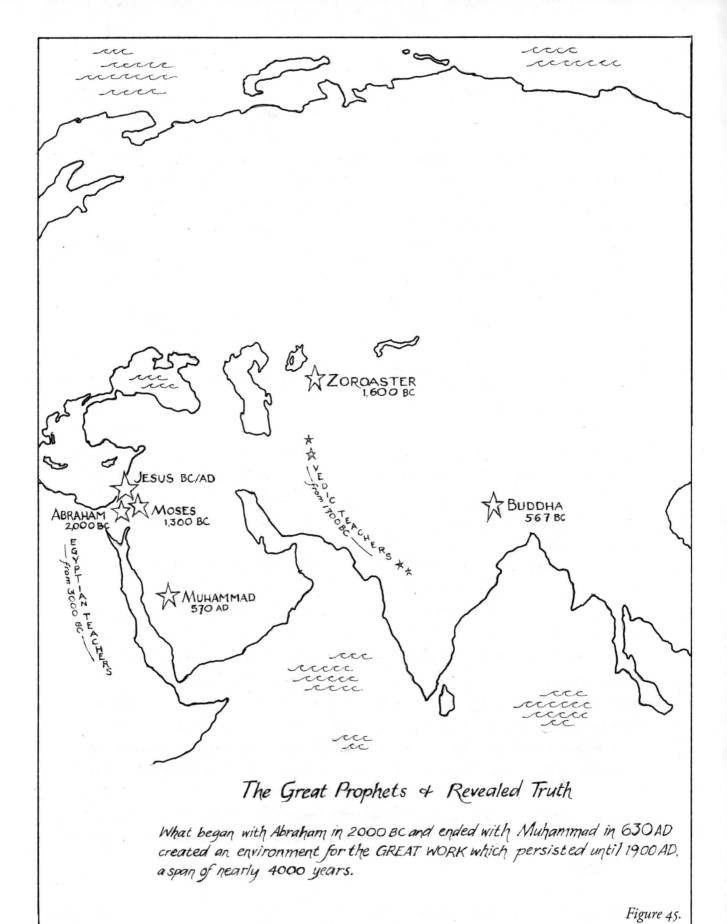

ZOROASTER
1,600 BC

VEDIC TEACHERS
from 1700 BC

JESUS BC/AD

BUDDHA
567 BC

ABRAHAM
2,000 BC

MOSES
1,300 BC

EGYPTIAN TEACHERS
from 3000 BC

MUHAMMAD
570 AD

The Great Prophets & Revealed Truth

What began with Abraham in 2000 BC and ended with Muhammad in 630 AD
created an environment for the GREAT WORK which persisted until 1900 AD,
a span of nearly 4000 years.

Figure 45.

certain disciplines. The transcendence of Nature is thus taken a step further; the New Religion demands a new way of life. Where the Original Religions placed a single God over Nature, the Prophetic Religions took Man completely out of the cyclical time that rules the natural order. The Prophet takes Man into irreversible time, and *presence must be now sustained in that time*. Virtue is now independent of changing circumstances, and with that comes an ever-greater pressure to achieve the Cosmos of Man.

With respect to the Buddha, who did not explicitly attempt to teach in irreversible time, his negation of the decadent Brahmanic Religion and the artificial strictures of Brahmanic society is nevertheless clear. He stated human potentials objectively, not in terms of the traditional religious myths, and he gave the paradigm of social order in the Kalachakara Tantra.

In our story, the outline of the Prophetic Traditions that follows will historically overlap the material given in Book III. This is because new prophetic teachings often arose within the older Spiritual Traditions and ran parallel with them. The seeds of the prophetic period were sown deep within the previous period, and, at the same time, the influence of the pre-Prophetic period continued well into the Prophetic. Yet the two remain distinct.

The first of the great Prophets was Abraham.

CHAPTER 26

Abraham

Abraham was born in the Sumerian city of Ur in about 2000 BC and migrated to Canaan to become a patriarch to the Israelite, Ishmaelite, Edomite, and Amorite peoples. He taught that there was only one God. Little is known about his actual life and the substance of his teaching, as the written records were heavily revised in ancient times to provide a historical framework for monotheistic belief.

The Islamic, the Christian, and the Judaic Traditions each defined Abraham as a Prophet for their peoples. These traditions also characterized the many lesser figures who succeeded Abraham as prophets. While the successors in Abraham's line may have reached a high level of development, they did not play the formative role that we attribute to a 'Prophet' in this study.

Abraham's monotheistic teaching was presented in opposition to the polytheistic beliefs of the Chaldees, the Babylonians, the Canaanites, and the Elamatics. It is interesting that the line of teaching that followed from Abraham's son Ishmael descended, over the centuries, into an anthropomorphic polytheism very similar to that which Abraham criticized. Muhammad, several millennia after the death of Abraham, invoked his own Prophetic teaching against the polytheism that had developed amongst the descendants of Ishmael – who were, of course, the Arab peoples. Apparently the original elements of Abraham's monotheistic teaching were discernible to Muhammad in the corrupt polytheism that had developed from it. In the same way, it is almost certain that the Mesopotamian polytheism that Abraham originally spoke against was also polytheism at the level of popular religion, which had developed out of the practical requirements of the Babylonian imperial system. The core teaching of the Spiritual Traditions is ever the same. The inner teaching of the Mesopotamian/Sumerian Tradition continued through the Babylonian period and survived Abraham, just as the esoteric teaching of the ancient Egyptian Tradition survived both Abraham and Moses.

It is not unusual for Spiritual Traditions to run parallel in this way and to contradict each other in their outer form, as the inner teachings may be strengthened and vivified by the uncertainty so created. The conflict itself places pressure on people to distinguish the real from the unreal. We see moments of direct conflict between the Egyptian and the Hebrew Traditions, the Vedic and the Buddhist Traditions, and the Christian and the Islamic Traditions.

About four centuries after Abraham the second Prophet came. He probably taught in Central Asia, and he taught without any reference to the teachings of his predecessor.

CHAPTER 27

Zoroaster

Zoroaster was born in Persia in about 1600 BC and was a *Magus*, or a member of the ancient Aryan/Avestan priest caste. On having received the revelation that defined him as a Prophet he began to teach, and his teachings immediately divided the *Magi*. In the wake of this split, those *Magian* priests who accepted his prophecy became the priest caste of the new religion. Thus, just as Jesus divided the Jews, Buddha divided the Brahmins, and Muhammad divided the Quraiysh, Zoroaster split the ancient Aryan priest caste in a long forgotten drama.

What we do know is that – like Moses and Muhammad – Zoroaster initiated an inner teaching, a community to support that teaching, a religion, and a civilizational order within his lifetime – the blueprint for the Pyramid of Man. He is, then, the 'classical example' of a Prophet.

While we do not know the form of the early Zoroastrian community, it seems to have been similar to the Vedic community in being guided and governed by its priest caste. The *Magi* themselves were to persist for more than two millennia, and survived by many centuries the social order of which they were originally a part. We have clear records of the *Magi* as a governing priest caste into the time of Sassanid Persia (224-651 AD), and if that is true the Zoroastrian Religion was a Living Religion for a very long time.

Zoroastrianism had a marked resurgence in and about 600 BC, in the time of the Achaemenid line of Persian kings. There were probably great teachers amongst the *Magi* at this time who converted the Achaemenid princes. This new generation of teachers initiated a 1200-year period in which Zoroastrianism was the dominant faith of Persia, Mesopotamia, and much of Central Asia. As evidence of its spread, the traditional Religion of Tibet – the Bon Religion – is a blend of Zoroastrianism and Shamanism. It was only the coming of Islam, some 1200 years later (651 AD), that brought to an end this period.

Zoroaster's teaching is the first Prophetic teaching of which we have a clear record, and when the Story of Man is done his teaching will surely be known as one of humanity's greatest teachings. Zoroaster distinguished his teaching from the prehistoric polytheistic religion of the Aryan peoples by stating that there was only one God, of which all other Gods were derivative. Many of the sacred texts carrying these teachings were destroyed at the time that Alexander the Great invaded Persia and many more when the Muslims conquered the same territory nearly a millennium later. Thus we have the Zoroastrian teaching only in traces, and only as reconstructed at later points in time. Nevertheless it is clear that the Zoroastrian theology was formative in the line of western Spiritual Traditions, powerfully influencing the Judaic, Christian, and Muslim theologies. For this reason we will outline it in detail, as it gives the flavor of an age, and – indeed – of the whole Prophetic period.

The Zoroastrian name for the Deity is **Ahura Mazda** (Figure 46). He represents Being in its purity: endless light, omniscience, and goodness. Ahura Mazda had, from the time before he created the visible universe, an antagonist who was chaos, evil, and death: endless darkness and a bent will. His name was **Angra Mainyu**.

The existence of Angra Mainyu, as an element of the universe which Ahura Mazda had not himself willed, is an indication of Ahura Mazda's finitude. He is not, then, what we have called the 'True Infinite,' for there is a Being that is 'outside' of him. Ahura Mazda is infinite in Time but not in Space. He is nevertheless a fully actualized Being, and has immanent within himself that transcendence of Being, which we have, in Chapter 2, called 'Beyond-Being.' Angra Mainyu, his opponent, is the 'flaw' in the universe; he is that aspect of Not-Being which is not encompassed within the will of the Deity. He is the active opponent to cosmic harmony.

While both of these spirits are in themselves finite, Ahura Mazda's transcendence of Time allows him to know the measure that exists between himself and Angra Mainyu, both within and outside of Creation. The story of the cosmic struggle between these two figures is, then, the story of the perfecting of an imperfect God; it is the transcendence of perfected Being to the True Infinite. This transcendence yields what the Zoroastrians

Figure 46. **Transcendent Ahura Mazda**

called the 'Final Body' of the Universe. We note that this is a particular perspective on the triadic nature of the Absolute.

In the immaterial state of the universe that pre-existed creation, there was no context in which Ahura Mazda could resolve his struggle with Angra Mainyu. His evil opponent was formless and therefore invisible to him. In order to resolve this struggle Ahura Mazda brought Creation into being. This he did in two stages. The first stage, known as *immaterial creation*, included the archangels, the angels, and the spiritual embryos of all men. The second stage was known as *material creation:* a transparent world radiant with light and beauty, perfect in every detail.

Angra Mainyu, being inherently evil, immediately attacked material creation. But the moment he entered it he became tangible and visible within it, and once having entered he was unable to extract himself. Thus, from the moment Angra Mainyu entered material creation, the struggle between Ahura Mazda and Angra Mainyu was defined and had to be worked through to its conclusion.

On having entered Ahura Mazda's perfected Creation, Angra Mainyu merged his evil will with it, and so corrupted it. He turned sea water to salt, he created deserts, he withered plants, he released plagues, poisonous snakes, and insects, and sullied fire with smoke. Yet the original perfection of Creation continued to shine through. It was still

Ahura Mazda's Creation. The Zoroastrians say that after Angra Mainyu's attack, Creation became a 'mixed' place.

Locked within Creation, Angra Mainyu became finite in both Space and Time, yet he became very powerful within this time/space manifold. Creation is, then, his natural home: he is the Dark Lord of the Temporal World for as long as it lasts.

Ahura Mazda, on the other hand, as the incarnation of Eternal Being and Eternal Wisdom, can never be at one with the physical universe he created. The core of his being exists independently of it, and he himself cannot violate the laws by which it functions. For this reason he cannot make a direct assault on Angra Mainyu within Creation. From one point of view Ahura Mazda is trapped on the outside of Creation while Angra Mainyu is trapped within it, their relation being determined by the very laws that govern Creation itself.

Thus, in order to engage in the struggle with Angra Mainyu, Ahura Mazda needs assistance. This brings us to the third figure in the Zoroastrian macrocosm, **Spenta Mainyu**. Spenta Mainyu is the self-revealing activity of Ahura Mazda within Creation. He reconciles the unchangeable nature of the Deity with the change and transformation of Creation. He also makes Creation into a cosmos, or organized hierarchy, to the extent that is possible. From another point of view he is the manifestation of Ahura Mazda's creative will – his goodness, his compassion, and his justice – within Creation. It was Spenta Mainyu who created both the Archangels who manage Creation (the six **Amesha Spentas**) and the retinue of Gods who serve them (the **Yazatan**).

This brings us to the final character in the cosmic drama, **Man**. Humanity, unlike the Archangels and the Gods, was the direct creation of Ahura Mazda, and was intended, from the very beginning, to be his ally in the struggle against Angra Mainyu. What immediately strikes our attention is that Man exists in that part of the universe where Angra Mainyu is lodged and where the force of his illusion is most compelling. Thus Mankind serves Ahura Mazda on the lowest level of Creation and is most directly subject to the onslaughts of the Dark Lord. Angra Mainyu is freely able to enter the minds and hearts of men and to sustain himself in their being. He is, indeed, the very Master of Illusion. He can control the medium of Man's imagination and use all his involuntary thoughts, feelings, and sensations to subvert prolonged presence. With the intervention of Angra Mainyu, Man's internal world becomes, quite literally, a battleground. And the battle is a desperate one, because Angra Mainyu can only win this struggle by corrupting the souls of men.

THE STORY OF MAN

But, as we know, Man was created with special possibilities. Where the being of Spenta Mainyu, the Archangels, and the Gods, is fixed, the being of Man is open to change. He is a microcosmos with the capacity for self-transcendence. While the legions of the Gods exist in a balance of stalemate with Angra Mainyu and his demonic retinue, Man – by achieving a transformation of consciousness – can change that balance and so change the Universe.

Man's duty is to represent Ahura Mazda and to confront the forces of Angra Mainyu through good words, good thoughts, and good deeds – summing to a Good Life. The good words, good thoughts, and good deeds are, in their highest form, the activity of the Steward, and the Good Life is a life of prolonged presence. Each man begins under the power of Angra Mainyu's deception and, to that extent, is subject to the most acute internal divisions. Angra Mainyu is known as 'the Lie,' and he manifests himself in every man and woman as a series of negative thoughts, feelings, and sensations. Rather than fighting each of these individually, the Good Man transcends them by creating a presence that is beyond them.

On the level of the inner teaching Angra Mainyu represents the Black Queen, and he is present in all men through the Black Queen that resides in each one. Spenta Mainyu, Ahura Mazda's lieutenant within Creation, is present in men as the White Queen. Ahura Mazda himself is present in the human sphere as the potential for fused Higher Centers. At the same time, and on a different scale, he is the representative of the emergent Absolute Spirit. The Zoroastrian Creation is, then, the battleground of 'Truth,' and the principal field of battle is the human psychology. Truth is the White Queen, the Nine of Hearts serving consciousness. 'The Lie' is the Black Queen, the Nine of Clubs utilizing imagination, negative emotions, and identification to keep Man locked in the world of the Lower Self.

In fighting on the side of Ahura Mazda, Man is fighting both for the conscious aspects of creation *and* for his own immortality. Should Ahura Mazda conquer Angra Mainyu he will complete himself as Absolute Spirit, becoming infinite in both Time and Space. He will then achieve what we have called the 'True Infinite' and what Zoroaster called the 'Final Body.' He will know his own opposite, and can 'will' cosmos on every level of Creation, so creating a coherent Macrocosm. Man will then take his place in the Final Body. Thus, in the Zoroastrian view, Man is in a very bad situation; the Deceiver has entered the most intimate places of his being, but, at the same time, he is called to a very high destiny. None of the later Religions have given Man such dignity.

We will now outline the Zoroastrian view of the drama of human history, which brings out – in a most remarkable way – what Zoroastrianism passed on to Judaism, Christianity, and Islam. It is, at the same time, a remarkable map of what was to follow for humanity over the next three and a half millennia.

Zoroaster taught the doctrine of the Four Ages of Mankind. Each age lasts for approximately 3000 years.

1) THE FIRST AGE: This begins with Ahura Mazda and Angra Mainyu co-existing in eternity. At a certain point Angra Mainyu attacks Ahura Mazda directly. He is defeated and Ahura Mazda casts him into an abyss where he remains for the next 3000 years. Ahura Mazda is aware that his victory is not permanent and that Angra Mainyu will recover himself.

2) THE SECOND AGE: During the 3000 year span to follow Ahura Mazda calls into being **1) immaterial creation** including Spenta Mainyu and – through him – the six archangels, and **2) material creation** including sky, water, earth, plants, the primeval ox, and the primeval Man – named 'Gayomart.' Gayomart lives for the duration of the Second Age as a pure spirit. After having created him, Ahura Mazda proceeds to create the pre-existent souls (or *fravahrs*) of all men. These fledgling souls have the choice of staying forever in the embryonic state or entering material creation and assisting in the struggle against Angra Mainyu. Only if they consent to descend to earth to carry on the struggle will Ahura Mazda be assured the final victory. The *fravahrs* of all men choose to serve Ahura Mazda in this way. Their choice gives them a special potential and at the same time opens them to great suffering.

In the meantime Angra Mainyu, at the bottom of his abyss, is not inactive during the Second Age. He creates six archdemons to counter the six archangels, and an entire demonic retinue to confront both angels and men.

3) THE THIRD AGE: Angra Mainyu, having recovered from his overthrow, attacks Ahura Mazda's Creation. Gayomart is deceived by one of Angra Mainyu's demons, who appears as the negative side of the eternal feminine, the 'Great Whore.' As a result of accepting her false teachings, Gayomart is forcefully incarnated, with only thirty more years to live. Before he dies his seed mixes with the earth, and from the earth arise Mashye and Mashyane, the first couple, from whom the human race is descended. The *fravahrs* of all men then incarnate through the descendants of Mashye and Mashyane. Thus Mashyane, the 'second woman,' is the opposite of the Great Whore, and represents the positive side of the eternal feminine. We note here the idea of an evil 'first Eve,' which is found in both the Sumerian/Babylonian and early Israelite traditions. In both of these traditions her name is Lilith. It is the 'second Eve' that is the mother of Mankind.

While the now-embodied Gayomart begins to suffer his thirty years of incarnation, Angra Mainyu befouls material creation, bringing rot and decay where there was once perfection. The Gods respond to this, and, at the behest of Spenta Mainyu, enter material Creation and do battle with Angra Mainyu and his demons. The Gods rout the forces of the Dark Lord and cast them into Hell, which is the physical underworld of material creation. Thus, while Angra Mainyu remains the master of Creation, he is confined in the part of it called Hell, and from this part he cannot escape.

When Gayomart finally dies, humanity continues in the 'mixed' and partially spoiled environment of earth, and Angra Mainyu ceaselessly attempts to corrupt it – for the control of the *fravahrs* of Man is essential to his ultimate success. The now-embodied human souls are, however, able to remember the vows they gave at the beginning of the Second Age, and so gather themselves to resist. But they do not yet have the True Religion, and over the next 3000 years Angra Mainyu is able to corrupt them.

4) THE FOURTH AGE: Ahura Mazda then sends Zoroaster, the first Prophet (*Saoshyant*) with the True Religion, to help Mankind. A regeneration of the human race occurs. But because Angra Mainyu rules Creation, he is again able to introduce corruption into both the True Religion and Mankind. By the end of a thousand years the situation has reached a point where Ahura Mazda sends a second *Saoshyant*, and the same pattern repeats on a slightly higher level. At the end of the second thousand years Ahura Mazda sends a third *Saoshyant*, and at the end of the third thousand-year span he sends the final *Saoshyant*, who is the ultimate redeemer of Mankind.

Before completing the review of the prophecies concerning the Fourth Age, which is our own age, let us review the situation of humanity.

Man is a finite being within Creation who dies at the end of a relatively short life. At the end his life he faces a Judgment, which occurs at the peak of the legendary Mount

Hara, on the span of the Chinvat Bridge. This is a bridge between Earth and Heaven, which has one end on the top of the sacred mountain and the other end on the road that leads up to the Sphere of Sentient Being, where the Angels and Archangels abide.

After the death of man's body his soul is brought to face judgment at the Chinvat Bridge. At the entry to the bridge are three angels who weigh the soul's merits, and in the chasm below the bridge Angra Mainyu's demons wait for those who are judged and found wanting. The bridge itself spans the abyss of Hell. For the good souls the bridge is broad and even, and the good man passes easily to the far side where he enters the realm of Endless Light. The wicked man finds the bridge as narrow as a knife edge, and after a brief struggle pitches headlong into the gulf below.

The individual judgment of the soul at death is a prelude to the Final Judgment at the end of time, when the 'body' of the man is resurrected and reunited with his soul. And here we must pause.

What, exactly, does it mean that the body is reunited with the soul?

It is useful to clarify the original understanding that was behind the idea of the 'resurrection of the body,' because this Zoroastrian teaching was directly taken up by both the Judaic and the Christian Religions – and in each case the original meaning was soon lost in the teachings of the popular religion.

The Zoroastrian teaching actually describes a relation between three different 'bodies.' Firstly there is the **physical body**, which is on a level with the system of Nature. Secondly there is a **psychological body**, internal to the physical body, which is the source of virtuous 'thoughts, words, and deeds.' In an evolving being these 'thoughts, words, and deeds' are directed towards spiritual development. Finally there is the **soul** (*fravahr*) which is the Higher Centers, whether **1)** in their latent form, or **2)** fully awake and self-sustaining. We can distinguish these three bodies more clearly with the help of the Hermetic terminology introduced in Book III.

> THE PHYSICAL BODY is comprised of cellular matter. It is the 'carrier' or vessel for both the psychological body and the soul. In itself it differs little from the body of an animal.

> THE PSYCHOLOGICAL BODY is comprised of molecular matter in an unconcentrated state. The finest molecular matter of the psychological body is what we have called in Chapter 3 'essence.' As a person becomes more focused in 'good thoughts, good words, and good deeds,' that molecular matter becomes more concentrated and refined, and – at the same time – the person develops a

Steward. When a person has truly entered the Work of the Steward, that work penetrates his essence and so becomes a part of it. In this regard, both essence and the Work of the Steward are part of what we have called the 'psychological body.'

THE SOUL is more difficult to characterize because it exists in both latent and active states.

- **When the Higher Centers are latent**, the soul is passive. The physical body and the psychological body then govern our behavior. In this condition we are subject to all the deceptions of Angra Mainyu.

- **When the Higher Centers are active,** the soul becomes the control center of both the psychological body and the physical body. In this condition we are no longer deceived by Angra Mainyu and can repel him. When the soul is in an active state, it is comprised of **1)** fine molecular matters, concentrated to the point of self-consciousness, and **2)** electronic matters. At the level of the active soul, the electronic matters have begun to concentrate the molecular matters.

The Zoroastrian idea of RESURRECTION, then, pertains to both the psychological body and the soul. It is the regeneration of **1)** the latent Higher Centers, which move from their passive to their active state, and **2)** essence, which fuses with the active Higher Centers, and **3)** the Steward, which becomes passive, entering service to the now-active Higher Centers.

When the Higher Centers fuse with essence – with the person who we really are – the result is a kind of identity which did not exist before. The Higher Centers are no longer latent abstract/universal principles, but are united with a particular human essence to form a new angel in the retinue of the Ahura Mazda. Our physical body is incidental to this process and unaffected by it. When the physical body finally expires, it is relatively easy for the 'resurrected' elements of the psychological body to disengage from it.

When the physical body of a person who has not experienced resurrection dies, things are a little more confusing. The unprepared individual will be unable to voluntarily disengage his molecular field from the physical body because his identity is too deeply rooted in it. Yet circumstances force the disengagement, leaving that person in a disoriented state. Most people are nevertheless able to retain a kind of molecular identity based on the natural cohesiveness of essence. Essence can carry forward the essential qualities (and weaknesses) of the person's molecular being into another form or embodiment.

When an individual has been engaged in the work to awaken Higher Centers, the molecular energies connected with that work will penetrate essence and so carry forward with it into a sphere where the work can be renewed and completed – for the soul (*fravahr*) must be in its active state before the individual can pass the Chinvat Bridge and enter the realm of eternal life.

For every human being we can say – with some confidence – that when death comes, the physical body simply decomposes. It does not carry forward into any other sphere, but returns to Nature as 'compost.'

Thus the idea of the resurrection of the body at the end of time, which the Judaic and Christian religions took from the Zoroastrian, refers to the molecular (psychological) body. The idea of the resurrection of the physical (or cellular) body is simply absurd. It expresses a need, deeply felt at the level of the popular religion, to preserve familiar reference points.

We note that these ideas concerning the 'psychological body' and the 'soul' parallel exactly the Egyptian concept of the interdependent development of the *ba* and the *ka*, as that is elaborated in the *Amduat* and *Journey Forth by Day*. The obvious influence of the Zoroastrian myth on the Judaic and Early Christian Traditions would have been supported by the similar Egyptian teachings, which were a 'background' for initiates of both Traditions.

Having said all of this, we must remember that – for Zoroaster – the resurrection of humanity is not an end in itself, but the means to a greater end. Should humanity achieve resurrection and all of the *fravahr* enter the active state, they would become completely inaccessible to Angra Mainyu and, at the same time, capable of fighting him. This would change the cosmic balance between Good and Evil in such a way that the defeat of Angra Mainyu would become a real possibility.

As we noted Zoroaster explained that he was the first of four *Saoshyants*. From the time of his coming, Mankind had the help of both a Prophet and the true teachings. After his passing, Mankind will also have the *Magi* – his priest caste – who are never completely corrupted and who are always preparing themselves to serve the new *Saoshyant* in the age to follow. We may remark that something like this did indeed occur.

In the Zoroastrian myth each of the three prophets to follow will come at a time when Mankind has reached a state of moral degeneration, such that it appears to have fallen to the forces of evil. Each *Saoshyant*, when he comes, adds a particular teaching or a particular development of the True Religion which is appropriate to its time in history. Each one represents the qualities which fit with the next stage of the Ahuric way. The final *Saoshyant* in the series is *Soshyans*, and it is he who leads Mankind in a definitive struggle against Angra Mainyu.

We come, finally, to the prophecies of the Fourth Age. The *Soshyans* redeems Mankind and prepares the way for the resurrection of the dead. He does this in three stages.

1. He regenerates the True Religion and defeats the forces of Angra Mainyu within Creation.

2. He then raises the bodies of the dead from all the ages past and reunites them with their souls. The resurrected bodies, both those who were resurrected from Heaven and those who were resurrected from Hell, must then endure a three-day ordeal – passing through a river of molten metal. This is the final punishment that the damned must endure before they enter into the Eternal Light which is the ultimate destiny of Mankind. The ordeal causes no discomfort to those who have already passed the test of the Chinvat Bridge.

3. In the final stage of this cosmic drama the *Soshyans* leads a regenerate humanity against the forces of Angra Mainyu and succeeds in pushing the entire demonic army outside of Creation where, finally, Ahura Mazda and the Archangels can directly engage them. Each Archangel seizes his own predestined enemy and destroys him. Finally only Angra Mainyu remains. It is now Ahura Mazda's turn to make a sacrifice of his opponent, to ensure the utter elimination of the fundamental flaw in the universe.

Ahura Mazda now becomes the True Infinite, achieving the Final Body forever and ever. The universe becomes a coherent macrocosm, integrated with the will of Ahura Mazda.

It is remarkable to consider that this vision of Man in the universe was first presented 3,600 years ago, before Moses, before Buddha, before Christ, and before Muhammad. It contains a remarkably accurate symbolic representation of the difficulties of pursuing the Great Work on this level.

The Zoroastrian Religion and Civilization differ from the Judaic, the Christian, and the Muslim in that Man is seen as the completion of nature and the natural manager of the medium of Organic Life. Both Creation and the Order of Nature are the work of Ahura Mazda. While they have been corrupted by Angra Mainyu, who continues to exercise a certain control over them, they are intrinsically beautiful and good.

Evil, in the Zoroastrian Creation, is not a mystery nor is it identified with matter. The world is unjust because its ruler, Angra Mainyu, is corrupt. The material world is itself the handiwork of God, and Man's role in it is to co-operate with Nature and to lead a virtuous life in service of God. Zoroastrianism is unusual in the extent to which it makes a positive virtue out of agriculture. Both the Earth itself and Nature are viewed as sacred. Agricultural activity makes the earth fruitful, strong, and abundant, as it must be in order to resist the onslaught of the Enemy – who brings blight and rot. The Zoroastrians took green to be a sacred color, representing the oasis in the desert that Man has surrounded with irrigated lands. It is both the symbol of a virtuous life and of the inner harmony of Man and Nature.

Man is also given quite specific guidelines as to creating the ideal human community. And so we see that, in order to follow the Ahuric Path, Man has been asked to create cosmos out of chaos in every aspect of his life.

As we noted, there was a great renewal of Zoroastrianism in the time of the Achaemenid Kings (late seventh and sixth centuries BC), and it became – at that time – the religion of the Persian Empire. The Zoroastrian teaching survived the conquests of Alexander (334-326 BC) and continued through the periods of Macedonian and Roman rule. With the rise of the Persian Sassanids (228 AD), there followed a full revival of Zoroastrianism as the state religion, and this continued until the time of the Islamic invasion in 642 AD.

Over the centuries different tendencies developed within Zoroastrianism. In the fourth century BC, after the Persian conquest of Mesopotamia, a sect of the *Magi* integrated the teachings of the Chaldeans, who carried the ancient Sumerian/Babylonian Spiritual Tradition. This lead to a refinement in the understanding of the first triad of the Absolute and a moderation of the dualist tendency which had developed in the interpretation of Zoroaster's teachings. There was a clarification of what we have called the relation between Being, Not-Being, and Beyond-Being, which emphasized the transcendent nature of Beyond-Being. From this refinement the Zurvanite sect of Zoroastrianism arose. Zurvanism, the confluence of two Traditions, survived for 1,400 years, disappearing from the pages of history in about the tenth century AD. The markedly dualistic teachings of Mani (c. 250 AD), which developed into the Manichaean religion, were also inspired by Zoroastrianism – but while Manichaeism was derived from elements of Zoroastrianism, it developed quite independently from it.

For the story of the third Prophet in our series, we return to Egypt and the Holy Land.

CHAPTER 28

Moses

Moses, the prophet who defined the Judaic Tradition, lived in and about 1300 BC. The Hebrew peoples had an existing relation to the previous Prophet Abraham and to the line of patriarchal figures which succeeded him, but they had neither the Religion nor the Civilization that they acquired during the time of Moses. The early Judaic scholars carefully assimilated the pre-Mosaic past into post-Mosaic Judaism, but the world of Abraham was a different world from the world of Moses, precisely because the Hebrews had not yet undergone the severe formative process of which Moses was the human agent.

Moses belonged to one of the Tribes of Jacob, which emigrated to Egypt in about 1700 BC. The Hebraic tribes had been in Egypt for about 400 years by the time that Moses was born. They were a client population to the Egyptians and assisted them in their vast construction projects. The Hebrews were not enslaved to the Egyptians, and while their fortunes changed with the changes in the Pharaonic order, they were not oppressed to the degree that tradition sometimes represents. They certainly experienced phases of prosperity, and individual Hebrews rose high in the hierarchy of Egyptian society – as the Old Testament makes clear. By the time of Moses' birth the Hebrew peoples would have been deeply permeated by Egyptian culture.

Almost certainly a circle of Hebrews made a connection with the Spiritual Tradition of ancient Egypt. They themselves, as the 'children of Abraham,' would have sustained the First Work and may have supported a Tradition of their own. The recognition between true initiates is immediate, and communication – when it occurs – is sincere and open. The Egyptian Tradition probably had the most direct connection to the teachings of prehistory of any Spiritual Tradition of its time. In other words it had, through direct transmission to prehistory, a vision of the responsibility of Men to Gods and a corresponding vision of the realization of human potential on all its different levels. The

Hebrews almost certainly incorporated certain of the Egyptian teachings into their own religion.

The story given in the Old Testament is that Moses left Egypt after having slain an Egyptian overseer who was beating a Hebrew worker. He fled to the Sinai Peninsula where he was, after a time, able to establish himself as a shepherd. Revelation came to him in the deserts of Sinai, as stated in Exodus 3:1-4.

> And the angel of the Lord appeared unto him in a flame of fire out of
>   the midst of a bush:
> and he looked, and, behold, the bush burned with fire, and the bush
>   was not consumed.
> And Moses said, I will now turn aside, and see this great sight, why
>   the bush is not burnt.
> And when the Lord saw that he turned aside to see,
> God called unto him out of the midst of the bush,
> and said, Moses, Moses.
> And he said, Here am I.

The burning bush that is not consumed is presence prolonging itself through time, independently of the four lower centers. Moses comes into Being and states: "Here am I." There is, then, Being sustaining itself without reference to anything on earth: "I am that I am." Here, suddenly, is the Higher Intellectual Center and the unity of Man with the level of creation that controls human destiny.

In his revelation Moses was commanded to lead the Tribes of Israel out of Egypt, to the 'Promised Land' of Canaan. He was also, on another level, commanded to lead the Israelites out of slavery to the Lower Self.

These two tasks were to become one in the line of time, as Moses guided the Israelite people through a series of tests and trials that were to last more than forty years. In guiding the Israelites through these trials Moses became the human instrument for the creation of a nation. As the father of the Judaic Civilization he communicated to the Israelites their laws and their conventions. As a Prophet of the Judaic Tradition he provided the Covenant which unites men in the presence of God.

On having received the revelation at Sinai, Moses immediately returned to Egypt, where he was accepted by the Israelites as a Prophet and as their natural leader. Moses then began to negotiate with the Pharaoh for the release of the Israelites from Egypt. The Pharaoh listened to Moses' requests, but refused to grant them. Upon this refusal, a succession of ten plagues fell upon Egypt, and at the end of the tenth plague the Pharaoh gave Moses permission to lead the Hebrews out of Egypt. This departure was called the *Exodus*, or the 'going out.' Within a few days of having given Moses this permission the Pharaoh changed his mind, and sent an army after him. The Egyptians came upon the Israelites by the Red Sea and cornered them at the shoreline. Moses then raised his staff and caused the sea to part, allowing the Israelites to pass. But when the Egyptians followed after them, the sea closed over them. The crossing of the Red Sea is symbolic of the Israelites permanently and irreversibly leaving behind the Egyptian/Abrahamic/pre-Mosaic culture that they had known for so many centuries.

Having escaped the Egyptians, the Israelites went into Sinai, where Moses was fated to receive the Ten Commandments. He first received the commandments by direct oral transmission and was then instructed to climb Mount Sinai to receive the stone tablets on which they were written. Moses climbed Mount Sinai in the company of a circle of elders, and instructed his older brother Aaron to stay behind with the remainder of the Israelites. While Moses and the elders made their expedition, the Israelites asked Aaron to make a visible image of the God who had delivered them from Egypt. Aaron made them the image of a Golden Calf, and many of the Israelites worshipped this image. When Moses returned from Mount Sinai with the tablets, he rebuked the Israelites for worshipping the idol, and a general upheaval broke out. Moses then demanded: "Who is on the Lord's side? Let him come unto me." The tribe of Levi, including the ambiguous figure of Aaron, immediately came to Moses, who then "ordered them to go from gate to gate slaying the idolators." The slaying of the idolators is almost certainly a symbolic representation of the 'slaying' of the thoughts and feelings that corresponded to the pre-Mosaic culture. We see the Israelites, under enormous pressure, having left the life that they knew, in a state of complete insecurity, being subject to the first of a series of defining trials.

The Israelites eventually passed through Sinai and came to the country of Canaan, their prophesied destination, which was – as the prophecy had stated – a rich and fertile land. But it was already inhabited by the Canaanites and the Amalekites, and many of the Israelites feared to force entry into that land. When the Israelites refused to advance on Canaan, Moses stated that, because of their fear, the children of Israel would not enter Canaan for forty years, until all of those who had refused were dead. In other words, he would not lead them into Canaan at that time but back into the desert. That evening there was a rebellion against Moses, and on the following morning an army of the Israelites marched on the Amalekites and the Canaanites. They were sharply repulsed. This incident of self-will followed by retribution was the beginning of forty years of desolate trials that the Israelites were to face wandering in the desert. This episode demonstrates that the Israelites were not psychologically ready to 'enter the Promised Land'; they had not yet internalized the Great Work that Moses had given them. The 'forty years in the desert' was the painful completion of this process.

Finally it came time for the Israelites to enter the 'Promised Land.' Having crossed the border into Canaan, Moses saw that Hebron, its chief city, was too strong for them to take, and decided to go east around the Dead Sea, passing through the lands of the tribes of Edom, Moab, and Ammon. These peoples were considered by Moses to be the descendents of Lot, and thus Hebrew peoples whom the Israelites were forbidden to attack.

Having passed through the lands of the Edomites, Moabites, and Ammonites, the Israelites came upon and defeated the Amorite people and occupied their lands. They were then able to acquire the land of Bashan, which bordered on the land of Moab. The King of Moab, not unnaturally, feared that the Israelites would attack him also. The Moabites were worshippers of Baal, a traditional god of all Semitic peoples, and the religion of Baal still exercised a strong attraction on the Israelite people. It was one of the original pre-Prophetic Religions, in a close link with the older shamanic practices; as such it offered all the comfort of established ritual, and its practices gave 'contractual' assurance with respect to crops, to rain, to fertility, and to personal well-being. In the Old Testament it represents Dead Religion, divorced from Tradition, in service to secular interests.

The King of Moab asked his chief prophet Balaam for advice with respect to the Israelites. Balaam made three divinations, and each one favored the Israelites – which was disconcerting both for himself and the King. Balaam then went to the neighboring Midianites, who also feared the Israelites, and gave them instructions as to how to defeat them. They were to send beautiful women into the Israelite camp, to seduce the young men into practicing forms of idolatry. The Midianites were successful in their attempt, and the incident was called the Midianite seduction. Phinehas, the grandson of Aaron, saw what had occurred and acted promptly to put an end to it, slaying the two most prominent offenders. A plague then came to the Israelites, killing many thousands of them. Moses proclaimed that the remainder of his people had been saved only because Phinehas had averted the wrath of God, and he gave Phinehas and his descendants the pledge of everlasting priesthood. The Israelites then attacked and conquered the Midianites.

This episode was yet another in the series of tests given the Israelites to separate Living Religion from Dead Religion: the test of the Exodus, the test of the Golden Calf, and the test of the first entry into Canaan. In the records given in Exodus, Leviticus, Numbers, and Deuteronomy, these tests were numerous, severe, and prolonged. The Gods arranged trial after trial to impact different segments of the Israelite population in different ways, according to the level at which each group was working. We can only imagine the pressure that Moses was under, as the human agent of this process.

When the Midianites were finally defeated, and the Israelites were ready to settle Canaan, Moses was warned that he himself would not be permitted to lead the people of Israel across the river Jordan but would die on the eastern side. He then assembled the tribes and delivered his parting address, in which he recapitulated the law that God had given them. He pronounced his blessing on the people, climbed alone to the top of Mount Nebo, looked at the country spread before him, and died at the age of 120. In Deuteronomy 34.10 it states: "And there arose not a prophet since in Israel like unto Moses, whom the Lord knew face to face." The 'face to face' metaphor – which appears in almost all Traditions – is a reference to World 3.

In dying before the Israelites entered the Promised Land, Moses mirrored the sacrificial action of the Steward, which ceases its activity in order that Higher Centers may emerge. Like Moses, it ends its patient and untiring effort in perfect humility.[1] Moses was followed by a line of prophets, who replicated his role in relation to the Israelite people, but whose vision was never so complete or authoritative.

The Covenant (*berith*) between God and the Israelites had been established with the giving of the Ten Commandments at Sinai. It was given form by the laws which Moses gave the Israelites before they entered Canaan. These laws were based on the Commandments, but extended to what were called the Ordinances and the Judgments. The latter dealt with all the issues of social life, including taxation, marriage, divorce, inheritance, military service, and slavery.

The idea of the Covenant is important in the Judaic Tradition, and it must be understood in its most general meaning. In the pre-Mosaic world, God had attempted many times to establish a Covenant with Man, and there had been a series of failures – beginning with the 'fall' of Adam and Eve, continuing with the great flood, and concluding with the dissipation of the teachings of Abraham. After these failures God turned to a particular segment of humanity, with the idea that they should become a 'kingdom of

---

1. We have described this action, known to all Spiritual Traditions, as the 'Death of the Steward'. See the Glossary entry.

priests.' The Israelites, under the guidance of the Prophet Moses, were *to realize a social order established in accordance with divine law*, and this social order was to be a model for the human race. The term the 'Kingdom of God' was, at that time, understood to mean the community of the Chosen People which had – at long last – taken root in Canaan. To use the language of Chapter 4, the 'pyramid' of Tradition, Religion, and Civilization having been established, there was the hope that a living relationship to the cosmos above the Cosmos of Man could be realized in a particular place by a particular people, and that this could be a model for Mankind.

From the Life of Moses to the Judaic Tradition

The Hebrew settlement of Canaan probably occurred in the years 1250-1225 BC. As the Israelite people attempted to realize Moses' vision in practice, they found themselves beset with many difficulties. There were struggles between the tribes of Israel, and there were problems with the assimilation of the Canaanites – who continued in the traditional worship of Baal. In the beginning there was not an Israelite 'kingdom,' but a cluster of settlements. There was some resistance to the settlers from their neighbors, and there was struggle amongst the settlers themselves. While there was no longer the towering figure of a prophet of Moses' stature, there was still the white heat of the Mosaic vision. Following Moses' injunctions each Israelite settlement formed a Sanhedrin (assembly) to consider religious matters.

We have evidence of this difficult period in the *Book of Judges*. The 'judges' were the elders who interpreted Moses' laws, created new laws as necessary, and passed judgments on the basis of those laws – all with the aim of sustaining the way of life that Moses had shown them. They were, in effect, the principal agents of Civilizational Order. The chaotic 'settlement period' in which the judges played this role continued for a full two centuries. The judges did what they could to preserve Moses' vision, but they were not themselves possessed of prophetic insight. There were certainly minor prophets during this period, such as the prophetess of the *Song of Deborah*, but little is known of their exact role. They did not exist in a defined relationship to a king or leader who could be held responsible for the state of the Covenant – because there was no such person. Nevertheless, the prophets of the first centuries were, in some way, a mirror to the people, a symbol of the Covenant, and a spur to right action.

Finally, in 1020 BC, Saul was able to establish himself as the single king of the twelve tribes of Israel, and David and Solomon followed directly in his line. This new phase saw the development of a stable relation between the Prophets and the Kings. This stability was necessary because **the Covenant** between God and Man – given by Moses – cannot be the work of the Kings alone; it must equally reflect the presence and the words of the Prophet. The role of **the Prophet** was then defined as *the guardian of the vision of the Covenant*. The last of the Hebrew judges, Samuel, became the first of the Prophets of the Kingdom of Israel, acting as the prophetic counterpoint to King Saul. The Prophet Nathan then acted as counterpoint to King David, and the Prophet Ahijah, to King Solomon. The rule of King David is generally seen as the time when the Kingdom achieved a mature and coherent form, and David himself is taken to be the author of the Psalms of the Old Testament. The new relationship between the Prophets and the Kings was symbolized by the 'First Temple' that David's successor Solomon constructed in Jerusalem as a center for the transmission of religious truth.

The achievement of **the Kingdom** brought with it a popular 'triumphalism,' an anticipation of the 'great day' when the Israelite nation would lead the other nations of the earth by setting an example for them. This is the idea of 'the Empire,' based on the assumption that the Mosaic Covenant could become a covenant for all humanity. The Prophets, in the meantime, carefully warned against false confidence, and against corruption in government.

The tensions between the tribes, controlled and moderated under Saul and David, came again to the fore in the years after Solomon's death. The ten northern tribes refused to accept Solomon's son, Rehoboam, as king, and took another, named Jeroboam, to be their king. The Kingdom of the Hebrews was thus divided into Israel in the north and Judah in the south, and the two remained, for some time, in a more or less open state of war.

With the split of Israel and Judah in the ninth century the idea of the 'Empire' could no longer be sustained. The triumphal period was over, and there came a period of acute questioning. The code-makers and historians returned to their sources to re-establish standards of order by which deviation from the Covenant could be measured. The Prophets, on their part, no longer referred to the preparation for Israel's day of victory over the nations but to 'a terrible day of judgment' that would be visited by God on the Kingdoms of Israel and Judah. The attitude of the Israelite and Judaic Kings towards the teachings of the Prophets would then determine the fate of those nations in relation to the judgment.

After the split between Israel and Judah, the corrupt Omride dynasty came to power in Israel, and with the Omrides came a re-emergence of the cult of Baal. The prophetic community of Israel spoke against the Omrides, and at a certain point the Omride King Ahab had the entire community massacred. A single individual, by the name of Elijah, survived.

Having escaped with his life, Elijah did not cease to challenge and confront the priests of Baal. At one point, when their public sacrifices had failed to bring to an end a long drought, he himself asked God – before the people – to accept the sacrifice. The sacrificial fires immediately lit and the rain began to pour down. In this way he proved the priests of Baal false before the people. Hearing of this incident, King Ahab's wife Jezebel threatened Elijah, and he fled into the wilderness.

After a day's travel Elijah stopped to rest under a juniper tree. An Angel came to him in his sleep, and told him to 'wake and eat.' He awoke and found food at hand. He ate and slept again. On awakening for the second time (and on having established a certain stability in World 12) he was told that he must make a forty-day journey to Mount Horeb.

Elijah travelled forty days and forty nights to reach the base of the mountain, and there sought shelter in a cave (Kings 19:19). A voice then called to him, asking him to step outside the cave and 'stand before the Lord.' He did so, and immediately experienced a violent wind, the shaking of an earthquake, and the searing heat of fire, but he did not experience the Lord God in any one of these. What this passage describes is the chaos that is created in the lower centers in the immanence of Worlds 6 and 12. And then, suddenly, in the wake of this chaos, Elijah was possessed by 'a sound of gentle stillness.' This is the stillness of World 6: a stillness deeper and more profound than any known in the normal course of life. In the New Testament this is described as 'the peace that passeth all understanding.' After he had spent a time in this space of stillness the voice said to him, 'What doest thou here, Elijah?' There was a presence within the space; the 'here' that Elijah had entered was the place in which men can communicate directly with the Gods, and from this place the God delegated to guide Elijah gave him the task of returning to Israel to re-establish the line of prophetic succession.

On his return Elijah was accepted as the prophet to King Ahab of Israel and, in time, became the prophet to his successor King Ahziah and to King Josaphat of Judah. In this role he acted as a direct representative of the Gods and as the opponent of both Dead Religion and material culture. At the same time he was 'the great restorer' of the vision of the Covenant.

After the reforms of Elijah, sometime in the early eighth century, there came a change of emphasis in the teachings of the Prophets. Their messages were directed not

THE STORY OF MAN

so much to the Kings as to the people themselves, showing in what way they were at fault. The idea of restoring the Covenant was still central to their message.

The next major Prophet in this line was Isaiah, a prophet of Judah who was active in the years 740 to 698. He prophesied for fifty-two years, during the reigns of Uzziah, Jotham, Ahaz, and Hezekiah. During Isaiah's youth the King of Assyria conquered Israel, and then threatened Judah. Before undertaking his attack the Assyrian King proposed, in 720 BC, a particularly compromising alliance. King Hezekiah of Judah, on considering the terms of this alliance, decided to oppose the Assyrian King. As an immediate result Judah was conquered by the Assyrian armies. Despite this defeat Isaiah called on King Hezekiah to continue his resistance against the seemingly insurmountable Assyrian forces. In a great act of faith Hezekiah gathered his troops and marched on the Assyrians. It states in the Book of Kings that 'the judgment of God now fell on the Assyrian army and wiped out 180,000 of its men.' The House of Judah had affirmed the word of the Prophet and so strengthened the Covenant. Isaiah stated that under these conditions the 'chosen people' and the 'knowable divine plan' required nothing for its embodiment but the 'unbounded trust in the House of Judah.' Thus, in the time of Isaiah, there was still the idea of the transformation of the Judaic Civilization and the restoration of the Covenant.

It is said of Isaiah that, like Elijah, he 'had a vision of the throne of God.' Moses, Elijah, and Isaiah represent, then, the connection of the Judaic civilization to World 3.

For the next 150 years, from the defeat of the Assyrians in 750 BC to the early sixth century, there was relative stability. However, in 623 BC the Babylonians allied with the Egyptians and drove the Assyrians out of Babylon. In 586 BC the Babylonians, under Nebuchadnezzar II, conquered first the Assyrians and then both Judah and Israel. The Babylonian onslaught culminated in **the Destruction of the First Temple** and most of the city of Jerusalem. There followed what has been called the period of **Babylonian Exile**, where the Babylonians deported the Jews *en masse* to Babylon. Estimates of the emigration vary, and some say that the majority of the population remained in place, with significant groups dispersing to Egypt and the surrounding Levant. Whatever the case, both the leaders of the Judaic Civilization and its line of Prophets were transported to Babylon. This was the beginning of the Jewish diaspora. The forty-seven years of the Babylonian Exile were a disaster for the Judaic Civilizational Order, but – amazingly – they brought renewal for both the Spiritual Tradition and the Living Religion. From the standpoint of Religion, the captivity was seen as a punishment given by God and as a challenge to the Israelites to change themselves internally. At the same time, the Men of the Tradition found themselves in contact with the initiates of the ancient Mesopotamian Spiritual Tradition, for Babylon was the seat of the Chaldean priest caste. This ancient priest caste was continuous with the Sumerian Tradition, which extended back at least 3,000 years. The *Song of Solomon*, which is a product of that period and which has a different flavor from anything that came before, very likely reflects a contact with the Mesopotamian Spiritual Tradition through its extension, the Chaldean priest caste. This would be the second contact of the Judaic Tradition with an older Spiritual Tradition, the first being the contact made possible during the long years of the Egyptian captivity. In each case, at the level of Civilizational Order there is conquest and control, at the level of Religion marked tension, but at the level of Tradition there is easy recognition and a natural communication of 'first things.'

We must emphasize that the contact of the Judaic Tradition with the Mesopotamian Tradition did not result in any cultural or religious syncretism. The Prophet of the period of Babylonian Exile was Ezekiel, who was as active in Babylon as his predecessors had been active in Judah and Israel. It was a period of concentration and refinement of the Religious teachings, which began to be written down and which produced, amongst other things, a more theologically precise monotheism. During the period of captivity theology, law, and custom were also consolidated and made coherent.

The destruction of the First Temple, with the resulting geographical dispersion of the Jews, was shocking in its implication for the Judaic Civilization. Scripture had ordained very specific guidelines for the worship of God: worship was to be conducted in only one sanctified location – the Temple in Jerusalem – and any decentralization was prohibited. For the first time in the life of the Jewish Nation there was no Temple in Jerusalem and the Jewish people themselves were decentralized. There were now three distinct centers of population: one in Babylon, one in Judea, and one in Egypt.

Ezekiel, recognizing the implications of this, prepared both the Spiritual Tradition and the Living Religion for the post-exilic stage, where there was to be no independent Judaic Civilization. He actually redefined the vision of the Civilizational Order, showing how the Jewish people might still be 'chosen,' in accordance with Moses' original Covenant, without their 'Promised Land' of Canaan and without their own appointed king.

A clarification is necessary at this point. From the time of the Assyrian conquest (722 BC), the temporal Kingdom of Israel disappeared from the pages of history. From the time of the Babylonian conquest (586 BC), the line of the Kings of Judah was broken, and consequently the second of the two kingdoms that were once Moses' Israel came to an end. During the Babylonian occupation of Israel and Judah, the term *Judea* came into use to describe the 'place' of the Jewish people, which is no longer a sovereign kingdom. The term *Judea* continued in this usage through late classical times, thus: Babylonian Judea, Persian Judea, Hasmonean Judea, Herodian Judea, and Roman Judea. Over the centuries the use of the terms *Israel* and *Judea* becomes inexact. The term *Judea* is often used to refer to the physical 'place' of the Jews while the term *Israel* – which never went out of use – is used to refer to the Civilizational Order, linking back to the connection of the Jewish people to Elijah, Moses, and Abraham.

The period of Babylonian Exile ended in 539 BC when the Persian King Cyrus (the first of the Achaemenid line) conquered Babylon. As a result of his victory the Persian Empire immediately absorbed the entirety of the Babylonian Empire – including Israel and Judah. Cyrus was a Zoroastrian, and his generation had produced some of the highest Magi since the time of the Prophet himself. The Magi had a tolerant attitude towards Judaism, and Cyrus promptly ended the Babylonian captivity, allowing the Jews to return to their homeland. It is estimated that 40,000 out of a total of 100,000 exiles did so. While the Jews were free to return to what had once been Israel and Judah – now 'Persian Judea' – to pursue their traditional faith, many remained in Babylon. One remarkable result of the period of exile was that Aramaic, the language of the Babylonians, became the spoken (not the sacred) language of the Jewish people. Babylon itself was to remain a center of Judaism, and was to contribute significantly – in late classical times – to the creation of the Talmud, one of the major sacred texts of the Judaic Tradition.

With the end of the Babylonian captivity the Israelite Civilization found itself in a state of disorder. There was a leaderless population centered around Jerusalem, perhaps 50,000 exiles remaining in Babylon, and different groups of refugees dispersed throughout Egypt and the Levant. Of the Jews dwelling in Persian Judea it is estimated that 50 percent practiced the 'new' post-exilic monotheism, and 50 percent practiced the old Canaanite religion. Under these conditions there could not be the pyramidal relation of Tradition, Religion, and Civilization that had previously existed. The Prophet could no longer show how the Covenant, as realized in the Kingdom – divided by faith and private interest of different kinds – measured against the original Covenant given the Israelites by Moses.

The renewal of the Jewish Religion that occurred during the period of the Babylonian captivity was the one compensation for this general disorder, and the return of the exiles, with their scrolls of sacred scriptures, saw the emergence of scribes and sages as the leaders of the Jewish people. Where before the captivity the Israelites had been organized by tribe, at the cost of great contention, in the period following they organized themselves by clan – with only the Levite tribe continuing in its special role as a priest caste.

Despite the effective destruction of 'the Kingdom,' the work of the Hebrew Prophets did continue in the period after the captivity, but the statements of the post-exilic Prophets became – increasingly – bleak existential appeals to humility, acceptance, and faith. For the fifth-century prophet Malachi, the judgment threatened by the eighth-century prophets had already come to pass. It was now part of the very texture of history. Thus by the fifth century BC, the Civilizational Order had been damaged (or significantly disordered in relation to its own archetype), the Religion greatly strengthened, and the Tradition placed in a situation that was both tense and ambiguous. It is amazing that the Civilization itself survived, and was to survive in the context of conquering 'host' Civilizations for many centuries to come – Persian, Ptolemaic, Seleucid, Roman, and, after the final stage of the diaspora, Byzantine, Islamic, Ottoman, and British. This survival reflects the strength of the Spiritual Tradition and the perseverance of the Living Religion within the Popular Religion.

The renewal of the Religion was symbolized by the creation of **the Second Temple** in Jerusalem. The original Temple – King Solomon's Temple – had been destroyed by the Babylonians in 586 BC. With the return of the exiles and the reconstruction of the city of Jerusalem, the Temple was rebuilt. It soon became a center for the transmission of the oral teachings that were at the heart of both Religion and Tradition.

Under 'Second Temple' Judaism (520 BC to 70 AD) the priests of the Temple establishment practiced a theologically rigorous monotheism. As we noted, in 520 BC about 50 percent of the Jews in Persian Judea practiced the old Canaanite religion. At the level of the Jewish popular religion there were a variety of cults: El, Asherah, Yahweh, and Baal. Cult worship itself was now supplanted by a highly developed monotheistic theology, which acknowledged the existence of both angelic and demonic figures in a defined relation to the Absolute. It was under the Second Temple that the authority of religious scripture was established, the practices of circumcision and Sabbath-observance initiated, and the institution of the synagogue made central to religious practice. Public readings of the 'scrolls' of *Torah*, which had been written down during the Babylonian Exile, created a new sense of unity and renewed trust in the priests themselves. The Covenant was now 'seen' rather than simply heard, and could be read by anyone at any time. It was in this period that the study of the *Torah* began in the synagogues, initiating a process that would allow the Jewish Religion to become both more personal and more portable. Thus, from 'the people of the Temple,' the Jews redefined themselves as 'the people of the book.' This period also saw the passing of the dual institutions connected with prophet and priesthood and the firm establishment of the institution of the Sanhedrin – or regional council of elders – which decided questions pertaining to religious law.

It was from this point that the *Torah* took on a central role in Jewish life.

The Torah is the five books of Moses, or *Pentateuch*. It also comprises the first five books of what is known to the Christian World as the *Old Testament: Genesis, Exodus, Leviticus, Numbers,* and *Deuteronomy*. According to the Judaic Religion the Torah was revealed to Moses at Sinai, but most modern scholarship agrees that its composition took place over many centuries, as a compilation of writings and oral tradition from different sources. Most modern scholars see the final composition as having occurred in the period immediately after the Persian conquest of Babylon in 539 BC. This would be a reflection of the intensity and focus of inner work that occurred within the members of the Spiritual Tradition during the period of the Babylonian captivity.

During the two centuries of relatively tolerant Persian rule that followed the Babylonian captivity, the Israelites were exposed to the influence of the Zoroastrian Spiritual Tradition. This would be the third ancient Tradition to which Judaism was exposed. This influence is revealed in the collection of sacred texts that later became known under the name of the *ƒ*, a secret oral tradition that was published and made public only in the thirteenth century AD. The Zoroastrian idea of a 'dark side' of creation – the sphere of influence of Angra Mainyu – is found in the Kabbalistic concept of the *Sitra Achra* (the 'other side'). The Zoroastrian idea of an evil 'first Eve' (Jahi) through which the 'dark side' enters humanity is represented in the Israelite figure of Lilith. Just as Jahi is the direct agent of Angra Mainyu, Lilith is the direct agent of Samael, the angel of the Dark Side. Here we see again that the Spiritual Traditions, at their points of contact, possess a kind of universality: a shared perception of the oneness of Mankind in relation to the level that is above it.

The sympathetic period of Persian rule, in which the Second Temple teachings took form, ended as abruptly as it had begun in 332 BC, when Alexander the Great conquered the Persian Empire. Judea, as a part of the Persian Empire, was annexed into Alexander's empire. After the death of Alexander in 323 his conquests were divided amongst his chosen followers, the *Diadochi:* the Antipatrids in Greece and Macedonia, the Attalids in Anatolia, and the Seleucids ruling most of the rest of the Levant. The lands of the Israelites were integrated into the Ptolemaic Empire, which was based in Egypt.

When the Seleucid king, Antiochus III, defeated Ptolemy V in 200 BC, Judea became part of the Seleucid Empire. This was yet another disaster for the Jewish people: the Second Temple was looted, its services stopped, and Judaism effectively outlawed. Both the Religion and the Tradition were forced underground.

After thirty-six years of Seleucid rule (in 164 BC) Judas Maccabee led a revolt which established the Maccabean line of priest-kings. These kings ruled Judea from 164 BC to 63 BC. The Maccabean revolt was, initially, a civil war between the Hellenized Jews and Orthodox Jews within Judea, which, with the victory of the Orthodox Jews, turned into a war of national liberation. The Maccabean Kingdom saw a certain reconstitution of the Civilizational Order, but it does not seem that this took place under the direct guidance of the Spiritual Tradition. Instead there was an ever-increasing connection of the Jewish Religion to Jewish ethnic identity – rather than to the universal esoteric practices of the First and Second Work established by the Judaic Tradition. Under these circumstances God (as the Absolute) ceases to be the God of all men – as this was understood at the beginning of the First Temple period – and effectively becomes the God of the Jews, all other Gods being simply false. The Religion, then, becomes ever more directly connected to the instinctive sense of identity that inheres in any ethnic grouping. The persecution of a race of people who share a single religion often produces this result, which is usually expressed – at least in certain elements of the population – in a tendency towards extremism or fanaticism. This extremism, when it occurs, is directly associated with the Religion, but never with the Tradition.

In the time of the Maccabean Kings, the work of the Second Temple, in all its different aspects, and on all its different levels, was accelerated. The Maccabeans had indeed won a 'second independence' for Judea, but they had won it in the power vacuum that existed at the end of the Hellenistic period. The rise of Rome and her conquest of the Carthaginian and Macedonian empires sounded the death knell of the independent Maccabean Kingdom.

In 63 BC the Roman general Pompey conquered Jerusalem, and Judea became a Roman province. In 66 AD the Jewish population rebelled against Roman rule, in what was called 'the Great Revolt.' In the first year of the revolt 6,000 Roman troops were massacred. In 70 AD the Roman legions under the Emperor Titus retook and destroyed much of Jerusalem, including the physical edifice of the Second Temple. It is said that a total of 1,100,000 Jews were killed in the siege of Jerusalem, although the Jewish people still continued to inhabit the ruined city.

Titus' razing of the city was a severe reprisal, but not an attempt to destroy Judaism itself – which continued to flourish under the uneven rule of his successor Domitian. The Nerva-Antonine emperors who followed Domitian, Nerva and Trajan, were not at all anti-Semitic, and Hadrian was, at least at the beginning of his reign, sympathetic to Judaism. At one point he actually spoke of rebuilding the Second Temple. Unfortunately, however, Titus' initial act of repression, and his successor Domitian's egocentric style of ruling, had aroused religious extremism amongst elements of the Jewish population. In the reign of Hadrian, a Jewish leader by the name of Simon ben Kosiba became the focal point for a channel of messianic extremism. The Jewish sage Akiva ben Joseph gave Simon ben Kosiba the new name of Simon *bar Kokhba*, meaning 'son of a star.' He was presented to the people as the messiah and connected with the Star prophecy verse from Numbers 24:17: "There shall come a Star out of Jacob, and a Scepter shall rise out of Israel, and shall smite the corners of Moab, and destroy all the children of Seth." But Simon bar Kokhba was neither a conscious being nor a prophet; Higher Centers were not active in him. From the standpoint of the Spiritual Traditions it is a great crime for a man without any working connection to a higher level to put himself forward as a messiah. For a people to follow a false messiah, driven by ambition, spiritual pride, and the simple affirmation of racial identity, is to depart from the spirit of the prophetic injunctions that were given in the beginning.

In 132 AD the **Bar Kokhba revolt** broke out, and in the following year the Emperor Hadrian reconquered Judea and razed the city of Jerusalem to the ground. This was the definitive end of the original Judaic Civilizational Order and the defining moment of **the Jewish diaspora**. The land of Judea was almost completely depopulated. The majority of the Jewish population were either killed, exiled, or sold into slavery. Judea itself was merged with Syria and renamed Syrian Palaestina. Jerusalem was renamed Aelia Capitolina and Jews were forbidden to live in that city.

The remaining Jewish population resettled in many different parts of the late-classical world, eventually sorting into three major groups: **the Ashkenazic Jews** who immigrated to Central and later Eastern Europe, **the Sephardic Jews** who settled in Iberia and later North Africa, and **the Mizrahi Jews**, who were descended from the Jews who had remained in Babylon after the destruction of the First Temple. And, despite everything, a small population remained in Syrian Palaestina.

But this was not the end of Judaism. Its greatness is marked by the fact that it was able to use this appalling repression to regenerate itself. This act of transformation is marked by the *Talmud*, the third major testament of Judaism – after the ancient oral teachings of the *Kaballah* and the First Temple teachings connected to the *Torah*. The Talmud integrated and organized the oral teachings of Second Temple Judaism so that they could be put into writing. The impulse to do this was given by Judaism's loss of a geographic center. Without the physical edifice of the Second Temple – as a recognized focal point of teaching and study – the old system of oral transmission and oral scholarship could not be sustained. The Second Temple teachings were thus put into writing in the centuries that followed the great diaspora of 136 AD (excepting those of the Kaballah). But the Talmud is more than a record of the traditional oral teachings; it clearly addressed the spiritual needs of its own times and anticipated the spiritual needs of the future. It is comprised of two major parts, the *Mishnah* (c. 200 AD) and the *Gemara* (c. 500 AD). Together they comprise sixty-three tractates of over 6,200 pages, consisting of writings on law, ethics, philosophy, customs, history, and theology – and this is the basis for all codes of Rabbinic law.

RABBINIC JUDAISM

With the priesthood of the Second Temple gone forever, the Talmud defines – from that point forward – the Judaism of the diaspora; it signals the beginning of Rabbinic Judaism. It is a document of Civilizational Order that has been – at the very least – influenced by a living Spiritual Tradition. Amazingly, it is without bitterness or resentment; it includes an admission of fault, in the form of a deviation from the teachings of the prophets. Simon bar Kokhba is defined as a false messiah, the text itself refers to 'bar-Kokhba' as 'bar-Kozeba,' a subtle play on the original name of 'ben Kosiba.' Simon 'bar Kozeba' means – literally – Simon 'the son of deception.'

The Talmud was certainly the work of men possessed of foresight and wisdom, but it is hard to tell to what extent it was directly the work of the Judaic Spiritual Tradition. And here, a few words of context and clarification are in place. The books of the *Torah* and the scriptures comprising the Hebrew Bible (*Tanakh*) had been canonized as sacred texts during the period of Persian rule. After this consolidation of the prophetic legacy, many Jews felt that they would no longer produce sacred works; that period was over, and they accepted the fact. Many also came to believe that the period of true prophecy had come to an end, and this belief was strengthened – in the fourth century – with the coming of Alexander the Great's all-encompassing cultural revolution. These changes of outlook were not in any way a weakening of the prophetic legacy; they were rather an inducement to focus and refocus energy on the study, interpretation, commentary, and endless literary refashioning of the sacred scriptures. There is an implicit recognition here that the end of the prophetic period was not at all the end of consciousness or spiritual enlightenment. It was in this framework that the Jewish people developed an amazingly rich literary expression, always grounded in the *Torah* and always ingenious in its interpretation, symbology, and self-revealing humor.

The *Talmud* is the effort of the Jewish people to maintain a 'national' spiritual activity within a state of diaspora that would connect the Religion and the Civilization to all that had been given in the beginning by the Gods, the Prophets, and the originating Spiritual Tradition. The integrity of the *Talmud*, its fundamental balance and its accurate anticipation of future developments, do suggest that the now-ancient Spiritual Tradition was still involved and so survived the holocaust of 136 AD. But if the Jewish Spiritual Tradition survived, it did so 'in retreat' – just as the Egyptian Tradition of the Tarot survived the end of Pharaonic Egypt 'in retreat.' The strategic retreat of the Judaic Tradition is also evidenced by the parallel decision to make the oral teaching of the *Kabbalah* secret, for the context that made these ancient teachings stable (not subject to extremist interpretation) disappeared with the destruction of the Second Temple.

In all of this one sees incredible effort, made with both humility and foresight, 1) to counter the instinctive messianism that had come to the fore in the Second Temple period and 2) to neutralize the despair that followed the destruction of the Second Temple. There is a timeless equanimity in the *Talmud*. It provided a general template that allowed for conscious work, of one kind or another, to continue for more than a millennium.

In sum, the Jews of the second century showed great spiritual maturity in accepting the savage persecutions of their time and engaging in intelligent self-criticism while continuing undaunted in their essential faith. With the publication of the *Talmud*, Rabbinic Judaism became a portable religion, centered around synagogues, with the ultimate scriptural authority of the *Torah*. The Jews kept these books, these laws, and these teachings, and dispersed throughout the Roman world and beyond.

Thus the Living Religion, so firmly entrenched and established, continued, but the links to Civilizational Order had been irretrievably broken. In a sense the Judaic Civilization had 'packaged' itself so that its culture might survive in the context of other host civilizational orders. It appears that this 'packaging' was the work of the now-ancient Judaic Spiritual Tradition, but the history of the Tradition itself – in the centuries following this final diaspora – is hard to trace. It appears that, after a period of time, the Tradition eventually split into different lines of Group work, which remained connected with the Judaic Religion, and to the work of individual conscious beings – who continued to appear and to teach for many centuries to come.

In summary, from the Prophet Moses came a Spiritual Tradition, a Living Religion, and a Civilizational Order. He saw clearly into the archetype of the Judaic Civilization, as that exists outside of time and space, and he acted in such a way that the archetype might be realized. Time and again, under his leadership, we see the testing of the Israelite peoples and the distillation of the different levels of Moses' teaching. We see the unity of Tradition, Religion, and Civilization in the 'white heat' of the Prophetic period. With the passing of Moses, the Kings of Israel and Judah were paired with a line of prophets – down to the time of the Babylonian Conquest. That 850-year span was to have a formative impact on all the western civilizations to follow. The Prophets Elijah, Isaiah, and Ezekiel were each given to see deeply into the archetype of the Mosaic Civilization, and each of these renewed the Mosaic vision of the 'Pyramid of Man.' But in the period after the Babylonian Exile this vision could no longer be sustained – for without the Kings, and without the Kingdom itself, it was impossible to implement.

Ezekiel, the prophet of the Babylonian Exile, actually reformulated the vision of the Judaic Civilizational Order, and during the period of captivity, theology, law, and custom were consolidated and made coherent. With the passing of the centuries, Second Temple Judaism became increasingly textual and formal. It made explicit things that were implicit, which on the one hand is limiting but on the other forces a more correct 'standard' expression. In the period after the destruction of the Second Temple, we see, at one and the same time, the agonizing descent of Civilizational Order and the resolute work of the Spiritual Tradition to prepare the ground for the future. After the destruction of Second Temple Judaism there is again an increase in textual definition and in the development of religious form, to compensate for the loss of an 'external' social context. At this time many of the esoteric teachings are given more sophisticated expression and symbolic representation. We must thank the men and women who did this work. Conscious work undertaken in a time of descent is a special service to Mankind, because it is undertaken – from the very beginning – without ambition or illusion.

What remained oral, even after the second phase of the diaspora, was the *Kaballah* – which was a direct development of the original oral teaching of the Mosaic Spiritual Tradition. In theory the Kabbalistic teachings were once open; those who could understand them did and those who could not simply left them alone. While the essential teachings of the *Kaballah* reach back to the time of Moses, the detailed teachings and complex cosmology of the published *Kaballah* were probably elaborated in the time of the Babylonian captivity, for they show the influence of Persian Zoroastrianism. They were almost certainly further integrated and consolidated under Second Temple Judaism. At the time of the post-bar Kokhba diaspora, the Sanhedrin decided to place this oral teaching under a seal of secrecy, fearing that it might be misused and misinterpreted in a scattered population without the necessary guidance to understand it. When the *Kaballah* was eventually published in the thirteenth century, it had a considerable impact on Judaic culture as well as Western European esotericism of that age. We treat this development in the section on The Judaic Tradition in Chapter 41 of Book VII.

Now we leave the Judaic Spiritual Tradition and move east to northern India, at a time which corresponds approximately to the period of the Babylonian Exile. In India we find ourselves in the atmosphere of the already ancient Vedic Tradition, in the midst of a Brahmanic society with a fully developed caste system. By the sixth century BC both the Brahmanic Religion and the Brahmanic Civilization had reached a phase of decadence.

CHAPTER 29

Gautama Buddha

The Life of the Buddha (567-483 BC)

Siddhartha Gautama, who was to become 'the Buddha,' was born in 567 BC. He was the son of King Suddhodana of Kapilavastu, in what is now Nepal. Siddhartha was a prince, and the Brahmins of his father's court prophesied that he would become either a Universal Monarch or a Great Sage. His father, fearing that he would become a sage, arranged that he should live a confined life, receiving exactly the education that was necessary to become a great king while having no exposure to the influences that would lead him to become a sage. He was married to his cousin Yasodhara, and his day was filled, from morning to night, with pleasurable and instructive activities.

One day, however, the young Siddhartha went out into the city and saw **1)** a sick man, **2)** an elderly man, **3)** a corpse, and **4)** a wandering sadhu (or holy man). The effect of these impressions was to shatter the illusion of life presented in his father's court, and Siddhartha left the palace in search of liberation from the vicious wheel of existence. He studied under two teachers, Arada Kalama and Udraka Ramaputra, before retreating to the Deer Park at Benares to work on his own. The Deer Park was a place where ascetics gathered, and Siddhartha went, with five other disciples of Udraka, to practice extreme forms of asceticism. After six years he concluded that one cannot find liberation through ascetic practice alone. He left the five other disciples of Udraka, washed himself in the Nairanjana River, dined, and then went to the great Bodhi tree on the banks of the Nairanjana, with the aim to awaken or perish.

Siddhartha remained under the Bodhi tree for six days. On the night of the sixth day something changed within him.

- *On the First Watch of the night* he saw all his former births.

- ***On the Second Watch of the night*** he understood the principles of karma; he saw that both life and death depend on the pattern of our actions and their results. He understood the laws of cause and effect as they impact human destiny, and he saw – with certainty – that there is no security in the cycle of becoming.

- ***On the Third Watch of the night*** he perceived the twelve conditioned links which, on the one hand, begin with ignorance and lead to old age and death and, on the other, begin with the cessation of ignorance and lead to the end of ignorance, old age, and death.

- ***On the Final Watch of the night***, just before dawn, he received what has since become the core of Buddhist teaching: the Four Noble Truths and the principles of the Eightfold Path. On the morning of the seventh day he realized the full enlightenment which is the birthright of every human being.

The Four Noble Truths are **1)** the truth of suffering, **2)** the truth of the origin of suffering, **3)** the truth of the cessation of suffering, and **4)** the truth of the Eightfold Path – which is the transcendence of suffering. The elements of the Eightfold Path are correct view, correct intention, correct speech, correct action, correct livelihood, correct effort, correct mindfulness, and correct concentration of the attention. Implicitly contained within these Truths are all the truths of the Great Work.

For seven weeks the Buddha enjoyed the freedom of complete liberation. At the end of the seventh week Brahma, the lord of all the worlds, ordered him to go forth and teach. He went first to the five disciples of Udraka, who were still practicing asceticism in the Deer Park. They recognized the change in his being, and they joined him in forming the first Buddhist spiritual community or *Sangha*. The teaching that he gave at this time was called **the first turning of the wheel of dharma**.

DHARMA

In ancient Sanskrit the term *dharma* means 'natural law,' referring to the natural order of things. It was a universal principle of law, order, and harmony. It is the natural pattern of things. With reference to human beings it was used to refer to one's real personal obligations, to one's calling, and to one's familial and social duties. The highest *dharma*, and the one to which all others refer, is the call to realize one's Higher Centers. The Buddha, when he came, was taken by his disciples to be the epitome of this *dharma*. After his death the word was used by Buddhists to refer to the body of his teachings. Thus, in a Buddhist context the term *dharma* means 'the teachings,' the truth, the way things really are. Buddhism itself is the practice of this *dharma*.

This was later to form the basis of Theravadin Buddhism. The group then traveled through northeastern India and many thousands of monks came to join them. The Buddha – in a marked break with Brahmanic convention – taught anyone who came to him: beggars, merchants, knights, kings, or peasants.

While traveling in the northeast of India he spoke of *Shunyata* – the Divine Void – and of the spiritual qualities needed of a true aspirant, which he called the six paramitas, or 'perfections.' This was **the second turning of the wheel of dharma**, and it was later to form the basis of Mahayana Buddhism.

After a number of years the Buddha decided to return to his father's kingdom in Kapilavastu. His father initially thought he was returning to rule his kingdom and joyously sent messengers to receive the returning heir, but the Buddha converted all of the messengers who came to him. His enlightenment was so powerful and so definite that he converted the entire kingdom, including his father and his stepmother, the queen. His stepmother asked permission to form an order of Buddhist nuns, which he granted, stating that women were capable of full enlightenment. His wife, Yasodhara, had taken ascetic vows at the time the Buddha had left his father's court. She did not approach him on his return, feeling that if her action was truly virtuous, he would come to her, and if not, she would continue her practice. She entered the order of Buddhist nuns formed by the queen and, with the help of the Buddha's instruction, achieved enlightenment.

On leaving Kapilavastu the Buddha traveled to Shravastri, just south of Nepal. Here he taught the doctrine of the 'Buddha Nature,' which was to become the basis for Vajrayana Buddhism. This was later called **the third turning of the wheel of dharma**.

Some time after this, at Kushinagar, the Buddha predicted his own death and three months later died at the age of eighty (as it is recorded in the Mahaparinibbana Sutta of the Pali canon). He had sown seeds that would continue to come to fruition for centuries and millennia after his death. He presented a teaching of great purity and force in a decadent phase of Brahmanic India. He illuminated the laws governing Man and the universe, and spoke with authority about the place of Man within the universe. He laid down directions for life that have been generally accepted as objective truth by millions of people for over 2,500 years.

The Buddha stated that he was not the first Buddha nor would he be the last. There was one Buddha yet to come. The Buddhas who had preceded him had lived in the distant past, and the Buddha to follow would take birth only when the true dharmic teachings had been completely forgotten. His successor would be named the Maitreya, and he would reconstitute the true dharma, leading both Gods and Men across the ocean of becoming deep into the Divine Void (Shunyata). There would then be an end of the 'middle time' in which humanity presently resides, and the creation of a New World. We may note that this parallels exactly the prophecy of the Zoroastrian Saoshy-ant and the prophecies that would later be made – by both Jesus and Muhammad – concerning the Second Coming of Jesus.

During the Buddha's lifetime a large circle of advanced disciples formed around him, and in the generations after his death his followers focused on practicing and communicating his teachings. During his lifetime the Buddha taught on different levels and did so in such a way that the different teachings would converge and cross-fertilize after his death. Of all the Prophets, he gave least in the way of external directive, and at the same time, his internal teaching was perhaps the most explicit. The Four Noble Truths and the Eightfold Path are among the most explicit internal teachings ever given, and they were given with the Buddha's assurance that all men could awaken, just as he himself had awakened through applying these principles. As a result, the unique aspect of the Buddhist Tradition was the focus with which his spiritual teachings were actually practiced and developed. The Tradition was strong, relative to the Buddhist Religion and the Buddhist Civilization.

The Buddhist Teaching

Two great councils were held after the death of the Buddha, in which the community of Buddhist practitioners – the *Sangha* – attempted to define and integrate the essential teachings.

First Council: c. 460 BC This occurred in the years immediately following the Buddha's death. The attempt was made to collect and consolidate what was genuine in the legacy of his teaching and to create unity in the Buddhist Religion.

Second Council: c. 360 BC This occurred a century later. Its purpose was to resolve the disagreements which had developed between the different Buddhist schools. At this Council the Buddhist community split according to different interpretations of the Buddha's work – just as the Christian and Islamic communities were to split after the deaths of their respective Prophets. The Theravadin Buddhists held to a strict interpretation of the Buddhist vows. The Sthaviravada, Mahasanghika, and Sarvastivada schools advocated a more open style. And there were also Buddhist practitioners who worked completely independently of these groups called the Siddhas. These were 'forest renunciants' who followed what was later to be called the Vajrayana path.

The result of the Second Council was that the great majority of Buddhists were expelled from the Sangha by the Theravadins. From this group there eventually arose the teachings of Mahayana Buddhism. All of the major tendencies that developed from this split were to bear rich fruit and to cross-fertilize in later centuries.

The Second Council defined 'the lay of the land' for the different Buddhist schools, and on this basis Buddhism spread through Asia. At the same time it continued to undergo rich developments in India. These were the three most important strands of Buddhism:

Theravadin Buddhism

Known as 'the Ancient Teaching,' its claim was always to be the closest to the original teaching of the Buddha. As it is hard to keep the severe tenets of Theravadin Buddhism outside of a monastic environment, the Theravadins developed a monastic focus. They adhered closely to the monastic vows, or *vinaya*, given in the *first turning of the wheel of dharma*. Much of the expansion of Theravadin Buddhism occurred under the Mauryan Kings in the third century BC. At this time important bases were established in Sri Lanka, Cambodia, Laos, Burma, and Thailand. The Theravadins of Cambodia produced the great temples at Angkor Wat, which are a tribute to the work of the Spiritual Traditions in all times and places.

Mahayana Buddhism

This developed from the more open approach that had been the counterpoint to Theravadin orthodoxy at the Second Buddhist council. It allowed, for example, a Buddhist to handle money or to work for a living.

The Mahayana path was outlined by the great Buddhist saint Nagarjuna, who came to his maturity in about 200 BC. His presentation of the Mayahana teachings was based on the teachings of the *second turning of the wheel of dharma*, the *prajnaparamita* sutras, given in the northeast of India during the middle years of the Buddha's life. Nagarjuna emphasized that the potential for awakening existed in all men, and he defined a Middle Way, uniting what was real in the teaching of various Buddhist sects. He also defined a middle way between ascetic renunciation, monasticism, and full involvement in the affairs of the world.

It was Nagarjuna who initiated the *bodhisattva oath* – the vow to refuse entry into *paranirvana* (World 6) until all sentient beings had achieved the awakened state. This vow was designed to take the self-centeredness out of awakening, and it represents an attitude which – however stated – is necessary to complete enlightenment. Nagarjuna also developed the teaching of Shunyata, or the divine Void, and his works on the subject became core teaching for all Mahayana Schools.

While Nagarjuna's teaching had a monastic emphasis, it was not exclusively monastic. After his death, however, the Indian Mahayanists developed a very elaborate structure of monastic life.

Vajrayana Buddhism

The term Vajrayana was first applied to the work of forest renunciants, the Siddhas who left the Buddhist community to work in solitude. These men and women, working in retreat, might gather a few followers, and from these small teaching circles came different lines of transmission. There were also Vajrayana practitioners who were not ascetic, and who worked independently of the monastic community, developing practices related to their immediate life circumstances. These practitioners were sometimes called 'householders.' They might work in the conditions of everyday life and even support a family. These independent practitioners were 'something different' from the normal world of the Buddhist monk, and – increasingly – they were treated with respect. Generally, if they took students, they took only those who came to them through the line of their fate, or – in the Buddhist terminology – through a definite line of karma. Both the renunciants and the 'householders' worked outside the traditional set of monastic vows that was called the *vinaya*.

The word *vajra* means literally 'thunderbolt' – something that is indestructible, that can pierce through or penetrate anything else. The word can also imply adamantine hardness combined with clarity or translucence, and in this regard it can refer to the qualities of a diamond. Indeed, the Vajrayana path is sometimes called the 'diamond vehicle.' From the standpoint of the material presented in Chapter 3, the Vajrayana teaching is focused on the working unity of the Steward and the infant Higher Centers. In other words, it does not address the Buddhist philosopher or the apprentice monk, but speaks directly to the Steward of a mature spiritual practitioner and to the Higher Centers that lie behind it. Indeed, the Vajrayana teaching begins at the very point where Higher Centers can be directly addressed and where the psychological structures that have built around them (including the activities of the Steward itself) can fall away without the practitioner losing orientation. But the Vajrayana teachings are equally addressed to the Steward, for every time the Steward 'falls away' it must be reconstituted – at least until such time as the Higher Centers can sustain themselves by themselves. This only occurs in the most advanced practitioners. In Buddhist terms this stage of development normally coincides with the permanent entry into *paranirvana* (World 6) which occurs at the death of the vehicle. As long as there is still a 'vehicle,' there is an instinctive center, and as long as there is an instinctive center there is active resistance to awakening. We come again to the division of the instinctive center which we have called the Black Queen and which the Buddhists call *Mara.* As long as she is able to recreate herself in the line of time, there is need of the Steward. We could say that the Vajrayana is the extreme reduction, and thus the extreme empowerment, of the Steward. The smaller the Steward, the more effective and the more powerful it is. For this reason the Vajrayana path has been called the path of awakening in this lifetime.

From very early times Tantric practices were associated with the Vajrayana Tradition. These can involve the controlled use of drugs, the sexual act, and occult techniques of different kinds. The most developed of these techniques were drawn from the yogic practices of the ancient Shamanic-Taoist Tradition. In the true Vajrayana these are only used by those who have achieved the highest discipline in meditation and who can sustain presence through the internal experiences that the Tantric techniques will evoke. The actual techniques are, in themselves, of the lower centers, and are initiated from the lower centers. If they are correctly applied they bring the lower centers to a receptive state and, at the same time, stimulate consciousness. Consciousness then becomes present to the lower centers while they are in a heightened state, and this allows for a very profound separation between what we have called 'consciousness' and 'functions' described in Chapter 3. In this condition consciousness knows the lower centers as separate from itself, and – above all – knows itself for what it is.

Because of the methods used and because of the promise of a quick path to enlightenment, there have been many abuses of Tantra. The techniques used to bring the lower centers into a heightened state can equally be employed by beginning practitioners. In this context they may have the beneficial effect of 'loosening' psychological rigidities or bringing to light hidden fears and desires. But when these practices are used without proper supervision, they can have effects which are far from beneficial. They touch the 'core area' of the Black Queen, and they can very easily be used by the Black Queen to reinforce the wrong feeling of 'I.' The most concentrated, powerful, and simple manifestations of the Black Queen can appear to have certain of the qualities of non-ego, although in a negative or destructive form. Even the most advanced spiritual practitioners need guidance in distinguishing Real 'I' from the manifestations of the Black Queen. Thus, when there were wrong applications of the Tantric techniques casualties were common!

We may note that the Vajrayana practice does not replace the Mahayana practices. It normally takes place on the foundation of those practices. In other words, if someone does not have the being to implement the bodhisattva vow, he should not attempt the Vajrayana path, and if he does have the being to implement the bodhisattva vow, the Vajrayana practice will strengthen his understanding of what this vow means.

Historically, the interaction of the Vajrayana and Mahayana schools helped to ensure a dynamic relation between the work of the Buddhist Traditions and the Buddhist Religion. The Vajrayana teachings continued for many centuries as 'secret' lines of transmission, known only to those who became involved with them. They came to the public eye in the seventh century AD at a time when the dominant Mahayana Schools of northern India had developed problematic tendencies. There was a tendency for monks to identify spiritual development with place and position in the monastic hierarchy and with the outer forms of monastic life. At the same time there was a tendency for the monasteries to accumulate wealth and to become lax in the practice of the monastic vows. And finally there was a philosophic tendency, focused on Nagarjuna's teaching of Shunyata, which defined the Divine Void intellectually, as a kind of dead space. This philosophy has a close parallel in Western nihilism, which, under the claim of destroying all that is false, encourages a particular development of the Black Queen. Both nihilism and purely philosophical Buddhism are always attended by a particular kind of self-importance.

The enlightened Mahayanists of the seventh century began to draw on the Vajrayana teachings to regenerate the mainstream Mahayana schools. They pointed to the vigorous disciplines of the Vajrayana practitioners. At the same time the Vajrayana Masters revealed the positive substance of Shunyata, by themselves existing in the state of prolonged presence – and so demonstrating the nature of the Void in a way that transcends concepts. They identified Shunyata with what they called the 'Buddha Nature.'

Thus, where the sterile Mahayana scholastics had emphasized that the absence of a unified self reveals a Void, the Vajrayana Masters emphasized a Voidness that is neither sterile blankness nor meaningless emptiness. The Buddha Nature is not frozen space, but clarity, light, and dynamic potential. This became *the doctrine of Clear Light*. When an individual has had his impurities removed, he is like a polished mirror, and Clear Light can manifest through him. Within this clarity the forms of the phenomenal world are revealed as expressions of a Dynamic Void. The nature of this Void is compassion itself, and in it the enlightened activity of the Buddha Nature can manifest. Thus, in the regenerated Mahayana teaching, Clarity, the Void, and dynamic Compassion were re-united, and the union of these is understood as the essence of all the Buddhas.

Philosophically, there is no difference between the Mahayana and Vajrayana teachings, it is simply that Vajrayana is more focused on what we called in Chapter 3 'direct work on Higher Centers' and on the moment of transmission between teacher and student. This is not something that can be pinned down by a particular conceptual formula or a particular yogic technique. But at the same time it is true that a correct conceptual representation of reality can help a person to make the transition through to the Divine Void. And here the Buddhists began to see how the Mahayana and Vajrayana practices could work together.

The problem with the Vajrayana path was that there were always many 'rogue' practitioners, and casualities were frequent. The Mahayana path could prepare students for Vajrayana practice and at the same time create a discipline which minimized the abuse of Vajrayana techniques. In turn the Vajrayana could correct the negative tendencies of the Mahayana. The challenge was to establish a right balance. This process was begun in India, but was taken further in later centuries in China, Tibet, and Japan.

In closing we must emphasize that each of the main Buddhist schools – Theravadin, Mahayana, and Vajrayana – were in their origin Living Spiritual Traditions, and each contained the tendencies of the others within itself. Having spoken of Buddhism as a Spiritual Tradition, we must now turn to the Living Religion in its relation to the Civilizational Order.

The Development of Buddhist Civilization

Buddhism began its life as a World Religion and a Civilizational Order more than two centuries after the death of the Buddha around 480 BC. This occurred in the historical moment when King Ashoka, the ruler of the Mauryan Empire in India, converted to Buddhism. King Ashoka ruled between 268 BC and 232 BC. Following his conversion he attempted to establish a government on Buddhist principles, reconciling the different Buddhist sects that had developed and initiating a phase of missionary work. In the time of the Mauryan kings, Buddhism expanded into Thailand, Burma, Laos, Cambodia, Vietnam, and Sri Lanka. Fifty years after King Ashoka's death the last Mauryan ruler was assassinated by one of his Brahmin generals, who then took the throne. The Buddhist teaching nevertheless continued to develop, and a precedent had been set for Buddhist civilization that had strong implications for the future.

Thus the Buddha's teaching was actualized in a civilizational order only two and a half centuries after his death, and with this 'grounding' Buddhism developed as a World Religion. We note the similarity to Christianity, where a Christian social order came into being only three centuries after the death of the Prophet.

Theravadin Buddhism eventually became predominant in Southeast Asia. The Mahayana teachings spread to China, Japan, Korea, Mongolia, Tibet, Nepal, and Bhutan. A Vajrayana style of teaching integrated with Mahayana-style monastic practice developed in both Tibet and Japan.

Chinese Buddhism

Buddhism first came to China by an indirect route. In 260-232 BC King Ashoka sent missionary monks deep into Central Asia, and Buddhism became established in what is now Afghanistan, Iran, Syria, and eastern Turkey. These were all stops along the line of the ancient Silk Road, and gradually merchants travelling the Silk Road brought tidings of these new teachings to China.

The Chinese proved receptive. Eventually the merchants brought Buddhist missionaries into China, and they were enthusiastically received. The first reference to Buddhism in China occurs in official records, which note the creation of a Buddhist temple under Imperial patronage in 64 AD. The translation of the Buddhist sutras into Chinese was underway by the first century AD. By the end of the second century a prosperous

Buddhist community had formed at Peng-cheng under the patronage of a brother of the Chinese emperor.

In 148 AD a Central Asian Buddhist missionary, An Shi-kao, established Buddhist temples in Lo-yang and there organized the translation of Buddhist scriptures. This began a wave of Central Asian Buddhist missionary work that was to last several centuries.

But, in certain ways, Buddhism was not a natural fit for China. Most of the Chinese gentry were indifferent to the Central Asian travelers and their religion. The concept of monasticism and the idea of a 'retreat' from social life directly contradicted the core Confucian principles of family and emperor. Chinese officials questioned how a monk's personal attainment could benefit Chinese society. However, Buddhist meditation was close in spirit to the traditional Chinese Taoist practices, and it provided a coherent vision of the universe that Taoism lacked. The Taoists proved quite open, both to the Buddhist meditation practice and to the Buddhist cosmology.

Chinese Buddhism, as opposed to Central Asian Buddhism or Indian Buddhism, began to develop in a way compatible with Chinese life. Indeed, the successful implementation of a spiritual teaching in a different culture, which is able to preserve the inner spirit of that teaching, indicates the breadth of vision that we associate with the Spiritual Traditions. Those Indian sutras which advocated filial piety became core texts in China, and it was argued that the enlightenment of the individual monk was of direct benefit to the society that had produced him. The spirit of the Mahayanist bodhisattva vow — selfless service — was important to the socially conscious Chinese.

The collapse of the Han dynasty in 220 AD and the centuries of unrest that followed greatly assisted the spread of Buddhism in China. (See "Chin through Tang Dynasties" in Chapter 30 for details of that period of Chinese history.) The upheavals of that time broke down cultural barriers. In the chaotic period of the Sixteen Kingdoms (304-439 AD), both the southern and the northern dynasties gave state support to Buddhism in non-Han areas. Buddhism was established principally in northern China and from there went to Korea and Japan.

Thus from 50 AD to 400 AD a base was laid. At the beginning of the fifth century the great Indian master Bodhidharma came to China and reinforced the standard that we associate with the work of the Great Spiritual Traditions.

BODHIDHARMA

Bodhidharma was an Indian Buddhist teacher, active between 420 and 534 AD. He is best known now as the father of Japanese Zen Buddhism, but this comes from a very

Figure 47. **Statue of the Buddha at the Lung-men Grotto – full figure**

long line of paternity. Although he may have been the source of the Zen Tradition, he lived his mature teaching life in China seven centuries before Zen came to Japan. Little is known of his early life, and much of what survives is myth. Bodhidharma was, like the Buddha, an Indian prince who renounced his birthright to become a monk – a disciple of the great Indian teacher Prajnatara. He came to China to teach 'special transmission outside the scripture' which 'did not stand on words.' He worked principally in northern China. When he arrived he found that the Buddhist practice he encountered was a kind of devotionalism backed with little spiritual insight. He combined his 'transmission outside the scripture' with the teachings of the Buddha and with certain of the Taoist practices he found in China. Bodhidharma emphasized that the awakening taught by the Buddha came primarily through meditation practice – direct work on wordless presence – and that it is primarily through meditation practice that one can awaken. We know that he taught the Mahayanist doctrine of Shunyata – the Divine Void. He originated what came to be called the tradition of Chan Buddhism. The original historical records of Chan Buddhism no longer exist, but as it developed it integrated within itself various currents of Mahayana thought. It presented the idea that spiritual, intellectual, and physical development are an indivisible whole and that enlightenment can only be achieved where these are in balance. Bodhidharma's name became particularly connected with traditions which specialized in the martial arts.

Figure 48. **Statue of the Buddha at the Lung-men Grotto – face**

Beginning from the time of Bodidharma we see many scripture-filled caves and the remains of extensive monastic structures. This is accompanied by great Buddhist art, particularly in the form of the gigantic statuary that we find in the caves at Dun-huang, Lung-men, and Le-shan. By the beginning of the sixth century Chinese Buddhism had grown to rival Taoism in popularity. In the open atmosphere of the early Tang Dynasty (618-907) Buddhism flourished, and it was in this time that Chinese Buddhism re-sourced itself in the original Indian Spiritual Tradition.

Three great Indian Masters – Subhakarasimha, Vajrabodhi, and Amoghavajra – were the source of the remarkable regeneration of Buddhism that occurred in the late seventh and eighth centuries. They knew one another, and they worked together. They took residence in the Chinese temple of Da-hsing Shan-si, established in the Tang capital of Chang-an, today's Hsi-an (Xi'an).

SUBHAKARASIMHA (637-735) was a renowned Vajrayana practitioner who arrived in Chang-an in 716, at the age of eighty, and taught for another nineteen years – completing the translation of the Mahavairocana-Sutra from Sanskrit to Chinese.

VAJRABODHI (671-732) was a Mahayanist graduate of Nalanda University, who had received transmission from Nagabodhi, who in turn received transmission from Nagarjuna – who was perhaps the greatest Indian Buddhist teacher after Gautama Buddha. He combined the Vajrayana teachings with the Mahayanist teachings of Nalanda. He continued the translation work of Subhakarasimha and focused on the production of esoteric art. He was able to make deep connections within the Chinese Imperial court.

AMOGHAVAJRA (705-774) was a disciple of Vajrabodhi. After Vajrabodhi's death he made a pilgrimage to India and worked for several years with his Teacher's Teacher, Nagabodhi. On his return to China he developed a strong connection to the Imperial family and served under three Tang Emperors. He became one of the most politically powerful monks in Chinese history.

This was a golden century for Buddhism in China. The result of this work was that Buddhism entered deeply into the essence of the Chinese people, spreading rapidly through the ninth century and achieving the most remarkable external expressions. The colossal statue of the Buddha which is found in the Feng-hsien cave (at the Lung-men grottoes, Figure 47 and Figure 48 on pages 400 and 401) – which reaches the level of World 6 – came at this time of regeneration.

But a Spiritual Tradition's principal realization is always internal, and, once firmly established, it can sustain itself strongly through very adverse conditions. The 'golden century' prepared the Tradition to survive the persecutions that were to follow.

The turning point for Chinese Buddhism came in 845. The Tang Emperor Wu-tsung, feeling that Buddhist monasteries were creating a drain on the economy, and acting under the influence of a Taoist monk, outlawed all 'foreign religions.' There followed a period of extreme repression of Buddhism. Wu-tsung ordered the destruction of 4,600 Buddhist monasteries and 40,000 temples. He had the most prominent Buddhist monks executed, and it is estimated that about 250,000 Buddhist monks and nuns were forced out of monastic life.

Following this disaster Buddhism went underground for more than half a century. At the beginning of the tenth century the Tang Dynasty dissolved into the 'Five Dynasties and Ten Kingdoms' and the open practice of Buddhism became possible once more. The principal surviving Spiritual Traditions at that time were Chan Buddhism and Pure Land Buddhism.

Chan Buddhism grew to be the dominant school of Chinese Buddhism and flourished through the Sung Dynasty (960-1279). Despite its 'transmission outside the scripture,' it produced the largest body of literature of any Chinese sect or tradition. Chan Buddhism coexisted with, and was taught alongside, Pure Land Buddhism.

Pure Land Buddhism began with the frank acknowledgment that it is very difficult to achieve permanent nirvana through meditative practice. All practitioners find meditation to be difficult, and particularly those who have gone far enough to become aware of the Divine Void. Additionally, very few people have the opportunity to practice meditation in retreat or under controlled conditions. Pure Land Buddhism teaches that through devotion to the *Amitabha Buddha* one can be reborn in a Pure Land, which is a heavenly realm ideally conducive to meditation. Should a person, through devotion, create a karma for himself causing rebirth in the Pure Land, then enlightenment is ultimately guaranteed. This refers to the First Work, which is the purification of the lower centers which must precede direct work on Higher Centers. Pure Land Buddhism was popular amongst peasants and merchants, as it provided a straightforward way of establishing themselves as Buddhist. It was also popular amongst social outcasts, prostitutes, and beggars, who – though denied the conditions of meditative practice – could still have a religious life.

Many masters taught both Chan and Pure Land Buddhism, and in time the distinction between the two was lost. Pure Land Buddhism became the Religion which corresponded to the Chan Spiritual Tradition.

Both Chan and Pure Land Buddhism flourished in the Sung Period (960-1279) and in the Mongol occupation of China which followed, which was known as the Yuan Dynasty (1271-1368). This was the time of Ghengis and Kublai Khan. The Mongols themselves, however, embraced Tibetan Buddhism, and Chan Buddhism began to feel competition from the Tibetan teaching. When the Yuan Dynasty was succeeded by the Ming (1368-1644), Chan Buddhism became so firmly established that almost the entire Buddhist clergy were affiliated with lineages claiming descent from Bodhidharma.

Then came the Manchu conquest of China in 1644, which led to the establishment of the Ching Dynasty. The Manchus kept themselves distinct from the Han Chinese and made Tibetan Buddhism their own official religion, just as the Mongols had done during the Yuan Dynasty. This preference relates to **1)** the great spiritual credence of the Tibetan Traditions, **2)** the powers which many of the Tibetan lamas could display at will, and **3)** the successful practice of Tibetan medicine as a tangible demonstration of openness and human compassion. While they themselves adopted Tibetan Buddhism, the Manchus promoted Confucianism as the Religion appropriate for the Chinese. They sharply suppressed Chan Buddhism, as they feared the independence of mind that it cultivated in the Han Chinese.

In Nationalist China, in the early twentieth century, both Chan and Pure Land Buddhism saw a brief resurgence, but they, along with all other forms of Buddhist thought, were severely repressed in the Communist period to follow, and most decisively during the years of the Cultural Revolution.

Beginning from the late Sung period (c. 1200 AD) the Mahayana form of Chan Buddhism spread southwards to Vietnam and eastwards to Korea and Japan. There was a Chan Buddhist renaissance in Korea from the seventh century to the late fourteenth, when it was severely repressed by the Yi Dynasty. Thereafter it remained marginal. In Japan, however, Buddhism became permanent. The Japanese pronunciation of 'Chan' is 'Zen' and this form of Buddhism developed in Japan from the twelfth century AD.

Japanese Buddhism

Buddhist monks came to Japan from Korea as early as 372 AD, and by the sixth century Buddhism had become a popular teaching. By the eighth century numerous Buddhist temples and monasteries had been constructed, and the government sponsored paintings and sculptures on a regular basis. Being at the eastern end of the Silk Road, Japan was able to preserve many aspects of Buddhism which were actively suppressed – at different times – in India, Central Asia, and China. The creation of Japanese Buddhist art was both rich and prolific from the eighth century onwards.

Then, in the twelfth century, came Zen.

Despite Zen's firm avoidance of theology and scholasticism, all of the early Zen masters were well-versed in the Buddhist scriptures. Zen is a form of Mahayana Buddhism, and the Zen Masters were men of wide and far-ranging vision. The Masters taught the Eightfold Path, the bodhisattva vow, and the combination of labor, service, and meditation. Japanese Zen perfected the technique known as 'koan inquiry.'

There were three main schools of Zen in Japan: **Rinzai**, **Soto**, and **Obaku**.

Figure 49. **Soto Zen temple at Eiheiji**

Zen came to Japan in the twelfth century when a Japanese monk by the name of Myoan Eisai traveled to China and connected with the Chan Lingji School, which was oriented towards the martial arts. He returned to Japan to establish a lineage, which became known as the **Rinzai**. The martial arts speciality had a strong appeal to the Japanese Samurai class, and from that time forward there was a strong connection between Zen Buddhism and the samurai.

In 1215 Dogen, a younger contemporary of Eisai's, travelled to China to become the disciple of the Chinese master Tiantong Rujing. On his return, Dogen established the **Soto** school.

The **Obaku** lineage came into being much later, in the seventeenth century, when – following the Manchu invasion of China – a Chinese monk by the name of Ingen traveled to Japan. His teachings became the basis for a school distinct from the Rinzai and Soto.

Zen flourished in Japan. In its Mahayana aspect it linked naturally with the traditional Shintoist teachings. Shintoism was a shamanic religion with an ancient and atavistic connection to the land and to the spirit of the Japanese people. It had probably been the vehicle for a Shamanic Spiritual Tradition in ancient Japan.

While Zen Buddhism did not have a direct connection to the Japanese Imperial House, it did attract many members of the nobility, or *daimyo*, and – more generally

– the members of the *samurai* warrior class. Zen became central to Japanese culture at the time the Japanese Imperial House was 'displaced' by the Togukawa Dynasty.

In the late sixteenth century Japan was deeply divided by dynastic civil war, based on conflicts of interest amongst the nobility. The emperor was powerless to mediate these intense conflicts. In 1603 General Togukawa Leyasu reunified the country by destroying those of the nobility who were his enemies and reuniting what remained of the *daimyo* under his leadership. He established himself as the *Shogun*, or commander-in-chief of the *daimyo*, and thus established the *Tokugawa Shogunate* – which was to endure until the late nineteenth century. The Shogunate sidelined, but did not eliminate, the old Imperial House. The newly-unified *daimyo* were the very heart of the *samurai* class, and the ethos of that class permeated the Tokugawa Shogunate. While the Japanese emperor continued to reside at Kyoto, and was still formally the head of state, Japan was ruled by the *Shogun*. The emperor himself remained the central figure of the old Shinto religion, to which Buddhism had almost perfectly adjusted itself. Thus, under the Tokugawa Shogunate, Buddhism and Shintoism became complementary aspects of the Religion of Japan.

Given the admiration that the *samurai* class had for Zen, the Zen form of Buddhism did penetrate the nation more deeply at this time – but at no point did the Zen Spiritual Tradition allow itself to become an 'official religion' for the Togukawa Shogunate. The Zen Masters were able to retain their autonomy and so the spiritual integrity of their teaching.

Japanese society came to a crisis in the mid-nineteenth century as Japan began to realize that she was a feudal nation in a world that was undergoing the first industrial revolution. She was entirely vulnerable. The ethnocentric and honor-fixated *daimyo* where quite unable to adjust to the rapidly changing outer circumstances, and the rigid class structure of the Shogunate made industrialization impossible. The hold of the *daimyo* on the traditional structure of society had to be broken, and it was broken by a new social movement, the **Meiji Restoration**. This revolutionary movement, which involved people from all classes and walks of life, led to a restoration of the ancient imperial line in 1867. The Emperor Meiji was used as a symbol of Japanese unity by a new regime, capable of responding to the demands of a new age, which demonstrated both great openness and ecumenical vision.

Zen practitioners were deeply involved in the Meiji Restoration and were largely responsible for the vision of *Dai Nippon*, or 'Greater Japan,' which was to define that movement. One might think that the ascendance of the traditional imperial house signalled a predominantly Shinto influence in the new regime, but the vision of Japanese unity was one in which the whole completely transcended all its component parts. Only the formless openness of Zen could accommodate such a vision! While Zen was quite capable of incorporating the spirit of Shintoism, Shintoism could not itself incorporate the formless openness of Zen. The vision of *Dai Nippon* encompassed what the Buddhist Tradition called *Shunyata*, or the Divine Void, and what we have here called World 6, in a way that transcended any single Buddhist or Shinto form. The social faction which carried this vision was an emergent service nobility, drawn from all walks of life, which subsumed within itself the traditional *samurai* values of honor and service. For this new nobility the open dimension of *shunyata* was realized in simultaneous service to the level one above and the level one below. But the vision of *Dai Nippon* was greater than the vision of the service nobility who carried it, greater than the Emperor, greater than the *samurai*, greater than the merchants, greater than the peasants – an ecumenical vision of a New Age for Japan, developing through deliberative assembly and the involvement of all classes in decision making.

This was a 'golden hour' for Japanese Zen, which – in its inner spirit – is totally formless. We have again a glimpse of the possibility of a completed Cosmos of Man. But only a glimpse. The process of rapid industrialization that the new regime initiated created direct links between the emergent military/industrial complex, the traditional *samurai* class, and the restored Imperial House. True deliberative assemblies, on a large scale, soon faded, and the 'centering' of *Dai Nippon* in the formless Void became, for the most part, a religious idea. Decade by decade the link between nationalism, industrialism, and militarism undermined the original Zen-based vision. As the spirit of Japan became increasingly connected to specific material goals, the inner spirit of Zen itself suffered. The living inner current of the teaching became more rare, and the external forms of Zen practice, more pronounced and more separate from their inner meaning. The link between militarism and industrialism hardened during the Showa Period (1926-1989), which corresponds to the lengthy reign of the Emperor Hirohito. Certain Japanese Zen teachers, such as Daiun Harada and Shunryu Suzuki, have criticized Japanese Zen practice of this period as being a formalized system of empty rituals in which very few practitioners ever attained realization.

Non-Zen Mahayana Buddhism also flourished in Japan. Indeed Zen Buddhism is better known in the West only because of the effect that it had on the West. A second source of Vajrayana teachings in Japan was the lineage of **Shingon Buddhism**. This was an integration of Mahayana and Vajrayana which flourished between 800 and 1600.

In neither China nor Japan was Buddhism a 'state religion,' but in both countries it was – arguably – the most coherent system of religious belief. In China, where Taoism had very deep roots, Buddhist practice acquired a marked Taoist coloration – particularly in relation to the martial arts and healing. In just the same way Japanese Buddhism linked naturally with the native Shintoism. This same pattern repeated again in Tibet, as Tibetan Buddhism took on the coloration of the older Bon religion. The Tao, the Shinto, and the Bon religions constitute the original shamanic cultures of China, Japan, and Tibet. When a Spiritual Tradition takes deep roots in a country, it penetrates and interacts with the existing culture – for it must engage its people on the level of their deepest hopes and fears.

Tibetan Buddhism

We move now to the 'roof of the world' – the high Tibetan plateau – flanked on the west by the Hindu Kush, the Pamir, and the Karakorum Mountains, on the north by the Kunlun and Altyn Tagh Mountains, on the east by the Yun Ling range, and along the south by the towering ramparts of the Himalayas. The southern rampart includes all the highest mountains in the world; titans such as Everest, Kanchenjunga, Lhotse, Makalu, and Annapurna. Such a landscape instills a sense of awe – of the vastness of nature and of the smallness of Man. Here we find the circumstances of life that force the mutual dependence of a community and at the same time foster – from earliest child-hood – the hardihood and self-reliance of each of its members. The Tibetan plateau was very gradually settled in the period before recorded history, the great majority of immigrants entering from Central Asia in about the eighth century AD. It is likely that, as Central Asia slowly turned to desert, the Central Asians emigrating to the northeast became the Mongols, while those emigrating to the east – over the Karakorum and Altyn Tagh Mountains – became the Tibetans. John Bennett believed that the principal settlements of the ancient Shamanic-Taoist Civilization were in the Hindu Kush and Altyn Tagh Mountains, so the movement onto the Tibetan plateau would have been a natural choice for these people. Thus the original population of Tibet were almost certainly carriers of the ancient Shamanic-Taoist Religion, which was one of the Original Religions surviving from the prehistoric period of Mankind. Somewhere in the second

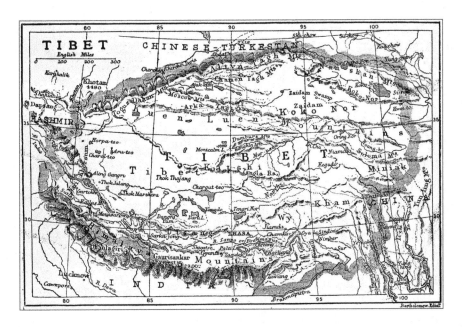

Figure 50. **Map of Tibet from 1906**

millennium BC this shamanic religion picked up traces of the Zoroastrian teaching, and the result was the Bon religion, which then became – until the ninth century AD – the popular religion of Tibet.

When Buddhism came into Tibet from India, beginning from the ninth century AD, it was overwhelmingly successful. The high Tibetan plateau became a place where prayer flags filled the sky and the spire-topped reliquaries of the Buddhist saints dotted the mountainsides. The landscape itself turned into a living tapestry of sacred sites, united by a never-ending flow of pilgrims.

Tibetan Buddhism is perhaps the closest that Mankind has come, at least in its recorded history, to a Civilization governed by a Spiritual Tradition. It is the closest historical example we have to a completed Pyramid of Man, where each level serves, at the same time, the level immediately above itself and the level immediately below itself. It is our view that the individual Tibetan Orders – the Nyingma, the Kagyu, the Sakya, and the Gelug – were each distinct Spiritual Traditions, working in relative harmony, with one or another playing the ruling role.

INTRODUCTION

In our overview of Buddhism we noted that the Spiritual Tradition – the innermost current of the Buddha's teaching – was most strongly represented in the Vajrayana lines of transmission. These were based in India, from the time of the Buddha's teaching to the time of the Mughal invasions, which began in the late twelfth century. By the beginning of the thirteenth century the Mughals had extinguished the light of the Buddha's teaching in India, and after that time – it is our belief – the Vajrayana lines were most strongly represented in Tibet. In Tibetan Buddhism, however, there was an integration of the Vajrayana and Mahayana teachings that had never occurred in India. These two were again integrated with the body of teachings that we have called the 'first work' and the Tibetans called the 'Hinyana' path. Indeed the unique feature of Tibetan Buddhism was the unity of its different levels: Hinyana, Mahayana, and Vajrayana.

The story of Tibetan Buddhism is well-recorded and constitutes one of the most remarkable chapters in the Story of Man.[1] We have spoken of the 'archetype' of a civilization, and the Tibetan Traditions – for much of their active life – actually worked in the conscious awareness of this archetype. In order to tell this story – with reference to the archetype that was behind it – we must be able to relate the vocabulary that the Tibetans used to the vocabulary that we have chosen to use here. Thus we shall begin by clarifying **1)** the idea of the 'Buddha Manifestations' and **2)** the concepts of Mahayana and Vajrayana Buddhism, as they were practiced in Tibet.

1) THE BUDDHA MANIFESTATIONS

In Tibet the term 'the Buddha' was often used in the same way that we have used the term 'the Absolute.' The modifying term 'Vairocana,' as in 'Vairocana Buddha,' can be an indication of this usage. It is the Buddha-aspect representing the principle of the Whole, which is now, always has been, and always will be. From this point of view the historical Siddhartha Gautama is one manifestation of the Buddha, and there have been others.

We noted that there are spiritual entities who were created directly from the Absolute, who never were embodied, at least as we understand embodiment. We referred to these beings as the Archangels. They were instrumental in the creation of the archetypes for both Tradition and Civilization, and they are, in that regard, deeply concerned with

---

1. The history of the individual Tibetan orders is well recorded, but it is nonetheless difficult to develop an overview of the history of the Tibetan civilization. Some helpful sources have been: Laird, Thomas, *The Story of Tibet, Conversations with the Dalai Lama*, Grove Press, New York, 2006; Powers, John, *Introduction to Tibetan Buddhism*, Snow Lion Publications, Ithaca, New York, 1995; Ray, Reginald, *Indestructible Truth, the Living Spirituality of Tibetan Buddhism*, Shambhala, Boston, 2000; Ray, Reginald, *Secret of the Vajra World, The Tantric Wisdom of Tibet*, Shambhala, Boston, 2001.

the pattern of human history. They are concerned with the relations of Tradition, Religion, and Civilization that will enable the realization of a particular archetype.

The term Archangel, which we have drawn from the Christian and Islamic Traditions, corresponds approximately to the Tibetan term 'Buddha Manifestation.' In the Tibetan view there were 'manifestations' of the Buddha that long pre-date humanity and that so far transcend the human race that they cannot be known directly by individual men, even by conscious beings. Yet in some very advanced practitioners, in whom the two Higher Centers have firmly locked, these 'manifestations' of the Absolute can make themselves known and, in so doing, leave a permanent imprint. When this occurs they make the person to whom it happened – at least in some degree – a reflection of the archetypal manifestation. In this way the Archangel can leave a direct impress on history. We shall follow the Tibetan Teacher Atisa in calling those individuals who receive the impress of a Buddha Manifestation an 'incarnation' of that Buddha Manifestation.

There is a certain amount of confusion concerning the names given to the Buddha Manifestations, because these names can be used in quite different ways. At the level of the Buddhist Religion they may be like a list of 'popular saints' that can be individually petitioned for favor. On a higher level they are sometimes used – in their aspect of representing different 'dimensions' of the Buddha – to portray different pathways through to the fully awakened state. But on the highest level they are real spiritual entities, of whom we can hardly conceive but who are nevertheless formative of Tradition, Religion, and Civilization.

These are the names most commonly used in Tibet for the Buddha Manifestations:

Avalokitesvara, more popularly known in Tibet as 'Chenrizi.' This is the dimension of the Buddha that is compassion – the will to work for humanity and to never, under any circumstances, give up. Avalokitesvara is often depicted in the feminine. Her compassion is so great that she is capable of manifesting in many different places and at many different times at once. For this reason she is often depicted with a thousand arms. The idea of the bodhisattva vow is deeply connected to the ideal of allegiance to Avalokitsvara. For all her compassion, she cannot change the quality of the material that she has to work with, but she never gives up.

Manjusri is often equated directly with the Divine Void, or Shunyata. Manjusri is, then, the dimension of the Buddha that relates Mankind to the wisdom of the Divine Void. On our own level he has an 'intellectual' quality; his impress may produce an 'incarnation' who is a great metaphysician or philosopher. He can make use of the intellect both to destroy ego and to reveal the nature of reality. He is usually depicted carrying the two-edged sword of wisdom, cushioned on the lotus of compassion.

Vajrapani represents the energy of the Buddha. We noted that in Sanskrit *vajra* is 'thunderbolt' or 'diamond,' and *pani* is 'in the hand.' The corresponding quality on the human level is fierce determination and unrelenting effectiveness in combating everything that obscures Man's latent Higher Centers. This is not the teachings but the decisive actions of a great teacher. Examples of this energy familiar to a Western student of religion would be Christ's overturning the tables of the money lenders or the advance of Muhammad's army on Mecca.

The Maitreya Buddha is the manifestation of the Buddha who will come into the world when the teachings of Siddhartha Gautama have finally been forgotten, and the line of conscious beings extending from him has finally come to an end. The Maitreya represents, in some way, the destiny of Mankind. He inspires Mankind in its darkest hours, when there seems little hope left in the individual life or when the work of a given generation appears to have come to an end, with still no light on the horizon. The Maitreya Buddha is like a fixed point, outside of time and space, towards which our efforts tend and cumulate.

2) MAHAYANA AND VAJRAYANA BUDDHISM

In the introductory section on the Buddhist Teaching we described the three forms of Buddhism that developed in the century after the death of the Gautama Buddha: Theravadin, Mahayana, and Vajrayana. Theravadin Buddhism was never established in Tibet, but the Tibetans retained the three-term set by introducing the term *Hinyana* to describe the spiritual practices which comprise what we have called the 'first work.' In other words the Hinyana path is the work to purify the lower centers and familiarize the aspirant with presence. Thus while Theravadin, Mahayana, and Vajrayana are historical terms, the term 'Hinyana' was coined in Tibet to describe the preliminary work that is the foundation for both the Mahayana and the Vajrayana paths.

We noted that in India the Mahayana and Vajrayana lineages had developed relatively independently of each other and were sometimes, in the general culture, viewed as being in contradiction. When we think of these teachings practically, and not in the abstract, it can be said that each has a positive and a negative face. The 'negative' face is revealed in the misapplication of the teaching, which is inevitable – at least in some degree – on a level where the Lower Self is prevalent. By clarifying the positive and the negative face of these two teachings and by looking at the relationship between them, we can understand something of the remarkable nature of the Tibetan synthesis.

MAHAYANA BUDDHISM

Negative Face In eleventh-century India, Mahayana Buddhism had become, to some degree, identified with the formal hierarchy of monastic life. In other words the preoccupation with 'place and position' in a monastic order usurped the pursuit of the Eternal Present. Mahayana practice implies a commitment to the *vinaya* (the set of spiritual rules given by the Buddha) and students may mistakenly equate strict adherence to these rules with spiritual development. Additionally, a purely philosophical Mahayanism developed, which understood Shunyata as a nihilistic 'dead space.'

Positive Face In its true application the Mahayana path transcends 'work on oneself.' The Bodhisattva vow brings a compassion and a universality that enables service to the level one above and the level one below. The 'form' of the Mahayana teaching is compatible with enabling a Civilizational Order and with a path of awakening that takes place in the world of everyday.

VAJRAYANA BUDDHISM

Negative Face The idea of having 'special' practices and techniques can lead to a preoccupation with one's own awakening, in the sense of believing that one is on a 'fast track.' (Indeed, it is this very idea that has made the Vajrayana teachings popular in the West today.) This deviation often involves a fixed desire to master certain techniques and to be known to have mastered them. There is a tendency to overvalue those techniques used to heighten the state of the lower centers by infusing them with the energies of World 12. These techniques include the use of drugs, the sexual act, and a wide range of yogic and shamanic practices. Generally speaking, the negative face of the Vajrayana reveals a tendency towards the eccentric and the bizarre.

Positive Face First there is the sublime art of the direct, wordless transmission of Higher Centers. Secondly there is the acknowledgment of Shunyata as the 'Buddha Nature' and the attending doctrine of Clear Light. From this point of view the Buddha is in everyone. True, Vajrayana Buddhism transcends the rigid, hierarchical structures of monastic life and the sectarianism of formal religion while supporting and enhancing the universality and compassion of the Mahayana.

The originators of Tibetan Buddhism saw that in the particular environment of eighth century Tibet a fusion of Mahayana and Vajrayana was possible, which would minimize the 'dark face' of each while at the same time actually enhancing their positive sides. The self-preoccupation and eccentricity of the Vajrayana would be neutralized by the service and compassion of the Mahayana. The institutional hierarchy and formalism of the Mahayana would be neutralized by the immediate sense of higher reality fostered in the Vajrayana. Such a unity within a single Spiritual Tradition would produce an 'inner circle' capable of linking that Tradition to Living Religion to Civilizational Order and so enabling the Pyramid of Man.

The story of Tibet began, then, when the Buddha Manifestations[2] – who carefully watch Mankind from one millennium to the next – recognized the exceptional potential existing in the peoples of this mountain kingdom. According to the traditional Tibetan story, Avalokitesvara – in her great compassion for humanity – worked to prepare the ground for the coming of Tibetan Buddhism many centuries in advance. During this period Tibet was a growing empire, governed by the line of Yarlung kings. It extended from Bengal in the south to Mongolia in the north and included parts of Central Asia and much of what is now China. Avalokitesvara first made herself known to the last rulers in the Yarlung line at a time when the Imperial phase was near to its end, somewhere in the seventh century AD. She awakened several successive kings, and they in turn drew around themselves great Buddhist teachers from India, who, with the support and patronage of the kings, initiated teaching lineages. Indeed we can imagine the archetype of Eternal Tibet – outside of time and space – as a particular pattern of archangelic entities and enlightened beings, molding and giving life to the civilization as a whole. On the human scale, which is the scale of our story, the development of the Traditions in Tibet is directly related to the spread of the Buddhist Religion. Indeed the unique relation between Mahayana and Vajrayana Buddhism that developed in Tibet would have been part of the archetypal 'seal' that defines both Tradition and Civilization.

---

2. The Buddha Manifestations are here taken as equivalent to the Archangels of Judaism, Christianity, and Islam.

In the pages that follow we shall use the temporal history, known to scholars, to suggest the pattern of the archetype. First we shall make a brief sketch of the entire span.

In 640 AD – through the direct intervention of Avalokitesvara – the thirty-third king in the ancient line of Yarlung kings embraced Buddhism and achieved full enlightenment. He and his immediate successors invited Indian Buddhist Teachers into Tibet, and so began what came to be called the **First Buddhist Dissemination** – which took place under the patronage of the last Yarlung kings. The Teachers who came from India quickly recognized that something in the essence of the Tibetan people was uniquely attuned to monastic life. In the ninth century the line of Yarlung kings was overthrown by representatives of the traditional shamanic religion, known as the Bon religion, and there followed a **Period of Repression**. This in turn was followed by a century of general civil strife. Beginning from the late tenth century Buddhism began to seep back into the Tibetan plateau, and so began the period of the **Second Buddhist Dissemination** – which saw the growth of the great Tibetan Buddhist Orders. Regional princes once again summoned Indian sages and the various 'underground' lineages that had survived the years of repression came again to the surface. In this period the Tibetan Buddhist Orders, as they were later known to history, began to take form. In the eleventh century all of Asia was profoundly impacted by the rise of the Mongol Empire, and Tibet was no exception. Just at the time when the transmission of the Buddhist Vajrayana teachings to Tibet was more or less complete, the Mughals (Central Asian Islamic Mongols) conquered northern India and destroyed Buddhism there. The Shamanic Mongols of northwestern Asia threatened to, but did not, conquer Tibet. When the Mongols became aware of the level of religious life that existed in this mountain fastness, they accepted the lamas as their 'priests,' and a Patron/Priest Relationship developed between the Mongols and the Tibetans. This 'external' relationship, managed as it was by the high Tibetan lamas, had the effect of **Unifying Tibet as a Theocracy**. There followed a phase of **the Development of the Orders under the Theocracy**. However, the increasing involvement of the orders in governance led to rivalry and to competing alliances with the different Mongol tribes – for the Mongols themselves were not a unity. These rivalries were resolved by the coming of the Dalai Lama known as the **Great Fifth**, and under his leadership a real **Unification of Tibet** ensued. This centralization was an acknowledgment of 'Tibet' itself, and it was at this time that the great palace of Potala, at Lhasa, was created. Following the seventh Dalai Lama there came a time, in the years between 1757 and 1895, when five successive Dalai Lama 'tulkus' (reincarnations) died before reaching maturity. This was the period of **the Rule of the Regents**, during which the office of the Dalai Lama was not properly filled. The Orders continued their work through this period, but Tibet itself did not develop in relation to the other nations around it. In other words it became increasingly isolated. In the nineteenth century an anti-sectarian reform movement sprang up, known as **the Rimé Movement**. It focused on reforming the increasingly introverted practice of the Orders and the consequent rigidity that had been built into the Tibetan religion. It brought out again the 'positive face' of both the Mahayana and the Vajrayana. The principles of this movement were embodied in the **Thirteenth Dalai Lama** who, on reaching maturity, recovered the 'vision' of the Great Fifth and attempted **a Reintegration of Tibet**. In the interregnum that followed the death of the thirteenth Dalai Lama **the Chinese Invasion** occurred, and the newly-ordained fourteenth Dalai Lama was forced to flee the country in 1950. From this time we have the diaspora of Tibetan Buddhism.

This is the shell; let us try to give it some content!

THE FIRST BUDDHIST DISSEMINATION: THE YARLUNG KINGS

The First Dissemination of Buddhist teachings occurred under the last three kings of the Yarlung Dynasty, known as the 'Dharma Kings.' We will recall that *dharma* means 'the true teaching.' From 755 to 806 Tibet was a conscious monarchy.

The thirty-third king of the Yarlung line, **Songsten Gampo**, converted to Buddhism in 648 and achieved full enlightenment. He is a seminal figure in Tibetan history and the first Tibetan Buddhist considered to have achieved full consciousness. We might liken him to the Christian Saint Paul, a man of strong will awakened through the direct intervention of Higher School. Songsten Gampo was, at the time of his conversion, the ruler of a great empire, extending into Central Asia, Bengal, and China, but after his conversion the priorities changed. He determined to create a script for the Tibetan language, modeled on the ancient Sanskrit in which the Buddhist texts had originally been written. He then invited a number of prominent Buddhist scholars to Tibet, including Acharya Kumara and Brahmin Shankara from India and Acharya Shilmanju from Nepal. These men began the propagation and translation of the Buddha's teachings. Although the Tibetan people were not, at this stage, engaged in the study of the Buddhist teachings, the king himself and the sages around him were able to give instruction to many. In the Tibetan Spiritual Tradition, Songsten Gampo is seen as an 'incarnation' of Avalokitesvara.

Songsten Gampo's successor, the thirty-fourth Yarlung king, was **Trisong Detsen**, who ruled from 755 to 804. He was not only able to continue the project that Songsten

Gampo had initiated but to actually take it to a new level. He invited a number of the best-known Indian sages of his time to visit Tibet, the first being the Mahayana Teacher Santaraksita. Once Santaraksita arrived in Tibet and developed a sense of the essence of the Tibetan people, he made a deep commitment to teaching there. Trisong Detsen provided him with all the material support that was needed to create the first Buddhist monastery, and this he did, at a chosen site called Samye. Santaraksita himself was to oversee the construction, according to a plan of his own making, but as work proceeded the monastery repeatedly collapsed, and the workers were terrified that the local Bon deities were the cause of these disasters. Santaraksita then advised that it would be good to have the assistance of the renowned Indian Vajrayana practitioner **Padmasambhava** to consecrate the ground of Samye. Trisong Detsen contacted Padmasambhava, and he immediately agreed to come to Tibet. When he arrived, however, he did much more than consecrate the ground at Samye. Like Santaraksita, he immediately saw the potentials that existed in the Tibetan people, and he stayed to teach them. Needless to say he was successful in taming the spirits at Samye, and the first monastery in Tibet was quickly completed. Padmasambhava then continued throughout the country, and, according to the traditional story, openly and fearlessly challenged the spirits of the land wherever they were found, transforming molecular energy fields resistant to Buddhism into molecular energy fields conducive to meditation. He used the context of these confrontations to discredit the traditional Bon religion and to teach the population something of the Buddha Nature. His exploits became the stuff of legend.

After Songsten Gampo, Padmasambhava was a second 'incarnation' of Avalokitesvara. He existed then – just as he exists now – outside of time and space. He was one of the pivotal figures in Tibetan history, and he, perhaps more than any other, understood the archetypal pattern from which Tibet was to develop. Having seen the full span of Tibetan history, he formulated teachings that would be appropriate to each stage of its development and encoded these as 'terma.' The terma were texts and images, hidden throughout Tibet, that were to be rediscovered at a later date. Each terma was said to be guarded by a spell that connects it to the one who will find it, and each would be found at the time when it was needed. Thus each age finds the terma appropriate to its particular needs. Some of these were indeed recovered physically while others were revealed to the appropriate individual in the depth of meditative practice. One of the best-known of the terma is the manuscript now entitled *The Tibetan Book of the Dead*. In this way the great Tibetan Orders, which were to emerge from the eleventh century onwards, experienced the involvement of Padmasambhava through the full span of their existence.

Padmasambhava, Trisong Detsen, and Santaraksita complemented one another perfectly. In the working relationship that developed among them, Trisong Detsen founded the monasteries, Santaraksita ordained the *vinaya* monks, and Padmasambhava removed the psychological obstacles that the Tibetan people had to the development of Buddhism while firmly establishing Vajrayana lines of transmission. This was the beginning of the unique combination of Mahayana and Vajrayana teachings that was to characterize Tibet. One form this combination took was the coexistence of the highest level of Buddhist scholarship with advanced yogic technique, two things which had always existed separately in India. As it became clear that the experiment of Tibetan monasticism was succeeding, Trisong Detsen backed ever larger projects for the translation of Buddhist scriptures.

At the same time, in the period of Trisong Detsen's leadership, the external (physical) Tibetan Empire began to collapse. The new theocracy was less aggressive than the traditional kingship had been, and the energies of the Tibetan peoples had begun to flow in different channels. This loss of temporal power evoked firm resistance from those whose livelihood was directly connected with the material doings of the Empire.

In 806 Trisong Detsen was succeeded by the thirty-fifth Yarlung king, **Ralpacan**, who ruled until 838. He was a cultured and discerning patron who invited the best artists, craftsmen, scholars, and translators from Nepal, Kashmir, and Khotan. He continued his predecessor's heavy investment in translation and developed a detailed Sanskrit-Tibetan lexicon. Indian and Tibetan scholars worked together to translate the Tripitaka, the Commentaries on the Sutras, and the ancient Tantras. Ralpacan continued with the construction of Buddhist temples, implemented the *vinaya*, and defined the different classes of monks. He was, however, a much better priest than he was a politician, and his undoubted faith did not protect him from his political adversaries. The line of the Yarlung kings suddenly came to an abrupt end when Ralpacan was murdered by two of his pro-Bon ministers.

THE PERIOD OF REPRESSION

After the murder of Ralpacan in 838, a local prince, Lang Darma, usurped the Tibetan throne and so ended the line of Yarlung kings. Lang Darma reinstituted the traditional Bon religion and initiated a period of Buddhist persecution that was to last 136 years.

With the accession of Lang Darma, the Indian Masters fled back to India, the temples were looted, and the Buddhist libraries destroyed. There was a determined and largely successful attempt to destroy Buddhist monastic institutions in Tibet. The teachings of the First Dissemination survived through underground lineages, derived from the Vajrayana lineages that Padmasambhava had initiated in eastern Tibet. Here, particularly in the provinces of Kham and Amdo, where the control of Lang Darma was weakest, the Great Work continued in secret.

In 842 a Buddhist monk shot Lang Darma between the eyes with an arrow and, from that moment, Tibet was divided as Lang Darma's successors struggled for the throne. The years of active repression were followed by a long period of chaos, often verging on civil war.

THE SECOND BUDDHIST DISSEMINATION: THE GROWTH OF THE ORDERS

The sources of the Second Dissemination were **1)** the *vinaya* monks gradually moving back to Central Tibet from the eastern provinces and **2)** a second generation of Buddhist Teachers coming from India. From the new Indian sources three entirely new lines of transmission opened up which were to define the Tibetan Buddhist Orders. Each of these lines began from the transmission of an established Indian saint, who was then backed by Tibetan disciples who, working with their teacher, achieved full enlightenment.

1. **Atisa** (980-1054), through the Tibetan Drontompa to the formation of **the Kadam Order**.

2. **Naropa** (956-1041), through the Tibetans Marpa, Milarepa, and Gampopa to the formation of **the Kagyu Order**.

3. **Shantipa** (960-1030), through the Tibetans Drogmi Lotsawa and Sakya Pandita to the formation of **the Sakya Order**.

The first of the newly-opened lines of transmission, and the one which began the Second Dissemination, was that initiated by Atisa (Figure 51). While Atisa was born slightly after Naropa and Shantipa, he was actually in Tibet when he taught and when he introduced the principles that would define an Order. The lines of transmission running from Naropa and Shantipa passed through several generations before reaching this stage of development.

Figure 51. **Atisa Dipankara Shrijnana**

The story of Atisa's line of transmission shows the payment the Tibetans were willing to make to secure their connection to the Gods.

THE LINEAGE OF ATISA

In 978 Tsenpo Khore, the king of the province of Guge in western Tibet, was able to re-establish a Buddhist monarchy. He announced that he had become a Buddhist monk and changed his name to Yeshe-O. He then selected twenty-one young monks and sent them to India to pursue Buddhist studies. All but two of these young men died in India. When the two surviving monks returned they brought with them several Indian scholars, and so the Second Dissemination began.

Yeshe-O then sent an invitation, with a large sum of money, to the Indian sage, **Atisa**, asking him to reintroduce the dharma in Tibet. Atisa, who was then attempting to reverse the decline of the Buddhist practice in northern India which had occurred in the wake of the Mughal occupation, refused the offer and returned Yeshe-O's gold. Believing that the amount he had sent was insufficient, Yeshe-O set about to raise a much larger sum. While traveling to raise funds, he was captured and imprisoned by a regional prince, who demanded a ransom equal to Yeshe-O's weight in gold.

Yeshe-O's nephew determined to pay the ransom and amassed all the gold that he could. When he brought the gold to the prince who held his uncle captive and had it weighed in a balance, the sum was found to be less than the weight of the King. Nevertheless Yeshe-O now had proof of the dedication of his nephew and secretly told him to keep the money and use it to make a second offer to Atisa. The nephew followed the king's command, and shortly after that Yeshe-O died in prison. The story of what had happened moved Atisa, and so he agreed to travel to Tibet. Yeshe-O's personal sacrifice, combined with the sacrifice of the nineteen young monks who died in India, was the psychological payment for the re-establishment of Buddhism in Tibet. They were acts in the very spirit of Avalokitesvara.

Atisa was to become a seminal figure of the Second Dissemination. He was an Indian prince, who had pursued Vajrayana and Tantric practices until the age of twenty-nine, when the Buddha appeared to him in a dream and advised him to become an ordained monk. He then applied himself to Mahayana studies. This reversal of the usual order gave Atisa a special understanding of monastic life and of the possible place of Vajrayana Buddhism in a Mahayana context. Once in Tibet Atisa focused on the Mahayana teachings, on monastic practices, and on the adherence to the *vinaya* rules. Yet he taught the Vajrayana teachings – which he understood well – in the Mahayana context. He felt it necessary to emphasize the Mahayana teachings in order to offset the effects of certain renegade Vajrayana lineages that had developed during the Period of Repression. The renegade lineages had propagated fantastic techniques with the promise of quick results, but the kind of results they produced only strengthened the Lower Self and arrested any real possibility of spiritual development. From Atisa's work came the Kadam Order, which was noted for the purity of understanding that lay behind its application of the *vinaya* rule.

And at this point we are in a position to clarify our theme.

VISION OF ATISA: ARCHETYPE OF TIBET

Atisa spoke of a particular vision in which he had seen seven shining images of the seed-syllable, representing Manjusri alongside the seed-syllables representing Avalokitsevara and Vajrapani. (In both the Tibetan and Sanskrit languages single syllables or 'seed syllables' can be used to condense the infinite meaning of the *dharma* into a point. The Buddha Manifestations are each associated with a seed-syllable.) Atisa told his attendants that the appearance of the seed-syllables indicated that seven 'incarnations' of the Buddha Manifestation Manjusri were to manifest in Tibet. By 'incarnation' Atisa meant an individual who had reached the level of locked Higher Centers, such that they could be given the direct impress or 'seal' of an Archangel (Buddha Manifestation) and retain what they had been given. This was later interpreted by the Sakya Order to refer only to the Sakya lineage, but it can also be interpreted – as we shall interpret it here – to refer to Eternal Tibet. The history of the Tibetan Traditions shows us that the 'incarnations' of Manjusri were to include Sakya Pandita, Tsongkhapa, and Lonchenpa – for each of these claimed that Manjusri had manifested directly to them in a vision. With respect to the manifestations of Avalokitesvara, Atisa recognized Songsten Gampo and, of course, himself. To his list we might add the fifth Dalai Lama and the very distinguished Karmapa and Dalai Lama lines of reincarnating lamas, both of which claimed to be grounded in the being of Avalokitesvara. With respect to the incarnations of Vajrapani, we stand on more uncertain ground, but they would include teachers of the 'type' of Marpa Lotsawa, of which there were many.

We can imagine, then, an archetype for Tibet comprised of Avalokitsevara, Manjusri, and Vajrapani, and the human 'incarnations' of these beings – beginning from **Songsten Gampo**, continuing with **Padmasambhava** and **Atisa**, and following through to **Sakya Pandita**, **Milarepa**, **Gampopa**, **Tsongkhapa**, the **Fifth Dalai Lama**, and **Longchenpa**. This image is brought to completion by the reincarnating Karmapa and Dalai Lama lines.

While we have, with hindsight, 'filled in' Atisa's pattern, he would have seen many things that we do not. Literally, as a conscious being with fully developed Higher Centers, he would have seen *several dimensions* that we do not! Both Atisa and his 'incarnate' successors saw deeply into the essential signature of Tibet, as it exists outside of time and space. Atisa's full name, *Atisa Dipankara Shrijnana*, means 'He Whose Deep Awareness Acts as a Lamp.' The lives of the great lamas in the generations to follow became attempts to make the archetype that Atisa had perceived fully manifest.

We are now in a position to look more closely at the Four Orders of Tibetan Buddhism that existed before the reunification of Tibet which occurred under Sakya Pandita in 1235.

We note that the three orders based on lines of transmission from India (Kadam, Sakya, and Kagyu) were each actually founded and given their organizational form by Tibetans. These were fully-developed conscious beings attempting to resolve the practical problems of the Second Dissemination by creating an environment where people working together on different levels could reinforce one another's efforts. In other words they were people who had a working vision of the Pyramid of Man and who gave their lives to serve that vision.

THE KADAM ORDER

After Atisa's death in 1054 his disciple **Dromtonpa** formed the Kadam Order, which became a model for *vinaya* monastic practice in Tibet. Atisa had written, translated, or edited more than 200 books which formed the basis for the library at Reting Monastery, which Dromtonpa founded in the Reting Tsampo Valley just north of Lhasa.

The Kadam conception of monastic life was one of great purity, carefully balancing the 'positive face' of the Mahayana and the Vajrayana. The Order transmitted the Mahayana teachings openly but transmitted the Vajrayana teachings in secret. When an initiate was perceived to be ready, he might be introduced to the more advanced practices – but the Vajrayana path was not open to monks unable to master the *vinaya*, and it was certainly not open to the general public.

The Kadam School did not survive the sixteenth century. The Order was split in 1419 when the great teacher Tsongkhapa formed a new Order, based largely on the Kadam teachings. The 'Old' Kadam Order lacked the patronage, the political grounding, and the kind of leadership that an Order needed to sustain itself in the fifteenth and sixteenth centuries. Nevertheless the organization and the practices that Atisa had created continued to influence Tibetan Buddhism, as Tsongkhapa's new order – the 'Gelug' – rooted itself firmly in Atisa's teachings. Additionally, the originators of both the Sakya and Kagyu Orders were profoundly influenced by Atisa's teachings.

THE SAKYA ORDER

Drogmi Lotsawa (993-1077) was a member of one of the First Dissemination family lineages which had been initiated by Padmasambhava. He had been exposed to Vajrayana technique but felt the need for a more general context of work. He sought out the Indian teacher **Shantipa**, who had combined Mahayana and Vajrayana teachings. On returning to Tibet he implemented Shantipa's teachings, and worked together with a circle of monks who had struggled to keep the teachings of the First Dissemination alive. After Drogmi Lotsawa's death this circle built the **Sakya Monastery** in 1073. It was in south-central Tibet, between the Brahmaputra River and the fertile Shigatse valley. The work undertaken at this monastery established the balance between the Hinyana, the Mahayana, and the Vajrayana paths that were to define the Sakya Order. Within a generation a great Teacher emerged from this monastery; he was a Sakya monk who, at an early point in his development, had a direct vision of Manjusri and was recognized as one of the 'incarnations' of Manjusri prophesied by Atisa. He became one of the few great philosophers of Tibetan Buddhism. In his maturity he was known as **Sakya Pandita** (1181-1251) and through him – as we shall discover – the first theocratic government of Tibet was established.

THE KAGYU ORDER

The beginning of the Kagyu order was the now-famous journey of **Marpa Lotsawa** (later known as *Marpa the Translator*) into India to seek the Vajrayana teachings. There he encountered the Indian Teacher Naropa and received Vajrayana transmission from him. He returned to Tibet with a great many Indian Buddhist texts and began to translate them. To sustain himself he worked a small family farm with his wife, and as disciples began to come to him, he involved them with the work on the farm – which gave his teaching a particular external form. Marpa taught in a non-monastic Vajrayana 'householder' style.

At this time a young peasant boy, **Jetsun Milarepa** (1052-1135), was, with his mother, disinherited from his family lands and reduced to penury. On his mother's encouragement the boy studied sorcery, and when he came of age, Milarepa wreaked a terrible vengeance on his persecutors. Realizing the bad karma he had incurred with his ferocious deeds, he sought a spiritual teacher who could help him to neutralize these destructive tendencies. He found the great Vajrayana teacher Marpa Lotsawa, who tested him with the most exacting rigor over many years before finally giving him full initiation into Vajrayana practice. At a certain point Milarepa went into retreat in a mountain fastness to pursue his practice without distraction. There the Gods brought him to a level parallel with that of the highest Teachers in the Tibetan Tradition. Because of his humble origins, his many setbacks and failures, and the beauty and profundity of the poetry he produced (*The Hundred Thousand Songs of Milarepa*), he became Tibet's favorite monk. *The Life of Milarepa* became one of the most widely read religious texts in all the Orders and is still popular today.

Were it only for Milarepa's achievement the Kagyu Order would not have come into being. A third figure was needed to provide organization and form. Gampopa Sonam Rinchen, known as **Gampopa** (1079-1153), came from a rich peasant family and married when he was quite young. His wife and four children died in a plague while he was still in his twenties and he then became a Kadam monk, working in the tradition of Atisa. While Gampopa admired the Kadam principles and was permanently influenced by them, he did not find the direct source that he needed in Atisa's successors. When he heard of the great yogi Milarepa, the monks of the Kadam Order gave Gampopa permission to study under him.

After testing Gampopa sharply, Milarepa accepted him as his student, and under Milarepa's guidance Gampopa achieved enlightenment. Milarepa then sent Gampopa out on his own, advising him to continue his practice in certain solitary mountain retreats. Gampopa, however, returned to the Kadam Monastery at Sewalung. He found, over time, that he was unable to integrate Milarepa's Vajrayana teachings with the practices of the monastery. He then went into solitude for three years, by the end of which time he had attracted a circle of disciples.

When the disciples came, Gampopa taught each according to his level: the Hinyana practices to some, the Mahayana to others, and to others yet the Vajrayana teachings that had come down from Marpa and Milarepa. In this mixed context he taught the Vajrayana teachings more openly than the Kadam Order did. By combining the Vajrayana teachings with the established monastic practices of the Kadampas, he made it possible to develop an organization that could meet the needs of spiritual seekers on different levels, and in this way the **Kagyu Order** was formed. The Kagyus proved outstandingly successful in transmitting the Vajryana teachings within a monastic framework.

THE NYINGMA ORDER

In eastern Tibet, where the control of Lang Darma had been weak, certain of the lines of transmission established by Padmasambhava were able to survive, concealed and preserved in loosely knit family lineages. These lineages began to re-establish themselves in the chaotic interim years of 842 to 978. As the large, landowning Orders took form in the early twelfth century, these more traditional lines became collectively known as the Nyingma or 'Old School.' Thus we can say that the **Nyingma Order**, as it eventually developed, was the only Order to have its roots in the First Dissemination. It had the privileged role of being able to save and to copy many of the original, supervised Tibetan translations of the ancient Indian texts, which by then had been destroyed in both Tibet (in the ninth century AD under Lang Darma) and India (in the eleventh century AD following the Mughal invasion).

Unfortunately the Nyingma lines were discredited by the general abuse of Vajrayana that took place in eastern Tibet in the period following the ascendance of Lang Darma, but – we must remember – these were not the abuses of the Spiritual Tradition itself but what happened in its proximity. Having been forced to work in secrecy, the Tradition could have no control over what happened outside of its immediate sphere of influence and thus had a much reduced capacity to control any deviant figures that emerged from within.

We must also remember that the Nyingma Order had both Vajrayana and Mahayana influences in its origin, from Padmasambhava and Santaraksita respectively. When the Nyingma teachings went underground there was great difficulty for the *vinaya* practitioners because monasticism tends to be visible. But somehow the *vinaya* practices did survive, and in the time of the Second Dissemination, *vinaya* monks came from the eastern provinces of Kham and Amdo to the central province of U-Tsang to renew the *dharma*. Over time the Nyingma Order acquired an external form loosely approximating that of the other orders.

UNIFYING TIBET AS A THEOCRACY: SAKYA PANDITA AND THE PATRON/PRIEST RELATIONSHIP

Understanding how the Orders came into existence, we are now in a position to understand how the link of Spiritual Tradition to Civilization was created in Tibet. Yes, the individual orders came into existence with the Second Dissemination and, yes, they were able to stabilize themselves in the twelfth century. But there was still no centralized government in Tibet, and there had been none since the time of Lang Darma's repressive regime. After the chaotic century that followed the Buddhist persecution, what grew back were elaborate monastic organizations which began to wield real power. With this came – from the middle-lower levels of the Pyramid of Man – a fixation with ever-bigger monasteries, ever-taller statues, and ostentatious displays of dharmic art. There also came rivalries and power struggles between the orders. In all of this there was little concern for Tibet. The link to Civilizational Order, which had been strong in the time of the three dharma kings of the Yarlung line, was now relatively weak. A greater concern for Tibet – and a greater awareness of what we have called the Pyramid of Man – came with the centralization of the country under the rule of the new Buddhist Orders, first the Sakya Order and then the Gelug.

To understand these matters more clearly, we must look again at Tibetan history.

In 1240 the grandson of Genghis Khan, Godan, invaded Tibet, killing monks and destroying and looting monasteries, villages, and towns. He asked his generals to bring him the highest Buddhist lama they could find, and their choice was **Sakya Pandita**, who we will recall from our description of the Sakya Order. Having been generally recognized as the 'highest Buddhist lama' of his time, he received a 'letter of invitation' to the Mongol court. He was being invited to negotiate the conditions of the submission

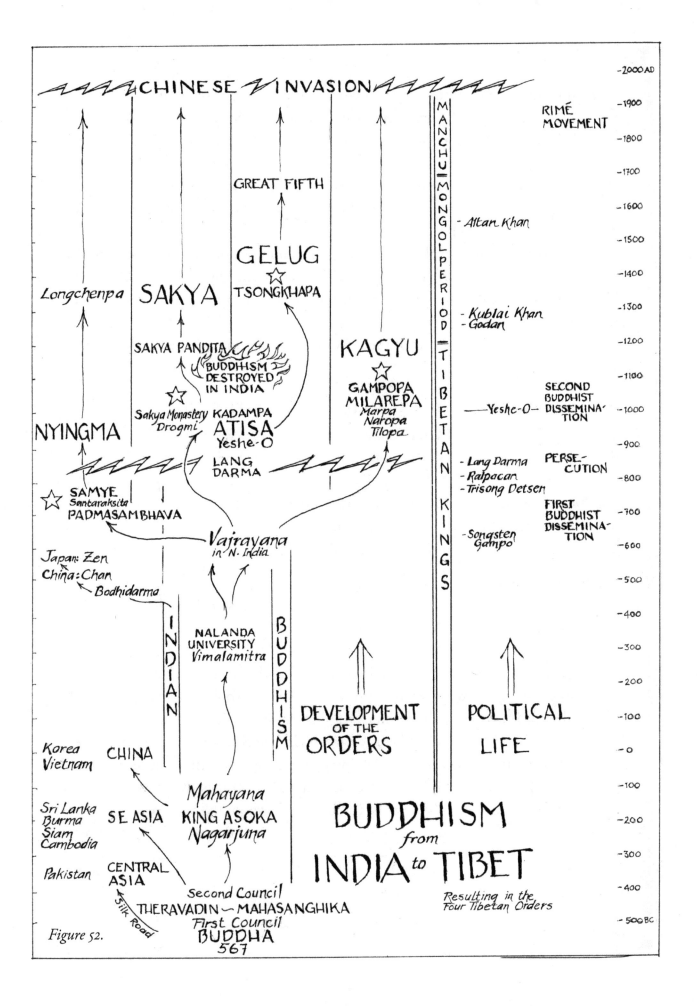

Figure 52.

BUDDHISM
from
INDIA *to* TIBET

Resulting in the
Four Tibetan Orders

of Tibet. At the time when Sakya Pandita met Godan, the prince was suffering from a debilitating illness. Sakya Pandita cured Godan, and in the period of his recovery converted him to Buddhism. Godan then became a disciple of Sakya Pandita and, as a consequence, decided not to invade the provinces of Tibet; instead he made Sakya Pandita his regent. This initiated the first patron/priest relationship between Mongol temporal might and Tibetan spiritual authority. The Tibetans supplied the religious guidance and the Mongols provided military support. This was, in fact, the foundation of the Tibetan theocracy: a nation ruled by an order of priest-kings.

When Sakya Pandita's nephew Pakpa succeeded him, he formed a relationship with Godan's successor Kublai Khan. Pakpa gave Kublai Khan Vajrayana initiations, and Kublai Khan gave Pakpa the whole country of Tibet, which until then had not been united.

From 1235 to 1358 the lamas of the Sakya Order were the acknowledged rulers of Tibet.

DEVELOPMENT OF THE ORDERS UNDER THE THEOCRACY

Tibet received many benefits from unification under the Sakya Order. At the same time there was an unavoidable politicization of the Orders. The Kadam Order, which lacked political grounding, faded. The final Tibetan Order, the Gelug, emerged as a direct reaction to the increasing Mongol influence in the Sakya Order. It drew its principal texts and teachings from the old Kadam School. Let us review, then, the Orders as they developed under the patron/priest relationship during the rule of the Sakya Order.

The Sakya

Being the ruling order the Sakyapa became directly involved in the management and administration of the country. The choice of the site of the Sakya Monastery proved fortunate as it was located at a nexus of trading routes connecting the fertile lands of the Shigatse valley, the rich agricultural land of Nepal, and the lands of the nomads who supplied the rest of Tibet with butter and wool. The Sakyapa were able to take full advantage of the commercial opportunities their site provided.

Both politically and commercially powerful, the Sakya Order became subject to the corruptive influence that wielding power brings, at least at the level of their religious and administrative practice. The material fortunes of the Order fell in 1368 when the Chinese defeated the Mongols with whom the Sakyapa were linked, bringing the Order onto a level playing field with the other three Tibetan Orders.

With this adverse turn of fortune came spiritual renewal, for the Sakyapa returned to the ideals and reform principles of Sakya Pandita, becoming a 'scholarly' order known for the rigor and clarity of its teaching and the firmness of its monastic rule.

The Kagyu

The Kagyupa developed a focus on the arts and emphasized the place of art in awakening. They were also the first Order to develop the 'tulku,' or reincarnate lama, system, and from this came the famous *Karmapa* lineage of tulkus. They had developed this system in the period before Sakya rule, but it was in the thirteenth century that it came into real prominence in Tibet and was adopted by all the Orders. It solved the problem of succession and of who the 'real Teacher' was. Under the tulku system, the 'real' teacher was literally an embodiment of the Bodhisattva vow – a perfected example of selfless service. There was, then, no limit to the development that could take place under this leadership.

The idea of reincarnating though a chosen tulku is based on the principle of the Mahayanist 'bodhisattva' vow. We will recall that under this vow an aspirant will forgo entry into *paranirvana* and work indefinitely for the realization of all sentient beings. Under the tulku system the head of an Order (or even of a monastery) would determine to be reborn as a human as many times as he considered necessary to fulfill his bodhisattva vow. Having determined to be reborn, the lama would then give clear indications as to where this would occur, who his parents might be, and how he could be recognized. The members of the order would then, after his death, recover the child and compensate the parents. This manner of determining succession brought with it the necessity of a regent, active in the period between the lama's death and the coming-to-maturity of the young tulku. Normally a lama would select his own future regent while he was 'still alive.'

The Kagyu lama **Dusum Khyenpa** (1110-1193) initiated this form of succession in Tibet. He died in 1193 and was reincarnated as Karma Pakshi in 1204. The Kagyu Order eventually formed the **Karmapa** line of tulkus, which was one of the most prominent in Tibet.

Thus it became accepted that great teachers might remain within the human world for many generations and, in this way, give continuity to the teachings and to the institutions of which they were a part. Each of the four Tibetan Orders eventually adopted this system. After the centralization of Tibet under the fifth Dalai Lama in 1637, it was allowed that a tulku could inherit the estate of his previous incarnation. This allowed the great estates of the Orders to continue unbroken. The disadvantage of this system lay in the period of regency it created. Normally the reincarnating head of the Order should select the regent, but if a tulku died before reaching maturity, a regent would have to be decided by other means, and in the extended interim period many difficulties and confusions could develop.

The Gelug

The Gelug Order emerged in the period of Sakya rule as a reaction to the corruptive effects of temporal power on the inner work of that Order. It was founded by **Tsongkhapa** (1357-1419), a Sakya monk born at a time when the Orders were in conflict over their respective alliances to different Mongol princes. Tsongkhapa felt that the Sakya Order, of which he was a part, was being drawn into purely political disputes. He was also concerned with the general ethical decay he saw in Tibet and with the abuse of the Vajrayana practices that had become prevalent. Against the advice of his lama he went into a period of extended retreat. In this retreat he had a vision of the Maitreya Buddha in eternity and encountered the disembodied manifestation of the Buddha whom the Tibetans call Manjusri. Manjusri taught Tsongkhapa directly, counselling him to teach the systems of Nagarjuna and Atisa. At a point when he was focused on studying the texts of Atisa, a multitude of Buddhas appeared before him. All the Buddhas then dissolved into Atisa, and Tsongkhapa was able to directly question this great master. At the end of the exchange Atisa placed his hand on Tsongkhapa's head in blessing. In 1419, on the basis of his visions and his studies, Tsongkhapa founded the Gelug Order, first known as the 'New Kadam.' He carefully laid out the relation between Hinyana, Mahayana, and Vajrayana practices that was to define that Order. In the process of founding it, he initiated the great monasteries at Ganden, Drebung, and Sera.

The Nyingma

What then of the original Buddhist lineage that had survived the repression of Lang Darma? This set of linked family lineages came under increasing pressure to define themselves in relation to the emerging Orders of the Second Dissemination. The Nyingma had both *vinaya* and *non-vinaya* monks, but there was a preponderance of *non-vinaya* 'householder' monks and ascetic solitaries. Another way of looking at this is that the Nyingma were those who did not follow the new forms created by Atisa, but drew most deeply on the traditions originally established by

Padmasambhava. They were accomplished experts in the old Vajrayana techniques. The centralization of Nyingma practice and the development of more elaborate organizational forms only began from about 1600.

The forerunner of this process was the very great Nyingma Teacher, Longchen Rabjampa, or **Longchenpa** (1308-1363). Longchenpa first received the Nyingma transmission which came to him through his family line, and then proceeded to study with the great teachers of his day without regard to sect. He received both the Kadam and the Sakya teachings, and then entered the monastic college of Sangpu Neutok, where he was able to study the range of Tibetan Buddhist texts. After the period at Sangpu Neutok he went into solitary retreat. In this phase of his existence he had a vision of Padmasambhava, who presented him with the Dzogchen teaching, a complementary set of Vajrayana techniques designed to help the practitioner bypass conceptual mind and directly realize the primordial, formless awareness that is Higher Centers. This became particularly precious to both the Nyingma and the Kagyu Orders.

Longchenpa was the third embodiment of Manjusri that Atisa had predicted. It is timely that the Archangel whom the Tibetans called Manjusri – with his special capacity to make use of the energies of the intellect – manifested within the Nyingma Order, which was known for its mastery of yogic technique. This enabled that Order to achieve balance, and the teaching that was to result ultimately influenced all Buddhist teaching in Tibet.

THE GREAT FIFTH AND THE UNIFICATION OF TIBET

From 1235 to 1358 the lamas of the Sakya Order ruled Tibet, but, as their rise to power was tied to the Mongols, when Mongol power diminished so did that of the Sakyapa. Sakya rule finally ended with the collapse of Mongol control of China in 1360, and a difficult period of rivalry between the Tibetan Orders followed. From 1450 onward internal struggles of one kind or another became almost continuous within Tibet. While the individual Orders were able to sustain their spiritual life and the Buddhist Religion continued to receive life from them, the civilization of Tibet did not fare so well. Again, we make the point that rivalries originate at the level of Religion and Civilization. The inner Traditions are, then, constantly forced to redefine themselves in light of these 'external' deviations – and they are constantly and very considerably challenged to give their internal works clear priority over their external activities.

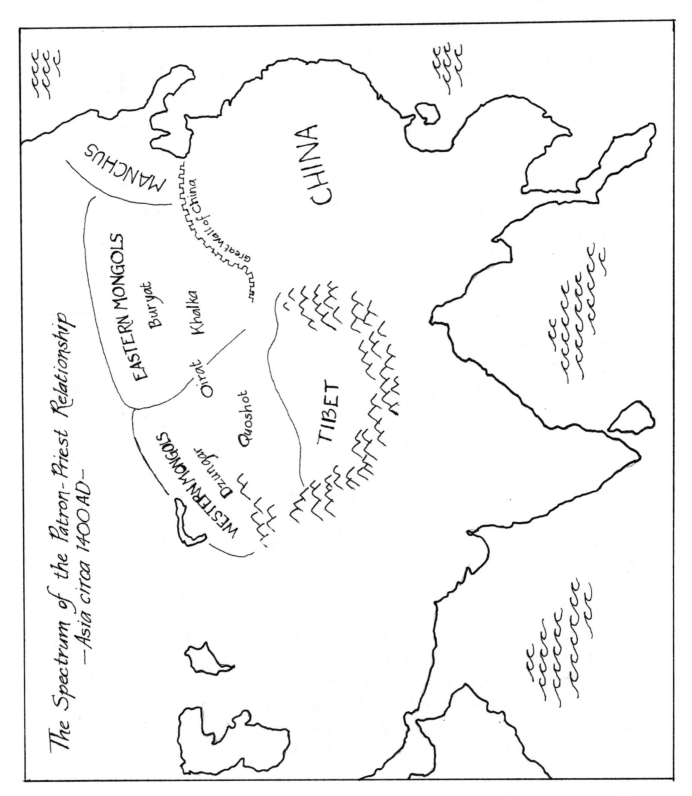

The Spectrum of the Patron-Priest Relationship
—Asia circa 1400 AD—

MANCHUS

CHINA

great Wall of China

EASTERN MONGOLS

Buryat

Khalka

Oirat

WESTERN MONGOLS

Dzungar

Quoshot

TIBET

Figure 53.

In 1550 **Altan Khan**, prince of the Tumed Mongols, recaptured the Mongol capital of Karakorum and established a general peace with the Chinese. In so doing he became the foremost Mongol leader of the Western Mongol Empire.

The patron/priest relationship was now to be re-established between the Gelug Order and the Tumed Mongols, and this coincided with the creation of the 'Dalai Lama' tulku lineage. But to understand how this happened and why the 'first' Dalai Lama is actually the 'third,' we must make a brief aside.

The Gelug Order had emerged in the period of turmoil that followed the weakening of Mongol, and hence Sakya, power. Part of its credo, coming from the experience of Tsongkhapa under Sakya rule, was that it was apolitical. In 1419 Gyalwa Gendun Drup (1391-1474) succeeded Tsongkhapa as the head of the Gelug Order. As an extension of his bodhisattva vow he determined to take birth again, and in that incarnation continue his work as the head of the Order. He explained to the members of his Order that, while he had been meditating by the sacred lake Lhamo, the female guardian spirit of the lake, Palden Lhamo, emerged and promised that she would protect the reincarnation lineage of the Gelug Order. He then prophesied his own re-embodiment and determined his regent. The re-embodiment, Gendun Gyatso, formalized the system of the reincarnation lineage, and since that time the Gelug regent has gone to Lake Lhamo to receive the signs that will reveal the next reincarnation.

In this third embodiment, as Sonam Gyatso, the head of the Gelug Order was invited to visit Altan Khan, the freshly triumphant leader of the Western Mongol Empire. When the two met Altan Khan immediately recognized in Sonam Gyatso a great Teacher and conferred on him the title of Dalai Lama. The word 'Dalai' is the Mongol world for 'great ocean.' Sonam Gyatso accepted this title, for both the Mongols and for the Tibetan people, and applied it to his previous two incarnations – thus becoming the 'third' Dalai Lama. He was given temporal authority in Tibet, and in the following decades he had great success in converting the Mongols to Buddhism.

While Sonam Gyatso successfully established the central authority of the Dalai Lama, trouble with Mongol alliances continued. When the Manchus began to make war on the Mongols, attacking them from the north and the east, the situation within the Mongol clans changed, and the Tumed Mongols ceased to exercise leadership. This changed the relation between the Orders in Tibet. The Kagyu Order had strong connections with the Khalkha Mongols in the central-north area of Tibet and to different regional princes within Tibet, particularly the king of the province of Tsang. At one point the King of Tsang actually tried to forbid the Gelug Order's search for the tulku of the fifth Dalai Lama.

This is the kind of politics and history with which we are all too familiar, but for the Men of the Tradition it was a dark hour. Many of them found themselves drawn into secular conflicts from which it was almost impossible to extract themselves – for they had taken vows and had real responsibilities to the members of their respective Orders. They would have known that figures like Padmasambhava, Milarepa, Tsongkhapa, and Sakya Pandita could never disagree, but on the levels just below even highly evolved people can be drawn into conflict, particularly when it affects those people and those causes that are nearest to them. For the inner circle of the Orders such a period would have instilled a deep wish to create the circumstances under which these destructive conflicts could never recur.

Fortunately the King of Tsang was unable to stop the Gelug Order from retrieving their tulku, and in 1637 Ngawang Lozsang Gyatso became **the fifth Dalai Lama**. By this time only the Western Mongols remained unconquered by the Manchu invaders. The regent for the fifth Dalai Lama had sought out the rising prince of the Khoshut ('Quoshot' in Figure 53 on page 432) Mongols, Gushri Khan, and asked him to defend the young Dalai Lama. We cannot say what it was that caused Gushri Khan to back the young boy, but back him he did. In 1640 he brought an army into Tibet, quickly defeating the Kagyu Order and their Khalka Mongol supporters and ended the factional struggles within the country. Gushri Khan then spent the remainder of his life in Tibet, and, in fact, became a Tibetan.

We can say, in retrospect, that the first four Dalai Lamas devoted their lives to building monasteries and realizing the principles established by Atisa and Tsongkhapa, despite the political chaos that raged around them. But the fifth Dalai Lama was something quite different. As he reached maturity even the Mongols looked at him in awe. He was a *Mahasiddha*, born enlightened, and a direct expression of Avalokitesvara. He saw the vision that Songsten Gampo, Atisa, and Gampopa saw; *he saw into the archetype of Eternal Tibet*. In his youth he received the Gelug, Nyingma, and Sakya teachings, and he had strong family ties to both the Sakya and Nyingma Orders. He himself followed – throughout his life – a nonsectarian path.

He was able to unite the central, southern, and western provinces of Tibet for the first time since the assassination of Lang Darma. He arranged Tibet in districts with regional ministers and provided a uniform set of laws for the country. He made Lhasa into its capital and had the great palace of Potala (Figure 54) constructed there. This

Figure 54. The Great Monastery of Potala, at Lhasa

magnificent example of Tibetan architecture became the image of a priest-kingdom linked to the Gods in its mountain fastness.

On another level he integrated the Hinyana, Mahayana, and Vajrayana practices in a way compatible with a Conscious Theocracy, where Living Religion and Civilization are guided by Spiritual Tradition.

The Great Fifth was the crown of eight centuries of Buddhist activity in Tibet; he represented the triumph of the metaphysical over the physical. True, he came to this position because there had been a struggle between the Orders, and his own regent had resolved it by summoning the Khoshut Mongols. True, he was a Gelug, and while he carefully studied the teachings of the other Orders, he could not be a Gelug, a Nying-ma, a Kagyu, and a Sakya all at the same time. True, there was a degree of 'bad karma' amongst the Tibetan Orders in the century before he came to power. But the Great Fifth also, and at the same time, represented eight centuries of 'good karma' finally coming to fruition. Just what this good karma was may not be so clear to us, because good karma does not provide the material for history – but we can presume that it was there. The point is that he did it, or 'it happened' – the archetype of Eternal Tibet became manifest.

One can think of the Great Fifth as a special 'organ' in the larger body of Tibet. This special organ being complete and ready, the larger body somehow adjusted itself to enable the regenerative function that it was equipped to perform. Thus the Great Fifth transcended the karma of his immediate past, and his influence, and the various influences that were realized through him, neutralized the other lower influences that existed in those circumstances. The transcendent beauty of the great palace of Potala is a symbol of this.

Of course with the passing of such a man the function that he represented would have to be sustained, and sustained by men who had not – perhaps – attained the same level of development. Success would require a special kind of positive intent: a will capable of letting go of the baser side of human nature and carefully positioning the higher functions and faculties so that they might control it. And this, not in one, but in many people. To our present knowledge humanity has never been able to accomplish this. Thus, when an event such as the Great Fifth takes place, and a higher function is activated – not just in an individual, but in the extended body of community – we should not be surprised if the 'bad karma' that was latent in the original situation wins through over time. These considerations aside, the vision of Tibet realized by the Great Fifth was a benchmark not only for Tibet, but for all humanity.

The seventeenth and early eighteenth centuries were a high water mark in the work of the Tibetan Orders. The relation of Tradition, Religion, and Civilization was finally complete.

THE RULE OF THE REGENTS

We step back a moment, then, from the function actualized by the Great Fifth to review the context. Viewed externally, the role of the Dalai Lama had been based on a patron/priest alliance with one or another of the Mongol powers surrounding Tibet. The 'patron' received the current of Living Religion while the 'priest' received military protection. The Mongols – with whom the patron/priest relationship had developed – were to remain a force in Tibetan life. From the seventeenth century there was a series of alliances with the different Mongol tribes, particularly the Khoshut and the Dzungar. During this time the Manchus, who were at war with the Western Mongols, also developed an interest in Lamaism. Like the Mongols they were without a religion of their own, and like the Mongols they were aware of the presence and value of the Great Religions of the World.

From the time of the Great Fifth the Gelug Order remained the center of government in Tibet. The sixth Dalai Lama was, however, a controversial figure. His regent was a Nyingma monk, versed in Tantric practices, which he communicated to the young

Sixth at a very early age. From the time of his maturity the Sixth ignored the monastic rules in a way quite uncharacteristic of a Gelug monk. Laizang Khan, the Khoshut Mongol prince who succeeded Gushri Khan, took him to be a false Dalai Lama, not a true incarnation of Avalokitesvara. He killed the Sixth's regent and deposed the Sixth himself, who then died while traveling into exile in China. On his last journey the sixth Dalai Lama composed a poem, revealing the essential details of his next incarnation, and on this basis the Gelug Order was able to find the tulku of the seventh Dalai Lama. In the meantime Laizang Khan established himself as the King of Tibet and installed a tulku of his own! Having secured the true tulku of the Seventh, the Gelug Order made an alliance with the Duzungar Mongols, who promptly seized Lhasa and forced out the Khoshut Mongols. This was a mixed blessing as the Duzungar Mongols ruled Tibet harshly. Within a few years the Gelug made overtures to the Manchus, who obligingly sent an army into Tibet. The Duzungars immediately fled, and the traditional patron/priest relationship now devolved onto the Manchus.

The Manchus at this time ruled China, while remaining racially distinct from the Chinese population. The Manchus saw the Chinese as a distinct subject-people and forbade intermarriage with them, directing the Chinese to continue in the practice of Confucianism while they themselves embraced Tibetan Buddhism. They created a special Buddhist shrine in the Forbidden City. They never attempted to govern Tibet, never attempted to collect taxes there, and never interfered with the tulku system. In short, they were not materially interested in this distant sparsely populated country with few natural resources.

Thus, after the overthrow of the Duzungar Mongols the theocracy re-established itself along the lines laid down by the Great Fifth. Unfortunately, after the seventh Dalai Lama, there came a period when five successive tulkus died before reaching maturity, and for 138 years (from the death of the seventh in 1757 to the maturity of the thirteenth in 1895) the country was ruled by regents who had not been selected by a mature Dalai Lama. Central authority in the country weakened, and there was much corruption. The regents themselves had little or no experience of what was going on in the outside world, and no one thought of the place of Tibet in the international theater. The regents tended to think, as Tibetans generally tended to think, that the Buddha was with them in the Sacred Land of the Dharma. The country remained loosely centralized and monastically oriented, but was increasingly subject to forms of social rigidification. The individual Orders amassed a great deal of wealth, and used it to create a wonderful religious life, but not to develop the country itself.

In this we see the 'Religion' of Tibetan Buddhism resisting the influence of the inner Tradition, and, at the same time, failing to cultivate the Civilizational Order which was the very fabric of Tibet. In the Pyramid of Man that was outlined in Chapter 4, each level must serve the level one above and the level one below. At the level of Religion, this would have involved an 'inspired' Tibetan Buddhism bringing the more gifted and motivated lay people into politics, administration, and law. It would have meant creating an enlightened theater of civic life, in which, perhaps, new 'secular' lineages might develop. Thus, while the internal life of the Orders continued, there was a weakness in the service to the level one below, and so in the ability to serve the life of the whole. There also developed, within the Orders, a marked preoccupation with the acquisition of occult and yogic powers. Thus there was a falling away from the vision of 'Eternal Tibet' as seen by Songsten Gampo, Padmasambhava, Atisa, and the Great Fifth. Nevertheless, much that had been established was preserved, real values were widely recognized in society, and this was – in many ways – a Golden Age for humanity.

One significant result of the rule of the Regents – over time – was a very weak foreign policy. When Tibet first adopted Buddhism it was surrounded by other Buddhist civilizations, but by the seventeenth century it was the only country in the region in which Buddhism was predominant. During the seventeenth, eighteenth, and nineteenth centuries Tibet became increasingly isolated from its neighbors. Internally, there was a growing conviction that Tibet was the only country in which the true dharma flourished. Thus the life of the country in the late eighteenth and nineteenth centuries centered increasingly around the individual Orders, and the Tibetan Civilization itself experienced a period of relative stagnation.

In the eighteenth century the Far East began to feel the presence of the European powers, and the eastern rulers became concerned to defend their territories and to extend them where possible in order to create buffer zones. At this time China began to eye Tibet. However, in 1799 China itself was plunged into social chaos by the first of a series of internal revolts. The Manchus were able to retain their hold on power but they were greatly weakened, and due to this the Manchu Emperors showed little interest in Tibetan affairs. This was a respite for Tibet.

THE RIMÉ MOVEMENT

In the mid-nineteenth century, from the 1860s, the Rimé movement developed within Tibet. This was an ecumenical and non-denominational attempt to regenerate Buddhist practice, presenting itself as an embodiment of the ancient ideals and principles of Buddhism in Tibet.

After a century of regent rule the religious and social climate in Tibet had again become partisan, and rivalries again developed between the Orders. These rivalries produced two things: **1)** the tendency towards narrow doctrinal purity within each Order and **2)** a diminished general concern for Tibet. We consider again the principal criteria for the Pyramid of Man – that each level serve the level one above and the level one below. In the rivalry of the Orders both forms of service were weakened. We mentioned above that a third result of the 'absence' of the Dalai Lama function was an increasing fascination with the development of occult and psychic powers. Within the Orders there was, on the part of some, pride in the display of powers – as though they proved a direct connection to the Gods, when in fact such displays represent the very opposite.

Thus, in early nineteenth-century Tibet, you did have something approximating the Pyramid of Man, but the place of the 'ruling principle' – the Dalai Lama – was vacant, and those who 'filled in' often had hidden agendas. The ruling position is, in any society, a natural focal point for ambition and greed of every kind, and it attracts individuals who are without conscience. When such an individual gains control it is very easy for things to go wrong. However, if Tradition and Religion retain their integrity it may not go far wrong, and corrective action is always possible.

The Rimé movement was initiated in eastern Tibet by Jamgon Kongtrul (1813-1899, Figure 55) and Jamyang Khyentse Wangpo (1820-1892).

The movement was not a new Order, but an ecumenical movement of like-minded men in each of the Orders. It emerged from within the Orders, and it was first directed at the substance of their teachings. In each of the Orders there was an established tradition of oral debate, and such debate easily leads to the conviction that the doctrine of one's own school represents the best or highest approach and that the others represent a flawed understanding. This situation was much exacerbated by the political and economic rivalries of the regent period. The Rimé Movement was vigorously opposed to the sectarian tendency that had developed. In its view each of the teachings is true and none are in contradiction. Yet the unique quality of each one must be understood. As Jamgon Kongtrul put it, "One must see all the teachings as without contradiction, and consider all scriptures as instructions." To ignorantly criticize other Orders was wrong, and any misunderstanding so created should be immediately rectified. The men of the Rimé emphasized that the Buddha himself had categorically forbidden his students

Figure 55. **Jamgon Kongtrul Lodro Taye (I) of Sechen**

to criticize the teachings of other teachers and other religions. The Rimé recognized, at the same time, that it was important to preserve the original style and methods of each teaching lineage and so preserve the power of the lineage experience. For these teachings are not abstract, but something you must respond to with the whole of your being. They are, in their highest expression, anything but rote learning. The great Rimé teachers were capable of presenting the teachings of each Order clearly and forcefully, without in any way confusing them with the teachings of the other Orders. At the same time they were capable of demonstrating that the essence of these teachings is the same, in the sense that they are all vehicles for the transmission of higher consciousness.

All of this reveals the spirit of the Great Work, and – as we shall see – the Rimé Movement had implications not only for the Orders but for Tibet itself.

THE THIRTEENTH DALAI LAMA AND THE REINTEGRATION OF TIBET

The situation changed in 1895 when Thubten Gyatso (1876-1933, Figure 56), the thirteenth Dalai Lama, came to his maturity. He was the first Dalai Lama in 120 years to survive past the age of twenty, and he recovered the vision seen by Songsten Gampo, Padmasambhava, Atisa, and the Great Fifth. *He saw that the vision of Tibet itself had been forgotten.*

Figure 56. Thubten Gyatso, 13th Dalai Lama

Here a clarification is necessary. The reincarnation of a tulku line is not something that can be understood in 'linear' fashion, for it includes dimensions which are outside of time as we know it. The inexactitude of the study of reincarnation is given by the fact that it relates to several different dimensions of time at once. Having said this, the fourteenth Dalai Lama, the successor to the thirteenth, said that he remembered something of the thirteenth Dalai Lama's life and of his aims and projects. He did not 'remember' the child incarnations at all but had again a strong 'memory' of the Great Fifth and a partial memory of some of the figures before him. We may presume, then, that the thirteenth Dalai Lama also had a 'weak' relation to the child incarnations and a 'strong' relation to the Great Fifth. Understanding this we can see that something that went 'off' during the period of Regent Rule 'came back' with the coming-of-age of the thirteenth Dalai Lama.

The thirteenth Dalai Lama was exposed to the Rimé Movement early in his life and became a Rimé teacher himself. What were the implications of this? Let us consider again the sectarianism of the Orders that the Rimé Movement strove to counteract. These Orders governed the country; thus sectarianism amongst the Orders was a sure sign that the vision of Tibet had been lost. The universal, non-sectarian view of the Rimé had clear implications both for the teachings of the Orders and for the administration of the country, for in a theocracy spiritual and material things are inextricably linked:

without openness on one level, you do not have it on the other. The Rimé attitude was a key to opening up the idea of service to the level one above (which transcends any specific teaching) and service to the level one below (which is the earthly foundation of all the teachings). Thus, at the beginning of the twentieth century, the success of the Rimé Movement was the condition of realizing the archetype of Tibet.

Additionally to this, as the thirteenth Dalai Lama reached maturity, he recovered the Great Fifth's vision of Tibet, but he recovered it *in an entirely different context*. In the time of the Great Fifth, Tibet had been surrounded by countries in which Buddhism was practiced and in which enlightenment was given great objective value. The very fact that the Tibetan monastic theocracy even existed was of great significance. But Tibet was only able to sustain this independence through what was called the patron/priest relationship. From the time Ghengis Khan had united the Mongol Empire, some five centuries before, Tibet – like all the small countries of the region – had to maintain a system of alliance and tribute payment in order to keep its independence. For Tibet the 'tribute' given was religious teaching, with military protection received in return.

The patron/priest alliance became a kingpin of Tibetan polity. It was initially formed with the Mongol Empire itself, under Ghengis Khan's grandson Godan. As the Empire gradually came apart, it devolved onto the different Mongol tribes: firstly the Tumed, then the Khoshut, and then the Duzungar. Finally – in the time of the seventh Dalai Lama – it transferred to the non-Mongol Manchus, rulers of Ching Dynasty in China. The Manchu placed such a high value on their relation to the Tibetan theocracy that they themselves embraced Lamaism, while encouraging the subordinate Han majority to focus on the Confucian teachings. The Manchu even created a Tibetan sanctuary at the heart of the Forbidden City in Beijing, named the Hall of Central Righteousness. Such was the situation in the seventeenth and eighteenth centuries.

But by the mid-nineteenth century the industrial revolution had thoroughly disrupted the traditional world of the eastern empires, and the Great Game played by the European powers – vying for the control of the eastern world – was well underway. The Manchus became more concerned with maintaining their territories than with securing the spiritual well-being of their dynasty. Thus, at a time when the patron/priest relationship was becoming irrelevant, the world outside of Tibet was being transformed into a field of struggle between the great industrialized nation states and ancient imperial empires aspiring to industrial status.

The fact that the vision of Eternal Tibet came alive with the thirteenth Dalai Lama was indeed a miracle, but this vision needed to be reimplemented.

In 1904 the British, who had established control of India, Nepal, Sikkim, and Bhutan, sent a military expedition into Tibet with the aim of establishing a loose protectorate. They wanted control, without a real commitment to defending the country. When the British invasion came, the thirteenth Dalai Lama – then twenty-eight – fled into exile in Mongolia, where he opened negotiations with Tsar Nicholas II, petitioning him for support. But the Russians were unwilling to directly confront either the British or the Chinese. As the dust settled, Thubten Gyatso felt himself able to work with the British on their own terms and returned to Lhasa. The British invasion, however, had terrified the Manchu. When they determined that the British were not prepared to defend Tibet, they sent one of their generals – Chao Erh-feng, known as 'the butcher' – with an army to occupy Tibet and to directly assimilate it into China. The Manchu army entered Tibet in 1909, killing, raping, and pillaging as it came. On its arrival in Lhasa, the soldiers began shooting Tibetan officials. The Dalai Lama escaped to Darjeeling, where he began actively networking with both the British and the Russians. But it seemed that he was coming to the end of his rope. Then, in 1911, the Chinese Nationalist party overthrew the Manchu dynasty. The Nationalists proclaimed sovereignty over Tibet, but it was a sovereignty they were completely unable to enforce, for the Manchus still controlled Tibet. When the Dalai Lama heard of the destruction of the Manchu power base in China, he immediately began working, through a system of couriers, to organize the overthrow of the occupying Manchu forces. Under his leadership the Tibetan people united to cast out the Manchu army. In 1912 Thubten Gyatso returned to Lhasa, and in June of that year he proclaimed Tibet's complete independence, both from China and from the European powers. This reprieve was the Indian summer of the Tibetan Civilization. From that point onward the reinstated Dalai Lama was able to play off British, Russian, and Nationalist Chinese interests to ensure Tibetan sovereignty. He created a Tibetan army, and began a process of modernization which included increased representation in government, legislation against corrupt officialdom, a centrally-run police force, rational taxation, a postal system, and a system of hydroelectricity in Lhasa.

The thirteenth Dalai Lama was concerned that Tibet be able to establish right alliances with the nations of the outside world. He knew enough of the Gods to know that when they worked closely with men, they brought great uncertainty – and in that uncertainty they expected men to find solutions for themselves. Help comes, then, when men have completely extended themselves, and so are psychologically ready to accept help in the form that the Gods choose to give it. And so the Dalai Lama extended himself on all fronts. As a member of the Rimé movement he worked for the inner reform of the Orders. At the same time he worked for the reform of the nation. It is the tragedy of Tibet that his vision came at a very late stage in the game.

Yet most Tibetans continued to rest secure in the idea that they were under the protection of the Gods, the deities, and the realized lamas. The recent Manchu occupation was simply a passing storm cloud. To them Tibet was the sacred land of the dharma, invulnerable to the onslaughts of the outside world. This attitude reflects the false sense of security given by Religion. But the end was not yet imminent. Beginning from 1920 the Chinese Nationalists were seriously challenged by the Communists under Mao Tse-tung, and this gave a final extension to the Tibetan Indian summer.

The Dalai Lama determined to use this time to bring Tibet into the international community, to seek allies against China, and to create a standing army at home. The great monasteries, however, were deeply resistant to change, and the international allies that the Dalai Lama sought – including England, Russia, and the United States – did not want to make a commitment to protect Tibet against China. In 1933, in a famous statement made shortly before his death, Thubten Gyatso warned his people of imminent danger from foreign invasion, and predicted that unless Tibet adopted his modernization policies it would be overrun, its people killed or enslaved, and its religion destroyed. He prophesied that "the great works of the Dharma Kings of old will be undone, and all our cultural and spiritual institutions persecuted, destroyed, and forgotten." This echoed Padmasambhava's prophecy, made more than a thousand years before, that, "when the iron bird flies and horses run on wheels, the Tibetan people will be scattered like ants across the face of the earth."

Thubten Gyatso died on seventeenth December 1933. We cannot follow the amazing story of his life without feeling compassion for this man and for all he represents. Yet this life is typical of one lived in direct service to the Gods: shocks, sudden reversals, visions of extraordinary possibilities, threats on every side – all threaded through with moments of complete transcendence. This is exactly what it is like to work directly with the Gods. Every vestige of security and human comfort is taken away. One lives in a state of complete vulnerability … and one realizes that this is the price of being asked to become one of them.

THE CHINESE INVASION

In 1939 the Second World War broke out, forcing a kind of alliance between the Chinese Nationalist Party and the Communists. At the end of the war the Chinese Communists, under Chairman Mao Tse-tung, made a successful bid for power. On 1st January 1950 the New Year's broadcast from Beijing announced that the People's Liberation Army would "liberate Tibet from foreign imperialists and reintegrate it with the Motherland." In August of that year a massive earthquake shook the country, and the sky over southeastern Tibet glowed an ominous red. On 7th October 1950, 20,000 combat-hardened Chinese troops with modern weaponry, backed by five million soldiers, invaded Tibet. The Tibetan militias were quickly overcome.

The state oracles of Tibet announced that the new Dalai Lama should replace his regent immediately. **Tenzin Gyatso**, the fourteenth Dalai Lama, assumed full temporal and religious control of Tibet on 17th November 1950, at the age of sixteen. He attempted to mediate with the Chinese and to preserve the forms of Buddhism that he knew. But it soon became clear that this was impossible, as the Chinese focused on murdering the highest lamas as they found them. From this point the lamas began to flee the country. Buddhism as they knew it was no longer possible in Tibet. Alexander Solzhenitsyn wrote that "China's rule in Tibet was more brutal and inhumane than any other communist regime in the world." The 'cultural revolution' that the Chinese imposed on the Tibetans cost 1.2 million lives (one-sixth of the total population) and destroyed 6,250 monasteries, the repository of 1,300 years of Tibetan Civilization. The Dalai Lama himself escaped to India in the guise of a young soldier and became the center of a Tibetan community in Dharmasala. Of him we shall say little, as this wonderful man has written of his own life, his aims, and his struggles much more eloquently than we can detail here. The persecution of the Tibetan people intensified as China consolidated her control of Tibet.

Tens of thousands of Tibetans fled the country to join the Dalai Lama in exile, hoping for a better life in India, Nepal, Bhutan, or Sikkim. The Kagyu Order formed important bases in Bhutan and Sikkim, the Nyingma in Bhutan, and the Gelug and Sakya in India. A number of teachers, trained in the traditional way under enlightened lamas, came to teach in the West or continued teaching in the East while accepting Western students. In the late 1960s, and through the 1970s, there was a noble attempt to establish the vision of Mahayana and Vajrayana Buddhism in the West. By now, however, the generation of teachers that began the great transmission to the West has passed away: the sixteenth Karmapa died in 1981, Chogyam Trungpa Rinpoche in 1987, Kalu Rinpoche in 1989, and Dilgo Khyentze Rinpoche in 1991. The fourteenth Dalai Lama himself still survives and teaches.

One can only hope that something may yet come of the selfless and well-intentioned attempt to re-establish the great Tibetan Orders outside of Tibet. Yet we may be the living witnesses to a fate already shared by the Sufi Orders of Islam, the Christian Monastic Orders, or the great Zen Schools – where the religious forms survive and Group Work may continue, but the Spiritual Tradition itself has come to an end. The problem for the Great Work in our own age is that any conscious teacher is increasingly isolated. In the general culture of our time there is not even an approximately accurate idea of what a conscious being is or what kind of authority naturally corresponds to a conscious role. Living Religion itself has become a thing of the past, and the true understanding of myth and symbol has faded into obscurity. To complete this picture we must note that the core of understanding required for the Work of the Traditions is very, very difficult to reconstitute. Ultimately it is not something that any human being, or any group of human beings, can 'do.' It requires the intervention of the Gods.

Here, in the drama of Tibet, we see all the tensions and contradictions that have characterized the work of the Traditions through history. In this tiny mountain kingdom the strain created by the close proximity of temporal power and the Great Work was neutralized and transformed, century after century, in a truly remarkable human achievement. It is hard to believe that something of such great promise could pass into history before our very eyes.

As we have noted, the crises that come to the Traditions, and to the Civilizations given life by Traditions, are never purely the result of external factors. Such crises are always, in some degree, the result of internal problems which have their place in attracting the crisis. The story of Tibetan Buddhism, which is undergoing crisis in the historical present, gives us a measure by which to understand the crises of the Spiritual Traditions as being both internal and external. In the Tibetan instance, Religion came too much to the fore, at the expense of both Civilization and Tradition. The individual Orders, then, were limited in their ability to serve the Civilizational Order to which they were connected. Had the internal order of each of the four Orders been closer to that of the archetype of true individuality and collective life, the rigidification of the dharma at the level of Religion might not have occurred. Each level might then have served the level one above and the level one below in a more direct and meaningful way. It is this relationship that neutralizes the tendency to self-preoccupation, which is endemic on each level. More importantly, the realization of this 'two-edged' service allows the lower level to see the higher level for what it is, to the extent that this is possible. Under these conditions Tibet might have achieved an 'enlightened' civic life, developing independently

THE STORY OF MAN

of the patron/priest relationship and drawing in people of ability and goodwill from outside the monastic community. This in turn might have enabled the Tibetans of the nineteenth century to make the trade relations and the political alliances that would have allowed them to preserve their independence through the twentieth century. Such a Tibet might then have been able to provide some guidance for the rest of humanity in the profound spiritual crises of the late twentieth and early twenty-first centuries.

This raises a more general point, at the 'theme' level of the Story of Man.

No matter how far one goes in the realization of human potential – as an individual, as the member of a Spiritual Tradition, or as the representative of a Civilizational Order – one is tested. Tests provide the opportunity to overcome certain obstacles which cannot be overcome in any other way. Of course a severe test may end in failure. It may bring about the collapse of the entire edifice, whether it be the Steward of the spiritual aspirant, the lineage of the Spiritual Tradition, or the fabric of the Civilizational Order. The test of Tibet was the twentieth century. It brought an end to the patron/priest relationship, it saw the global isolation of the country, and it saw the coming-into-being of Communist China. At the same time it saw a sudden re-emergence of the vision of the Great Fifth, and it felt the regenerative influence of the Rimé Movement. The failure to pass this test was not simply the failure of twentieth century Tibetans, but the karma of Tibet and the karma of Mankind over the last 1,200 years. By the time the turn of the nineteenth century came, what happened in the twentieth was probably inevitable. But we must keep in mind that failure in this test was the failure to achieve what humanity has never yet achieved, and it represents the most concerted attempt to establish the Pyramid of Man in recorded history. Many favorable circumstances supported Tibet's emergence as a theocratic state: geographic isolation, the proximity of India's greatest teachers, and the historical development of the patron/priest relationship. Tibet may well stand as more of a credit to humanity in the eyes of the Gods than any other polity known to history. Also, the struggle of the Tibetan Traditions to pass this test produced many permanent and significant results, which are simply not visible to us in the line of time that we are in.

CHAPTER 30

Confucius and the Chinese Spiritual Tradition

Eternal China shows us a refinement, depth, and radiance that reflects the workings of Enlightened Mind. The enlightened state is essential to Imperial China, and resonates through it; it is inscribed in its ceramics, its architecture, its painting, its poetry, its literature, its statuary, and even its furniture. Viewed over its nine millennia lifespan China has the semblance of a cosmos, and the teachings of Confucius are a reflection of that. At the same time, Confucius' teachings are an attempt to instill the principle of cosmos ever more deeply into the Chinese social order. Thus, we cannot understand Confucianism without understanding something of China. But with China – so ancient and vast – it is hard to generalize in a meaningful way. Its history has been over-written and re-written innumerable times, particularly in the last century. Nevertheless the Chinese experience is such a significant part of the Story of Man that we must make the attempt.

China always brings with it a feeling of centrality; it has been its own reference point since the beginning of recorded history. The Chinese, like only the Sumerians and the Egyptians before them, developed written language without reference to any other previously known script. The basin of the Yellow River was one of the two places on our planet where we have evidence of agriculture before 7,000 BC and the first to be able to support a substantial population. Thus, since before the beginning of recorded history, there has been an expanse of fertile agricultural land, supporting millions upon millions of people.

While China is vast and populous, it is potentially unstable. Because of its prosperity and the concentration of wealth in its great cities, it has always been vulnerable to pillage and conquest by the nomadic tribes to the north and west. At the same time, China has always been subject to periodic internal upheavals. It is hard to secure a single governmental form over such a large population, and regional dynastic struggles were common.

The recorded history of China begins from the great social 'consolidation' of the dynasties, starting with the Hsia (2100-1600 BC) and the Shang (1600-1046 BC) and taking more definite form with the Chou (1045-256 BC). There followed a succession of centralized, bureaucratic empires, punctuated by chaotic interim periods, arising from both internal strife and external conquest. Chinese history is the history of these imperial regimes, and at the same time it is the unfolding drama that took place between the native Han Chinese and the other peoples surrounding them; these were the Mongols, the Manchus, the Tibetans, the Japanese, and the Vietnamese. China has been periodically conquered by these surrounding peoples and, in turn, has attempted to assimilate and conquer them. The legendary Great Wall of China, which was erected along its northern border, was easily breached and only effective when defended by a single, centralized regime. Given that China was subject to periodic outbreaks of internal strife, it remained vulnerable to invasion.

Returning to the theme of the Story of Man, whatever plan the Gods may have had for China, Confucius' teaching was certainly part of it. He provided an ethical and social code that fitted with the centralized imperial system that was appropriate to China, and this code was universally accepted by the Chinese as their own. His teaching proved – over the centuries – to be an essential element of the Civilizational Order. Confucianism spread, historically, in the periods of relative stability when the vast bureaucratic empires took form. These were the empires of the Han, the Tang, the Sung, the Yuan, the Ming, and finally the Ching.

Confucius, who lived from 551 to 479 BC, meets many of the conditions of being a Prophet. His teaching was unique and it permanently changed the spiritual landscape of China. While it was not widely accepted during his own lifetime, it marked the beginning of a definitive Spiritual Tradition, and it became – over time – one of the great World Religions. Confucius' frequent references to Sky, Heaven, and Nature link him to the ancient Shamanic-Taoist Tradition which had deep roots in China's past. Confucius taught in an environment where Taoism was practiced in conjunction with the traditional Chinese polytheistic religion. He did not break with these more ancient

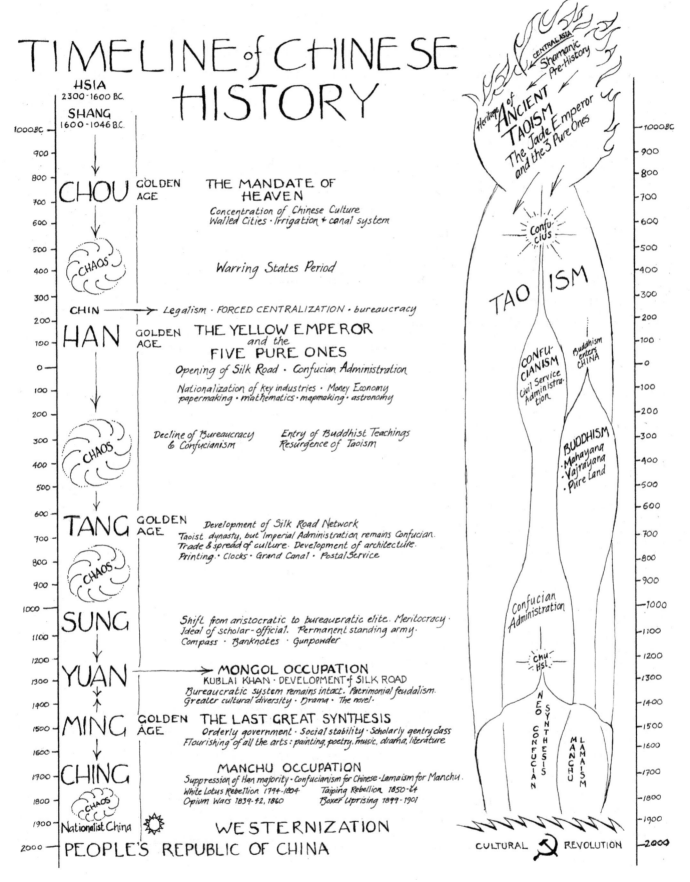

TIMELINE of CHINESE HISTORY

HSIA
2300-1600 B.C.

SHANG
1600-1046 B.C.

CHOU — GOLDEN AGE
THE MANDATE OF HEAVEN
Concentration of Chinese Culture
Walled Cities · Irrigation + canal system

CHAOS

Warring States Period

CHIN → Legalism · FORCED CENTRALIZATION · bureaucracy

HAN — GOLDEN AGE
THE YELLOW EMPEROR
and the
FIVE PURE ONES
Opening of Silk Road · Confucian Administration
Nationalization of key industries · Money Economy
papermaking · mathematics · mapmaking · astronomy

CHAOS
Decline of Bureaucracy   Entry of Buddhist Teachings
& Confucianism   Resurgence of Taoism

TANG — GOLDEN AGE
Development of Silk Road Network
Taoist dynasty, but Imperial Administration remains Confucian.
Trade & spread of culture. Development of architecture.
Printing. · Clocks · Grand Canal · Postal Service

CHAOS

SUNG
Shift from aristocratic to bureaucratic elite. Meritocracy.
Ideal of scholar-official. Permanent standing army.
Compass · Banknotes · Gunpowder

YUAN → MONGOL OCCUPATION
KUBLAI KHAN · DEVELOPMENT of SILK ROAD
Bureaucratic system remains intact. Patrimonial feudalism.
Greater cultural diversity · Drama · The novel.

MING — GOLDEN AGE
THE LAST GREAT SYNTHESIS
Orderly government · Social stability · Scholarly gentry class
Flourishing of all the arts: painting, poetry, music, drama, literature

CHING
MANCHU OCCUPATION
Suppression of Han majority · Confucianism for Chinese · Lamaism for Manchu.
White Lotus Rebellion 1794-1804   Taiping Rebellion 1850-64
Opium Wars 1839-42, 1860   Boxer Uprising 1899-1901

CHAOS
Nationalist China

WESTERNIZATION

PEOPLE'S REPUBLIC OF CHINA

CENTRAL ASIA
Shamanic Pre-History
Heritage of ANCIENT TAOISM
The Jade Emperor and the 3 Pure Ones

Confucius

TAOISM

CONFUCIANISM
Civil Service Administration

Buddhism enters CHINA

BUDDHISM
· Mahayana
· Vajrayana
· Pure Land

Confucian Administration

Chu Hsi

NEO CONFUCIAN SYNTHESIS

MANCHU LAMAISM

CULTURAL REVOLUTION

1000 B.C.
900
800
700
600
500
400
300
200
100
0
100
200
300
400
500
600
700
800
900
1000
1100
1200
1300
1400
1500
1600
1700
1800
1900
2000

Figure 57.

traditions, but created a social ethic that was in conformity with them. Indeed he provided extensive commentaries on the ancient Taoist Book of Changes, known as the *I Ching*. Confucius drew much from China's past, but, in relation to the principle of Civilizational Order, his teachings were much more focused than anything that preceded it.

To understand the continuity and development of the Confucian Tradition, we must look a little more closely at the cultural situation from which it emerged.

Through the early dynasties (the Shang and the Chou periods, 1600-256 BC) China had loosely embraced a Taoist folk religion. This had developed in a spontaneous, unstructured way from the teachings of a series of ancient masters, Taoist and otherwise. It seems likely that, through the centuries, there were several enlightened emperors who were able to give the Taoist folk religion meaningful form and impress it on the pattern of Chinese life. The ancient masters of Chinese prehistory were similar to the Vedic masters of Central Asia, in that – while we know little of them – they made the world different from what it was before.

In the traditional Chinese religion **the Jade Emperor** was the ruler of Heaven and Earth, Lord of the living and the dead, of the gods, of men, and of demons. Behind the Jade Emperor was the First Principle of the Universe, which had no beginning and no end; it was self-existent, changeless, limitless, and invisible. This First Principle was divided into an upper purity, named the *Shang-ch'ing*, and a great purity named the *T'ai-ching*. These two 'purities' combined with the Jade Emperor, who was also called the 'jade pure' – or *Yu-ch'ing* – to become **the Three Pure Ones**. In this there is, perhaps, some echo of a triadic conception of the Absolute.

An important principle that developed during the Shang dynasty – the dynasty just before the Chou – was the principle of **the Mandate of Heaven**. This principle became central to the Chinese world view over the entire dynastic period. The belief was that the Jade Emperor would bless the authority of a just ruler but be displeased with a despotic one. Heaven would thus 'withdraw its mandate' from a despotic or corrupt ruler and transfer it to the one who would rule best. The principle of the Mandate of Heaven emphasized the performance of the ruler, and it did not require that the legitimate ruler be of noble birth. And indeed the Han and the Ming Dynasties were founded by people of modest birth. Evidence of a divine repeal of the Mandate of Heaven might include continued internal strife, severe floods, famines, or plagues. The principle of the Mandate of Heaven was well-accepted by the common people of China, as it encouraged the removal of incompetent or despotic rulers and provided an incentive for rulers to rule well. It even legitimized a certain level of social dissent.

However, as the Chinese population grew into the largest on earth (50 million by 1,000 BC) and the Chinese civilization began to take form, the precepts of the traditional religion were not enough to ensure social order. The teachings of the religion were not easy to put into practice, and they were invariably subject to superstitious interpretation. In order for a great emperor to preserve the Mandate of Heaven some new influence had to enter the social fabric – and so the stage was set for Confucius' contribution.

CONFUCIUS' TEACHING

Confucius was born at the end of the Chou Dynasty. The Chou was an immensely long period of relative stability (1045-256 BC) which saw the origin of the Chinese written language and the foundation of much of Chinese culture, literature, and philosophy. However, from the sixth century BC internal strife began. At the time Confucius was born, in 551 BC, China had entered the Warring States period, and the early Chou was already viewed as a golden age.

Confucius wanted to 'restore the Mandate of Heaven' and to bring peace and prosperity to the Chinese people. He had the vision of a unified imperial state whose rulers would succeed to power on the basis of merit and personal integrity rather than on the basis of family connection. The ruler should be devoted to his people and should aspire both to personal perfection and to the social perfection of his kingdom. The moral influence of such a person would affect all those around him. The virtues of the ruler would then communicate through his personal example, rather than by the imposition of an explicit code of behavior. A central principle was "The sage values human beings over property." Confucian ethics gave priority to the attainment of a certain state of being – which included the cultivation of discerning judgment and an understanding of the play of human energies – over the simple memorization of rules.

A central principle of Confucius' teaching was that of *jen* (*ren*), which was a combination of altruism, benevolence, and conscience. *Jen* is an innate impulse in Man which can be developed through his participation in the community. One should develop one's responses of *jen* to the point where they can guide right action intuitively. *Jen* also means 'relationship,' and implies benevolence where appropriate, but remains always sensitive to context. In some cases real compassion might imply stern reprimand. When one was unsure of the appropriate action to take – when one's *jen* was insufficiently developed – one should refer to the rules of *yi*, the established guidelines for proper conduct. To develop one's *jen* one must first internalize the Confucian Golden Rule – to always treat others just as one would wish to be treated oneself. Virtue, then, is based on a principle of harmony with other people, produced through ethical practice and by a growing identification of the interests of self and other. This field of activity is the ethical life of the community, and its development is the development of a people's natural morality. The other becomes a mirror for oneself. Thus Confucianism relates directly to Civilizational Order, and is developed out of Civilizational Order. From another point of view, it is a development of the 'social' side of Taoism.

Jen is energy: patterns of energy and flow of energy. The focus is always on the experience of different qualities of energy and on placing the higher energies over the lower. Like classical Taoism, the Confucian 'way' is not a defined set of principles but a path ... a never-ending journey. With respect to its view of our internal energies, Confucianism is very close to Taoism. With respect to its view of external life, however, Confucianism emphasizes correct social relationships, justice, and sincerity.

To understand the impact of Confucianism we must understand that the Chinese are a 'relational' people; they are relationship-oriented. They understand that life is comprised of a combination of different kinds of relationship: family, personal, economic, and political. Confucius described the five archetypal human relationships in the terms appropriate to his time: **1)** father to son, **2)** subject to king, **3)** friend to friend, **4)** brother to brother, and **5)** husband to wife. To keep all of these relationships healthy and alive requires a high degree of self-knowledge and a generally selfless attitude. Confucianism understood the need to manage human relationships carefully and intentionally, both the necessity of fulfilling social responsibilities and the very real obstacles to achieving this. In fact, to actually achieve consistency in this area requires that one live in the present, taking the moment of NOW as the reference point for every human interaction.

Confucius presented the principle of benevolent well-being in all contexts of life, in a way that penetrated the heart of the Chinese people. His teachings were recorded in the *Analects*, which were written by his followers in the generation after his death.

Was Confucius a Prophet? Was he a person who brought the message of God to Man, authoritatively initiating a Tradition, a Religion, and a Civilization, and presenting a clear view of the priorities that exist between these three? Confucius did not claim to bring the word of God to Man, and he did not make clear distinctions between the

Work of a Tradition, the work of a Religion, and the work of a Civilization. Nevertheless, what survived from his teaching became universal to Chinese culture for nearly two millennia. It is, taken on its deepest level, a teaching of how the internal work can impact external life and the government of men. Confucius' inner teaching was based on the traditional principles of Taoism. He then provided an 'outer' teaching which was capable of supporting the 'inner' teaching, while at the same time receiving inspiration from it. To use the terminology of Book I, he formulated the First Work in such a way that it could be connected to the practices of government and administration. The practice of Confucius' inner teaching (the Work of the Steward) could then animate the First Work and so penetrate society at large. Later, as we shall see, Neo-Confucianism developed, with a sophisticated presentation of the relationship between these different levels.

It is likely that Confucius regenerated an existing Spiritual Tradition. This Tradition was to endure and to reassert itself in different forms through the long life of Imperial China. The Tradition at work in the formation of the Chinese Civilization, more than a thousand years before, was probably similar to the Vedic Tradition in India in that there was not the defining figure of a single Prophet, but a Tradition working through a series of Masters, some visible and others invisible. In this way an environment was created where the realization of human potential was possible and where the vision of the archetypal China was reflected in its social life over several millennia. These potentials were, of course, realized only to a degree; they coexisted – through Chinese history – with all of the weaknesses and limitations that the human psyche reveals in whatever phase of history we find it.

In studying the history of Dynastic China we find clear evidence of the Pyramid of Man. We see, time and again, the living link between Tradition, Religion, and Civilization. We see the Tradition adjusting to changes in the regime and giving a sense of continuity to Chinese history while at the same time supporting the spiritual aspirations of the Chinese people. Looking at the full span of Chinese history we see an intelligence at work behind the many changes of regime. Through the rebellions, the restorations, the phases of bureaucratic corruption, and the periodic reforms, we see evidence of the *credo* of the Spiritual Traditions: to serve the level one above and to serve the level one below. The simultaneous awareness of the Gods above and the general state of Mankind below brings both profound commitment and great uncertainty while revealing ever-deeper layers of meaning. For those who can bear such an awareness, everything comes

Figure 58. Tai-nan Confucian Temple, Chuan Tai Shou Hsueh

into the present. We shall see, then, how the Story of China developed as the exploration of one of the main themes of the Story of Man.

To understand how Confucianism developed and how Neo-Confucianism – the philosophy of the late Tang, Sung, and Ming dynasties – took form, we must first understand something of the older Taoist teachings, which are the very essence of China.

THE TAOIST CONTEXT

Taoism is better understood as a way of life than as a religion. It is behind Chinese art, astrology, medicine, martial arts, alchemy, *feng-shui*, and cuisine. We can generally associate it with the most remarkable refinement in the arts, wherever that is found.

The Western idea of Taoism developed in the romantic or counter-cultural atmosphere that existed from the 1930s to the 1960s. It became connected with the idea of a retreat from society and the achievement of a mysterious unity with nature. In fact the Taoist teachings were usually addressed to the gentry and provided guidance in all the different walks of life, including statecraft and administration. Political figures influenced by Taoism advocated humility in leadership and a restrained approach to administration. We could say that Confucianism, when it came, transformed and perfected this side of Taoism. While Taoism instructed the 'civilized person' in the practice of the arts – particularly of music and of poetry – it carried within itself the ancient yogic practices which had originated in Central Asia, and these became a permanent part of Chinese life and culture.

The literary legacy of ancient Taoism is the *I Ching,* or Book of Changes, which is supposed to have been written by a Chinese ruler in 2800-2737 BC.

The best-known historical teacher of the Tao was **Lao-tzu** (551-479 BC), who may have been a contemporary of Confucius. According to the traditional belief he was the keeper of the Archives at the royal court of Chou. He was versed in the classics of his time, and there are several versions of a story about Confucius consulting with Lao-tzu concerning rituals. It is said that, towards the end of his life, Lao-tzu grew weary of the moral decadence of city life, in an era which saw the decline of civilizational order. He decided to travel 'into the West' and live as a hermit on the unsettled frontier. At the western gate of the city he was recognized by one of the guards. The sentry asked the aged Master to leave a record of his wisdom, and this was the legendary origin of the *Tao Te Ching.* In fact the *Tao Te Ching* is a multilayered commentary on many traditional sayings. There is not strong evidence for a single author, but there is an underlying thread of conscious influence and conscious involvement. It is the work of an entire Tradition over many centuries.

In the text of the *Tao Te Ching* the word *Tao* means literally 'path' or 'way,' and on the deepest level it refers to the flow of the universe itself. The Tao is the unseen source of all existence; it is immensely powerful yet utterly humble, at work in the very roots of all things. Humans have no special place within the Tao, being just one of its 10,000 manifestations. The man who enters this inner current returns to a natural state of calm transcendence. From within the Tao he does not assert himself 'against' his environment, but acts spontaneously in relation to the pattern of events that flowers all around him. He moves with the flow of the greater river. When people are in contact with the Tao, their decisions will be right; when they become one with the Tao they will become immortal. Lao-tzu was considered by the Chinese an immortal being instructing men in how to become themselves immortal.

This side of Taoism was further developed in the works of **Chuang-tzu**, who lived a century later, in the very depths of the **Warring States** period. Chuang-tzu's teachings give a peculiar pre-eminence to personal awakening, and their timing may reflect his response to the changing Tao. Put bluntly, "If society is in a shambles, you go back to the bamboo grove." Chuang-tzu's reputation was such that, after his death, the Taoist tradition was often called the Lao-Chuang School.

In the Lao-Chuang School view, the universe works naturally and harmoniously according to its own laws. The essential energy of the universe is *chi*, which is manifested on the human level as 'existence' or 'being.' Human life itself was a natural flow of *chi*, which, in its connection with the outer world, results in an ongoing pattern of action and reaction. The blockage of *chi* leads to aggression, fear, illness, and insanity; the enhancement of *chi* leads to transcendent existence.

Compassion, moderation, and humility are principles of behavior that enable the flow of *chi* in a human being. In acting according to nature, Man is accepting his place in the living cosmos. A central principle arising from this understanding of *chi* is *wu wei,* or effortless action. This signals unity with the Tao itself. The core values of Taoism are spontaneity, naturalness, vitality, detachment, flexibility, receptiveness, emptiness, and a complete relativity about all human custom, habit, and thought.

More generally, the Taoists believe that Man is a microcosm of the universe. The human body, like the universe that contains it, is comprised of five essential elements. While Lao-tzu did not teach the theory of the five elements, the majority of Chinese Taoist teachings incorporated this principle. In the Taoist view Man gains knowledge of the whole by understanding how the five elements work within himself. To this end many techniques were utilized which we have characterized as 'yogic.' These would include the practices of *Nei Gung, Chi Gung,* five-element acupuncture, and certain of the practices now associated with *Tai Chi Chuan.* All of these techniques were ultimately the heritage of the ancient Shamanic-Taoist Tradition of Central Asia, and they were to give a firm base to the Confucian spiritual teachings of the Imperial period. Here we see an exact parallel to the yogic techniques associated with the ancient Vedic religion in India, which were perpetuated to give a firm base to the Vedantic and Buddhist teachings in the age that followed.

It was part of the 'plan' of Chinese civilization that the Confucian teachings appear on a Taoist base, to enable the transition through the Warring States period. The elements that we have described – Taoist, Confucian, and yogic – came to fruition in the Han Dynasty, which then provided the basis for the Tang, the Sung, the Yuan, and the Ming.

CHIN THROUGH TANG DYNASTIES

Having noted that Confucius began his teaching during the relative chaos of the Warring States period, let us see how the 2,400-year drama of Confucianism unfolds.

In the late third century BC the **Chin Dynasty** (223-206) was able to assert control over China. Chin rule was based on a vision of stability and centralization through force. It was linked with the philosophy of **Legalism**, which asserted that the state should be centralized around the ruler and that the individuals who comprised the social body had no personal rights or civil freedom. The Legalist thinkers advocated a strictly enforced code of law which applied equally to everyone.

While the Chin period was brief, it was a time of tremendous concentration, and it had a permanent effect on China. To ensure the new-found stability and to enforce the new code of law, there was a tremendous destruction of the past. This included a reaction to Confucianism, for Confucianism encouraged relativity towards the letter of the law and accommodated the traditional Chinese ancestor-worship and the system of property inheritance connected with that. The Chin program of "burning the books and burying the scholars" saw a destruction of culture and philosophy that is now difficult to measure or estimate. And it was too much. This severe and authoritarian regime came to an end only seventeen years after its creation. The forces of the Chin Emperor were defeated by the peasant rebel leader Liu Pang. Yet its legalist ideology had a deep impact on all regimes to follow. It was in the Chin Dynasty that China first achieved its fully developed imperial/bureaucratic form, and this it retained – through periodic upheavals and renewals – until the twentieth century. Then the pattern of "burning of the books and burying of the scholars" recurred – with even greater violence – during the Chinese Cultural Revolution.

The Chin Dynasty forcefully centralized China, on the basis of real need, with reference to radical new principles. Yet these were not objective principles but imperfect human 'ideas' applied with great rigor. The rebel leader who overthrew the Chin regime – Liu Pang – was a member of the largest ethnic group in China. This was the vast population which had resided in the Yellow River basin and the fertile lands adjoining it since before the beginning of recorded history. This prosperous and industrious people was constantly threatened by **1)** the different nomadic peoples who surrounded them and **2)** the difficulty of integrating their own kingdoms into a workable system. Liu Pang represented the interests of this people, and when he named his dynasty the Han, they took their name from that. While the Han dynasty was eventually overthrown, the Han Chinese people remained the basis of every great Imperial Tradition that followed in China.

The **Han Dynasty** (206 BC to 220 AD), once firmly established, brought great prosperity to China. It saw the arts and sciences, which had taken form during the Chou

Dynasty, come to their full flower. These centuries were also the golden years of the Han Chinese. The traditional Taoist religion was regenerated, with the Jade Emperor of antiquity now supplanted by **the Yellow Emperor** of the Han Period. The Yellow Emperor is the human embodiment of the rule of heaven, based on the historical, though half-legendary, figure of Gung-sun Hsuan-yuan (2497-2398 BC) – who was taken to be the ancestor of the Han Chinese. At the same time the myth of **the Five Emperors** came into being. This set of complementary archetypal figures included **1)** The Yellow Emperor himself, **2)** Chuan-hsu, **3)** the Emperor Ku, **4)** the Emperor Yao, and **5)** the Emperor Shun. The Five Emperors are a mix of mythological figures and culture heroes who appear, in retrospect, as a lineage of great sages – embodiments of the core values of the Han people.

It was during the Han period that Confucianism first gained real pre-eminence in China. It was the philosophy that supported the bureaucratic centralization of the Han Empire. The works of Confucius were made required reading for civil service examinations, and this tradition continued, broken only by the chaos of the inter-dynastic periods, until the end of the nineteenth century.

After four centuries the Han Dynasty split into a variety of dynastic and regional governments, and social order began to dissipate in war. The next 'great integration' of China was not to come for another 400 years. First the Han split into the Western Han, the Eastern Han, and the Xin Dynasties. Then came the Period of the Three Kingdoms – Wei, Shu, and Wu (220 AD to 280 AD). This was in turn supplanted by the Chin (Jin) Dynasty (265-420) and the Sixteen Kingdoms (304-439). Finally there was a general division between the Southern and the Northern Dynasties (265-420), followed by the brief and unstable Sui Dynasty (581-618).

In terms of religion, much happened during this lengthy inter-dynastic period. With the reduced focus on bureaucratic careers, Confucianism declined. The traditional Taoist practices to some extent supplanted the Confucian, and the yogic practices connected to Taoism became – for the first time – directly connected to the idea of retreat. Buddhism entered China in the first century AD. It then gained a strong foothold wherever the Han bureaucracies were displaced, and this occurred particularly in northern China. Huge Buddhist statutes, temples, and monasteries were erected in the centuries to follow.

But how, we may ask, did Buddhism 'fit into' China? How did a monastic culture develop in a highly relational society? We must remember that the essence of China, the ancient Taoist base, was responsive to the ever-changing Tao. Buddhism was actually adopted in this spirit; its strict meditation practices were seen as a natural response to the loss of dynastic stability. Chinese Buddhism itself adapted to the change of circumstances; Chan Buddhism, with its 'transmission outside the scripture,' incorporated the Taoist distrust of metaphysics. At the same time Chinese Taoism incorporated Buddhist principles, such as monasteries, vegetarianism, the prohibition of alcohol, and the doctrine of Shunyata, or the Divine Void. Of course the Chinese people wished peace and prosperity, and they knew – even in the midst of social chaos – that the Confucian ethic was compatible with justice and harmony in a stable, established regime. In the inter-dynastic period Taoism, Confucianism, and Buddhism deeply influenced one another. Each had its strengths, and each had its aberrant forms.

We could make a quick caricature of the three religions:

TAOISM: On the one hand, it represented focus and single-mindedness, the transcendence of all ideology, and complete freedom of mind. On the other hand, it often led in practice to crippling superstition and an unhealthy preoccupation with magic.

CONFUCIANISM: On the one hand, it represented true, balanced commitment to one's fellow man in all walks of life. It contained a universally recognized social ethic. On the other hand, it easily descended to bureaucratic idiocy and the extremes of ancestor worship.

BUDDHISM: On the one hand, it provided a coherent view of the universe and a strict practice of meditation in relation to that view. On the other, it produced vast, introverted monastic structures that were subject to corruption.

As the short-lived Sui Empire began to collapse, the Li family seized power and was able to initiate the **Tang Dynasty** (618-907 AD). Under the Tang Emperors, China once again achieved unity and marked prosperity. Taoism was reinforced, as the Imperial family claimed direct descent from Lao-tzu. Buddhism flourished, as the teachings of the inter-dynastic period underwent a great renewal. Chinese Buddhism re-sourced the Mahayana and Vajrayana teachings from the original Indian wellspring, and Buddhism became, for a time, the predominant religion. Confucianism continued to exist in a more 'passive mode,' but the Chinese knew that it was Confucianism and not Buddhism that instructed you how to sustain presence in service of the state.

In the middle of the Tang Dynasty came a very harsh period. The Emperor Wu-tsung, a zealous Taoist, found the Imperial finances in a desperate state. Most provinces had stopped paying their taxes, and the vast Buddhist monasteries were entirely tax-exempt. Wu-tsung responded by seizing the monasteries and drastically repressing not only Buddhism but all non-Chinese religions – including Christianity, Manichaeism, and Zoroastrianism. While Buddhism eventually recovered from this persecution, the other religions did not.

During this time Neo-Confucianism began to make its appearance, as a unique synthesis of Confucianism, Buddhism, and the traditional Taoism. The values that Buddhism brought to China were given expression in a Confucian context, compatible with both the Imperial state and the essentially Taoist culture. Under the Tang Dynasty Neo-Confucianism was a proposed 'solution' for the problems of China. It was not yet the Imperial philosophy but a new and growing system of thought striving for clarity. It was the formula of Neo-Confucianism that was to give stability in the Sung Dynasty to follow, when China made many of its greatest social and technological advances.

The isolationist and xenophobic tendencies initiated by Wu-tsung were the beginning of the end of the Tang Empire. In the early tenth century it finally dissolved into the strife of the Five Dynasties and the Ten Kingdoms.

THE SUNG DYNASTY

The Sung Dynasty (960-1279 AD) was initiated by the Emperor Tai-tzu of Sung, who was able to unify China through conquest, ending the ongoing upheaval of the Five Dynasties and Ten Kingdoms. There followed a shift from the many aristocratic elites of that period to a universal bureaucratic elite. The civil service developed accordingly, and Confucianism developed with it.

While Sung China was strong and centralized, it was under the constant threat of war from the competing Chin Dynasty and from the Mongols to the north and west. Perhaps for this reason it saw a marked development of technology. China became the first country to make use of gunpowder and to print bank notes.

It was during the Sung period that Neo-Confucianism became the officially recognized creed of the Imperial civil service. The Chinese mind, in its search for harmonious order, increasingly embraced this synthesis of Confucianism, Taoism, and Buddhism. There was still tension between the three Religions, but Neo-Confucianism was able – to some extent – to subsume Buddhism and Taoism to Confucianism. Having said that, many Neo-Confucians were critical of the Taoists and the Buddhists, but their criticism was a pragmatic criticism; they were principally critical of the anti-social (or a-cosmic) side of Buddhist and Taoist practice in their own time. We must remember that, whatever sectarian disputes may occur, men of a higher level understand one another, and all of the Spiritual Traditions agree on a vision with the interests of the whole in mind. What exactly happened in the time of the emergence of Neo-Confucianism has been lost to history, but we emphasize that Neo-Confucianism was more than just a social ideology; it was a revival of the original vision of Confucius. It had its own essential insight, both into the present and into the archetype of China. Let us look at this vision in greater depth.

NEO-CONFUCIANISM

The principal figure in the creation of this new synthesis was the Sung philosopher **Chu Hsi** (1130-1200 AD). He used Confucius' commentaries on the *I Ching* to reproduce or recreate the **lost Tao of Confucius**. In this view the Tao of Heaven is expressed in the spiritual principle of *li*, which, on the cellular level, is always sheathed in matter, or *chi*. *Li* is in all things and in perceiving *li* one is perceiving the inner spirit of what one observes. There is an 'external' science of *li*, but *li* is also in the human heart, and this is the most important place in which to find it. *Li* in itself is pure and perfect, but with the addition of *chi*, base emotions and conflicts arise. Human nature is originally good, but, once immersed in matter, it cannot become so unless action is taken to purify it. It is imperative, then, to purify one's *li*. Because *li* is primal life energy, it is sought – not by reason – but by intuitive self-awareness.

Chu Hsi wrote on 'the way' in Taoist style, on ethics in Buddhist style, and on customs and social protocol in Confucian style. Thus, in the philosophical atmosphere of his time, he clarifies an 'internal' Confucianism, transcending logic, whose deeper current of life itself gives life to all ethical activities in the social sphere. And it is in the social sphere that traditional Confucianism prevails. This synthesis entered the popular religion and the popular culture in the centuries to follow. There is a well-known Neo-Confucian motif showing Confucius, Buddha, and Lao-tzu all smiling and drinking out of the same vinegar jar, with the caption "The three teachings are one!"

Chu Hsi's four-book presentation – *The Great Learning*, *The Doctrine of the Mean*, *The Analects of Confucius*, and *The Commentary on Mencius* – became the official canon of Ming Dynasty Confucianism, and the material for its official curriculum of civil service examinations.

The criticism that can be made of Chu Hsi is that he drew on the past to regenerate the present, and in so doing lost something of the originality of his source philosophies. Nevertheless his own thought is original; it does sum in a completed vision, and this vision did come to fruition later in the Ming Dynasty. Thus Chu Hsi helped to create an environment where human potential could be realized in the different theaters of life that exist within an integrated social whole. And of course both Chinese Buddhism and Chinese Taoism continued to develop independently of Chu Hsi's Neo-Confucianism.

The Sung Dynasty came to a sudden end with the rise of the world-historical figure of Ghengis Khan. The era of Mongol conquest began, and in 1271 Genghis Khan's grandson, Kublai Khan, conquered China.

FROM THE MONGOL INVASION TO MODERN CHINA

The Mongol government of China was known as **the Yuan Dynasty** (1271-1368 AD), and during this period Tibetan Buddhism, which the Mongols themselves had embraced, made inroads in China. The Mongols took over the existing civil service, and Confucianism was strongly reinforced as the social belief appropriate to the Chinese. The Mongols themselves focused on trade, and developed the Silk Road trading network – which became extremely profitable to China. Confucianism, Buddhism, and Taoism continued to develop, each in its own way.

In 1368 a number of Han Chinese groups united to overthrow the Mongols, and **the Ming Dynasty** (1368-1644) began. This was the apogee of orderly government and social stability in China. *The Ming period saw the highest phase of achievement of Chinese culture and civilization.* With the re-establishment of an indigenous Chinese ruling house, there was again court patronage of the arts. Temple building flourished, and the Imperial Painting Academy was established, encouraging spontaneity and freedom of expression while at the same time achieving great refinement of technique. Ming furniture, Ming tapestries, and Ming calligraphy surpassed all work that had been done previously. Ceramics, porcelain sculpture, and lacquerware reached an exceptional level of refinement. The decorative arts generally benefited from the new uses made of jade, ivory, and cloisonné. At the same time there was a remarkable development of the Chinese theater and the Chinese opera.

The Ming period saw the recreation of the Grand Canal and the Great Wall, the creation of a standing army, a fleet, and the building of the infrastructures required to support large urban centers. The Forbidden City was constructed at this time. The enemies of China, on all sides, were walled out and a strong and complex bureaucratic machinery put in place. Once again Confucianism, in the form of Neo-Confucianism, became the status quo. Economic policy focused firmly on self-sufficiency, and favored agriculture over trade. However, without the support of the Mongols, the Silk Road network languished. It ceased to bring huge revenues into China, and the Ming saw the beginning of a new isolationism.

Towards the end of this period a series of disasters befell China. Altan Khan, the Mongol prince, successfully breached the Great Wall and began to assert his control over large parts of the country. At the same time the Japanese made a series of successful assaults on the eastern coast. In 1556 the Shan-hsi earthquake took 830,000 lives, and had a devastating effect on the Chinese economy. Beginning from the 1650s what has been called the 'little Ice Age' shortened the growing season, devastating agriculture and bringing both famine and plague in its wake. And in this time the Manchurians to the north began to prepare an imperial venture of their own. From 1558 to 1626 the Manchus conquered the Mongols (which the Chinese had never been able to do) and then began to expand into Imperial China itself. By the end of the seventeenth century the Ming Dynasty was unable to resist the Manchus, and the Han Chinese were forced to submit to Manchu Rule.

The Manchu period is known as **the Ching Dynasty** (1644-1911). The Manchus, like the Mongol overlords of the Yuan Dynasty, made use of Confucianism, while discouraging the relative 'individualism' of Taoism. Many great Taoist texts, including almost all copies of the *I Ching*, were destroyed at this time. The Manchu rulers distinguished themselves sharply from the Chinese population; they themselves adopted the religion of Tibetan Buddhism while actively promoting Confucianism for the masses. But only the more functional aspects of Confucianism were encouraged; the greater vision of Neo-Confucianism was suppressed.

In some sense Eternal China died with the passing of the Ming because its essential vision was not preserved or developed by the Manchu in the period to follow. The Manchu ruling class had no Spiritual Tradition behind them; they were invaders who held the Han Chinese as a subject population. During the Ming Dynasty the 'World of China' was still intact, but during the Ching it gradually came to pieces. Acute social tensions developed in the late Manchu period; there were many social rebellions, and these combined with the general impact of the emergent industrialized West to undermine the social fabric. There was, however, such a deep current of life in China that it continued to find expression in many different forms. Throughout the Ching period there were still superb achievements in all of the arts. Yet it was during this period that *the inner work of the Traditions became dissociated from the Civilizational Order*, and the Great Work began to break into different forms of Group Work.

In the nineteenth century the European powers began to make definite inroads into the Chinese sphere of influence. It was in part the involvement of the European powers that sparked a series of social rebellions, at a huge cost of human life: the Taiping Rebellion, the Punti-Hakka Clan Wars, the White Lotus Revolution, the Opium Wars, the Nien Rebellion, the Panthay Rebellion, and the Boxer Rebellion. One result of these rebellions was that the will of the Han Chinese people to overthrow the Manchus was strengthened. Additionally, and parallel to this, there developed a general fear of Western invasion. The Chinese perceived clearly the modernizing effect of the first Industrial Revolution on the European powers and on the Meiji Republic in neighboring Japan. They saw also that the Manchus were incapable of leading them towards modernization.

In 1911 the republican general Sun Yat-sen initiated a revolutionary uprising, and a long period of civil war began. In 1921 the Chinese Nationalist party (Kuomintang) joined forces with the emergent Chinese Communist Party (CCP). In 1925 Sun Yat-sen died and power transferred to his lieutenant Chiang Kai-shek. Shortly after, in 1927, the Kuomintang Party split into Communist and non-Communist elements. The split soon developed into open military struggle. Through the late 1920s and 1930s Mao Tse-tung emerged as the dominant figure in the CCP, yet Chiang Kai-shek was able to keep the Communist forces generally in retreat. However the outbreak of the Sino-Japanese war in 1937 forced a strategic alliance between the two factions. This war continued into the global conflict of World War II, which pitted the Chinese against Axis-allied Japan. After the defeat of Japan the Chinese Communist army, under the leadership of Mao Tse-tung, was able to defeat and disperse the Nationalist forces. In 1949 China became the People's Republic of China.

Thus China adopted a Western ideology as a means of rapidly achieving its first industrial revolution and attaining internal solidarity in face of foreign incursion. Both of these aims were related to the fundamental fear of foreign control. In the Manchu period, Russia, Japan, England, France, and the United States became progressively more involved in Chinese affairs, and the Chinese wanted an end of this. The forced centralization and radical redistribution of property and power that came with Communism recreated the tense atmosphere of the Chin Dynasty in the third century BC – and indeed there is a remarkable similarity here to the Chin adoption of Legalist ideology. In each case the ruling party achieved its aims, and in each case much of traditional Chinese culture was destroyed, but in the latter case the destruction was far more complete. Whatever short-term benefit the Chinese Communist Party may have brought the Chinese people, *it was the death-knell of the Traditions*. The hope for their regeneration finally disappeared. The most acute phase of this destruction was the Cultural Revolution, which occurred between 1966 and 1976, and in which the Chin Dynasty's 'burning of the books and burying of the scholars' was exactly replicated. The second destruction took the form of a war against 'the four olds' – old customs, old culture, old habits, and old ideas. This quickly turned into a war against the people who represented 'the four olds,' and as a result between 25 and 40 million people lost their lives. This is one of the greatest holocausts in human history. In ten short years there was a fervent destruction of the past that has probably never been equaled.

In the beginning the Chinese Communists had ideals, based on certain socialist beliefs and certain convictions about class consciousness, but after the slaughter of the Cultural Revolution there was only social pragmatism. You have, then, Han ethnicity searching for stability and prosperity and the CCP leadership viewing religion only as the potential vehicle for ethnic and social dissent.

OVERVIEW OF THE WORK OF THE TRADITIONS IN CHINA

The unity of Taoism and Confucianism, which later extended to Chinese Buddhism, created a magnificent social fabric and a fertile ground for the work of the Traditions. Confucius was able to integrate the traditional Taoist culture with a social philosophy appropriate to the imperial form – thus allowing the inner work of the Traditions to find expression in social practice. This in turn allowed the influence of the Traditions to penetrate Chinese society very, very deeply, and so to generate an incomparably rich and varied culture.

It appears that, in China, a single Prophet did not initiate a Tradition and a Living Religion at the same time. It is likely that Traditions pre-existing China's imperial phase recreated themselves through its successive dynasties, and tried – at many different points – to influence the development of Chinese society in such a way that it might achieve a high level of Civilizational Order.

At least until the end of the Ming Dynasty we see evidence of the Pyramid of Man described in Book I: the delicate linkage of Tradition, Religion, and Civilization which enables the relation between Men and Gods. That we see a continuous thread of life behind all the changes in regime stands as testimony to this.

We turn, then, from the vast territories of contemporary China to the little kingdom of Judea in the southeastern corner of the Mediterranean – as it was 2000 years ago. While dynastic China had a vision, supported by a current of conscious life, it did not have the form of prophethood. The tiny kingdom of Judea was the home of one of the greatest Prophets given to Mankind, but the civilization that was to come from his teaching was not specific to Judea, and was not tightly tied to the fate of any one people.

CHAPTER 31

Jesus Christ

THE LIFE OF JESUS

Jesus of Nazareth stated clearly that he had been called by God to testify before men, and that he was guided in all his actions and decisions by a higher agency. His life and teaching are reconstructed from the four gospels of the New Testament, which were written between 70 and 100 AD, as teaching manuscripts.

Jesus was born in the town of Bethlehem in Judah. At the time of his birth three *Magi* came 'from the East' to visit his birthplace. The *Magi* were members of the Zoroastrian priest caste, and they claimed to have determined that the Messiah – who for them would be the next *Saoshyant* – was to be born at this place in this time. They wished to receive the Messiah and to that end they 'followed his star' to Bethlehem. The reports of the *Magi* came quickly to the ears of Herod, the king of Judah, and he became concerned, fearing to lose his throne to the child. He determined, then, to kill the infant. However, shortly after the arrival of the *Magi* in Bethlehem, Jesus' parents were advised in a dream to flee into Egypt and remain there until they received word that it would be safe to return. This they did. Herod died within a year, and the family was able to return to Judah, where they settled again in Galilee. Here Jesus grew to manhood, working at the trade of his father, who was a builder or carpenter. He continued with this work until he reached his thirtieth year. Many speculate that during his early adult life Jesus studied with the Essenes, a Jewish sect noted for its ascetic rigor, who were active throughout Judah at this time.

While Jesus was still in his twenties an apocalyptic preacher named John the Baptist began to preach in Judah and developed a following of many thousands. John preached of the coming of a new messiah, and, in anticipation of this, asked his followers to repent of their sins and to be baptized (a ritual water purification common amongst the peoples of Palestine at this time). One day Jesus went to John, who was preaching at the Jordan River, and after hearing him speak volunteered to be baptized in the river. As Jesus rose from the water his first prophetic revelation came to him. Following this experience he made a retreat into the desert, where he fasted for forty days and forty nights. During this time "Satan came to him" and repeatedly tempted him, and Jesus showed himself able to resist these temptations. In the language of the Traditions the temptation of Jesus refers to a definitive confrontation with the Lower Self: the last assault of the Black Queen, in whatever form that may take.

Having passed this test and achieving the internal clarification that would result from this success, Jesus returned to teach in Galilee and in Jerusalem. Many thousands responded to his prophetic teaching. He stated that he was the son of God, that the world known to humanity would suddenly come to an end, and that he would – at some point in the future – return to judge that world. He also said that "this generation would be given no sign," which placed his prophecies in a longer time frame.

Jesus taught the highest practices known to the Spiritual Traditions, for the symbols and the parables that he used beautifully illustrate the teachings of the Second Work. It is also clear that he taught different disciples on different levels, and that the simple, forceful way in which he did so left a body of well-integrated material, which provided the basis for 1) a Spiritual Tradition, 2) a Living Religion, and 3) a Christian Civilization. Jesus taught not only the Jews, but also the Samaritans and probably the Greek-speaking people in Antioch. While his native tongue was Aramaic he almost certainly spoke Greek and very likely spoke Hebrew.

After several years of teaching Jesus selected twelve disciples, who had achieved the level required to communicate the inner spirit of the teaching, and so to perpetuate it after his death. These disciples were to become – after Jesus' death – the twelve 'apostles,' with the exception of the disciple Judas, who was later replaced by Paul. Of the apostles, Peter, James the Greater, and John were assigned a special status by Jesus during his life, and of those Peter was the leader. The apostle Paul, who never knew Jesus in the flesh, acquired a special status after Jesus' death.

Near the end of Jesus' period of active teaching, he led Peter, John, and James to the top of Mount Tabor to pray. Once they had climbed the mountain Jesus appeared before them transfigured, with the prophets Moses and Elijah appearing on either side of him. A bright cloud overshadowed the three, and a voice from the sky said, "This is my beloved son, with whom I am well pleased." It was one of the formative visions of a

Great Tradition. From the time of this revelation Jesus began to tell his disciples of his future death and resurrection.

Shortly after the experience on Mount Tabor Jesus traveled, with many of his disciples, to Jerusalem. A large crowd came to meet him crying out, "Hail, King of Israel." Jesus did not discourage the crowd, and his presence created great consternation in the city of Jerusalem. Later in the week Jesus celebrated the Passover meal with his disciples, which was subsequently known as the Last Supper. During this supper Jesus prophesied that he would be betrayed by one of his disciples and that he would be executed. He stated, "Whither I go thou canst not follow." Peter then said to him, "Though all men shall be offended because of thee, yet will I never be offended." Jesus replied to him, "Verily I say unto thee, that this night, before the cock crows, thou shalt deny me three times." (Matthew 26:34).[1] The Last Supper was, in many ways, a turning point.

In the teaching of the Last Supper, as given in John 15: 1-7, Jesus describes the spiritual community capable of supporting the Great Work. These passages can only be understood with reference to the supra-personal dimension of Jesus' nature. As a man in whom the Higher Centers have emerged and locked, Jesus had embraced World 6, and at the level of World 6 human consciousness passes into the divine and the cosmic. In John 15, Jesus refers to the Christian community as 'the vine.' Sometimes he refers to the vine as a community of discrete individuals, emphasizing the 'branches of the vine,' but at other times he refers to the World 12 consciousness that exists within each of these individuals – and at this level there is a harmony that transcends individual human differences. The vine, in this latter context, represents a single current of higher understanding. Beyond this, Jesus sometimes speaks of World 6 – the purely cosmic – in which the community is sourced. This transcends human individuality as such, reaching deep into the cosmos above the Cosmos of Man. While from one point of view this would be distant from the daily experience of most of the members of the community, the fact of a connection to World 6 – in this case through the higher consciousness of Jesus – determines the nature of the events that befall such a group, as well as the people who can and cannot be in such a group.

More generally, in the teachings of the Last Supper, Jesus sometimes speaks of himself as a single member of the nascent Christian community and sometimes as the embodiment of the transcendent state which unites that community. This state is shared by all of its members, although in different degrees according to their level of

---

1. All bible quotations are from the King James Version, unless otherwise noted. All KJV references to the 'Holy Ghost', as a translation of the Greek πνεῦμα (pneuma), have been changed to 'Holy Spirit.'

development. When Jesus refers to something that transcends the community, and so the individuality of its members, he uses the term 'the Father.' As a Man Number Eight, Jesus is one of the few complete embodiments of World 6 in our history.[2] His entire being was centered in this level and this was the level from which he acted. He is an extraordinary combination of real personal identity and cosmic impersonality.

In the passage from John 15 quoted below, Jesus makes a delicate play on the use of the term Father to bring out the cosmic dimension of his nature. He also uses it to refer – in a general way – to the action of World 6 on the worlds that are below it and, at the same time, contained within it, as subordinate worlds. World 6 stands in a privileged relation to World 1; it directly serves World 1. A person who enters World 6 for extended periods of time may have glimpses of World 3. Once a person has entered World 3 the Absolute may contact them directly, for will of the Absolute reaches World 3. In other words, such a person might speak, from first hand experience, of the authority of the Absolute. Thus Jesus' references to "my Father" probably range from World 6 to World 1, depending on the context. Throughout the following passage Jesus uses the pronoun 'I' most artfully, to refer to all of these different levels and to bring them together as the elements of a unified vision. The following passage represents the inner structure of one of the few highest Spiritual Traditions known to history.

> I am the true vine, and my Father is the husbandman. Every branch in me that beareth not fruit he taketh away: and every branch that beareth fruit, he purgeth it, that it may bring forth more fruit. Now ye are clean through the word which I have spoken unto you. Abide in me, and I in you. As the branch cannot bear fruit of itself, except it abide in the vine; no more can ye, except ye abide in me. I am the vine, ye are the branches: He that abideth in me, and I in him, the same bringeth forth much fruit: for without me ye can do nothing. If a man abide not in me, he is cast forth as a branch, and is withered; and men gather them and cast them into the fire, and they are burned. If ye abide in me, and my words abide in you, ye shall ask what ye will, and it shall be done unto you. (John 15: 1-7)

These themes are elaborated in the other teachings given at the Last Supper. Note again the amazing play that Jesus makes on his own identity, which is sometimes given as that of an embodied human being, at the level of World 12, and sometimes presented as a direct expression of World 6 (e.g., 'the Father'). These discourses would have been

---

2. George Gurdjieff stated that only the prophets, whom he designated as Man Number Eight, function from World 6 for any extended period of time, and in this critical moment of Jesus' life it is likely that he was functioning from this level. See the Glossary entry for 'Man Number Eight.'

immediately understood, in all their implications, by the people to whom they were addressed.

> If ye had known me [HJ: the man in World 12], you should have known my Father also [World 6]. (John 14:7)

> Believe me that I am in the Father [World 6], and the Father in me: or else believe me for the very works' sake. (John 14:11)

> At that day [the day of my passing] ye shall know that I am in my Father, and ye in me, and I in you. (John 14:20)

Here Jesus links the disciples to the Absolute. When Jesus is 'in my Father' (Worlds 6 and 3) in a disembodied state (after his death), he stands transparent before World 1, the Absolute. When the embodied apostles remain in contact with the disembodied Jesus while he is in a direct connection to the Absolute, and are able to maintain the standards of prolonged presence which that relationship implies, that is a special moment in history. The Pyramid of Man has been completed in quite a special way and infused with quite a special kind of life. When "I am in my Father, and ye in me and I in you," humanity has reached one of the few highest moments of its 40,000-year span. The Cosmos of Man has been linked to the Celestial Hierarchy that is above it, and, on every level, there can be service to the level one above and service to the level one below. The realization of Jesus' prophecy of continued contact with the Apostles explains why the formative period of the Christian Church began from the time of Jesus' death and continued until the death of the youngest apostle John – for this was the short but electric period of time in which the living experience of "I am in my Father, and ye in me and I in you" could be realized.

> If a man love me, he will keep my words [HJ: he will successfully sustain presence through a fully developed Steward]: and my Father will love him [World 6 will be disposed towards his development], and we [World 12] will come unto him, and make our abode with him [thus making him into a conscious being]. (John 14:23)

> I will not leave you comfortless: I will come to you. (John 14:18)

When a disembodied prophet is able to sustain a relationship with an embodied man, who could not himself endure a direct experience of the Absolute, that man is nevertheless able to work in the light of the Absolute, and so able to convey something of that level to the stratum of humanity who have matured in the First Work or who achieved the Work of the Steward.

But the comforter, which is the Holy Spirit [HJ: in this context the Higher Emotional Center or World 12], whom the Father [World 6] will send in my name, he shall teach you all things, and bring all things to your remembrance [unbroken, prolonged presence in all its aspects], whatsoever I have said unto you [including all of Jesus' relevant teachings]. (John 14:26)

At the Last Supper, Jesus consistently teaches from the level of World 6, for in the deepest reaches of World 6 one is at the point of transition to the disembodied state: one is on the thin edge of Life and Death. When teachings such as these are taken literally, with great fervor, by those who do not understand their inner meaning, then all the schisms of the Church are soon to follow. Jesus' teachings were understood by his disciples because the presence of the Prophet himself raised their consciousness to the required level. It is amazing to consider that, in the moments that Jesus spoke these words, he knew that schism and misunderstanding would follow from them. He knew that his words would later fall on unenlightened ears, and he accepted this in order to give the highest truth he could to those capable of receiving it. He gave freely to those "who have ears to hear," so destroying the complacency of the Men of Religion in the ages to follow. He had to do this because, unless the understanding of the Spiritual Tradition is secure, there can be no Living Religion.

After the Last Supper, Jesus and his disciples went to pray in the Garden of Gethsemane. While they were in the Garden the temple guards came to arrest Jesus, on the orders of the Sanhedrin (the circle of Jewish elders) and the high priest Caiaphas. The Sanhedrin had condemned Jesus for blasphemy because he had stated that he was the Son of God. This he did not deny. He was tried by the Roman procurator Pontius Pilate, who found him guilty of no crime against the Romans. It was the custom at Passover for the Roman governor to free a prisoner. Pilate offered the crowd a choice between Jesus of Nazareth and an insurrectionist named Barrabas. The crowd chose to have Barrabas freed and Jesus crucified.

During and immediately after the trial, Jesus' closest followers were sought out by the Pharisees. In the course of their search and interrogation someone accused Peter, and, almost before he knew it, Peter heard himself deny his connection to Jesus three times, so fulfilling Jesus' prophecy at the Last Supper.

Jesus was crucified at Calvary and died before the late afternoon. Pilate gave permission to the Christians to bury Jesus' body in a tomb, and so they took it to a sepulcher outside of Jerusalem. This, then, was the site of his resurrection.

Of all the Prophets, Jesus is remarkable in that much of the formative impact of his teaching was realized after the death of his physical vehicle. We may remember that there was no Christian Church when Jesus died! According to Paul (1 Cor. 15:5-6) Jesus appeared to more than 500 people after the resurrection, and his appearances and manifestations had an authority and impact which is hard for us to understand or reconstruct – for the disembodied Prophet works directly in the light of World 3. These appearances galvanized and united the people of Jesus' community to achieve otherwise impossible aims. It was in the period after the crucifixion that Jesus empowered the Apostles to teach and that he made the clearest distinctions between the Work of the Spiritual Traditions and the Work of the Religion. Thus the Christian Church, as we know it, was largely the result of Jesus' teachings between the time of his resurrection and the death of the last of the Apostles.

Because this material relates directly to the theme of the Story of Man and to the theories of the Spiritual Traditions that we introduced in Book I, we will review the nine appearances of which we have record, in the order in which they occurred.

1) TO THOSE AT JESUS' SEPULCHER

On the third day after the crucifixion Mary Magdalene went with a friend, who was also named Mary,[3] to the sepulcher. What happened there is described in Matthew 28: 1-10.

> In the end of the Sabbath, as it began to dawn toward the first day of the week, came Mary Magdalene and the other Mary to see the sepulcher. And behold, there was a great earthquake: for the angel of the Lord descended from heaven, and came and rolled back the stone from the door, and sat upon it. His countenance was like lightning, and his raiment white as snow: And for fear of him the keepers did shake, and became as dead men. And the angel answered and said unto the women, Fear not ye: for I know that ye seek Jesus, which was crucified. He is not here: for he is risen, as he said. Come see the place where the Lord lay. And go quickly, and tell his disciples that he is risen from the dead; and behold, he goeth before you into Galilee; there shall ye see him: lo, I have told you. And they departed quickly from the sepulcher with fear and great joy; and did run to bring his disciples word. And as they went to tell his disciples, Jesus met them saying, All hail. And they came and held him by the feet, and

---

3. This is 'Mary mother of James', the 'James' referring to either of the two apostles named James.

worshipped him. Then said Jesus unto them, Be not afraid: go tell my brethren that they go into Galilee, and there shall they see me. (Matthew 28: 1-10)

From the statement given in Matthew 28:16 it is clear that the meeting place in Galilee was a particular mountain.

2) TO THE TWO DISCIPLES ON THE ROAD TO EMMAUS

Shortly after the appearance at the sepulcher, in the afternoon of the same day, Jesus appeared to two disciples who were walking from Jerusalem, where they had seen the crucifixion, to Emmaus. One of these was named Cephas. The two men were filled with sorrow. A stranger joined them on the road and asked about their grief. The stranger was Jesus himself. Without telling them who he was, he reassured them by interpreting his own death in terms of the prophetic teachings of the Old Testament.

Then beginning with Moses and all the prophets, he interpreted to them the things about himself in all the scriptures. As they came near the village to which they were going, he walked ahead as if he were going on. But they urged him strongly, saying, "Stay with us, because it is almost evening and the day is now nearly over." So he went in to stay with them. When he was at the table with them, he took bread and broke it and gave it to them. Then their eyes were opened, and they recognized him and he vanished from their sight. (Luke 24: 13-15)/Mark 16: 12-13)

3) THE APPEARANCES AT JERUSALEM (LUKE 24:33-53)

As soon as Jesus vanished, Cephas and his friend returned to Jerusalem and sought out the eleven Apostles, who were gathered together there. As they told their story Jesus himself appeared in their midst (Luke 24:36). He spoke with them, reassured them, and even dined with them. Jesus appeared twice to the Apostles in Jerusalem, and these two appearances were in close succession. In the second he asked the 'doubting' Apostle Thomas to touch one of his wounds. In these appearances he demonstrated the reality of his embodiment and the realization of the prophecies. (This has been taken as evidence of the 'resurrection' of the body, but it is not that. It demonstrates the capacity of a highly developed being to synthesize bodies – of the kind that we have – at will. It is a power that other men have exercised at other points in history, usually with the aim of placing a definitive emphasis on a life's teaching. Peter Ouspensky did just this in the days after his death in 1947.) [4]

In Jesus' second appearance in Jerusalem one of the disciples asked him, "Lord wilt thou at this time restore again the kingdom to Israel?" He replied:

> It is not for you to know the times or the seasons which the Father hath put in his own power. But ye shall receive power, after that the Holy Spirit is come upon you: and ye shall be witnesses unto me both in Jerusalem, and in all Judah, and in Samaria, and unto the uttermost part of the earth. (Acts 1:6-8)

This makes it clear that the authority to teach, on the level of a Spiritual Tradition, is not something given by one man, or even by a group of men. It comes as the result of many things, but the prerequisite is an inner transformation, coming from the presence of the Holy Spirit within. All of the Apostles were teachers of the Spirit (World 12).

Shortly after Jesus' appearances to the disciples in Jerusalem, perhaps the following morning, Mary Magdalene arrived in the city with the news of Jesus' appearance at the sepulcher and Jesus' instruction to meet them in Galilee.

In reviewing these first appearances, we see that the Gods are masters of the unexpected. First the angel says to Mary that Jesus has risen and gone. Then, immediately after, Jesus greets Mary. Just as Cephas and his friend describe Jesus' appearance to the Apostles, he stands before them. Just after Jesus has spent time with the Apostles, and demonstrated the fact of his resurrection, Mary appears before them with the news that they must meet him in Galilee. A living Tradition is full of such disarming shocks and sudden turnarounds, which bring sharply into question the illusion of a unified 'I.' Religion, by contrast, gives a sense of continuity, reinforced by ritual.

4) THE APPEARANCE AT THE MOUNTAIN IN GALILEE

On receiving Mary's message (Matthew 28:16), "… the eleven disciples went away into Galilee, into a mountain where Jesus had appointed them." At the meeting in Galilee Jesus went beyond the demonstrations and proofs of his resurrection. He acted in such a way as to define the Tradition and the Religion which were to come from his work. When the disciples had assembled, he appeared to them and spoke these words:

---

4. See Rodney Collin, *The Theory of Eternal Life*, Watkins, London, 1974, pp. 115-116. Collin describes how his own Teacher, Peter Ouspensky, created a body of electronic matter, independent of time, capable of appearing in both the future and the past. He then describes the appearances of this 'electronic body' that occurred immediately after Ouspensky's death.

All power is given unto me in heaven and in earth. Go ye therefore, and teach all nations, baptizing them in the name of the Father, and of the Son, and of the Holy Spirit: Teaching them to observe all things whatsoever I have commanded you: and, lo, I am with you always, even unto the end of the World. (Matthew 28: 18-20)

The disciples – now Apostles – were then left to digest this experience. They had been traveling for many days, and they needed to find sustenance, so they went down from the mountain to the Sea of Galilee. Peter found a boat with fishing nets near to hand and decided to go fishing. The others joined him. And suddenly – completely unexpectedly – there came a second revelation to complement the first.

5) THE APPEARANCE AT THE SEA OF GALILEE

John in 21: 1-14 states that Peter and the Apostles cast the net on the left side of the ship and found nothing. A stranger then called to them from the shore, saying, "Cast the net on the right side and ye shall find." When they cast the net on the right side, they were not able to draw the net in for the multitude of fishes. Peter realized the stranger was Jesus. Jesus asked them to bring the fish in and then to dine with him. In the course of their conversation Jesus asked Peter three times, "Lovest thou me?" The first time Peter replied, "Yea Lord; thou knowest that I love thee." Jesus then said to him, "Feed my lambs." The second time, when Peter again affirmed his love, Jesus said, "Feed my sheep." And on the third time when Peter said, "Lord thou knowest all things; thou knowest that I love thee," Jesus replied, "Feed my sheep." John then closes his account of the episode: "And there are also many other things which Jesus did, the which, if they should be written every one, I suppose that even the world itself could not contain the books that should be written." (John 21:15-25)

Jesus injunction to "Feed my lambs" refers to the Living Religion, the twice-repeated injunction "Feed my sheep" refers to the Spiritual Tradition. A teacher of Peter's level must focus first on those students who can understand him best; he must never put Living Religion before the Spiritual Tradition.

6) THE APPEARANCE AT PENTECOST

On the fiftieth day after Jesus' resurrection came the feast of Pentecost. At a time when the Apostles were gathered together with many other Christians, they were all filled with the Holy Spirit (World 12); they were "all in one accord on one place." (Acts 2:1) This was attended by many wonders and signs (Acts 1:6-11) which were given as the condition that "ye shall be witnesses unto me both in Jerusalem, and in all Judea, and in

Samaria, and unto the uttermost part of the earth." The appearance at Pentecost is the "rounding out" of the cycle of appearances that began with the appearance at the sepulcher. After this Jesus' appearances are fewer and focused more directly on the Apostles.

7) THE APPEARANCE TO PAUL ON THE ROAD TO DAMASCUS

More than a year after his resurrection Jesus revealed himself, in a remarkable way, to a man who was to be the representative of the new Tradition and its Living Religion to the gentiles. Jesus suddenly appeared before Saul of Tarsus, who was an orthodox Jew, then involved with persecuting the nascent Christians, because they were considered to be heretical Jews. Saul was, at the time, traveling on the road to Damascus. The tremendous impact of this event immediately converted Saul, and from that point forward his name was changed to Paul.

As he (Saul) neared Damascus on his journey, suddenly a light from heaven flashed around him. He fell to the ground and heard a voice say to him, "Saul, Saul, why persecutest thou me?" (Notice the use of 'me.' Jesus is still speaking as part of the extended body of the Spiritual Tradition.) "Who art thou, Lord?" "I am Jesus, thou persecutest.... Arise and go into the city, and it shall be told thee what thou must do." (Acts 9)

Paul was physically blinded by Jesus' appearance, so it was with great difficulty that he made his way to Damascus. Immediately after this, and before Paul's arrival, Jesus appeared to Ananias, a Christian healer in Damascus, and asked him to receive Saul of Tarsus and relieve him of his blindness. On receiving this instruction Ananias pointed out the harm that Saul had done to the Christians.

> The Lord said to Ananias, "Go! This man is my chosen instrument to carry my name before the Gentiles and their kings and before the people of Israel. I will show him how much he must suffer for my name." (Acts 9:15)

Ananias received Saul and relieved him of his blindness, saying simply "Brother Saul, receive thy sight." Paul was then shown what work he had to do. Paul states in his letter to the Galatians:

> For I want you to know ... that the gospel that was proclaimed by me is not of human origin: for I did not receive it from a human source, nor was I taught it, but I received it through a revelation from Jesus Christ ... But when God, who had set me apart before I was born and called me through his grace, was pleased to reveal his Son in me, so that I might proclaim him among the Gentiles, I did not confer with any human being. (Galatians 1:11-13)

8) THE APPEARANCE TO PETER, GOING FORTH FROM ROME

Jesus appeared to Peter twenty-eight years later, in 61 AD, in what was to be the last year of Peter's life. We may remember that when Jesus said to the disciples, at the Last Supper, that he would not be with them for much longer, Peter immediately asked (John 13:36), "Whither goest thou?" Jesus replied, "Whither I go, thou canst not follow me now; but thou shalt follow me afterwards." Jesus' revelation to Peter is the fulfillment of this enigmatic prophecy. Peter was then living and teaching in Rome, as the bishop of that city. The persecutions of Nero had just begun, and, as these persecutions became more extreme, Peter's followers suggested that he leave the city.

> But Peter said unto them: Shall we be runaways, brethren? and they said to him: Nay, but that thou mayest yet be able to serve the Lord. And he obeyed the brethren's voice and went forth alone, saying: Let none of you come forth with me, but I will go forth alone, having changed the fashion of mine apparel. And as he went forth of the city, he saw the Lord entering into Rome. And when he saw him, he said: Lord, whither goest thou? And the Lord said unto him: I go into Rome to be crucified. And Peter said unto him: Lord, art thou crucified again? He said unto him: Yea, Peter, I am crucified again. And Peter came to himself [HJ: World 6]: and having beheld the Lord ascending up into heaven, he returned to Rome, rejoicing, and glorifying the Lord, for that he said: I am being crucified: the which was about to befall Peter. (Acts of Peter 37:2-4)

9) THE REVELATION TO JOHN AT PATMOS

Finally, in about 95 AD, Jesus came to the last living Apostle, John, who was then exiled on the Island of Patmos, and gave Revelation, prophesying both the Second Coming and the End of Time.

> And I saw a new heaven and a new earth: for the first heaven and the first earth were passed away. (Revelation 21:1)

He spoke of the seven angels of the apocalypse and of the seven plagues that they would bring. He then spoke of the final Armageddon of humanity, the second coming of Christ, the binding of Satan, and the redemption of humanity.

In the Revelation he also addressed the Seven Churches of Asia: the churches of Ephesus, Smyrna, Pergamon, Thyatira, Sardis, Philadelphia, and Laodicea. To the Church at Ephesus he said:

> I know thy works, and thy labour, and thy patience, and how thou canst not bear them which are evil: and thou has tried them which say they are apostles, and are not, and

hast found them liars: And hast borne, and hast patience, and for my name's sake hast laboured, and hast not fainted. Nevertheless I have somewhat against thee, because thou hast left thy first love. Remember therefore from whence thou art fallen, and repent, and do the first works; or else I will come unto thee quickly, and will remove thy candlestick out of his place, except thou repent. (Revelation 2:2-5)

The 'first love' is the love of the Spirit, and the 'first work' – in this case the higher work – is what we have called the Work of the Steward, or the work to directly enable Higher Centers. The congregation at Ephesus have persisted in their work to purify the lower centers, and in all the external works of the Christian Church, but they have fallen away from the glory of direct work on Higher Centers. To 'remove the candlestick' is to remove the connection to the light of Higher Worlds. This does not, of course, need active intervention; it simply happens when the experiment is left to run its course – for the lower centers can never produce the pilot lights to guide man towards World 6 and 12.

In these addresses to the Seven Churches of Asia we see the breathtaking standard of the Great Spiritual Traditions, and we understand that they were very different from the churches of today. Each of the Seven Churches is measured directly by the standard of the Work of the Steward. Knowing this we can imagine the wonderful developments that occurred here in the generation of the Apostles. Similar developments were certainly occurring in Rome, in Jerusalem, in Antioch, and in Constantinople. So many seeds were sown in the first century, yet by the third century these 'lamps' were dimmed, and the flame passed to the fledgling monastic communities.

John was the last of the generation who knew Jesus personally, and this was the last of a certain kind of revelation.

We provide two timelines in the following renderings. The first gives an overview of the time of the Apostles and the Church Fathers: the time of Early Christianity. The second provides a view of the development of Eastern and Western Christianity taken as a whole, to the present time. The former timeline will shed light on the remainder of this chapter, and the latter will also be helpful with reference to Book VI, The Middle Ages and the Rise of the West.

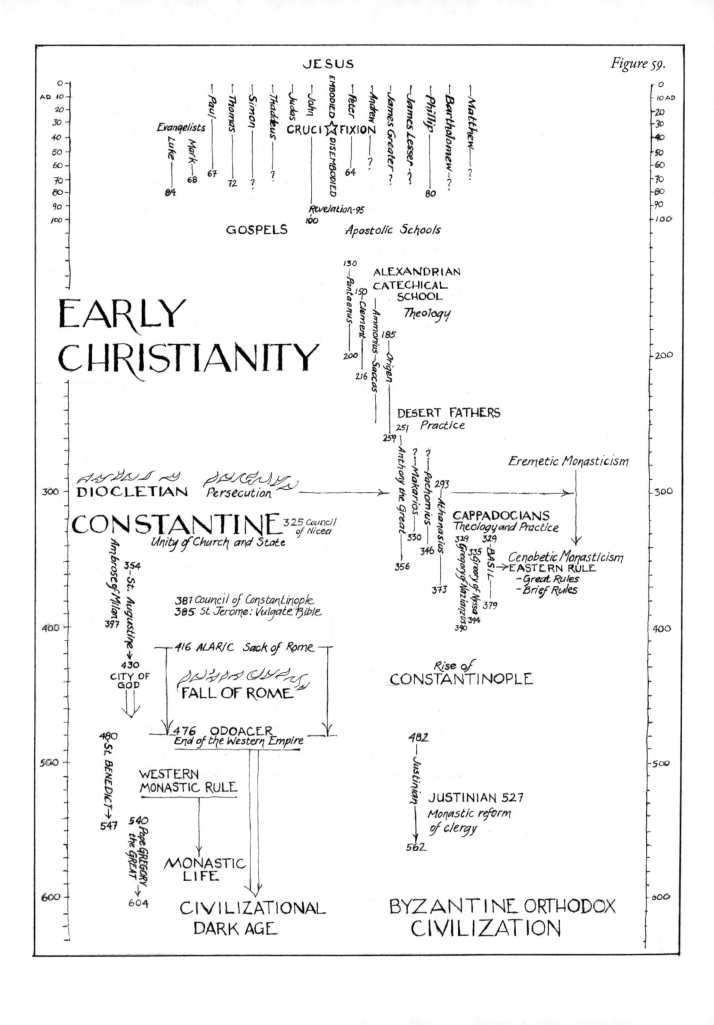

Figure 59.

EARLY CHRISTIANITY

JESUS

AD 0
10
20
30
40
50
60
70
80
90
100

Matthew —?—
Bartholomew —?—
Philip — 80
James Lesser —?—
James Greater —?—
Andrew —
Peter — 64
CRUCI ☆ FIXION
EMBODIED
DISEMBODIED
John
Judas —?—
Thaddeus —?—
Simon — ?
Thomas — 72
Paul — 67
Mark — 68
Luke — 84
Evangelists
Revelation-95
100

GOSPELS   Apostolic Schools

130
Pantaenus — 150
Clement — 200
Ammonius-Saccas
Origen — 185
216

ALEXANDRIAN CATECHICAL SCHOOL
Theology

DESERT FATHERS   Practice
251
259
Anthony the Great — 356
Makarios — ?
Pachomius — 346
Athanasius — 373
293
330

DIOCLETIAN   Persecution

CAPPADOCIANS
Theology and Practice
329 329
335 BASIL
Gregory of Nyssa — 394
Gregory of Nazianzus — 390
379

Eremetic Monasticism

300

CONSTANTINE 325 Council of Nicea
Unity of Church and State

Cenobetic Monasticism
EASTERN RULE
- Great Rules
- Brief Rules

Ambrose of Milan — 397
354 — St. Augustine →
430
CITY OF GOD

381 Council of Constantinople
385 St. Jerome: Vulgate Bible

400

416 ALARIC Sack of Rome

FALL OF ROME

Rise of CONSTANTINOPLE

476 ODOACER
End of the Western Empire

482
Justinian — 562

480 — St. BENEDICT →
547

WESTERN MONASTIC RULE

500

JUSTINIAN 527
Monastic reform of clergy

540 Pope GREGORY the GREAT → 604

MONASTIC LIFE

600

CIVILIZATIONAL DARK AGE

BYZANTINE ORTHODOX CIVILIZATION

From Jesus to Christianity: the Work of the Apostles

Like Moses, Jesus taught different people on different levels. Unlike Moses he did not found a Religion and a Civilization in his lifetime, although he clearly sowed the seeds for the Christian Religion in forming and guiding the work of the Apostles. He certainly understood the implications of his teaching for a Christian Civilization, although we have no record of his thinking on this subject. This was to be the work of Peter and Paul.

It appears that Jesus' followers had a firmer grounding in the First and Second Work than the followers of Moses, for they achieved more in a shorter period of time. Additionally, there was less time in Jesus' life given to 'civilizational modeling,' and it is apparent that he modeled his disciples intensely in the time that he had.[5]

As we know, the essential teachings of Jesus developed, in the generation after his death, into the religion of Christianity. The Christian Civilization came several centuries after the death of the Prophet, beginning with the establishment of a Christian kingdom in Osroene in 201 AD, and developing rapidly from the time Constantine established himself as the first Christian Roman Emperor in 306 AD. From the moment that Christianity became the state religion of the Roman Empire, many integrations and consolidations were forced upon it. Early Christianity, as it was before Constantine, was comprised of many different currents of influence, all stemming directly from Jesus' teaching, but each developing along its own lines. The Christian Religion, as it developed in the first century AD, was largely the work of Men of the Tradition, who – in their attempt to create a coherent form and a coherent theology – drew freely on Egyptian ritual and Zoroastrian mythology. This was all given a homogeneous gloss by the theologians of later centuries.

---

5. By 'civilizational modeling' we mean connecting the emergent Higher Centers of the Prophet's closest disciples to a particular way of being with respect to the external world, making them into the ideal of a Christian or a Muslim, or an Israelite. The modeled first-generation ideals are very close, across Traditions, with particular differences accumulating in the generations to follow.

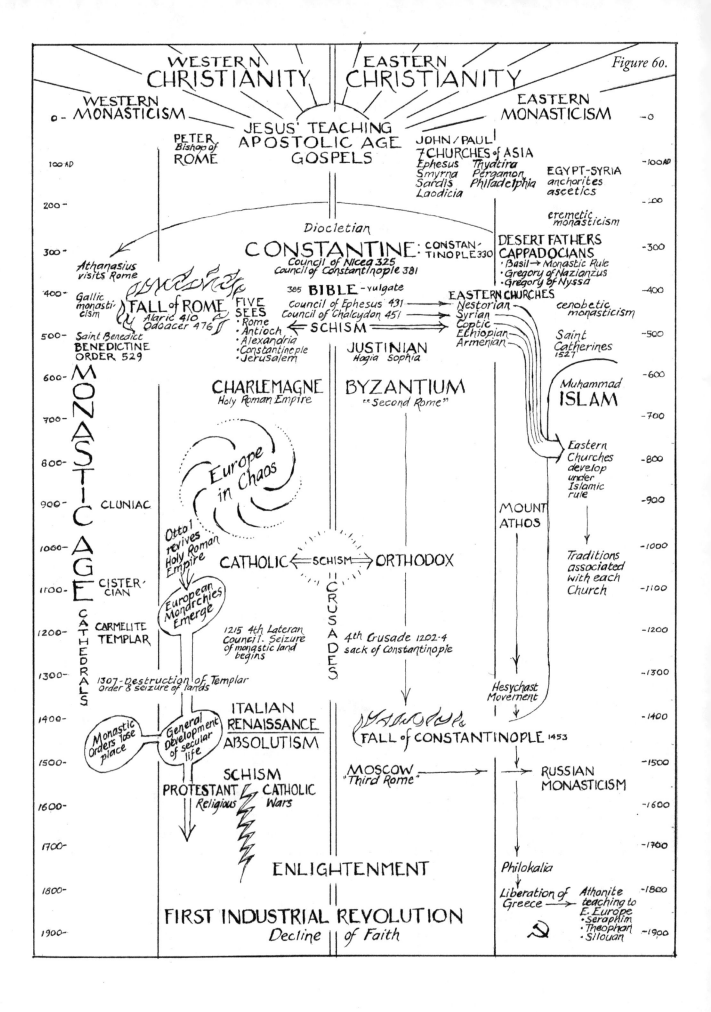

Figure 60.

The period of Jesus' life, and that of the generation to follow, was one of extraordinary charismatic force. The few sources that we have from this period can only be understood in this light. The impact of Jesus' life and teaching on his own generation and the generations to follow is very similar to that of the Buddha. The timing of the emergence of the Christian Religion and Christian Civilization is also quite similar to that of the Buddhist. Both Religion and Civilization were undefined in the lifetime of the Prophet, with the Religion taking form in the generation after the Prophet's death and the beginning of the Civilization several centuries later.

Let us focus, then, on the work of the Inner Tradition of Christianity in its relation to the development of the Christian Religion. In Jesus' lifetime the twelve Apostles were tasked both with spreading Jesus' teaching and establishing a Christian community. We may note that all were martyred but John, and all lived their lives as men who expected, and did not fear, martyrdom.

The Apostles taught and established churches in the Holy Land, Egypt, North Africa, Parthia (now part of Iran), India, Mesopotamia, Asia Minor, along the northern coast of the Black Sea, and generally throughout the countries of the northern Mediterranean – including Greece, Rome, the Italian peninsula, and Spain.

Peter, the senior Apostle, began teaching in Palestine, in the cities of Jerusalem and Caesarea. He traveled extensively through the eastern Mediterranean, becoming for a period the Bishop of Antioch, in what is now Turkey, and finally establishing a permanent base in Rome, where he continued to teach until he was martyred. The group that produced the New Testament probably originated directly from Peter's work in Rome.

Paul, the Apostle whose role it was to bring Christianity to the gentiles, traveled throughout Palestine, Syria, Asia Minor, Greece, and Italy. His work, along with that of John, was central in founding the Seven Churches of Asia. Like Peter, he was martyred in Rome.

James, son of Zebedee (or James the Greater) was one of the senior Apostles, yet we know little of him. He taught in Palestine and Spain and was martyred in Jerusalem by Herod Agrippa.

Matthew, who was reputed to be a witness of both the resurrection and the ascension, preached to the Jewish community in Judea before – according to Clement of Alexandria – 'going forth to other countries.' We have no record of what these countries were.

John, brother of James, taught with Peter in Palestine and with Paul throughout Asia Minor.

Bartholomew went into Armenia, Ethiopia, Mesopotamia, Parthia, and Lycaonia.

Thomas taught in Asia Minor, Syria, and India.

James, son of Alpheus (called James the Lesser or James the Just) taught in Palestine and Egypt, and was made the Bishop of Jerusalem by Peter, becoming a central figure in the developing church.

Jude, sometimes called Thaddeus, taught in Judea, Ethiopia, Armenia, and Caucasian Georgia.

Mark traveled with Paul on his first journey through Cyprus and Asia Minor and was said to have been the first Bishop of Alexandria. His influence in Egypt was great.

Andrew is of particular interest. Eusebius quotes Origen as saying that Andrew preached in Syria, in Asia Minor, in Scythia, along the southern shores of the Black Sea, and even up the Dnieper to Kiev – so becoming a patron saint of the Ukraine, Romania, and Russia. Settling in Constantinople he founded the Bishopric See of Byzantium, which was later to become the center of the Orthodox Church. Later he taught in Thrace, Epiros, and the Greek Peloponnese, and was finally crucified in Patras, Greece. His story, of which we have only the vaguest outlines, is one of the many unknown dramas of the first two centuries of Christianity.

The First Three Centuries of the Church

It is clear that the Apostles extended themselves to their limit, and that everywhere they went they received a strong response, whether positive or negative. From the earliest apostolic teachings came the church in **Jerusalem**, the church in **Antioch**, the church in **Alexandria**, and the church in **Rome**. From the work of Paul, John, and Andrew came the Seven Churches of Asia, and there were certainly many other apostolic churches in the first century. Peter was the senior apostle and so Rome was the leading bishopric, but it was only the first amongst equals. A miracle was unfolding all over the Mediterranean basin into the Levant, North Africa, and Asia Minor.

Indeed, the early days of Christianity were filled with a sense of the miraculous; the dark hour of the crucifixion had passed, Jesus had ascended, and he was working openly and directly with his followers. This phase lasted for more than sixty years after his death. There were now many conscious beings working on many different levels, in a general atmosphere that we can only imagine. Tradition, Religion, and fledging Civilization were still closely knit. Wherever the Great Work was found, there was more of Christianity, and many, many seeds were sown during the apostolic period. The standards demanded of the Seven Churches in Asia in the Revelation to John, were the standards of the Great Work – standards to which no contemporary Christian Church, or even monastic order, could hope to uphold.

How the Great Work continued, both within and parallel to the development of the many regional churches, we can only surmise. We can be certain that the Apostles succeeded in initiating this work in many centers in Asia Minor, the Levant, and Mediterranean Europe.

In these early years, where so much has been lost to history, the term 'Gnostic' was often used in relation to particular groups of Christians. We need to clarify this idea, firstly because doing so reveals something about the teachings of the apostolic period and, secondly, because it allows us to clarify certain aspects of the Spiritual Traditions generally.

GNOSTICISM

The term was originally derived from Plato's use of *gnosis* (γνῶσις) in the *Politicus* dialogue, as a combination of knowing and seeing. Beginning from about the second century BC it was used to describe a radical stance that was taken in relation to a number of different religions. The term is in no way exclusive to Christianity, and by the third century AD it had been used in at least three different ways:

1. Gnostic can refer to a person who is entirely focused on the inner meaning of a religion or of a teaching, someone who has achieved a concentrated inwardness

and who is undistracted by any external factor. It was used in this way, at least from the second century BC, to describe Judaic ascetics such as the Essenes.

2. Gnostic has been used to refer to a general view that there is something radically wrong with our world as we know it. There was an error or fault at the time of the creation of the world, and as a result human beings are trapped in what is, in effect, a false reality. This fundamental fault cannot be resolved from within the world itself, and therefore Man's only hope is to escape it. Thus the world itself is seen as evil, and the state of continuous imagination to which all its inhabitants are subject is seen as a reflection of that evil.

   This severe view of the human condition is usually combined with a dualistic view of the universe, pitting good against evil even at the highest level. The world is thus a theater in which Good and Evil struggle for mastery, in a contest that has not yet been resolved. Such a perspective can lead to a dark and fearful view of the human situation, and can bring motivations of fear and self-hatred into the work itself. This kind of radical dualism developed amongst certain neo-Zoroastrian, Judaic, and Christian sects.

3. Finally, there were the people who called themselves Gnostics. There was a school of Gnosticism which developed in the second and third centuries AD, on the basis of Egyptian, Platonist, Zoroastrian, Chaldean, Manichaean, and other occult teachings. These were integrated in the early third century AD under the name of Hermes Trismegistus in what we described as the aftermath of the work of the Egyptian Spiritual Tradition. (See Book III, Chapter 16.) Hermetic Gnosticism survived for many centuries, and, like Christianity, survived the Classical World. But while the Hermetic Gnostics were open to the Christian teachings, and the Christian Gnostic sects were certainly open to the Hermetic teachings (the Nag Hammadi library includes both Hermetic and Christian texts), the Roman Church itself ultimately rejected Hermetic Gnosticism.

Having said this much, we acknowledge that Gnosticism has often been equated with early Christianity, and that some early Christians actually called themselves Gnostics. Therefore it is important to clearly distinguish Gnosticism from the work of the early Christian Spiritual Tradition. As we noted, Gnosticism of types **1)** and **2)** is not unique to Christianity, and existed also in Judaism. Yet many of the early Christians were identified as Gnostics of type **1)** – that is, people with an exclusive focus on the inner life. Jesus and the Apostles were certainly like this, but to be 'like this,' and to have succeeded in connecting one's essence to Higher Centers, is not to be less human, but to be more human in a deeper way. This 'deeper humanity' distinguishes the early Christians from most Gnostics of type **1)** and all Gnostics of type **2)**. Early Christianity is quite unlike the Gnosticism of type **2)** in that Jesus taught the love of the world. He taught that the world was ultimately good, and that Mankind was worthy of redemption. Gnosticism of type **3)**, which developed after the Christian Church had taken form, was rejected by it.

To understand the significance the term 'Gnostic' had for the early Christians, we must keep in mind that the majority of Christians were Christians at the level of belief only, not initiates of the inner work. When these people encountered other kinds of Christians, who were attempting to establish themselves in a state of prolonged presence, they may have been taken aback and labelled them as Gnostics – simply as a way of dismissing them.

On the other hand, some of the early Church Fathers used the term Gnostic in an entirely positive way to refer to Christians who were succeeding with the Work of the Steward. But as the first meaning of the term Gnostic (exclusive focus) became more and more closely linked to its second meaning (belief in a dualistic universe), this positive usage gradually disappeared, and it became inappropriate to call a Christian a Gnostic. By the third century only the negative usage of the term survived within Christianity, and this was used to brand heretics.

Here we must make it clear why Gnosticism of the second type does not conform to the view of the Great Spiritual Traditions. Gnosticism of type **2)**, taken in the strong sense, lacks the conception of simultaneous service to the level one above and the level one below. Taken by itself it becomes a kind of negative self-preoccupation: 'my' attempt to escape from 'them.' The vision of the celestial hierarchy, lifting level on level, so well described by Dionysios the Areopagite, is alien to this view. Dualistic Gnosticism tends to cut itself off from the level one below and, in so doing severs itself from Living Religion and from humanity at large. It also, at the same time, severs its practitioners from the real purposes of Higher School.

The practitioners of the Great Work do not have this kind of exclusive self-centeredness. They are simple, focused people, with clear priorities, who do whatever they are doing in an open, unpretentious – yet totally undistracted – way. Jesus' teaching was indeed radical. It does represent a concentrated inwardness, undistracted by any external factor. But his stance, and the stance of the Spiritual Traditions generally, is also much more than that. Because the Great Work is confident in its connection to Higher School, it embraces a love of the world. The particular kind of fear, or the sense of something sinister, that is connected to Gnosticism of type **2)** is utterly foreign to it.

In early Christianity the tendency towards withdrawal and self-preoccupation was completely overridden by the commitment to the level one above and the invocation from that level to serve the level one below. Jesus said to Peter, "Feed my lambs." This positive universalism with respect to humanity is the very opposite of Gnostic withdrawal. But there is truth in both the Gnostic stance and the open stance that embraces all men and all things. The balance in the presentation of these truths at any particular point in history is related to the historical requirements of the time and the plan that was given an individual Tradition to actualize. Either of these poles, taken to its extreme, signals only the absence of the Great Work. The Great Work itself is an enigma, an extremism that transcends extremes.

More generally, the counterpoint to **Gnosticism** in classical times was **Humanism**, in both its Christian and its pagan forms. Humanistic thought had developed considerably in the cosmopolitan atmosphere of the Hellenistic World, beginning from the late fourth century BC. It came to its full flower in the first centuries of the Roman Empire. The weakness of Humanism is that it takes humanity – on its own level – to be something real and permanent, and to be a worthy end in itself. Within Christianity this kind of humanism becomes the deviant expression of Jesus' positive universalism. Classical Humanism established firm roots in Christianity with the popular view that the crucifixion had (at least potentially) redeemed the human race, and that all men and women who accepted Christianity were automatically 'saved.' The rest, then, were either waiting to be saved, or might potentially be saved. Their evil was simply ignorance. What is implicit in this view is that human beings are fine as human beings, and do not need to fundamentally change themselves. They just need to become 'good' human beings as opposed to 'bad' human beings. What is lost in this popularization is the fact that each human being has been given a unique potential to transcend his organic or embodied state, and it is his first duty to realize this potential. This is what it originally meant to be a Christian.

While both the Gnostic and the Humanist positions have truth in them, they are both false in themselves, for both positions lack (albeit in different ways) a transcendent element, without which there can be no true understanding of Man as a microcosm.

Having clarified the phenomenon of Gnosticism, we can now look more closely at the historical origins of the Christian Religion, and the relation of this Religion to the Spiritual Traditions that were connected with it. Again, and not surprisingly, we see the contact with non-Christian Traditions.

From the eleven fully conscious Apostles who taught throughout the Mediterranean and the Levant, from the conscious evangelists Mark and Luke, and from a host of other conscious beings who are now unknown to us, the Christian Spiritual Tradition took root and developed in its main lines of transmission. In the beginning these lines of transmission were closely linked: the Church of Rome with Peter, the Church in Byzantium with Andrew, the Seven Churches in Asia with Paul and John, and the Church in Egypt with James the Lesser and Mark. However, over time the churches that developed out of the apostolic teachings diverged. It is interesting to see, time and again, the Men of the Traditions breaching divisions that emerged at the level of the Popular Religion. It was in Egypt, in the work of the Desert Fathers, that the monastic practices were to develop which were to bring some stability to the relation of Tradition and Religion throughout the Christian world. The basis for this work in Egypt was:

1. A continuity of work that began from the teachings of James and Mark and developed through the Coptic Church in Egypt and the Catechetical School of Alexandria

2. The formation, in the deserts of Egypt, of a refuge from persecution, where many Christians sought safe haven.

Thus, in many ways, Egypt became a natural destination for Christians. Although it had been a Roman province since Caesar's conquest in 48 BC, the capital city, Alexandria, was quite cosmopolitan and very tolerant. It was, in the first century AD, a major center of trade and culture, where many races mingled. And here the most remarkable fusions and syntheses were to take place, for Alexandria was not only a center for Christians but was also the home of fledgling Neoplatonism, which was to supply the mature Classical Civilization with a fresh stream of conscious beings. This strange confluence of Christianity and Classical philosophy was ultimately the source of Christian theology, which was necessary to the Christian civilization as it developed. How, then, did this synthesis come about?

In the early years of the century, the Apostle Mark, who became the Bishop of Alexandria, founded a school for training novice Christians. This was called the Catechetical School of Alexandria. In the generation after Mark three key figures – **Pantaenus**, **Clement**, and **Ammonius Saccas** – became involved with the School, and changed its character and function. Pantaenus was a prominent Stoic philosopher who converted to Christianity and became the head of the School following Mark. He took, as his senior student, a young Greek by the name of Titus Flavius Clemens, or Clement (c. 150 to c. 215). Clement eventually succeeded Pantaenus as the head of the School. In the generation of Pantaenus the Catechetical School had begun to change, becoming more like an open university than a training school for Christian novices. A significant part of the role of the Catechetical School, as it developed, was to present Christianity to the non-Christian population of Alexandria. Since Alexandria was a major cultural center of the Classical world, these people were often highly educated with a firm grounding in the First Work. Indeed, prior to the coming of the Apostles to Egypt, there had existed an Alexandrian School, which taught Jewish theology, Greek philosophy, and a variety of Gnostic doctrines. It had as a resource the Library at Alexandria, which was then the greatest library in the world. The positive dialogue that developed between the Hellenistic Alexandrian School and the Catechetical School brought many new converts to Christianity. **The School of Alexandria**, as the Catechetical School became known, thus provided an environment in which Christians, Gnostics, Neoplatonists, and Jews could mix and debate. We will remember that Christianity was then in its charismatic phase. No one doubted that it was a living force, but it was a force that needed to articulate itself and to develop all that was implicit in Jesus' teachings.

We make the point that there was no Christian theology in the first century AD; there was no generally stated Christian view of Man in the universe to put against the other prevalent views of the age. In this time the potential for a unity of Tradition, Religion, and Civilization was clearly felt – even presumed – and a coherent theology was one of the elements necessary for its realization.

Greek philosophy was, in the Classical world, the common denominator for cosmic speculation and the direct correlate of classical science. It was originally based on the insights of Higher Centers, and many early Christians found it quite amenable to expressing the new understandings that came to them. What the early Christian thinkers took from Platonism was 1) the precedence of the invisible over the visible, 2) the attitude that all things temporal and material were a secondary reality, and **3)** the conviction that what was real and eternal in the universe was connected to the Good, or the triadic Demiurge, which we have called the Absolute.

The three key figures in the development of the Catechetical School were Clement, Ammonius Saccas, and Origen.

THE CATECHETICAL SCHOOL IN ALEXANDRIA

Clement, as we noted, succeeded Pantaenus as the head of the Catechetical School. While he was born an Athenian and in his youth acquired a full classical culture, he converted in his early adult life and was always first and foremost a man of the Church. He died as a Christian martyr in 215 AD when the Catechetical School was subject to one of its periodic Roman persecutions. In his lifetime Clement succeeded in uniting the Greek philosophical doctrines with those of the Christian teaching. Having said this, we must note that Clement always placed a first value on *gnosis* that could be held by Christians specially chosen by God. At the same time he pursued a more popular Christian teaching actively, clarifying it with 'gnostic' insight. He freely used the term Gnostic to describe Christians who had attained the Second Work – the work of the Christian Spiritual Tradition. In the early Middle Ages his writings were used by the monasteries as guidelines for combining classical culture with the Christian teachings.

Ammonius Saccas was the most prominent teacher of his generation in the open School of Alexandria. He was an enlightened being, who taught directly from the experience of Higher Centers. He was also, and at the same time, the greatest philosopher of his age. The Christians (St. Jerome and Eusebius) claimed him as a Christian. The Neoplatonists (Porphyry) claimed him as a Neoplatonist. But no one now knows exactly who he was or what he taught because he left no writings, and his inner teachings were given under a vow of secrecy. We know from Porphyry that his teachings were the source and origin of classical Neoplatonism. He argued for an original idealist interpretation of Plato (over the skepticism of the second Academy) and he argued that the Platonic and Aristotelian doctrines were essentially the same. It is possible that he taught that all the great religions and teachings were one, and demonstrated the way in which the Christian teaching summed these different expressions of the truth. The first Christian theologian, Origen, studied under Ammonius Saccas, and from him came Christian theology as we know it. The greatest classical philosopher after the death of Aristotle, Plotinus, studied under him for twelve years, and from him came Neoplatonism as we know it. It is remarkable that the first Christian theologian and the greatest philosopher of the Classical World were students of one and the same teacher in Alexandria, friends under the same vow of silence. This shows us something about the early Christian World.

Origen (185-254) was an Egyptian who joined the School of Alexandria in his teens. He was first a student of Clement and then of Ammonius Saccas. It was he who revived the Catechetical School after the persecution of Clement and who succeeded him as its head. In this position he had to respond to the many questions and challenges that were put to the School, and in the course of formulating these responses he became the father of Christian theology. However, history was to repeat itself, for Origen – like Clement – was persecuted and forced to flee the city of Alexandria. Demetrius, the Patriarch of Alexandria, felt threatened by Origen's growing influence, and claimed that Origen had been ordained without his permission. On this basis he expelled Origen from the city. Origen then relocated in Caesarea (in modern Israel), where he was persecuted and tortured, either by Demetrius or by the Roman Emperor Gaius Decius. Accounts vary. He survived these persecutions and continued to teach and to publish. He was deeply loved by his students, both in Alexandria and in Caesarea. His impact on Christian theology, as that developed, was such that we shall summarize his teaching here.

ORIGEN'S TEACHING

In defending the unity of God against the Gnostic dualists, Origen taught the complete subordination of all creation to God. **God**, then, is perfect unity, invisible and incorporeal, transcending all things, and therefore both inconceivable and incomprehensible to Man. We note that in Origen's teaching, the world 'God' is understood to be the equivalent of the Absolute, as presented in Book I. **Creation** is the revelation of this perfect unity; it is the spontaneous self-emanation of God. The act of Creation itself is continuous, in the sense of continuing even now.

Origen called the self-expression of God in Creation the *Logos*. He was using the term in the Greek sense of 'cosmic utterance,' and this we must clarify.

- While God's BEING is centered in itself, it has an outward-turning face, and this face is the **Logos**. In the pre-Socratic/Stoic use of the term, the *Logos* is the ongoing utterance of Creation: the spawning of all that is. But the *Logos* is not simply a chaotic outpouring. The multiple beings that are generated out of the *Logos* are all, as they come to their maturity, realizations of this more centered state of BEING – at whatever degree of remove from their source. In other words BEING is somehow behind everything, but is more completely expressed in some things than in others.

- Thus the *Logos* includes all the discrete objects, events, and relations that we see around ourselves, but – when these things are viewed from the cosmic center – they all appear in their essential connection. Let us clarify. As embodied beings, we perceive our immediate surroundings in only three dimensions, and for this reason the things that we perceive appear before us separately. We can, for example, see a cat, but we cannot see 'all cats at all points in time,' yet the entity that is 'all cats at all points in time' certainly does exist. If you remove the limitations of space and time, you see an essential felinity, or archetypal cat, that is alive in all its extensions. And the same principle applies to everything! Creation, as the *Logos*, is **the unity of the many archetypes** that are realized in the objects, events, and relations that we see around ourselves. And – taking a step inward – the *Logos* includes the originating outward-facing aspect of BEING itself. We could say, speaking more generally, that the *Logos* represents the conscious aspects of Creation. It is below God (as he is in himself) and above Man, and **it includes Man's latent Higher Centers.**

- When we look at Creation in this way – from the inside out – it is fundamentally a unity. This is how God views it, and this is how it was created. In fact the higher influences that reach men come not directly from God himself but from the *Logos*, and from the hierarchy of Angels that are active in different levels of the *Logos*. Thus the inner unity that is behind the 'outer shell' of visible Creation is a unity which comprehends multiplicity, and for this reason Origen termed it an "essence of essences" or "idea of ideas."

- From the standpoint of Creation, the *Logos* is the conscious purpose that is behind it and that reveals its unity.

Because God's six-dimensional revelation-through-Creation is not visible to men (who normally perceive in only three dimensions), he was obliged to make a more specific revelation to men through the person of Jesus Christ. Origen described this embodied revelation "as an incarnation of the *Logos*." Thus Jesus Christ was not one of the multiple entities spawned by the *Logos*, but an incarnation of what it is. *He is a direct incarnation of the essence of the Logos*, and so is prior to the multiplicity of created things. As the Prophet, he is – to use Origen's term – the 'essence of essences.' To understand how this is true we must clarify the principle of 'incarnation.' There could not, by definition, be an incarnation of God, because God (the Absolute) is beyond incarnation. If something has become incarnate, it is not God. So Jesus Christ cannot be an incarnation of God. But there can be an incarnation of the *Logos* that is **1)** relevant to the specifically human experience of Creation, and **2)** has known God face-to-face. In other words there can be an incarnate being who understands the essence of the *Logos*, and so understands something about how everything is connected, and – beyond this – understands how all of this exists in relation to God. According to Origen, Jesus Christ was such a person.

Before proceeding further with the history of the Christian Tradition, we must be clear how Origen's theological usage of the term *Logos* is grounded in a particular usage of the Greek term λόγος (*Logos*) in the gospels. This is necessary to understanding the idea of the Holy Trinity, which we shall come to shortly.

THE DOCTRINE OF THE LOGOS

Origen's use of *Logos* as 'cosmic utterance' is substantiated by the opening lines of the Gospel of John, which relate the *Logos* to the 'creation of all things that were made.' The Greek 'λόγος' (*Logos*) in John 1:1 has traditionally been translated into English as 'Word' (rather than 'cosmic utterance'), yet the context seems to demand the pre-Socratic meaning that Origen gave it.

We shall reproduce the opening passage from John (1:1-1:3) replacing the English translation of *Logos* as 'Word' with the original Greek *Logos* (implying 'cosmic utterance'). We shall then follow Origen's advice and translate the second reference to God (which has no article) as 'divine Being.' Origen pointed out that John always uses the definite article when he refers to the uncreated cause of all things. Thus when John says *the* God (ὁ θεός/*ho Theos*), he refers to the first cause (the unknowable Beyond-Being), and when he says simply God (θεός/*Theos*) he refers to God in his Being-aspect. It is the Being-aspect of God that engenders the *Logos*. Thus the first three verses can be rendered:

> In the beginning was the *Logos* and the *Logos* was with God [HJ: the uncreated first cause], and the *Logos* was divine Being. The same [divine Being] was in the beginning with God. All things came into being through him, and without him not even one thing came into being that has come into being. (John 1:1-1:3)

The passage makes perfect sense when we use the pre-Socratic meaning of λόγος (cosmic utterance). The BEING aspect of God flowers into the *Logos*, which, in its manifest forms, constitutes Creation. The *Logos* is directly related to God but not identified with him, and so the unknowable dimension of Beyond-Being is preserved.

But traditional theologians, who interpreted 'ὁ λόγος' as 'the Word,' came to very different conclusions. They translated the passage from John 1:14 as … "the Word was made flesh and dwelt among us." They took this to mean that Jesus was the Word, and from this they concluded that 'God,' 'Jesus,' and 'the Word' were the same thing. But identifying the Prophet directly with God creates a host of problems. What John is actually saying in this passage is that the *Logos* (the cosmic utterance) took human form in Jesus Christ. In other words, Jesus Christ had a level of consciousness that could know the essence of the *Logos* independently of Creation, and so see the intention of the *Logos* in Creation.

The strange series of logical links that results from interepreting 'ὁ λόγος' (the *Logos*) as 'the Word' was made the basis of official Church doctrine at the Council of Chalcydon in 451, and has been accepted by the Western Church ever since! But using the pre-Socratic meaning of the term, as Origen did, relieves us of the awkward identification of 'the Word' with Jesus, and at the same time frees us from the direct (and quite inaccurate) identification of Jesus with God.

There is no reason to think that a person as adept in self-expression as John (who was the one Apostle who authored his own gospel) would choose to make Jesus equal to God, when he records Jesus saying "My Father is greater than I." (14:28) Additionally Origen, having been born only a century after John wrote, and having done extensive work of translation, was a master of the 'common dialect' Greek that was in use between 300 BC and 300 AD and was known as the *koiné*. He was familiar with the Greek usages of that time in a way that no fifth-century theologian could be, for by the fifth-century AD Classical Greek was no longer a living language in the Western Roman Empire.

According to Origen the bodily incarnation of Jesus Christ was necessary because Mankind lives almost exclusively through the flesh (its four lower centers) and God, as the Absolute, has no means of communicating directly to Man's dormant Higher Centers. Because Jesus Christ was both embodied and an incarnation of the *Logos*, he could address men through their lower centers, while trying to awaken their dormant Higher Centers. As the essence of the *Logos* he could see their Higher Centers **from the inside**, and so was quite expert at nursing and stimulating them to life. When Jesus succeeded in this – even slightly – he could communicate to men something of their real place in the universe and something of their real possibilities. He could also communicate what God required of them at this particular point in history. And this was precisely the role that Jesus Christ was created to play.

The philosophers and the gnostics at Alexandria questioned the remarkable place that the Christians claimed for their Prophet. Origen responded to them by formulating **the Doctrine of the Trinity**, based on Jesus' use of the terms **the Father, the Son,** and **the Holy Spirit** – which is found principally in the teaching of the Last Supper. Using this doctrine he explained the different aspects – divine and human – of Christ's existence. We note that *there is no doctrine of the Trinity* in the New Testament. The terms the Father, the Son, and the Holy Spirit are used many times in quite specific ways, but their relationship is never clearly defined. Origen's Doctrine of the Trinity became part of the essential creed of the Christian Religion, and in order to proceed we must have some understanding of it. We keep in mind that the man who formulated this doctrine was intimately familiar with 1) the Greek doctrine of the *Logos*, and 2) the Egyptian myth of Ptah-Creation – one of the first known expressions of the doctrine of 'cosmic utterance.' Origen's presentation of the three essential terms of the doctrine can be summarized as follows.

THE DOCTRINE OF THE TRINITY

The Father

The Father is the deity himself who is unknowable to Man and who is, in some way, 'behind' the person of Jesus Christ. Relating this to the terminology of Chapter 2, we could say that the Absolute is God as he is in himself, unknowable to Man. The BEING that generates the *Logos* is the dimension of God that is recognized – at whatever distance – by the popular religion. This exactly parallels the Vedic presentation of Brahma as the Absolute, with the derivative Brahmā as the 'face' of the Absolute that can be recognized by Man.

The Holy Spirit

The Greek word that the term Holy Spirit is based on is πνεῦμα/*pneuma*, which translates as 'spirit,' 'breath of life,' or 'inspiration.' For some reason it has often been translated as Holy Ghost, which – given the current English usage – is a mistranslation. Jesus made one defining statement about the Holy Spirit in John 14:26: "But the Comforter, which is the Holy Spirit, whom the Father will send in my name, he shall teach you all things, and bring all things to your remembrance, whatsoever I have said unto you." The word 'comforter' is a translation of the Greek word παράκλητος (*parakleitos*), which means literally 'friend,' 'someone who comes to help you,' or 'someone who intercedes on your behalf.' In this context the term Holy Spirit clearly refers to the Higher Emotional Center, for in the moment that it comes it is suddenly there 'under your skin,' supporting everything in you that is most real. The Sufis used the term 'the Friend' in exactly the same way. But the Holy Spirit is *more* than the Higher Emotional Center. How can we understand this?

- Origen used the term Holy Spirit in relation to his understanding of the *Logos*. As we noted, the *Logos* is the deity taking form in such a way as to give expression to Creation. It is thus both the actual multiple forms of creation that we see and the 'ideas' which are the 'essence' of those multiple forms.

- While God himself (as the Absolute) is unknowable to Man, different aspects of the *Logos* can be known by embodied human beings, because embodied human beings have higher faculties latent within themselves which may, under certain circumstances, be brought to life. But Origen did not have – as part of the inheritance of the 'first generation' of Christian teachings – the concept of Higher Centers with which to clarify these matters. Jesus did not need the concept of Higher Centers, because he taught from the Higher Centers and referred to them directly in a symbolic way. Origen – speaking to people who never knew Jesus – made use of the first-generation concepts that came closest to suiting his needs. He placed the Higher Centers within the realm of the *Holy Spirit*, and used this term (and others) to refer to them. Having made this point we can now make the point that Origen's Holy Spirit is *more* than our latent Higher Centers. The Holy Spirit is not only something within us, it is also something in the essence of the *Logos* itself, and in the conscious purposes that are realized through the *Logos*. So the Holy Spirit is both inside of us and outside of us. (As Jesus states, in the recently discovered Gospel of Thomas, "The Kingdom is inside of you, and it is outside of you.") The *Logos* that is inside of us is, for almost all of us, latent or potential, while the *Logos* that is outside of us is 'active' (whether we are aware of it or not).

We can now be more explicit about how Origen used the term Holy Spirit. It refers to a direct perception of the invisible *Logos* that is behind physical creation by an embodied human being, through their Higher Centers. It refers both to the Higher Centers themselves and what they open us to. But of course this kind of knowledge must begin with a knowledge of our own, latent, Higher Centers, for without this our perceptions of the *Logos* – as it is in itself – cannot be integrated. The development of the latent Higher Centers is, then, the critical point and the beginning of everything.

The Son

The Son (of the Father) is the physical embodiment of Jesus Christ. According to Origen this physical embodiment was necessary for two reasons: **1)** in order that the *Logos* might be made known to men and **2)** in order that Christ himself might be a man and suffer everything that men suffer. In this way he could be both God and Man, and so redeem humanity by revealing its divine nature. This is very similar to the redeeming role of Osiris in the Egyptian Tradition. In Jesus, the Holy Spirit was developed to such a degree that he was completely transparent to the level above himself and could transmit the light of that level to the level one below. As the essence of the *Logos*, he is in some way 'behind' Creation.

We noted above that there is no Doctrine of the Trinity in the New Testament. In Jesus' original, oral teaching the term Holy Spirit was often used to refer to the Higher Emotional Center, and the term Father was used to refer either to a profound experience of World 6 or to the Absolute. Jesus himself most frequently uses it to apply to World 6. But Jesus' precise usage (whatever it was) was lost in the generation that came after the Apostles. Origen formulated his Doctrine of the Trinity to address the questions that the interested, but still sincerely questioning, prospective Christians were asking. After Origen's death the Doctrine of the Trinity became a principal point of contention in debates that arose within the Church. These became known as the Christology debates. Origen's doctrine soon became subject to all the pressures of sectarian dispute. Indeed, for at least the next millennium, every schism in the Church defined itself in terms of the Trinity.

Origin's original presentation of the relation of the terms of the Trinity was significantly refined, in the spirit in which he formulated it, in the Council of Constantinople of 381. This was the work of three enlightened beings – Basil of Caesarea, Gregory of Nyssa, and Gregory of Nazianzus – but we shall come to this later.

Why, then, did the Doctrine of the Trinity became such a contentious issue?

One great difference between the teaching of the Christian Spiritual Tradition and the creed of its emergent popular Religion was in the conception of God. The Man of Religion wants to feel that he 'knows' what God is, that he knows what he is talking about when he says "I believe in God." This can be quite a deep emotional need because the popular religion envisions a personal relationship to the deity. The Tradition, however, knows God, as the Absolute, to be transcendent and incomprehensible to Man.

The popular religion – which included most of the senior clergy – wanted an idealized Christ-Super-Man with an absolutely authoritative God backing him up. It wanted a simple Trinity where, in effect, Jesus *was* God. This interpretation finds support in a superficial interpretation of passages like John 14:10: "Believest thou not that I am in the Father, and the Father in me?" But the assertion of a direct identity between Jesus and God is explicitly denied in John 14:28, where Jesus stated: "Ye have heard how I said unto you, I go away, and come again unto you. If ye loved me, ye would rejoice, because I said, I go unto the Father: for my Father is greater than I."

In the second, third, and fourth centuries the Men of the Tradition used the Doctrine of the Trinity to explain Mankind's relationship to an utterly transcendent God. They wanted to open up the sphere of reference to Higher Centers, to the *Logos*, and to that BEING which is below the God who encompasses Beyond-Being. They were concerned to elucidate the three terms in a way that would allow them to refer to what we have called the world of Higher Centers. On this basis we can make some clarifications:

In popular Christianity a simple, unitary God is good, and so God's creation must be good. Humanity does not live in a world of illusion, but in the world that God intended. While some men are evil, humanity itself is all right in the condition that it is in. Some are Christians and some are not; the ones who are not can join the Church anytime. Men can pray directly to God just as they are, and Christian communities can choose to do God's will. The Christians do not, like the early Judaic communities, need second-generation prophets to keep them on course. When individual men err, it is their own fault and the individuals in question must correct their ways.

This is a form of theism, and it is this view to which Christian theology became increasingly committed. The official 'discrediting' of Origen's work by later theologians was done to preserve the simple, unitary theism that developed in the popular religion.

From the standpoint of the Christian Spiritual Tradition things look very different. Mankind is fundamentally under an illusion, and this includes converted Christians.

Mankind itself has missed the mark, and Christians – even after their conversion – have a responsibility to find that mark, to release themselves from the hold of the Lower Self, and to find the God within. To become a Christian is to commit to profound internal change, or *metanoia* (μετάνοια). Jesus often asked his disciples to "wake" or "sleep not" (γρηγορεῖτε/*gregoriete*). As these men were *already* in the normal waking state, Jesus was clearly asking them to enter the higher state of consciousness in which he himself existed. We can be certain that this approach to Christian teaching was quite alive in the first century, and that the early Christians were much more adept at this kind of thing than they were at theology. Not surprisingly, the term *gregoriete* (γρηγορεῖτε) is now usually translated into English as 'watch,' as though Jesus had a recurring need for an external lookout or sentinal.

When Christians of the first century – through diligent effort – came to know the God within, they would achieve a kind of 'natural' teaching authority: an authority grounded in the direct experience of Higher Centers. But as the institution of the Church developed and complex regional politics built up within it, there was a very great reluctance on the part of the clergy to recognize this kind of authority. There was an instinctive resistance to acknowledging an achievement that can only come quite independently of church politics and that does not – by its very nature – respect institutional protocols.

The Church, as it developed into an established institution, naturally wanted to control who had teaching authority. We can sympathize with this because there were – at that time, as in our own – hosts of false prophets and false teachers making spurious claims. But ethnic and regional considerations, combined with the all-too-human will to power, began to skew the ability of the clergy to make clear judgments in this regard. One of the regional churches might find an enlightened man in its midst and want to acknowledge his leadership in matters of faith. The people around this man might be able to distinguish the truth of his teaching from the institutional theology of the time. But this man's recognition quickly brings into question the established relation between the different Churches and the formal structure of authority. There is the potential, then, for many misunderstandings, and when these are combined with ethnic and regional rivalries you have all the schisms of the Church.

It is a tragedy that Christian theology was rent, for more than a millennium, with heated debates about the 'person of Christ,' simply because the popular Religion could not articulate the different levels of Man.

Leaving these matters aside and returning to the Catechetical School in Alexandria, we must emphasize that the first aim of men like Clement and Origen was never to counter pagan objections with a perfect theology, but to show how the life of a Christian – a life dedicated to realizing a state of prolonged presence – was superior to that of a pagan or to that of a merely speculative philosopher. Origen always taught that the only road to perfection was through the imitation of Christ, and it was the example of his life that won him the love of his students and led him, in the end, to martyrdom. It is often forgotten now that Christianity's first theologian was a direct inspiration to the originators of Christian monasticism, who came in the generation to follow.

And so – as the result of the labors of men like Pantaenus, Clement, and Origen – Christian theology came into being. It was part of the working unity of Tradition, Religion, and Civilization, and it must certainly have existed in the archetype of the Christian Civilization. Initially theology was the work of Men of the Tradition. Having said this, we must emphasize that *the inner teaching of the Christian Spiritual Tradition was complete in the time of Christ*, and continued just as it was even into the nineteenth century. Theology was, in the beginning, a working link between Tradition and Religion. It kept the doctrinal teachings of the Religion open to the set of higher meanings which were behind them. Indeed, theology's highest calling would have been to serve Worlds 6 and 12 in the life of the Church. But with the passage of time, and the tremendous growth in the temporal power of the Church, theology became increasingly tied to all the issues and concerns affecting particular groups of Christians in particular places. To some degree it transcended these issues and brought unity, but more frequently it was distorted by them.

As a result of the work of the Catechetical School, the city of Alexandria became, by the third century, one of four Apostolic Sees, second only to Rome. But the Catechetical School was, at the same time, part of the beginning of Christian monasticism. Origen himself deeply influenced two of the founders of Christian monasticism – Basil the Great and Gregory Nazianzus. One thousand seven hundred years later, when the monks of the Orthodox Spiritual Tradition compiled the first edition of the *Philokalia,* they included a collection of Origen's works. In Caesarea where Origen's personal influence lived on, he was viewed as the father of Greek monasticism.

Having said these things, we must note that in the politics of the Church, as that developed over time, Origen's theology was eventually discredited. While much of Origen's theology was taken for granted – as though it had been taught by the Apostles themselves – the fact that he taught the transmigration of souls was anathema. People wanted their guarantee of Heaven in one lifetime. Origen also taught that the 'purification of souls' was an eternal process which continually adapted itself to new cycles of history. This was intolerable to the consensus of opinion in the fourth-century Roman Church. In the Synod of Constantinople in 543, Origen was declared a heretic. While this judgment was later rescinded, Origen never recovered the place that he had held in the more open and dynamic world of Early Christianity.

The Emergence of Monasticism

While so many promising developments occurred in the first centuries of the Christian teaching, they were counterbalanced by **1)** internecine strife, **2)** the popularization of Jesus' teaching, and **3)** the increasing temporal power of the Church. It was – in the end – the Spiritual Traditions of Christian monasticism, both Orthodox and Catholic, that leave us with the clearest and most consistent traces of the Great Work. Orthodox and Catholic monasticism came from a single source, from circumstances which developed in the late third and early fourth centuries in Egypt and Syria. These developments corresponded to a change in the very complexion of Christianity. Many of the initiatives taken by Men of the Tradition in the first century did not develop in the way they had expected, because the very nature of Christianity changed in its transition into a 'state religion' at the beginning of the fourth century. To understand how the work of the Christian Spiritual Traditions developed in the fourth and fifth centuries, we must review the general situation.

The Early Christians had – at least to a degree – a 'martyr' psychology. Their Prophet was a martyr, and all of the Apostles were martyred, except John. The martyr is a symbol of one who places the reality of the next world over the reality of the world that we can see and feel and touch. And he is a poignant reminder of the temporal nature of our existence.

When, in the struggle to secure his position as Roman Emperor, Constantine defeated Maxentius at the Battle of the Milvian Bridge, the world of Christianity changed. Constantine converted on the field of battle, and Christianity became the state religion of the Roman Empire. Between Constantine's victory in 312 AD and his death in 337 there was a direct alignment of Church and State, and the Church began to wield great temporal power. It then attracted men capable of wielding that power, and these men became subject to all of the temptations that come from its exercise. The role of the martyr began to recede into history. Many Christians of that time felt there was a decline of the faith and that the rejection of this world – symbolized by the martyr – had been forgotten by an increasingly worldly religion.

Parallel to these developments, however, a second chain of events took place. In the early centuries of the Church, when Christians were actively persecuted, many took refuge in the deserts of Egypt and Syria, forming small communities called *sketes*. These were independent from the major regional churches and were comprised of clusters of anchorites, or solitaries. There was certainly a relationship between the early *sketes* and **1)** the line of apostolic teaching transmitted in Egypt through James and Mark, and **2)** the first Christian theologians who taught at the Catechetical School in Alexandria.

When the Emperor Diocletian's active persecution of the Christians began, just after the year 300, these communities grew rapidly. It was in this period that many of the Christians inhabiting the deserts, already steeled in hardship and poverty, began to realize that they could work better together.

At the very time that Constantine succeeded Diocletian, and succeeded in establishing Christianity as the official religion of the Roman Empire, certain of the solitaries – known as **the Desert Fathers** – were beginning to form monastic organizations. They did this by defining monastic rules. Saint Anthony gave the Anchorite Rule in about 310, and Saint Pachomius produced a Cenobetic or communal rule in or around 318. The rejection of the world through martyrdom was thus replaced by the rejection of the world through monastic life. The monk became the living reminder that the teaching of Christ was to transcend the Lower Self and to know God directly through Higher Centers. These men and these rules became the ultimate source of both the great monastic orders of the West and the tradition of Eastern Orthodox monasticism. The Western orders were destined to carry the torch of Civilizational Order through the Dark Ages, while Eastern Orthodox monasticism became the very backbone of Byzantine Civilization in Eastern Europe.

To be clear about how monasticism evolved from this point, we must clarify the terms that were originally used to describe it.

The hermit (or anchorite) is a monk living in solitude.

Eremetic monasticism came into being as groups of hermits began to live under monastic rules in *sketes*, which afforded the monks a degree of mutual support and security. As *sketes* were without any kind of patronage, they had to be self-sustaining, and the monks often manufactured and sold baskets, ceramics, or other goods. After the emergence of monasteries in the fourth century, the *sketes* formed a kind of bridge between the monastic community and those monks who continued to work as hermits. Often the three forms of monasticism could be found in close proximity.

Idiorrhythmic monasticism developed out of the *skete* in the Eastern Church. Idiorrhythmic communities were larger than the *sketes*, but, as with the *sketes*, the monks were self-sustaining. The individual monks could hold private property and might have a developed professional life. While these monks lived separately from each other and cooked for themselves, they engaged in common worship.

Cenobetic monasticism is full-fledged monastic life, with a monastery, communal worship, communal meals, and private cells. An abbot or abbess leads the monastic organization. Cenobetic monks are not themselves self-supporting, although the monasteries might – and usually did – undertake practical work of different kinds.

Saint Anthony, the author of the anchorite rule, had a student **Athanasius**, who eventually became the Bishop of Alexandria. As a Bishop, Athanasius lived by the cenobetic rule. In about 340 he traveled to Rome. His presence in Rome must have been a strong statement of what the monastic life can achieve, for his influence was tremendous. From the time of his visit the rule of monastic life was everywhere studied and admired. It was, in a way, the beginning of a new age in Western Christianity.

The work of the Desert Fathers continued. In 358 **Saint Basil of Caesarea** (Basil the Great), after having studied Christian monastic practices throughout the Eastern Mediterranean, created a Monastic Rule which was to be the basis of all monastic life in Eastern Christianity. Basil was a pivotal figure; he was a formative influence on Saint Ambrose of Milan – the proponent of Christian universalism – who was in turn a formative influence on Saint Augustine.

The Rule of Basil the Great was directly implemented by a monastic order at Sinai, located at the foot of Mount Horeb, the very place where Moses had received the Ten Commandments. Because this part of Sinai was a wilderness, the monks of the order were periodically threatened by brigands. When the Emperor Justinian became aware of the monks' situation, he created the walled monastery of Saint Catherine's, which was completed in 527. Saint Catherine's became a major center of monastic practice for Eastern Christianity, and with the Islamic conquest of the area in 635, it became a model of how Christian monastic practice could be sustained under Islam. Saint Basil's rule was preserved and was eventually implemented (ca. 860) at Mount Athos in Greece. It must have been implemented in the same spirit in which it was created, for, from about that time, the Holy Mountain became the center of Eastern monasticism.

While the monastic practice of Eastern Christianity found an early and enduring model in Basil's rule, the situation with Western monasticism was more problematic. Because the circumstances of life were different from those of Eastern Christianity it was hard to find a definitive monastic form. Many experiments ran parallel – all following upon Athanasius' initial inspiration – but with varying degrees of success. Finally, in 520, **Saint Benedict** created the **Benedictine Rule**, which was specifically tailored to the situation of Western Christianity. From the application of this rule, and from the reaction to its application, comes all of Western monasticism. (We shall return to Benedictine monasticism in Chapter 38, on the Middle Ages.)

The Divisions of the Church

As we noted, the different Christian Churches developed from the work of the Apostles in widely separate regions and in very different cultural contexts. While we have emphasized the development of monasticism in the first centuries of Christianity, different branches of the Christian Spiritual Tradition were alive in both the churches and the small monastic communities. In the beginning these two streams ran parallel. The point at which the Great Work faded from the Churches is hard to determine. Whatever the case, before the coming of Constantine, the idea of what a Christian was varied widely. The Spiritual Tradition was relatively stronger while the Religion itself was less unified. There was a greater unity of faith and, at the same time, a greater diversity of theological schools. Early Christianity thus presents a colorful and varied tapestry.

There was – as we noted in our discussion of Origen – a particular dispute over the idea of the Holy Trinity. The concepts of the Father, the Son, and the Holy Spirit were central to defining what a Christian was, yet they could not be correctly understood without reference to what we have called Higher Centers, and hence they were defined differently in different places by different men. As soon as the men of one place and generation held tightly onto a dogma of words, others resisted them.

This debate took place largely through the Ecumenical Councils. The Councils were meetings of the different Christian Churches with the aim of resolving outstanding issues and bringing unity to the faith. Their hope was to preserve the spirit of Pentecost, when, it is said, the Holy Spirit descended on an assemblage of Christians. Many became one in mind and heart, and the truth was revealed. These Church Councils were accepted as significant reference points in both the East and the West.

We shall review the formative Ecumenical Councils of 325, 381, 432, and 451.

COUNCIL OF NICEA: 325

In 325 the Emperor Constantine called the Council of Nicea to bring a uniform interpretation to Christianity. One of the aims of the Council was to address the creed of Arianism, which had developed out of the teaching of Arius, a presbyter in the city of Alexandria. Arius allowed that Christ was more than human, but did not allow that he was 'of one nature' with God. What Arius said was – like so many things – true in one way, but not in another. The essential (and legitimate) concern of Arianism was that Christianity not fall to the level of the cult worship of a man and that it acknowledge an infinite and unknowable God. Arius did not, in other words, want a God who was a bearded old man in the sky and a Prophet who was worshipped like a pagan cult image. Arianism had the effect, however, of reducing the special nature of Jesus Christ and so the significance of his appearance amongst men. The Council – in opposition to this – defined *orthodoxy* as the belief that Christ 'proceeds from' or 'is one in essence with' God, with the caveat that the nature of Christ was the unity of the Father, the Son, and the Holy Spirit. This doctrine became known as **the Nicene Creed**.

COUNCIL OF CONSTANTINOPLE: 381

The Nicene Creed was elaborated in greater depth in 381 at the Council of Constantinople. This Council was able to draw on the understanding of some of the greatest theologians of Early Christianity: Saint Athanasius and the three Cappadocian Fathers – Gregory of Nazianzus, Gregory of Nyssa, and Basil of Caesarea. Basil – as we noted – was the original author of the cenobetic rule of Eastern Monasticism. While he died just before the Council of Constantinople, it is almost certain that he drafted the version of the Nicene Creed that was presented there. All four of these men were monks under vow, and all four were men of the highest spiritual attainment. The result of their work, the Nicene Creed of 381, was a masterful representation of the relation between God, the Prophet, and Mankind.

To understand this achievement we must understand the context in which it was formulated, particularly the theological problems which arise from a theistic view of God – which was then becoming general in the popular faith. Theism conceives God as the active ruler of the universe. He rules in the same way that a king rules, in other words, an individual subjective identity who makes decisions based on that identity. Like a king he can be petitioned, and like a king he will acknowledge the subjective nature of those he rules. From the standpoint of theism God is an enlargement of human subjectivity: a superhuman subject.

This belief is a kind of anthropomorphism; it makes God less than what he is by imposing a human form of subjectivity on him. God, as he is imagined by men, can never be what he is in himself. We distance ourselves from God in every moment that we impose a human conception of 'self' upon him. The Nicene theologian Gregory of Nyssa addressed this problem when he stated: "The true knowledge and vision of God consist in this – in seeing that He is invisible, because what we seek [HJ: in God] lies beyond all knowledge – being wholly separated by the darkness of incomprehensibility." [6] Reducing God to the form of a human subject – even if a super-subject – forces a like reduction of the other elements of the Trinity. This lesser 'Son' of God then becomes an embodied image of the super-subject. In this context, the more closely the Son can be identified with the Father, the better. The Holy Spirit then becomes a kind of 'second intermediary' between God and Man. Jesus Christ, the 'first intermediary' is no longer in our midst, but the 'ghostly' secondary intermediary remains with us now, just as in apostolic times. The conception of the Holy Spirit as an intermediary 'person' allows a connection to the divinity that does not threaten human subjectivity, and so leaves both the Black Queen and the Lower Self in place. In this way the theistic view allows us to believe that we can communicate with God just as we are, concealing the difficult truth that God – as he is in himself – is utterly anathema to the subjective sense of 'I.' Thus the Holy Spirit, which was taken in apostolic times to refer directly to the Higher Centers and to the utterly open-ended *Logos*, was fast becoming the ghostly 'third person' of the Holy Trinity. Indeed it was increasingly referred to as the 'Holy Ghost.'

We emphasize that the Nicene Creed of 381 was formulated by people who understood these problems. They understood that the basic statement of what it means to be a Christian had to be meaningful to people who were capable of only a theistic view, but that, at the same time, the Creed had to open the door to a higher view of God. The theologians of Constantinople were challenged to present a view of the Trinity in which the Father was transcendent, the Son both transcendent and genuinely human, and the Holy Spirit at least commensurate with the conscious aspects of the Creation. We shall try to summarize the Creed of 381 and to bring out its implications.

---

6. Gregory of Nyssa, *Life of Moses*, II, 163 (377A).

THE NICENE CREED

The Council of Constantinople defined Jesus Christ as "the only-begotten Son of God, begotten of the Father before all aeons, God of God, Light of Light, very God of very God; begotten, not made, being of one in essence (ὁμοούσιος/*homo-ousios*) with the Father, by whom all things were made." Christ was thus begotten of God before Creation; he pre-exists Creation. At the same time the 'Son of God' was born a man, within Creation, and was crucified in the flesh. After his crucifixion he rose from the dead, so demonstrating **1)** God's forgiveness of humanity and **2)** something of what is possible for every human being. Jesus Christ will come again to humanity, at the end of time, to judge both the living and the dead.

Clarifying the idea of the Holy Spirit, the Council stated it was "the Lord and Giver of Life; who proceeds from the Father; who with the Father and the Son together is worshipped and glorified." This is entirely compatible with Origen's *Logos*. (Origen did not become a 'heretic' until 543 AD.) The Holy Spirit is worthy of our reverence because it is inclusive of the original ground of BEING, that is behind the multiplicity of Creation. It thus represents conscious purpose, as that can be known within Creation. The Council affirmed that the Holy Spirit spoke through the Prophets, including Moses, Elijah, Isaiah, Ezekiel, and Jesus.

COMMENTARY ON THE NICENE CREED

The Creed of 381 emphasized the special relation that Jesus Christ has to God, without diminishing Christ's humanity. At the same time it carefully avoided the formulation of the Holy Spirit as a 'person.'

The critical term used to clarify the relation between the Father and the Son was the Greek word *homo-ousios*, which we can translate as "being of one essence." *Homo-ousios* has, as its root word, *ousia* (οὐσία). The Greek word *ousia* refers to the being of any created object or entity. Because every object within Creation is an expression of the *Logos* it has transcendental BEING immanent within it, and it is this being to which *ousia* ultimately refers. *Ousia* is best thought of as the being of a thing, sustained through time, independently of all that is external to it. This usage of *ousia* – the depths of which we cannot plumb here – is entirely consistent with Aristotle's usage in the *Poetics*. The term has often been translated into English as 'substance,' but this is a poor fit, because the English word 'substance' is intuitively grounded in what we call 'solid matter.' The simplest literal translation of *homo-ousios* is "same being," and the most appropriate English word that has been used to translate the Nicene text is 'essence.' Being "one with the Father in essence" does not imply "being the same as God." One can have something within onself that is continuous with God without being God himself.

We can understand how this is so by remembering the context for the relation between Father and Son – what Origen called the *Logos*. The *Logos* is Creation viewed as a hierarchy of interpenetrating Worlds which are defined by their different vibrational frequencies. One level can penetrate and infuse the level immediately below it, and thus something in the lower level can be continuous with something in the higher level. In other words, something in the BEING of the Father can be continuous with something in the BEING of the Son, without claiming identity between the two.

The presentation of the Council of Constantinople of 381 is compatible with the idea presented in Chapter 3 of the highest level of man. In a Prophet – who George Gurdjieff designated as a Man Number Eight – there is a connection to World 3 in a microcosm that supports Worlds 6 and 12. When the two Higher Centers are developed, and the link between them has developed to a point that enables a certain access to World 3, then a connection to the Absolute is possible. This is quite a special situation because World 3 is not – like Worlds 6 and 12 – latent in us. It can be known only by the grace of God. Because it exists entirely outside of our own space and time, we can say that it pre-exists Time. So, in this way, we can say that the Prophet pre-exists both Time itself and Creation-in-Time. We need not assert, as many Early Christians felt impelled to do, that the man Jesus Christ was somehow outside of time from before the moment of his physical birth. We need only understand that *the apex of his developed being was outside of time* – for 'the beginning,' 'the middle,' and 'the end' have an entirely different relation to one another with respect to World 3. With reference to World 3, it is the apex point that defines both the beginning and the end. And from here the Absolute may connect with Man.

We can also think of this problem in terms of the concepts introduced in Chapter 2. The Prophet was an implicit element of the Absolute's decision to effect Creation (as a means of generating consciousness not derivative of his own consciousness). He is thus pre-created in the purpose (the will) that informs his existence, although he must, like all men (and through his own will), enable the fused Higher Centers that will support a connection to World 3. The connection to World 3 is, then, 'given.' It transcends and pre-exists the Prophet's planetary life. This same connection is possible for all men, but, at the same time, it represents something that no man can do. The Prophet's connection to World 3 is a grace given even in the Absolute's act of Creation, reflecting his love for

Man. The Prophet Jesus Christ, in his turn, reflected this love, and affirmed it with his great sacrifice.

Thus all Prophets, in all the different times and places, can be seen as a system of multiple World 3 links to the Absolute in the hierachical structure of the macrocosm. These links are an essential part of its transformative machinery, and they were taken into consideration in the Absolute's original plan for a negentropic (or syntropic) whole: a whole that is continuously regenerated out of its own negative entropy.

The Absolute holds within himself both **1)** the inconceivable vastness of Creation and **2)** a latent self-transcendence to a dimension that is utterly beyond our capacity to imagine or anticipate. No Archangel, no Prophet, no God-Man can know the Absolute as he is in himself. Yet the Prophet can know (as Origen first demonstrated) the place from which Creation proceeds, in the moment when it turns from a latent potential (a kind of blueprint) into the actual opening forth of the *Logos*. The Prophet may see Creation – as the Absolute sees it – from the inside out. He can thus know the purpose behind Creation in a way that no other man can.

COUNCIL OF EPHESUS: 432

While the 'solution' of 381 was intelligible and simply put, it was – in its inner spiritual meaning – beyond the understanding of the great majority of the clergy. It had been formulated by four Men of the Tradition – who could see directly from their own Higher Centers into the invisible order of things. The clergy – taken as a whole – were not prepared to receive this vision in its depth and could not understand all of its implications. And so, in the next fifty years, theological controversy raged on.

At the Council of Ephesus, in 432, the Patriarch of Constantinople, Nestorius, argued against the most recent formulation of the Nicene Creed. He emphasized that no union between the human and the divine was possible; Christ could not be co-substantial with God and co-substantial with Man at the same time. Christ was thus of two natures, part Man and part God. This belief is known as Diophysitism. While Nestorius emphasized that a part of Christ was one with God, there was, in his presentation, no necessary relation between the divine part and the human part. Thus Nestorius' statement of the Trinity failed to convey the true impact of Christ's presence on Earth. The subtle implication of *homo-ousios* was lost, or – better put – left undeveloped. Nestorius' arguments, which did raise many legitimate questions, were not given the response they deserved. In other words no one was able to clarify what was implicit in the well-formulated Nicene Creed of 381; Nestorius was simply labeled a heretic and his teaching defined as a heresy. Thus the followers of Nestorius proceeded to establish **the Nestorian Church**, independent of the leadership of Rome. The Church of the East, then perhaps the largest church in Christendom, adopted this view.

SECOND COUNCIL OF EPHESUS: 449

At the second council of Ephesus in 449, Dioscorus of Alexandria produced a response to Nestorius' arguments, the substance of which became known as **Monophysitism**. It allowed that Christ is 'from two natures' but held that after his incarnation there was 'only one incarnate nature': one single will. Christ's human nature was thus absorbed into his divinity, to such an extent that the Prophet would be immune to human suffering. This absorption of the lower into the higher erased the drama of the Via Dolorosa and the great sacrifice that Christ made for Mankind, just as though it had never been. To take away this sacrifice is to take away an important link that exists between humanity and the cosmos above the Cosmos of Man. This is from the point of view of the higher level 'looking down.' From the point of view of the lower level 'looking up,' there is another issue. The critical significance of the Prophet is that he is a man who has raised himself to a point where the Gods can make demands upon him. This is precisely what men – in their natural state – cannot do, and this is what makes the Prophet so rare and so precious to us. Thus where Diophysitism weakened the link between the Prophet and God, Monophysitism obscured the relationship between the Prophet and Mankind.

COUNCIL OF CHALCYDON: 451

The debate on the nature of Christ intensified, and at the Council of Chalcydon it was declared that Monophysitism (like Nestorianism) was a heresy. This alienated the Egyptian and Syrian Churches where the Monophysite tendency was prominent.

The Council of Chalcydon stated that Christ represented both perfect divinity and perfect humanity. Christ was to be considered "in two natures but not of two natures." He was made known to Mankind in two natures; these natures were without mixture but – at the same time – without separation. The difference between the two natures is not removed by their union, but the property of each nature is preserved in it. Thus the two natures coalesce in a single being. Jesus Christ is both perfect God and perfect Man.

The 'solution' of Chalcydon is weak theologically, for it conceives the identity of the two natures as the identity of two things that exist on the same level. It is a logical play on words. In fact the Father and the Son represent different levels, the lower contained within the higher. The lower level can reflect the existence of the higher level, but it cannot BE that level itself. When these two levels are conflated the original Greek understanding of *ousia* (essence) grounded in *onta* (BEING) is lost.

We recall, then, the understanding of the different levels of man that is known to the Spiritual Traditions. The fused Higher Centers of a fully conscious being – even in the light of World 3 – do not give you a 'perfect man.' They give you a man who has all the human weaknesses but who always works in the light of something higher and so behaves differently from other men. This gives you the human side of Jesus Christ, and it gives you his terrible suffering, which would have been heightened by the sensitivity of his nature.

While the solution of the Council of Chalcydon did reflect a sincere wish to preserve unity within the Church, it was not based on insight. It reflected only the need for doctrinal consistency.

The Syrian, Coptic, Ethiopian, and Armenian Churches could not accept this position, and so could not accept the leadership of Rome. They broke off and became the Monophysitic churches. While the Churches of Constantinople and Antioch accepted the statement of the Council of Chalcydon, their tendency was to acknowledge a transcendent deity, and for this reason they were closer to the Monophysite position. But both the Monophysite position and the official position of the Council of Chalcydon were theologically weaker than the version of the Nicene Creed presented at Constantinople in 381.

Thus, truths which can be easily grasped with reference to the different levels of man were not given adequate expression by the theologians of Chalcydon. This was not because they did not have the proper terminology, but because there were no theologians amongst them at the level of the Spiritual Traditions who had the support of both the Eastern and Western Churches. The theology of the fifth century was not that of the fourth. Yet, while there was a growing distance between Tradition and Religion, we emphasize that the Spiritual Traditions were still alive within the different Churches.

These theological disagreements were directly related to regional and linguistic differences that were developing as a result of the gradual dismemberment of the Roman Empire. Nevertheless these disagreements were not, in the fourth century, beyond the possibility of reconciliation. The concerns behind both Monophysitism and the Creed of Chalcydon were real, and parties on both sides still sought reconciliation.

But the schism went much deeper with the *Filioque* controversy, which occurred in 1053, six full centuries after the Council of Chalcydon. What exacerbated the slowly descending situation was that the single world of the *Pax Romana* no longer existed; there was a Greek-speaking Byzantine Civilization in the East and an emergent Medieval-Latin Civilization in the West. In this context the schism, which had gone unresolved for so long, became a full-fledged schism between the Catholic Church in the West and the Orthodox Church in the East.

The roots of the socio-political division between East and West go back to the death of Theodosius the Great, the last Emperor to rule a united empire. He died in the year 395, and after this time the Empire was divided into its Eastern and Western halves; Latin was spoken principally in the West and Greek in the East. There later developed a convention to call the Eastern Empire *Byzantium*, or **the Byzantine Empire**, using the original Greek name for that region – in order to distinguish it from the Empire which included the city of Rome. We shall follow this convention here. It is necessary for us to understand something of the Byzantine Empire, for it is relevant not only to the divisions of the Church but also to the history of the Eastern Monastic Tradition, which we shall explore in Chapter 39. More generally, it is an important chapter in the Story of Man.

THE BYZANTINE EMPIRE

Byzantium did not survive the Western Roman Empire by a thousand years simply because it was successful in perpetuating an established classical governmental form in a Christian context. At a certain point, what we call Byzantium ceased to be the Eastern Roman Empire and became a Civilization of its own, with an important role to play in history. Charles Diehl makes this point well:

> Not by some freak of fortune [HJ: did Byzantium survive Rome], but gloriously, governed and administered by great emperors, brilliant statesmen and diplomats, and fine generals under whose guidance the Empire accomplished tremendous things. Before the Crusades, Byzantium was the champion of Christendom against the infidel, and perhaps surpassed the Crusaders in tenacity of purpose; surrounded by barbarian neighbors, it developed a superb civilization, fine and more highly cultivated than any the Middle Ages knew for a long time. Byzantium was the tutor of the Slavic and the Asiatic East, and its influence spread into the West, which learned more from the school of Constantinople than can well be estimated. [7]

---

7. Charles Diehl, *Byzantium: Greatness and Decline*, Rutgers University Press, 1957, p. 13.

Down to the end of the eleventh century, the Byzantine Empire was the center of civilization in Christendom. It had a highly developed system of law and a remarkable administrative machinery that allowed it to maintain order over the vast tracts of land that comprised it. The very fact of its survival in the midst of a world of pillage and violence is a testament to its greatness. It created a center of peace and prosperity affecting all of Eastern Europe and the Levant, and this allowed both civilization and Christianity to penetrate the Slavic World. The Byzantine Empire passed on its own cultural forms to the Russians, the Serbs, the Bulgars, and the Croats. Through trade, intermarriage, and the spread of the Christian Religion, it made nations of them, teaching their princes to govern, and transmitting written language and literature. In all of this the monks were active, and in all of this we see the traces of the Great Work.

Now we can return to the developing political division and the eventual schismatic split of East and West. After the initial division of the Roman Empire, with the death of Emperor Theodosius in 395, the respective cultures of East and West changed more rapidly.

The Byzantine Civilization consolidated itself in relation to threats from both the Slavs and the Persians. The Roman Church also consolidated itself, but its civilizational base was eroding.

When, after the initial division of the Empire, the differentiation of Greek-speaking and Latin-speaking Christians occurred, most educated people in the Eastern and the Western Empires were bilingual, at least until the fifth century AD. But when, in 476, the Germanic chieftain Odoacer deposed Romulus Augustulus, the last Emperor of the Western Roman Empire, linguistic differences became more pronounced and so did problems of communication. In the Western Empire there was a complete loss of the Greek language and even a weakening of Latin usage. Additionally, while Rome remained the principal bishopric of the Christian Church, the city of Rome was no longer the greatest city of the civilized world. In this context the Eastern and Western churches began to split along doctrinal, theological, linguistic, political, and geographical lines.

The Byzantine Emperor **Justinian**, who ruled from 527 to 565, changed the course of events by reconquering the Western Empire. He was in many ways similar to Constantine, and just as devout a Christian. He neglected no opportunity to secure the rights of the clergy and to extend monasticism, and became known as the 'nursing father' of the Church. Indeed, he was known as 'the emperor who never sleeps' – although as a person he is said to have been open and easily approachable. He sincerely attempted to reconcile Monophysitism with the version of the Nicene Creed presented at Chalcydon in 451.

In 536 Justinian's armies seized Rome from the Ostrogoths, and by 540 Justinian had become the first Emperor of the Eastern and Western Empires since the death of Theodosius in 395. While, as the Western Emperor, Justinian was not above pressuring the Pope, he did work consistently for Church unity and decried 'merely theological' disputes. He built the Hagia Sophia in Constantinople, which was unquestionably the most magnificent church in the world until the coming of the Gothic Cathedrals six centuries later. He provided support for the Eastern Churches and constructed Saint Catherine's monastery in the Sinai, the first of its kind. Justinian himself was close to Monophysitism in his beliefs, and so was quite sympathetic to the Nestorian, Syrian, Coptic, Ethiopian, and Armenian Churches (the Oriental Churches) which had split at the Councils of Ephesus and Chalcydon. He worked diligently, and with some success, to create an accord with the Oriental Churches.

However, the Byzantine control of the West lasted only a generation, with the Lombards conquering most of Italy in 568. From this time Western Europe descended into a more barbaric state, which made the Greek-speaking East – with its direct connection to classical civilization and culture – all the less willing to accept Western leadership.

Greece itself remained under Byzantine control, and strong Orthodox monastic communities began to develop – particularly at Mount Athos, on the northern peninsula of Chalcidyce, and later at Meteora in Thessaly.

After 600 the great bishoprics of Antioch and Alexandria came under Islamic rule, and this tended to polarize the bishopric of Rome in the West and the bishopric of Constantinople in the East. We note that at this time the Nestorian, Syrian, Coptic, Ethiopian, and Armenian Churches also came under Islamic rule, yet all continued as Christian Churches.

The differences between the Roman Church and the Eastern Churches continued to develop over the centuries until, in 1053, a theological dispute turned into an issue of heresy. The Roman Church changed the Nicene Creed (which had originated in the ecumenic agreement at the Council of Nicea in 325 and stood relatively stable since the Council of Chalcydon in 451) by inserting a short passage known as the *Filioque*. This insertion strengthened the person of Christ in the Holy Trinity in a way that would provoke resistance in any Eastern Church. The impulse to do so came originally from Charlemagne, who wanted to claim for himself the title of Holy Roman Emperor. The idea was that the inserted passage would antagonize the East, bring the Pope closer to

Figure 61. Hagia Sophia

the West, and so ensure that the title Holy Roman Emperor was not contested by the Byzantine Emperor. Members of Charlemagne's court pressed the insertion on Pope Leo III, who refused to alter the Nicene Creed in this way. Yet the use of the *Filioque* persisted in the West, and was eventually accepted by the papacy, without an Ecumenic Council of the Church having been called to affirm it.

THE FILIOQUE

Originally the Nicene Creed ran: "I believe … in the Holy Spirit, the Lord, the Giver of Life, who proceeds from the Father, and with the Father and the Son together is worshipped and together glorified." But the papacy inserted "and from the son" (in Latin *filioque*) so the Creed came to read, "I believe … in the Holy Spirit … who proceeds from the Father and the Son." The idea that the Holy Spirit might proceed from the Father and the Son would have been unacceptable to all participants in the Council of Constantinople in 381, at the time the Nicene Creed was formulated.

COMMENTARY ON THE FILIOQUE

The Prophet represents a precious and irreplaceable link to World 3, and so to the Absolute. It is absurd to think that Creation proceeds from him. We must remember that the Absolute, as the True Infinite, is the only real and complete individual in the universe. He contains within himself both the Not-Being of the Universe and a latent self-transcendence – to a dimension that no Archangel or Prophet could imagine. The original will to Creation came from this unimaginable and inscrutable source. While the Prophet may perceive the essence of Creation, as that emerges from its original ground of BEING, he is completely unable to know the source from which this essence arose, far less to will that essence himself.

At a certain point Rome noted that the Byzantines had omitted the *Filioque* in their practice and determined to assert its authority. In the summer of 1053 three legates of Pope Leo IX entered the church of the Hagia Sophia (Figure 61) and placed a Papal Bull on the door excommunicating the Patriarch of Constantinople. They left for Rome two days later, leaving the City of Constantinople in a state of riot. The bull was burnt and the schism between the Orthodox and Catholic Churches had officially begun.

Still, on both sides, there was a deep memory of all that had gone before, and the two churches vacillated between schism and reconciliation through the eleventh and twelfth centuries. The definitive rupture came with the Fourth Crusade, which was launched in 1204. The Crusade was initiated to 1) reverse the expansion of Islam, 2) repossess the Holy Land, and 3) unite the Catholic and Orthodox Churches. None of these aims were realized, and the outcome was something that no one expected or even imagined.

The initial aim had been for the combined forces of Western Europe and Byzantium to invade Egypt and then the Holy Land. But when the Latin armies entered Byzantium, they saw a level of civilization they had never known before; here was more wealth than existed in all of Europe put together and an urban culture descended directly from the great cities of the classical world. The project of the Fourth Crusade had been set in motion with insufficient resources to meet its costs, and immediately, as the Crusaders became aware of the riches of Constantinople, the Venetian Doge persuaded them to take the city itself. At this point the project fell into the hands of adventurers, and the original intent was quite forgotten.

Constantinople fell after three days of siege. Once the walls had been breached there began an orgy of violence and looting not known since the Visigoth sack of Rome. Bishops, priests, and nuns were slain indiscriminately, and women were violated in the streets. The Hagia Sophia was looted, and fires were started throughout the city. In the weeks and months that followed, the looting and destruction were systematized, and there began a steady export of Byzantine artifacts to Western European cities. And so it was that the greatest works of art of the ancient Byzantine Civilization were either destroyed or shipped abroad.

Pope Innocent III was distressed when he heard of these outrages and excommunicated some of the perpetrators. But as he saw the possibility of the church being reunited under the papacy, he went along with the reality of what had been done.

Having taken Constantinople, the Crusaders proceeded to occupy northeastern Asia Minor, pushing the Byzantines into the south. A Latin kingdom was established in the north, and Baldwin of Flanders was placed on its throne. Within the new kingdom the Orthodox Patriarch was replaced by a Venetian Bishop, and all the Orthodox bishops were deposed and replaced by Roman prelates. Pressure was put on the Orthodox priests to submit to the papacy, but this they firmly resisted. Innocent's support of the Latin Kingdom thus became a direct attempt by the Western Church to absorb the Orthodox Church by violent force, and while it was not successful, it sanctioned sixty years of the open pillage of Orthodox relics and art. The schism of the two churches was final. How could it not be?

We are describing here the work of Dead Religion, and it stands as good evidence that people will do the worst things when they are most sure that God is behind them. In the Western Church there was still both Living Religion and Living Tradition, but the link between Church and State was so strong that much of what went under the name of Religion was driven by purely temporal concerns. It was also true that a strong link between Church and State existed in Byzantium and had, to a degree, weakened Byzantine Orthodox Christianity as a Living Religion. Indeed, it may be that the temporary break of the official relation between Church and State that was caused by the Fourth Crusade, allowed for a reemergence of the Orthodox Religion.

In 1261 the Byzantine Emperor Michael VIII Palaiologos drove the Latins out of northern Asia Minor and recaptured the city of Constantinople. And so the Byzantine Empire was given its Indian summer, but the Byzantines were now less able to resist Islam. The Crusaders had demonstrated that the unbreachable Theodosian walls – which for 800 years had held against the Avars, the Arabs, the Rus, the Bulgars, and the Huns – could indeed be breached. In 1453 the city finally fell to the armies of Mehmed II, and the Byzantine Empire fell with it. By 1460 the Turks had conquered adjoining Greece and their occupation of Byzantium was complete. Both Orthodox Christianity and Orthodox monasticism were tolerated by the Muslims, as representing 'people of the book.' Indeed the Greek monastic communities at Meteora and Mount Athos fared better under Islamic rule than they had under Latin rule. At the same time the center of gravity of the Orthodox Church shifted to Russia, and Moscow succeeded Constantinople as 'The Third Rome.'

Under Islamic rule the Eastern Churches in Asia Minor and the Levant continued to develop, but as the churches of a conquered people. Their temporal power was sharply limited, and perhaps for this reason corruption was less pronounced than it was in Rome.

In the Western Church the papacy became increasingly subject to control by the noble families of Europe, and it was the monastic orders which served as a natural corrective to this. We may remark that the fact that there was corruption in the Church does not mean that the majority of its administrative officials were also corrupt. Nevertheless it was the monastic orders that maintained the integrity of Christianity in the West from the eighth through the fourteenth centuries – and they were able to do this because of the stream of conscious life that continued to flow through them.

Thus it was that the work of the Christian Spiritual Traditions now continued on either side of the Great Schism. Looking back, from the break finalized by the Fourth Crusade, we can see the different lines of influence which formed the different Churches.

The Catholic Church began directly from the work of Peter in Rome and from the tremendous support the Church received from the Romans. Where the Kingdoms of Israel and Judah did not, on balance, embrace Christianity, the Romans did, and the city of Rome became, in the first century, the core area of the Christian Religion. With the fall of the Western Empire and the coming of the Dark Ages, the Western Monastic Traditions showed tremendous vitality, first the Benedictines, then the Cistercians, Carmelites, Carthusians, Dominicans, Cluniacs, Templars, and finally the Freemasons or Cathedral Builders. Monasticism literally carried Western Christianity from 700 through to 1000, and we must acknowledge its extraordinary achievement in preserving civilization in Western Europe. In the period following the European Renaissance the Western Church then suffered the schismatic split of Catholic and Protestant.

The Orthodox Church: What is now called the Orthodox Church was initiated by the work of the Apostles Paul, John, and Andrew. As we noted the Eastern Churches were profoundly influenced by the monastic work of the Desert Fathers in Egypt, culminating in the monastic rule of Saint Basil. The Bishopric of Constantinople was integrally connected to the great monastic centers that developed in Syria, in Cappadocia, and later at Mount Athos. These were to distinguish Eastern Christianity for nearly two millennia. After the schism of 1053 the Orthodox Church became formally separate from the Roman Catholic, and Constantinople became its center. As we noted, following the Islamic conquest the center of the Orthodox Church shifted from Constantinople to Moscow. In the Eastern Church the divisions of clerical and lay, monastic and pastoral, were less distinct than they were in the West.

The Eastern Apostolic Churches, Nestorian, Coptic, Syrian, Ethiopian, and Armenian, were all founded by Apostles. While they lacked the universality of Catholic and Orthodox Churches, it is certain that Living Monastic Traditions were connected with each one of them. After 600 they came under Islamic rule, but they continued, with tremendous life and vitality, for one century after the next.

Having related the Christian Spiritual Traditions to the work of the Prophet and his Apostles, and having distinguished the Work of the Church from the Work of the Traditions, we shall postpone our further discussion of Christianity to Book VI.

We turn now to the last of the great Prophets. The place shifts from the Mediterranean Basin to the Arabian peninsula, and the time to just after the death of the Emperor Justinian. It is interesting that the last Prophet came when Chrisitanity was only 600 years old and had many of its greatest works yet to do. The Gods had intended a certain tension for the people of the Traditions.

CHAPTER 32
Muhammad

The Life of Muhammad

Muhammad was a Prophet who came to the Arab peoples at the beginning of the seventh century AD. The Arab tribes were of a single ethnic origin and spoke the same language, but they were not united politically, and were only vaguely united with respect to religious belief. There was no generally established system of law, only accepted custom and an unwritten code of honor. They were often at war with one another. At the time of Muhammad's birth the Arab tribes inhabited what is now the Arabian Peninsula, eastern Syria, and western Iraq, up to the shores of the Euphrates River. In the northern parts of their domain they cohabited with the Syrian Christians and with the Jewish tribes who had settled in the diaspora following the Babylonian captivity. Both the Christians and the Jews were devout, and both – at that time – lived in the expectation of a messiah. We could say that the anticipation of a Prophet was part of the atmosphere of that place and time.

The Arab peoples carried the remnants of an Original Religion, either as a collection of beliefs borrowed from neighboring civilizations or as the remains of an original transmission that occurred in ancient times. This Original Religion was overlaid by a very patchy record of the teachings of the Prophet Abraham. The result was a hybrid religion which the Arab peoples practiced simply because 'it had always been there.'

To provide a more complete context for Muhammad's teaching we must go back some thousands of years. By the late third millennium BC the Original Religion of the Arabs – whatever its source – had descended into an eclectic polytheism. Sometime in the nineteenth century BC the Prophet Abraham and his son Ishmael came to the Arabian Peninsula to present a monotheistic Prophetic Religion to the Arab peoples.

Abraham and Ishmael erected a temple to the One God in Mecca, which became a center of pilgrimage for the new monotheistic faith. This temple was called the Kaaba, and it still stood when Muhammad was born. Indeed, it still stands today. However, over the centuries, the more ancient polytheistic beliefs gradually usurped the Abrahamic teaching, until only traces of the Prophetic Religion remained. The Arab religion of the sixth century AD was thoroughly heterogeneous, to the point where different tribes worshipped different gods. Nevertheless, all of these gods were represented, in one way or another, at Mecca, in the vicinity of the Kaaba. The Kaaba itself was still seen as sacred, and still remained a center for annual pilgrimage for all the Arab tribes.

Muhammad was born in 570 AD and lived into his sixty-third year, completing his life in 632 AD. As a Prophet, he stated, just as Jesus stated, that he had been called by God to testify before men, and that he was guided in all his actions and decisions by a higher agency. Strangely, he came at a time when the preceding Prophetic World Religion – Christianity – was far from being a Dead Religion. Indeed, Christian Monasticism, both Eastern and Western, was in its most dynamic phase of development. The tensions that were inevitably to develop between Christianity and the new Islamic Religion stimulated the Spiritual Traditions internal to each Religion to ever-deeper life. While there was often strife between the two great Religions, there was – at every point – communication between initiates. Indeed Muhammad was first recognized as a Prophet – when he was still a boy – by an orthodox Syrian monk. Later, when Muhammad's armies conquered the Sinai Peninsula and the great monastery known as Saint Catherine's came under his jurisdiction, he bade his people treat the monks with respect and deference. He viewed their monastic rule as legitimate and the spirit of their practice as worthy of emulation.

Muhammad was born in the city of Mecca, which is in the western part of the Arabian Peninsula, near the Red Sea. His parents died while he was still in his infancy and he was raised by his uncle, Abu Talib, who was a merchant. Muhammad worked with his uncle in the family business, married, and raised a family. We noted that Mecca was the center of the eclectic traditional Arab religion, and Muhammad's tribe, the Quraish, provided the priest caste for the polytheistic religion.

While the Meccans were to a degree lawless, and many lived by piracy, they had a firm sense of honor, and, lacking a revealed code of law, tried to establish standards for themselves. As a young man Muhammad revived a traditional organization which had been created to arbitrate disputes and repress lawless behavior. He became universally respected as an arbiter. When he was in his thirties, he divided his time between working for his uncle and helping to arbitrate disputes. In this period he would periodically retire to a cave in Mount Hira to meditate.

When he was in his fortieth year, during one of the retreats to Mount Hira, the Archangel Gabriel appeared to him and made certain requirements of him. The contact with Gabriel had many aspects, and it is impossible for us to describe all of them here, but what came from it, and what Muhammad communicated to his fellow Arabs, was that **1)** there is only one God, **2)** Muhammad is the chosen Messenger of God, **3)** there is a coming day of Judgment for humanity, and **4)** every man who lives according to God's will will enter Paradise. Muhammad understood himself to be a messenger from God to the Arab peoples, who had not had a Prophet since the time of Abraham. The Arabic word for God is Allah (*al ilah*), literally "the deity," and this term became the reference point for the fourth great Prophetic Religion.

When Muhammad stated, "There is no god but God," he was affirming a fundamental Unity of Being which annihilates the apparent multiplicity of creation. In his view nothing exists outside of God. God comprehends the Many in the One, and to the extent a Man becomes godlike – raising himself to mirror-like transparency – he is able to see the One in the Many; he is able to perceive this fundamental Unity of Being directly, both within himself and within Creation. In affirming himself as 'the Prophet of God' Muhammad is placing himself in a certain relation to the rest of Mankind. He is a part of the Created World, yet he can directly relate this World to the uncreated, pre-existent aspect of the elements that comprise it, to the 'ideas' of things as they were originally given in the Mind of God before Creation. The Prophet has fully realized the archetypal form of Man, as it was originally uttered from that level. He is thus an archetypal Being, a Man who has realized his 'all possibilities' and is capable of seeing the One in the Many. He sees the potential that exists in every man and woman, and he is seen by the Gods who are immediately above him. He is thus capable of relating Mankind to the Unity of Being which is its original ground. And this Muhammad did, throughout his teaching life, according to the indications and instructions given him by Higher School.

Muhammad stated that, from the moment of his first revelation, God communicated to him through the Archangel Gabriel. The record of these communications was kept from 610 AD until Muhammad's death in 632 AD, in the **hadith** (collected sayings of Muhammad) and in the single unified text of the **Koran**. These texts were and are respected as the revealed truth for all Muhammad's followers.

Muhammad began to preach in Mecca, asking the Meccans to abandon their idolatry, and to change their inner lives. He warned them of the fate that had overtaken past races, who had not heeded the preaching of former Prophets. A small number of followers gathered about him, one of the first being his father-in-law Abu Bakr. At the same time, the senior Meccan tribe, the Quraish – who were the proponents of the existing religion – began to persecute Muhammad and his followers. He did not waver in his mission and continued to preach in a gentle and unfanatic manner. The Quraish then organized a system of persecution, and many of the first Muslims were forced to emigrate to the Christian kingdom of Abyssinia (now Ethiopia), on the other side of the Red Sea. There they won many converts. Other followers of Muhammad emigrated to Syria. Through these emigrants, Muhammad's name soon became known in all parts of the Arabian penninsula. He himself emigrated to Taif, some sixty miles east of Mecca, but was soon forced by the people of that city to return to Mecca where he continued to preach. In the twelfth year of his mission (620 AD), at a time when his followers were subject to the most acute persecution by the Meccans, the Archangel Gabriel came to Muhammad and brought him a second revelation. Gabriel took him – in the spirit – on a 'Night Journey' from Mecca to Jerusalem, and there the two ascended through the seven heavens to God. At each level Muhammad met the earlier Prophets of other Traditions: Adam, Abraham, Moses, and Jesus. Beyond the seventh Heaven he passed through the veils covering that which is hidden, until he reached the veil of Unity and looked directly on the Face of God. This is a reference to World 3. After this vision, the pressures on Muhammad increased.

In 622 Muhammad had a prophetic dream concerning the city of Medina, which was 210 miles north of Mecca. On the basis of this dream the Prophet directed his followers to seek refuge at Medina while he remained in Mecca with Abu Bakr and his young son-in-law, Ali. At this time the Quraish decided to assassinate Muhammad. Muhammad and Abu Bakr became aware of this plot only when the house they lived in was already surrounded. They arranged that the young Ali pretend to be Muhammad by sleeping in his bed, and so they made their escape. When the assassins found only Ali in the house, they let him go, and he was able to join Muhammad and Abu Bakr in Medina.

Muhammad's teaching was well received in Medina; he was accepted as a prophet, and he gave the city a written constitution, or charter, which included freedom of

Figure 62. **Muhammad's Night Journey**

religion. For the Muslims this charter is taken as the beginning of the Muslim era. And indeed this moment is the beginning of the Muslim Civilization: the Prophet is united with his people just as Moses was united with the Israelites. He claimed that his teaching was the pure faith of Abraham, who, through Ishmael, was the ancestor of the Arab peoples. It was Abraham who had first preached pure monotheism, and Muhammad was renewing his monotheistic teaching. The teachings of Moses and of Jesus, which had since been distorted by the Jews and the Christians, would come alive again in Islam. The word 'Islam' means literally 'voluntary submission to God,' and the term Muslim is 'one who surrenders to God.'

In 624 the Meccans determined to conquer Muhammad's little city-state. Amazingly, the untrained and outnumbered Muslim army was able to defeat the Meccans at the

Battle of Badr. The Muslims treated the conquered Meccan army with a humanity quite contrary to Arab custom, and this brought them many converts. In the year following the Meccans came to Medina with a much larger army and were again defeated at the Battle of Uhad. In the third year, 626, the Meccans combined their forces with those of the Jewish tribes to the north and fielded an army of 10,000. The Muslins numbered only 3,000. A Persian Muslim by the name of Salman (who had previously been one of the Zoroastrian Magi) suggested building a trench about the city, and this they did. The Meccan army tried for thirty days and thirty nights to breach the trench, but were unable to do so. When the siege was lifted Muhammad signed the Treaty of Hudaybai with the Meccans and a truce was established.

Throughout this period the citizens of Medina were in the 'white heat' of existence: they put into practice Muhammad's many teachings and injunctions, they implemented a new code of law, they fought battles with the Meccans, and they managed the city under siege while facing acute shortages of food and water. The people of Medina were the emergent community of the new faith living in direct contact with the Prophet, who had received – and who was still receiving – direct instructions about how to live according to God's will. Throughout this formative period there were sharp internal divisions within the city, as Muhammad insisted on giving the Jewish population – who were exempt from his religious injunctions – full civic freedom. Under these challenging conditions he was able to create a community at a very high level. At all times he radiated complete self-confidence, complete certainty, and complete calm while gently asking the Meccans to do the impossible. He was, like Moses, the human vehicle through which a people were tested, molded, and formed. He raised his community to a level where the Pyramid of Man came into existence, lifting – level upon level – from Civilizational Order, to Living Religion, to Spiritual Tradition, to Higher School. He gave one of the greatest demonstrations in history of the measure of what is possible for Man.

Muhammad chose ten companions to whom he gave special responsibility. Abu Bakr was the leader and principal administrator, as Peter was to Jesus, and Muhammad's son-in-law Ali was the principal teacher, as Paul was in the decade after Jesus' death.

From the time of the Treaty of Hudaybai, Muhammad began to preach outside Medina. In 628 he sent emissaries to the rulers of Byzantium, Persia, Egypt, and the leaders of the Ghassanite Arab tribes in Syria inviting them to embrace Islam. These letters were the basis of an international vision of Islam, and they described or mapped out what would be the eventual field of influence of the Prophet. It was clear that the World of Islam went entirely beyond the scope of the Arab people. The king of Persia, Khusro Parvis, was enraged, while Heraclius, the Emperor of Byzantium, treated the Muslim ambassador with great respect and questioned him carefully about the new faith. The Ghassanite Arabs simply murdered the envoy.

In the meantime the Meccans repeatedly violated the terms of the treaty of Huday-bai. In 630 Muhammad sent them an ultimatum – to respect the treaty or to call it null and void. The Meccans chose to void the treaty and shortly after found 10,000 Muslims marching on their city. The Meccans offered no resistance. Their leader, Abu Sufyan, came out to negotiate a surrender with Muhammad and, on meeting the Prophet, immediately converted to Islam. Abu Sufyan then returned to prepare the city for the entry of Muhammad. Muhammad pardoned all of the elders of the city and preached a sermon on the brotherhood of Man. Most of Mecca then embraced Islam. The acceptance of Muhammad in Mecca brought the question of Arab Unity immediately to the fore. The Quraish of Mecca were the senior tribe of the Arab world and the reputed descendants of Ishmael. They had submitted to Muhammad and were satisfied that it was not within their power to oppose him. Historically this was a critical moment. Both the Christians and the Jews had received indications of a messiah coming in this time. Had such a Prophet come to the Arab people? The embassies from the different Arab tribes streamed into Medina to make submission to Muhammad, and there was, for the first time, a feeling of Arab unity. Then the Prophet dispatched disciples in every direction to preach Islam.

In his role as representative of the Arab people, Muhammad moved between the cities of Mecca and Medina. In this phase of his teaching Muhammad placed an emphasis on organizational and institutional problems. He created all the principles and laws needed to give form to an Islamic Civilization. In the first years in Medina, Muhammad had established a Spiritual Tradition, and the Religion that came from that Tradition was a Living Religion. Following the conquest of Mecca a Civilizational Order began to emerge from the Religion.

In 631 Muhammad – at the age of 63 and in perfect health – gave a farewell sermon to a crowd of 124,000 Muslims, stating, "I will not be with you for long." A few months later, in the year 632, he fell ill and died. He made his senior companion, Abu Bakr, the leader of Islam. Muhammad had stated before his death that he would be the "last of the Prophets."

MUHAMMAD'S LEGACY

Muhammad created an intense center of esoteric work in the community which formed around him during his lifetime. While he asked his inner circle to perform night vigils and to employ periodic fasting, he curbed the extremes of asceticism that developed when his followers began to take their sense of identity from these practices and not from presence itself.

The seeds of **1)** the Islamic Spiritual Tradition, **2)** the Muslim Religion, and **3)** Islamic Civilization were all sown during the ten years when Muhammad governed Medina. It was hoped that the caliphs (or successors) who would follow Muhammad, beginning with Abu Bakr, would continue to develop the standards achieved in that Community – which would then become the permanent core of an Islamic Civilization.

Throughout Muhammad's teaching life his words and actions were carefully recorded. The record of his sayings, his actions, and his declared principles of practice is called the *sunnah*. The principles of Islamic law that were derived from these – some of which were given directly by Muhammad – were called the *sharia*. Where the *sharia* were not explicitly given by Muhammad they are carefully derived from the *sunnah*. The *sharia* then became the legal framework for both public and private life within Islam, and they were the object of constant study and revision in order that they conform to the spirit of his teaching. The more detailed principles of Islamic jurisprudence were known as the *fiqh*. A class of Islamic scholars formed, called the *ulama*, who continuously studied the *sunnah* and *sharia* in relation to the practical problems of daily life. The *ulama* were an important working part of the Islamic Caliphate. Of course, for this system to preserve the spirit of Muhammad's teaching, the current of living presence initiated by Muhammad must be nurtured by the Spiritual Tradition, and the Tradition must be acknowledged by both the Living Religion and the Civilizational Order. In other words the Pyramid of Man must be complete.

Muhammad is like Jesus Christ and Gautama Buddha in that the span of his teaching life, and the life of his Companions, was one of extraordinary charismatic force. One cannot understand the early history of Islam without understanding this, and it is not something we can easily reconstruct today. Muhammad is unlike Jesus and the Buddha – and like Moses and Zoroaster – in that the Spiritual Tradition, the Religion, and the Civilization that derived from his teaching all took germinal form within his lifetime.

From Muhammad to the Sufi Orders of Islam

The original Islamic community, formed during Muhammad's years in Medina, did not survive the rapid transition of Islam to world religion and worldly empire. Within a single generation the civilizational order that had developed out of this community expanded into the Middle East and the Mediterranean Basin. But the inner teaching that Muhammad gave, and the people to whom he gave it, came to crisis, particularly after 650. The decades that followed were a dark hour for the Spiritual Tradition.

The first four caliphs were all drawn from the circle of Muhammad's companions; they were known as the Rashidun (or 'rightly guided') Caliphs. Each one of them would have been part of the same original community.

ABU BAKR (CALIPH 632-34)

When Abu Bakr assumed the Caliphate, the Arabs were already at war with both Syria and Persia. When Persia entered a state of civil war, Khalid bin Walid, Muhammad's greatest general, proceeded to conquer the entire country. The Byzantines then raised an army against Islam. Khalid routed the Byzantine army, and this victory set Islam on the road to worldwide expansion. At the same time the war with Syria was actively carried forward. During this period Abu Bakr was scrupulous in setting standards for the Caliphate. He did not select his relatives for high public office, but always selected those most fit for service. He distributed the spoils of war amongst the entire community, and he did not allow his generals and administrators to own land outside of their own native cities.

UMAR (CALIPH 634-644)

Umar was appointed by Abu Bakr. Under Umar the city of Damascus, the capital of Syria, was taken in 635. Egypt was conquered in 639-44, and Israel and Palestine in the same year. Khalid bin Walid then completed the conquest of Persia. But problems began to grow out of the enormous incoming wealth. The traditional Arab families became increasingly powerful, and they adopted their own rules for the distribution of spoils and the ownership of land. When Umar attempted to reform these practices, he was murdered in 644.

At this time the name of **Ali Ibn Abi Talib**, Muhammad's cousin and son-in-law, was put forward for the Caliphate. He was one of Muhammad's

Companions, a great general, and a part of the teaching line of Muhammad's community. He both practiced and taught the surrender of Self to God in action. Ali refused the Caliphate because it was offered to him on the condition that he retain the now-corrupted status quo with respect to the distribution of wealth and the ownership of land. Ali retained the ministerial and advisory role that he had under both Abu Bakr and Umar. Ali and his close associate **Salman the Persian** were part of the Spiritual Tradition that had been at the very core of Muhammad's Community.

UTHMAN (CALIPH 644-656)

Uthman Ibn Affan then became Caliph. He was a member of the Umayyad clan, the leading family of the Quraish. Uthman was elderly at the time he became Caliph, and the rising generation of generals and administrators were able to take advantage of him. In response to the pressures that they placed upon him, he put members of his own family in positions of responsibility, and he allowed his officers to settle in conquered territory and to own property. The leading families of the Quraish thus spread out into different cities and built up separate centers of power. Power rivalries soon began to develop between the great Arab families. At the same time revenue began to flood in on a scale previously undreamt of. At a certain point the remnants of Muhammad's Community rebelled, and uncontrollable rioting broke out in Medina. There was a call for Ali to replace Uthman. Ali sent the rioters away, showing solidarity with Uthman, but in return asked Uthman's promise that in the future he would be guided more by his own advice than that of his relatives. Uthman gave his promise, but it was of little avail as he was murdered by the rioters shortly after having made it. Ali's name was again put forward for the Caliphate. He refused it under these circumstances, but the chaos continued to grow. Soon the very civilization of Islam was in jeopardy.

ALI (CALIPH 656-661)

Finally Ali accepted the Caliphate. The Umayyads, who now based themselves in Syria, immediately placed pressure on Ali to bring the murderers of Uthman – who was an Umayyad – to account. In the meantime the riots continued, and the state of social upheaval was such that it was impossible for Ali to punish the murderers of Uthman. The punishment of the murderers of Uthman became, then, the battle cry of the Umayyads. The rioters, on the other hand, saw their only hope for survival was continuing the state of unrest, and soon it became impossible for the Caliph to govern from Medina. Ali shifted his capital to **Kufa**, a garrison town in Persia, which was much better situated to administer the growing Islamic empire. Ali's supporters, and many of Muhammad's original Companions, congregated there.

Ali then instituted a set of radical reforms to bring the Caliphate into alignment with the principles that had governed Muhammad's Community. He replaced all the provincial governors, established equity of salary, disallowed landownership outside of Mecca and Medina, and returned all Uthman's gifts to the treasury. As a result, civil war broke out. Ali was challenged by the Umayyad leader **Muawiyya**.

Civil war represents the opposite of everything that Muhammad had taught. The causes of it came from the failure to realize his teachings on many different levels by many different people. The war came to a climax in 657 with the Battle of Siffen. At a point when Ali's forces were clearly winning, Muawiyya submitted to arbitration. Ali, remembering always Muhammad's injunctions against civil war, accepted this. A segment of Ali's partisans were outraged and seceded, naming themselves the Kharijites. In 661 the Kharijites sent out assassins to murder both Muawiyya and Ali. They succeeded only in murdering Ali.

Before going further we shall provide a graphic representation (Figure 63 on page 534) of the expansion of Islam in the time of the Rashidun Caliphs. The emergent Islamic Empire entirely changed the context of the development of the Caliphate.

What was to happen following the murder of Ali? Ali had had two sons from Muhammad's daughter Fatima – Hasan and Hussain. Both of these men were the grandsons of Muhammad, and both had been raised in his household. Both were trained in the teaching line of Muhammad's original community.

Ali lived for a few days after having received his death wound. He appointed **Hasan**, who was then thirty-six, as the next Caliph. Muawiyya refused to accept Hasan as Caliph and met him with a large army near Kufa. As Hasan's forces confronted Muawiyya's army, Hasan saw clearly – to his chagrin – that a large part of the original Islamic Community would be killed in the conflict. When the two armies confronted one another Muawiyya again sued for peace. Negotiations opened and a deal was made that Muawiyya would rule, and Hasan would assume the Caliphate after his death. Hasan

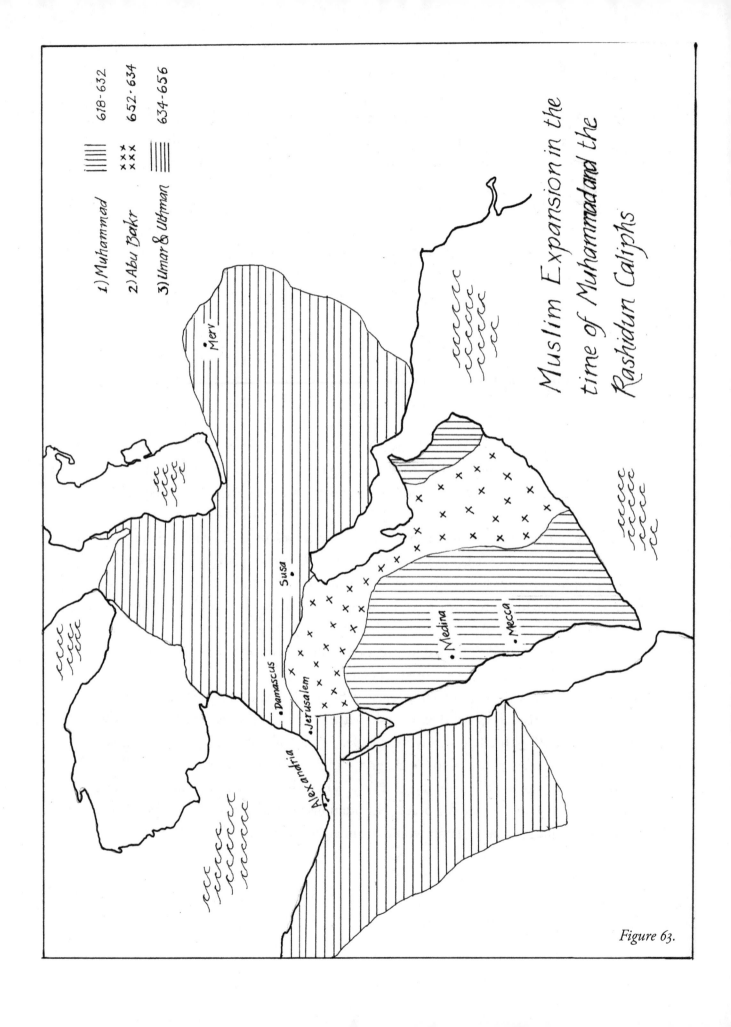

Muslim Expansion in the time of Muhammad and the Rashidun Caliphs

1) Muhammad   618-632
2) Abu Bakr   652-634
3) Umar & Uthman   634-656

Merv

Susa

Damascus
Jerusalem

Alexandria

Medina
Mecca

Figure 63.

then returned from Kufa to Medina, where he attempted to create a School embodying the principles of Muhammad's community.

Muawiyya shifted the capital of the Caliphate from Kufa to Damascus, an Umayyad stronghold where the traditional Arab values prevailed. The Umayyads made a distinction between Arab and non-Arab peoples and sharply repressed the Persians. They continued to extend the borders of Islam and accumulated staggering wealth.

When the Caliphate shifted from Kufa to Damascus, Medina became a center of faith – filled with the memories of a golden age – but with little real political power. At the same time the majority of Ali's followers remained in Kufa, including almost all of Muhammad's surviving Companions: Salman the Persian, Ibn Abu Waggas, Abu Musa, Abd Allah ibn Masud, Ammar ibn Yasir, and Juzayfa ibm Yaman. Kufa became a center of Islamic studies and all the practices that Muhammad had encouraged amongst his immediate circle – including prayer, fasting, and night vigils – were continued there. It became, to some extent, an ascetic reaction to the excesses of the Umayyad regime.

In the meantime Muawiyya's rule was fast turning into a reign of terror. The official *ulama* associated with his regime (the Islamic scholars, jurists, and theologians) began a fabrication of *hadiths* (recorded sayings of the Prophet) with the aim of removing any favorable mention of Ali or of the particular standards that Ali had attempted to enforce. In 680 Muawiyya broke his agreement with Hasan and arranged that the Caliphate pass to his own son Yazid, who was a thoroughly corrupt individual.

Hasan refused to re-enter politics to combat Yazid, fearing that he would create war amongst the Muslim peoples. His younger brother **Hussain**, however, determined to pursue reform and to preserve the original intentions behind the Islamic community. He remembered that his grandfather Muhammad had stated that a Muslim is obliged to strike out against a false regime, and that his own father Ali had done so at the cost of his life.

The nobles of Kufa immediately pledged their support to Hussain, who was at that time in Mecca. Hussain then set out for Kufa with his family and a party of seventy. An Umayyad army of more than a thousand intercepted Hussain in the desert just outside of Kufa and killed him and all of his family, which was the family line of the Prophet. This was the infamous battle of Kerbala (680 AD), which became the basis for the split between Shiite Muslims (supporters of Hussain) and Sunni Muslims (supporters of the Caliphate) which continues until this day.

Following the battle of Kerbala the remnants of Muhammad's original community – the heart of the Islamic Spiritual Tradition – found themselves gathered in the vicinity of Kufa, completely divorced from the official Caliphate. And *here followed the struggle of a Great Tradition for its very life*. The true terms of this struggle were clear to the combatants; victory was not the control of the Caliphate but the control of the Lower Self. A victory for the Tradition would mean a continuity of prolonged presence, radiating forward from the being of Muhammad to the future generations of Islam. But this greatest of struggles has been lost to history, and the major players of the ninety-year period between the death of Ali and the overthrow of the Umayyad regime are now unknown to us. Because the inner teaching of the Islamic Spiritual Tradition was forced underground, we are only able to reconstruct events from the scattered external reports that have survived.

We know, for example, that night vigils and ascetic practices were initiated in Kufa from the time of Ali's first residence. Later, in the difficult years of Umayyad rule, a succession of saintly ascetics appeared, and these were held in general respect. These ascetics were sometimes asked to serve as emissaries to foreign governments or to act as arbiters in local disputes. People of this class began to adopt a simple costume of white wool, probably in imitation of Christian monks. They were known by a variety of names, including *zuhhad* (ascetics), *mussak* (devout men), *qussas* (preachers), *qurra* (studious ones), *ruhhan* (monks or hermits), or *bakka-un* (penitents). These were the 'parents' of the Sufis.

Al-Qushayri, in his *Principles of Sufism*, stated – without any reference to the history of Ali's following in Kufa – that **the first Sufis** came from that city. According to Al-Qushayri (writing in the eleventh century AD) the term Sufi was first used with regards to an inhabitant of Kufa, Abu Hashim, who died at a ripe old age in the year 777. The term was then applied to a second Kufan, Jabir, a Shiite alchemist who was slightly younger than Abu Hashim. If these two men reached their teaching maturity by the year 750 – which seems likely – their presence within Islam as Sufis would correspond exactly with the coming of the Abbasid Caliphate, and with the general opening of society that occurred in the years following the Umayyad repression. The simple, generic name 'Sufi' comes – finally – from the white wool *hirka* or cloak that they wore. Before the overthrow of the Umayyads, any practitioners of the Great Work would probably have avoided a generic name or identity and would have concealed themselves as harmless renunciants or ascetics.

But the legacy of Muhammad's teaching was not limited to the activities of his followers in Kufa. The Civilization and the Religion also, in different ways, attempted to regenerate themselves, and there may even have been conscious beings involved in this work. It would nevertheless have been impossible for them – under the circumstances that existed – to return the Caliphate to the state of Muhammad's Original Community. Yet they did much to raise it from the abyss of Umayyad rule.

During the reign of Yazid, there developed a general dissatisfaction with the Umayyads. In 749 a descendent of the Prophet's uncle, Abbas, received wide backing – especially from the Persian peoples – to overthrow the Umayyad family. He executed a coup and established the Abbasid Caliphate. The new ruling family attempted to prove its legitimacy by proper adherence to religious law, the *sunnah* and the *sharia*. But the Umayyads had destroyed those *hadiths* (sayings of Muhammad) that directly contradicted their own practices, and these were never recovered. The Abbasids followed Muhammad in emphasizing that their empire was not meant to be Arabic, but Islamic.

Abbas transferred the capital from Damascus back to Kufa, and then recreated the Persian capital city of Ctesiphon – which had been leveled in the Arab conquest of that country – as **Baghdad**. The city of Baghdad became the new center for the new Caliphate, and this opened the door wide to Persian cultural influence. The Persians and the Arabs were the two principal peoples of Islam at this time, and the Persian culture was much more ancient and developed than the Arabic. The Abbasid alliance with the Persians represented the beginning of a shift in Islam from Semitic to Persian culture.

The Abbasid Caliphate returned to a close study of the Koran, the *hadith*, the *sunnah*, and the *sharia*. In their attempt to coordinate a fast-growing global empire, they drew generously on the understanding of the older civilizations of the Hellenistic World, particularly Greece (for philosophy, mathematics, and geometry) and Rome (for law, engineering, administration, and architecture). In this context the Abbasid *ulama* – the community of lawyers, scholars, and theologians whose duty it was to clarify the basic principles of Islamic life in a changing world – developed to an entirely new level.

One result of this was that the Abbasid Caliphate saw the flowering of Muslim science. A central theme of Muhammad's teaching was the categorical unity of God with everything in the world. With this reference point he counseled his community to seek knowledge, for knowledge of the world was, ultimately, the knowledge of the unity of God. The Umayyads – more intent on conquest than on science or theology – did not make this task a high priority, but the more devout Abbasids found themselves in a position to acquire the most remarkable knowledge. The Abbasid family had originated in the Persian East, where the general culture had long been penetrated by Greek philosophy. The Abbasids arranged that the Greek philosophical and scientific works that had been preserved by Eastern Christians in Mesopotamia, Syria, and Egypt, be translated

Figure 64. **Al Aqsa Mosque, Jerusalem**

into Arabic. The translators were principally Nestorian and Syrian Christians, who were possessed of real philosophical acumen and who had themselves struggled to keep Aristotelian theology and science alive. The translations were good. In the Abbasid period Muslim scholars were thus able to acquire the full classical legacy of Neoplatonist and Aristotelian philosophy, which was to deeply penetrate Islamic theology. They were also able to assimilate almost all of classical science, including mathematics, geometry, astronomy, medicine, and proto-chemistry (or alchemy). Beyond this they found and studied the alchemical and Hermetic material of the ancient world: Sumerian/ Chaldean, Egyptian, and Greek. The alchemical studies, combined with the study of mathematics and geometry, triggered Islamic science, which reached its fullest flowering during the Abbasid Caliphate. We may add that the end of the Abbasid Caliphate, which came with the Mongol invasions of the thirteenth century, was also the end of the active development of Islamic science.

By far the most important development of the Abbasid period, however, was the resurfacing of the teaching line of Muhammad's Original Community in the Sufi teaching lineages, which then became the 'hidden heart of Islam.'

Figure 65 shows the maximum extent reached by the Muslim Caliphate, though not all of these territories were under the control of the Caliphate at any one time.

THE STORY OF MAN

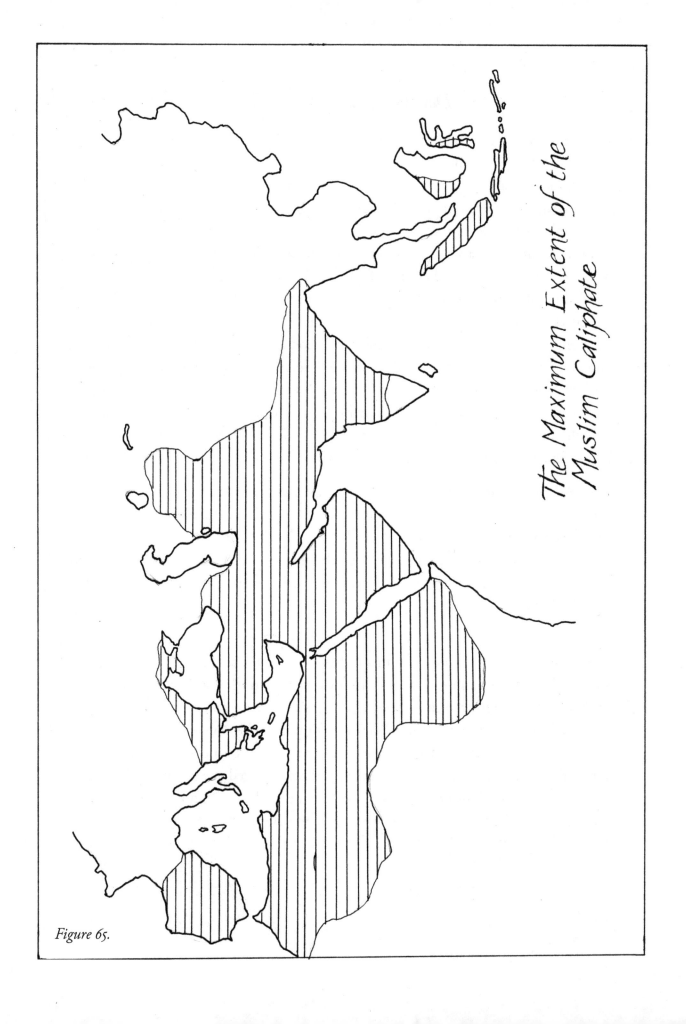

The Maximum Extent of the Muslim Caliphate

Figure 65.

The Development of the Sufi Orders

In the early centuries of Abbasid rule (800-1000 AD) a dynamic relationship developed between the Caliphate and the Sufi Orders. The challenge for the Abbasids was to realize the unique relation of Spiritual Tradition, Living Religion, and Civilizational Order that had existed for a few intense decades in the Original Islamic Community in Mecca. The simple faith and humility, the compassion and benevolent egalitarianism of early seventh-century Mecca would have been extremely difficult to achieve in the context of the now-massive imperial edifice of Islam, reinforced by its official *ulama*. And the Abbasid family understood the challenge only in part, perhaps because there were no conscious beings in their number. They had a sense of the Tradition, but not the inner experience of what that was. In the Abbasid period the absence of Muhammad and his Companions was balanced, as much as it could be balanced, by the teaching lineages of the early Sufis. We must be clear, then, who these Sufis were and where they came from.

Sufism is many different things. What it began from, in the century after the death of Muhammad, was very different from what it ended as, in the last years of the Ottoman Caliphate. Speaking generally, we could say that there were five stages of Sufism.

The origin of Sufism was in the Great Work practiced by Muhammad's Community in Medina. After Muhammad's death and the evacuation of Medina by his Companions, this work was recreated by groups and individuals working in the city of Kufa. We emphasize that there was a direct lineage of teaching between the work in Medina and the work in Kufa, although the term 'Sufi' was not used to label that work until it was well into its second phase.

The second phase of Sufism, which saw the consolidation of Sufi practice, began with the overthrow of the Umayyad regime. Abbasid rule stabilized the Islamic Civilization, and small Sufi communities were able to form within it. The earliest Sufis gathered in the home of a master or in the home of one of his students, and such a gathering place was known as a *zawiya*, or 'corner.' With the coming of the Abbasids, the Sufis were allowed to inhabit – without charge – the defensive outposts of the Islamic empire, which were called *ribat*. In the next few generations there emerged the spiritual teachers who are remembered by history as the first Sufis. Four of the best known were **Rabia** (d. 801), **Muhasibi** (d. 857), **Dhu-I-Nun** (d. 861), and **Bayazid Bistami** (d. 874). Each of these teachers represented landmarks in the spiritual life of Islam. In the generation to follow came **Al-Junayd** (d. 910) and **Al-Hallaj** (d. 922), who introduced principles of spiritual development that were studied seriously and applied practically for more than a millennium. In the eighth and ninth centuries the majority of the Sufis were close to the community of the *ulama* (Islamic scholars), and many of them actually came from that community. A minority, including al-Hallaj, directly challenged the more rigid teachings of the *ulama*. Both aspects of Sufism were necessary to its survival as a living teaching. There was some persecution of Sufis during this period, but generally speaking this aspect of things has been exaggerated.

The third phase of Sufism saw the emergence of spiritual communities, where teachers and students lived together in larger centers, which might also function as hostels or hospices. Increasingly these communities had links – official and unofficial – to the Islamic government. It was in this stage that people came to refer to the teaching places of the Sufis as **khanaquah**. This transition occurred with the shift in the center of gravity of Sufism from Baghdad to the Khourasan region of Persia. Indeed the Persian **Abu Said** (d. 1049) was instrumental in creating the new form. There was a movement away from a strict, reverent relation between the *murid* (student) and the *murshid* (master or guide) to a larger, looser organization which served the Islamic community in many ways, both charitable and artistic. While the *khanaquah* – or in Turkish **tekke** – was used exclusively for spiritual work, the Sufi community might invite the general public to certain of its activities or put on public performances, either within the *khanaquah* itself or in other locations that the Sufis found suitable. It was in the *khanaquah* phase that Sufism became directly associated with art, music, poetry, and dance. It began to shift away from its early monastic and ascetic emphasis, to develop forms and techniques which could be practiced in the circumstances of everyday life. Sufism took on what has since been called a Fourth Way dimension.[1]

During this period Sufi teachings became established in Andalusia, North Africa, and Egypt.

The fourth phase of Sufism arrived as different spiritual paths or 'ways' were defined, and connected lineages of teachers were established. The word for 'way' is **tariqa**, and this was the name given to the new phase of the teaching. Thus the individual *tariqas* were not groups of Sufis associated with particular places (towns or villages), but the Sufis who followed a particular path of spiritual development. A great teacher would define a path, and the teachers in his line would then pursue and develop that path. It

---

1. See the entry for 'Fourth Way' in the Glossary.

was in relation to this that the *tariqa* lineages used the term **silsilia**. This word literally means 'chain' and was used to symbolize the linked succession of masters that comprise a 'golden chain' of conscious life. Over the years the outer form of the *tariqa* became more connected to the institutional structure of Islamic Society and the members of the *tariqa* were more directly concerned to serve that social order. Formative figures here were **Yusuf Hamadani** (d. 1140), **Ahmad Yesevi** (d. 1166), and **Abdul Khaliq al Ghujdawani** (d. 1180).

The *tariqa* lineages emerged in the century immediately before the disruption of the Mongol Invasion (1210), in just the same way that the Christian monastic orders emerged in Western Europe in the century before the collapse of the Western Roman Empire. In both instances one sees the evidence of a larger plan.

The fifth and final phase was that of the ***taifa*** organizations, known popularly as the Great Dervish Orders. These began to take form in the fourteenth century, but to describe their development in the Islamic world as it existed after the Mongol occupation, we must return to our historical narrative.

Figure 66 provides a graphic representation of the development of the Sufi Orders of Islam. The phases of the development of Sufism are shown on the left and the corresponding phases of the Islamic Caliphate on the right.

Tracing the History of Sufism

We shall now go back to the beginning of Sufism and trace the inner spiritual line of its development. In the early eighth century the acts of extended prayer, asceticism, or retreat carried out by the 'proto-Sufis' were – at the same time – a rejection of the Umayyad Caliphate, which had clearly abandoned the principles of Muhammad's Community. These acts of asceticism were thus a renunciation of society, in the form that it had taken. We noted, in the early decades of Abbasid rule, the rise of organized Sufism and the shift of its center from Kufa to Baghdad. At the same time the Islamic studies which had been undertaken in Kufa (under Ali's direction) developed into the more expanded studies of the new *ulama* in Baghdad. However, for the Sufis of the eighth century, the background flavor of 'renunciation' remained. Beginning from the

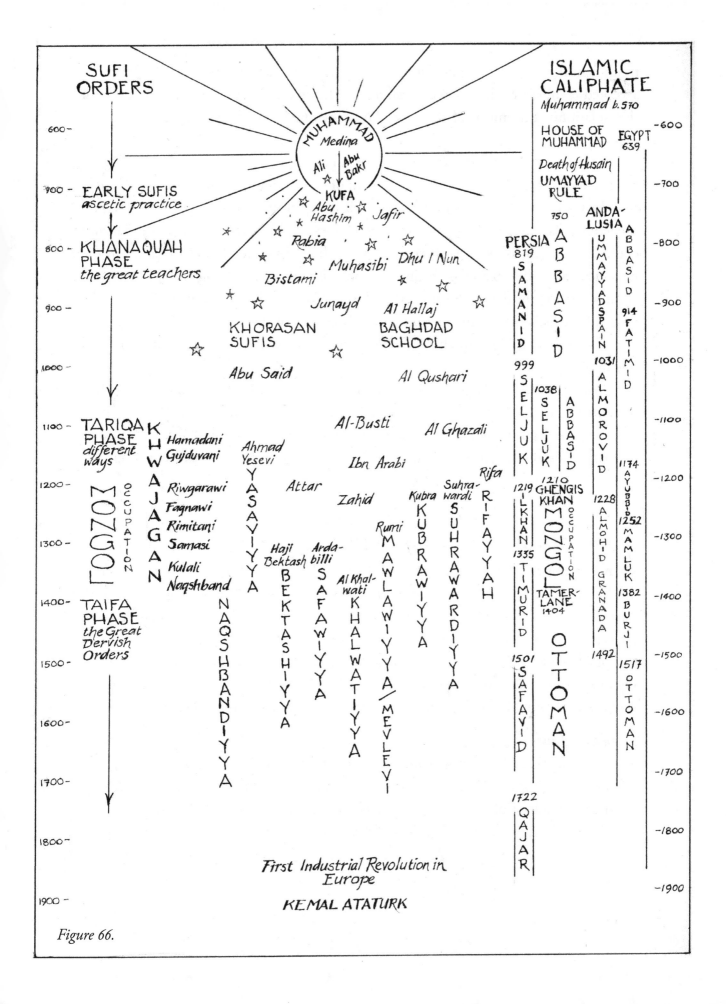

Figure 66.

ninth century, however, the position of the Sufis changed; they came into full view as accepted members of the Islamic community. They were firmly centrist, rejecting both the isolationist extremism of the proto-Sufis and the legalistic professionalism of the *ulama*.

While there still existed a degree of tension between the Baghdad Sufis and the Abbasid *ulama*, there was now a definite element of mutual reinforcement between Sufism and the Caliphate. The Sufis understood well the spirit behind the *hadith* and behind the letter of Islamic law. They set a very positive example of what an orthodox Muslim could be. The Abbasids, in their turn, allowed the Sufis to teach and to gather in the mosques and public places of Baghdad. They also encouraged the formation of Sufi communities in the defensive outposts that were erected throughout the Caliphate. The new Sufi Schools that formed in and around the city of Baghdad were – for the most part – small, tightly-knit teacher-student groups, following closely defined forms and practices.

How, then, did the Baghdad Sufis see their relationship to the Islamic society? This is an important question to ask, because something of the vision of the Baghdad School became permanent in all forms of Sufism to follow. The teacher who gave the clearest original vision of Sufism was Al-Junayd (d. 910), perhaps the greatest of the Baghdad Sufis.

AL-JUNAYD'S VISION OF SUFISM
AND OF THE RELATION OF SUFISM TO ISLAMIC CIVILIZATION

Junayd presented six basic concepts which defined both the work of the Sufi Spiritual Tradition and the relation of that Tradition to the Islamic Civilization. These concepts were **fana**, **tawhid**, **baqa**, **sahw**, **mithaq**, and **khawass**. In Junayd's teaching these concepts were clarified and completed by the practice of the **zikr**. To understand what this practice meant we need also to understand the terms **nafs** and **Satan/djinn**. Having understood these nine terms, we will be able to relate the original practice of Sufism both to the Islamic Caliphate and to the material presented earlier in Chapter 3.

Fana and *Tawhid*

The concepts of *fana* and *tawhid* are best understood together. *Fana* is personal annihilation; it is not the death of the body but a profound psychological death. In the terminology of Chapter 3, *fana* is the annihiliation of the Lower Self, and *tawhid* is the unity with God that may follow from it. Passing through *fana* does not, however, guarantee *tawhid*. You can only reach a unity with God when **He claims you** in the vacuum created by the annihilation of the Lower Self. People can have the experience of *fana* without the experience of *tawhid*, in which case they enter what the medical profession calls a state of shock. *Fana* is completed in *tawhid* when the shock has been created – not by accident or violence – but by the intentional act of the Master or by the forces of destiny. The right result comes only after the aspirant has struggled for many years against the Lower Self, so that the different levels of his or her being have been loosened and separated. The crisis of *fana* then brings the final rupture, disengaging the lower levels of your being from whatever it is that you really are. Then, in annihilation's waste, you are pulled near God by God himself.

As Junayd puts it, "You do not reach Him through yourself but you reach Him through Him."

Baqa

The completion of *fana* in *tawhid* can lead to a state of 'abiding in God' or *baqa*. This is a higher state of consciousness, independent of the four lower centers, which is self-sustaining. It is sometimes attended by a degree of disorientation in the four lower centers. A person in *baqa* often appears to be in a trance state.

In Junayd's definitions of *tawhid* and *baqa* we see the same double use of the term 'God' that was employed in the Christian Monastic Traditions. The final state of *baqa* is abiding and continuing in God, **but not as God**. Junayd is firm that, "even in this divine state it is not possible for him (the spiritual aspirant) to approach the Ultimate Reality which now possesses him." Junayd's 'Ultimate Reality' refers to what we have called the Absolute. So there is a relation to God – as the Self – in *baqa*, and then there is God as the Absolute, which is a different thing.

Mithaq

The sequence of *fana-tawhid-baqa* is, at the same time, a dissolution of the subjective sense of 'I.' At the end of this sequence we find ourselves in an entirely new place. Junayd described this journey as the return to a primordial state known to all human beings in the time before their embodiment. He called this primordial state *mithaq*. Junayd said that Mankind had existed in this state on the day of the first covenant between God and Adam. He often spoke of *mithaq* as the Primordial Covenant and described it as selfless existence in God. It is nevertheless not a state of pantheistic unity, but a higher form of individuality than that which is common amongst men. This higher form of individuality was incomplete in the souls that pre-existed the embodiment of Mankind, but it can be completed by embodied men and women who undertake the work of the Spiritual Tradition. When any man or woman has success in this work, the state of the Primordial Covenant is re-attained on a level higher than it had been originally known, and those who achieve this are, in their innermost nature, Companions. Junayd made it clear that the state of *mithaq* is a type of existence which only God knows and only He is aware of. Those who share this state of consciousness are his elect.

Sahw

Those who pass through *fana*, and are claimed by God, do not remain in a state of selfless absorption but are eventually returned to their senses and reconstituted as 'renewed selves.' In other words, they do not remain in *baqa* but reintegrate with the life of the four lower centers and return to their work on a new level. They return to a **state of sobriety**, or *sahw*, which 'looks back' on the created world as something outside of itself. The state of *sahw* is, then, the natural state of the reconstituted self.

Junayd says, of the reconstituted self:

> He is present in himself and in God after having been present in God and absent in himself. This is because he has left the intoxication of God's over-whelming victory, and comes to the clarity and sobriety, and contemplation [HJ: the Work of the Steward] is once more restored to him, so that he can put everything in its right place and assess it correctly. Once more he assumes his individual attributes ... His personal qualities persist in him and his actions in this world; when he has reached the zenith of spiritual achievement vouchsafed by God, he becomes a pattern for his fellow men. [2]

Having understood *fana, tawhid, baqua, mithaq*, and *sahw*, we can understand what Junayd means when he says that the combination of *fana* and *sahw* is difficult. It is difficult because there is not a single veil separating Man from God but many veils, and thus the cycle of *fana-tawhid-baqua-sahw* will be repeated in any evolving be-ing. The aspirant must balance the periodically deeper 'annihilations' and periodi-cally deeper states of absorption into God with the continuity needed to sustain the 'reconstituted' self. Junayd said that this balance is almost impossible to achieve and that God must send a series of tests, or **bala**, to keep the aspirant on track. Given

---

2. Quoted by Abdel-Kader, *The Life, Personality and Writings of Al-Junayd*, p. 90 (Risala, No. 8).

this challenging situation we see why the balancing principle of 'service to the level one below' – a leitmotif for all the Spiritual Traditions – was adopted by the Sufis.

Khawass

Those who have been 'reconstituted and returned' in a state of *sahw* are what Al-Junayd called the *khawass*: those who have been given the special mission of guiding others to God. They are a tightly-knit brethren who operate as God's instruments on earth. Effectively they are the inner circle of humanity, and the very fact of their existence is significant. They help the members of the Sufi circle towards self-realization, and they also help in the Islamic community as scholars, helpers, guides, and instructors. They set an example, and in so doing they bring the entire community closer to God. Ali Hassan Abdel-Krader, paraphrasing Al-Junayd, describes the role of the reconstituted brethren of the *khawass*:

> In this state of sobriety [*sahw*] ... the Sufi is, so to speak, released to return to the community and to serve God's creatures. He will be able to spread the gifts he has from God to his fellow men, to each according to his degree of capacity; he will support the simple people through his piety; he will help those who have embarked on theological study as a theologian; he will lead and teach the young; and he will be a companion to the initiated, to his fellow mystics, and will share with them his most sublime experience ... he will not be isolated ... he will continue to help others. [3]

Here we have the exact substance of the Buddhist *bodhisattva vow*. However, the role of the Sufi in the ninth and tenth centuries AD was more circumscribed than that of the Mahayana Buddhist of the third century AD, for the *khawass* could not provide service – past a certain point – without competing with the official *ulama* of the Islamic Caliphate and so with the authority of the Caliph. For this reason the Baghdad Sufis carefully monitored themselves, taking a firm centrist position – between that of the total rejection of society by the proto-Sufi renunciant and the self-confident professionalism of the *ulama*. Those who broke with this centrist position – and there were some – broke the working connection that was developing between Sufism and the Caliphate and so undermined the real possibility of serving the level one below, which the Baghdad Sufis wanted to preserve.

---

3. Abdel-Kader, *The Life, Personality and Writings of Al-Junayd*, p. 91.

Having defined what unites the Sufi circle to the Islamic community, we can now define what unites the *khawass* itself – the inner dimension of its work. This inner work is in turn defined by what resists it. For the work to be defined by its internal resistance is, in a way, quite natural, because this resistance was designed into the Archetype of Man – from which the multiple embodiments of humanity were generated. The internal resistance is represented, in the Sufi teaching, by the two related terms, *Satan/djinn* and *nafs*.

Satan/Djinn

We mentioned that the crisis of *fana* is repeated on different levels, and that with a succession of such crises one's penetration of the Sphere of Sentient Being is deeper and more complete. This process – from its very inception – **needs right resistance**. Man needs to develop his will, corresponding to the depth of the annihilation that he experiences, or he will soon lose his way. It is *Satan* who provides the foil to the development of conscious will, and his presence was given as part of the original design for Man.

The principle of the *Satan/djinn* comes directly from Muhammad's teachings. In the hadith from Jabir (C 18: V 50) he said to his companions, "Satan is present in all you do." In the Sura 17 of the Koran, which discusses the creation of Man, Satan tells God what he will do to the fledgling human souls, once they are embodied:

> I shall lurk in ambush for them on Thy Right Path. Then I shall come upon them from before them and from behind them and from their right hands and from their left hands, and Thou wilt not find most of them beholden unto Thee. (Sura 7, verse 17, trans. Pickthall).

Muhammad later clarified this by stating that Satan's presence in the human soul was realized not directly but through a race of genii or *djinns*. Some of the *djinns* were good, but many more were evil. Satan ensured that an evil *djinn* was attached to the soul of every single human being at birth, like a small black spot in his heart. From this concealed place the *djinn* continuously manipulates Man's thoughts and feelings; he whispers those thoughts that will deflect Man from God. This is a vivid depiction of the function of the Black Queen.

But to understand more practically how Satan sets upon us "from before and behind, from right and from left," we must understand the principle of the *nafs*.

Nafs

The *nafs* are the "many 'I's" of the four lower centers as they are under the control of the Lower Self. The *nafs* are not the four lower centers *per se*, but the four lower centers under the control of the *Satan/djinn*. In this condition each center will be in a state of continuous imagination, and the person subject to this imagination will be in a constant state of concern about his relation to other people and to the external world.

In Chapter 3 we described the resistance to the Work of the Steward as the process by which the many 'I's of the Lower Self are continuously manipulated by the Black Queen to deflect consciousness. The Sufis understood this resistance just as we have described it. The many 'I's of the Lower Self are, exactly, the *nafs*, and the Black Queen behind the many 'I's is *Satan*.

Finally, then, we come to the practice by which Man transcends this internal resistance and realizes his highest potentials.

Zikr

All of the Baghdad Sufis made use of exercises and techniques that fall collectively under the name of *zikr*. These were prayers of repetition (of the names of God or of carefully timed phrases) combined with breath awareness. The prayers of repetition served as a 'forcing house' for the development of the Steward. They helped to create the necessary balance between the continuity of effort needed to pre-empt the Lower Self and the absence of effort needed to enable Higher Centers. What does this balance entail?

In all Spiritual Traditions the Work of the Steward serves to bridge a major interval in human evolution. This interval is the point at which the aspirant's Higher Centers have become intermittently active, but are still unable to sustain themselves independently of the lower centers. They do exist, but they are unable to realize themselves. It is a point of despair, a point at which the aspirant sees that he has very little control over his own evolution – for the functions cannot, by their very nature, sustain this kind of presence.

Having reached this impasse the aspirant must **1)** somehow develop a much greater *continuity* of effort and **2)** distinguish these efforts from the emergent reality of the Higher Centers.

Greater continuity comes from the awareness of the unsleeping internal foe, the *Satan/djinn*. The *Satan/djinn* was always there, but at a certain point in the development of the Steward, it begins to resist and so one begins to become aware of it. This in turn spurs greater effort.

The greater continuity of effort is the very thing that creates the necessity of distinguishing the emergent Self from the efforts made to enable it. The danger is that the efforts to bring the lower centers into presence may override the emergent self-consciousness of the Higher Centers. It is like the athlete who, in his ambition to win the race, overtrains and so defeats himself. For this reason one must acquire the ability to surrender the entire edifice of 'effort making' to the emergent Self. It is an art, and it is an art that is learned through the practice of the *zikr*. The moment of surrender – or meditative pause – is given, either in the *zikr* or between its repetitions.

The interval given in the *zikr* is usually measured by a set number of breaths. What fills this interval at the beginning of practice is the simple 'presence' of the four lower centers, but the 'space' of the interval may – and increasingly does – attract the emergent Self. The *zikr* is repeated hundreds of times a day and each repetition contains the interval in which, in the words of Al-Junayd, "God may claim you."

Because the *zikr* is initiated from the functions, it cannot ensure that the emergent Self will appear in the timed pause. An experienced practitioner, however, knows how to create the ideal space, and knows how to remember the emergent Self so that it comes ever nearer to the surface and 'claims its own' in an ever-greater number of the intervals. It then begins to 'claim its own' not only in the timed interval but whenever it has the power to do so. And whenever it comes one must know to bow to it. Once this process has gotten underway a man experiences what the Greeks called *metanoia* or inner transformation. From that point forward he is 'formed from within' rather than being formed by his responses to the external world.

The aspirant's work then becomes a balance of doing and not-doing. The 'not-doing' side of it is no holiday because it must be based on the most rigorous and accurate observation of a new kind of presence. When the Higher Centers are there, you allow them to sustain themselves. But you must watch vigilantly to determine the moment when they fade. Only the most practiced observer can determine the exact moment when the presence of Higher Centers has been exhausted, and one is left with the simple 'presence' of the four lower centers. There is nothing the matter with this lesser presence, except that it is helpless to withstand the onslaughts of the Black Queen. And she does not wait long! Thus, when the quality of presence

THE STORY OF MAN

changes one must immediately re-engage the line of effort one has been trained in – bringing the lower centers out of imagination and pre-empting the Lower Self.

Each of the Great Spiritual Traditions employed special techniques for 'holding together' the doing and not-doing (or effort and not-effort) aspects of the work. For the monks of Mount Athos it was the prayer of the heart, for the Tibetan Orders it was the use of mantra, for the Sufis of Baghdad it was the *zikr* – which they refined and developed at great length.

Having provided this overview of the work of the Baghdad Sufis, we will review its implications for the place of the Sufi circle, in relation to both the level one above and the level one below.

Given the awkward relationship between the *khanaquah* and the Islamic Caliphate, and the primary responsibility that the *khawass* had to the Gods who knew it 'from within,' the Sufi circle needed the balance beam of service to the civilizational order. We know that the inner circle of 'reconstituted selves' needed service to stabilize the state of *sahw*. The majority of the *khanaquah*, however, did not exist in the state of *sahw*. Their experience of Higher Centers came principally through the influence of their conscious brethren. Although such experience is derivative, it is genuine, but because it is triggered from without, the tendency to desire it – as something external – is strong. The Lower Self easily inserts itself into this desire because it is – in itself – no different from the desire for sex or money. Thus it is even more important for the novices to serve than it is for the *khawass*. Of course in the service to the level one below there is the additional danger – for both the *khawass* and the novices – of spiritual pride. In their service they may simply be gratifying a romantic picture of themselves as Sufis. The Teacher, then, gives tasks and disciplines, combined with his own personal observations, to ensure that his students are sincerely trying to counteract their Lower Selves in their external works and in their interface with society. When the correct balance is achieved, the presence of the Sufi *khanaquah* affects the community which contains it in such a way as to complete the Pyramid of Man.

Following these principles the Sufis penetrated deeply into the social fabric of the Abbasid Caliphate. They were, as a rule, politically inactive and quietist, with a few notable exceptions. In the beginning they were a distinctly urban phenomenon; they usually came from the artisanal or merchant classes and sometimes the nobility. Some were gainfully employed and had children; others lead a strictly ascetic life. Generally the groups were small, the organizations tight, and the requirements on the students great. There were certain places of gathering; there were special initiation practices; there was the study of Islamic texts; there was pilgrimage and travel in groups; and above all there was the practice of different forms of the *zikr*. These might take the outward form of a sacred ritual, visible to the entire Islamic community, or they might be entirely invisible. But whatever form they took, they were directly intended to sustain the Work of the Steward.

Despite what we have said about the wish of the Sufis to serve the Islamic community, there always remained an element of ambiguity between the Baghdad Sufis and the Abbasid *ulama*.

The Sufis carefully maintained a distance from the *ulama*, but this distance was not based on contempt. The Sufis had a profound respect for the *sunnah* and *sharia* given by Muhammad, and these were acknowledged to be the building blocks of true civilization. But discursive knowledge of the *sunnah* and *sharia* could only be the beginning of true service to God. This must be completed and consummated in *fana* and *tawhid* and realized in *sahw*.

And this same distance was observed by the *ulama*. Many of the official theologians looked upon the Sufis as well-intentioned eccentrics, and some saw them as arrogant charlatans. Yet there was real dialogue between the two groups, and some of the greatest *ulama* were self-proclaimed Sufis.

Towards the end of its third century, around 1000, the Abbasid Caliphate entered a decadent phase, and the Caliphate itself became more and more exclusively focused on the court life in Baghdad. In the Eastern Islamic world the Seljuk Turks began to replace the Abbasid family as a dominant force, and by the year 1000 the Seljuks were governing much of Persia and Central Asia. This was the homeland of Persian Sufism, which had steadily evolved from the ninth century, both as a Spiritual Tradition and as part of the organization of society. It was here, in Persia, that the *tariqa* phase of Sufism came into its own.

The links that developed between the Seljuk princes and the Persian Sufis were strong because the official *ulama* was proportionately weaker than the *ulama* of Baghdad. The Persian Sufis were thus able to perform many of the functions that the *ulama* had performed in Baghdad. At the same time they showed themselves able to present a coherent Religion to the Persians and the Turks. For these reasons the early *tariqas* of Persia and Central Asia were often directly supported and backed by the Seljuks.

Thus, while the inner work of the Persian Sufi Orders flourished through the eleventh century and the *tariqas* prospered, the decadence and division that was developing within Islamic Civilization as a whole was the signal of catastrophic change.

In the year 1210 Ghengis Khan and his Mongol hordes conquered most of the Islamic world. The highly mobile, well-coordinated Mongol cavalry were, in their own time, unstoppable. They had the strength, the speed, and the sudden impact of a force of nature. The Mongol armies razed Baghdad to the ground, massacring more than 500,000 people in a few days. They rolled the Abbasid Caliph into a carpet and marched camels up and down the roll until only a stain remained. The Mongols conquered all of Persia (what is now Iran, Turkmenistan, and Uzbekistan), Mesopotamia (Iraq), and the Caucasus. Outside the sphere of the Islamic Caliphate they conquered China, Tibet, and Pakistan, much of Eastern Europe, and most of Russia. Their policy was to ruthlessly massacre all those who resisted their advance and to embrace those who came over to their side. For two centuries they occupied the majority of the lands that comprised the old Abbasid caliphate.

The Mongols were a Great Spirit people, the nomadic descendents of the ancient shamanic civilization of Central Asia. While they were guided by their Shamen, they had begun to feel the want of a Religion of the kind that the other civilizations of that time possessed. As a people they had a complete disregard for pretension of any kind and placed very, very little value on human life. For the Mongols, the Islamic Caliphate and the *ulama* were both artificial and intrinsically meaningless. By contrast, they immediately related to the Persian Sufis as being men of wisdom and treated them with the same respect that they treated their own Shamen.

The Mongols soon found themselves quite unable to govern and administer the territory they had conquered. They were not an urban culture, and they had no experience in maintaining the infrastructures of society: the roads, the trading centers, the schools, and the irrigation systems that the Abbasids and the Seljuks had maintained. It was at this point that the Sufi Orders undertook a special role, quite similar to the role played by the Benedictine monks in early Medieval Europe. First the Sufis converted the majority of the Mongols to Islam, and then they guided them in the management and administration of the empire they had won. During the period of Mongol rule, the Sufi *tariqas* became fully fledged Schools of the Fourth Way.

In order to understand how this development occurred, we must step back a few years. In the period immediately before the Mongol invasion, from about 1100, there appeared a truly remarkable line of Teachers in the Persian Khourasan, known as the Khwajagan Masters. The Khwajagan were not an order but a succession of very high teachers, each one of whom had both Higher Centers open and fused. These men were in contact with one another and worked together to realize shared aims. With the Khwajagan Masters the most important things did not need to be spelled out or negotiated; they were known and understood. In all of Sufi history the time of the Khwajagan suggests most directly a period of direct and continuous contact with Higher School.

THE KHWAJAGAN MASTERS

We can characterize the Khwajagan by comparing them with the Sufis of the Mesopotamian region. The traditional Baghdad School relation between *murid* and *murshid* was one of complete subservience and personal reverence. The Master dealt with those outside his circle through his students, who, of course, spoke of him with complete respect and reverence. The Khwajagan Masters entirely rejected this path. They would never allow their pupils to show them personal reverence, referring to the example of Muhammad. They encouraged an atmosphere of openness, of acceptance, and of the brotherhood of all men.

Following the Persian Sufi Tradition the Khwajagan particularly emphasized the principle of *fana*, or annihilation. This is the path of liberation through death of the Lower Self. Another major theme of their teaching was the transformation of suffering. If one takes the suffering of life as coming from a higher level, one can use it to awaken a higher level within oneself. This doctrine complements the doctrine of *fana*, as both concern the death of the lower and the birth of the higher. On the level of technique the Khwajagan made extensive use of the *zikr*, or prayers of repetition, that had originated with the Baghdad Sufis. These they combined with many kinds of breath control and fasting. The Khwajagan developed the *zikr* in many different forms; some were adapted to public gatherings, some were internal to the *tekke*, and some were wordless – mastered individually by the aspirant who had reached the requisite stage of development. The Khwajagan Masters required long periods of apprenticeship and encouraged service through physical work. Their history is unique in its lack of doctrinal dispute and sectarianism, as the Masters knew that rivalries and divisions are completely foreign to the world of Higher Centers.

The first of these Masters was **Yusuf Hamadani**, from the city of Hamadan in western Persia. He was born in the year 1048, during the time of Abbasid decadence when the Seljuk Turks held power in that area. In his early years he was deeply influenced by both Christian and Zoroastrian teachers. When he was eighteen, he traveled the 260 miles to Baghdad to study Islamic jurisprudence, in which he excelled. At a certain point he changed course and began to teach from his own understanding. Taking this as his vocation, he returned to Hamadan and taught for five or six years, attracting a considerable following. At the end of that time he decided to move permanently to Bukhara, 900 miles to the northeast, on the far side of the Amu Darya. The spoken language of the area was Turkish, and Yusuf spoke only Persian and Arabic. On what his decision was based we can only speculate, but it proved fateful in many ways.

In 1080 Yusuf and eleven of his closest companions set out on foot on the long and dusty road to Bukhara. It is said that Yusuf carried with him the walking stick of Salman the Persian. This journey was symbolic of a change in Sufism. From this time forward, young men in search of the miraculous went not to Baghdad, but to Herat, Merv, Balkh, Tashkent, and Bukhara. It also signalled the rise of **Persian Sufism** and of the coming of a distinctively **Turkish Sufism**.

In moving to Bukhara, Yusuf left behind the more rigid forms of Mesopotamian Sufism. He was open and tolerant to men of all faiths, and he kept carefully out of politics. He distinguished four different classes in the population of the region: 1) the princes and the sultans, 2) the Turkish mercenary army, 3) the orthodox Muslim priesthood, and 4) the general population of merchants and farmers. He advised his follower to "be loyal to your authority" and at the same time "maintain the same language and behavior to all four castes." Then, "if everyone knows that you always speak the truth, no one will touch you." Holding to these principles he became – with a completely passive bearing – a legendary figure and attracted many of the greatest spiritual practitioners of his time.

In 1114, when Yusuf had taught in Bukhara for thirty-four years, the Seljuk Turkish Sultan, Sanjar, encouraged him to move from Bukhara to Merv, which was then the largest city in the world. Yusuf decided to accept the invitation, and the major figures of his Bukhara circle went with him. While Yusuf was in Merv, one of his greatest disciples, **Ahmad Yasavi**, reached his spiritual maturity and went to teach in Tashkent. This was the beginning of a uniquely Turkish Sufism.

When Yusuf died in 1140, many of his students returned to Bukhara. The senior people of his circle agreed to ask Ahmad Yasavi to return from Tashkent to Bukhara. At the same time it was agreed that Yusuf's foremost disciple, **Abd al-Khaliq Ghujdawani**, should go to Tashkent to take the place of Ahmad Yasavi.

Ghujdawani, the Khwaja to follow Yusuf, was one of the eleven who had originally gone from Hamadan to Bukhara. In Tashkent he introduced the famous eight principles of Khwajagan practice. Each of these principles was to be studied, internalized, and practiced until it became like a single point thought which the aspirant could engage at will, independently of – and in opposition to – the never-ending train of discursive thought that runs through the human mind.

Conscious breathing (*Hosh dar dam*)

Literally: 'mind in breath.' Take no breath without the remembrance of God. Do not let your attention wander for the duration of a single breath.

Singlemindedness (*Baz gasht*)

Literally: 'returning.' Return, travel one way; be single minded – for we have within ourselves the goal of our striving.

Watchfulness (*Nigah dasht*)

Literally: 'watch the heart.' Be attentive to what engages your feelings. Do not allow the heart to connect with thoughts unrelated to awakening. Struggle actively with all alien thoughts and desires.

Recollection (*Yad dasht*)

Literally: 'safeguard the heart.' Do not allow the Nine of Hearts to forget God's Presence. Take action to pre-empt the Lower Self. Keep the heart in a state where it is capable of recognizing a kind of consciousness that exists independently of the functions.

Journey Homeward (*Safar dar watan*)

Literally: 'travel to your homeland.' Constantly travel from the world of appearances to the world of unity and transcendent reality.

Solitude in the crowd (*Khalwat dar anjuman*)

Khalwat refers to the seclusion of the renunciant. Sustain your solitude in all the activities of the world. In the midst of the marketplace, in the noise and bustle of the crowd, in the circle of the extended family remain totally centered in awareness. And, taken more internally, the Steward maintains its single will to presence in the midst of the colorful proliferation of 'I's that continuously issues forth from the four lower centers.

Watch your step! (*Nazar bar qadam*)

Keep your intention before you at every step. Remember where you came from and where you are going.

Remembrance (*Yad kard*)

Literally: 'the essence of remembrance.' You use the *zikr* not for its own sake, but to remember who you really are. Always remember what your efforts serve – not the presence of the functions but the presence of the Self.[4]

We note that these one point injunctions are all internally connected and well adapted to spiritual practice in the midst of everyday life.

Ghujdawani continued Yusuf Hamadani's personal example of openness and humility, and taught the techniques of the transformation of suffering. In these and many other ways he prepared his people for the task that was to come with the Mongol invasion.

Over the decades the Khwajagan won the respect and trust of all classes. They were not in the least concerned with acquiring authority – religious or secular. But following their own path they became consummate leaders of men. After Ghujdawani the line of the Khwaja continued through Arif Riwgari, Mahmud Anjir Faghnawi, Ali Azizan-i Ramitani, Muhammad Sammasi, Amir Kulal, and finally Bahauddin Naqshbandi, who died near the end of the period of Mongol occupation in 1389.

---

4. This listing of the eight principles is based on two sources: Hasan Lutfi Shushud, *Masters of Wisdom of Central Asia*, Inner Traditions, Vermont 1983, pages 32-33, and Mawlana Ali ibn Husain Safi (compiler), Muhtar Holland (trans.), *Beads of Dew from the Source of Life*, Al-Baz Publishing, Inc., Florida, 2001, p. 17-25.

At the time of the Mongol invasion, the Khwajagan Masters were both well-established and independent of the existing political structure. Here again we see the evidence of a larger plan, for the Masters found themselves in just the right position to influence the Mongol invaders when they arrived.

The Mongol invasion itself came in the time of Ghujdawani's successor **Arif Riwgari**. There is a story of Arif's first meeting with Ghengis Khan. The Khan was passing through the city of Riwgari on his way to Bukhara; the citizens had all fled, but Khwaja Arif remained working at his loom. Ghengis Khan came up to him and asked why he sat weaving in the empty city. He replied, "My outer attention is on my work and my inner attention is on the Truth, so I have no time to notice what is happening in the world around me." Ghengis Khan was so pleased with his answer that he ordered the Mongols to spare the inhabitants of Riwgari, and invited Arif to go with him to Bukhara to advise him as to who he might be able to work with. When the siege of Bukhara came to an end, one week later, the defending soldiers were killed, but there was no general massacre in the usual Mongol style.

The Mongols related to Arif Riwgari just as the Turks and Persians had related to Yusuf Hamadani, with profound respect. This created a sphere of openness around the Master and enabled him to exercise real leadership and influence. The example set by the Khwajagan Masters allowed the orthodox Turkish Muslims to respond to the occupation with greater openness and less fanaticism than they otherwise would have done. This was important because the Mongol conquest had devastated and impoverished huge areas of the country, and a full century of reconstruction lay ahead. Cooperation between the different elements of society was necessary. The Khwajagan took an active part in organizing the projects of reconstruction while remaining aloof from the inevitable political and religious quarrels that developed. The Masters and their pupils worked steadily to house the homeless, to build mosques and schools, and to train people in practical skills. It was in their tradition that every candidate had to do hard physical work.

By the time of Bahauddin Naqshband, in the late fourteenth century, Islam was again dominant in Anatolia, Persia, and Central Asia, and the Ottoman Caliphate – based in Turkish Asia Minor – was rapidly taking form. The role of the Masters changed as the Naqshbandi support of the Ottoman Caliphate took new and different forms.

Where the Khwajagan had begun with a *khanaquah* style of teaching, they developed the *tariqa* to its full potential, and by the end of the Mongol period – with the backing of the Seljuks and the Ottomans – their lineage developed into the *taifa* form, which was the basis for what we know today as **the Great Dervish Orders**. But to understand this development we must return again to our general history.

Over the two centuries of Mongol rule, divisions emerged amongst the descendants of Ghengis Khan and the representatives of the different Mongol clans. Basically it was the Mongol system of inheritance that created these divisions, which ultimately undermined the ability of the Mongols to rule the lands they had conquered. As a result, beginning from the early fourteenth century, the Seljuk Turks turned the tide on the Mongol Princes. In 1370, however, the Turko-Mongol Prince Tamerlane suddenly appeared on the stage of history and launched his extraordinary campaign to restore the Mongol Empire. By 1405 he had established control over an area extending from southeastern Turkey – through Syria, Persia, and all of Central Asia – into northwest India and eastern China. This was achieved at an estimated cost of seventeen million lives. Tamerlane united these lands as an incarnation of the eternal warrior; he left no polity, no stable governmental forms, and no possibility of organized succession. After his death his empire dissolved in a single generation, and so did the hold of the Mongols on Central Asia.

To understand what followed Tamerlane we must take a step back. Before the rise of Tamerlane, at the beginning of the fourteenth century, a minor Turkish chieftain by the name of Otham had united the Turkish-speaking people of Asia Minor in an Ottoman Confederation. When Tamerlane came he decisively defeated the Seljuk Turks, but the Ottomans were able to survive his onslaught, and – after the collapse of Tamerlane's empire – they established themselves as the natural leaders of Islam.

By the late fourteenth century the Ottomans had been able to re-establish the approximate geographic boundaries of the Islamic Caliphate as it had been before the Mongol conquest, but they were only able to achieve this with the help of the Dervish Orders. Whereas the Umayyad and the Abbasid families, both of which were Arabic, were able to claim direct descent from the Prophet, the Ottoman Turks could in no way be construed as his descendants. Thus they derived their legitimacy from the Sufi Orders, who had been – for centuries – the carriers of the Spiritual Tradition and who had become increasingly the center of the Islamic Religion. So it was that the Sufis, who had proven themselves in service and who had linked strongly with the lives of the ordinary people, in many ways replaced the traditional *ulama* class – thereby gaining the authority that the *ulama* had possessed within the Abbasid Caliphate. The relationship between the Caliphate and the Great Dervish Orders naturally deepened at this time.

Where the Sufis had greatly expanded their range of activity in the reconstruction period that followed the Mongol conquest, they expanded still further under the Ottomans who replaced them. The vehicle for this expansion was the emergent *taifa* orders. Having made this point we are able to elaborate the fifth and final phase of Sufism.

The Great Dervish Orders

The pressures that attended Mongol rule made the entire period a forcing house for the inner work of the Spiritual Traditions, and their external form developed accordingly. At the end of the period the traditional *tariqas* were able to enter the service of Islamic Civilization on an entirely different scale. With the vast resources of the Ottoman Empire behind them, the traditional *tariqa* developed into the Great Dervish Orders of the *taifa* phase. In so doing they revealed the color, the breadth, and the cultural depth of mature Sufism.

The principal orders were the Yasaviyya (Yesevi), Bektashiyya (Bektashi), Naqshbandiyya (Naqshbandi), Mawlawiyya (Mevlevi), Safawiyya, Kalwatiyya, Kubrawiyya, Suhrawardiyya, Rifayya, Quadiriyya, Badawiyya, Shadhiliyya, and Khalwatiyya. The first three orders mentioned emerged directly from the work of the Khwajagan Masters.

The emergence of the *taifa* from 1350 to 1450 was the development of an organization rather than the work of a single teacher. While the *taifa* orders contained a *silsilia* (a linked chain of conscious masters) and were the expression of a particular *tariqa* (way or approach to awakening), they had a much expanded organizational form, with orders and sub-orders, associations and associates, and multiple connections running throughout. Here we must pause to note a problem that faces all researchers in this area. As links were forged between the Sufi Orders and the Ottoman Caliphate, the newly-formed *taifa*, anxious to assist in the legitimation of the Ottomans, boldly traced their lineages back to Muhammad, Ali, and Abu Bakr. In doing so they used considerable creative license and linked teachers together who had lived generations and even centuries apart. The histories and records of the Sufi Orders before this time go back only to the first teachers of the *khanaquah* phase, somewhere in the beginning of the ninth century: Al Junayd, Bistami, and Dhu-I-Nun. Thus the *taifa* rewrites entirely obscured the dark century between the death of Ali and the coming of the Abbasids, and we have – in these pages – done our best to shed light on this period.

In many ways the *taifa* were closer to being religious organizations than they were to being the direct expressions of the work of Spiritual Traditions, but we must remember that the *tariqa* (the way) continued to exist within the *taifa*. The Naqshbandi order provided the model for this pattern, sustaining its inner line of spiritual work with great rigor while engaging in many forms of cultural and social work. Indeed, the *taifa* orders became part of the management of society in post-Mongol Islam, as the new organizational form allowed for the existence of a very large outer circle. This created a situation where many could engage in the Work of Religion on a relatively high level, and those who aspired to enter the Work of Works were free to do so. Thus the *taifa* organizations eventually merged with the Ottoman Civil Service to become the unofficial religion of Islam in the Ottoman Caliphate. They came to own vast properties and to manage the guild organizations behind most craft and industrial work. Under the influence of the *taifa* orders, the activity of each guild became a way.

This was not to say that there was no orthodox Islamic *ulama* under the Ottoman Caliphate. There had to be an *ulama*. The ongoing review of the *sharia* and the *fiqh* in light of the *sunnah* is a necessary task for any Islamic community. The Ottomans tried, quite conscientiously, to reconstitute the *ulama* class which the Mongols had decimated. They created great *madrasas* (theological colleges or universities) for the *ulama*, but the *ulama* themselves – as they became installed in these *madrasas* – proved quite unable to provide a Living Religion for the masses. In the period of Mongol occupation the Sufi shrine, the dervish house, and the little circle of *zikr*-reciters had become the popular religion of the Persians, the Turks, and the Tartars. The Orders had won the respect and trust of the general population. When the *taifa* orders came, they were able to retain this parochial character, providing village religion, a system of lodges, and an education for youth which instilled real values. Through their rituals and their spiritual guidance they provided for the religious needs of the people while, through their art, they both instructed and enthralled. In Persia a Sufi dynasty, the Safavids, recreated Isfahan as the most beautiful city in the world of its time, showing Islamic architecture at its finest.

This brings us to a particular point with respect to the *taifa* orders – their creation of art at the highest level and their ability to link art to awakening. In the *tariqa* phase Sufism had become directly involved in the development of Islamic art and culture. This was particularly connected to the cultural influence of Persian Sufism and the emergence of a Persian Sufi literature in the work of Attar, Hafiz, and Rumi. In Persian Sufism there was an integration of esoteric understanding from many sources, and this found expression in a variety of art forms. In the *taifa* phase this was taken a step further. The Mevlevi Order, which specialized and excelled in art, brought the dervish

Figure 67. The Grand Square of Isfahan

dances and Sufi theater to the level of enchantment. Throughout the *taifa* orders there was a development of poetry, music, storytelling, dancing, painting, calligraphy, and carpet weaving. Both art and craft were raised to the highest level. Architecture and the decorative arts were infused with symbolic geometric designs which were unparalleled. Often many art forms worked together in a seamless unity, and the guild organization of the *taifa* orders greatly facilitated these cooperative projects. On the one hand, it was the Spiritual Traditions raising the level of the Civilization and, on the other, it was the expression of a unique understanding of the relationship between art and awakening.

We are finally in a position to give a characterization of the major Sufi Orders, without which any history of Sufism is incomplete. But because these Orders were so widely differentiated in space and time and so varied in form, these characterizations can be no more than sketches. We break the Orders into three principal groupings: **1)** the Mesopotamian Orders, centered around Baghdad, **2)** the Orders of Egypt, North Africa, and Spain, and **3)** the Orders of Central Asia.

Figure 68. The Safavid 'Imam' Mosque

The Mesopotamian Orders

We begin by remarking that Kufa ceased to be a center of activity as nearby Baghdad became the seat of the reformed Abbasid Caliphate. Mesopotamian Sufism was centered in Baghdad, embraced Syria, and extended into Egypt.

SUHRAWARDIYYA

Founded by Diya al-din Abu n-Najib **as-Suhrawardi** (d. 1168), the organization of the Order was developed by his nephew Abu Hafs Umar **al-Suhrawardi** (1145-1234). This is a typical example of the *tariqa* being defined in its first two generations, with the actual organization developing in the third and the fourth. The Suhrawardiyya followed the firm teaching style of Al-Junayd. A strong emphasis was placed on ascetic practice, but there were definite links with Islamic politics and the Caliphate. When the thirty-fourth Abbasid Caliph an-Nasir (1158-1125) attempted to revive the spiritual life of Islam and unite the Islamic peoples in face of the Mongol threat, he engaged the Suhrawardi-yya Order to create an Islamic youth movement, the *futuwwa*. It has been suggested by some that an-Nasir organized the *futuwwa* movement in order to more broadly diffuse Abu Hafs Umar al-Suhrawardi's teachings. The ideals of the *futuwwa* went directly back to early Sufism and even to Muhammad's community: the brave youth who is both generous and faithful, the young man who never says 'I' but 'my community.' The *futuwwa* groups came to constitute an important part of social life throughout Islam. Their ideals were maintained through the centuries and their work became connected to the work of many Sufi Orders.

Abu Hafs Umar al-Suhrawardi, through his pupils and his works, influenced almost every Sufi of his day. He traveled extensively, staying at many *khanaquahs* in many different cities, and so the Suhrawardiyya became an Order known to all the other Orders.

QUADIRIYYA

Al-Gilani (1088-1166), the source of the Quadiriyya teaching lineage, was one of the most popular saints in the Islamic World. He began his development with the study of Hanbalite law (one of the four schools of Islamic law) and after a time entered the Sufi school of Abu'l-Khair Hammad ad-Dabbas. After a few years with this teacher, he spent twenty-five years as a wandering ascetic in the deserts of Iraq. Only in 1127, when he was over fifty years old, did he return to Baghdad and begin to teach. A Quadiriyya *tariqa* formed in the generation after his death. Al-Gilani himself left no system and no path, but in the course of time a body of rules, teaching, and practices formed around his inner teaching. Although Al-Gilani was a popular saint, the order itself was never popular in Mesopotamia. Its expansion belongs to its own *taifa* stage, when it took root in both Egypt and India.

RIFAIYYA

Ahmad ibn Ali ar-Rifai (1106-82) was born into an Arab family and spent the whole of his life in the Basran marshlands of southern Iraq, leaving only once to go on pilgrimage. The Basran marshes were a forbidding location, known as the haunt of outlaws. Nevertheless ar-Rifai's marshland retreat became a focus of attraction for migrant Sufis. The Rifaiyya were known as the 'howling dervishes' because of their loud *zikr*. We recall that the *zikr* is a prayer or rhythmic meditation combined with breath awareness, which can be practiced in many different forms, silent or vocal. It often rises to a vibrant humming noise, but it can crescendo in something much louder. The Rifaiyya were known for their howling *zikr* and for performing spectacular yogic feats, such as rolling in flames, eating burning coals and poisonous snakes, and cutting themselves with swords and lances without afterward showing signs of injury. The order eventually spread to Egypt and, from there, throughout Islam. Despite the very colorful reputation the Rifaiyya acquired, ar-Rifai himself was always regarded with respect by the other Sufi teachers.

The Orders of Egypt, the Maghrib (Algeria, Morocco, Tunisia), and Spain (then Andalusia)

These orders tended to develop along regional lines, contributing little to the larger currents of Sufism that ran throughout Islam. Having said that, a number of the most prominent Sufis were Egyptians, and the most widely read Sufi writer – Ibn Arabi – was a product of Spanish, or Andalusian, Sufism. The Sufi Orders of Egypt, the Maghrib, and Spain had the advantage of being untouched by the Mongol invasion, and as a result Egypt became a bastion of Islam in the thirteenth and fourteenth centuries. Egypt was effectively defended against the Mongols by a Mamluk army, formed of Islamic captives of war. They distinguished themselves as the first army to definitively repel the Mongol hordes. The nominally enslaved Mamluks soon rose to high social status in Egypt, becoming a powerful military caste. An intimate relation developed between the Mamluks and the Egyptian Sufi orders.

BADAWIYYA

Based in Egypt, their festivals regularly attracted the Mamluk officers and soldiers. The Badawiyya was a rustic order and adopted a considerable number of pre-Islamic esoteric practices and techniques, of which there was a huge variety in Egypt. Whichever of these practices the Badawiyya adopted they mastered, and this made them colorful in the extreme. As a *tariqa* it produced no great teachers or writers but was rather known as a people's cult. Indeed, it was sometimes called the 'beggars order.' It was at all times subject to the censure of the *ulama* – which never in the least affected its popularity.

SHADHILIYYA

Abu'l Hasan al-Shadhili, born in Spain, became fixed on a search for the *Qutb*, or pivot point of the universe, which he eventually found in the master Abd as-Salam ibn Mashish of Fez. On the advice of this teacher, he went into retreat in a cave near Shadhila, from which the order takes its name. He had the style of a vagabond ascetic, and was the leader of many long and demanding pilgrimages. Yet he always showed a strong concern for the welfare of his followers and kept in close touch with his inner circle. In his mature life Shadili settled in Egypt. The Order took its finished form under Shadili's successor, Abu al-Abbas Ahmad al-Mursi (1219-1287), and this was unexpectedly different from the vagabond lifestyle of its founder.

In its *tariqa* and *taifa* stages the Shadhiliyya did not emphasize pilgrimage, or ascetic retreat, or poverty. Nor did it encourage the vocal forms of the *zikr* which can create a feeling of esoteric identity. The Shadhiliyya appealed, rather, to a middle class of officials and civil servants who were trained to fulfill their duties with conscious intent. The Order became an intrinsic part of Egyptian life, and its members were recognized by their tidy attire and modest bearing. The distinctive feature of the order is that each member is taken to have been predestined and believes that the *Qutb*, or the head of the spiritual hierarchy, will always be a member of the Shadhiliyya. We note in passing that the Shadhiliyya were credited with having invented the use of coffee as a means of prolonging their litanies and vigils, and that the general popularity of coffee grew from this.

The Khourasanian Orders

The Sufi Masters of the Khourasan, in northeastern Persia, expressed a great individualism of style, embracing a wider range of doctrines and techniques, and succeeded in establishing the link between art and awakening. The Khourasani Sufis developed the principle of *sama*, which understands artistic inspiration as a free act of divine grace. The practice of Sufism became inseparable from the arts from this time forward. We may note that the Khourasan was the ancient heartland of both the Magi and the peoples of the Great Spirit Religion. The Persian and Turkish Sufis who practiced there drew freely from a library of ancient techniques that reached back into prehistory.

KUBRAWIYYA

The Order was founded by **Najmuddin Kubra** (1145-1220) who was born in Khwarezm, near the delta of the Amu Darya river just to the north of the Persian Khourasan. He began his search by following a course of ascetic discipline in Egypt, under the sheikh al-Wazzan al-Misri. He then traveled to western Persia and studied under Baba Faraj of Tabriz and Ismail al-Qasri of Desful. It was in Persia that he began to teach. He was a scholar, excelling in metaphysics, and understood the universe as an ascending scale of cosmoses. He presented the view that Man, as a microcosmos, contained every potential existing in the macrocosm. He also developed the concept of an angelic 'other self' who might appear before an aspirant at certain stages of his development. After his death the Kubrawiyya developed an elaborate color symbolism, with 'black light' representing the experience of *fana* or annihilation and the color green symbolizing eternal life. They also developed a *zikr* which, when practiced in retreat, was intended to work not only on the breath but even on the blood and so transform the disciple's entire being. At the time the Kubrawiyya transformed into a *taifa* organization, the sheikh as-Simani emerged as an important teacher. He was orthodox in his literal interpretation of the Koran and his adherence to the *sharia*, but at the same time he adopted *zikr* practices that integrated the yogic techniques of ancient Central Asia. He also taught a form of contact, through concentration, with the spirits of the great Sufi Masters of the past. This practice was later taken up very seriously by the Naqshbandi and the Bektashi. Over time the Kubrawiyya spread from Central Asia to Turkey and India.

YASAVIYYA (YASAVI)

Ahmad Yasavi (1093-1166) was a Turkish pupil of Yusuf Hamadani. He was from Yasi, later known as Tashkent, and was renowned as the father of Turkish Sufism. He initiated a *tariqa* of wanderers, and the *taifa* Order that developed from that always stressed retreat. He was also a master of the sacred dance. The Yasaviyya did more than any other Sufi community to develop music and exercises that acted directly on the physical body and the emotions of Man. The Yasaviyya were the main repository of the science of vibrations, expressed partly through dance and music and partly through sacred rituals that had been handed down from the Persian Magi. They incorporated many of the techniques of the older shamanic traditions of Turkey and were regarded by the *ulama* as unorthodox for their use of magic.

MAWLAYIYYA (MEVLEVI)

More commonly known as the Mevlevi Dervishes, this Order derives from the legendary **Jalaluddin Rumi** (1207-1273), a Persian immigrant to Anatolia, who was a product of classical Khourasanian culture. He was, perhaps, the greatest poet of Islam, and his mystical poem the *Mathnawi* became known throughout the Islamic world. The Mevlevis themselves regard the *Mathnawi* as a revelation of the inner meaning of the Koran. Rumi's father, **Bahauddin Walad**, was a Khourasanian *ulama*: a theologian and jurist with a very significant poetical output. Bahauddin was also considered to be a fully enlightened being, working outside the formal structure of the Khourasanian Orders (while nevertheless retaining an informal connection to the Kubrawiyya). He had acquired a small circle of disciples by the time the Mongols began their conquest of Persia in 1215. Bahauddin, his family, and this spiritual circle fled the country, passing through Mecca and Baghdad, before reaching Seljuk Anatolia, where they settled in the city of Konya. Here Bahauddin was able to establish himself as a teaching member of the local *ulama*, and here the young Rumi trained and practiced as an *ulama*. During his years of training Rumi had exposure to Anatolian Sufism under the influence of Burhan ud-Din.

In his young adult life Rumi achieved preeminence in the Konyan community and was acknowledged as a person of significant spiritual stature. He was, however, completely overwhelmed in 1244 by his contact with a wandering dervish named **Shams ad-din of Tabriz**. Shams was to be the greatest formative spiritual influence in Rumi's life. This enigmatic and inscrutable dervish had acquired, through his extensive travels, a profound body of knowledge, yet he completely transcended this knowledge in his moment-to-moment practice. In 1248 Shams suddenly and completely disappeared, but only after having brought Rumi through to this own level. Through Rumi, and through Rumi's art, Shams' understandings were to pass into the Mevlevi Order. But they did not do so directly. We must note that the Mawlayiyya developed as a self-perpetuating Order only after Rumi's death. In Rumi's life the transmission was only to the several circles of people that spontaneously formed around him. It was Rumi's son and spiritual successor, Sultan Walad, who first gave the Mevlevi Order form. As Rumi's family had developed a close network of associations amongst the Seljuk ruling class, the Mevlevi Order developed along aristocratic lines, under the direct patronage of the Seljuks, and eventually became a very wealthy corporation. The Mevlevi were to exercise an enormous cultural impact on all of Turkey, becoming famous for their elaborate *zikr* exercises, their devotion to music, and their mastery of the dance. The Mevlevi dances were symbolic of the universal life of the spheres, varied and complex in form, yet reflecting an essential unity. The dances were designed to bring one into an awareness of the all-embracing presence in which the movement of the spheres – and so of all earthly life – takes place. The Mevlevi were known in Europe as the 'whirling dervishes.'

As an organization the Mevlevi *taifa* was restricted to Asia Minor and the Ottoman European provinces.

NAQSHBANDIYYA (NAQSHBANDI)

Bahauddin Naqshband (1318-1390) distilled the wisdom of the Khwajagan Masters, of which he was the last, to produce a single *tariqa* which became the basis of the largest and most influential *taifa* Order that ever existed. Thus Shah Naqshband was both the end of one era and the beginning of another. As a Sufi teacher his influence was second only to that of al-Junayd, 500 years before.

The Naqshbandi *taifa* established the principle of a strict inner line of conscious teaching existing within a larger organization: a *silsilia* of masters supported by a focused inner circle as the living heart of the larger organization. This standard then became a measure for the other *taifa*.

The Naqshbandiyya, like the Shadhiliyya, had a vision of celestial hierarchy in which there is always a *Qutb*, or supreme spiritual pivot. They also employed the Kubrawiyya practice of 'direct contact' with the past Sufi teachers of their own line. For the Naqshbandiyya this practice linked them directly to the Khwajagan Masters, from whom they did not distinguish themselves. Several of the Khwajagan Masters had spoken of a hidden prophet, **Khidr**, who was associated with the Archangel Gabriel and who – although disembodied – was capable of working directly with spiritual aspirants in any dimension of time. The Naqshbandi sheikhs continued to experience the direct involvement of Khidr in their spiritual development. Thus, this otherwise very strict and focused tradition had an open idea of the Gods and of the involvement of the Gods in the development of their order.

The Order itself spread from Central Asia to the Caucasus, Turkey, Kurdistan, and south into India.

BEKTASHIYYA (BEKTASHI)

The Bektashi Order took the name of a semi-legendary Sufi of the Khourasan called **Haji Bektash**. The Bektashis began as a Turkish Order, emerging during the period of Mongol occupation (ca. 1350). They stemmed ultimately – as did the Yasavi Order – from the teaching of Ahmad Yesevi, a student of the great Yusuf Hamadani.

The Bekatashiyya developed into one of the largest *taifa* orders, but were limited to Asia Minor and its European provinces. Like the Naqshabandiyya they had a vision of the *Qutb* and the perpetual spiritual hierarchy, and claimed a special relation to the hidden prophet Khidr.

Haji Bektash received his initiation in the Khourasan from the tradition of Ahmad Yesevi before emigrating to Asia Minor. He helped to synthesize the pre-Islamic religious and shamanic elements, which still prevailed in Turkish culture with orthodox Islam. The Order itself became versed in different kinds of shamanic magic. They also emphasized the teaching of Ali, and thereby gave Shiite Muslims something that the

Ottoman Caliphate had denied them. These unusual aspects of the Bektashi teaching were crowned by the fact that they accepted both men and women. What cannot be denied is their popularity. The exoteric teaching of the Bektashis became the accepted religion of many Turkish Muslims.

Despite their unorthodox practices the Bektashiyya had surprisingly strong connections with the Ottoman Caliphate. This came from their close relationship with the Janissary Corps. The Janissaries were infantry units originally formed by Sultan Murad I (Caliph from 1359 to 1389) from renegade prisoners and non-Islamic children (mostly Christian). The Bektashiyya were made directly responsible for the spiritual education of the Janissaries. The Janissaries were celibate, as were sections of the Bektashiyya, and they held to many of the rules of the Bektashi Order. But when, in the nineteenth century, the Ottomans faced the combined military threat of Western Europe and Russia, they realized the need to modernize and reform their own forces. One result of this was that they decided to eliminate the Janissary Corps, and the Bektashi Order fell with them. The orthodox *ulama*, who had long castigated the Bektashiyya as heretics, took this opportunity to initiate a general persecution of the Order. The properties of the Bektashi Order were officially transferred to the Naqshbandi Order, and many of the Bektashi members were executed or imprisoned. The Bektashi teaching, which went underground at this time, was able to survive into the early twentieth century.

KHALWATIYYA

The Khalwatiyya was a popular Order based on reverence for the teacher. It was known for the strictness with which it trained its dervishes. At the same time it did encourage a certain individuality of expression. The Khalwatiyya traced their origin to semi-mythical Persian, Kurdish, and Turkish ascetics. The Order placed a firm emphasis on retreat and had strong links with the cult of Ali, so making itself open to Shiite Muslims. It was based in the Khourasan region and later established branches in Egypt.

Sufism and Islamic Civilization: Al-Ghazali and Ibn-Arabi

Having sketched a history of the great Sufi Orders, we must balance our picture by re-emphasizing the relation of Sufism to the Islamic Civilization. This is embodied in two figures in particular.

AL-GHAZALI

Al-Ghazali (1058-1111) defined the place of Sufism in Islam in such a way as to **1)** give it credence with the Caliphate and the *ulama* and **2)** justify the trust and sympathy given the Sufis by the broad masses of Islamic people.

Al-Ghazali was a Persian, of Sunni persuasion, from the Khourasan region. There were strong Sufi links in his family line, and he grew up in the context of the Sufi teachings. He came to maturity at a time when the Sunni theology was facing intense criticism from Shiite Ismaelite theology and from the Arab-Aristotelian school of philosophy (*falsafa*) that had grown up around the Abbasid caliphate. As a young man he entered the great madrasa at Nishapur where, after studying under several prominent Asharite theologians, he made criticisms of both Shiite theology and the Arab-Aristotelian school.

To understand Al-Ghazali's criticisms we must go back to the attempts of the early Abbasid scholars – following Muhammad's injunction to seek knowledge – to integrate the corpus of classical philosophy and science. These scholars did translate the principal classical texts, but – for the most part – they understood them on the level of method, epistemology, and 'content-as-information.' In other words, the Abbasid *ulama* who had done this work were only scholars. Lacking the insight of Higher Centers, they were unable to interpret classical philosophy in relation to Muhammad's original teaching. Because both classical philosophy and the theology of Islam derive ultimately from the experience of Higher Centers, there are points at which they clearly have the potential to illuminate one another. This potential, however, was not exploited by the eleventh-century *falsafa* scholars They were satisfied with their intellectual mastery of what appeared to be the most remarkable accumulation of knowledge in the world of their time. The sense of possessing a unique and comprehensive knowledge made many of the *falsafa* forgetful of the inner spirit of Islam and inclined to neglect its religious laws and duties. It had, of course, the same effect on the people who studied its philosophy.

Al-Ghazali's best known work, *The Incoherence of Philosophy*, was a refutation of the *falsafa* philosophy. He argued that demonstrative proofs of logic could not have precedence over revealed truth (truth received directly from a higher level). He was in effect saying that the Arabic *falsafa* were 'incoherent' in the use they made of Aristotelian logic as Muslims. He was not trying to demonstrate that they were incoherent as Aristotelians, for Aristotle himself placed the *nous* (the self-transparency of the cosmos) over *phronesis* (practical reason). But inevitably, in the popular culture of eleventh-century

Islam, Al-Ghazali's critiques were taken to imply that he opposed Aristotelianism and rejected its teachings. While Al-Ghazali did criticize Aristotelian logic as a defining context for the Islamic *sunnah* and *sharia*, he developed a complex response to the Aristotelian *corpus*, rejecting certain of its teachings while accepting others. In affirming the truth of revelation over the proofs of discursive reason, he asserted that there was no way to revelatory truth except through Sufism; that is, through the practices which lead directly to the opening of Higher Centers. Thus, in the course of his refutation of the *falsafa*, he provided a profound and moving theoretical justification of Sufism.

Al-Ghazali's obvious genius soon attracted the patronage of the Seljuk Sultan Malikshah (r. 1071-92), and as a result he became closely connected to the caliphal court in Baghdad. In 1091 he was made head of the Nizamiyyah College of Islamic jurisprudence at Baghdad, and, in that role, became – undoubtedly – the most influential Islamic scholar of his time. In this position he attempted to reconstruct Islamic theology and science on the basis of the priority of revealed truth.

However, after four years as the head of the College, he came to an internal crisis. He found that he could not deepen his understanding of revealed truth while in the service of the sultans, viziers, and caliphs. In 1095 he renounced his position as the head of the college to re-embrace Sufi practice. This was not at all a rejection of the principles of Islamic law, which he continued to defend until the end of his life. When he felt stable at a new level of *fana* – after about ten years in retreat – he resumed teaching for a few years at the Nizamiyyah College in Nishapur, where he had first studied.

Al-Ghazali's resolution of the apparent contradictions between reason and revelation – and so his attitude towards Sufism – was accepted by almost all later Muslim theologians. At the same time his dissection of pseudo-Aristotelianism brought the study of Aristotle to a new level within Islam. As a result Greek science and philosophy were finally integrated – at a deeper level – into both Muslim theology and Sufi discourse.

While Al-Ghazali's teachings did not end sectarian dispute they did register a change in the general relation of the Sufi Orders to Islamic Civilization. *Islam began to realize that it needed the Sufis to keep on the path that Muhammad had originally opened.*

Looking back over the span of Islamic history, Al-Ghazali's role within it seems fateful. He died a century before Ghengis Khan's conquest initiated two centuries of Mongol rule. Through his work he **1)** set the stage for the final flowering of Abbasid philosophy and theology that occurred in the work of Averroes and Ibn Arabi, and **2)** prepared the ground for the Sufi-backed Ottoman Caliphate that was to emerge in the wake of the period of Mongol rule.

Thus, 500 years after the death of Muhammad, when the Islamic Civilization was in a very different phase of its development, Al-Ghazali rediscovered and restated the intentions of the Prophet as clearly as could have been done in his century. In thinking of him we cannot but think of Muhammad's prophetic statement: "My brethren are amongst those who have not yet come."

IBN ARABI

Ibn Arabi (1165-1240) made a definitive statement, for the Islamic world, of Man's place in the universe with reference to the individual, the community, and the structure of civil society which holds the two together. Carefully reassessing the classical legacy of both Aristotelianism and Neoplatonism – in relation to a profound working of the Higher Centers – he clarified Islamic theology, transcending the many controversies of his time. He embraced the Greek doctrine of the *Logos* (as cosmic utterance), but stated this in a way that did not contradict Muhammad's categorical assertion of divine unity. In a way he represents the supreme culmination of Abbasid theology, on the very eve of the Mongol invasion.

Ibn Arabi taught a **unity of being** in which all things pre-exist as ideas in the Mind of God. All things emanated from this prior existence and all things will return to it. Muhammad, however, pre-existed the ideas behind the things. He was the first particularization of the Universal; he was the image of God as light incarnate. God himself pre-exists light, but Muhammad mirrors to God the light that is in him. All other particularizations follow from this first particularization. Muhammad is, then, the light from which the World was created.

This was called the doctrine of **Muhammadan Light**, in which the Prophet is seen as the first mirror image of God in the state of pre-creation. The Created World, then, is a manifestation of the Muhammadan Light, becoming incarnate in Adam, Abraham, Moses, Jesus, and every individual who achieves the degree of transparency required to allow the light of a higher level to shine through him. The doctrine of Muhammadan Light resolved many contradictory views that had emerged in the first three centuries of Islam. At the same time it provided a theological basis for the (often very particularized) worship of the many Islamic saints who had become an intrinsic part of the Islamic Religion. The Dervish Orders of the *taifa* phase (from about 1350) drew extensively on Ibn Arabi's theology in their definition of the *silsilas* or the golden chains of masters that

MUHAMMAD'S COMMUNITY, SUFISM AND THE ISLAMIC CALIPHATE

In Muhammad's community conscious beings had real authority. The word 'sufi' was not used, and there were not 'sufi' roles separate from the Islamic community.

In Islamic civilization conscious beings did not exercise authority. The Sufis attempted to preserve the inner teachings of Muhammad, in opposition to certain tendencies within Islam. In the beginning the proto-sufis were passive critics of Umayyad Islamic orthodoxy. At a later date the Sufi Orders supported Islamic Civilization and gave it life.

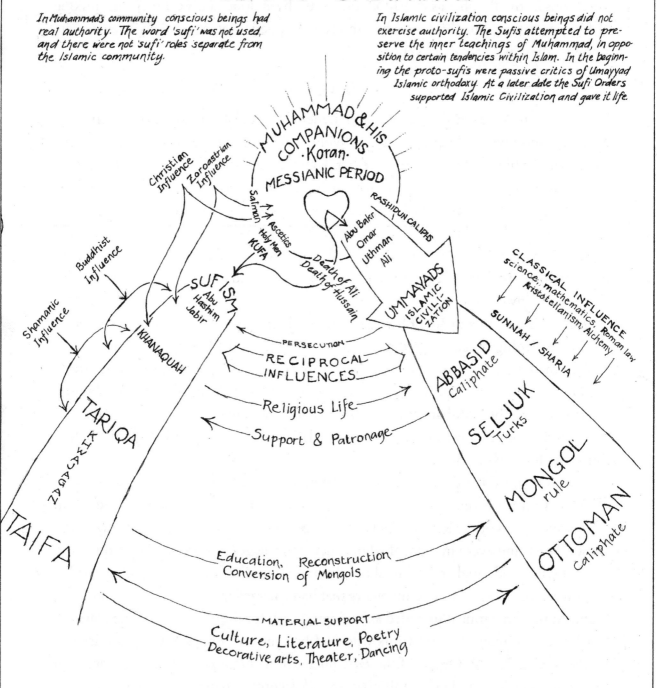

MUHAMMAD & HIS COMPANIONS
· Koran ·
MESSIANIC PERIOD

Christian Influence
Zoroastrian Influence
Buddhist Influence
Shamanic Influence

Salman
Ascetics
Holy Men
KUFA

Death of Ali
Death of Hussain

RASHIDUN CALIPHS
Abu Bakr
Omar
Uthman
Ali

UMMAYADS
ISLAMIC CIVILIZATION

CLASSICAL INFLUENCE
science, mathematics, Roman law
Aristotelianism, Alchemy

SUNNAH / SHARIA

SUFISM
Abu Hashim Jabir

KHANAQUAH

TARIQA

TAIFA

PERSECUTION
RECIPROCAL INFLUENCES
Religious Life
Support & Patronage

ABBASID Caliphate

SELJUK Turks

MONGOL rule

OTTOMAN Caliphate

Education, Reconstruction
Conversion of Mongols

MATERIAL SUPPORT
Culture, Literature, Poetry
Decorative arts, Theater, Dancing

The Sufis remained distinct from 'orthodox' Islam, yet at the same time they needed to remain in an open relationship to it. On the one hand they were in danger of becoming absorbed into the religion, while on the other they were in danger of becoming divorced from both the religion and the civilization, and so failing in service to humanity.

Figure 69.

define the different lineages. The *silsila* is a chain of transference of the Muhammadan Light.

We mentioned that the Prophet is, in some way, the archetypal Man. In realizing his 'all possibilities' he has become an incarnation of the luminous, transparent archetype for Man that was originally created in Higher School. In this respect he is the prototype for all men, and can understand all different types of men and women as variant expressions of himself. The Prophet unites all individualities and transcends all contradictions in the infinite and universal nature of the pre-create Self, which lives in the radiance of the Muhammadan Light. Hence assimilation to the Prophet as universal prototype becomes the means through which the artisan or architect can display the splendor of Creation: the lawmaker, its necessary equilibrium; the healer, its benevolence and compassion; and the musician, its harmonies.

From the perspective of the Light behind Creation, Ibn Arabi wrote on law, ethics, government, art, and education – but above all on the realization of human potential. It is a tribute to the level of Islamic Civilization in his time that it more or less accepted his teaching. Only a Sufi – only one with a working experience of Higher Centers – could have attempted to reconnect Islamic Civilization to the essence of Muhammad's teaching.

There is one point to note in passing. Ibn Arabi describes God as being both immanent and transcendent, and in this view the 'Not-God' or 'Not-Being' aspect of what we have called the Absolute tends to disappear. As a result there is the philosophical tendency towards a flat pantheism. In Book I we presented an Absolute which was – in its Beyond-Being dimension – utterly and permanently transcendent, presiding over a macrocosm which – under the law of the Heropass – was self-sustaining. The transcendent Beyond-Being of the Absolute is not immanent in the macrocosm. The Absolute is presented as the only complete and self-created individual in the universe. As the entities under the Absolute evolve, they acquire – in stages – new forms of individuality, which approximate ever more closely that of the Absolute. The Gods who inhabit the macrocosm are the intermediaries between a transcendent Absolute and his Creation. Creation, then, contains Not-Being, Time, and Death. Man has been called upon to emulate God in his act of self-transcendence and so to generate the consciousness necessary to stabilize Creation.

To view God as both immanent and transcendent *in the same way*, or in a way that is undifferentiated, de-emphasizes the tensions that exist at every level of the Macrocosm and that ceaselessly drive all forms of conscious life to emulate the Absolute's original act of self-transcendence. The mix of immanence and transcendence encourages an 'emanationist' view, which leaves us unable to conceive the independent integrity of the Macrocosm. And Muhammad himself – we note – was not an emanationist. He refers often to Creation. In fact it is very hard to pin him down under a particular label; he presents a number of enigmatic statements which stand in a certain relation to one another. While the work of Ibn Arabi is the product of a very high degree of spiritual enlightenment, it is less than the teaching of Muhammad himself, which – without theological underpinning – conveys the awe, wonder, and uncertainty that we find in the teaching of all the Prophets. For the Prophets are beings who have known the Absolute face to face. As the apostle Paul reminds us, "One cannot testify to the great truths except through the Holy Spirit."

Both Al-Ghazali and Ibn Arabi were, at the same time, Sufis and *ulama*, and their work was more or less accepted by the *ulama* of their time. They became part of the very fabric of Islamic Civilization, and contributed as much to that Civilization as they did to the Sufi Orders. The social space which supported this kind of ecumenic activity disappeared after the overthrow of the Abbasid Caliphate. The formulations of both of these men nevertheless remained spiritual reference points throughout the Ottoman period to follow.

In the course of Islamic Civilization there were also direct experiments in government by the Sufis. The great Sufi teacher **Khalil Ata** governed Bukhara for six years in the mid-fourteenth century. He attempted to create a new society based upon the teachings of the Kwajagan Masters and for a time succeeded, but he was eventually overthrown by the noble classes, who were incapable of living by these principles. The head of the Safaviyya Order, **Shah Ismail Safavid** (1487-1524), initiated the Safavid Dynasty in Persia, which began as a Sufi-governed state, but was soon absorbed by the established Islamic political and military interests that existed within it.

We provide a graphic overview of the relation between Muhammad's original Community, the Sufi Orders, and the Islamic Caliphate over thirteen centuries in Figure 69 on page 574.

A Recapitulation of Muhammad's Prophecies

Having followed the work of the Islamic Spiritual Traditions over more than a millennium, let us review the prophecies that Muhammad made in the beginning. These, like Zoroaster's prophecies, relate not only to his own Tradition but to the entire line of Prophetic Traditions. They are taken directly from the *hadith*, the collected sayings of the Prophet Muhammad.

Muhammad understood that the community he formed in his lifetime would not transcend itself; he understood that the Islamic Civilization would be less than what this community was, because his teaching would be taken at its highest level only during his own lifetime. He stated,[5]

> The best of my people are my generation; then they that come after them; then they that come after them:
>> [Muhammad ibn Ismail al-Bukari, collections of sayings of the prophet, LXII, I]

Muhammad warned his people that they eventually would follow the Jews and the Christians on the path of degeneration; that is, they would lose the Work of the Steward:

> Ye will follow them that were before you [HJ: the Christians and the Jews] span by span and cubit by cubit until if they went down the hole of a poisonous reptile you would follow them down.
>> [Muslim ibn al-Hajjaj al-Qushayri, collections of sayings of the prophet, XLVII, 6]

He spoke then of the Dark Age, the lowest ebb which would be reached by Mankind before the End of Time.

> Islam began as a stranger and will become once more as a stranger.
>> [Muslim ibn al-Hajjaj al-Qushayri, collections of sayings of the prophet, I, 232]

Having stated these things he saw that Islam would have a long life, and that the Religion of Islam would be regenerated by a succession of Living Teachers.

> God will send to this community, at the head of every hundred years, one who will renew for it its religion.
>> [Abu Daud as-Sijistani, collections of sayings of the prophet, XXXVI, I]

---

5. Here we have used the English translations of Martin Lings, from his book *Muhammad, His Life Based on the Earliest Sources*, Inner Traditions, Vermont, 1983, Chapter LXXXII, 'The Future', pages 329-331.

There is a second prophecy of this nature, which is, perhaps, a vision of the great Sufi Masters of the next millennium. It was given on an occasion when several of his companions heard him exclaim, "O my brethren!" As this spontaneous exclamation was obviously not directed towards themselves, one of them asked: "O Messenger of God, are we not thy brethren?" and Muhammad answered:

> Ye are my companions. But my brethren are amongst those who have not yet come.
> [Abul Husain Muslim bin al-Hajjaj al-Nisapuri, II, 0482]

He made several prophecies concerning the End of Time. He predicted that a great teacher would come, the Mahdi – or rightly guided one – who would renew Islam for a period of seven years. At the end of that time the Antichrist would appear. The true Muslims would resist the Antichrist, but many would come under his influence.

> In the darkest hour Jesus Christ will come again and redeem humanity.
> [Muslim ibn al-Hajjaj al-Qushayri, collections of sayings of the prophet, LII, 9]

He gave a further prophecy concerning the Dark Age. This was reported by his companion (and later Caliph) Umar. When Muhammad was asked of the hour of the Last Day he replied: "The one being questioned knows no better than the questioner." He was then asked, "Tell me of its signs?" He answered:

> That the slave-girl shall give birth to her mistress; and that those who were but barefoot naked needy herdsmen shall build buildings ever higher and higher.
> [Muslim ibn al-Hajjaj al-Qushayri, collections of sayings of the prophet, I, 1]

This prophecy seems to point to familiar patterns in modern culture. The woman who gives birth to a daughter, to whom she will in turn become a 'slave-girl,' refers to a woman allowing herself to be influenced by her daughter's immature values. We think, then, of a 'youth culture,' which has no Spiritual Tradition and which looks forward only to the biological future of a rising generation. (In our own time the 'rising generation' determines taste simply by becoming the principal consumer market.) The second part of this saying refers to a traditional Arab distinction between the discipline and hardihood of nomadic life in the desert and the more sedentary way of life of herdsmen, who never travel in the desert. The herdsmen, or those lacking in real internal discipline, "shall build buildings every higher and higher." While Muhammad's companions would not have understood this strange proclivity, we can easily understand it today.

Truly, Allah does not remove Sacred Knowledge by taking it out of his servants, but rather by taking back the souls of Islamic scholars [HJ: in death], until, when He has not left a single scholar, the people take the ignorant as leaders, who are asked for and who give Islamic legal opinion without knowledge, misguided and misguiding.

[Fath al-Bari, 1.194, hadith 100].

This shows clearly that Muhammad had hoped for a conscious inner circle of *ulama*. Allah does not 'take away' awakening from those who have it; it is rather that the line is not sustained. And this is what has happened.

Muhammad had seen into the archetype of Islam and into the trajectory of Islamic civilization in history. We think again of his exclamation, "O my brethren," referring to the great Sufi teachers to come. He was surprised at both the number and the level of the teachers that were to follow. And they came in an unexpected form; they came not from the ranks of the *ulama* but from the Sufi Orders of Islam. It is certain that the greatest of the Sufi Masters participated in Muhammad's vision and saw into the archetype of Islam. And in relation to that, they saw into the archetype of the Spiritual Tradition of which they were a part. We consider here Ibn Arabi's unique vision of Islamic Civilization, Rumi's interpretations of Muhammad's legacy in the Mathnawi, and the youthful Shah Naqshbandi's vision of his *silsilia*. Visions such as these were central to the work of the Great Dervish Orders.

We also note that the original Spiritual Tradition of Islamic Civilization – which developed directly out of Muhammad's community – experienced a dark period in the first century after the death of the Prophet. This is quite similar to the crisis faced by the original Spiritual Tradition of the Tibetan Civilization, which experienced the persecutions of Lang Darma, followed by a century of chaos. The final organizational form of both the Sufi and the Tibetan Buddhist Orders emerged in the wake of a century of persecution. The Christian Tradition also experienced persecution in its second and third generations, but this was prior to the formation of a Christian Civilization, so its impact and its consequences were different.

The Age of the Prophets: In Summary

As we conclude the Age of the Prophets – Abraham, Zoroaster, Moses, Buddha, Confucius, Jesus, and Muhammad – we see that each one of them initiated both Spiritual Traditions and World Religions. Because one figure was the source of both esoteric and exoteric teachings, esotericism was able to justify its existence in relation to the source figure and to survive – not without difficulty – within the fabric of the Religion. While the parameters of our world have been defined by the work of the Prophets, the Age of the Prophets has now passed. The general context for both Religion and Tradition has changed dramatically, and patterns of secular life now dominate in both spheres.

It is interesting to note that the teachings of Zoroaster, Moses, and Muhammad were realized in a Religion and in a fledgling Civilization within the Prophet's lifetime. Jesus' teaching was actualized in a Religion in the generation after his death and in a Civilization three centuries later. The Buddha's teaching was realized in a Religion in the century after his death and in a Civilizational Order two and a half centuries later.

◆◆ BOOK V ◆◆

Civilizations Derived from the Classical World

Although we have examined the Prophetic Traditions, our review of the Great Work remains incomplete. We have spoken, to this point, of Civilizations derived from **1)** the prehistoric Shamanic Spiritual Traditions, **2)** the Spiritual Traditions behind the Original Religions, and **3)** the Spiritual Traditions initiated by the Prophets. But now we shall speak of Civilizations derived from a different archetype: the Greek and Roman Civilizations. These are the civilizations that defined the Classical World, and they are the parent civilizations to modern Western Civilization.

To understand the Greek and Roman Civilizations, we must first understand the classical idea of an archetype, as that applies to the human condition.

CHAPTER 33

The Classical Archetype and the Cosmos of Man

We recall from Chapter 1 that an archetype is an essential form, existing outside of space and time, which is the cause of the multiple forms that we see. At the time humanity came into being, the Gods created two different kinds of archetypes.

On the level of the individual human being they created a blueprint for the transformation of energies, which – if implemented – would enable the individual to transcend himself. We see evidence of this blueprint in **1)** Man's latent Higher Centers and **2)** the internal alchemical pattern which enables a man to transform energies of a lower vibrational frequency (entering his system from food, air, and sensory impressions) to energies of a higher frequency (capable of sparking the latent Higher Centers into life).[1]

On the level of the human community the Gods created the archetype of the Cosmos of Man, which gives – at least potentially – the ability for a society to form itself into a completed cosmos and so to serve the cosmos one above.

These two archetypes are necessary to the human experiment. They are actually interdependent. It is clear that the second archetype requires the first, but it is less clear

---

1. The classification of energies relevant to human development includes four general categories: cellular energy, molecular energy, electronic energy, and mineral energy. This classification originated in the ancient alchemical schools, and it was brought to its highest level of refinement in the work of Peter Ouspensky and Rodney Collin, which we follow here, particularly regarding terminology. (See the biographical notes in the *Subject Bibliography*.) For an in-depth discussion of these energies see Rodney Collin's *Theory of Celestial Influence* and *Theory of Eternal Life*. See also the Glossary entries for each of the four types of energy and a brief explanation of 'alchemy,' as the term is used in this book.

how the first requires the second. Put simply, the opportunity to realize one's personal potentials is related to the state of the society in which one lives. When a society falls below a certain level of civilizational order, the opportunity for individuals to evolve within it is much reduced.

Both of these archetypes are comprised of a set number of connected processes. In both, the process by which conscious energy is generated out of the organic energies of nature governs the other processes. It is, for this reason, sometimes called the process of regeneration. How can we recognize this ruling process?

> ***In the individual*** it is (in its highest form) the development of the Steward in service to Higher Centers. In this process the energies normally connected to the working of the organism are transmuted – via the action of the Steward – to a finer quality of energy, capable of stimulating and enabling the latent Higher Centers.

> ***In the human community*** the ruling process is more difficult to describe. However we label it, the process for the development of consciousness in Man must rule the other social processes. The necessary precondition for this is a relatively high proportion of conscious cells in the social order. The achievement of a 'high proportion of conscious cells' is connected to the work of the Spiritual Traditions: their ability to link with the Civilizational Order and their ability to create – within the Civilizational Order – a balance between True Individuality and Collective Life.

As there are actually different kinds of social order, we would expect there to be variant forms of the second archetype. In Book I we speculated that there might have been an original archetype, which embodied the ideal relation of True Individuality and Collective Life, and that on that model variant archetypal forms, appropriate to different historical circumstances, were created.

By understanding the variant forms of the 'social archetype' we can better understand the difference between the Graeco-Roman Civilizations and the Civilizations that preceded them.

In the Civilizations we have studied to this point – the Shamanic, the Prophetic, and those connected with the Original Religions – civilizational order was achieved under the leadership of a Tradition. In other words the original vision of the Civilization came from the Spiritual Tradition that was behind it. Additionally, at least in its formative years, the Civilizational Order reflected a unity of Spiritual Tradition and Living Religion. The way in which these two were united would then define the principal social forms of the Civilization in question.

In the Graeco-Roman Civilizations neither of these two conditions hold. While they appeared in an age when the Prophetic Civilizations were in full flower, they were of a different nature: they represented a new pathway through to the Cosmos of Man. How can we understand this?

Whereas a Prophetic Civilization develops directly out of the Prophet's vision of the archetype and reflects a unity of a Spiritual Tradition and a Living Religion, the Graeco-Roman Civilizations developed out of an existing Civilizational Order, without the intervention of a Prophet and without the context of a Prophetic Religion. In other words they were Civilizations designed to be realized in two stages: 1) a preliminary stage where an 'originating' Spiritual Tradition is involved but not leading, and 2) a 'realization' stage where a Tradition takes leadership.

In their first stage the Graeco-Roman civilizations were influenced and shaped by the work of non-Prophetic Spiritual Traditions. This influence was exercised through the involvement of conscious beings – representative of those Traditions – in the process of civic life. In this way certain ideals were instilled into the social fabric.

Thus, while Greece and Rome were each created with the potential to form a School Civilization,[2] they were not, in the beginning, ruled by a Spiritual Tradition. Rather these civilizational orders were prepared, both by their originating Traditions and by Higher School, to give birth to a Ruling Tradition at a later point in time. In both of these experiments the originating Tradition developed a vital theater of civic life that was conducive to the emergence of a Ruling Tradition. Once such a theater has been established, the Gods can selectively introduce conscious roles until it assumes the semblance of a conscious hierarchy. Such a hierarchy, established in a single generation, can be sustained through a particular combination of aristocratic and democratic forms, and when this occurs a Ruling Tradition may emerge from it. Under the leadership of a Ruling Tradition the civilizational order might then form itself into a completed Cosmos of Man. It is not the particular aristocratic or democratic forms that produce this result, but the involvement of the Tradition in civic forms that have evolved to a certain level. Unfortunately, in neither Greece nor Rome was the originating Spiritual Tradition able to establish stable and enduring rule such as we have seen in Old Kingdom Egypt, First Temple Judaism, India under the Guptas, and Tibet under the Dalai

---

2. See Glossary and Book I.

Lama lineages. Nevertheless the Classical Traditions became, at different points, central to the life of the Greek and Roman Civilizations – and this had the longer-term effect of permanently elevating the cultural and intellectual level of the entire family of Western Civilizations. While we do not see a Ruling Tradition emerge in Greece or Rome, we see the same traces of the completed Cosmos of Man that we have seen when Ruling Traditions have been in place. Here we keep in mind that a Ruling Tradition may indeed rule, while being unable to form the completed Cosmos of Man.

In the Prophetic Civilizations, the link between Spiritual Tradition and Living Religion is vital, and the relation of Tradition to Civilizational Order occurs through the Living Religion. However, in the mature Classical Civilizations, the relation between Spiritual Tradition and Civilizational Order was direct, and all else depended on this direct relation. Because this was by its very nature a more tenuous link, the experiments of Greece and Rome were not ultimately successful. But while they did not – in the end – succeed in producing a Ruling Tradition, they nevertheless realized something of the special archetype that was behind them. These partial realizations of the archetype of a School Civilization, based on a developed theater of civic life, left traces which inseminated the entire family of Western European Civilizations.[3] So, beginning from about 700 BC, they represent a new chapter in the Story of Man.

To understand the story of the Classical Civilizations, we must understand the principle of the Cosmos of Man in greater depth. In other words we must understand how it would apply to a School Civilization. By understanding it in this way we will be able to understand something about the whole family of Western Civilizations, for Greece and Rome are the parents of this family.

The Cosmos of Man

Firstly we must review the idea of a cosmos. We will recall from Book I that a cosmos is a system with its own internal coherence which is capable of self-development. It is made on a universal pattern and contains within itself all possibilities. Pythagoras called a cosmos *a self-perfecting whole*. The created universe itself is a cosmos on the highest scale. We have called it – following the Classical Hermetic writers – the Macrocosm: an interlocking system of cosmoses, each one contained within the next. Each lower cosmos is contained within – and created out of – the cosmos immediately above it. From the standpoint of the higher cosmos, the cosmos immediately below it is a microcosm,

---

3. See Glossary entry for 'School Civilization.'

and from the standpoint of the lower cosmos, the higher cosmos that contains it is a macrocosm. But however far down the chain you go, the microcosm carries the signature of the whole. Because the universe was created from the top down – and not from the bottom up – the possibility always exists for a microcosm to transcend itself and to enter into the life of the cosmos that contains it. Through successive acts of transcendence it can enter consciously into the life of the whole. In so doing, it remains true to its original creative principle.

Now we must look more closely into the internal workings of a cosmos. For this, we will refer to the invaluable work of Peter Ouspensky and Rodney Collin, who took up and developed the ancient knowledge of the three substances and the six processes that comprise a cosmos.[4]

On every level of the universe, a cosmos takes into itself three different kinds of sustenance. These three kinds of sustenance, or foods as Ouspensky and Collin named them, are transformed through six processes to generate all of the energy, consciousness, and insight that are possible for the cosmos in question. The process of transformation of the three foods, via the six processes, develops according to the same law that applies to the development of musical octaves. (Pythagoras was the first person to connect the simple pattern of the musical octave to cosmic laws.) We could say that the six processes stand for the full notes in the musical octave and the three incoming foods represent the half tones which bridge the intervals between the notes. Through the progressive transformation of the three incoming substances, a cosmos develops, or fails to develop, the potentials given in the moment of its creation. Let us try to clarify the idea of the substances and the processes.

THE THREE SUBSTANCES

In the individual man the three substances are **1)** food, **2)** air, and **3)** the impressions taken in by the four lower centers (emotional, intellectual, moving, and instinctive). Each substance enters at a different point. The progressive transformation of these substances in a Man, can – under special conditions of School work – be taken to a point where they spark the latent Higher Centers. Through constant stimulation of this kind the Higher Centers can learn to sustain themselves independently of the physical body.

---

4. See particularly Peter Damian Ouspensky, *In Search of the Miraculous*, Routledge & Kegan Paul, London, 1977, pp. 181-193, and Rodney Collin, *The Theory of Celestial Influence*, Watkins, London, 1980, pp. 172-203.

THE SIX PROCESSES

These processes have been called by many names. On the scale of the human organism, Ouspensky and Collin called them growth, healing, regeneration, digestion, elimination or destruction, and crime or disease. Each of these processes leaves the incoming matter on which it works at either a higher level or a lower level than it was when the process began. The ruling process, which completes the development of a cosmos, is the process of regeneration. In a man this is his spiritual life; it is everything that leads to and supports prolonged states of presence. If the process of regeneration is weak, the life of the cosmos will be driven in an arbitrary way by the other five processes. If the process of regeneration is strong enough to regulate the other five processes, the microcosmos will ultimately transcend itself. In the case of a Man this means that he will make the transition through to the Sphere of Sentient Being.

The idea of the three substances and six processes was developed in great detail by Ouspensky and Collin. It was based on material drawn from many different sources and from their own personal experience. While these principles are not stated as directly in any other source, it is clear that they were understood – at least in their general working principles – by many different Spiritual Traditions and at many different times in history. For our present purposes we do not need to understand these ideas in detail, but we shall try to make them a little more tangible.

We begin with the examples of an individual man, a Spiritual Tradition, and a Civilizational Order (in this case a School Civilization).

An individual man is a complete microcosmos, exhibiting all six processes.

A Spiritual Tradition is a kind of intermediary or artificial cosmos, which bridges the very considerable gap between Mankind and the cosmos of Higher School, which is comprised of molecular – rather than cellular – beings.

A School Civilization is a Civilization which has been prepared by Higher School, from the very beginning, to be governed by a Spiritual Tradition. A Civilization governed by a Tradition connects Mankind both to the level one above and the level one below. It enables Mankind to serve Higher School directly and to actualize the purposes of Higher School on earth. It completes Mankind in

THE STORY OF MAN

its relation to the medium of organic life and so ultimately changes the relation of the earth to the other planets – in such a way that the earth can serve the development of the sun and the solar system as a whole.

The transition from an individual man to a fully conscious being has often been achieved. The creation of an intermediary cosmos, in the form of a Spiritual Tradition, has intermittently been achieved. But a School Civilization, in its complete and final form, has never, as far as we know, been achieved. As we have seen, in the Living Civilizations known to history, there is some evidence of the process of regeneration, but only in periods where there has been the direct conscious influence from a Spiritual Tradition, such as the Sufi Tradition with respect to Islamic Civilization or the Egyptian Tradition with respect to ancient Egypt. In no Civilization has the process of regeneration actually developed to the point where it regulated the other five cosmic processes over any significant period of time.

But, we may ask, if a complete civilization has never been achieved, what is civilization as we know it? The great civilizations of history, including the Greek and Roman civilizations, are social orders in which the process of regeneration is active but not dominant.

It is not hard to find evidence of the six processes in human society. (In pursuing this study we are expanding on the work done by Rodney Collin in *The Theory of Celestial Influence*.) Let us take the six processes – digestion, growth, healing, destruction, crime, and regeneration – and make the analogy to the same processes in the human body. Farmers, agricultural workers, and people involved in the processing and preparation of food are like the cells in the digestive system. Builders, architects, engineers and town planners are like the glands controlling growth. Doctors, nurses, and counselors of different kinds are like the immune system, which works to heal diseased tissue. Soldiers and policemen are like the secretions of the adrenal gland, ready to come to the defense of the organism and to destroy what threatens it. Criminals are like the poisons or bacteria which attack the organism at its weak points and are the cause of disease. Finally there are those men and women who regenerate the whole order and allow it to develop on a new and better footing. They are the statesmen of will and vision, the great artists, the philosophers, and the saints, who transform their experience of the whole into wider vision and higher life.

A civilization, which is usually ruled by groups of people representing one or another of the six processes, takes its general tone from that process. For example, ancient

Sparta took its general tone from the warrior caste which ruled it, Tibet took its tone from its ruling priest caste, and contemporary America takes its tone from the life of its business classes.

Having considered civilization in terms of the six processes, we may reflect again on what a School Civilization might be.

Just as we think of a man as being more developed if he is ruled by the more refined processes within himself – such as healing or regeneration rather than crime or digestion – so we think of a civilization as being more developed if it is ruled by its higher processes. The most developed civilization would be that in which the six processes were arranged in a hierarchy according to the intrinsic quality of the energies with which they worked.

As the finest energies generated by the human organism are those connected with the process of regeneration, it is clear that the highest potentials of civilization would be realized when the other five processes are governed by the process of regeneration. For a civilization this would occur when one of the great Spiritual Traditions worked not in isolation or through a Living Religion but by directly managing the workings of society.

George Gurdjieff put it this way, making a parallel to the development of the Steward in the individual:

> The process of evolution … which is possible for humanity as a whole, is completely analogous to the process of evolution possible for the individual man. And it begins with the same thing, namely, a certain group of cells gradually becomes conscious; then it attracts to itself other cells, subordinates others, and gradually makes the whole organism serve its aims and not merely eat, drink, and sleep. This is evolution and there can be no other kind of evolution. In humanity as in the individual man everything begins with the formation of a conscious nucleus. All the mechanical forces of life fight against the formation of this conscious nucleus in humanity, in just the same way as all mechanical habits, tastes, and weaknesses fight against conscious self-remembering in man.[5]

What applies to the whole of a cosmos applies on the scale of the individual processes which comprise it; the finer energies should regulate the coarser energies. Thus, in a civilization ruled by its warrior caste, the inherent coarseness of the energies associated with war should not disorder the energies of the supporting processes. Regeneration and artistic creation require the finest energies of the human organism. The process of healing proceeds at a slower speed, needing great patience and care. The process of the

---

5. Quoted by Peter Damian Ouspensky, *In Search of the Miraculous*, p. 308.

education of children – which combines growth, digestion, and regeneration – requires a high degree of receptivity. Each process should work with the energies appropriate to it, and on every scale the finer energies should govern and organize the coarser, for this is essential to the primary purpose of a cosmos – to enable the transmutation of energies, level upon level, to the next highest cosmos. It was the city-states of ancient Greece and of the Italian Renaissance which understood this principle best, and it was these Civilizations that left us with the highest levels of artistic expression in almost every field of endeavor.

While the principle of the control of the coarser by the finer is not democratic, it allows the life of the whole to pervade its parts equally. We have seen how, in the original moment of Creation, the Absolute placed the higher energies of the universe over the lower energies in such a way that the higher might manage and orchestrate the lower and thus preserve Value throughout the macrocosm of Creation. This is not to denigrate the lower – or coarser – energies, for every energy is correct in its place. A metaphor on a smaller scale illustrates the point. A great cathedral is comprised of tens of thousands of stones. The capstone of a great arch or the relief work on the façade might seem more important than the paving stones in the crypt, yet each stone – precisely placed – is necessary, and each stone participates in the purpose that informs the whole. The cathedral, taken as a whole, transcends itself in symbolizing the relation of Man to God. Each stone, then, participates in this transcendence. A yard of unplaced capstones signifies nothing; even the smallest paving stone intentionally placed in the crypt of a cathedral has a greater significance.

There is a second aspect in which the analogy of the cathedral applies. There is an optimal number of stones needed to realize a particular type of cathedral. When this number is achieved, each stone has its necessary place. When false dividing walls are created around the apse and the choir or when outbuildings are attached to the side of the cathedral, the number of stones increases but the power of signification is weakened. In like manner both a Tradition and a Civilization have an optimal size. To exceed this lessens the degree to which each member senses the purpose of his or her individual life.

We return, then, to Classical Civilization, as a context for the development of the Cosmos of Man. We noted that for this to occur the theater of civic life had to be raised to a point where a Spiritual Tradition might emerge from it.

In order to begin from the level of Civilizational Order, rather than from the high vantage point of a Prophetic Spiritual Tradition, the Gods had to very carefully pre-arrange a number of conscious roles, so that each would have the necessary effect on the entire social order. While there are always invisible conscious roles in society – and these have their own critical function – the strategy here would be to inseminate the visible social fabric with conscious leaders, conscious artists, and conscious writers, until a true civil service aristocracy could emerge. This enlightened civil service aristocracy might then become the inner circle of a mature Spiritual Tradition. When we look at the Classical World, we see the conscious roles which suggest such a plan.

1. In the Greek period: Herakles (the historical figure from which the myths of Hercules originated), Homer, Lycourgos, Solon, Pythagoras, Parmenides, Heraclitus, Phidias, Aeschylus, Sophocles, Socrates, Plato, and Aristotle.

2. In the Hellenistic period: Zeno, Cleanthes, Chryssipus, Panaetius, and Posidonius.

3. In the Roman period: Cornelius Scipio, Scipio Africanus, Virgil, Horace, Plotinus, Epictetus, and Marcus Aurelius.

The medium of Classical society, however, did not prove adequate to support a governing Spiritual Tradition. The institutional forms required to support an enlightened service aristocracy did appear intermittently but never congealed. In relation to a civil service aristocracy, or to conscious roles in public life, we see evidence of Groups and Schools aspiring to rise to the level of a Spiritual Tradition rather than the Spiritual Traditions themselves. Had the Classical Experiment succeeded, the history of Western Civilization – culminating in the modern world and in our own lives – would have been quite different. For this reason it is important to understand the legacy of the Classical World.

What is unique about the Graeco-Roman vision is that it envisages the work of a Spiritual Tradition developing out of a secular society through the medium of civic life and then – in a second step – raising the level of that society so that it can function as a School Civilization. This would require that the society in question possess forms whereby the processes of growth, healing, digestion, destruction, and crime could be coordinated with the process of regeneration. There would have to be real communication between the people responsible for managing these processes and the governing body of the society itself. This implies that there would have to be – within the society – representative forums that worked effectively. The Tradition could then monitor the development of each one of the processes, according to the quality of energy needed to sustain it and according to how it worked with the others. We see the traces of this in the golden age of the Greek *polis* and in the Roman *cursus honorum* (course of honors) of the first, second, and third centuries AD. In each case we see great civic projects undertaken with the aim to form Man in such a way that he might realize his potentials.

The core of a School Civilization is a service aristocracy, as exemplified by Plato's *archon* (philosopher king) and the several circles of the guardians. Those who prove themselves in service have the privilege of leadership. At every level there is **1)** the living example of a higher level and **2)** the duty to serve – and so to raise – the level one below. The man of highest virtue can then make the demands of virtue on those who aspire to his level of service.

This vision of a School Civilization is, from one point of view, greater than the vision of a civilization kept spiritually alive by the firm unity of Living Religion and Spiritual Tradition – for it involves the entire community in a system which makes direct demands on each person to be more than what they presently are, and so promises to lift them, level on level, to the point where there is a general, and direct, convergence with the goals of Higher School.

We know that in Classical times two great experiments were initiated, each of which produced a level of civic life with the potential to support the Great Work. They each had, at different times, conscious beings as head of state and many conscious beings prominent in civic life. They were each capable of the highest and most discerning level of patronage of the arts.

CHAPTER 34

Greece

Figure 70. The Athenian Parthenon

The potential for School Civilization found its first expression in Classical Greece, where civic life developed to a level previously unknown. The city-state became, effectively, the religion of the Greeks. School, then, arose in the medium of civic life. Plato summed this vision brilliantly in *The Republic*.

Initially we have the religion of the Olympian Gods, as it was presented in the epics of Homer. There was almost certainly conscious leadership of the Greek community in the few generations after Homer, in the late ninth and early eighth centuries BC, when the form of the Greek *polis* consolidated, and *poleis* sprang to life along the shores of the Aegean Sea, the Black Sea, and throughout the Eastern Mediterranean. There were, perhaps, a number of conscious statesmen, who combined a vision of the *polis* with a certain presentation of the Homeric myths. The vision of these first magical years, like the vision of the first years of Mankind, has been lost to us. What can be said is that the Greek city-state was a group of people who governed and were governed in turn and who shaped every aspect of their existence through participating in the different theaters of a shared civic life. There was both a high degree of individuality and a highly developed civic sense. There was the potential, then, for the Greek city-state to embody the ideal relation between True Individuality and collective life – to become, in fact, the first School Civilization.

We shall take the trouble to introduce a few Greek terms to describe the public life of the *polis*. We do so for two reasons: firstly because they are more appropriate than any terms in the English language and, secondly, because they best describe the ideal which has been a measure for Western Man in all the phases of his development.

arête (ἀρετή)

Arête was a value handed down from pre-Homeric Greece. It was originally the combination of a proud and courtly morality with valor in war. The term itself means excellence or virtue, but it was unlike the contemporary idea of virtue in that it was something recognized in the moment. It was a quality of energy that revealed itself only in the moment. As the civilization of the Hellenes developed, *arête* was recognized in many different forms; it was revealed in gracious gestures, in acts of generosity, in the capacity to state the truth, and in acts of artistic creation.

From the standpoint of the terms introduced in Book I *arête* represents the presence that can be achieved by the opening and purification of the four lower centers. It is excellence; it is the authentic experience of life in all its intuitive depth. And of course certain of the Greek conscious beings extended this to include the highest form of excellence attainable by Man – the presence of Higher Centers.

paideia (παιδεία)

Paideia refers to the whole cultural education, beginning from earliest childhood, which enables Man to rise to moments of *arête*. It enables him to discover an ideal of *arête* within himself and teaches him to serve that ideal.

morphosis (μόρφωσις)

Morphosis derives from *metamorphosis*, or transformation. To experience *morphosis* is to be changed in your innermost being, to be transformed or transfigured. The *paideia* which enables *arête* leads to a *morphosis* of Man's inner being.

to kallon (το κάλλον)

To kallon is a central value in Greek *paideia* and a dimension of all the different expressions of *arête*. It refers directly to beauty: not any kind of beauty but beauty as an inner quality that directly reflects a nobility of nature and so endures through time. The Greeks were unique in their understanding of the formative power of beauty on the human psychology. George Gurdjieff and Peter Ouspensky understood beauty as being connected to the third of the three substances (food, air, and impressions) that a man might use to develop something higher in himself. This ancient alchemical understanding has been lost to the art of the modern world.

From one point of view the achievement of Greek Civilization was the discovery of the *paideia* which produces *arête*. Each citizen was educated to rise to an ideal of *arête*, which included both his inner nature and his outer acts. It addressed the whole man; it was the education of what he was. In archaic times this process was concentrated and refined in the nobility; in Classical times – the fifth century – it became more general, if perhaps more diffuse.

We have spoken of the *paideia* of ancient Greece, relating it to the participation of the individual in the life of the city, but to understand how this *paideia* related to the *polis* itself we must understand the Greek word *es meson*.

es meson (ἐς μέσον)

The word means literally 'middle space.' The *es meson* was the dynamic space where decisions were made and actions initiated. Homer says, again and again, that the warriors gathered in the *es meson* to make their plan. It is a space in which honor was valued and in which performance was expected. There is a kind of dynamic equivalence between those who enter that space.

The Archaic Greek hero sought to shed all mortality through achieving *arête* in the *es meson*. His actions were visible not only to other men but to the Gods themselves. The desire to achieve honor in the space of public life was thus intense. Indeed, the Greeks had a special word for this, *philotima* (φιλότιμα), meaning the love of honor.

Having understood the relationship between *arête*, *paideia*, and the *es meson*, we can understand the most important thing about the civilization of the city-state. The Greeks had the idea that the city is a living thing, a process of communication and regeneration in which the Gods themselves directly participate. The Gods of the city come directly into contact with men in the space of the *es meson*. When the Gods inspire the action of virtuous men in the *es meson*, it is the gods themselves who become the ultimate source of *arête*. The Greeks believed that one could achieve a kind of immortality by merging with the larger life of the city; that is, by contributing to the life of the *es meson*. Great words and great deeds would resonate forward through time, enabling greater words and greater deeds by others in the future. To become one with the life of the city in this way is to achieve both *to kallon* (the beauty that endures) and *to eu* (τό εὖ – perfection/completion).

The living current of *arête* in the *es meson* ran continuously from the time of Homer until the end of the life of the Greek city-state. The forms surrounding this social space may have changed, but its life was continuous until some time in the fourth century BC. With the destruction of the internal dynamic of the *polis*, this current could not be sustained in the same way. It was, nevertheless, understood by individuals and groups through the Hellenistic and Roman periods, remaining a part of Classical culture until late Roman times.

The historical challenge for the Greek city-state – in relation to its archetype – was to expand the *es meson* to include more and more of the population of the city while preserving the *paideia* which produces *arête*.

From one point of view the Religion of the ancient Greeks was the city itself – the *polis*. The Gods were the gods of the city, and one came close to them by the quality of service rendered in public life. Honor, or *arête*, in public life was the measure of a Man. Performance in public life created a service aristocracy, based on feeling for the city itself and for the life of the Gods in the city. There was no higher honor than to die for one's city.

Having tried to represent something of the civic life of the *polis*, we may note that this life was supported by sacred mysteries. The mysteries included all members of the *polis*, even those who did not participate in civic life, such as the house servants and slaves. They involved special initiations relating to **1)** the transition between life and death and **2)** the art of transforming suffering. These initiations provided the basis for Greek tragedy as we know it. While the different *poleis* favored different Gods and specialized in different mysteries, the great mysteries – Eleusinian, Dionysian, and

THE STORY OF MAN

Orphic – were general to the Greek Civilization as were the great oracles at Delphi and Didyma. Thus, while participation in the mysteries and in the oracles was part of the life of the city, it was also a cyclical dimension of the life of Greece. While the mysteries and the oracles were not always and everywhere the regeneration of a cosmos – falling often into corruption – they were clearly intended to support the process of regeneration on a pan-Hellenic scale. The sacred rituals behind the mysteries and the great Hellenic oracles helped to center and concentrate the moments of *arête* that arose from the theater of public life in each of the *poleis*.

Of course the Greek *polis* had its tragic flaw. Only if the different classes of society were able to perceive their common interest would they see the life of the city as a larger life in which they could realize the potentials that existed in themselves. If the division of interest between social classes or the rivalry between noble families became too strongly marked, the integrity of the *es meson* would be reduced. Enlightened civic life would become an idea only, and not a living thing. The Greek city-state thus tried to inculcate in its members the idea that they stood or fell together. The Gods would be with them in the *es meson* only if they became more than just a collection of individuals with different material interests.

The Greeks had a very special understanding of the place of beauty and art in the formation of Man. The tiny Greek city-states produced the greatest epic poetry, the greatest philosophy, the greatest drama, the greatest sculpture, and much of the greatest architecture in the history of the West. Each one of these art forms, in its maturity, modeled Man as a citizen. Additionally, each art form influenced the others, reacted to the others, and so helped to form the others. In this there was an understanding of the principles of harmony and symmetry which was unique to the Greek civilization.

In the final hour of the Greek city-state came Plato's brilliant statement, *The Republic*. This was both a direct representation of the ideal of the Greek city-state and the most developed vision of a School Civilization of which we have record.

To understand *The Republic* in its historical context, we must think back to the World of the Original Religions, with its elaborate rituals of cyclical time relating all human activity back to a 'sacred center.' We remember, then, the 'terror of history'[1] that comes with the entry into irreversible time, where everything is in a state of constant change, and nothing returns to its point of origin. From the standpoint of the Original Religions this is a loss of relation to the divine origin of things – a loss of the sacred. When a people experience a loss of the sacred, it is, at the same time, a loss of the

---

1. From Mircea Eliade. See Book II, Chapter 11.

relation to the archetype that informed the World of the Original Religions. They cease to be the people that they were!

Greek mythology had its beginnings deep in the cyclical time of the Original Religions. The Olympian mythology of the Mycenean Greeks was an adaptation of older Minoan myths, and we can say that the Mycenean Greeks inherited their sense of the sacred from the Minoans. But in the Homeric period the Greeks went forward into irreversible time. The character of Odysseus is that of a fully modern Man. We could say that Homer adapted the Olympian mythology to the situation of the Greeks in the eighth century BC. Both Archaic and Classical Greece existed, more or less, in irreversible time, and this is one of the bases of Greek tragedy.

Plato, writing in the time of the decline of the *polis* (the early fourth century), took Homer's adaptation a step further, compensating for the further erosion of meaning that had occurred in the intervening four centuries. He did this by developing the archaic Greek idea of the archetype. This has been called Plato's 'theory of ideas.'

Plato's archetypes are different from the archetypes of the Original Religions: 'great builder,' the 'great warrior,' or the 'great mother.' These relate the acts of everyday life to the acts of the Gods at the beginning of time. Rather, Plato's archetypes are the 'forms' of the created world, as they appear when viewed from the Sphere of Sentient Being. They are the inner forms of things, existing outside of time and space, that inform – and so give meaning to – the discrete objects, events, and relations that we see in the stream of time. By entering into the Sphere of Sentient Being, one sees the archetypal forms – of things, of men, of civilizations – and so one reacquires essential meaning.

Plato saw directly into the archetype of Classical Greece itself. His vision of the city-state reveals the inner potential of the Classical *polis*, and presents the ideal of civic life with conscious purpose. We could say that – in his presentation of the archetype – he blends the objective content of the ancient myths with ideals of civic life, to produce a superb exposition of the *paideia* which produces *arête*. The great warrior and the great builder are replaced by roles which serve the archetypal form of *The Republic:* the *archon*, the guardians, the warrior-guardians, and the citizens.

The *archon* – the philosopher king – is a cosmic being, with direct insight into the realm of the archetypes. The guardians are those who are closest to him. They have given their lives to **1)** serve the inner principle of *The Republic* and **2)** achieve entry – with the *archon* – into the Sphere of Sentient Being. They are the guardians of the connection that the City has to the Sphere of Sentient Being. They aspire to become like the *archon*, and they are engaged in direct work on Higher Centers. The warrior-guardians, who defend the city externally and who have a range of civic duties, aspire to the more concentrated state of the 'best of the guardians.' They are the practitioners of the First Work, the work on virtues (ἀρετή/*arête*). They live a life of duty on a very limited income, yet they are deeply penetrated by *to kallon* (το κάλλον), the beauty that reflects an inner nobility of nature. They receive this beauty from the very development of the City that they serve. The citizens – the merchants, the freehold farmers, the builders, the craftsmen – have all the freedoms of the archaic city-state, including the freedom to participate in civic life. They have fewer responsibilities than the guardians or the warrior-guardians, and they have pleasures and freedoms that the former groups have not. At the same time they are inspired and positively influenced by the example of the life of the guardians and warrior-guardians – into which they may enter if and when they have the desire. The ticket for entry (and for upward movement at every point on the scale) is *morphosis* (μόρφωσις) or change of inner being. Each level serves the level one above and lifts the level one below, and so there is a 'lift on lift' movement running throughout the City. The *archon* serves the Gods face to face and lifts the guardians who are immediately below him. The citizens, at the other end of the scale, serve the guiding principles that the *archon* has given for the City and lift the entire way of life that is realized in the external form of the City. The solutions to the problems of the City are, for the most part, practical and pragmatic – coming from the level of the citizens and the warrior-guardians. But they are solutions decided upon in light of the cosmic insight of the *archon* and with respect to the evolutionary aims of the guardians.

Plato thus retains the zone of the sacred in a society that has entered irreversible time. He is able to succeed with this because he retains cyclical time, not in relation to a particular mythical story but in relation to the archetypes and the Sphere of Sentient Being.

In summary, Plato's theory of the archetypes (or the Ideas) is not a conceptual device for solving philosophical problems; it is the expression – in philosophy – of a direct insight of Higher Centers into the working of the universe. Because concepts are, in themselves, inadequate to represent the insight of Higher Centers, their use will always produce a vision of the universe which opens certain doors while closing others. Given clear vision into the workings of the universe, a master is needed to undertake the task of giving optimal expression to what Higher Centers see and so produce something of real and enduring value. In *The Republic* Plato succeeded in describing an archetypal social form which actually exists (outside of time) but which had not been realized at the time that he wrote and which has not been realized since.

Ten years after the death of Plato, in the year 338 BC, the armies of Philip II of Macedon conquered the combined forces of the Greek city-states at the Battle of Chaeronea. This was the hour of the passing of the *polis*, and in the pre-dawn light that followed the darkest hour, came two teachings that would carry the ideals of the city-state into the age to follow: **1)** Aristotle's ethics, politics, and metaphysics and **2)** the teachings of the Stoic philosophers.

Aristotelianism and Stoicism were not really new philosophies; they were restatements of what had been understood before, in a changed social context. And what was this changed social context? With the containing shell of the *polis* broken, the Greek-speaking peoples found themselves a component part of the vast Macedonian Empire, which was becoming the Hellenistic (post-Hellenic) world and which would, in its turn, dissolve into the all-embracing Roman Empire. Both Aristotle and the Stoic philosophers anticipated, in different ways, the needs and the hidden potentials of the new age. They would, in effect, translate the ethos of the *polis* – with its *paidea* that produces *arête* – into teachings that would reach past the Classical Age into the Early Christian, Medieval, and Renaissance worlds.

In examining this pre-dawn transition we see clear evidence of the Spiritual Traditions that were at work behind it, Traditions that served the entire Classical Family of Civilizations. These Traditions did not lead as the Islamic Tradition (during Muhammad's lifetime) led the Muslim world. For centuries the Classical Traditions anticipated and inseminated, as circumstances allowed – yet they did so accurately and with considerable foresight. They never appear under their own name, yet we see their unmistakable influence in literature, in art, in architecture, and in philosophy.

There certainly was a Greek Spiritual Tradition, which probably found its clearest expression (before our historical records begin) at the time of the origin of the *polis*, in the eighth and seventh centuries BC. We see its direct influence again in the late Archaic period and in the flowering of the golden age of Athens. This same Tradition, in a very difficult transition, was able to carry its work forward into Hellenistic times and, through the Hellenistic period, set the stage for Rome, where – in the age of the Antonines – it came very close to becoming a ruling Tradition. But, somewhere in the Hellenistic period, we probably come to a reformation or renewal of the Tradition.

THE STORY OF MAN

We hazard that there was **1)** a Greek Spiritual Tradition, which survived into the late fourth century BC and **2)** a derivative Hellenistic/Roman Spiritual Tradition, which developed in two stages. These Classical Traditions were not connected to a Prophet or to a defining Religion, and they cannot be known from any particular philosophical work or from the activities of any particular philosophical school. They were quite adept – like the Egyptian Tradition – at operating behind the scenes, and they could be active behind several nominally-different philosophies or schools. Plato, who authored the best-established body of philosophical work in Classical times, gives us clear evidence of this independence of form in his *Seventh Letter*. This letter was written to the friends of Dion, the associates of a pupil of Plato's who had just been assassinated. Dion himself had attempted to realize the ideal of *The Republic* in the city of Syracuse and came near enough to success to be assassinated for his troubles. Following his assassination his associates sought Plato's guidance – so the concerns of the *Seventh Letter* go considerably beyond matters of philosophy. In this letter Plato speaks about the nature of his first interests and his teaching of them.

> One statement at any rate I can make in regard to all who have written on or who may write with a claim to knowledge of the subjects to which I devote myself ... Such writers can, in my opinion, have no real acquaintance with the subject. I certainly have composed no work in regard to it, nor shall I ever do so in the future, for there is no way of putting it in words like other studies. Acquaintance with it must come, rather, after a long period of attendance on instruction in the subject itself and of close companionship [HJ: with a conscious being], when, suddenly, like a blaze kindled by a leaping spark, it is generated in the soul and at once becomes self-sustaining.[2]

This light, 'kindled in the soul,' that 'leaps up and sustains itself' is prolonged presence. Further on in the *Seventh Letter* Plato assures the friends of Dion that they will not find his inner teaching recorded anywhere in writing.

> Nor can he [HJ: who has understood the matters of the 'first concern'] have written them down for the sake of remembrance; for there is no danger of their being forgotten if the soul has once grasped them, since they are contained in the briefest of formulas.[3]

---

2. Letter VII 341 c, d/trans. L.A. Post, from *The Collected Dialogues of Plato*, ed. Edith Hamilton and Huntington Cairns, 1980, pp. 1588-1589.
3. Letter VII, 344 d, e/trans. Glenn R. Morrow, from *Plato: Complete Works*, ed. John M. Cooper, Hackett Publishing Company Inc, 1997, p. 345.

These words, coming from the man who left the greatest written legacy in Western philosophy, show that his deepest understandings were grounded not in concepts but in the direct experience of Higher Centers. Plato's first commitment, then, was to the teaching and transmission of Higher Centers, for without this the philosophy will become divorced from the deepest insights that inform it. Plato was able to use philosophy, without placing his identity in any particular philosophical expression, and thus preserve the intuitions that were behind it. This relativity shows us how the Men of the Traditions were able to use different philosophical expressions, according to the needs of the historical present, while sustaining a single inner teaching. They were able to nurture the flame 'that leaps up and sustains itself' in different philosophical contexts, while sustaining themselves in prolonged presence using the most practical and simplest of methods, or as Plato says – 'the briefest of formulas.'

With these understandings it is clear to us that the work of a Classical Spiritual Tradition was behind the difficult transition from the Hellenic to the post-Hellenic – or Hellenistic – period. Both the philosophy and the cultural ideals that informed the Hellenistic and Roman Civilizations were seeded in fourth-century Athens, in the atmosphere created by Plato's *Academy*, Aristotle's *Lyceum*, and the prominent post-Socratic philosophers who worked in that environment. The two philosophical threads most important to us are Stoicism and Aristotelianism, which originated independently of one another but which fused two centuries later in the work of the Middle Stoic school at the time of the ascendance of Rome in the Eastern Mediterranean.

To be able to follow this process, we must first paint a picture of the Hellenistic World.

CHAPTER 35

The Hellenistic Period

The Hellenistic age began from the moment that Philip of Macedon defeated the combined forces of the Greek city-states on the field of Chaeronea, for from that moment the ethos of the *polis* was dead. The final and irreversible defeat of the independent city-states occurred just ten years after Plato's death, at the time when Aristotle – then aged forty-six – had reached maturity as a teacher. While individual Greek *poleis* survived the Macedonian conquest, the magical nexus of civic life that made them the unquestioned reference point for all their citizens was gone forever.

The death of the ethos of the *polis* was the beginning of the Hellenistic age. Hellenic culture was the culture of the Greek city-state. Hellenistic culture was Hellenic culture divorced from the vital nexus of civic life that sustained the city-state. It was Greek culture taken independently of the *polis*.

Into what 'new world' was the culture born from the *polis* launched?

In the thirteen years after Philip's death, his son Alexander conquered and occupied the entire Persian empire. The new Macedonian Empire that succeeded it was based, at least in Alexander's mind, on the ancient Hellenic ideals – although these were freely adapted to the high and ancient cultures of the conquered lands. The result was a series of varied and syncretic forms, in which a vibrant Hellenistic culture flourished. When Alexander died in 323 BC, he bequeathed to his generals – who were known as the *diadochi* or 'successors' – empires embracing most of the known world of that time. The Antipatrid Dynasty, based in Pella, ruled Macedon and northern Greece. The Ptolemaic Dynasty, based in Alexandria, ruled Egypt. The Seleucid Dynasty, based in Antioch, ruled vast territories – extending from eastern Anatolia and Syria through Mesopotamia to all of Persia and much of Central Asia. After another forty years of struggle (in 283 BC) the Attalid Dynasty, based in Pergamon, came to rule most of Anatolia. Shortly after this, in 276 BC, the Antigonid Dynasty replaced the Antipatrid in Macedon and Greece.

These empires were not based, like the *poleis*, on an unspoken bond or 'social contract.' Nor did they have a common pantheon of gods. They were based on the ability of their leaders to have and to hold power and to effectively administer vast tracts of land populated by many different peoples. These were vast cosmopolitan empires visibly subject to the tides of chance and fortune. Thus the Hellenistic Age brought a feeling of insecurity, and there was a general dissolution of familiar reference points. This was accompanied, on the one hand, by an attitude of cynicism, and, on the other, by a growth of real humanistic feeling – vividly depicted in the comedies of Menander. Also, there is no doubt that – within this vast and colorful theater – great experiments and noble polities were pursued. Particularly we think of the philosopher kings of Pergamon and the great libraries created at Pergamon and Alexandria.

In this context the Seleucid and Ptolemaic Dynasties adopted the Oriental god-king religions that were native to their regions. Neither the Stoic nor the Aristotelian visions of Man were relevant to this form of state religion. Yet Stoicism and Aristotelianism were relevant to the cosmopolitan populations, who, for the most part, took the 'state religions' casually. Additionally, whatever the form of rule, the device used everywhere for implementing centralized government was 'the city' – formed after the Greek pattern with a council, an assembly, duly elected magistrates, and a fiscal system. This development of cities carried the tide of the Hellenistic Empires, where, in many ways, the old coexisted with the new.

In this way the Hellenistic Empires created the context of civilized life throughout the Eastern Mediterranean, the Levant, and Central Asia, until, in 31 BC, Augustus Caesar initiated the Imperial phase of Rome with his victory at the battle of Actium.

For the transition of Hellenic culture to these immense post-*polis* Hellenistic Empires, two things had to occur:

1. The Hellenic values related to character formation, which had been instilled into the Archaic Greeks from childhood – as the *paideia* which produces *arête* – had to be individualized. They had to be articulated in such a way that they could be recognized, chosen, and applied by individuals raised outside of the archaic Greek *polis*. This work was initially done by the Cynics and later by the Stoics.

2. The Hellenic ideals of civic life, the different forms of excellence achievable in the *es meson*, were specific to the *polis*, and so had to be stated in other terms.

This second work was done, and done brilliantly, by Aristotle and the Stoics – yet this second work only came to its fruition in the Roman phase of Classical Civilization.

In the transition to the Hellenistic and Roman phases of Classical Civilization the work of Aristotle and the Stoics was complemented by the direct impact of Greek art, architecture, and drama. These art forms had originated from the Greek Tradition and carried – within themselves – the understandings of Higher Centers. They were a direct source of the highest of the three foods that enter the Microcosmos Man – impressions. And they often radiated impressions at the level of World 12. These great works were literally 'in-formed' by *to kallon* (το κάλλον), the beauty that reflects a nobility of nature – as the artists of the Tradition had created this beauty in the direct presence of Higher Centers. In the Hellenistic period the Greek-speaking peoples carried the art of the *polis* to the farthest reaches of Alexander's empires, and it had an immediate effect on all who saw it. The impact of the Hellenic visual arts was equal to or greater than that of Greek philosophy, because the arts can bypass the intellectual center and touch Higher Centers directly.

Thus the inner life of the Greek city-state was extinguished, but a powerful, centered, and specifically Greek culture survived it. What is surprising is how portable this culture proved and how quickly it was accepted and adapted over such a large part of the world. It is as though – at the moment a large portion of humanity was disposed to receive it – the Hellenistic culture appeared. The empires that Alexander had conquered were old and often isolated civilizations that were given new life by the energetic spread of pan-Hellenic values. The young left the rural areas in great numbers to seek higher education in the new Hellenistic cities.

Excepting the regenerative impact of Greek art, the work of the transition from Hellenic to Hellenistic – as that seeded in fourth century Athens – was two-sided: the work of Aristotle on the one hand and the work of the Stoics on the other. We shall examine each of these in turn.

The Platonic school was able to sustain itself through this period, but it was only in Roman times, when Hellenism had completed its transition from polis to empire, that the Classical World was again able to take Platonism on its own terms. We take Neoplatonism, initiated by Plotinus in about 245 AD, to be a genuine recrudescence of Plato's teachings. Serious and original work was done by Platonists through to the end of the fifth century, as evidenced by the work of Proclus (412-485 AD). In the late

Classical period then, both Neoplatonism and Stoicism had a profound and formative effect on the teaching of the Christian Religion.

THE WORK OF ARISTOTLE

We noted that, although Plato wrote in the first half of the fourth century, his philosophy had deep roots in the archaic *polis* and in the *paideia* which produces *arête*. Plato knew he was writing in the twilight of the city-state, which was signaled clearly in his own time by the destructive nature of the Peloponnesian War. He wrote to revive the ideals of Archaic Greece and give them philosophical form, and in doing this he used myth to deepen, balance, and compensate his philosophical expression. Aristotle's philosophy, by contrast, originated in the latter half of the fourth century and was published after the Macedonian conquest. Indeed Plato's foremost pupil was himself a Macedonian, known in the court at Pella, and chosen to be the tutor of Philip of Macedon's son Alexander. Aristotle was a guide and mentor to Alexander the Great in his early adult life, and predeceased him by only a year. Thus it is literally true that Aristotle saw the formation of the Hellenistic world occur before his eyes.

We could say that Aristotle liberated the spirit of Platonism from the container of the *polis*, preserving and developing what was essential in it. Aristotle simply 'turned about' to face a new audience, who were confronted with a new set of problems, and re-translated Plato's core teachings into different terms. In so doing he intuitively anticipated the whole change in civilizational order, through to the Roman Empire. While, as a philosophical idealist, he remained Plato's student, his expression is rooted in the direct insights of his own Higher Centers, and in certain ways he went further than Plato. In many ways he sowed the seeds of modern science and of modern Western civilization.

To understand the implications of Aristotle's critique for the Hellenistic world we need to know a bit more about the difference between Aristotle and Plato, and so we delve into a brief examination of how a conscious teacher, Plato, and his conscious student, Aristotle, each saw into the celestial hierarchy, and – from that same vision – derived philosophies appropriate to two different worlds. We shall attempt to sketch how Aristotle translated Plato's most important ideas into terms accessible to the rising Hellenistic world.

Aristotle criticized Plato's theory of the archetypes ('forms' or 'ideas') by asking how the 'idea' of a thing could exist 'in relation' to the thing itself, or how the idea could somehow 'correspond' to the thing without being the thing itself. The 'thing' is real, clearly. And we must base our empirical studies on the things themselves. What, then, is the 'idea' that is not the thing? For Plato, by contrast, it is the idea or archetype that is real and the 'thing' that is less real or derivative. We do not begin our study with the 'thing' but raise our souls to a point where we can see into the archetypes of things.

As a philosopher Plato understood the irreconcilable opposition of Being and Not-Being (he tortures us with this in the *Parmenides*) and he had a clear conception of Beyond-Being.

In the famous passage in the *Timaeus* (52d) Plato presents us with

1. Sentient self-existing Being, [(ὄν/*oun*), neuter gender of ὤν (participle of the verb εἰμί)]; Space (χώρα/*chora*) as the 'void' container of Being;

2. Generation (γένεσιν εἶναι/*genesin einai*) or 'generated being;' and

3. The Good (τὸ Ἀγαθόν/the *Agathon*), which transcends Being, Space, and Generation.

The Good is the cause of Being, Space, and Generation. In relation to the act of creation Plato sometimes speaks of the Good as the Demiurge (δημιουργός/*demiourgos*). But at other times, when he is in myth-making mode, he speaks of the *Demiurge* as a single creating subject, equivalent to God (θεός/*Theos*). All of this is legitimate because Plato's conception of the Absolute is not fixed. He considered reality, at the level of the Absolute, to be utterly inexpressible, and he gestured towards it in different ways at different times – using both philosophy and myth. The balance that he strikes is very similar to the Vedantic, recognizing three forces but often emphasizing a single one as representative of those three in relation to Mankind. Like the great teachers of the Vedanta, Plato never forgets that the Absolute exists quite independently of Mankind, and that it relates to many different levels of sentient being simultaneously. Plato's *Theos* (θεός) is, then, close to the Hindu *Brahmā* (as a dimension of triadic *Ishvara*), which is the Absolute seen in its relation to Mankind. By using terms such as 'the Good,' 'the Demiurge,' and 'God,' in an intentionally inexact way, Plato was able to preserve the enigma that lies behind them while, at the same time, describing the space that is the ultimate source of the archetypes.

Plato had a clear awareness of the limitation of the principle of Being as an ultimate principle or reference point, and it is certain that he understood the Good (the *Agathon*) to be Beyond-Being. While the *Agathon* creates from necessity, that necessity is not specified except in a very general way. So, at the level below the *Agathon*, all Being has the correlate of Void, or Not-Being, which is sometimes the philosophical concept of space or void (χώρα) and sometimes the mythological god Erebos (Ἔρεβος – son of primordial Chaos, representing darkness without reference to light).

When we come to the level of generated being we have, then, 'Creation' at the level of the 'ideas' or the archetypes. On a level below this are the discrete, independent, physical objects that comprise the world that we know. For Plato the idea or archetype behind the physical 'thing' is more real than the 'thing' itself, because the idea neutralizes Not-Being (and its correlate time) more completely. In other words the identity of the archetype is more complete and permanent because the discrete object that is before us is always coming into being and passing away in the stream of time, while the archetype behind it endures. In its turn the *Agathon*, which is never at any point different from itself, is more real than the archetypes.

Aristotle is more a philosopher of Being than Plato, but Aristotle's 'Being' must be understood as pure activity – unqualified and unlimited existence, sustained without any moment of break or pause. Aristotle's representation of the highest level in the universe is the Prime Mover Unmoved. Aristotle specified 'unmoved' because movement is a process, and the Prime Mover is not a process but immediacy itself; it is complete fruition, pure activity with no remaining moment of potentiality. It is so dynamic that it is always the same; it is such a complete incarnation of activity that no change is possible.

In this context, what was for Plato the realm of the archetypes becomes for Aristotle the world of 'final causes.' The principle of cause can 'inform' the inner form of the 'things' that we see because Aristotle's creation is the downward (or centrifugal) thrust of higher sentience. It is hard to summarize Aristotle's creation because he adopts the stance of logic, beginning from two complementary points: **1)** God must exist as the necessary first cause of the world and **2)** if God exists he could not cause a world significantly distinct from himself. The being of the 'things' of this world are thus derivative of the being of God; they are different 'derivative aspects' of God's Being and this is reflected in their innermost form, which is only imperfectly embodied in their physical presence, as that is realized in the time-space manifold.

For Aristotle the defining inner 'form' of a thing is its 'final' or ultimate cause, immaterial and outside of time. Thus, as part of a natural expression of what he is, the Prime Mover Unmoved generated a hierarchy of Being. The form of each individual 'thing' within that hierarchy is not separate from the thing itself, but is its integral structure, which is not – ultimately – material. But, for Aristotle, the immaterial 'final causes' of things are not more real than the 'things' that we see. They exist in the things that we see, but at the same time they have been 'created from' the Prime Mover Un-moved. The 'final causes' of the things are the simplified, inner principles, which can be likened to Plato's archetypes. Unlike the archetypes they do not exist 'in themselves'; they exist in relation to the perfected Being of God, and they can be either more or less perfectly realized in the stream of time. On this basis Aristotle elaborated the impulse to self-perfection as the impulse to realize one's own final cause in the stream of time. He applied this both to Man and to nature in a way no other thinker has. In the entire tradition of Western thought only Leibniz and Goethe have been able to take up and develop this idea.

In conclusion, for Aristotle the 'thing' before us is real and the point of departure for study. But for Plato the 'thing' is not-quite-real; it is never the same for two successive moments, and at a certain moment it is not-at-all. For Plato it is the archetype of the thing that is real. But you cannot investigate the archetype directly. You can only investigate it by being continuously present to the 'things' of this world from your Higher Self (ὄν, Being), which is capable of perceiving the relation between things as the dimensions of itself. That is, you can only investigate the archetype by awakening your own Higher Centers.

Plato chose the vantage point of philosophical theology while Aristotle chose the standpoint of logic or philosophical science. It is our opinion that Plato grounded his philosophy in a higher conception of the Absolute, but he never pinned down his conception; he merely gestured towards it in different ways. He did not feel it could be pinned down! His conception of the archetypes is derivative of his conception of the Absolute, and in many ways it is inspired. But by Aristotle's logical standards Plato's conception of the archetype is not justified. With respect to the difference between the two thinkers, our attitude is that you could see it either way, depending on what you wanted and on how you understood the needs of the historical present. But Aristotle's 'way' enabled science as we know it. Platonic ethics – by contrast – spurs a man to work on Being as a first priority, with insight into the created world derivative of that and, in a way, incidental to it. Aristotelian ethics, as we shall see, is fully compatible with the independent development of science.

Yes, in the end Aristotle rejected Plato's notion of the archetypes, but we must be clear that he did so without sacrificing the vision of a sentient universe, comprised of a hierarchy of different levels where the higher levels are the 'cause' of the lower levels. The idea of the archetype is thus transformed into the Aristotelian idea of form as final cause. The way in which Aristotle effected this transformation empowered the emergent sciences.

More generally, Aristotle's reformulation of idealist philosophy led to an ethics relevant to the Hellenistic world. Plato's ethics was not immediately relevant to the world outside of the *polis*. Taking a very great liberty, we could describe Plato's ethics as the *paideia* which produces *arête* directly applied to the realization of human potential, both in the individual and in the community. The *archon* of the Republic, its acknowledged and accepted leader, has raised himself to a point where he has the capacity to look directly into the world of the archetypes and to understand our own world from that vantage point. In Plato's city the social issues would not need to be debated at all because the full citizens of the Republic (those who understood the level the *archon* had attained) would agree on how they saw the problem. The 'solution' would then be based on the full citizen's best understanding of the practical dimension of the problem, taken in the light of the *archon's* cosmic insight. The challenge of the citizens (on all levels) would be to raise themselves to a point where they could actualize that solution. Plato's *Republic* is thus based on an ethos of service, and Plato's audience were men and women who understood the *ethos* of the late-Archaic *polis*.

But we could not speak in these terms to the peoples of Antigonid Greece, or Seleucid Persia, or Ptolemaic Egypt. There was not the same consensus on 'first things,' and, at the same time, there was a host of practical problems to be addressed. With the end of the age of the *polis*, ethics needed a new set of reference points, and Aristotle provided this. He began by breaking ethics into 'virtues of the intellect' and 'virtues of character.'

> ***Virtues of the Intellect*** (*dianoia*) are at the heart of ethics. These are ultimately rooted in the understanding of the *nous* (νοῦς), which is the part of the human soul that can comprehend Being independently of time and space. Clearly, the *nous* can work quite independently of concepts, for the *nous* of Man is connected to the *nous* of the Prime Mover Unmoved, and as such it represents part of Man's realization of his final cause. Aristotle once described the *nous* as the self-transparency of the cosmos. When the human intellect digests the experience of the *nous*, the result is **1)** *sophia* (philosophical wisdom) and **2)** *episteme* (science).

But when *sophia* and *episteme* are turned practically towards the outside world, they become *phronesis*, or what we would call practical wisdom. It is a kind of practical wisdom which is tempered by the experience of Higher Centers.

Virtues of character (*ethikos*/ethics) have an entirely different basis. Our character begins from our working relationship with the community of other men and women. There are good and bad 'states of character.' We have, or have not, liberality, courage, good temper, justice, temperance, truthfulness, taste, and tact. Our states of character relate to our desires, which may be worthy, unworthy, or a mixture of the two. Our desires – of which we are only very partially aware – drive our action or *praxis*.

So, if our character contains virtues of the intellect, our actions (*praxis*) will be tempered by *phronesis* (practical wisdom tempered by Higher Centers). If we are developing ourselves (realizing our final cause), our desires will increasingly include 'ends' given from the *nous*, and our character, taken as a whole, will increasingly be subordinated to *phronesis*. A character subordinated to *phronesis* will serve the *nous*. Our virtues of character will thus be increasingly colored by virtues of the intellect. But, from another point of view, the virtues of the intellect cannot be developed unless we develop our character in such a way as to become a suitable vehicle for this work. So we must work on our character, as it is, and work on the flaws which exist in it, as these are revealed in our relations with other people. Aristotle called a life which successfully integrates virtues of character with virtues of intellect a life of *theoria* (contemplation). Thus Aristotle's ethics relates both to our potential and to the current mix of who we actually are in relation to other people.

On the basis of these distinctions Aristotle introduced two principles that were instrumental in translating Plato's core understandings into terms accessible to the Hellenistic world: the Doctrine of the Mean and the Doctrine of *Philia*.

The Doctrine of the Mean is to be understood at the level of the virtues of character. We have arguments and disagreements more because of conflicting states of character than because of different reasoned understandings about how to reach a defined goal. Virtue, then, consists of finding an appropriate middle ground between two extremes. The virtue connected with each state of character has not one opposite but two – its excess and its deficiency. For example, the opposite of courage is both cowardice (the want of courage) and rashness (the excess of courage). The Doctrine of the Mean would counsel us to seek the balance between cowardice and rashness. The Doctrine of the Mean always emphasizes the importance of moderation. We achieve virtue by finding a middle ground, not by aiming at an extreme. We keep in mind here that the great weakness of Religion – to the extent that it is based on simple belief – is that it tends to produce extreme solutions, and thus extreme conflicts.

The Doctrine of Philia begins from 'states of character' but refers to 'virtues of the intellect.' When two human beings each recognize that the other is someone of good character, and when they spend time together engaged in activities that exercise their virtues, they form a special kind of friendship. This friendship is based on two characters which support *phronesis* (practical wisdom) and so have a (potentially) common background of noetic insight. *Noesis* is, ultimately, the self-transparency of the universe. The two characters, then, begin to awaken to the fact that their friendship is grounded in the self-transparency of the universe. This strengthens the love of like for like, and introduces – as that becomes possible – higher and more noble ends into the activities that they share. As more than two people are needed in most activities, we can extend this same principle to the group. Ultimately, people working together in a state of *philia* are able to balance their striving for a life of *theoria* (contemplation) with **1)** *phronesis* (practical wisdom) in relation to the problems they confront and **2)** the Doctrine of the Mean in their *praxis* (action).

This, then, would be a basis for enlightened government. In a shared state of *philia* people could address a range of scientific, legal, administrative, and other problems – acknowledging the reality of these problems and the need of coming to a real solution amongst men who are imperfect. If Aristotle's circle, working together in a state of *philia*, was able to enter a shared life of *theoria* (contemplation), we would then have – exactly – al-Junayd's company of the *khawass*: the tightly-knit brethren who operate as God's instruments on earth and who are known by God himself from the inside. Those who live a shared life of *theoria* are, at the same time, participant in the level one above and the level one below.

We noted that Aristotle's Prime Mover Unmoved is the ultimate cause of all things. The Prime Mover is fully actualized; he is fully perfected actuality and so part of the essential nature of all things, which, according to their degree of reality, attempt to assimilate themselves to him, so rising to his own level of intelligence and activity. Man is closest to the Prime Mover in his moral activity, because moral goodness in some measure resides in the effort itself, independent of the result and so independent of time, process, and accident. Thus, as Man comes to know God, and to serve what is Godlike in other men, he begins to become transparent to himself.

The fusion of true ethics (which integrates the 'states of character') with the practical reason (partially deriving from *noesis*) brings a recognition of the real ends of human activity. To bring all of one's faculties to the highest ends of human activity is what Aristotle called the *ergon anthropon* (the Work of Man). This can be developed, with the development of *philia*, in each different sphere of society. Accomplishments in different spheres reinforce one another as the expressions of a single final cause. The ultimate final cause is the Prime Mover Unmoved, which can be experienced by, and which itself inspires, the *nous* in Man. Thus, to the degree that enlightened action is involved in the work of a community, it may feel the action of the *nous*, or higher mind, in its midst. In a city or state with a developed polity, the *nous* itself acts as final cause, mirroring the final cause which gave form to the created universe.

There is a beautiful quote from Aristotle's *Nicomachean Ethics* which summarizes his peculiar balance of the ideal and the real.

> But such a life [HJ: θεωρία/*theoria*, life of contemplation] would be too high for man; for it is not in so far as he is man that he will live so, but in so far as something divine is present in him; and by so much as this is superior to our composite nature is its activity superior to that which is the exercise of the other kind of virtue. If reason is divine, then, in comparison with man the life according to it is divine in comparison with human life. But we must not follow those who advise us, being men, to think of human things, and, being mortal, of mortal things, but must, so far as we can, make ourselves immortal, and strain every nerve to live in accordance with the best thing in us; for even if it be small in bulk, much more does it in power and worth surpass everything. This would seem, too, to be each man himself, since it is the authoritative and better part of him. It would be strange, then, if he were to choose not the life of his self but that of something else ... that which is proper to each thing is by nature best and most pleasant for each thing; for man, therefore, the life according to reason is best and pleasantest, since reason [*dianoia*] more than anything else is man.[1]

Aristotle anticipated man's needs for an ethics that would allow him – as an individual in a newly ecumenical (or cosmopolitan) crowd – to still connect his actions to a final

---

1. McKeon, Richard (ed.), *The Basic Works of Aristotle*, Random House, New York, 1941, p. 1105, from the *Ethica Nichomachea* (1177b25-1178a8), translated by W.D. Ross.

cause in a universe of spirit. He related *theoria* (θεωρία), or the contemplation of God, to *praxis* (πρᾶξις), or intelligent action in the external world, in such a way as to define the *ergon anthropon* (ἔργον ἀνθρώπων), or the Work of Man.

Now we move to the second initiative in the transition through to the post-Hellenic world, the Stoics. The Stoic teaching developed in three stages: the Early Stoa, which developed in Greece following the Macedonian conquest, the Middle Stoa, which is directly connected to the emergent Roman Republic, and the Late Stoa, which is a product of Imperial Rome.

The Stoics

In order to explore the second initiative in the work of transition from the passing of the *polis* to the opening of the new age, we must return to the years immediately following Philip of Macedon's conquest of Greece. In the mid-fourth century BC, an environment of high philosophic debate developed between Plato's Academy, Aristotle's Lyceum, and the community of post-Socratic philosophers who gathered in the Athenian *stoas* (public colonnades). New things came out of a new environment; firstly, the Cynic thinkers and then the Stoics.

PRELUDE: THE CYNICS

The Cynics were not what we think of today as cynical men. They were men of high *arête*, who, having been deprived of the core values of the Greek *polis*, internalized that *arête*, transforming it into a determined and often ascetic drive to self-perfection. The aim of the Cynics was to free themselves of any dependence on social norms and to become completely psychologically self-reliant, which they referred to as a state of *ataraxy* or 'self existence.' This independence of social context made them immediately equivalent to all other men. Thus the man who achieves *ataraxy* is, in that moment, a citizen of the larger *polis* which embraces the *cosmos*; he is, in fact, a cosmopolitan citizen of the world. Thus, while the Cynics were marked individualists, and usually critical of society, they had a social conscience and a firm regard for their fellow human beings.

The Cynics took the goal of life to be happiness, which they found by living in accordance with nature. This meant to live in harmony with the way 'things naturally are.' Suffering and unhappiness are the result of false judgments of value which, by creating expectations and desires that are unrealistic, lead to unhappiness. To become happy one must free oneself from any influence that has no value in nature, such as wealth, fame, power, or any social needs which are the result of convention. The man who is the master of himself is the man who is capable of adjusting his own judgments of value to 'the way things naturally are,' and so mastering unhappiness.

Perhaps the most famous Cynic was Diogenes (412-323 BC), who begged for a living and slept in a tub in the marketplace of Athens. It was he who first said, "I am a *cosmopolites* – a citizen of the world."

THE FIRST STOIC THINKERS

The Stoics followed from and developed out of the Cynic School. Where the Cynics were concerned with the happiness of the individual rather than the well-being of the community, the Stoics thought primarily in terms of the community, insisting that nothing could be injurious to the individual if it was good for the community of which that individual was a part.

Stoicism followed Cynicism in its focus on *ataraxy* (individual self-sufficiency) but added to this the emphasis on a single World Spirit animating all men as fellow beings. Stoicism had a marked egalitarian aspect. Its ethical code was manly, rational, and temperate, insisting on justice and virtue, complete self-discipline, and unflinching fortitude. In many ways it echoed the archaic *arête*. It promised both clarity of vision and freedom from the storms of passion.

Having characterized Stoicism we can follow the transition from the Hellenistic period to the Roman period by following the three phases of Stoicism: the Early Stoa, the Middle Stoa, and the Late Stoa.

THE EARLY STOA

Stoicism was founded by Zeno, a native of Citium in Cyprus (334-262 BC) who eventually settled in Athens. The doctrine takes its name from the *stoa* or colonnade in Athens where he was accustomed to discourse. His chief disciple was Cleanthes (331-232 BC), who was in turn succeeded by Chrysippus (279-206 BC). The doctrines of the Early Stoa received their final formulation at the hands of Chrysippus, and it is principally from his work (and principally at second hand) that we know them. The philosophy of Chrysippus became Stoic orthodoxy for many centuries to follow.

Chrysippus emphasized that one's mental conception of reality must fit with one's direct experience. One must remain in touch with the first-hand experience of the senses and adjust mental conceptions and attitudes to fit with it. And one must do this continually. The aim of the philosopher is to live in harmony with nature (φύσις/

phusis). Nature is not – in this view – the combined plant and animal kingdoms. It is the way things are in themselves; it is a reference to the inner nature of things. One accepts things as they are in themselves. This means that **1)** one does not impose one's own mental constructs on reality and **2)** one does not see things in relation to one's personal desires.

What drives the unfolding pattern of 'things as they are in themselves' is the *Logos*. The *Logos* is the utterance of the mind of God. This usage of *Logos* as 'cosmic utterance' is completely consistent with the earlier usage of Heraclitus and Plato and derives from it. The Stoics likened the mind of God itself to an unimaginably rarified and ethereal fire, which is possessed of consciousness, purpose, and will.

From the principles of nature and the *Logos* came the doctrine of tension, which is important for us to understand. From the observation that heated bodies expand, the Stoics concluded that heat produces pressure. Pure Spirit – or the 'ethereal fire' – expanded outward by the force of its own pressure, and as it cooled, tension diminished. As tension diminished the elements of air, water, and earth became visible. A hierarchy of cosmoses then formed, one contained within the next, gradiated by their intrinsic fineness of energy. You have, then, the gradual emergence of a universe of life forms.

In the course of this process the ethereal fire throws countless thousands of 'sparks' and these form into the 'centers or consciousness' which – in their embodied form – are men. Thus men are, in their innermost essence, sparks thrown from the mind of God. There are levels of created beings both above men and below them. The levels above men are the Gods.

After the emergence of a developed hierarchy of life forms, the ethereal fire begins to reassert itself, reintegrating everything that has developed out of it. This process begins, not from the ethereal fire itself, but from the life forms created out of it. Each individual life form is possessed of a creative impulse to 'return to the source,' which takes different forms in different species and different individuals. The ethereal fire – either latent or manifest – is the force which guides and directs every kind of growth or development towards its ultimate perfection. It is alive, purposeful, and intelligent. The life impulse of the myriad of created beings eventually completes the pattern of creation by generating the entire complex order of nature that we see around ourselves. Human civilization is the crown of nature, and human reason is at the center of civilized life. In the highest of civilizations the impulse to return to the source is consistently fed by human activity and the spiritual fire begins to be recognized for what it is. It begins to win its way!

As it becomes increasingly manifest, the ethereal fire begins to shape men and their various activities towards their destined ends. The Gods on the level above our own become involved in helping the most advanced of the men. There is a commonwealth of Gods and men. At a certain point the ethereal fire begins to take on the attributes of a World Soul. The World Soul has the same relation to the Created Universe as the soul of an individual man has to his physical body. With the passing of the millennia there comes a time when the World Soul begins to absorb its own creations: water evaporates into air, and air is finally consumed by fire. Finally everything reintegrates into what we have called Worlds 12 and 6!

Thus, the created universe is periodically consumed by its spiritual center, from which, in due course, a new world order emerges. The world year ending in the general conflagration was called the *magnus annus*. This great cosmic cycle recurs endlessly in the unfolding pattern of the universe. There is something wonderful to understand about the *magnus annus*. The 'commonwealth of men and Gods' is not specific to the living generation, but is an expression of the spread, development, and expansion of the ethereal fire through the body of humanity, over the full span of the *magnus annus*. The commonwealth of Gods and men thus includes those presently living, those already dead, and those not yet born. In joining the 'great commonwealth' the individual is not joining something limited to his own slice of time and space; he is joining a company which is alive over the span of the *magnus annus*.

Thus, in the Stoic view, Man is an image or microcosm of the universe. His physical body is comprised of the same four elements and, to the extent spirit develops in him, the element of fire controls his behavior. The coordinating fire is continuous with Higher Mind in the universe, and by leading the Stoic life a man can make his spirit consciously continuous with Higher Mind. When a man dies the elements of earth, air, and water are dispersed while fire is reintegrated into Higher Mind. The original doctrine of Cleanthes was that, after the dissolution of the body the soul lived on in the upper regions of the air and was not resolved into the world fire until the final conflagration (in the *magnus annus*). The later doctrine of Chrysippus was that only the souls of the good and wise preserve their personal identity until the end of the world.

Because all men are the various manifestations of this single spiritual force, they are, in this regard, brothers. The entire universe could be likened to one great city where beings on different levels serve the interests of the whole, either consciously or unconsciously. Here the vision of the Early Stoa took up one important theme that Cynicism had relinquished – service to the level one below. Man is essentially a social being, committed to his fellow creatures. Stoicism is, thus, both aristocratic and egalitarian. As men live increasingly according to their inner nature, they become increasingly aware of what is spiritual in one another. While all men are sparks generated by the divine fire, in a few the fire has come into its own.

THE MIDDLE STOA

The Stoic middle school was both Greek and Roman, or 'between the two.' It reintegrated themes developed by Plato and Aristotle in the context of the emergence of Rome as a world power. It came into particular focus in the time of the Second and Third Punic wars (218-146 BC), in which Rome confronted and defeated its arch rival Carthage and Carthage's principal ally Macedon. The Middle Stoa fortified the rising world empire, infusing it with its ethics and its vision of the universe. To the Middle Stoa emergent Rome seemed a natural stage in the integration of the World Soul. Zeno of Tarsus, a pupil of Chryssipus, who became the head of the school in 206 AD, is usually given as the first of the Middle Stoa, but the two greatest figures of the middle school were Panaetius (185-109 BC) and his pupil, Posidonius (135-51 BC).

PANAETIUS (185-109 BC)

Panaetius was a native of Rhodes, who traveled to study in Pergamon, Athens, and Babylon before moving to Rome, where he lived for more than a decade. In 129 BC he returned to the center of the Stoic school in Athens to become its head. He was thoroughly familiar with Plato and Aristotle and taught their doctrines as much as he did the Stoic. Indeed, his ethics were principally Aristotelian. He brought the existing Stoic ethics under the Aristotelian division of *ethikos* (practical ethics) and *dianoia* (the contemplation of the *nous*). Another Aristotelian doctrine that filtered through to Stoicism at this time was the realization of Sentient Being (the Prime Mover Unmoved) as pure activity – which fits perfectly with the Stoic doctrine of reintegration into the ethereal fire. Panaetius also questioned the original Stoic doctrine of periodic world conflagration.

More generally Panaetius softened the harsher ascetic doctrines of the Early Stoa, without departing from their principles. He modified the extreme individualism of Zeno and Cleanthes so that it might be related to the conduct of life in an empire which promised to be the next stage of manifestation of the World Spirit. In this way he adapted Stoicism to the needs of statesmen and soldiers, and it was through his doctrines that Stoic philosophy gradually became a part of the life of the Roman nobility.

In this context we can see why he chose to develop the Stoic idea of the Celestial City. The Celestial City is the universal city, of which all the cities of Man are but different rooms and apartments. When a man raises his being to the point where he begins to participate in the ethereal fire, he acquires a degree of universality. He becomes a citizen of the whole. Panaetius saw Rome as beginning to embody the principles of the Celestial City, and, in this regard, he saw Roman law as an expression of the *Logos* – the utterance of the Mind of God.

Panaetius' teachings greatly influenced the Roman consul Scipio Africanus and his circle of friends. This circle was influential in late Republican Rome and, in a way, prepared the ground for the transition to Rome's Imperial phase. Panaetius was active through several generations of the Scipionic circle. While known as an associate, he was actually a central figure in the group, which included many of the most prominent figures in Roman public life. We note that, while Posidonius was Panaetius' student, he operated independently, and while he was certainly connected with the Scipionic Circle – and would have been directly involved with it while he lived in Rome (87-86 BC) – he lived principally in Rhodes and Athens. We shall deal briefly with the activities of the Scipionic Circle here.

- *Scipio Africanus* was (as we shall later see) one of the greatest generals of Classical times. He was the Roman general principally responsible for the defeat of Carthage, which was an important precondition for the emergence of Augustan Rome. As the greatest general of his age, he embodied Stoic ideas in the very forefront of public life. The Scipionic Circle began to meet at his villa, and developed – over time – into a Stoic school, which evolved over several generations. It was comprised of both Greeks and Hellenized Romans; indeed it was the beginning of the transference of the center of the Stoic School from Athens to Rome.

- In the second generation of the Scipionic Circle came Scipio Africanus' nephew, *Scipio Aemilianus* (185-129 BC), who was the Roman general responsible for the final defeat of Carthage.

- Another member of this circle was the historian *Polybius* (200-118 BC) who saw, in the general convergence of the peoples of the Mediterranean world, a kind of cosmic drama – the emergence of an ecumenic (or universal) humanity. He did not take Rome to be the center of this drama, but the agency through which a great plan was being realized.

- In the third generation came the liberal reformers *Tiberius* and *Gaius Gracchus* (active 133-120 BC). They were the grandsons of Scipio Africanus and they ardently took up the egalitarian side of Stoicism, linking this with its ethos of service.

- The last great Republican politician, *Cicero* (106-43 BC), was a late member of the circle. In his writings, he tried to unite the Stoic teaching with Aristotelian ethics, and both of these to his own political practice as a Roman senator. The outstanding value of Cicero for posterity was that he was an example of a man who tried to evolve spiritually as a citizen, through service to his city. Following Panaetius and Polybius, he viewed Roman law as an expression of the *Logos*.

Probably figures like the Gracci and Cicero were only in the sphere of influence of the Scipionic Circle, yet they give clear evidence of what was happening within it. Stage by stage, the outlines of the Augustan principate seem to have been drawn by Stoic theorists.

POSIDONIUS (135-51 BC)

Posidonius studied under Panaetius in Athens and then traveled to Rhodes to study the sciences (and possibly to contact the school from which his teacher Panaetius had come). He became a citizen of that city and soon was promoted to high political office, which brought him into contact with the great Roman statesmen and generals of his time. He was closely associated with both Cicero and Pompey. In Posidonius we see clearly both Aristotelian ethics and Aristotelian science.

He related the daily tides to the moon's orbit, determined that tidal heights vary with the cycles of the moon, and hypothesized that yearly tidal cycles synchronized with the equinoxes and the solstices. He calculated the Earth's circumference, with reference to the star Canopus, at 24,000 miles, which is very close to today's calculation of 24,901 miles. He wrote on physics, astronomy, seismology, geology, mineralogy, hydrology, botany, ethics, logic, mathematics, history, and natural history – but he saw the emergent sciences (*episteme*) as subordinate to philosophy (*sophia*), as philosophy most nearly conforms to the reason of the World Spirit.

Posidonius emphasized the traditional Stoic doctrine that all men were equally members of the cosmos, and so equally a part of the divine plan. He felt, as did the members of the Scipionic Circle, that this plan was being realized in the growing *ecumene* created by the emergent Roman Empire. His most important contribution was to conceive the role of the ruler as servant to the plan. In his teaching the ruler was the 'housekeeper' of the emergent Celestial City; he was the servant and not the master. He had to do what the unfolding pattern indicated, and not what he himself wanted. To serve the plan both he and the ruling classes who worked under him had to overcome their personal desires and ambitions. This theme survived Posidonius to be taken up again – some two centuries later – by the Late Stoa and by the Nerva-Antonine emperors.

THE LATE STOA

The late Stoa we shall discuss in the context of Rome itself. With the *Pax Romana* that followed the Battle of Actium (31 BC) and brought Augustus Caesar to the place of the 'first citizen,' Stoicism entered more deeply into the veins of Roman civic life and became connected to the inner workings of the *cursus honorum*. Its greatest representatives are Epictetus and the Roman emperor Marcus Aurelius. What strongly suggests the influence of the Great Work in the work of the Late Stoa is the final refinement, simplification, and perfection of its teaching. It lets go of science and the more elaborate attempts at cosmology and theology to focus directly on the internal work and on duty in service both to the level one above and the level one below. The context for this double service did exist for a golden hour in Nerva-Antonine Rome (96-180 AD).

And so we see how the Stoic fusion of Platonism and Aristotelianism potentiated the Roman *ecumene*. What was seeded in the vital nexus of the archaic Greek polis now became part of the integument of the empire. By the time that Julius and Augustus Caesar took Roman polity to an imperial or international level, both Stoic philosophy and Hellenistic art had gone deeply into the fabric of the Roman civil service.

CHAPTER 36

Rome

The ancient Romans tell us that they were originally immigrants from Troy who fled the city in the wake of the Mycenaean conquest, which was so vividly described in Homer's *Iliad*. The Trojan prince Aeneas led his people to Latium, in the eastern-central part of the Italian peninsula, the area which surrounds what is now Rome. Just north of Latium was Etruria, the land of the Etruscans, which extended north to what is now Florence and east to what is now Venice. At first, there was normal trading and cultural exchange between the two peoples, but as their fortunes changed, rivalry and a struggle for control developed. Eventually they effectively merged under Roman leadership.

We know that the early Romans of Latium were shepherds and farmers and that their religion appears to have been a form of animism, where impersonal spirits were seen to inhabit rocks, trees, birds, heavenly bodies, human homes, and even individual men and women. The household gods were called the Lares, the goddess of the hearth was Vesta, and the list of gods extended to include all the experiences that made up a normal human life. These spirits were called collectively *numen*, and the spirit of a man himself was his *genius*.

A list of the early Roman kings in Latium survives, from the year 753 BC onward. Each of these kings ruled in conjunction with a circle of senators. At the end of the seventh century BC, an Etruscan dynasty of kings established itself, and from this period there was a tremendous influence of Etruscan culture and religion. Indeed in some ways the Etruscan civilization was a parent civilization to the Roman. This influence was most strongly expressed in architecture, which directly reflected the Etruscan religion. The Etruscans had an obsession with divination and prophecy and particularly with the art of reading the will of the gods through signs in the skies, such as lightning or the flight of birds. However it came about, the observance of omens and the offering of sacrifices became an integral part of Roman life. The Romans were naturally prone to the practices of sympathetic magic, augury, and astrology, and remained so for the entire life of their civilization. Generally stated, they were extremely sensitive to patterns of energy.

It is likely that the Roman success in war, and their remarkable capacities in town planning and law, derived from this sensitivity to patterns of energy and from their consequent ability to relate to changing patterns of energy in the affairs of the outside world. They learned quickly from each people with whom they came into contact.

Perhaps because the early Romans had little sense of a unifying deity, they were particularly open to the religion and culture of other peoples. The Greek city-states had begun to influence Rome even in the time of the Etruscan kings. The fact that the Romans internalized the elements of other religions never caused them to question the rituals of their earliest religion, which seems to have proven itself as an effective approach to life.

In 510 BC the Romans overthrew the Etruscan dynasty and established a Republic. In the period of the kings – both Roman and Etruscan – two distinct social strata had emerged, the patricians (aristocratic landholding families) and the plebians (small farmers, tradesmen, and servants). It is likely that the plebians worked together with the patricians to overthrow the Etruscans on the condition that a Republic be established, and it is likely too that the example of the Greek city-states was an influence. The new Republican government was comprised of three popular assemblies and a senate. Of these the Roman Senate was the most enduring and influential body. The Republic itself was an extremely complex system of checks and balances, and the government was the site of the most intense rivalries. While the government was predominantly patrician, all classes were directly involved.

In the newly formed Republic the 'conflict of the orders' – patrician and plebian – continued unabated. This struggle led ultimately to a system of universal law, known as the Valerio-Horatian laws. The Romans displayed a genius for law, and this has been one of their greatest gifts to Western civilization.

In the meantime, as the population of the city of Rome expanded, it came into conflict with its neighbors. Rivalries and systems of alliances developed, involving the other kingdoms of the Italian peninsula, which were, one after another, drawn into the general conflict. Rome was the victor, and, without having planned to be so, or even wanting to be so, became the master of Italy. As the city of Rome extended its holdings, it also extended its system of law and ultimately Roman citizenship itself.

At the time Rome began its expansion into the Italian peninsula, in the late fourth century BC, Philip of Macedon conquered Greece. His son Alexander then conquered the whole of the eastern Mediterranean, much of North Africa, and the whole of the Middle East. In so doing he conquered the great Phoenician cities of Asia Minor. The Phoenicians, however, regrouped in their stronghold city of Carthage in North Africa (modern Tunisia), just south of Italy. From this base, in the period after Alexander's death, they built an empire to rival and surpass the Macedonian, and from this point forward history knows the Phoenicians as the Carthaginians.

Carthage had interests in southern Italy and Sicily, and as Rome became the controlling power in that area, she found herself in conflict with the greatest power of the age. As this conflict between Rome and Carthage developed, a system of alliances formed throughout the eastern Mediterranean, and Macedon, at a certain point, decided to side with Carthage. Ultimately Rome triumphed over both Macedon and Carthage, sacking the city of Carthage in 149 BC.

As we noted, the Middle Stoa was deeply involved with the key players (on the Roman side) in the formative struggle between Rome and Carthage. We speak again of the Stoic Circle which included Scipio Africanus (who conquered Carthage while showing clemency to its people and to their general Hannibal) and Scipio Aemilianus (who finally defeated and destroyed Hannibal's forces). Thus, at a critical point, when everything hung in the balance, we see an infusion of conscious values into Roman public life.

Victory in the conflicts with Carthage and Macedonia, each an empire, suddenly left Rome in control of vast territories, inhabited by many different peoples. But the government of the Roman Republic had been designed to neutralize conflict in a small sixth-century city. It was not adequate to governing an empire which extended into Central Asia. In the early years of the empire, the conflict of the patricians and the plebians, now called the Social War, had continued unabated and weakened Rome's imperial polity. There were unceasing factional struggles and a succession of *coups d'etat*. Finally the strongman Cornelius Sulla (138-78 BC) accrued power to himself and was able to stabilize the city. This allowed Rome to perform internationally and to generate a set of provisional solutions for the Social War. Sulla was then followed by a triumvirate of generals: Pompey, Crassus, and Julius Caesar. Each of these men had a presence, both within the empire and in the city. Conflict developed among the three, and a struggle ensued which raged through the entire Mediterranean basin. Julius Caesar emerged as the victor, and Caesar then replaced Sulla as the single head of state. He was a remarkably gifted man who developed a complete administrative system for the city of Rome, whose population had now reached the one-million mark. He launched architectural projects, created a fire department, a police department, and a system of famine relief. At the same time he stabilized the empire and won the respect of many of its subject peoples. Yet he incurred the hatred of the Republican senators whom he had effectively displaced, and he was murdered by a group of them in 44 BC. Civil war then followed, and eventually Octavian (63 BC to 14 AD), Caesar's grand nephew and adopted son, triumphed.

In 27 BC Octavian took the title Augustus Caesar, and he ruled for forty-one years, until 14 AD. He showed a genius equal to that of Julius Caesar, but of a different kind. He was the supreme statesman. He knit the elements of Roman society together and laid the foundation for an imperial civil service. It was Augustus who initiated the *Pax Romana*, bringing peace to the entire Mediterranean basin for the better part of three centuries. Trade became possible on a scale that had never been known before; regional economies of scale emerged, and craft production of different kinds flourished in all parts of the empire. Augustus Caesar had defined a new order and so established Rome as the Universal City.

Augustus, and the men around him, formulated the program under which the Empire was to be established under the influence of Posidonius' teachings. They accepted the Stoic doctrine of the 'divine plan' and the idea of the role of the ruler – and of the ruling classes – as the 'housekeepers' to that plan. The establishment of Rome was, in their view, a turning point in the reassertion of the 'centrality' of the ethereal fire. The mission of Rome was to pacify and civilize the world so that Mankind might return to its source. In this view the destiny of Rome becomes a central concern of providence.

The poet Virgil – almost certainly a conscious being – was a close friend and confederate of Augustus and a direct participant in his vision of the Eternal City. In his epic, the *Aeneid*, he makes many direct parallels between its hero, Aeneas, and the Emperor Augustus himself. Whereas Homer's heroes – Achilles, Menelaos, and Hector – make their own tragic choices and must abide by the consequences that follow from them, Virgil's hero Aeneas is concerned to serve the emergent archetype of the Eternal City. He must constantly suppress his personal desires for the sake of a duty that has been imposed upon him. He must school himself and his men to the acceptance of destiny and to the service of a divine plan.

We have described the period of the end of the Republic and the beginning of the Empire, but let us look more closely at the cultural developments that occurred during this time. During the three Macedonian wars (221-168 BC), when Rome conquered

– one after another – the Greek city-states, she was herself conquered by the Greek culture that she discovered there.

The formative impact of Hellenic and Hellenistic art on the Roman Civilization began with the Roman conquest of the Greek cities on the Italian peninsula. As the Romans entered Tarentum in 272 BC they had their first close look at a complete Greek civic environment. They saw the calculated *symmetria* of Greek architecture and the superb marble representations of the archetype of Man – and from this date Greek art began to enter Rome in a steadily growing stream. Plutarch noted that the sack of Syracuse, in 211 BC, marked the beginning of a major cultural ferment in Rome.

At the battle of Pydna, in 168 BC, the Roman general Lucius Aemilius Paullus defeated the Antigonids and so brought to an end the Macedonian monarchy. Plutarch reports that when the Roman army returned with its spoils, "a whole day was barely sufficient to see the statues that had been seized and the paintings and colossal images." These included a statue of Athena by Phidias, which was one of the best-known pieces of the Greek high Classical period.

The Roman historian Strabo states that "the best of the public monuments of Rome" came from the destruction of Corinth in 146 BC. We speculate that this would have included many of the works of the renowned Greek sculptor Polykleitos.

In 133 BC came the integration of the Kingdom of Pergamon, which borders the Mediterranean in eastern Asia Minor. Its ruler, Attalus III, made a bequest to Rome of both the city and the kingdom of its name, which was – at that time – the greatest cultural center in the Hellenistic world. Many Romans discovered what it was like to visit and to live in one of the most artistically refined cities of all time.

As the interest in Greek art intensified, in what was fast becoming the largest city in the world, new patronage became available. Many Greek workshops relocated to Rome or established Roman branches. Copies of existing masterpieces could be created on request. By the first century BC Rome had become permeated through and through by Greek culture and Greek art, and had become itself an influential center of Hellenistic art. The ideal note that Greece sounded continued to resonate through the body of Roman Civilization throughout its longer life. In the remains of the Roman libraries that have been excavated, the greater part of the manuscripts are in Greek. While the exposure to Greek culture began with the conquests of the Republican period, the true integration of that culture began from the time of Augustus.

And all of this was incorporated into the great Augustan building plans. In the century that followed the Macedonian wars, Rome embraced the Hellenic way of life.

Figure 71. **The Roman Pantheon**

The patricians became effectively bilingual, and it became the custom that Roman aristocrats be raised by Greek nursemaids. Rome, then, carried Hellenistic culture into the entire Mediterranean basin. The combination of Hellenistic culture and Roman law created the social space in which the Christian Religion was later to develop.

The Stoic philosophers, who had been active in the Roman Republic, became a formative influence in the vast civil service which developed in the early years of empire. These years saw the birth of a true service aristocracy. The career path followed by a civil servant was called the *cursus honorum* or 'course of honors.' This was the sequence of military and administrative posts that a Roman official had to pass through in the course of his working life – and its defining values were Stoic. The *cursus honorum* was intended as a rounded education, a training in public services, and a selective test of ability. To the extent that it was possible, the space of the *es meson* was replicated in the course of honors. The emperor himself was the product of this system, but should the delicate system of checks and balances that made the system work fail, a deviant emperor was a very real possibility.

We know that Rome expanded by incorporating other cities and peoples into its own system and then extending the rights of Roman citizenship to all qualifying free men. The *Pax Romana* was thus conceived as universal; it was a network of self-governing subordinate cities, tributary kingdoms, and tribes, each living by its own customary

Figure 72. **Interior of the Baths of Diocletian, now Santa Maria degli Angeli**

laws in the context of the universal system of Roman law. The Roman Empire was pantheistic, acknowledging the different religious beliefs and cultures of its component peoples – providing only that they did not violate the principles of Roman law and Roman civic life.

Understanding the Stoic theory we can feel the force of the pantheon (all gods) as the precursor of the absorption of the universe into the ethereal fire (World 6).

The Roman civil service thus became the carrier of Hellenistic culture. The kind of educated artistic patronage that evolved in Greece continued in Imperial Rome, and many of the workshops of the Greek artisans actually relocated to Rome.

The Stoic philosophers, from the time of the Roman Republic, had defined a way of active service. Aristotelian ethics had combined the Doctrine of the Mean with the realization of Sentient Being as pure activity, unadulterated by any dross of matter. The Aristotelian doctrines fused with the work of the Middle Stoa, and this defined a path of awakening which could be pursued in the midst of the world and other men. The universality of the later Stoic thinkers combined with the universal principles implicit in Roman law to create a remarkable environment for Roman architecture and Roman town planning.

The rule of the Antonine emperors – Trajan, Hadrian, Antoninus Pius, and Marcus Aurelius – represents the Golden Age of Imperial Rome.

The foundations of the Age of the Antonines had been laid by the activities of the Late Stoa, from the time of Augustus. The most important Stoics of the first century AD were Seneca, Annaeus Cornutus, Musonius Rufus, and towards the end of the century, Epictetus. It was Stoicism that gave a philosophical basis to the aristocratic opposition to the succession of emperors who attempted to rule without the senate (Caligula, Nero, Galba, and Domitian). The principle opponents of Nero – Helvidius Priscus, Paetus Thrasea, and Rubellius Plautus – were all Stoics, as was Junius Rusticus, who was condemned to death under Domitian. But the most important figure of the Late Stoa was the Emperor Marcus Aurelius (121-180, ruled 161-180 AD), in whose being the ethos of an enlightened civil service reached supreme expression, and who himself left us an example of conscious service that is unmatched.

The following passages from Book XI of Marcus Aurelius' *Meditations* allow us to see what the *cursus honorum* of second-century Rome was – at least in certain moments – based upon. Book XI begins with a depiction of the Work of the Steward, and continues to describe the laws that govern the universe.

> The properties of the Rational Soul [HJ: the Steward] are these: it sees itself, dissects itself, molds itself to its own will, and itself reaps its own fruits [HJ: an ever-deepening presence], whereas the fruits of the animal and vegetable kingdoms are reaped by others. It always has its work before it, perfectly complete, and so is complete at whatever moment life reaches its appointed end. Unlike dances or plays, where if they are suddenly cut short the performance is left imperfect, the soul, no matter at what stage arrested, will have her task complete to her own satisfaction, and be able to say, 'I have to the full what is my own' [HJ: presence self-aware]. More than this, it can encompass the whole universe at will, both its structure and the void surrounding it, and can reach out into the infinitude of time, embracing and comprehending the great cyclic renewals of creation, and thereby perceiving that future generations will have nothing new to witness, even as our forefathers beheld nothing more than we of today, so that if a man comes to his fortieth year, and has any grain of understanding, he has seen – thanks to their similarity – all possible happenings, both past and to come. Finally, the properties of the rational soul include love of neighbors, truthfulness, modesty, and to prize nothing above itself – a characteristic also of law. In this way, then, the Reason that is right reason, and the Reason that is Justice are one.[1]

---

1. Author's translation of *Meditations*, Book 11, paragraph 1, with reference to Maxwell Staniforth's translation (*Marcus Aurelius: Meditations*, Penguin, 1964, p. 165) and the Loeb Classical Library translation of C.R. Haines, p. 293.

We may ask what contemporary head of state could speak in this way, from his personal experience? And it was Marcus Aurelius who left us with the leitmotif of the Great Work: "to have few tools, but to have them always close to hand and use them well." This is reminiscent of Plato's reference to "the briefest of formulas." Both refer to the 'concentration of the Steward' in the direct work to enable Higher Centers.

All of this is to emphasize that the Graeco-Roman experiment was a major watershed in the history of Mankind. Here, in the Mediterranean basin, there came into being – for the first time – an ecumenic humanity, transcending ethnic, regional, and cultural differences. There was open communication and trade between the peoples of Western Europe, the entire Mediterranean basin, North Africa, and the Levant. There was a universal system of law, and into that social space there came not one but a series of World Religions – Judaic, Christian, Manichean, Mithraic, and later Islamic.

Of course Rome fell in stages and over many centuries. As Imperial Rome slowly disintegrated, a new Christian Civilization began to rise in its stead. But for a long time the two coexisted, one within the other. Perhaps it was the unrealized potential of Roman Civilization to have raised its civic life to a level where it could integrate the work of the emergent Christian Spiritual Tradition, and through that Tradition regenerate itself as a School Civilization? We keep in mind that the Roman Civilization did ultimately accept the Christian Religion, and that, in the time of the Italian Renaissance, a profound fusion of Classical culture and the Christian values did occur.

We ask, then, could Classical Civilization and the Christian Tradition have merged in the ecumenic humanity of the second century AD? Could the magnificent cultural synthesis that we glimpse in the Italian Renaissance have been achieved 1,000 years earlier, when both Traditions were still in their prime? Could this have become the culture of Mankind's first School Civilization? And, as a result, could Western Man have been saved the long night of the Dark Ages?

There was rigidity and intolerance on both the Roman and the Christian sides, but there were also towering figures, like Augustine, who transcended the divide. Augustine's vision of the *City of God* had deep roots in Chryssipus' Stoic vision of the Celestial City, and – of course – in Plato's *Republic*. It was Augustine who said, so eloquently, that true civilizational order is "a group of people bound together by the common possession of the things which they love."

The possibility of a synthesis of Christian and Classical Civilizations did exist, but in the line of time that we are in, the elements were not in place for this synthesis to occur. The *cursus honorum,* as a formative influence in the Imperial civil service, disintegrated steadily after the principate of Marcus Aurelius (180 AD). The unrelenting pressure from the Visigoths, the Ostrogoths, the Vandals, and the Huns, weakened Rome economically and brought the military arm of the Empire to the fore. In the third century AD power politics permanently displaced the balanced training-in-service of the old *cursus honorum,* and as a result of this the civilizational order itself declined.

For all of these reasons the coming of Constantine as the first Christian Emperor in 306 did not represent a merging of the Christian and Classical worlds. Classical culture was already failing in the late second century, and by the time of Constantine there was no Classical center that could integrate Christianity into itself. Thus the fledgling Christian Civilization began to develop within the defensive fortress that was the 'shell' of the old Classical Civilization. In 410 Alaric sacked the city of Rome, and in 476 Odoacer displaced the last Western Roman Emperor, Romulus Augustulus. When the Classical order finally gave way, the fledgling Christian Civilization, which had just begun to replace it, was severely set back, and a general social regression ensued. The Greek language was lost, and even the use of Latin was increasingly confined to the Church.

By the sixth century the Rome of Augustus, Vespasian, and Hadrian was only a memory. At the same time the Civilization of the emergent Christian West was being significantly undermined by:

1. The disintegration of Classical civic life and the old Roman system of education, and

2. The rapid integration of vast numbers of 'barbarian' peoples into the Christian religion, with the subsequent dilution of its teachings.

With the decline in general intellectual culture Christian theology in the Western Empire was frozen until the time of Thomas Aquinas. Thus the cultural ideals of the Classical Civilization were destroyed before the embryonic Christian Civilization was able to integrate and reformulate them. By the late sixth century only the skeletal form of the Western Monastic Orders remained as the blueprint for a brave new world.

We are much the less for the collapse of Classical Civilization; many things were lost that were never recovered. This is not to denigrate the Medieval Christian Civilization that followed, but this first post-classical civilization only came into being after many centuries of social disorder. Medieval Christian Civilization has its own achievements and must be measured by its own lights. The loss of Classical Civilization was a loss for every Civilizational Order to follow in the Western line.

Humanity did not again come to the 'ecumenic feeling' that was intrinsic to the Classical World until the nineteenth century. This happened under the pressures of **1)** the first Industrial Revolution, **2)** an emergent world market, **3)** developing imperial systems, and **4)** the rise of the international socialist movement. While their political allegiances differed, nineteenth- and twentieth-century figures like Giuseppe Mazzini, Matthew Arnold, Abraham Lincoln, Jacob Burckhardt, Bernard Bosanquet, Benedetto Croce, Jan Smuts, Cordell Hull, Albert Schweitzer, Raymond Aaron, and Dag Hammarskjold were strongly resonant of the spirit of civic life in Classical times. And, indeed, each one of these men was well-educated in the classics.

✠ BOOK VI ✠

The Middle Ages and the Rise of the West

Post-Classical Western history begins in the line of the Prophetic Civilizations, with the Christian Civilization reaching its apogee in what we call the Middle Ages, and the Islamic Civilization appearing as its counterpoint. But, with the coming of the Italian Renaissance, the Western family of Civilizations sees a reawakening of the archetype that was first revealed in ancient Greece and Rome. Modernity, as we know it, has its origins in this Classical Archetype – where civic life plays a central role. Knowing this helps us to reconstruct the aims of the Spiritual Traditions of the Renaissance, of the Enlightenment, and of post-Enlightenment modern times. As we see the recovery of the Classical ideal, the trajectory of Western history reveals the penumbral image of a School Civilization.

CHAPTER 37

General Reflections on the West

We must begin by defining historical terms, for what is called the Middle Ages – the period between the end of the Roman Empire and the rise of the Absolutist Monarchies in Europe – spans a full millennium. Conventional historical periodization, which we accept, breaks it into three significantly different periods: The Early Middle Ages, The High Middle Ages, and The Late Middle Ages.

The Early Middle Ages (from the overthrow of the last Roman emperor by the Ostogothic King Odoacer in the year 476 to about the year 1000) reveal the tremendous struggle of the Western Monastic Orders to sustain the Work of the Steward and to secure Civilizational Order.

In fact it is problematic to begin the Middle Ages directly from the end of the Roman Empire. The first three centuries of the Early Middle Ages are better described as a transitional period, because the landholding system used under late the Roman Empire – the villa system – was still in place. This system was based on the classical institution of slavery, which was both inefficient and technologically sterile, becoming unworkable as the classical form of slavery became impossible to maintain. The real Middle Ages – as that is represented in our art and literature – came into being with the feudal system of landholding, and the new social order that was based on that system. This change did not occur until well into the ninth century.

In the High Middle Ages (1000-1300) we see the consolidation of the feudal way of life. A close working link developed between **1)** the monastically-based Traditions, **2)** a generally accepted Religion, and **3)** the various governments of Europe. It was the golden age of the Monastic Orders of Europe. There was also a growing connection between Europe and the world that existed outside of it.

In the Late Middle Ages (1300-1480) we see the increasing centralization of the European monarchies and the development of cities. There is also a great increase of mercantile activity and a stream of incoming influence from the Classical and the Islamic Civilizations. The Monastic Orders, and the Spiritual Traditions contained within them, lost ground, both within the Church and in the general theater of European life.

With the flowering of the Italian Renaissance, which actually occurred in the Late Middle Ages, an entirely new development occurred. We see, in the Italian city-states, a re-emergence of the Classical ideal of the Cosmos of Man, and, beginning from that, a remarkable development of secular thought and culture. And here there is an important qualification. By 'secular' we mean 'not religious.' We do not mean 'not sacred.' Secular thought, like the teaching of the Roman Stoics, or the works of Plato and Aristotle, is well capable of moving in the realm of the sacred. Examples of the sacred in Renaissance culture would include **1)** the recovery of the Classical theory of Eros, **2)** the ability to relate art directly to the experience of Higher Centers, and **3)** the ability to anticipate the conditions for the emergence of a School Civilization. This development of Western thought, at least in its higher range of expression, is the result of the work of a Renaissance Spiritual Tradition, which we shall call the School of the Renaissance. The School of the Renaissance coexisted with the Monastic Traditions of its time, and sometimes – although not consistently – found itself at odds with them. This School was to survive the Italian city-states and work to form the post-Medieval world.

Historically, it was the Absolutist Monarchies (1480-1914) which succeeded both **1)** the city-states of the Italian Renaissance and **2)** the Kingdoms and Duchies of the High Middle Ages. Under the Absolutist Monarchies the School (or Schools) of the Renaissance became more generally connected with the Life of Europe. But we must define the term 'Absolutist Monarchy' before going further, as it describes the stable form of post-feudal society which gives the context for the development of our theme from the sixteenth through nineteenth centuries.

The Absolutist Monarchies came into being at the point when the monarch, as representative of the national government, was able to assert clear supremacy over the nobility, enabling a centralization of power. This process began in the Late Middle Ages but took a more definite form from about 1480. It enabled the introduction of standing armies, a permanent bureaucracy, national taxation, codified law, and the beginnings of a unified market. The weakening of the nobility at the end of the High Middle Ages coincided with the disappearance of serfdom, the emergence of a 'free' labor force, and the consequent rise of the merchants and the business classes. The centralized monarchies, and the new infrastructures that they supported, enabled a new range of social classes to coexist. It also enabled many different forms of patronage, so that the maturation of the Absolutist Monarchies ushers in the Baroque Period in art from about 1600.

The Absolutist Monarchies came into existence at an interstice of history, where many of the elements of society could be united in a new way. It is part of the pattern of history that, in this period, unusually gifted individuals – like Henri IV of France, Elizabeth I of England, Peter the Great of Russia, or Frederick the Great of Prussia – sometimes came to play the role of monarch. Under such leadership certain of the new monarchical states became examples of what was called 'Enlightened Absolutism.'

Taken as a whole, the Absolutist Monarchies were a turning point in what is called the 'Rise of the West.' This period saw a marked decrease in the influence of the Church and a further expansion of secular life. It also saw a definite loss of place for the Monastic Orders of the Church. It is in the time of the Absolutist Monarchies – and partly as a result of the power struggles of the Absolutist Kings – that Christian unity is lost, and the wars of the Reformation (beginning from Martin Luther's 95 Theses in 1517) and Counter-Reformation (beginning from the Council of Trent in 1545) get under way.

In these pages we put forward the idea that the cultural 'Renaissance,' which began in the Italian city-states, took root and continued in the emergent Absolutist Monarchies, so that we can – without contradiction – speak of Renaissance Absolutism. From this point of view, the term 'Renaissance Civilization' can be applied to both Baroque and Enlightenment Europe, and in the same way we can say that the 'Renaissance' is still with us.

It may be that, in the original plan for humanity, the Italian Renaissance was a turning point, in which a new potential might – or might not – be realized. Perhaps the Spiritual Traditions that emerged in the Italian Renaissance might have merged more fully with the civic life of the Italian city-states, and, in a second phase of development, merged more fully with the emergent dynastic states of Europe. They might then have entered yet more deeply into the life of the Absolutist Monarchies, and particularly the Enlightened Absolutists. Here we see the potential for a full realization of the Cosmos of Man under the leadership of the Schools of the Renaissance.

The transition of the Renaissance Spiritual Traditions from the Italian city-states to the emergent Absolutist Monarchies of Europe was made possible both by **1)** the direct patronage of the nobility and the kings and **2)** the increasingly neutral social space created by the new forms of civic life. In this more neutral space unifying and socially integrating projects could be launched.

If the Enlightened Absolutist Monarchies had become integrated with the Renaissance Traditions, the principle of the Cosmos of Man might have been fully realized in this context as a means of creating an open or working connection to Higher School. This would have made possible a 'secular' religion, transcending previous religious forms, and so a School Civilization. Panaetius' vision of the Celestial City might then have been restated in a terminology appropriate to Baroque Europe. At this point we might expect a Tradition capable of integrating the work of other Traditions.

But for this to occur there would have to have been, somewhere in the Late Middle Ages, a handover from the Monastic Traditions to the Schools of the Renaissance. A handover of what? Of the developed techniques of the Work of the Steward, including the willingness to share literally centuries of experience in helping spiritual aspirants through the difficult transitions of the Great Work. Perhaps, in some line of time where more of our potentials are realized, the work of the Monastic Traditions would have burst its religious shell and – somewhere in the fifteenth century – infused deeper life into newly emergent forms of the Cosmos of Man.

If such potentials had been built into the Italian Renaissance, they were certainly not realized in the line of time that we are in. The Schools of the Renaissance never, at any point, became Ruling Traditions. While we do see the traces of the completed Cosmos of Man in Renaissance Europe, it did not achieve its completed form, either at this time or in the centuries to follow. In fact the failure to realize the Cosmos of Man in the Renaissance/Baroque period was accompanied by a weakening of the Monastic Orders of the Western Church and a radical decline of Living Religion. As a result we see a general secularization of society – to a degree never before known in history. And, particularly from the nineteenth century onward, as traditional societies were swept into the maelstrom of the Industrial Revolution, this process of secularization became the inheritance of humanity at large. Indeed, in the period since the first Industrial Revolution – from the mid-nineteenth century – we appear to have lost our sense of the sacred.

When we consider the unrealized potentials of the Italian Renaissance, we can see that the process of secularization that actually occurred in Europe differed greatly from the secularization that would have come from a full realization of the Cosmos of Man. We could say that the latter process would rightly begin 'from the top down,' whereas the process that actually occurred developed 'from the bottom up.' In the former you would have a kind of secularization that enabled new forms of the sacred, making formerly secular activities into vehicles for the Great Work. In the latter you have a secularization that is directly opposed to the sacred, and that is based on the will to power and the drive for material gain.

Simply put, Europe, in the fifteenth and sixteenth centuries, was not in a position to support the kind of civic life that would have enabled a completed Cosmos of Man. And in this regard it was not different from other civilizations at other times of history. The Cosmos of Man represents a level that humanity has never been able to sustain, even in dynastic Egypt and ancient Tibet. The fact that Europe did not succeed in no way diminishes the glorious accomplishments of the Renaissance and Baroque periods. The Renaissance in Italy was indeed the dawn of a new age, but – beginning from the French invasion of Italy – Europe faced a backlash from the unresolved contradictions of its feudal past. These came through with full force in the wars of the Reformation and Counter-Reformation, where the tensions between church and state reached their apogee. The increasingly independent monarchies wanted to define their own terms independently of the Church. And if the Pope did not serve their interests, they wanted a religion that would. The fragmentation of the universal church into competing churches and the weariness with religious strife greatly hastened the general process of secularization 'from the bottom up' that was to characterize the centuries to follow.

It was in this theater – and partly as a result of these religious and social crises – that the mercantile classes came to the fore, promoting a secular worldview based on purely practical considerations. This view was grounded, not on a new vision of public life, but on the expansion of the sphere of private economic practice. While it was 'progressive' and legitimate on the level on which it was conceived, it was completely divorced from any understanding of the true nature of human potential. It needed to be complemented by something else, and it wasn't. The secularization 'from the bottom up' that occurred from the fourteenth century onwards was not, however, simply the result of the self-interest of monarchs and the rapacity of the merchants. The Church itself abetted this process. In the Papal Schism of 1378-1417 and in the debilitating wars of the Reformation and the Counter-Reformation, faith in the Church began to fail.

As the Monastic Orders weakened Living Religion was increasingly replaced by a formalized system of belief reinforced with ritual. This sometimes reduced to simple religious ideology, which served the purpose of ensuring social stability. We are not here condemning Religion, or denouncing the economic motives that came to the fore with the development of the commodity markets. We are trying to describe a more fundamental social change, that is evidenced in both religious practice and economic life. Some sense of the connectedness of things, some intuition of the cosmic hierarchy, some feeling for the underlying unity of Man in Nature, was lost. It was replaced by a drab, flat, spread-out view of the world – comprised of disparate objects, accidental events, and arbitrary relationships. The world became, increasingly, an arid flatland in which it was 'every man for himself.' Causality in the created universe was no longer seen to work from the top down but from the bottom up. The poetry and the life of the world was thus reduced, and the intuitive sense of man's relation to a higher level was proportionately diminished. Something that had been carried forward from the traditional societies, through the age of the Prophets, was being gradually but certainly undermined and dissolved.

We emphasize that this is not a condemnation of Western European Civilization as it actually developed. For Renaissance Europe to have succeeded in making a 'secular religion' of the Cosmos of Man, it would have to have received a more definite legacy from the civilizations that preceded it. Both Classical Civilization and Early Christianity would have to have accomplished tasks they were unable to accomplish. We speculate that Europe's original potential was to integrate the culture of the Classical World and the work of the Orthodox and Catholic Traditions of Christianity with the first flower of the Renaissance in Italy. Its destiny – independently of its potential – was to allow the emergence of a theater of civic life, to enable the development of science, and to foster the first and second Industrial Revolutions. The achievement of this destiny, with a full recrudescence of the forms of civic life that existed in the Greek *polis* and a full development of modern science, would have been an achievement difficult to imagine. With such a synthesis behind it Western European Civilization would clearly have had the potential to assimilate all that had been understood by the Vedantic, Sufi, and Tibetan Traditions.

We do see the shadows of such a synthesis. We see evidence of an attempt to integrate Classical, Christian, and Renaissance culture in the work of men like Johann Goethe, Immanuel Kant, G. W. F. Hegel, Jacob Burkhardt, and Bernard Berenson. We see focused attempts to bring the 'wisdom of the East' to the industrialized West in the work of men like Narenda Vivekananda, Inayat Khan, George Gurdjieff, Peter Ouspensky, Meher Baba, and Chogyam Trungpa. While each of these men worked with considerable understanding, we can say, with hindsight, that Western Civilization was only able to integrate their work in a superficial way. Again, this is not a judgment of the West, because to have succeeded would have been to eclipse all human achievement to this point. The fact that this extraordinary synthesis did not occur is not simply the fault of Modern Europe, nor is it due to insufficient effort on the part of the individuals mentioned; it is the fault of all the failures that occurred in all the previous phases of Western Civilization.

These, then, are our questions and concerns. Let us review the history itself.

CHAPTER 38

The Middle Ages

We begin with the turning point, the fall of the Western Roman Empire in 476, understanding that this was only the beginning of a much longer period of decline, which reached its lowest point in the Dark Ages of the ninth and tenth centuries.

In the early ninth century, Charlemagne attempted to recenter the remains of the Western Empire in a Christian context. All across Europe there was a glimmer of hope for the return of the *Pax Romana* under a Christian ruler. Charlemagne behaved as a Christian king and strongly affirmed the Church in his actions, and as a result Pope Leo III crowned him Holy Roman Emperor on Christmas Day of the year 800. This act symbolized a unity of temporal and spiritual powers in Western Christianity. Charlemagne attempted to put this unity into practice in his relations with the papacy and – more specifically – by attempting to restore the education system to Classical standards, by preserving Classical texts, by establishing authoritative versions of the Bible and the liturgical books, and by developing a new script – the Carolingian miniscule – that became the standard for the next four centuries.

The vision of the unity of Christian church and state had been a central theme of Augustine's *City of God*, and it was part of the 'archetypal form' of Medieval Europe. But it was a vision that would not be realized in the ninth century for, within a generation of the death of Charlemagne, Europe slipped down into the depths of the Dark Ages. Yet the note sounded by Charlemagne was never forgotten: it was a true harbinger of the High Middle Ages yet to come.

With the collapse of the Carolingian Empire in the mid-ninth century, Western Civilization disintegrated into a multiplicity of baronial fiefdoms in a state of almost continual war. To add to this, the Norsemen, the Magyars of Hungary, and the Arabian Saracens surged over Europe in destructive waves. Byzantium continued to hold its own in the East, but the civilization of Western Europe almost completely disintegrated. It was the Monastic Orders who carried Spiritual Tradition, Living Religion, and Civilizational Order through this Dark Age, and to them we owe an incalculable debt.

Looking at the very lengthy transition from the Early Middle Ages, beginning in 476 to the stabilization of a Christian Civilization in the High Middle Ages around 1000, we can distinguish four phases of Christianity relevant to our study: **1)** Early Christianity, **2)** the Crisis of the Church and the rise of the Monastic Orders, **3)** the time in which Christian (or High Medieval) Civilization was actually achieved, and **4)** the retreat and retrenchment of the Monastic Orders in the period of the rise of the Absolutist Monarchies.

Preceding these four periods was the Apostolic period, from the year 30 to the year 100 when the Apostle John died. Following them there is the period of secularization which corresponds to the rise of the Absolutist Monarchies.

1. ***Early Christianity*** is dated from the year 100 to about 530. This is known as the period of the Church Fathers, or the Patristic period. Christian theologians normally close the period with the death of the last great classical theologian, Saint Augustine, in 430. But for another full century the shell of the Classical Civilization continued to provide a context for development of the Christian Religion. If we take Early Christianity to be the period in which the Christian Religion developed in the context of the Roman Empire, it does not come to a close until 530. The Early Christian period culminated in the Christian Religion becoming the state religion of the Western Empire, under the Emperor Constantine who ruled from 306 to 337.

2. ***The crisis of the Western Church and the development of Western Monasticism*** lasted from about 530 to 950. This corresponds, very approximately, to the Early Middle Ages. With the fall of the Roman Empire, the Civilizational Order itself rapidly deteriorated. The educational system broke down and Classical Greek went out of usage, which was a crisis for both the Civilizational Order and for the Christian Church. The Roman Civilization had failed without a defined Civilizational Order to replace it. Whereas, from its inception, the Church had attracted people with a Classical or Judaic culture, who fully understood the implications of their conversion, it was now faced with the problem of integrating many illiterate peoples without any such culture. These peoples came as conquering invaders and had to be negotiated with, from a postion of relative weakness. Would the teaching of the Church be significantly diluted in

the process of integrating these peoples? The Western Church faced a profound threat with the destruction of its civilizational base. It was the Monastic Orders who preserved the elements necessary to sustain the Spiritual Tradition and the Living Religion through a period of civilizational malaise. This Great Work began when Saint Benedict founded the monastery at Monte Cassino in 530.

3. ***The stabilization of the Christian Church*** and of Christian civilization corresponds to the High Middle Ages in Europe, which began with the emergence of the feudal social system – beginning from about 950 or 975. Here we see a much-expanded role for the Monastic Orders, which continued up until 1200 and then declined until the end of the period in 1350. The decline of the monasteries ran in parallel with a rise of Scholasticism, the Cathedral Schools, and finally the Universities. The High Middle Ages came to a close with the rise of the centralized European monarchies.

4. ***The period of retreat and retrenchment of the Monastic Orders*** began with the emergence of the great European nation states and the rapid development of secular life. The Church itself was increasingly fragmented in relation to national polity.

To follow the trajectory of the Middle Ages we shall begin by reviewing the achievement of Early Christianity, and continue through to the period of retreat and retrenchment. We shall then provide a brief outline of the life of the central Spiritual Tradition of Eastern Christianity in this same period.

Early Christianity

We have already discussed Early Christianity in our outline of the emergence of the Christian Religion. Our concern here is not with the 'golden beginnings' of the Christian Church but with what Early Christianity was able to leave to **1)** the institution of the Western Church and **2)** the Western Monastic Orders. As we noted, the period of Early Christianity begins with the death of the last Apostle, John, in about 100 AD and ends in about 530 AD. In this 450 years both the form of the Christian Church and its essential theology were defined. The most prominent Christians of this time are known as the 'Church Fathers.' They were the spiritual leaders of the church in Classical times and they were the first Christian theologians. This group would include Basil of Caesarea, Gregory of Nyssa, Pantaenus, Clement, and Origen, whom we discussed in Chapter 31. The theological achievements of this period continue through to the death of the last Church Father, Augustine of Hippo, in 430. During this time Platonism was central to Christian theology, and mystical experience (the experience of Higher Centers) was – within theological discourse – still given priority over rationalist logic and dialectical proof.

The Patristic thinkers claimed that the wisdom of Plato and the Greeks was a result of the inspiration of the *Logos*. It was therefore God's truth, as that found expression through pre-Christian minds. The highest wisdom of the Classical World was not seen to be in contradiction with the supernatural revelation contained in the Gospels. It was understood as having been given before the coming of Christ in order to create the context for the Christian Church. More generally, we find – in Basil, Origen, and Augustine – the idea that there are two orders of truth, the supernatural and the natural. It is the aim of the Church to bring these two orders into harmony; faith aids reason and reason aids faith. In their work the Early Fathers succeeded in integrating what had been given as the 'Classical' context of Christianity, and this was an important achievement – for this context was about to be stripped away.

The Patristic era ended in the sixth century, when, with the decay of the Western Roman Empire, humanities scholarship in Europe slipped down into 'survival mode.' The theology of the Church was then as complete as it was going to be for the next seven hundred years!

To understand this process we must understand the implications of the decay of the Roman educational system and the loss of the Greek language in the Western Empire. This was a disaster, because real scholarship of all kinds was in Greek – and so, in ancient times, nobody had bothered to translate Greek into Latin. They wrote either in Greek, for one purpose, or in Latin, for another. At the time when the Roman *cursus honorum* collapsed and the Classical *paideia* came to an end, most of the literature that was of interest to Christians was available only in Greek. Late Roman attempts to translate Greek writings into Latin had met with very limited success. With the coming of Constantine in 312, there was a further rigidification of cultural life. The open, tolerant, pluralistic system of the late Roman Empire was replaced by a system based on a rule of fixed authority. Education became both more limited and more formalistic. We note that, with the passing of Greek, real philosophical acumen passed out of the West for a full millennium – until the publication of Thomas Aquinas' *De Ente Et Essentia* (On Being and Essence) in 1255.[1]

After Emperor Constantine there began a real process of de-urbanization, which was attended by a marked decline in literacy. Justinian, in his time, actually suppressed Classical literature in the Western Empire, so relatively little came through to the High Middle Ages from the Western side. In the fifth century the schools closed, and there was only the Church. Within the Church there was **1)** the education that occurred within the Monastic Orders and **2)** the education provided by the Cathedral Schools, that is, lay Christians teaching young people. We will look at each of these in turn.

The Monastic education system preserved a treasury of the Gospels, the Old Testament, and the theology of the Early Fathers. It also preserved Latin as the universal European language, for even this was under threat. What, then, was the *corpus* of the Monastic Orders, going into the Dark Ages? Because Greek had fallen out of usage, any relevant texts had to have been already translated into Latin. (Had this not been the case the works of Plato and Aristotle would certainly have been included.) The principal works that were preserved were naturally those of the Church Fathers: Clement of Alexandria, Origen, Pseudo-Dionysius the Areopagite, Ambrose, and Augustine. There were also works by Boethius, a Christian writer of the late Empire (and for a time a Roman consul) who attempted to put the late Roman world of culture and philosophy into Latin. The works of Virgil, Cicero, and Livy were preserved as means of teaching Latin, representing the standard of excellence, and at the same time providing some moral content. Additionally to these Latin works, there were Latin translations of Plato's *Timaeus*, *Phaedo* and *Meno*, which were theologically significant, and Latin translations of Aristotle's *Categoriae* and *De Interpretatione*.

The Cathedral Schools were initiated by Christian bishops sometime after the fall of Rome to ensure that Christian children would learn to read and write and acquire a Christian orientation towards the world. While the Cathedral Schools

---

1. Thomas Aquinas recovered the Greek inheritance through reading Aristotle in the original Attic Greek. (Here we accept the argument of A.T. Drone in his work *Christian Schools and Scholars*.) Aquinas was able to separate the inner current of Aristotle's thought from the pantheism and rationalism of Averroes, whose 'translated translations' of Aristotle were popular in Aquinas' time. Since Thomas Aquinas, both Renaissance and Classical German philosophy have made legitimate contributions to the understanding of Man's place in the universe. Please see the entries for Immanuel Kant and Georg Wilhelm Friedrich Hegel in the Bibliography.

began as a means of providing a Christian primary education, they were to become significant – in later centuries – in the development of theology. By 520 there were many Cathedral Schools in Spain and France. In 597 Pope Gregory the Great sent Augustine of Canterbury to Britain, and in the wake of that journey many Cathedral Schools sprang up in Britain, as new dioceses were created. This process received a further boost in the time of Charlemagne, who reigned between 768 and 814. The Emperor – noting a decline of literacy – issued decrees requiring that education be provided at monasteries and cathedrals. Cathedral Schools sprang up in all the major cities of that time: Chartres, Orleans, Paris, Laon, Liege, Rheims, Rouen, and Utrecht. The system of Cathedral Schools again suffered decline in the darkness of the ninth and tenth centuries, until they were revived by the Emperor Otto I in about 960. From this point forward they were a stable part of Christian life through the Middle Ages. The Cathedral Schools taught the seven liberal arts: grammar, astronomy, rhetoric, logic, arithmetic, geometry, and music. Grammar included instruction in reading, writing, and speaking Latin. Logic included the mathematics known at the time.

The Crisis of the Western Church and the Rise of the Monastic Orders

The fall of Classical Civilization was the fall of Civilizational Order itself, for there was really no stable Christian Civilization until the tenth century. From 496 to about 950 there was a lengthy intermediate period in which the nascent Christian Civilization simply could not get off the ground. The Religion was there, but actual Civilizational Order did not congeal. The highlight of this long transitional period was a vibrant Christian monasticism.

Over five centuries of relative chaos the Monastic Orders were able to preserve themselves and to preserve the essentials of Civilizational Order. What are the essentials that the Monastic Orders preserved?

1. The corpus of work left by the Church Fathers, the command of the Latin tongue, the physical transmission of the literature of pagan and Christian Rome, and – in each generation – a preservation of the record of their own time.

2. More importantly, the Orders preserved a connection to conscious life: presence prolonged through time – charity, compassion, wonder, and conscious love. The

Monastic Orders gave the Christian World direct exposure – through service – to the people of the Great Work. They gave an example to a semi-barbarian world of what human beings could become.

Who was responsible for this Great Work?

THE WESTERN CHRISTIAN TRADITION DISCOVERS ITS ESSENTIAL FORM: THE BENEDICTINE ORDER

Western monasticism begins with Benedict of Nursia (480-547), the founder of the Benedictine Order. He was the son of a patrician family in Umbria, and he possessed the Roman genius for organization and administration. As a young man he was repelled by the chaotic social conditions in which he found himself, and took up the eremetic life in a cave in the forest near Subiaco.

To understand Benedict's achievement we must begin by outlining the problems faced by monasticism in the fifth century. Eremetic monasticism was originally an import from the East and retained the imprint of its Eastern origins. With it came a host of legends describing feats of extreme asceticism, miracles, and wonder-workings. These were reflections in the popular religion of the presence of a real Spiritual Tradition, but – from the standpoint of Tradition – these feats of asceticism and wonder-workings are of no more significance than stories of athletic prowess or simple conjuring tricks. The fascination with ascetic deeds was often combined with the latent self-hatred that is common in any period of civilizational decline. The result was an atmosphere unconducive to right monastic practice.

Egyptian eremetic monasticism did indeed follow an ascetic path, but it had developed in very different climactic and cultural conditions. Its direct connection to the Church Fathers and to the Apostles was stronger and its practitioners more mature. Transferred to Northern Europe, the same eremetic practices produced, on the one hand a reckless asceticism and, on the other, an overreaction to this recklessness. The overreaction could be described as a retreat into a secure communal life. The sum result of these two tendencies was the lack of any firmly implanted monastic ideal which could give guidance to life and which would inspire men to act in such a way as to affirm their deepest spiritual aspirations.

After three years in retreat the young Benedict acquired the reputation of being a spiritual guide, and many people sought him out for counsel. As more and more novice monks came to him, Benedict established a monastery at Subiaco and then twelve other monasteries in the vicinity. His own experience had shown him that eremetism was not for the novice but should be undertaken as the culmination of years of practice. Benedict saw that many of the people who came to him, and who wished to imitate him, would not immediately benefit from extreme asceticisms. Those who were ready for such practices needed a context in which they could work, not just for themselves but for the larger whole of which they were a part. In response to these needs he created a code of monastic laws applicable to the Western conditions, and he developed this, not in one, but in a whole family of monasteries. From his initiative came the basic monastic rule of the West.

In 529 Benedict, with a chosen group of men, went to Monte Cassino and founded a central monastery to his family of monasteries. Here, amongst a closed circle, Benedict assembled everything that was needed to realize the purposes of Higher School in the age to follow: the learning of the Old and New Testaments, the works of the Early Fathers, and the Latin texts necessary to achieve excellence in that language.

The Rule of the Order – independently of its inner teaching – can be summed as follows. The monk was given a full eight hours to himself, which included the time for sleep. The remainder of the day was divided into three portions:

1. The daily common service, chanted in the choir, to which was given four and a half hours;

2. Manual work in field or cloister, to which was given six or seven hours;

3. Reading of the Scriptures and the work of the Early Fathers, to which was given three to five hours.

Individual monks might work under different conditions than those given above, or spend time in retreat, as circumstances required.

The principle of monastic government was 'authority exercised after counsel.' The abbot was elected by the monks for life. He then appointed the officials of the abbey, but at the same time, on all critical issues, he took the advice of the senior monks. After that, all were to obey his commands. The authority given the abbot allowed each monastery to develop its own customs on the basis of the Rule. It allowed future abbots to implement new understandings and to respond to changing circumstances.

Novices entered the order under a vow of chastity, poverty, and obedience. But while an individual monk could own nothing, the corporate wealth of the abbey could become great. This was Benedict's insight into the future, for as the social order stabilized over the centuries, the monasteries accumulated endowments, which were then used to assist in the reconstruction of the Civilizational Order. Without the assistance of the monasteries, the civilization of High Medieval Europe could never have come into being. Even from the beginning of the Order – in the sixth century – some monasteries were founded as hospitals, some devoted to relief of the poor, and some established on the great roads to aid travelers so that Christians could make pilgrimage and monks could travel back and forth between the different monastic houses that were to be established throughout Europe.

One aspect of the Benedictine Rule particularly reflects its founder's genius. This was the vow of stability: no monk could leave the monastery where he had initially joined. A monk might travel, as needs required, but his membership would always be to the first monastery. The one exception would be if he were sent to initiate a new Benedictine house. This vow meant, effectively, that the monks had to make a commitment to each other, as partners in a life's work. They each had to work, for the duration of their lives, with other men who knew them well and who constituted their personal 'inner circle.' These men knew each other's human weaknesses and developed respect for each other's spiritual potentials. The vow of stability, combined with the flexibility that attached to 'authority exercised after counsel,' guaranteed the existence of each Benedictine house as a continuous, permanent society with its own traditions. This was explicitly designed to correct the weakness of the post-Roman world: a dissolute, crumbling society, in which men were often forced to flee from one place to another. In the midst of a world of passion, impulse, and violence, the monasteries became examples of peaceful, harmonious order; they reflected the internal reality of a steady transformation of energy from the level of World 96 to the level of Worlds 6 and 12.

The great Abbey at Monte Cassino became the center from with the Benedictine Rule spread. Benedictine houses soon formed through central Italy and particularly in Rome. When the Lombards sacked Monte Cassino in 580, many of the monks fled to Rome, where they were given residence by Pope Pelagius II in a monastery adjoining the Lateran Basilica. This act of random violence proved fateful. The Benedictines were now established under the very eyes of the Pope. Their merits were seen and this changed their relation to the Christian Church.

GREGORY THE GREAT:
THE FUSION OF TRADITION AND RELIGION

In about 574 a young monk named Gregory, who was to become Pope Gregory I, entered the Benedictine Order in Rome, where he spent – by his own admission – the three happiest years of his life. Gregory was very like Benedict himself. Born into a patrician family which had converted to Christianity some generations previously, he possessed the Roman genius for leadership, organization, and administration. He was one of those special cells in the social body capable of performing the coordinative functions necessary to Civilizational Order.

How was this sudden convergence of emergent Western Monasticism and the Church of Rome to develop? The story is revealing of the way that Gods work with Men.

Gregory's youth saw Rome in its most desperate hour. He was born in the year 540. In 542 the Justinian plague ravaged the city, drastically reducing its population. In 547 Totila, the Ostrogothic chieftain, sacked the city, and Gregory's parents were forced to retreat to their Sicilian estates. In 547 Totila vacated the ruined city, inviting those still alive to return to its empty streets. Gregory's parents returned to what was still, formally, the papal city and the seat of Western Christianity. The Ostrogoths then, acting on impulse, retook Rome in 550. In 554 Justinian, the Eastern Emperor, sent armies into Italy and Justinian's general Belisarius was able to push the Ostrogoths out. The Franks attacked in the same year, and again the city was successfully defended. However Justinian died in the year 564, and from that time Byzantium – now under attack from the Persians in the east and the Avars and Slavs from the north – was unable to send significant aid to Rome. In the meantime the Lombards had begun to make incursions into northern Italy, and by 568 they occupied much of its territory. They soon began to make regular assaults on the city of Rome itself. Between the attacks of the Ostrogoths, the Franks, and the Lombards, the dreaded plague came – time and again.

When Gregory entered the Benedictine Order in 573, at about the age of thirty, he had been fully exposed to all that was dark and confused in human nature, and he sought, with all his heart, to discover the essence of Christianity. In this, his fondest wish, he succeeded – penetrating deeply into the Christian Monastic Tradition, which was still in its first flush of life. Very soon after Gregory entered the Benedictine Order, its headquarters at Monte Cassino was sacked by the Lombards, and refugee Benedictines flooded into Rome, so Gregory would have met all the senior Benedictines of his time. He repeatedly described these years as the happiest years of his life, and he wanted nothing more than to continue as a monk. However, he had served the Pope Pelagius II (who had also been ordained as a Benedictine monk) actively before entering the Benedictine Order, and so his administrative abilities were known to the Pope. In 578 Pelagius called Gregory out of monastic seclusion to deal with a deep schism that was then rending the Church. Gregory spent the next six years in service to the Pope as the Western ambassador to the imperial court in Constantinople. In 585 he was forced to return to Rome to address new crises there, with the schismatic dispute still unresolved and Byzantium itself under pressure from the Sassanid Persians. Things had changed in Gregory's absence. The Lombards had conquered most of Italy, and the city of Rome had filled with refugees who – whatever their walk of life – had no means of sustaining themselves. At the same time the plague had repeatedly ravaged the city. In 590 Pope Pelagius II died of the plague and Gregory was elected to succeed him, becoming Pope Gregory I. He inherited a ruined city, filled with refugees, with the Lombards camped at its very gates.

In the conditions of duress that he found himself, Gregory spontaneously assumed temporal as well as spiritual authority. He assigned a tribune to the city, organized a system of charitable relief for the many homeless refugees, and set quotas for agricultural production for the extensive church lands that surrounded the city. He devised a sophisticated accounting system to measure agricultural production, and any surplus from the Church lands was immediately used for charity. Gregory then reorganized the Church itself on the basis of the order he had experienced as a Benedictine. He aggressively required his churchmen to seek out and relieve needy persons, reprimanding them if they failed to do so. He organized the resources of the Church into an administration for general relief, with the idea that the Church was only the steward for wealth that was to go immediately to those in greatest need. He maintained all of these responsibilities and fulfilled all of these duties, while his own health was weak, as he himself had been subject to the ravages of the plague. On having brought stability to the city of Rome, Gregory was able to negotiate a peace with the Lombards. In this more stable situation he was able to renew the Church's missionary activity in England, France, North Africa, northern Italy, and Croatia.

Gregory was the father of the medieval papacy. He was a leader of the greatest vision, a remarkably gifted and determined administrator, and a highly skilled diplomat. As Benedict was a high point for Western monasticism, Gregory was a high point for the papacy and for the Roman Church. Indeed the roles of the two men are intimately connected. Gregory applied the principles of Benedictine monasticism to his own life of active service. He was convinced that the monastic system had a special value for the Church and did everything within his power to propitiate it. He lived in a time when the Christian Spiritual Tradition was alive in the Benedictine Order, and he believed that the work of that Monastic Order and the Church were integral. And he was right. He knew the true measure as few have known it since.

THE SPREAD OF WESTERN MONASTICISM

Rome remained the center of the Benedictine Order for 140 years. It was from the Benedictine Monastery of Saint Andrew in Rome – under Pope Gregory's instruction – that Saint Augustine of Canterbury (to be distinguished from Saint Augustine of Hippo) set forth in 595 – with forty companions – on a mission to evangelize England. Christianity did have a foothold in England, but the Christian Church had developed in isolation since the withdrawal of the Roman legions in 410. Everywhere on their travels, on the long journey north to England, Augustine and his company spoke of the Rule that they lived by and left copies of the Rule itself. Soon after his arrival in England, in 597, Augustine established the first English Benedictine monastery at Canterbury, and many other monasteries were founded in its wake. It was said that Saint Benedict seemed to have taken possession of the country. From here the Rule spread with extraordinary rapidity and was adopted in most of the monasteries that had been founded by the Celtic missionaries from Iona. In the seventh and eighth centuries the Order spread from England to Germany and from there to Denmark and Scandinavia. It penetrated Spain in the ninth century, and by the end of the ninth century it represented the only form of monastic life in the whole of Western Europe.

The rapidity of the spread of such a strict monastic rule says much about the times. There was obviously a deeply felt need to secure the connection to a higher level. But in the darkness of these times men happily embraced the Benedictine Rule just as a means to be certain of their connection to God. In other words many joined the Benedictine Order as Religion only, and many abbots were only men of the First Work. For this reason it is now impossible to trace the history of the Spiritual Tradition, amongst the history of the many Benedictine monasteries that came into existence. But the evidence of the Great Work is clear.

The Benedictine Rule became the basis for a stable way of life that was to survive the chaos yet to come. The Order itself was a light in the darkness of the ninth and tenth centuries, when even the patterns of village life came apart in much of Europe. In these twilight years cultivated land returned to wilderness, and, in many areas, wolves roamed the streets. The Benedictines succeeded in preserving what was essential to Civilizational Order, but, beginning from the late tenth century, they provided something more.

The Stabilization of the Christian Civilization and the Expansion of the Monastic Orders

In the late tenth and early eleventh centuries the social order of the Middle Ages finally began to take form; the peasant, the priest, the knight, the merchant, and the noble began to emerge into the light of day. The opening note for this development had been sounded in the time of Charlemagne, and, although it was not realized at that time, it did not cease to resonate.

A first sign of the re-emergence of order in Europe came in the mid-tenth century when Otto of Saxony was able to establish jurisdiction over the host of principalities which comprised Germany and Italy, creating – for the first time since 814 – a centralization of power in continental Europe. Otto was a devoutly Christian ruler, and in 962 Pope John XII crowned him the Holy Roman Emperor and proclaimed him the successor to Charlemagne. Thus Augustine's vision of the City of God was affirmed a second time in the line of time.

Throughout Central Europe, Otto strengthened ecclesiastical authority at the expense of secular, endowing bishoprics and abbeys with large tracts of land, over which the secular authorities had neither power of taxation nor legal jurisdiction. He also reinstituted the system of Cathedral Schools, to the point where they became the first general system of education that had existed since the fall of the Roman Empire.

The Holy Roman Empire helped to give form to Central Europe in the Early Middle Ages, and in many ways helped to establish the culture of the High Middle Ages. The centralization of power enabled a parallel process of stabilization in the parts of Western Europe that were outside of Otto's jurisdiction – Normandy, Anjou, and Aquitaine.

Now let us examine the feudal system, which was the real, underlying foundation of this political stability. The fatal problem of the Carolingian Empire had been the inability to secure inheritance. Under the Carolingian system inheritance was divided equally amongst the different male heirs. Significant holdings and estates were thus broken up in the second and third generation, and strife inevitably followed. In the late tenth century the convention of inheritance changed so that the entire estate passed on intact to the eldest son. This was called the 'system of primogeniture' and it enabled the large estates to remain intact over generations. From the time of the establishment of primogeniture, the nobility was able to focus on the development of agriculture, and indeed a real agricultural revolution ensued. At the same time the Monastic Orders were able to develop their own land. The result was that Medieval agriculture actually advanced over the agricultural practices of the Classical World.

For the system to work the relatively small and independent noble houses had to form a stable system of alliances. The natural regional basis for this system was a king. We could say, therefore, that in the eleventh and twelfth centuries kings were necessary, but weak. The nobles did not want the kings to be strong enough to infringe on the activities of their own desmenes (great manorial estates). Nevertheless, it was through the kings that the emergent European nations existed: Norman England, Capetian France, and Hohenstaufen Germany. Throughout this same period, and independently of the nobility, towns formed, trade began to flourish, and banking houses were established. As a result of this there was a rapid expansion of the market for luxury goods, which again stimulated trade and reopened relations with the countries of the Levant. During this time both the Church and the Towns became able to sustain themselves independently of the great noble estates.

The bonds that united the different groups comprising feudal society into a living whole were forged by the Church under the close supervision of the Monastic Spiritual Traditions. In a great labor the Church sacralized secular functions, making all a unity under God. Not only did it sacralize the stages of life – birth, marriage, and death – but it sacralized the actual functions that society performed. We provide a brief sketch of the template that the Church created, carefully distinguishing this from the actuality of any particular medieval society.

THE SERF was a member of the lowest feudal class, legally attached to a section of land that was owned by his lord. He was required to perform labor on this land in return for certain rights. Thus the serf did possess rights, and from one point of view feudal society was actually based on this social class. Unless the serf was able to work the land there could be no society, and from this point of view the knight and the noble existed to help the serf continue his work. Additionally, in Early Medieval society, rural village life was the basis of every activity. The Church was able to link the idea of serfdom to the surrender of self-will: the yielding up of the passions through subjection to God. The serf, with no property of his own, had a childlike closeness to God, which the merchant, the knight, and the noble lacked. His station encouraged a deep acceptance of the ordained patterns of life – the change of the seasons, the succession of years of famine and of plenty. He had, in some ways, the most accurate sense of the place of Man in God's universe and a kind of humility which brought him close to reality.

THE FREEMAN was an intermediary in feudal life, between the agricultural world of the serf and the feudal court. Both guildsmen and merchants qualified as freemen, and both were under a system of obligations and laws that was much more complex and demanding than the laws which governed the serf. In the medieval view freedom was a quality to be realized in service, and it was articulated in specific duties – to the Lord, to the King, to the guild, and to the Church. The thrift, the honesty, and the quality of work that the freeman was capable of was the measure of his service to God. In travel and in commerce the freemen were, in many ways, the eyes and ears of the country. The guilds linked the members of each profession to a defined place in the social order, and it was the guildsmen who were responsible for the magnificent passion plays which entranced medieval society.

THE KNIGHT offered himself and his sword to the service of God. He embraced the established ideals of chivalry: unflinching courage, loyalty, courtesy, generosity, and fidelity to promise. His duty was to defend the Church and Christendom, revere the priesthood, and protect the weak, the poor, and the injured. He committed himself to putting his life at risk in the defense of others who were unable to defend themselves.

THE NOBLE bore the weight of many responsibilities. Noble status was not, after the tenth century, principally transmitted by blood line. It was rooted rather in the institution of landed property, by which a man entered into a set of relationships determining his place in society. In so doing he assumed both responsibilities and privileges denied to those in the other ranks. It was often the noble who, through his free will, funded the abbey or the cathedral. In the early Middle Ages nobles often determined the moment of transference of their title by taking a vow to enter a monastic order on reaching a certain age. In the High

Middle Ages the nobility were the principal drawing ground for the military orders, such as the Knights Templar, the Hospitallers, the Order of Saint George, and the Teutonic Knights.

THE KING was alone, under God. He was held accountable for it all, and this particularly included implementing and developing the law of the land. What the Church did not sanction was tyranny, the simple rule by force. Part of the king's duty was thus to determine just laws, approximating the will of God on earth – as nearly as that was possible. Nominally, of course, the king was under the pope, but in fact he was alone – to forge whatever alliances were possible for him, to make whatever wars were necessary, and to deal with the succession of crises that visited his realm.

THE MONK was God's own servant. It was a characteristic of medieval law that those who submitted to the duties of a station must do so by their own choice. There must be a personal act, an oath, a contract embodied in a public ceremony. And the highest law of all was that under which a man stripped himself of this world's goods and subjected himself to religious poverty and obedience. In this way the highest place, that of the Monk, began from the sacrifice of the serf, and was taken a step further. And thus the end is contained in the beginning. On a more practical level, the monks, as members of the Monastic Orders, were responsible for much of what we call 'social services' today: charity, health care, land reclamation, and the protection of travelers.

And so the Church was able to relate each of these social categories directly to the service of God, and, through that to specific duties to other men. In this way it united the parts in a living whole. The social categories thus formed a hierarchy, but at the same time each group was unique and complemented the others in a certain way. Each added some essential quality of life which the others could not provide, and so the different groups had a real regard for one another. While there were divisions between these groups, there was also a bond of a kind which does not exist in modern society, and so the Medieval Civilization – in its better moments – had a depth and resonance which is now hard for us to reconstruct.

However greatly individuals may have deviated from the ideals of their station and whatever forms of nepotism and abuse of power emerged, the template for society created by the Church was real. It was part of the working fabric of society. Indeed, the nostalgia for this 'original unity' remained, even into the nineteenth century.

This is the period in which the Monastic Orders flourished. The period of fragile balance between church and state (900-1250) was the golden age of Western monasticism. The Cluniac order made its appearance in 909 and the Cistercian in 1098.

The Benedictine Order had originally focused – quite strictly – on the spiritual awakening of its participants, and on preserving what was necessary for the Civilizational Order to continue once the 'container' of the Roman Empire had been shattered. But, as the monasteries grew in tandem with the great feudal landholdings, the commitment to serving the Civilizational Order took new and different forms. Abbeys were financed by noble founders, so an Order might be connected to a particular feudal desmene. The individual monasteries became centers of public intercession and prayer, performing services for their noble founders, for their benefactors, and for society in general. The monks had to intercede before God for the entirety of the outside world. And this was legitimate, as the world could not intercede for itself. The monasteries developed the land given them, gave succor to the sick and the poor, gave sanctuary to the persecuted, and took care of travelers at a time when inns could not be trusted.

As the medieval social order stabilized, the number of monasteries required – for literally thousands of fiefdoms – increased. It became impossible to staff the monasteries by voluntary recruitment, and so it became the duty of the noble estates – if they wanted monasteries – to provide men. This was not a particular hardship, as, in a time when birth control did not exist, many families had difficulties in providing for their own. Children were willingly, and often proudly, offered as novitiate monks. In effect the monasteries were filled with a conscript army, not unwilling or ineffective on that account. But the situation created a need to provide discipline of a very basic kind, and thus monastic rules evolved that were several times the length of the original Benedictine Rule – often specifying the activities of the entire monastic community in minute detail. In this way the standard of a meticulously organized and highly ordered life spread through Western Europe.

This phase of monastic life will always be associated with the reforms to the Benedictine Rule made under the name of Cluny – which became **the Cluniac Order**. The Order was unique in that a single center managed connected subsidiaries throughout Europe. Cluny became an immediate link between men of all nationalities in Europe.

The Cluniac Order exalted the range of daily activities. Life itself became an elaborate and beautiful religious ritual: mass with choral accompaniment, prayer, physical work, meditation, daily readings of large sections of the Bible, the study of the works of the Early Fathers and of Christian history. There was, at the same time, the company of distinguished men circulating in an international community and the permanent background of noble architecture. Together these things brought the sense of being on the crest of a new age and of setting an example of Christian life that would be respected throughout Europe. This was the large and unfanatical spirit of Cluny.

The process of expansion of the Monastic Orders was similar to that of the Sufi Orders in the *taifa* phase of development, and in like manner the Western Monastic Orders became themselves a source of Religion. The Spiritual Tradition, then, had to exist within the Order, just as the *tariqa* had to exist within the *taifa*.

There was a natural reaction to this expansion, in the new rules established by the Cistercian and Carthusian Orders. **The Cistercians** – from 1098 – sought to return to the original Benedictine spirit, giving a prominent place to physical work and emphasizing monastic self-sufficiency. Prominent figures here were Steven Harding (1110-1134) and Bernard of Clairvaux (1090-1153). **The Carthusian Order**, initiated in about 1200, was – within Christianity – the most solitary of all the forms of organized religious life. Later came **the Franciscans**, following from the work of Saint Francis of Assisi (1181-1226) and **the Dominicans**, following from the work of Saint Dominic (1170-1221).

And now we come to another aspect of the Great Work of the High Middle Ages. We recall that in the Dark Ages of the ninth and tenth centuries land went out of cultivation, and there was a general depopulation. We noted that, as the noble estates achieved stability and as the population increased, the nobles actively developed the land that was under their control. The monasteries did the same, but on a different scale, and this changed the countenance of Medieval Europe. The most radical development of the medieval economy in the eleventh and twelfth centuries came from the reclamation and conversion of uncultivated soil – the recovery of land for tillage or for pasturage. Between 1000 and 1250 there was a vast movement of reoccupation of land and of colonization of new lands. This took different forms. There were the reclamations by individual peasants, but these were piecemeal. There were the reclamations undertaken by the nobility, which were on a larger scale but were always subject to the changing fortunes of the noble house. It was really only the Monastic Orders that could envision land reclamations on the scale of generations, extending to include remote or intractable regions. The Cistercian and Cluniac Orders made this work their own, transforming the countryside, improving agriculture, planting vines, and stocking rivers with fish.

However, we must emphasize that the most important thing the monks gave Medieval society was not scholarship, or arable land, or intercession through prayer, but *themselves*: men and women who experienced, on a daily basis, the 'peace that passath all understanding.' We are not speaking here of the compassion and humility that comes from religious belief, for, to the extent this is based on an imagined God – rather than on the actual experience of Higher Centers – it is an artificial humility. We are speaking here of the compassion and humility of monks undergoing *morphosis* within a Spiritual Tradition. These are people who quite literally 'see themselves in others.' The author of *The Cloud of Unknowing*, an anonymous English monk, describes this difference vividly. Having characterized false humility, based on a concern to appear holy in the eyes of men, he describes the true humility that arises naturally from the practice of the Great Work.

> The work of contemplation will have a favourable effect on both the body and soul of anyone who practices it, and make him agreeable to everyone, man or woman, who sees him; so that the appearance of the most ill-favoured man or woman living on earth, if they could by grace be enabled to engage in this work, would be suddenly transformed into graciousness. Thus all good people who saw them would be glad and joyful to have their company, and would find that in their presence they were very greatly comforted in spirit and helped by grace towards God.[2]

This is what the Christian monks gave to Western Europe. It is also what the Sufis gave to Islam, what the Brahmins gave to Ancient India, and what the Buddhist monks gave to China, Tibet, and Japan. It was something that traditional societies had, and it is something that we no longer have today.

Having said all of this, we emphasize the centrality of the Church in the life of Europe in the High Middle Ages as perhaps never before and never since.

In the half century from 1100 to 1155 we have the three great pan-European clerics: the Abbot Suger, Bernard of Clairvaux, and Hugh of Cluny. The Abbot Suger (1081-1151), a Benedictine monk, launched the program of Gothic cathedral building, beginning with the cathedral at Saint Denis. Bernard of Clairvaux (1090-1153) was the central figure of the Cistercian reform, which literally covered the face of Europe with

---

2. *The Cloud of Unknowing and Other Works*, by Anonymous, and A.C. Spearing, Penguin, 2001, p. 79. British spelling has been retained in this quotation.

Figure 73. **Chartres Cathedral**

Cistercian monasteries. He also helped to establish the Rule of the Knights Templar and was, more generally, the most important public figure of his age. While the Cistercians and Benedictines gave Western Europe the stability that came from strict adherence to monastic rule, the abbots of Cluny were international statesmen. In the tenth century the Cluniac order surpassed the Benedictine as the principal monastic order of Europe. It was Hugh of Cluny (1024-1109) who first worked with anonymous freemasons in the construction of great abbeys. By the year 1000 the Cluniacs had secured the 'Truce of God' across Europe; fighting was prohibited on half the days of the week and during all religious festivals. By the mid-eleventh century there were Cluniac centers all over France: Chartres with its specialty of medicine, Rheims with its specialty of music, and Mont-Saint-Michel with its specialty of astronomy.

There are few more beautiful symbols of the place of Man in the universe than the great Gothic cathedrals, rising majestically out of the fields of Medieval Europe. The men of the twelfth and thirteenth centuries left us with a legacy that is unforgettable. The greatest physical structures of their time were not defensive fortifications or factories, but tributes to the living God. The achievement of the Gothic cathedrals changed the physical and spiritual landscape of Europe; in them architecture rises to great art, and their sculptures, relief works, and stained glass windows encode the highest knowledge of humanity in that time. Victor Hugo claimed that the cathedral was the 'book'

Figure 74. **Beauvais Cathedral**

of the Middle Ages and that it was only in the eighteenth century that the published book supplanted the cathedral.

On another front, the Monastic Orders were also responsible for initiating the nine great Crusades against Islam launched between 1000 and 1250. These expeditions did, temporarily, bring to a close the internecine struggles in Medieval Europe, but in many ways they bent the Church towards secular goals and placed stress upon the relation of Church to Spiritual Tradition. They led, ultimately, to a deepening of the schism between the Catholic and Orthodox Churches.

The Development of Medieval Civilization and Rise of Scholasticism

We noted that the coming of the High Middle Ages (1000-1300) saw the gradual emergence of the large centralized monarchies: kings with suzerainty over nobles, great standing armies, the growth of towns, and the creation of roads and infrastructures of trade. In this context the Church became increasingly caught up in the concerns of secular life and began to seek control over the Monastic Orders which had, in the past, given it life. The Fourth Lateran Council of 1215 placed a ban on the formation of new Monastic Orders and initiated the seizure of monastic lands.

Now a confusing point: the loss of place of the Monastic Orders runs parallel with the rise of Scholasticism and with a very real development of Christian theology. The new theology was a response of the Church to changes occurring at the level of the Civilizational Order. In other words the development of theology was driven by challenges originating from the lower levels of the Pyramid of Man. Medieval Civilization had entered a period of rapid growth and expansion, which impacted people in all walks of life. The challenges to the Medieval Civilizational Order were also and at the same time, challenges to the Christian Church. These challenges were well met by a brilliant theologian, Thomas Aquinas.

Aquinas was a gifted philosopher and a monk of high spiritual attainment – but his role was in service to the Church rather than in service to the Christian Spiritual Tradition. He was, perhaps, the first real philosopher in the Church since Classical times. His contribution was part of the development of the Scholastic movement, which began in the Cathedral Schools and culminated in the first European universities. That a man of his spiritual development should play such a role suggests that the Christian Spiritual Tradition did not have, as part of its task, the role of giving guidance in these new developments. This might be the reflection of a weakness in the Tradition, or it might be that the new developments were so entirely worldly that the Tradition could not – by its very nature – play a leading role. Whatever the case, it shows the Tradition in a lower relief than it was during the twelfth century.

To understand how the Scholastic movement developed out of lay – rather than monastic – scholarship we must return to the Cathedral Schools. Through the eleventh century the scholars of the Cathedral Schools endeavored to bring the teachings of the Patristic tradition into relation with the issues facing contemporary European

Christianity. But it was difficult for them to connect rightly to the spirit of the Patristic era, and to work from that. They were confronted with problems of psychology, metaphysics, cosmology, science, law, and ethics, which the Church Fathers had never addressed. We must remember that, for the High Medieval world, Nature was still a chaotic playground of supernatural forces. The worlds of politics and law were likewise riddled with folk wisdom and superstitions of different kinds, to an extent that rendered them almost intractable to thought. It was necessary to think about these areas in a different way. The scholars of the Cathedral Schools attempted, for the most part, to resolve their problems in a rationalist way – as the Church had to have something sensible to say about these different issues.

The one Early Father who was useful in this regard was Boethius. His surviving work, *The Consolation of Philosophy*, gave people of the eleventh century a glimpse of the most impressive body of systematic teaching available to the Classical world. The preview of Aristotelian logic given in *The Consolation* opened the vista of an orderly and systematic view of the physical universe. Boethius made an introductory presentation of the Aristotelian Categories: Quantity, Quality, Relation, Position, Place, Time, State, Action, Affection. These related the forms of human psychology and human perception to the structure of the living universe, establishing standards to guage thought in different areas. The types of argument that were valid in each area were strictly limited, and could be classified according to principle. Thus Aristotelian philosophy promised to organize and centralize a chaos of confused fact, folk wisdom, and outright superstition. In the face of the very real intellectual challenges of the eleventh century, these 'traces of the Classical Master' exercised a kind of fascination. We could say that, in terms of Christian thought, the eleventh century was the century of Boethius.

This process of digestion and assimilation was given huge stimulus by two events: **1)** the opening up of Andalusian Spain and **2)** the Fourth Crusade.

1. From about 1140 Europeans began to penetrate Islamic Spain (Andalusia) and gain access to the Classical texts, particularly Aristotle, Plotinus, and Plato. The Christian city of Toledo, in central Spain, became a center for the study and translation of texts coming from Islamic Seville, Granada, and Valencia.

2. In 1204 a body of renegade Crusaders – having been given privileged entry into Byzantine territory to support the crusade – sacked Constantinople, and proceeded to conquer much of Byzantium. As a result, for more than half a century, a Frenchman acted as the Byzantine Emperor and a Latin Patriarch was installed

at Constantinople. As a result of this situation – and of the expeditions of the crusades generally – Arabic and Classical Greek texts began to stream into the body of the Christian Church.

This influx of Arabic science and Classical philosophy created a crisis in the Church. As we noted, the Monastic Orders had been able to preserve only a few of the original texts of Plato and Aristotle. Christian theology of the eleventh century was essentially Platonist, but it was based on the 'second-hand' Platonism of Clement, Origen, and Augustine. Now the entire corpus of Classical Philosophy, on which this theology had originally been based, was coming into circulation. And with it came the commentaries of Islamic thinkers, who had already been working hard to make sense of it, and who – for the most part – had greater philosophical acumen than their Christian counterparts. At the same time the brilliant Jewish theologian Maimonides, who was able to make a close study of Aristotle in the Arabic translations available in Spain, began to publish. His students made criticisms of Christian theology that were hard for the clergy to answer. Thus, access to the original Classical corpus, which had been a source of inspiration to the Early Fathers, was both a threat and a promise to the Medieval Church.

The new texts, as they came to light, brought both illumination and confusion. The philosophies of Plato and Aristotle were grounded in the experience of Higher Centers, but they had not, of course, been 'adjusted' to the language of the Gospels. The fragments that had survived within the Christian Church had been adequately interpreted (or assimilated) by the Early Fathers and by Boethius. But the discrepancies between the two sets of teachings became more apparent as the entire body of Platonic and Aristotelian work came into view. The Early Fathers had not been bothered by this, because they could not anticipate what might appear as discrepancies to their Medieval counterparts. Christian theology had, over the centuries, been rigidified by a succession of schismatic conflicts, and many things that would never have seemed heretical in the first century AD were unacceptable to the Church of the twelfth century. Additionally the Islamic thinkers had carefully interpreted Classical philosophy in a way consonant with their own teachings, and this again did not correspond to Christian theology in the eleventh century.

Further to this, many acute confusions were created – both in Christianity and in Islam – by the inability of theologians, so distant from the Greek philosophical culture, to understand the scope and universality of the original Platonic and Aristotelian teachings. Both Christianity and Islam felt the need for a philosophically-grounded theology, and the Classical material exercised an undeniable attraction, but theologians were unable to understand how many things that appeared contradictory to them might be true at once. With respect to the original Classical material, there was a marked tendency – on the part of all theologians – to leave out the things they did not understand and to relate the parts that appealed to them to the theology they already had.

And all of this was only a part of the confusion. With Islamic science came all of Classical science: mathematics, astronomy, botany, medicine, and the proto-chemistry known as alchemy. Alchemy came to Europe not in the form of dusty manuscripts but in the form of actual experimental practice. For not only had Islam appropriated Classical learning, it had – in the Abbasid period – actively developed it. The alchemical 'science' could not but have a profound effect on Medieval Europe, because it was the state-of-the-art chemistry of the twelfth century. A knowledge of substances and their qualities was necessary to medicine, to metallurgy, to glassmaking, and to the production of inks, dyes, paints, and cosmetics. The very word 'alchemy' is the Greek word *chemia* with the prefix of the Arabic definite article *al*. The first rudimentary periodic tables came from the alchemical proto-chemistry of Islam. The doctors and metallurgists of twelfth-century Europe were painfully aware of the limits of their knowledge, and the Islamic alchemists revealed new methods and techniques that could be immediately put to work.

The first alchemical text entered Latin Europe through an Englishman – Robert Chester – who studied in Andalusia. His translation of the Arabic *Book of the Composition of Alchemy* was completed in 1144. As interest in Islamic alchemy grew, Toledo became a center for alchemical studies, and this center quickly connected to many other emergent centers in Europe.

The 'scientific' side of alchemy was laced, through and through, with the principles of Aristotelian science, particularly with the idea of the four primal elements – earth, air, fire, and water. It also carried **1)** the store of Hermetic knowledge that the Arabs had taken from Alexandria, the ancient center of Classical learning and **2)** the even more ancient Sumerian/Chaldean teachings, which the Arabs gained access to with the conquest of Mesopotamia. In the Hermetic teachings, taken as a whole, there had been a particular development of the Greek understanding of cosmos, of the idea of a hierarchy of cosmoses, and of the principle "as above so below." This was complemented – in European alchemical culture – by the Kabbalistic teachings, which became available in the thirteenth century. The Kabbalistic Sefirot, with its representation of the different levels of Creation, covered the same ground as the Hermetic study of the Macrocosm and was often studied in relation to it.

Of course this confluence of knowledge – scientific, occult, cosmological, and esoteric – does not, in itself, sum to anything more than a fascinating collection of parts. It is only when such information is organized and utilized by higher beings for higher purposes that it acquires real value. To some extent this did occur, but we must set this theme aside for the discussion of Renaissance Hermeticism in Chapter 40.

In the alchemical teachings that came to Europe in the twelfth century there was **1)** the vision of a 'spiritual science,' unlocking the secrets of God's universe, **2)** the basis for a 'science of charlatanism' that was to plague Europe until the coming of the Enlightenment, and **3)** the actual foundations of modern science as we know it.

All of this alchemical material directly entered the Church, which was – more or less – the only device for the integration of knowledge in Europe. Two of the best known early European alchemists were the Dominican Albertus Magnus (1193-1280) and the Franciscan Roger Bacon (1214-1294). Pope Innocent VIII (1432-1492) was actually a patron of alchemy and Martin Luther (1483-1546), in his break with Catholicism, emphasized that alchemy was entirely consistent with Christian teachings. But, at the same time, alchemy went deeply into lay society; it went into the guilds and into the workshops of independently funded masters.

But how does alchemical practice, so closely connected with occultism – both ancient and modern – relate to the Spiritual Traditions? As we have noted, alchemy and Hermeticism[3] directly penetrated both the Christian Religion and the Christian Civilization. The Christian Spiritual Tradition internalized it through the Monastic Orders (which, by the twelfth century, were not equivalent with the Tradition, but acted as its expanded 'containers'). It was natural for the Tradition to absorb the Hermetic material, because the study of the cosmoses, and of the relation of the different energies circulating within a cosmos, were directly related to its area of specialty. But the aspect of alchemy that was of greatest interest to the Spiritual Tradition was its very graphic understanding of what was involved in the dissolution of 'I'; of what it meant to break yourself up into parts and place the energies of the higher parts over the energies of the

---

3. See the Glossary entry for 'Hermeticism.'

lower parts. These alchemical teachings brought clarity to what the Tradition already taught, for this is, exactly, what the Work of the Steward entails.

Thus the spiritual side of alchemy was recognized and used by certain of the Monastic Orders, but – to run ahead of ourselves – it was universally used in the new generation of Traditions which emerged in the fourteenth century and which took the form of the Renaissance Schools. Of these we shall speak later. Having clarified these points, we must return to our story, as it was unfolding in mid-twelfth century Europe.

The bulk of the Aristotelian and Platonic theological material was taken into the Church through the Cathedral Schools, from which the Medieval universities were soon to develop. Not being subject to the monastic rule, these Schools were not subject to the same restrictions. This new information – particularly the philosophy – was also taken into the Monastic Orders, but it was the Cathedral Schools which opened it up, explored its implications, and made it controversial. The point to be made is that the drive to integrate and assimilate this new material *did not come from the Christian Tradition;* it came from **1)** the Christian Civilization, which had an acute need for new material and **2)** from the Roman Church, which needed to generate a coherent and defensible theology in face of questions and criticisms coming from both the Islamic and the Jewish quarters. These tasks were all the more pressing because the younger Islamic Civilization was actually ahead of the Christian Civilization in both its knowledge and its science, and the Christians felt this.

The key figure here was Aristotle, both theologically and scientifically. We could say that, as the digestion of Boethius was the task of the eleventh century, the digestion of Aristotle's logic was the task of the twelfth. Enigmatically, Aristotle's intention to create a philosophy for the post-Hellenic world was realized in Islam in the ninth and tenth centuries and in Europe in the twelfth century.

The key figures of the first phase of the assimilation process were those who had already assimilated it for Islam – Avicenna and Averroes.

Avicenna (Ibn Sina – Persian, 980-1037) was the most influential polymath of the Islamic Golden Age of scholarship and science. He was exposed to the opening world of science, mathematics, and the Islamic integration of Roman law. He was himself instrumental in the recovery of Classical Science, and felt that he had reconciled Aristotelianism and Neoplatonism with Islamic theology. He found that Aristotelianism placed science in a context that was compatible with the teachings of Islam and Muhammad's injunction to 'seek knowledge.' Aristotle's thinking was rational, and at the same time showed a profound insight into the structure of the universe.

Averroes (Ibn Rushd – Andalusian, 1126-1198) defended Aristotelian philosophy against the attacks made on it by traditional Islamic thinkers who were reacting to the popularity of Avicenna's work. They felt that Avicenna was making an illegitimate use of non-Islamic thinkers. Averroes focused more explicity than Avicenna on Aristotelian theology, ethics, and science, and was therefore of greater interest to the West.

Both Avicenna and Averroes elaborated Aristotelian logic and Aristotle's theory of the Prime Mover Unmoved. They were agreed on two doctrines, which they felt clarified aspects of Muhammad's teachings and which were in sharp contradiction to twelfth century Christian theology.

1. *There is one single intellect – or universal mind – for the whole human race*, and it is independent from the souls (or personal psychologies) of the individual human beings who comprise that race. A man's 'personal psychology' is mortal while his 'intellect,' at least in its developed form, is immortal. When a man whose intellect is developed comes to the end of his life, the intellect passes into the Universal Mind, merging there with other intellects. Islamic Aristotelianism can appear as a form of pantheism. In this view there is a single 'world soul,' a generally fatalistic view of life, the lack of any individual redemption, and even the lack of an individual soul to go to heaven and stay there. Finally there is the lack of a theistic God of the kind that was central to popular Christianity.

2. *The World is eternal*, it always was and always will be. This, of course, contradicts the Christian idea of Creation. (It also contradicts Muhammad's recorded teachings on Creation, but that is another issue.)

The theory of a 'single common intellect for the human race' is, in fact, a misinterpretation of Aristotle's theory of the Prime Mover Unmoved. Indeed, in this regard, Avicenna and Averroes were neither strictly orthodox Muslims nor strictly orthodox Aristotelians. But Aristotle did hold that the World is eternal, and so even Aristotle – the 'new authority on the world' – had to be treated by Medieval theologians with some circumspection. Philosophical acumen was obviously necessary.

In the last half of the twelfth century many Christians adopted different neo-Aristotelian ideas in different degrees, and held them to be compatible with the revealed truth of Christianity. This produced **1)** a range of eclectic thinkers and **2)** bitter struggle within the Church.

In the early thirteenth century (1210-1220) the eclectic neo-Aristotelians were suppressed. Augustinianism and Platonism were presented as orthodoxy, while Aristotelianism was seen to be lacking the Holy Spirit. This suppression came principally from the level of Religion, but it included the reaction of the Christian Spiritual Tradition to the general explosion of discursive thought. Let us look more deeply into this.

The sense of vocation of the monastic leaders of the twelfth century, reaching back to the Gospels and the teaching of the Early Fathers, was violated by the development of discursive theology in the form it took under the influence of Arabic-Aristotelianism. The atmosphere of the Early Church was the polar opposite of pantheism, which accepts rational activity as Man's highest calling, and understands reason as the manifestation of an impartial Univeral Intelligence working through different men at different times. The Early Christians believed that Man had sinned, that he was asleep, and that in his unregenerate state he did not possess the Holy Spirit. Under these conditions it is meaningless to say that God is everywhere and in everything. The Apostles and the Church Fathers had embraced a truth that could only be secured through internal struggle, and they had accepted this on authority. Jesus spoke for God, whom Man cannot hope to understand, and whom he had been called upon to represent. Only because Jesus was God's chosen son, and only because he spoke to Mankind, was there a relationship between Man and God. And it was the only kind of relationship that could exist, because God himself does not speak to men. The Prophet speaks to men, and God's angels may appear before Men. The Angels and the Prophets, by their very nature, convey the authority of God. And beyond this, any point of contact between Men and Gods makes a demand on Men to become like Gods. It is never casual, and this is always its first purpose.

This demand, which the Early Christians felt so clearly, was directly expressed in Jesus' teachings. We keep in mind that Jesus Christ was an incarnation of World 6; he was a concentration of molecular and electronic energies such that the normal sense of 'I' could not be sustained in his presence. When Jesus says, "Follow me; and let the dead bury their dead,"[4] it is the voice of World 6 saying 'accept my standard and leave everything else behind.' One feels the elemental force of his injunction to "Sell all that thou hast … and come, follow me."[5]

We note that the Early Fathers were themselves criticized for introducing themes that could be construed as pantheistic, or at least counter to the principle of individual redemption. They certainly carried within themselves the universality of Greek philosophy, which many of them knew from childhood. Yet the spirit of their work is profoundly aligned with the spirit of the Apostolic teachings, and many of them died as martyrs. Later theologians, with a much longer history of schismatic dispute behind them, were unable to directly understand Pantaenus, Clement, and Origen, because they were unable to see the way in which – for Higher Centers – many things can be true at once. Origen's casual acceptance of reincarnation does not contradict the principle of individual redemption or the need to radically distinguish the different levels of the human psychology, but a certain breadth of experience is needed to understand this.

The instinct of a man like Bernard of Clairvaux against the rationalist neo-Aristotelianism of his time is correct; God – as the Absolute – is authority incarnate. Our debt to him is infinite, and our obligation to serve him, in the universe he has created, is equally without limit. The fact that his direct involvement in our lives must occur though his angels actually heightens this sense of authority, for through the angels one comes into direct contact with an intelligence incomparably higher than one's own. And this intelligence serves an intelligence incomparably higher than itself. The poet Rainer Maria Rilke described this well. Speaking of the 'angelic orders' he says their beauty "is the beginning of terror we can still bear, and it awes us so much because it so serenely disdains to destroy us." It is this sense of awe, of direct contact with a higher level, and of the will to conscious service that is characteristic of the Spiritual Traditions. The Christian Tradition would naturally counter any view that relaxed the moment-by-moment effort of meditation, allowing it to slip back to the level of discursive thought and, by so doing, dissolving the intensity and immediacy needed to penetrate the Sphere of Sentient Being.

In sum, the Spiritual Traditions clearly sense the Absolute behind the Angelic, and they sense it intensely, as beings tasked from the Angelic level and held responsible to it. But they possess *an intensity that is without fanaticism*. Fanaticism comes only from the level of Religion, because it arises only from the level of the four lower centers.

---

4. Matthew 8:22.
5. Luke 18:22.

Fanaticism is, in itself, a passion which reinforces the wrong sense of 'I'; in fact it is the ultimate egotism, the most extreme form of self-importance. In the atmosphere of the Traditions one has intensity with compassion and with 'the peace which passeth all understanding.'

However, despite the firm reaction of the early thirteenth-century Church, the conflict with Eastern Aristotelianism was soon renewed, for it was not just the City of God that needed to be satisfied, but the City of Man. Until these questions could be settled on their own terms, the clamor they created would not be quieted.

It was **Thomas Aquinas** (1225-1274) who put all of the pieces together in a way that was workable for the Church. He attempted to harmonize 'intensity without fanaticism' with emergent science. Aquinas was able to read Aristotle in the original Greek and saw that what Avicenna and Averroes attributed to him was based on a peculiar interpretation of his work. It was Aquinas who first integrated the original Greek Aristotle into Christian theology.

But how did Thomas Aquinas, a Dominican monk who worked in an environment of monastic retreat, get dropped into the middle of all this heated debate? To understand how this happened we must go back to **the Cathedral Schools**. All of these studies, and all of the issues connected with them, were being debated there, and these debates were turning certain of the Cathedral Schools into the first European universities. It was in this open environment that Aquinas developed, refined, and honed the new theology. The situation of Aquinas was very similar to that which Origen faced at the time of the beginning of Christian theology. Indeed, the environment of the Catechetical School at Alexandria in the second century AD was very like that of the Cathedral Schools-cum-universities of the early thirteenth century. As head of the Catechetical School, Origen was forced to respond to new Christians, to Christians with firmly held beliefs, and to people outside the Church who had 'burning' questions. In this dialogue the guiding principles of his theology gradually emerged. It happened in a very similar way to Aquinas.

We will remember that the Cathedral Schools were run by lay, not monastic, clergy – and so were not subject to a monastic rule. As a consequence they had full access to the Greek and Islamic texts and commentaries that were entering Christendom at this time, and were fully caught up in the intellectual restlessness of the age. They were possessed by an ever greater desire for exact knowledge. Certain of these schools began to rise in stature, and individual teachers appeared whose mastery distinguished the school of which they were a part. Over time great Cathedral Schools emerged, whose reputation did not depend on a single master, or even a succession of single masters. The schools of Chartres, Tours, and Orléans were fast becoming the intellectual centers of Europe.

In the second generation of the twelfth century, universities began to develop out of the Cathedral Schools. It is hard to determine the exact date, but universities began to appear in Italy, France, and England. Professional scholars debated the metaphysical and scientific works of Aristotle and his Arabic commentators, and there was a larger view of many subjects, including mathematics and science. On the one hand, the traditional foundations of Christian thought were threatened and, on the other, new vistas for an ideal ordering of all of human knowledge opened up.

Understandably the Church was quite concerned with all of these developments. In 1268 the Dominican Order (as an arm of the Church) determined to combat the rise of Averroism and radical Aristotelianism in the universities. It assigned Thomas Aquinas to be regent master at the University of Paris – the best-known university in the world. The end-result of this was an orthodox Christian Aristotelianism and so we see, by implication, the importance that the universities had for theology.

What, then, was Aquinas' solution to the problems of his age?

Aquinas stated that there were two distinct sciences, philosophy and theology. Philosophy relies on reason alone; theology uses the truths derived from revelation. Aquinas argued that because God is the author of all truth, it is impossible to think that anything in the natural order could contradict what Jesus – God's representative – taught concerning the supernatural order.

We recall that the Early Fathers had seen enlightened Classical thought as an expression of the *Logos*, and so not in contradiction to the revelation of the Gospels. Their notion of the *Logos* was Classical; that is, it was the utterance or communication of a transcendent Being. The *Logos* was both the actual pattern of the world we know and – through the agency of chosen men – utterances concerning that pattern. With respect to understanding the Creation, the Early Fathers emphasized the need for change of being (*morphosis*). A man needed to change his inner being in order to know the truth. If a man succeeded in this, he would see what is real, and the rest would fall into place. Yet, in the world of everyday, they acknowledged that there was a need for human reason. Faith does need reason. It was just a matter of keeping harmony between the two, under the leadership of faith. The Patristic point of view gives clear primacy to supernatural revelation – or the direct insight of Higher Centers – over rational activity.

The thirteenth-century Aristotelians within the Church were, by comparison, more concerned to 'get things right' at the level of knowledge, so that they might successfully relate to rapid changes in the Civilizational Order. They hoped that, through their efforts, the Church might succeed in its discursive struggles with its multiple foes on the planetary surface. But would it retain the immediacy and awe of Early Christianity? Aquinas was – in some degree – able to answer both requirements, although in his writing the emphasis is on the conceptual side. In other words, he does not write as a teacher of the Great Work (what the Buddhists would call a Vajrayana teacher), but as a scholastic theologian who has some experience of Higher Centers (what the Buddhists would call a Mahayana scholar). While Aquinas did belong to a Monastic Order (the Dominican) he was not the product of a Christian Spiritual Tradition but an awakened being in service of the Christian Religion.

In his logic Aquinas more or less adopted the Aristotelian view. With relation to political philosophy (the organization of Christian Civilization), he did not reject the views outlined by Saint Augustine in *The City of God* – but he, and the other scholastics, created a new foundation for the study of political organizations based on Aristotle's definition of the purpose of civil society. Man is naturally a social and a political animal. By giving human beings a nature which requires cooperation of other human beings for its welfare and survival, God ordained Man for society. Man learns things that God wishes him to learn by participating in society. This view allows a relation between faith and more pragmatic thinking. Aquinas opened up the same relation between theology, politics, law, and science that Muhammad had opened up in the last ten years of his teaching life.

We note that in these reflections Aquinas is addressing the relation of the Church to the Civilizational Order, not the relation of the Church to the Spiritual Tradition. He solved many problems for the Church, and solved them with some degree of inspiration. In so doing he gave life to the Church at the very point where the Tradition was no longer able to do that.

To summarize the twelfth century, with the increasing power of the monarchies and the expanded role of the Church, the Monastic Orders – and with them the conscious lineages of the Christian Spiritual Traditions – were in retreat. The Church was, increasingly, fulfilling the needs of the Christian Civilization. The Church now began to play a leading role, but in leading – when it should follow – it did not receive the same current of life from the Christian Tradition. We must keep in mind that by this time there was no longer a direct equivalence between the Monastic Orders and the

Christian Tradition. The Tradition existed within the Monastic Order. The outer shell of the Monastic Order was Religion, or what we have called the First Work as that was practiced within the Religion. In the twelfth century the Christian Traditions (like the *tariqa* within the *taifa*) were doing everything they could to preserve what was real: prolonged presence and the techniques for the transformation of suffering. They did not need more knowledge in order to succeed with this. So, while the new universities announced themselves as centers of learning and the Scholastics disputed on many subjects, the Men of the Tradition pressed quietly onward into the Sphere of Sentient Being. In this, if in nothing else, they succeeded, for the Spiritual Traditions did survive the Middle Ages. But by the beginning of the twelfth century the nature of their service to the level one below was no longer as clear. At the same time they had – increasingly – to struggle for their very survival in the heated atmosphere of Church politics. And so they focused on their first priority and their area of expertise. But a Spiritual Tradition cannot be sustained with relation only to the level that it is on. This 'spiritual introversion' was the beginning of a gradual loss of place, both in relation to the level one below and the level one above – for the two are not separate.

The loss of place of the Monastic Orders was marked, rather dramatically, by the Fourth Lateran Council in 1213. Under pressure from the European monarchs, Pope Innocent III limited the number of the Orders and began the process of confiscating their lands. The Christian Tradition itself became ever more invisible, its central concern being to sustain its delicate lineages of conscious life. Through the Late Medieval period and into the Baroque era there was still a succession of saints, transmitting presence from one generation to the next with the inherited wisdom of centuries behind them.

Retrenchment of the Monastic Orders and Retreat of the Tradition

Let us return to developments in the secular world. Where the eleventh century saw the impact of Aristotle and Islam, the twelfth saw the beginning of the end of the feudal system. Beginning from 1348 the Black Plague reduced the estates of the nobility, and indirectly helped to increase the size and independence of the cities. This brought about an increasing centralization of finance, a development of international trade, and a rise of the mercantile classes generally. All of these factors again strengthened the Monarchy. Centralized authority and a national military force had become necessary to sustain the infrastructures of economic life.

By the fourteenth century the individual European nation states had begun to function more and more independently and to decide European issues amongst themselves rather than with reference to the Church. They were naturally resistant to the powers of the Monastic Orders, as these represented pan-European powers. The most dangerous of these was the Order of the Knights Templar, which had arisen during the Crusades, and was – at the beginning of the fourteenth century – the strongest military force in Europe. We noted the 'first shock' of the Fourth Lateran Council in 1213, which began the process of the confiscation of monastic lands. The definitive moment in the 'loss of place' of the Monastic Orders came, however, in 1307 with the papal bull of Pope Clement V who – acting under pressure from Philip IV of France – instructed all Christian monarchs to arrest all Templars and seize their assets. The Western European nations conspired to act in league to seize and execute the leading Knights Templar and to destroy the Order itself. As a result many hundreds of Templars were burned at the stake. Thus the increasingly independent and powerful nation states used the Church to reduce the scope and influence of the Monastic Orders.

From this point, however, the Church was increasingly forced to adjust itself to the separate national requirements of whatever country it was in. As Church politics had usurped the power of the Monastic Orders, monarchical power politics gradually usurped ecclesiastical authority. Italian and French dynasties struggled for control of the papacy itself, the seat of the papacy shifting to Avignon in France between 1309 and 1376. Following this there was an *actual papal schism*, where, between 1378 and 1417, rival lines of French and Italian popes coexisted. It was a discrediting of Religion that brought about a subtle yet fundamental change in the spirit of the age.

All of these developments led ultimately to the great split of the Protestant Reformation in the sixteenth century, the scope and impact of which were largely determined by those nation states who could not wield decisive influence in Rome to win independence from it. The religious wars of the Reformation period followed. The result of this was a split of religious denomination by country, under the governing principle 'let the subject conform to the religion of his sovereign.' This principle guided both the Peace of Augsburg in 1555 and the Peace of Westphalia in 1648. The religious life of Europe was being dominated by entirely pragmatic considerations. The split of the universal church into competing churches, and a century of the most dreadful religious wars, created a secular atmosphere in Europe that was constantly reinforced by the ever-expanding activity of the mercantile classes. The ascendant bourgeoisie were intelligent, educated, independent, and dynamic, and while they gave substance to the new Enlightened Absolutist regimes, they were at the same time cunning, rapacious, and self-centered.

The Monastic Orders did survive, but lost their central place in the working of things. The Spiritual Traditions within the Orders also survived, and while the fifteenth century saw a continuing secularization of life, there was – in the late fifteenth and sixteenth centuries – a reform and revival of Monastic Life. This reform came entirely from within, and it came out of the continuing current of the Great Work.

We think of figures such as Meister Eckhart (Dominican, 1260-1327), Julian of Norwich (Benedictine, 1342-1416), Catherine of Siena (Dominican, 1347-1380), Bernardino of Siena (Franciscan, 1380-1444), Teresa of Ávila (Discalced Carmelite, 1515-1582), and John de Ypres Álvarez, or Saint John of the Cross (Discalced Carmelite, 1542-1591).

Saint Teresa of Ávila gives us the best example of the spirit of the Catholic Counter Reformation. Her reform of the Carmelite Order was based on a purely apostolic notion of the contemplative life. Only if the Carmelites sustained themselves in prolonged presence, to the point of entering into the Sphere of Sentient Being, could they atone for the religious confusion of Mankind in the sixteenth century. Contemplative prayer was adopted as the center and the end of all activity. Saint Teresa's protégé, Saint John of the Cross, was probably the greatest Christian teacher since the end of the High Middle Ages.

The many Christian mystics, both Catholic and Protestant, of the fourteenth through seventeenth centuries – such as John Ruysbroeck (1293-1361), Johannes Tauler (d. 1361), Ignatius Loyola (1491-1556), Jacob Boehme (1575-1624), and William Law (1686-1761) – have left us with moving and original writings. Some are poetic, some visionary, some link with the ancient Hermetic teachings, some celebrate new discoveries of the relation of Man to God. Many of these people are unquestionably conscious beings, and some initiated Group Work that had an enduring effect on both the Christian Religion and the Christian Civilization. But this kind of teaching is not characteristic of the work of the Spiritual Traditions. The Traditions *already have* the state of consciousness and they *already have* the connection to Higher School, and they can understand these things directly, through the experience of Higher Centers. They do not need florid poetry, grandiloquent prose, or amazing visions, and even less a theology hardened by centuries of schismatic debate. The art of the Spiritual Traditions is to deepen the connection to Higher School and to communicate their experience of Higher Centers as directly as they can to those who can understand it.

THE STORY OF MAN

The role of the Christian Tradition in the time of the Early Fathers was to leaven the Christian world view, as expressed in theology, with the insights of Higher Centers. But by the Late Middle Ages theology itself had been mutilated by the unrelenting pressure of religious strife. Increasingly the Men of the Tradition were inclined to 'keep out of it,' for it was so easy to be distracted by the sectarian tensions of the age.

The style of the Traditions is epitomized by the work of the anonymous English monk who wrote *The Cloud of Unknowing*. His hypothetical student is instructed – with intensity and without fanaticism – in such a way that he will succeed with meditation on a moment-by-moment basis and never be deterred. He will know how to place all value on that, and not on something else.

The influence of figures of the Spiritual Tradition, like Meister Eckhart, Teresa of Ávila, and John of the Cross, was tangible and universal in pre-Enlightenment Absolutist Europe. The Christian Religion, despite the presence of many 'dead' figures in key positions, was still a Living Religion in the sixteenth century. From the sixteenth through the eighteenth centuries, we have evidence of the continuing work of the Christian Tradition within the Monastic Orders. But the upheaval of the French Revolution, and the wars that followed from it, had a disastrous effect on both Tradition and Religion. While Group Work, in different forms, survived into the nineteenth century, the Spiritual Traditions of Western Christianity did not.

CHAPTER 39

Development of the Traditions of Eastern Christianity

Having described the Monastic Orders of the Catholic Church, we must turn now to developments on the Orthodox side, and here we face a challenge. Where in Western Christianity there were distinct Monastic Orders, each with its own rule and history, in the East there were no distinct Monastic Orders. All monks followed the rule of Basil of Caesarea, and Basil himself founded no order. Thus, while monasteries sprang up everywhere, particular spiritual lineages and particular programmes of spiritual work are much more difficult to trace. Nevertheless we see clear evidence of the work of an Eastern Christian Tradition, both in relation to the Orthodox Religion and in relation to the Byzantine Civilization – and we must try to present this in the general way that we can.

To link the work of the Spiritual Traditions to Byzantium we must go back again to the beginnings of Christian monasticism. We know that the Christian Tradition was directly at work in Egypt, Syria, and the Sinai in the first, second, and third centuries. Its principal concern was to isolate the work on Higher Centers and to perfect the Work of the Steward in service to that. And there were certainly direct links between the apostolic teaching of Paul, Andrew, and John and the monastic communities that appeared in Egypt, Syria, Greece, and later Cappadocia, but the remarkable story behind these lines of transmission has been lost to history.

We noted that, at the beginning of the fourth century, Christianity became the state religion of the Roman Empire. This development was formally signaled in 325 when Constantine called the Council of Nicea to unify both the Church and its theology. From this moment forward the Christian Religion changed profoundly; its membership increased rapidly, its social responsibilities multiplied, and its clergy began to wield real temporal power. A world religion began to take form, fulfilling many important social functions: baptisms, weddings, funerals, the celebration of religious holidays, and counseling of many different kinds.

In response to the many new demands being made on it, the Church began to develop independently of the Spiritual Tradition. Increasingly high ecclesiastical office was given to men without presence and without the experience of Higher Centers – and these people were set to work in an institution that bore ever-greater temporal responsibility.

In reaction to this process of secularization there emerged a monastic movement within the Eastern Church. This movement was inspired by the example of the Men of the Tradition, whose example was visible in the *sketes* and in the related monastic communities. Certain of these monks seemed not to be subject to the secular influence and the 'pride of position' that had grown common in the episcopal hierarchy; these were men who knew the experience of Higher Centers from within and who lived a life unswervingly dedicated to the defeat of the Lower Self. The Christians who were in touch with these men were thus exposed to something of the essence of Christianity, and in contrast to this they saw a vast ecclesiastical structure developing that had little relation to the work of Christ and his Apostles.

The monastic movement developed in two phases. There was a first wave from about the time of the Council of Nicea (325) to the Council of Constantinople in 381. The presence of the Spiritual Tradition was evidenced by the formative influence of Athanasius and the Cappadocian Fathers in the Council of 381. After this Council the continuing expansion of the Church, and of its many social functions, caused the pendulum to swing the other way. Church positions were often sold (the practice of simony) and men without religious training were often raised to the episcopate. Additionally, as the employ of the Church increased, its need for revenues grew accordingly. There were constant financial crises, and Church lands were often sold off simply as a means of resolving financial problems. Some of the Churches were given rights of monopoly in certain industries and at the same time made exempt from taxation. Newly ordained clerics often had to pay considerable sums to the local priest, as a kind of admission fee. Former civil servants whom the Emperor wished to reward might be given Church Sees.

More generally, the tone was wrong. In the Byzantine East bishops might appear at theaters, horseracing shows, or gladiatorial fights, and senior ecclesiastics might be seen at the gambling houses.

In this context the monastic movement regained momentum, and there was a second wave which reached a kind of hiatus in the mid-fifth century. Of course it was not possible for the movement to demand that the high clergy show some degree of presence or some capacity to respond to Higher Centers. But it did demand a reform of all the abuses listed above, and asked that the high clergy engage in real spiritual work.

In the early sixth century Justinian (r. 527-565) established himself as the Emperor of Byzantium and reunited the Eastern and the Western Empires. He promoted a radical reform of the military, of civil administration, of law, and above all of the Church. This man had internalized, and made his own, the entire body of criticism put forward by the monastic movement. Whether the example of the Tradition had entered him through direct contact or whether the Gods used him as a tool to remold Byzantine Civilization, we cannot tell. We know only that he initiated a radical reform of the Church with the ideals of the monastic movement in mind. Whether he did it consciously or as a product of circumstance, *Justinian put the Spiritual Tradition forward* – and because of his reforms the monastic movement penetrated deeply into the life of the Church. From the second half of the sixth century men living under the monastic vow began to secure a firm footing in the ecclesiastical hierarchy.

This reform began in the East but soon spread to the Western Empire, which Justinian's armies were busy liberating. In 579 Pelagius became the first monastic pope, and he was followed by Gregory (r. 590-604), who was directly affiliated with and who actively promoted the Benedictines. In the Churches of Constantinople, Jerusalem, Alexandria, and Antioch, monks under vow became, at different times, Patriarchs.

Sometime after 568 the Byzantines lost their control of Europe west of Greece, but within the Eastern Empire ecclesiastical hierarchy came increasingly under monastic control. And Justinian's reforms were not restricted to the sphere of Religion; he took it upon himself to define the very paradigm of Civilizational Order by rewriting the Great Code of Byzantine Law and so redefining the relation of Church and State.

In the rewritten code Church and State were to form a single organism. Within this whole the priesthood (*sacerdotium*) and the imperial power (*imperium*) were distinct, yet interdependent. Neither one controlled the other; each had its own proper sphere and each was autonomous. Yet the close cooperation of the two was essential to realizing the polity of the Empire. Justinian stated that – between the two – there must be a relation of symphony, or harmony. This was the ideal, at least. Given the unregenerate state of humanity, a conflict of Church and State was unavoidable. We could say that this conflict was the destiny of the Byzantine Civilization – the engine that was either to drive it forward or destroy it.

Thus, in the formative years of the early sixth century *the Tradition was there*, at the very heart of things. We can be sure that it suffered setbacks and persecutions, that its lineages were interrupted, and that its enemies (internal and external) sometimes triumphed, but it existed, and over eight centuries it gave light to the whole!

Monasticism in Eastern Christianity was based on **1)** the monasteries, which existed throughout the Empire, **2)** privately formed *sketes* of monks, which were common, and **3)** the practice of hermits or ascetics under vow. Solitary monks were found everywhere – in the vicinity of monasteries, on the outskirts of villages, or sequestered in the forest.

One of the outstanding features of Byzantine monasticism, in all its phases, was its championship of the poor and the oppressed. The monks provided organized forms of charity, creating hospitals, orphanages, and hostels for the poor. Beyond this – and more importantly – they provided counsel and guidance that gave meaning to people's lives. Thus the Byzantine monks permeated the Byzantine Civilizational Order with the energies of regenerate Man.

Byzantine Civilization had its strengths and, undeniably, its weaknesses. Its powers of renewal were extraordinary, although – after eleven hundred years of carrying the torch for Christian Civilization – it finally exhausted itself, and succumbed to the ever-mounting pressure of its foes. Certainly there was a history of court intrigue, treachery, and cruelty; the vast Byzantine bureaucracy was sometimes corrupt and even despotic. But there were also men and women of great vision: able administrators, brilliant generals, civil servants dauntless and unswerving in pursuit of the common good. Additionally to this was the splendor of Byzantine art and architecture, with all of the refinement given by the most cunning craftsmanship, craftsmanship that had developed directly out of the craftsmanship known to ancient Greece and Rome. There was a beauty of ceremony and pageant that has never been recaptured, which left an indelible mark on the entire Medieval World. Beyond this there was a richness of common humanity: gentleness, charity, and grace, rounded by a depth of real culture. The whole, then, was leavened by the energies of men and women who gave their lives to the Great Work and who, in their daily activities, reflected the light of a higher level.

THE STORY OF MAN

After the fall of Constantinople in 1453 the Byzantine *sacerdotium* became simply the Eastern Orthodox Church, as it was able to sustain itself in Asia Minor and in Greece. The Orthodox Church of what had been the Byzantine Empire continued, intimately linked with the Orthodox Churches in Bulgaria, Serbia, and Russia. By the time of the Islamic conquest the center of the Eastern Monastic Spiritual Tradition had been firmly established – with some degree of self-sufficiency – at Mount Athos in Greece while the center of the Orthodox Church itself shifted to Moscow. And in the new period there came new generations of spiritual teachers. By the fifteenth century the tradition of the *starets* (Russian) and of the *gerond* (Greek) had been well-established. These were monks who had been called upon by destiny to the rigors of internal work; they were seasoned in retreat, mature in spiritual experience, and capable of guiding others – both in their lives and in their inner work. The *starets* were common enough to be a working part of the Orthodox community, and so contributed significantly to the spiritual culture of their time.

Thus there is a path – now lost to history – from the teaching of the Apostles to the practice of the early monastics of Eastern Christendom. It began in the lines of transmission that developed from the teaching of Paul, Andrew, and John, and came to fruition in the mature monastic culture of Egypt, Syria, the Sinai, and Cappadocia. It took one turn on the road to Alexandria, Antioch, and Constantinople (through Anthony, Athanasius, and Basil) and another on the road to Rome (through Benedict and Gregory).

While we can only speculate about the teaching lineages that existed within the Byzantine Empire and its Slavic extensions, we do know the story of the greatest Orthodox Monastic Tradition, that of Mount Athos. The 'Holy Mountain' was the center of Orthodox monasticism from the mid-ninth century to the late nineteenth. Its history is one of the central dramas in the Story of Man, for it is a history of the direct involvement of Men with Gods, extending over 1700 years.

The Story of Mount Athos

From the time of the Apostles, Greece had been a focal point for Christianity. Sometime in the second century AD monks began to settle on the northernmost peninsula of

Figure 75. **Mount Athos, Simonapetras Monastery**

Chalcidice, known as Mount Athos. These monks took up an eremetic style of life and lived in loosely organized *sketes*. These small but highly focused communities were able to sustain themselves, on the same physical scale, for the next five centuries. While the communities at Mount Athos did not represent a major center of monastic life, they were generally known throughout the Christian world.

With the Islamic conquest of Egypt and the Holy Land in the seventh century AD, the core area of Christian monasticism came under Islamic control, and many of the monks of that region sought the peace and security of Mount Athos. As the population grew a monastic city began to take form. This became, over time, a formal part of the Orthodox Patriarchate of Constantinople and so of the Byzantine Empire. The first monasteries were constructed in the ninth century and, in the year 885, the Emperor Basil I proclaimed Mount Athos a place exclusively for monks. In 962 the central church, the Protaton, was built, and in the following year construction began on the great monastery of the Megisti Lavra, which is still the largest of the monasteries. The community at Mount Athos soon became a pan-Orthodox community, including Georgians, Russians, Serbians, Bulgarians, and Romanians.

From the time Mount Athos became a part of the Orthodox Patriarchate the principal monk, or Protos, was chosen by the Byzantine Emperor himself. This choice was purely ceremonial, affirming the Protos already chosen by the monks of the Holy

Figure 76. **Meteora, Roussano Monastery**

Mountain. The jurisdiction of the Emperor did not in any way interfere with the long established right of the monks to manage their own affairs. The self-government of the monks of Mount Athos stands as a recognition – both by the Byzantine Civilization and the Christian Orthodox Religion – of the authority of a Living Spiritual Tradition, for if a Tradition cannot determine its own internal hierarchy, it cannot function. It is only Higher Centers that can know Higher Centers.

In the tenth century, Athonite monasticism branched out into a new system of monasteries that sprang up in Meteora in the mountains of Central Thessaly. The strange beauty of these monastic retreats is matched only by the monasteries of Tibet, Nepal, and Bhutan. By the end of the tenth century Meteora had become a second monastic state.

A severe trial came to the Athonites in 1202, with the advent of the Fourth Crusade. After the Catholic Crusaders sacked the city of Constantinople, they forcefully occupied Greece, and this gave the Western Church official jurisdiction over the Holy Mountain. There followed a phase of intense persecution. Many Athonite monks were burned at the stake and many more were tortured for their refusal to accept the supremacy of the Roman Bishop and the Catholic doctrine concerning the Trinity. These monks died with all the dignity of the Christian martyrs of the first century. When Pope Innocent III was made aware of this violence (and after the Athonite monks actively petitioned him), he allowed that they might keep their Orthodox faith. Despite this formal recognition the Athonite monks continued their work under the greatest duress.

In 1261 Emperor Michael VIII Palaiologos reconquered Constantinople for Byzantium, and by the time of his death in 1281 the Byzantines had retaken the north of Greece and the Aegean islands. Mount Athos regained its political autonomy and became once more a part of the Patriarchate of Constantinople. The monks were able to return to their traditional way of life, but the world outside of them had changed forever. Despite the Byzantine reconquest, the disaster of the Fourth Crusade marked the beginning of the end of the Byzantine Empire. The monks knew that it was now only a matter of time before one of the Islamic offensives would succeed. And so they worked on, knowing – with a certainty – that they would eventually lose their connection to the Orthodox Patriarchate and face either Catholic or Islamic rule. And in these uncertain years fresh hardships came upon them in the form of repeated assaults by Catalan mercenaries from the north and seagoing pirates from the south. Monks dedicated to formal retreat were periodically called out of their cells to repel invaders scaling the walls with siege ladders.

The Great Spiritual Traditions – with their more open connection to Higher School – are trained to use difficult circumstances as a kind of forcing house for changes that could not otherwise occur. In the last decades of the thirteenth century the Athonites were successful in transforming the hardships of their existence, and this found expression – just after 1300 – in the *Hesychast* movement. Hesychasm (ἡσυχασμός) means literally 'stillness,' or 'silence.' Practices known as Hesychast had been part of Orthodox monasticism from the fourth century, but the early fourteenth century saw a surge of practice based on a new inner competence, and this affected all of Mount Athos.

HESYCHASM

The technique of Hesychasm is a form of **the prayer of the heart** that employs a rigorous control of both breath and posture. We can relate Hesychast terminology (Orthodox monastic usage of Greek) to the language used in Book III. The Hesychast attaches *eros* (ἔρος – the love of the Nine of Hearts for what is higher) to the monastic practice of *sophrosyne* (σωφροσύνη – the exercise of the will in combating imagination). At a certain point the practitioner permanently overcomes **1)** the temptation to *akedia* (ἀκήδια – existing in a passive state with the attention scattered) and **2)** *philantia* (φιλαντία – self-love, whether in the positive form of spiritual pride or the negative form of self-deprecation). This leads him to the point where *the mind drops into the* *heart* (the Steward becomes continuously active under the Nine of Hearts), and the prayer begins to run automatically. Discursive mind becomes passive and the prayer is initiated directly from essence. This corresponds to a major – although not necessarily a final – defeat for the Lower Self. From the time the prayer begins to run automatically the practitioner spends much longer periods free of imagination (*phantasia* – fantasia). Once the ground has been cleared in this way, self-impelled or self-moving meditation (the opening of Higher Centers) begins to occur spontaneously.

In the first decades of the fourteenth century a new standard of work was established at Mount Athos, which soon attracted external resistance. In 1337 a prominent member of the Orthodox Church, Barlaam, was exposed to the practice of Hesychasm at Mount Athos, and immediately reported it as a heresy to the Patriarch at Constantinople, stating that the Hesychasts were claiming a direct knowledge of God. This is a perfect example of Dead Religion attacking Living Tradition. The strong sense of identity and self-importance that so easily attaches to religious office is profoundly threatened in an environment where the Lower Self is passive and the current of invisible presence is alive. In such circumstances the total self-assurance of the prelate can turn, in an instant, into the feeling of a thief caught in the night, and this the Lower Self cannot tolerate.

Following the report of heresy, an Athonite monk – Gregory Palamas – was called upon to defend the Hesychast practice by articulating the theology that was behind it. His first concern, as a theologian, was to "safeguard the direct approach to God." He presented a doctrine of negation, emphasizing God's utter transcendence of the human world. Gregory distinguished between God's essence – what he is in himself – and his energies. Man could not know the essence of God (the objective-universal) but an embodied man (a created being) could go so far as to know the uncreated energies, or uncreated light of the Holy Spirit (World 6, transcending time and space as we know it). God is therefore both unknown and known. The uncreated light is the indication of God's existence that we can know and experience directly, within Creation. It is what the Hesychast can actually aspire to. Indeed, it is the purpose of every Spiritual Tradition to produce men and women with developed Higher Centers who can sustain and prolong this experience.

A synod was held in Constantinople in 1341 and Gregory was asked to present his views. At its conclusion the synod voted to support Gregory and to condemn Barlaam. The controversy, however, continued, as Gregory's opponents attempted to slander him in different ways. In 1344 they secured a second condemnation for heresy. Three other synods on the subject of Hesychasm were held, and finally, in 1351, a synod under the presidency of the Emperor John VI Kantakouzenos *established the Hesychast doctrine as the doctrine of the Orthodox Church*. In 1353 John VI Kantakouzenos retired as the Emperor of Byzantium to practice Hesychasm as a simple monk!

We note the level of concern that existed in the Byzantine Civilization over the practice of the Athonite monks. It reveals a Civilization that has made the Work of a Tradition important to itself. Indeed, to this point in the history of Mount Athos, we see the Byzantine Civilization – in the spirit of Living Religion – supporting a Great Spiritual Tradition.

In the late fourteenth century the Athonite monks, realizing that the Islamic invasion was imminent and knowing of Muhammad's compassionate treatment of the monks at Saint Catherine's monastery in the Sinai, successfully opened a line of communication with the Ottoman Sultans. The Athonites did not harbor the false pride of formal religion; they knew the real importance – for themselves and for humanity – of perpetuating the work they were in, and of preserving the achievement of Hesychasm. They knew that in the Great Work there is always uncertainty, and that the Gods help only those who help themselves. When, in 1430, Sultan Murad II conquered Thessalonika, just north of Mount Athos, the Athonite monks pledged their allegiance. Murad, on his behalf, recognized the monasteries' ownership of their properties, and his successor Sultan Mehmed II formally ratified this when Constantinople fell in 1453. The fifteenth and sixteenth centuries saw relative peace and prosperity on Mount Athos. With the conquest of the Serbian Despotate by the Ottomans many Serbian monks came to the Holy Mountain. Sultan Selim I became a substantial benefactor of the Xiropotamou monastery. In 1517 he issued a *fatwa* stating that wherever Christian monasteries had been burned or damaged, they would be reconstructed. We note that these developments occurred at the same time that the Sufi orders were establishing themselves in Greece!

However, in the century following, circumstances changed and the Ottomans began to tax the land heavily. This culminated, in the seventeenth century, in a general economic crisis. And here again we see the great independence and vision of the Athonites. To face this challenge the monks determined to adopt an *idiorrhythmic* lifestyle. We will recall that under this form individual monks are self-supporting; they can own property and they may live separately. The *idiorrhythmic* lifestyle was taken up at first by a few select monasteries and then – as it proved successful – by all of them. The process was

THE STORY OF MAN

complete by the first half of the eighteenth century. As *idiorrhythmic* monasteries do not have abbots, they were governed by internally selected committees. This flexibility of form was possible because of the true hierarchy of being that was behind it. Mount Athos here reveals itself as a microcosm, in which the process of regeneration coordinates the other processes. And through this time of change the hermits, who lived in silent solitude on the alarming precipices of the southern tip of the peninsula, were allowed to continue their special work – to the benefit of the whole.

Once an economically viable *idiorrhythmic* system had stabilized it was decided that certain of the monasteries should return to the *cenobetic* form (communal lifestyle under a strict rule which governs all activities). Thus, in the second half of the eighteenth century, each of the three forms of monastic life that had developed originally in Egypt – hermit/anchorite, eremitic/idiorrhythmic, and cenobetic – were proceeding side by side in Mount Athos.

Beginning in the late eighteenth century there was yet another renaissance of Athonite monasticism. The Greek edition of the *Philokalia* – a compilation of Orthodox Christian monastic writings considered to be one of the world's great religious texts – was published, and the *Russian Philokalia* appeared shortly after. Missionaries from Mount Athos went into Moldavia, Wallachia, Serbia, and Russia itself to found new Athonite Monastic Orders.

This movement was the source of the nineteenth century revival of the Russian Orthodox Church. The teachings of Mount Athos came to Russia through the initiative of men like Pasius Velichkovsky, Archimandrite Makarius, Ignatii Brianchaninov, and John of Kronstadt. In the early nineteenth century the Russian tsars acknowledged the open connection between Mount Athos and Russian Orthodox Christianity by making large donations to the Holy Mountain. The Romanov family, through to Nicholas II, actively supported Orthodox monasticism both at Mount Athos and in Russia. The Russian Revolution, in conjunction with the impact of the First World War, brought this period to an end. We will review what happened in the years that followed in the section on the Decline of the Traditions.

CHAPTER 40

The Renaissance through Modern Times

The Italian Renaissance, which developed in the context of High-Medieval Europe, saw the resurgence of the vision of a School Civilization, initially within the northern Italian city-states. How did this come about?

As we noted, the stability of Europe in the twelfth and thirteenth centuries led to an increase in trade and an increase in the demand for luxury goods. The Italian craft guilds created the finest luxury goods in Europe: fabrics, dyed silk, brocades, tapestries, needlework, gilded leathers, furniture, glass, ceramics, chemicals, metalwork, fine armor, mosaics, jewelry, and printed books. At the same time Italy – in particular Venice – was the final western destination of the Great Silk Road, which stretched across three continents to China, and this added to what Italy could not herself produce. Additionally the Italian bankers were the most skilled financiers in Europe. Thus, as the medieval cities took form and the market for luxury goods accelerated, the Italian banking families and the associated trade guilds became ever more powerful. As a result certain of the northern Italian cities broke from the control of the local counts and took the form of urban communes. From these cities came the Italian city-states. They were based, like the Greek *poleis* of ancient times, on a certain quality of civic life. At the same time they preserved the forms of medieval court life, and integrated the life of the courtier into the new civic spirit. Yet in their institutions of government there was a much higher degree of transparency and accountability than there had been in the medieval world.

The city-states determined to model themselves on the Greek *poleis* and the early Roman Republic. The conviction that the individual grows towards maturity, both intellectually and morally, through participation in the life of the *polis* or the *repubblica* came to the Italians through the works of Aristotle, Cicero, and Livy. As the Italians were now in a position to study the original Greek and Roman texts, there was a direct awakening of the ancient civic spirit. A Classical conception of education arose, whose object was not only to train learned men, but to produce good citizens.

It was at this point that **the Schools of the Renaissance** emerged, independently from, but often in communication with, the existing Monastic Orders. It is hard now to distinguish just how these schools came into being, but the formation of the Platonic Academy by Cosimo de Medici was certainly a turning point. The Medici Circle rediscovered Classical Platonism: both the concept of the Cosmos of Man and the doctrine of Eros. The Cosmos of Man is the truth behind Plato's *Republic*, and the doctrine of Eros is – in its inner meaning – the love of the Nine of Hearts for the Higher Self. The art of the Renaissance is resonant with this theme.

We shall review, briefly, what the Renaissance Schools took from past ages.

We know that, in the twelfth century, the Scholastics recovered Aristotelianism and much of Classical Science. In the fourteenth century the Renaissance Schools rediscovered Platonism and Neoplatonism – the understanding of how the love of beauty can **1)** form the human essence in a manner conducive to the emergence of Higher Centers and **2)** actually open the gates of Higher Centers.

Further to this the Renaissance rediscovered the principles of art and architecture which implemented the classical 'love of beauty': harmony (*harmonia,* ἁρμονία), symmetry (*symmetria,* συμμετρία), structural order (*taxis,* τάξις), artistic composition (*diathesis,* διάθεσις), compositional patterning (*rythmos,* ῥυθμός), the perfection of style (*thematismaw,* θεματισμω), and the concepts of the archetype (*archetupon,* ἀρχέτυπον) and of the perfection of form (*to eu,* τό εὖ).

Additionally, the Men of the Renaissance were able to relate these principles directly to Aristotle's idea of civic life as a tool for the formation of Man. In an enlightened *politeia* one could create a social environment resonant with beauty, in which the arts exercised a formative influence on Man. In sum, the Renaissance Schools understood – **better than anyone has understood since** – Plato's conception of the formative power of Beauty on Man, and they were able to relate this to the formative power of civic life in a way that was entirely original.

We noted that the Arabic alchemical sciences, incorporating Classical alchemical science, entered Latin Europe in the twelfth and thirteenth centuries – largely through the Church. But these teachings were received by the Church in one way and by secular society in another. In a secular context, the men of the Renaissance were able to pursue this learning further than the churchmen, and indeed further than either the Islamic or

THE STORY OF MAN

the Classical Civilizations were able to do. The Hermetic side of alchemy – those studies under the name of Hermes Trismegistus – became an intrinsic part of the Schools of the Renaissance. This included the study of cosmoses, the relation of microcosm to Macrocosm, and the relation between the different cosmoses within the hierarchy of the Macrocosm. Renaissance Hermeticists drew heavily on the texts of Neoplatonism, with their representations of the Chaldean, Zoroastrian, and Egyptian mysteries - along with whatever other original traces of these ancient teachings they could find. The men of the Renaissance also had access to the teachings of the Kabbalah, and particularly the Sefirot, which provide a parallel description of the different levels of Creation, and themselves draw upon the older Zoroastrian myths.

Renaissance Hermeticism, in its most developed forms, preserved – ultimately from Pharaonic Egypt – the principle of a Triadic Absolute, who completely contains his own opposite and who is – for that reason – the only completely real individual in the Universe. The very act by which the Absolute embraces his own opposite, and so acquires a comprehensive individuality, necessitated Creation (or 'manifestation'). This vision fits *perfectly* with the Greek idea of the Macrocosm, self-sustaining under the Absolute, comprised of a hierarchy of cosmoses contained within cosmoses. Thus, within the Macrocosm, there are different levels of self-hood approximating – in different degrees – the self-hood of the Absolute. Transcendence at every level is driven by Not-Being in whatever form: time, death, entropy, or chaos. These ancient teachings counter the pantheistic tendency of 'Aristotelian' Islam, realized in the writings of Averroes and Avicenna or the 'Aristotelian' Judaism of Maimonides. It is true that, as a developing being acquires consciousness, there is an increase of universality, but this is attended by an increase of true individuality, approximating the individuality of the Absolute. As the Hermetic teaching states: "As above so below."

The alchemical focus on energies, the enhanced sensitivity to energies, and the principle of placing higher energies over lower energies fit perfectly with the Renaissance understanding of art. Indeed, the alchemical vision of a 'spiritual science' was at the very heart of the Renaissance. Leonardo da Vinci was as much an alchemist as an artist – bent on discovering the inner laws governing God's universe and making those visible in art.

The Franciscan alchemist Ramon Lull (1232-1315), who was condemned by the Roman Church in 1376, exercised a great influence on all of the Renaissance thinkers – particularly and very directly Giordano Bruno (1548-1600). Prominent masters of Renaissance alchemical science included Nicholas Flamel (1330-1417), Paracelsus (1493-1541),

John Dee (1527-1608), and Robert Fludd (1574-1637). But the greatest adepts of spiritual alchemy were probably men who remain anonymous, and were so even in their own time. We do know that certain of the fathers of modern Western science were practicing alchemists, including the astronomer Tycho Brahe (1546-1601), Sir Isaac Newton (1642-1727), and Robert Boyle, who first defined the scientific method (1627-1691). Thus the alchemical retort of the Renaissance was the source of modern Western science.

It is a wonder that the Renaissance was not buried under the weight of the legacy it inherited, but its innate creative force was so great that it transformed everything that came within its ambit, giving it the characteristic stamp of the Renaissance Mind and producing entirely original work.

Having said this we must emphasize that the Renaissance was rooted not in new knowledge, but in **a new vision of Man** – which the men and women of those times attempted to realize directly in their common life. As we noted, the Italian High Renaissance was seeded from the republican city-states of northern Italy, which emerged like so many reincarnations of the Greek polis. As we might expect, this development was immediately challenged. Once the medieval communes of Florence, Tuscany, Siena, and Luca had become established as city-states (by about 1390), the much larger monarchy of Milan, under the Visconti family, determined to conquer and then to control all of northern Italy. In 1400 the Visconti threatened to invade Florence and Bologna. Under the immediate threat of invasion the great banking families – the Medici, the Pitti, the Alberti, the Spinelli, the Bardi, the Frescobaldi – held all the more firmly to their Classical ideals. The invasions were repelled, and the Visconti were ultimately overthrown as the ruling dynasty of Milan.

The period of acute tension with Milan came at a time when the most important artistic figures of the early Renaissance were coming of age: Ghiberti, Donatello, Masolino, and Brunelleschi. Each of these men was inculcated with an intense republican spirit. In this atmosphere Classical civic ideals combined with the conception of Man as a microcosm to ignite an unfettered striving for the infinite – the Faustian ideal of the High Renaissance. Man's creativity was seen as a signal of his divine origin. It was this generation that fully recovered the Classical understanding of the formative effect of beauty on the human essence, not only in principle but in practice. And from this point forward there was not only patronage of the arts, but the most gifted patronage that post-Classical Western Civilization has known. It was based on an art which had risen to the level of World 12 and even – in moments of crescendo – to World 6.

With the overthrow of the Visconti, Milan briefly joined the family of republican states and then, from 1489, was ruled by the Sforza family – who were true Renaissance princes and patrons of the arts. Thus the Renaissance city-states of Florence, Venice, and Milan were conceived in the recreated context of Classical Civilization.

This time of new beginnings in Italy corresponded to the end of an age in the Byzantine Empire, which lay just to its southeast. Increasingly the Byzantines sensed their mortality in face of the rising Islamic Empire, and Byzantine scholars began to emigrate north, bringing with them Classical learning in an unbroken line of transmission from ancient Greece and Rome. By 1453, when Constantinople finally fell to the Ottoman Sultan Mehmed II, there had been a tremendous transfer of Classical learning to a class of pupils who could not have been more receptive.

However, the most important thing the Renaissance recovered from the Classical World was not its learning, but its understanding of the relation of Art and Beauty to the realization of human potential – and the related understanding of how the arts can work in concert to elevate Mankind.

Renaissance Christianity

Before Renaissance thought and culture could penetrate the emergent Absolutist Monarchies to the north, the unbridled passion for ancient art and literature had to be balanced with an acknowledgment of the real legacy of the Christian Spiritual Tradition. After Lorenzo Valla made the first critical revision of the New Testament, Marsilio Ficino and Pico della Mirandola, of the Florentine school of Neoplatonic philosophy, set to work on a new theology in a half-Classical, half-Scholastic framework. They drew primarily from the theology of the Early Christian period, for this was closer to the Platonism of the Renaissance School than the Scholastic teachings were. Yet within this framework both Ficino and Pico conceived the position of Man in the universe, his dignity and his creative power, in purely Renaissance terms.

The merging of Christian values with the Classical Vision of Cosmos – as expressed in art and in a certain vision of society – was an idea of almost hypnotic power for the Italian city-states. It was realized *visually* by Masaccio, Titian, Tintoretto, Leonardo, Michelangelo, and Raphael; *philosophically* by Petrarch, Nicolaus Cusanus, Ficino, Pico della Mirandola, and Pomponazzi; and *architecturally* by Brunelleschi, Bramante, and Palladio. It is symbolized by the magnificent edifice of Saint Peter's in Rome (Figure 77 on page 702). We note that this synthesis was potential in the late Classical World,

Figure 77. **Saint Peter's Basilica, Rome**

but it was not – at least in the line of time that we are in – realizable within it. This would have needed a more developed Stoic practice within the Roman civil service, one capable of recognizing and responding to the Christian Spiritual Tradition. It would also have needed a more open attitude within the Early Christian Church. The unified vision of Christian and Classical finally came, with the help of passionate antiquarian research, in fourteenth-century Italy. This vision, having arrived, now seems inevitable; one cannot imagine European Civilization without it.

It remains a source of wonder to us that the Renaissance Schools recovered the Classical idea of the Cosmos, not only in its philosophical aspects but in all its practical applications. They understood the idea of cosmos in relation to the arrangement of the fundamental social functions (cosmic processes) in a hierarchy, according to the intrinsic quality of energies which comprised each one (see Chapter 33). What we have called 'quality of energy' was very quickly recognized and placed in Quattrocento Italy. Here the great artists worked in studios, with a graded system of apprenticeship, so that foundation skills were transmitted forward and critical understandings preserved. Talent was immediately recognized and carefully nurtured. Statesmen and patrons of the arts were in open contact with both the great studios and with the artists themselves, and this led to truly discerning patronage. This pattern, which emerged in Renaissance Italy, was replicated in every European nation state in the century to follow.

The Renaissance under Absolutism

The conquest of Italy by France in 1500 signaled the absorption of the Renaissance, as a cultural movement, into the social dynamic of the rising European nation states. Although the Renaissance vision of civic life was brought to a close by the French invasion, its artistic and cultural ideals continued to develop within the fabric of the European Monarchies. And so, almost symbolically, in 1516 Leonardo da Vinci left the city of Milan for the court of Francis I of France, where he ended his life in service to the king. Although the Italian city-states had lost their precious centers of civic life, the understanding of the place of Art and Beauty in the formation of Man was preserved, and this was to inseminate the European Dynastic states in the centuries to follow. Thus the vital germ lived on, and the destiny of Western Man lived with it.

Before going further we must clarify what we mean when we speak of Absolutism.

We recall, from our study of Medieval Europe, the effect that the Black Death had on the Medieval Civilization: the depletion of the noble estates, the corresponding growth of towns, and the general development of the urban economy. But while there was a marked weakening of the nobility, this did not lead immediately to the preeminence of the mercantile classes. The towns themselves, the banks, the guilds, and the trade organizations were all dependent on centralized authority. They wished to exist independently of the nobility, and at the same time they needed infrastructures which they could not generate by themselves. Thus, as the noble estates weakened, the monarchies began to centralize authority within the nation. A standing army and a bureaucracy with extensive instruments of administration became necessary to each of the European nation states.

As trade flourished, cities grew and new forms of economic life developed. The noble estates became part of a national economy and the nobles themselves became permanently dependent on the monarch. The patchwork systems of noble estates, which had characterized the High Medieval monarchies, were integrated into unified kingdoms, and in the fifteenth century centralized monarchies emerged in France, England, and Austria.

While the term Absolutism implies the absolute power of a monarch, this phase of monarchism actually saw the opening up of a theater of civic life. Whereas Absolutist government was associated with the theory of the 'divine right of kings' and its rhetoric was 'absolutist,' in fact these monarchies were also constitutional. A condition of Absolutist government was that a working balance of power be created amongst its different social groupings, which the monarch could then mediate. Thus these governments were built on constitutions that would help to determine that balance. The constitutions enabled a secular civic space in which a working balance of power could be established. The bureaucracies which were created to manage the expanded infrastructures of the Absolutist nation states were connected to this same civic space. They became – in some ways – a working link between the monarchy, the nobles, and the rising business classes. From these bureaucracies projects could be initiated which united the interests of the different social classes.

We see the beginning of true Absolutist centralization during the reigns of: Louis XI of France (r. 1461-1483), Ferdinand and Isabella of Spain (r. 1479-1516), Henry VII of England (r. 1485-1509), and Maximilian I of Austria (Habsburg Holy Roman Emperor, r. 1486-1519).

The Absolutist States were then consolidated under the reigns of Henri IV of France (r. 1589-1610), Henry VIII of England (r. 1509-1547), Charles I of Spain (Habsburg Holy Roman Emperor r. 1519-1556), and Phillip II of Spain (r. 1554-1598), and Ferdinand I in Austria (Habsburg Holy Roman Emperor, r. 1531-1564).

Some of the most famous Absolutist rulers were exemplars of Enlightened Absolutism: Louis XIV of France, Peter the Great and Catherine the Great of Russia, Leopold I of Austria, John V of Portugal, Frederick II of Denmark, Charles XI and Charles XII of Sweden, Frederick the Great of Prussia, and Elizabeth I of England.

To understand just how the inspiration of the Renaissance carried forward into this new theater of life, we must review certain developments that occurred within the Absolutist Monarchies.

The weakening of the great noble estates and the centralization of the European nation states was not the demise of the nobility. This very reconfiguration created new opportunities, of a different kind, for the noble classes. The lower echelons of the nobility proceeded to make themselves indispensable to the new armies and the new administrations that were emerging. **The ethos of a service aristocracy** came into being, and court life acquired a new centrality. There was the echo of the Roman *cursus honorum*. New chivalric orders were created to integrate the lesser nobility of the provinces into the royal court, to launch royal projects, and to provide avenues for aspiring nobles and burghers to rise. In England there was *the Order of the Garter* (1348), in Austria and Spain *the Order of the Golden Fleece* (1430), in France *the Order of Saint Michel* (1469), in Hungary *the Order of Saint George* (1325), and a host of others. There were also orders of a different kind, such as the Freemasons or the Rosicrucians, which were independent of particular nation states, yet connected to the patronage of the great dynastic families of Europe. Certain of these pan-European orders, or even the sub-orders of these orders, could easily have been vehicles for Living Traditions or the means of providing the patronage for them. Many more of these orders would have been connected with Group Work of different kinds.

In the pattern of Renaissance Absolutism the balance that emerged between merchant and noblemen and between urban and chivalric culture was dependent on the polity of the individual court, and the results varied in each European country.

The civic life and culture of the early Italian city-states was recreated in this expanded theater of court life and civil service. What was preserved was the secular-classical tone and the idea of realizing one's Self in a shared common life. What was lost was the Ciceronian republicanism so prized by the city-states. The ideal of the Ciceronian citizen was replaced by the Augustan ideal of a service aristocracy, based on the principle of active participation in a living whole. In this new social space the assimilation of the Italian achievements in literature, in art, in education, in politics, and in science became the central task. It became, indeed, the passion of the age. From this moment forward the Renaissance became a movement of European scope, and the Schools of the Renaissance – once under the patronage of the bankers – were now under the patronage of an emergent service nobility.

The new Chivalric Orders, which we might call *the Orders of the Service Aristocracy*, fostered the cosmopolitanism of (what we now think of as) Old Europe. The rising Service Aristocracy helped to integrate the life of the European courts. This occurred even through the dreadful struggles of the Reformation and Counter-Reformation. The great dynastic houses continued to network amongst themselves, share a common social life, make alliances, and intermarry. Many of the Chivalric Orders had all of Europe as their recruiting base. But where the internationalism fostered by the Monastic Orders in the tenth century was unqualified, the internationalism of the Service Aristocracy was qualified by the material interests of the different nation states. Nevertheless the new cosmopolitanism facilitated patronage, and – more importantly – it allowed those who 'had ears to hear' to know when and where the Great Work might appear.

Under Absolutism the work of the Schools of the Renaissance ran parallel with that of the Western Monastic Orders, which were – after 800 years – in a phase of retrenchment. While the Monastic orders were a preservation of the values of the past, the Renaissance Schools were an anticipation of the future.

It is hard to make an assessment of the work of Spiritual Traditions in this time: group work attempts to rise to the level of a Tradition; there is a sudden politically-motivated purge, or loss of needed patronage, and activities come to a halt; word goes out of a new center of activity – in one of the German duchies or one of the Italian provinces – and the members of the inner circle begin to orient around that point; names change and new activities commence. The process is hard to track, and it is particularly hard to determine the different levels of activity. There was, for example, clearly something behind the work of the Masonic Order, but by the eighteenth century there were literally millions of Masons spread all over Europe, doing different things in different places. It became the fashion, in certain social circles, to become a member of a Masonic Lodge. In this context it is very hard to see what is real, when something that is real stops being quite so real, and when the essential forces regroup and regather. There is the additional difficulty that great art and great literature – which this period produced in abundance – are not certain signs of the Great Work. For these reasons we are not able to follow the development of the Schools of the Renaissance individually and in detail. Johann Goethe's *Wilhelm Meister's Apprenticeship* and Hermann Hesse's novels *Journey to the East* and *The Glass Bead Game* give us faint after images of this period.

What we can see in this environment is that there emerged titans, like Shakespeare, Bach, and Leonardo da Vinci, who were microcosmoses of the entire European Civilization and who were directly linked to the designs and purposes of Higher School. They were representatives of the transcendent inner life of Europe, and a gift from the Gods to Mankind.

The Schools of the Renaissance leave us with the faint but unmistakable image of **Tradition as architect of the Cosmos of Man**. They contain this potential, which is always only partly realized. Indeed this was the last great, formative cosmic vision for humanity of which we are aware. So they were, in some way, both less and more than their contemporaries.

The Coming of the European Enlightenment

There was, however, another side to the development of Absolutist Europe. With the rise of the Absolutist State there came, inevitably – generation by generation – the rise of an increasingly able class of bankers, merchants, and financiers. The commercial life of Europe flowered as the markets of the world opened up to it. At the same time the naked pursuit of material gain by the rising business classes displaced the ordained order of service that was at the heart of Medieval Society and the sense of the sacred that went with that. Through the seventeenth and eighteenth centuries secular thought and secular culture, coupled with the rise of science, culminated in the movement that we now call the Western Enlightenment.

The perspective of the Enlightenment is represented in the idea that 'Man is the measure of all things.'

This idea actually came from the older Renaissance Schools, where it was understood in relation to the ancient Hermetic idea of a hierarchy of cosmoses, microcosm contained within Macrocosm. Renaissance thinkers referred to this as 'the Great Chain of Being.' Man, then, was 'the measure of all things' because he is a microcosm of the living whole. The Renaissance view did not at all imply that there are no powers above Man in the universe.

But the Enlightenment thinkers understood the idea that 'Man is the measure of all things' to mean that Man is at the center of a mechanistic universe, where the higher life forms develop out of the lower, and Man himself develops by freeing himself from all that is primitive and superstitious. God may or may not exist on the outside of this vast, clockwork mechanism. Man's immediate goal is to establish mastery over the System of Nature to which he was previously subject. Man's 'good,' then, is the well-being and security of men. Service to the level one above is dismissed as superstition, and the focus shifts to a practical and effective 'self-service.' In this context the idea that 'Man is the measure of all things' becomes an insular and anthropomorphic view. This 'man-centered' vision of the universe was reinforced by the beginning of what we now call the population explosion.

And here we have the beginnings of the progressivism which has become so pervasive in the West. At the time of the first Industrial Revolution, it was principally a belief in progress, as a simple cumulation of practical achievements that would change our relation to Nature, and so allow us to overcome the problems of want. It carried within itself the Enlightenment belief that the development of human reason would eclipse the more primitive and superstitious forms of thought. At the same time it subtly internalized the Judeo-Christian sense of an immanently impending 'new heaven and new earth.' The unbounded optimism that was characteristic of the Enlightenment, and the faith that reason will solve all human problems, has now waned, but the current of progressivism still runs deep – for it touches upon Mankind's deep-seated need to believe that 'something good' is in the making for it. The Enlightenment replaced a sacred something good with a secular something good, but the background tone of expectation remains. Additionally, there is a backward-looking aspect to Progressivism. It is not only the faith that the future will bring something good, it is the conviction that our involvement with things of the past acts as a constraint on receiving this secular benediction. The past is, then, the source of all our problems, something that we need to purge ourselves of in order to receive the benefits that the future is waiting to shower over us. But this pending secular nirvana is – from one point of view – simply the complete freedom to exercise a will that is in service to biological life: in other words, the 'will to self-maintenance' that is the province of the Black Queen. It is a future of infinite self-expression and infinite self-gratification. Our true destiny is the polar opposite to this: to enter service to the cosmos above the Cosmos of Man.

The late eighteenth century brought the French and American Revolutions. The first Industrial Revolution came to fruition in the early nineteenth century, and the mid-nineteenth century saw the rise of bourgeoise-democratic political institutions throughout the Western World. At this time the idea that 'Man is the measure of all things' became a general attitude, related – in many ways – to the development of modern science. Enlightenment science was science uprooted from its alchemical base, divorced from the study of a living universe comprised of different levels and divorced from the science of *morphosis* which determines the movement between those levels. In short, Enlightenment science turned its gaze away from the inner transformation of the Microcosmos Man. The ethos of the Enlightenment was given the expression appropriate to its times by the nineteenth-century utilitarian thinkers and was considerably reinforced by the fact that it did appear that Man was now harnessing Nature to serve his own ends. There came, then, the idea – derived from nineteenth-century evolutionary theory – that we are now 'on the top of the heap of history,' and that we have achieved this by ourselves, each generation advancing on the work of the one previous. Having begun as monkeys we have gone from one triumph to the next, becoming the Masters of the World and all of Nature, with designs on the solar system and beyond. It was as though an *enfant terrible* had been released. In the late nineteenth and early twentieth centuries secular life developed a degree of independence and self-determination never before known in history. The positive face of this new-found independence was freedom from superstition and the attempt to take full responsibility for managing the conditions of material life. Its negative face was a loss of awe and wonder; loss of the sense of what is higher than Man; and loss of the feeling of unity with Nature.

The charts in Figure 78 allow us to reflect on the relationship between 1) the increase of population that occurred with the first and second Industrial Revolutions, 2) the

THE STORY OF MAN

POPULATION GROWTH
AND THE SPIRITUAL TRADITIONS

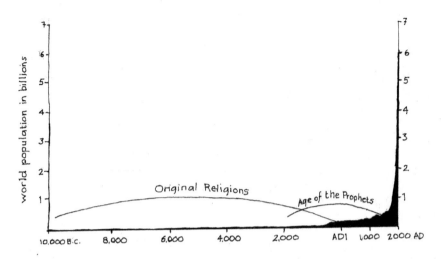

World population remained at less than one million until end of the last ice age.
The agricultural revolution that followed brought the population to five
million by 8000 B.C.

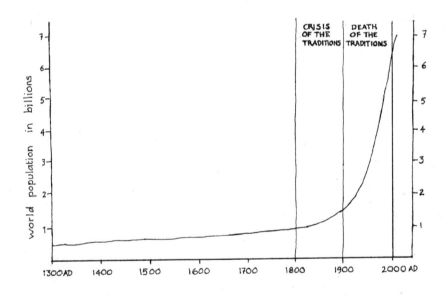

World population reaches one billion by 1800 and two billion by 1927. We mark
the crisis of the Traditions from 1800 to 1900, and the period of the 'death'
of the major Traditions from 1900 to 2000.

The 'crisis' corresponds approximately to the first industrial revolution, and
the 'death' to the second industrial revolution - taken as a combination of a
general use of electricity in conjunction with a certain development of the internal
combustion engine.

Figure 78.   Taken together these two charts suggest a drastic decline in the ratio of conscious
beings to the general population.

diminishing proportion of men and women considered to be conscious beings within their Spiritual Traditions to the total population, and **3)** the ascent of secular values.

BOOK VII

Conclusion

We step back, then, to review the fate of the Great Spiritual Traditions. The first Traditions that we studied – the Shamanic, those of the Original Religions, the Mesopotamian, and the Egyptian – each died a natural death. Each sustained itself for thousands of years, each achieved all that was possible in its own time, and each potentiated developments for the future.

The Prophetic Traditions were tied, in greater or lesser degree, to the peoples of their founders, and so connected to the destiny of those peoples in the changing tides of history. With the rise and fall of the Civilizational Orders the first Prophetic Traditions – the Zoroastrian and Abrahamic – were absorbed into the newer Prophetic Traditions, which followed from them. But the very age of the Prophetic Traditions – as a form of Civilizational Order – itself came to an end.

The second generation of Prophetic Traditions – the Buddhist, the Christian, and the Islamic – successfully defined the field of history for several thousand years, but when the first industrial revolution came they were unable to survive its many social impacts. And the Civilizations that supported these Traditions were not replaced by another order of Civilization capable of sustaining the Great Work in a new context. We emphasize here that many Christian, Islamic, and Buddhist Schools did survive, in the context of their respective Religions. But not the Spiritual Traditions, as we have defined them here. Certainly, there were determined attempts by the Spiritual Traditions to make this transition, as shown in the drama of the Tibetan diaspora in the last half of the twentieth century. In the West the secular Traditions that were spawned by the Italian Renaissance continued to develop in the context of the Absolutist nation states, but they failed with the fading vision of the Cosmos of Man in the nineteenth and early twentieth centuries. For neither capitalist democracy nor state socialism – in the forms that we know them – have shown themselves conducive to the formation of a Cosmos of Man.

Finally, having reviewed this decline, we must ask ourselves how it all sums? Where do we presently stand?

CHAPTER 41

The Decline of the Spiritual Traditions

Let us review the Prophetic Spiritual Traditions, one by one.

The Tradition of Abraham

Of the Tradition of Abraham we know little. His work profoundly affected the Judaic Tradition, and we see him principally through the eyes of that Tradition.

We see evidence of the original Abrahamic peoples in the Old Testament at the point where Moses and the Israelites enter Canaan. Not wanting to confront the Canaanites, they passed to the east of the Dead Sea, through the lands of the Amorites, Moabites, and Edomites. Moses instructed the Israelites not to attempt to occupy the lands of these people because they were the children of Lot, the nephew and disciple of Abraham. At the same time the Amorites, Moabites, and Edomites did not allow the Israelites to pass through their lands, forcing them to make a difficult passage through the deserts to the east. We can see that there was little sense of identity between these earlier Abrahamic peoples and the Israelites.

We see evidence of the remains of the Abrahamic Tradition again when Muhammad explains to the Arabs that the Kaaba in Mecca had been created by Abraham and Ishmael for the purpose of worshipping the One God. By the time of Muhammad the original Abrahamic monotheism had entirely deteriorated into a polytheistic religion that was little more than superstition.

The Abrahamic Tradition was the first Prophetic Tradition to expire, yet it was a beginning, and there were other notes to follow from it – in the Judaic, the Christian, and the Muslim Worlds.

The Tradition of Zoroaster

Zoroastrianism was the next Prophetic Tradition of which we know, and it was the next to expire. It was centered in Persia. The conquest of Persia by Alexander, and the rule of the Seleucid Kings who followed him, did not break the Tradition of the Magi. The Seleucids were eventually displaced by Parthian invaders, who did not have a religion of their own but espoused Hellenism, both as culture and religion. From 248 BC to 226 AD the state religion of Persia was a syncretic combination of Hellenism and Zoroastrianism. In 226 the Sassanid dynasty overthrew the Parthians and established a Zoroastrian kingdom which lasted for more than four centuries. This continuity of faith was broken by the Muslim conquest of Persia in 640. The Muslim conquest occurred at a time when the Sassanid government had been corrupt for at least a century and when Islam was at the height of its prophetic charisma. Many of the Persians recognized in Islam a Living Religion, and some of these came into contact with the Spiritual Tradition that was behind it. Many of the Magi decided to accept Muhammad as the next Zoroastrian prophet in the predicted cycle of the Saoshants. In the end the majority of the Persians converted to Islam, while a small community of the Magi sustained itself independently for many centuries. Some migrated to India and Zoroastrianism continued there, even into the twentieth century. By the twelfth century AD the Persian Magi appear increasingly as eccentrics, only indirectly related to the social order of which they were are a part. Zoroastrianism has continued as a peripheral faith down to the present time.

The Judaic Tradition

With respect to the Judaic Prophetic Tradition, we witnessed the rupture of Tradition, Religion, and Civilization that began from the end of the period of Babylonian exile.

With the end of both the Kingdoms of Israel and Judah, there was a separation of the Prophets and the Kings. The line of Prophets continued, in a much lower relief, but the line of Kings – and so the covenant – had ended forever. The Prophets that followed Ezekiel were not, then, part of a living cosmos in the way that their predecessors had been. Their vision of the Judaic Civilizational Order had changed, and their message took on much more of what we would call an existential tone. The Pyramid of Man had come apart. Nevertheless, the Judaic Spiritual Tradition survived the prophetic form.

Both Tradition and Religion were renewed in the period of the Babylonian Exile, and the work of the Tradition became centrally connected to Second-Temple Judaism.

With the destruction of the Second Temple and the suppression of Judaism that followed the Bar Kokhba revolt, the diaspora reached its final phase. While some Jews remained in the area around Jerusalem, most emigrated. Those who settled in Central and Eastern Europe became known as the Ashkenazic Jews; those who settled in Iberia and North Africa, the Sephardic Jews; and those who inhabited the area around Babylon, the Mizrahi Jews.

The original Civilization of the Israelite peoples – First and Second Temple Judaism – had come to an end, but both the Tradition and the Living Religion were able to sustain themselves. As we noted, the Talmud was a benchmark of this achievement. The various threats to the Jewish people, and to their way of life, made their Religion all the more precious to them. Behind this Religion were some of the greatest prophets ever given to Man and the hopes and strivings of a great nation over eight centuries. The Jewish culture was so strongly reinforced by its Tradition and its ancient Religion that the Religion itself was able to survive by making itself 'portable,' so that it might survive within a host civilization. It seems very likely that the Spiritual Tradition also survived the 'Roman' diaspora, to complete its final phase of work. For how many centuries it continued we do not know, but it eventually disappears from sight. However, just as the Judaic Prophetic Tradition was followed by a Second-Temple Tradition, the Spiritual Tradition itself was followed by a series of conscious teachers connected with the Religion. According to the theory advanced in Book III, a Religion, once divorced from a Spiritual Tradition, ceases to be a Living Religion. Yet the Judaic Religion was a central part of the life of the Jewish people, and it continued to be inseminated by conscious influence in the form of group work. It appears that it did survive as a Living Religion. One result of this was the careful preservation of the oral teachings of the ancient Tradition – the Kabbalah – for over more than a millennium.

As the centuries passed the Jews adjusted themselves to the different societies in which they were able to exist, but they remained periodically subject to persecution of different kinds. They lived a 'ghetto' existence, that is, segregated from the rest of the community with certain restrictions. However, their situation began to change in the late Medieval period, as Europe opened up to trade and mercantile activity. Cities began to develop independently of the feudal desmenes, and a more cosmopolitan urban culture came into being. The Jewish people became an essential part of the development of the great banking houses that emerged during this period. As a result the Jews of the diaspora found themselves increasingly integrated into the general economic life of Europe. It was at this time that many of them began to rethink their religious views. The great Jewish theologian Maimonides (1135-1204) began a more rationalist and humanist interpretation of Jewish theology, which was based – in some degree – on the actual experience of Higher Centers. Maimonides' philosophy itself was inspired by the revival of Aristotelian thought spurred by the Andalusian Muslim polymath, Averroes (1126-1198). Developing Aristotle's fundamental insights Maimonides made Jewish theology more universal and in that way brought it closer to the atmosphere of the teachings of the first years of the Kingdom.

However at the same time the Jews were being brought into the economic life of Europe, they were being more actively persecuted. In this general atmosphere there was the growing expectation of a Messiah. Additionally, amongst the orthodox European Jews, there was a growing a concern about the popularization of the religion which had begun with Maimonides. In these circumstances the orthodox inner circle decided to publish a set of secret teachings which had previously been transmitted orally – with scrupulous care – for 1,700 years. This was, of course, the Kabbalah. It had been transmitted forward by a conscious teaching that was the direct inheritor of the ancient Judaic Spiritual Tradition. The reaction of this conscious Group to neo-Aristotelian Judaism parallels exactly the reaction of medieval High Christianity to the neo-Aristotelian Christian theology that was appearing at the same time. There was the same concern that a rationalist universalism might displace the spiritual force and authority that always attends the actual presence of a higher level – and that always asks you to be more than what you presently are.

The Kabbalists presented these inner teachings with a prologue. They explained that when the diaspora first began, the Sanhedrin leaders were concerned that the Jews being deported, some of whom knew the Kabbalistic teachings, would be unsupervised by conscious teachers. Without the presence of a conscious teacher the oral teaching could easily be misunderstood and that might lead to deviant forms of practice. As a result it was decided that the Kabbalistic teachings would be made secret and transferred orally under closely controlled conditions. The European Kabbalists of the thirteenth century felt that, at the point of history they had reached, publication would do more good than harm.

We provide, then, a very brief review of the Kabbalistic material, as evidence – albeit at a distance – of the teachings of a very great Spiritual Tradition.

THE KABBALAH

The teaching of the Kabbalah represents God as being unknowable, utterly transcending the personal God of popular religion. The Created Universe is the revealed aspect of God, and it is at least partially accessible to human thought. God created the universe through ten sets of emanations, known as the *Sefirot*, which are presented in the diagram of the Kabbalistic tree. Each emanation is the expression of a spiritual quality: will, wisdom, understanding, mercy, strength, harmony, victory, glory, power, and dominion.

Although the Kabbalah affirms the unity of God, it states that there is an evil counterpart to his goodness. God would not be transcendent if he did not transcend an evil that was real. While the holy emanations of the *Sefirot* (and thus the inner structure of Creation) comes from God's right side, a negative mirror image of these emanations comes from the left side. The right side (and the transcendent reality embracing both sides) is the *Ein Sof*. The negative mirror image of the right side is the *Sitra Achra*. The point is that the Sitra Achra is fully alive within the divine structure of the *Sefirot*. (Sitra Achra is translated as the Other Side.) While it has no direct power over the *Ein Sof*, it does have direct power over Mankind, and hence the human condition of unceasing imagination, ever-recurrent negative emotion, and unknowing servitude to an illusory sense of 'I.' Under these conditions the medium of human experience is strongly colored by fear, greed, aggression, and individual self-preoccupation. Mankind inhabits a psychological world divorced from the objective measure of action. Man is never sure of himself. The Kabbalah teaches that this condition exists in order to give Mankind the capacity for choice, that he may learn to choose the good and to make it his own.

Thus, while Mankind does inhabit a kind of 'training ground' for the *Ein Sof*, it is still under Samael, the Angel of the Dark Side, and it is collectively unaware of this fact. We are literally held under a malignant spell, from which we can only extricate ourselves by the development of conscious will.

There is something in the Kabbalah which has the ring of very old objective truth. At the same time the texts of the Kabbalah are probably at some distance from the oral transmission of the Kingdom in the ninth century BC. They are colored by a kind of fear and a very dark picture of the human condition. They do not carry the 'great good tidings' of the Spiritual Traditions: that Man has the freedom to serve the level one above, and so the ability to serve the level one below – in a way that is both objective and true. The Kabbalistic teachings reflect – at least to a degree – the gnostic emphasis of the conscious beings and the groups who worked for so many centuries outside the Light of the original First Temple Spiritual Tradition. Indeed, divorced from the Pyramid of Man, objective knowledge does tend to produce a 'gnostic' stance. (Here we refer to the second definition of Gnosticism given in Chapter 31: the belief that there is an unresolved struggle of good against evil that reaches to the highest levels of the universe, and that – as a result of this – human beings are trapped in a false reality.) In the Great Work this emphasis on the dark side is always neutralized by the magic of a direct, working connection with the Gods in Eternity. This brings a flavor of joy and universality; it brings a white heat of existence embracing all men and all things. In relation to humanity at large, it brings not fear and revulsion, but the unpretentious compassion that is embodied in the bodhisattva vow.

Thus we see in thirteenth-century Judaism the same gnostic and humanistic tendencies that had existed in the first centuries of Christianity. Maimonides was almost certainly a conscious being working in relation to the Jewish Religion, who taught with a pantheistic-humanistic emphasis. The authors of the Kabbalah were part of a conscious group, descended from the Judaic Spiritual Tradition, who had acquired a gnostic emphasis.

The centuries to follow saw the success of the Jewish subculture within the body of Western Civilization, culminating in the rise of the great nineteenth-century banking houses of Warburg and Rothschild. The intensity of Group work faded proportionately, although conscious work of different kinds did continue. Indeed we see the traces of a conscious vision in the creation of the State of Israel (in the works of Martin Buber) yet the state itself was formed independently of a Spiritual Tradition. It was not, in any way, a replication of the Kingdom of the ninth century BC.

We move now to consider the fate of the Christian Tradition, which began out of the Judaic. The younger child survived its parent, continuing actively through the European Middle Ages into the early post-Renaissance period.

The Christian Traditions

By the eleventh century AD the Christian Religion had achieved a richness and universality to rival that of Brahmanic India. It supported many Monastic Orders simultaneously in Europe and in the Levant. The spiritual development of the Eastern Apostolic churches continued vigorously in the period after the Islamic conquest. Yet, as we noted, the development of Western Civilization, from the Renaissance through to the first Industrial Revolution, brought about a situation where secular life dominated religion.

The rise of secular values which began in the Baroque period, with the emergence of the great European nation states, brought a crisis to the Christian Spiritual Traditions, which we have described in Chapter 40.

We noted that, with the rise of the modern nation states, both the Church and the Monastic Orders were displaced as pan-European temporal powers. From 1307 there began a general seizure of church lands, and throughout the fourteenth century there was a decline of monasticism as a style of life. In the sixteenth century the great schism of the Protestant and Catholic churches occurred, and as a result each of the European nation states chose its own religion. From the sixteenth century onward all of the critical or formative developments in European Civilization occurred within the secular sphere.

The European Monastic Traditions were medieval. They had their beginnings in the late-Classical period and their greatest flowering in the tenth, eleventh, and twelfth centuries. They were distant from the movement of the European Renaissance, and culturally divorced from the Enlightenment, the emergence of democracy, and the first Industrial Revolution. Whereas in early medieval times the Monastic Orders led the Church, in the post-Renaissance period Church and State bonded, and the Monastic Orders were displaced. Yet the Orders managed somehow to survive, in their particular ecclesiastical niche, even into the twentieth century.

We mention in passing the great resurgence of Orthodox monasticism that occurred in eighteenth- and nineteenth-century Russia, through the influence of the monks of Mount Athos – and directly connected to the practice of the 'prayer of the heart.' This was a reseeding of Spiritual Tradition and a true renewal of the Russian Orthodox Religion – yet it suffered a devastating purge in the wake of the Russian Revolution. In the 1920s and 1930s more than one hundred bishops were murdered, along with tens of thousands of priests. In what seems like a sidelight of twentieth-century history, more Christians were martyred than were put to death in the Roman Colosseum.

More generally, the complete inability of Christianity to moderate the violence of the first Industrial Revolution or to prevent the devastation of the First and Second World Wars subtly undermined its credence in Europe. By the midpoint of the twentieth century, people still felt the need for the Church, but they stopped looking to it for the solution to human problems. Christianity now lacked the force of a Living Religion. It provided consolation and guidance, but it no longer challenged its adherents to change themselves internally. It was not a Living Religion.

As the sincere adherents of religion became fewer, the capacity for Religion to support Tradition diminished. The victory of science over religion in the nineteenth century was not compensated by any new and greater vision.

In the records of enlightened twentieth-century monks, like Thomas Merton or Silouan the Athonite, one increasingly senses isolation. Thomas Merton was more stimulated by his travels in Tibet than he was by the work of his colleagues. Silouan felt that his own Spiritual Tradition was at its end, and he expressed the hope that another kind of Tradition would follow it in the West.

The Buddhist Traditions

It was mentioned in Chapter 29 of Book IV that Buddhism was destroyed in India, the land of its origin, by the twelfth-century Muslim invaders. It was virtually extinct as a Religion in India by the beginning of the thirteenth century. By the nineteenth century there were pockets of Buddhist practitioners in India, and in the twentieth century Buddhism has seen a revival due to the presence in exile of the fourteenth Dalai Lama of Tibet and the development of Tibetan communities in the north of India.

We also noted in Chapter 29 that the rise of Communism in China had a disastrous effect on the practice of Buddhism in that country. The general development of secular life, under Western influence, radically undermined the Buddhist faith in Japan and Southeast Asia. The Buddhist Religion adapted to changing conditions, and the Spiritual Traditions internal to it struggled for their very life.

We studied the fate of the great Buddhist Orders in Tibet and the disasters that befell that country. The Tibetans were dispersed in a pattern exactly following that of the Jewish diaspora of ancient times. The fourteenth Dalai Lama is himself resigned to this situation, and has suggested that the office of priest-king be replaced with the institutional form of parliamentary democracy. He has also indicated the end of the *tulku* system, which the Chinese Communist Party has so strenuously attempted to co-opt. While this seems an absurd action for a political party which claims itself atheist, it reveals the unscrupulous nature of the CCP. At the time of writing the Dalai Lama is considering the selection of a living successor as the head of the Buddhist religion to circumvent Chinese politics.

It was the Dalai Lama himself who pointed out that crises, such as the invasion and occupation of Tibet, are never caused by purely external factors. There is always the extent to which problems internal to the Tradition (or Religion or Civilization) have attracted the external situation.

Examining the story of Tibetan Buddhism, with an eye to its possibilities, realized and unrealized, gives us a measure to understand the crisis of the Traditions in the late nineteenth and twentieth centuries.

In Tibet we clearly see the Religion of Tibetan Buddhism – which provided the ruling caste of the Civilizational Order – failing to receive sufficiently the inner truth of the Spiritual Traditions, and, at the same time, failing to actively cultivate the Civilizational Order for which it was responsible. In the Pyramid of Man each level must serve the level one above and the level one below. In the Tibetan instance Religion came to the fore, at the expense of both Civilization and Tradition. Had the internal form of each of the four Tibetan Orders (Gelug, Sakya, Kagyu, and Nyingma) been closer to the archetype of true individuality and collective life, the rigidification of the *dharma* at the level of Religion might never have occurred. It is the dynamic of service to the level one above and the level one below that neutralizes the tendency towards self-preoccupation, as that exists on every level, and allows the lower levels to see the higher levels for what they are. Under these conditions Tibet might have achieved an enlightened civic life, developing independently of the patron/priest relationship. The Tradition might then have been able to directly connect with talented and well-intentioned Tibetan lay people, working outside the confines of monastic life. These people would have enabled the ruling Orders to make the trade relations and political alliances that would have freed the country from dependence on the dated – and often treacherous – patron priest relationship. The thirteenth Dalai Lama might then have been able to realize his aim of bringing the country of Tibet into the modern world. The Rimé movement – coming in the nineteenth century to enable this transition from within – might then have regenerated Buddhist practice in such a way as to create more open, ecumenic forms – allowing Tibet to set an example to the world and so allowing the Orders to openly share their great understanding.

Such a Tibet might have been able to provide guidance for the rest of humanity in the crises of the late twentieth and early twenty-first centuries.

The Sufi Traditions

We noted that, in the generations after Muhammad, the Sufis became 'the hidden heart of Islam.' By the seventeenth century the Sufi Orders (in the form of the great Dervish Orders) had largely merged with the Islamic state, and by the eighteenth century they had themselves become Religions. The Sufi Orders organized all the major craft guilds and controlled and managed entire sectors of the economy. The very legitimacy of the Ottoman Caliphate rested on the Sufi Orders of Islam.

We mentioned that the Naqshbandi Order provided a model of how the inner teaching of a Spiritual Tradition might sustain itself in an organization containing as many as eight million members. The other Sufi Orders each followed this model, in one way or another, trying to create an order within an order. But the impact of directly wielding such vast temporal power was great, and by the nineteenth century different forms of corruption had become entrenched. This is, again, the story of the dominance of secular life over Religion, the weakening of Living Religion, and the increasing separation of the Religion from the Spiritual Tradition that informs it.

The First World War finally brought the collapse of the Ottoman Caliphate. In the chaos that ensued, the Turkish general Kemal Atatürk attempted to establish a democratic, secular, and unitary constitutional republic. In so doing he outlawed the Sufi Orders of Islam, stating that Civilization could not exist when a society was organized around sheiks, dervishes, and disciples, from whom a client population gained various material and spiritual benefits. In the historical circumstances in which he said this, he was right. Atatürk's criticism of the Orders, of their corruption and their intransigence, was not unfounded. He was, of course, criticizing the Religion of Sufism, not the inner Tradition itself, as he was completely unaware of this. Indeed the inner Tradition had come to exist in a very low profile, as it became more and more difficult for it to pursue the Great Work within the Orders as they were then established.

Thus on September 2, 1925 the 'institutional expression' of Sufism was made illegal in Turkey, the country which had previously been the seat of the Islamic Caliphate – and which had attained this status by taking its Islamic credentials from the Sufis. From this moment the Sufi Orders quickly disappeared from the Arab and Turkish world. Survivals of the Orders in Pakistan, Egypt, and North Africa continue to this day. Some of the organizations derived from the original Orders have managed to perpetuate themselves, and multiple claimants to the throne of Sufi Master exist, but it is doubtful that any of the Orders – which were once the inner light of Islam – have managed to survive. Group work, in different forms, certainly continued after 1925.

From the early 1960s, under the inspiration of men like Idries Shah, there have been numerous spurious revivals of Sufism in the West, but they lack any real connection to the *silsila* of the Great Sufi Traditions of earlier centuries. In 1953 Emin Chikou, a mature Naqshbandi teacher, who received his formative training before the Turkish Republic was established, said to J.G. Bennett: "I tell you that there is no longer any Islam – just as there is no Judaism and no Christianity. All has been spoiled."[1]

With respect to the Traditions generally, the rise of secular life that occurred throughout the nineteenth century, and the influence that this had on the Religions, made it increasingly difficult for the Traditions to work in conjunction with them. It was also increasingly difficult for the Traditions to sustain themselves within the fabric of civil society. As a result the twentieth century brought crisis to each of the major Spiritual Traditions: Tibetan, Hindu, Sufi, Zen, Orthodox, and Catholic. This was certainly not the end of activity under these names, but it was the end of strong, centered Spiritual Traditions, where a number of Men Number Five worked under the direction of a yet higher teacher, who was in turn directly answerable to the Gods. In relation to the Civilizations that were connected to these Traditions, it was the fading out of the faint, penumbral image of the Pyramid of Man. Indeed, the very taste of the Pyramid of Man has now gone from the pallet of humanity. Probably each of these Traditions began to come asunder in the early nineteenth century, and broke into groups, or disintegrated entirely, in the first half of the twentieth.

In our attempt to bring the Story of Man through to the historical present, we will now turn to the impulse towards School Civilization that had its beginnings in Classical Greece and Rome, and that reached its apogee in the Renaissance of Western Civilization that occurred from the fourteenth century onward.

---

1. Reported by J.G. Bennett in *Journeys in Islamic Countries*, Bennett Books, Santa Fe, New Mexico, 2000, p. 45.

The Fading Vision of the Cosmos of Man

While the vision of a Completed Cosmos of Man – where conscious beings emerge in an enlightened theater of public life, and a Ruling Tradition develops on this basis – has not been realized in the West, a step-down version of it is nevertheless integral to Western history. This vision was central to Greece and Rome, and became central to the European family of Civilizations after the time of the Italian Renaissance. While much of the impact of the Renaissance was neutralized in the religious wars of the Reformation period, the renewed vision of the Cosmos of Man did not die. What, then, was its fate?

Let us begin by remembering the kind of polity that supported the vision of the Cosmos of Man in Classical times. We noted that in both Classical Greece and Imperial Rome conscious beings made their appearance in the medium of civic life, and affected that medium profoundly. The polity of the Greek city-states included both aristocratic and democratic elements, while that of Imperial Rome was essentially aristocratic, with democratic forums at each level of society, and with an Emperor as mediator. In the Cosmos of Man there must be a relation between aristocracy and democracy; presumably it might emerge from either form.

For an aristocracy to support the kind of civic life which would engender the Cosmos of Man, it would have to be based on a true hierarchy of being. There would also have to be a high degree of accountability, a system of universal law, and public forums and representative bodies of different kinds. In other words, an aristocracy must have a high degree of transparency in order to work. Indeed, the whole idea of Plato's *Republic* was based on the principles of transparency and accountability. Additionally, the governing class must be able to recognize and recruit talent from outside of itself. This corrects the inherent tendency of aristocratic forms to rigidity and corruption. Both the Greek city-states and Imperial Rome achieved – for brief periods of time – a degree of transparency and an ability to recruit talent from without. The advantage of an aristocracy is that it is able to educate and develop a cadre in such a way as to raise the level of the whole. The fineness of energy required for particular functions of society can be connected to the skills and abilities of the people who are to perform them. The disadvantage of an aristocracy is that its most developed functions tend to become connected to particular family lines, and are then limited or distorted by them and – in that degree – divorced from the principle of service to the whole.

For a democracy to support the level of civic life that would engender the Cosmos of Man, it must be able to counteract the tendency to develop a polity which is a simple averaging out of the material interests of different groups. Under a democracy civic life all too easily becomes a matter of expedience and collective bargaining, which is – in one degree or another – manipulated by economic interest. A democracy must be able to bring men and women of natural ability to positions which make use of that ability, while holding them accountable for their use of the powers given. Most particularly democracy must be able to attract people of high moral caliber to positions of authority. This and this alone neutralizes the tendency of the democratic form to cater to the appetites of the numerical mass, and to powerful economic interests. While these appetites and interests are legitimate, and must in some way be fulfilled, human Civilization cannot be based on a vision of their efficient collective gratification.

The great strength of the democratic system is its accountability and transparency. But only under conditions where this system can consistently bring the best men and women forward can there be cultural ideals, leadership by example, discerning patronage in the arts, and a system of education which aspires to make Man more than what he presently is.

There is an idea which must be taken into account in any attempt to assess the potentials of aristocratic and democratic polities to form the Cosmos of Man. It is the idea that there is a natural hierarchy in Mankind. This can be understood with reference to the ideas of 'previous lifetimes' and of *karma*, two concepts often used to explain the varying capacities of individuals, but which can be understood quite independently from this by examining the way in which Mankind functions as a living and connected whole.

NATURAL HIERARCHY

Natural hierarchy is not a forced hierarchy of control, created by one social stratum to extract surplus from another; it is rather a hierarchy that is natural to the way we work together in groups. It is a precondition and a necessary component of the Cosmos of Man.

The hierarchy of a symphony orchestra provides a perfect example. When a conductor stands at the front of an orchestra and gesticulates, without actually guiding or inspiring the individual performers, the performers do not 'make music.' When the conductor is connected to each individual performer, is fully acknowledged by each one, and actually conducts the group of them, there is a very different kind of music. Each instrument plays better and more truly. The conductor and the orchestra are two connected levels of a hierarchy, which extends to include the audience as a third level. The hierarchy of conductor and orchestra acquires a fourth level when the conductor has made the phrasing of the music internal to his being, so that he remembers the entire piece of music 'all at once.' When this occurs the whole force and exact timing of the music emerge moment by moment, and are felt in every note. Thus the hierarchy of audience, orchestra, and conductor is extended upward into the 'idea' of the music in the mind of the composer. Inspired conductors like Wilhelm Furtwängler, Rudolf Kempe, Otto Klemperer, Nikolaus Harnoncourt, or Sergiu Celebidache can create a complete unity of music, orchestra, and listening audience – enabling a deeper current of life to pass through all. In some magical way, then, the whole of the musical composition exists in each performer, and each performer creatively and knowingly enhances this whole. Each part feels its participation in a whole that transcends it.

On the basis of this example we can generalize. A natural hierarchy is comprised of many complementary – but not identical – parts, and a process which unites those parts in action, in relation to the whole that they serve. It is a hierarchy which acknowledges general fitness and ability, and on this basis delegates responsibility for the different functions through which the whole realizes itself. When such a dynamic exists, each of the individual parts directly experiences its relation to a living whole, and so becomes more than what it otherwise would be.

This principle of hierarchy applies equally on the scale of human society. A society can function as a natural hierarchy when its parts or members recognize a common goal, and when they possess shared ideals in relation to that goal. Then *each part participates in realizing the potential that is in the Whole, and each part feels the whole* through this participation. When society is enhanced by the Work of a Living Tradition, this whole is extended through to the level of the Gods who, in their inscrutable way, monitor the activities of the human race. Under these circumstances, both society and each of the parts which comprise it are more real and alive than they otherwise would be.

The connection of the whole to the part that exists under these circumstances is the opposite of the connection of the whole to the part that exists in crowd emotion. A

THE STORY OF MAN

crowd emotion seals off the individuals who are subject to it from any kind of higher influence. A crowd experiences only 'a crowd,' which is less, not more, than an individual. While a crowd may, under certain circumstances, understand things that – for example – a corrupt dictator may not, its understanding is immeasurably less than that required to sustain true Civilizational Order.

Jean Jacques Rousseau presented what we have called a 'crowd' as the 'general will' of society. Rousseau's idea became central to the social-contract theory, which is the basis of much democratic political theory. Rousseau's general will is the expression of a population of equivalent individuals, who are all representatives of Man in his natural state. This natural state is hypothesized as a state of innocence, reflecting Man's original 'species being.' But Rousseau presumes that natural Man is somehow without a Lower Self, and that the general will is therefore essentially virtuous. This myth of the innocence of natural Man is something to which, in many ways, we are still subject. The truth is that – to use the Hermetic terminology – the 'vibrational range' of Mankind has always included, and will always include, the negative reality of Worlds 96, 192, and 384.[2] Thus, while William Wordsworth is right to say that we come into this world "trailing clouds of glory" (Worlds 6 and 12), we come also with a live connection to worlds lower than the human. And what if we each come – not for the first time – but carrying the mixed karma of previous lives? What Rousseau hoped would come out of the egalitarian crowd has never come out of any crowd at any time in history. The results he anticipated certainly haven't come out in the 250 years since he wrote. Neither authentic genius, nor sustained presence, nor real solutions to the problems of society can come out of a group of people that is no more than a crowd. The crowd members can feel 'the crowd,' but they have no real feeling of the whole that contains it. They simply imagine that the whole is 'themselves extended.'

In a natural hierarchy there is, by contrast, a realization of the potentials that exist, both in the individuals and in the social order. Each individual must adjust his or her will – which carries within itself the animal assertiveness of the nine of clubs – to the will of the other individuals involved and to the shared goals of society. As a result there is, for each individual, a gain in True Individuality. Each person absorbs, compensates, or otherwise neutralizes the dross of his own Lower Self in order to access something that is beyond it. In a true hierarchy the will of the individual is 'opened out' to incorporate something that is beyond the will of the Black Queen.

---

2. See the Glossary entry for 'World 96.'

We see evidence of the amended will of many individuals working in concert in the Sphinx, the Athenian Parthenon, the Hagia Sophia, the Gothic Cathedrals, and the Mesoamerican plazas. Each of these structures was created in an impossibly short period of time by many people working at once, and each gives evidence of profound inspiration. These structures are not the result of genius-level preplanning combined with almost unlimited material resource. They are the result of a natural hierarchy intuitively in touch with a living whole which includes Worlds 6 and 12. These natural hierarchies gave something not only to their own Civilizational Order, but to all of Mankind.

The fact of natural hierarchy does not imply that an aristocracy (or an aristocratic monarchy) is the ideal form of government. Monarchies and aristocracies can suppress natural hierarchy just as effectively as democracies, and democracy can and has supported natural hierarchy in many different forms. But radical democracy does have an intrinsic difficulty in enabling natural hierarchy, and this is painfully revealed in the failure of the democracies of the twentieth and twenty-first centuries to achieve intelligent and discerning patronage in the arts. Bourgeois democracy – always deeply engaged in the manipulation of public opinion – definitely tends to favor popular culture. But having made this point, and having emphasized that it does not exclude democracy from being a vehicle for the Cosmos of Man, let us return to the more general problem.

Both aristocracy and democracy have, as their highest potential, a developed civic life based on a true principle of service. Whichever of these two systems, in the conditions of a particular Civilization, allowed an enlightened community to rule would be the best. We speak not of the rule of one man for one generation – as has actually occurred – but of a system of enlightened rule sustained over many generations. Probably, in the majority of cases, a mixed system would be optimal.

If we take something of democracy and something of aristocracy and the resonance of the celestial hierarchy that comes to us from the Spiritual Traditions, we find the balance of True Individuality and Collective Life that reveals the Archetype of Man. When Man is able to model himself on the Archetype, there is transparency and accountability in relation to the level one above and the level one below. Here we have Plato's guardians! While no Tradition can succeed in government without some accountability to the Civilization that it sustains, the accountability to Higher School has an even greater objective value. It is, at the same time, much rarer. Plato is the only writer who has described it explicitly, and one cannot understand his *Republic* without understanding this, and all that it implies.

To understand how the vision of the Cosmos of Man was lost, we must consider another aspect of our situation.

In Classical times democratic forums did not exist in the context of a highly developed market economy. Since the early nineteenth century, a free-market economy has uniformly been the context of democratic polity. The difficulty of this combination is that a free-market economy has a marked tendency to cater to those human appetites which are the most widespread and the most constant; these are the appetites that we share with the animals. In a technological society, which is capable of producing a great range and diversity of products, the free market creates a psychological environment of consumerism, where people define themselves by what they are able to purchase rather than by the purposes that they serve. Consumerism reinforces the tendency of a market economy to expand the range of human 'needs' in a way entirely unrelated to the purposes Mankind was originally designed to serve. Additionally the manipulative marketing and promotional practices which develop in this context easily and naturally transfer into politics and into civic life.

The tendency to develop markets which are based on the lower range of human needs, and to cultivate the tastes which correspond to those needs, makes it very difficult – on the level of government – to implement enlightened policies with respect to the country as a whole. In other words it makes it difficult for Man's economic activities to serve and develop the higher range of human needs, *or even to define what those needs are*. Whereas the governing classes of Europe in the Middle Ages were able to allocate a significant part of their revenue to the creation of the Gothic Cathedrals, which embodied the highest values of their age, and which have elevated Mankind from that day to this, the modern European social democracies are hardly able to produce a public monument which is not a source of embarrassment. The problem of distinguishing and prioritizing the finer range of human energies has been made more difficult by the development of the mass media – for here there is the marked tendency to create a pseudo-reality, based on the hopes, needs, and desires of Man as he presently is.

We reflect briefly on the rise of the sciences in this context.

The development of the market economy, in conjunction with the sudden ascent of the business classes, brought about a radical development of the sciences. This has had both positive and negative effects. In considering this subject we must keep in mind that there is no 'science'; there are only sciences – particular practices of conceptualization and experiment, which may at times shed light on one another, but which are each defined by their own internal problematic.

In terms of the material presented in Book III, science is the use of the intellect, and to a lesser degree the motor function, to investigate the universe as known to the senses. The tools of science are conceptual; they rightly exclude or limit the perceptions of the emotional and instinctive centers, but they also exclude the special faculties which were given us for the purpose of knowing ourselves in relation to higher levels of the universe. It is right for science to define its own parameters in this way, but at the same time every scientist works in relation to what is outside his own discipline, and is influenced by what is outside his own discipline. A science practiced in the light of Higher Centers would be far more dynamic than a science driven by personal ambition or the desire for profit. And there are examples of what this might be: one is Aristotle's recognition of the role of form as 'final cause,' as that informed his empirical studies, another would be Johann Goethe's concept of the 'primal phenomenon' as a guide to biological research. Each of these discoveries opens an explicitly spiritual dimension to science; both are based on real understandings, yet both have been marginalized in modern research.

Viewed from this perspective, science represents a very partial view, makes use of a very limited set of tools, and is increasingly subject to rapid cycles of error and revision. The human intellect itself has been generated out of one of the lowest levels of the Created Universe. It functions very slowly, with relatively coarse energies, and is ill-adapted to accommodating – or even properly acknowledging – what is outside its own sphere. Additionally, in any individual, the intellect develops in a psychology that is controlled by Imaginary 'I,' and so is ultimately under the control of the instinctive center. It is thus integrally linked to the Man-centered view that holds our species in check. While, in the nineteenth century, science divested itself of religion, it did not divest itself from its immediate social context. Thomas Kuhn understood something of this when he spoke of the "tissue of tenacious error" which inevitably inheres in any science.[3]

While science did have the legitimate need to free itself from religion, and from its own alchemical bases, in order to establish – in each different sphere of investigation – the controls and parameters necessary to its method, it might have received something more from religion and alchemy than it did. Man has been given other faculties than the intellect for the investigation of the universe that contains him, and both the monk and the alchemist used faculties which are dormant in the modern scientist. There can and should be a cross-fertilization between the work of the monk, the alchemist, and

3. Kuhn, Thomas, The *Structure of Scientific Revolutions*, University of Chicago Press, Chicago, 1962.

the scientist, and there is no reason at all why this should destroy the integrity of their respective disciplines. Fritjof Capra (*The Tao of Physics*) and David Bohm (*Wholeness and the Implicate Order*) have marked the 'great divide,' but modern science – taken as a whole – remains true to its bourgeoise patrons and to the spirit of the age.

To presume that our intellectual and moving functions are adequate to make anything more than tentative generalizations about the whole is naïve. To believe that concepts can give us a comprehensive grasp of reality on levels higher than our own is absurd. The main point for Mankind is not to generate more complex and elaborate conceptual webs, but to develop the concepts that serve its needs while activating entirely different faculties for knowing, that is, Higher Centers.

Concepts themselves are quite inadequate to knowing the reality of Worlds 12 and 6. The Gods who reside in these levels make use of symbols rather than concepts, and acquire their knowledge directly through the Higher Centers. Science, then, is the specialty of Man, and – having said this – it is a legitimate specialty.

Yet despite the fact that the concepts of science are **1)** particular to specific sciences and **2)** limited in their relevance to the world of the five senses, individual scientists show themselves quite ready to step outside the parameters of their disciplines and present themselves as the secular gurus of a cult of 'concept-based' individualism. This splices perfectly with the bourgeoise myth of the 'self-creating individual,' triumphant over both God and Nature.

With respect to providing any real benefit to Mankind, science and scientific research are neutral, in the sense that they can be used for either good or evil. They have produced a great deal of both in the last two hundred years. The most extreme example of the misuse of scientific research has been, of course, the nuclear proliferation that has occurred in the last two decades.

Whatever the case, in the last two hundred years, science has become the carrier of many hopes and expectations. With the passing of Living Religion, the inarticulate hope that 'something good must be in store for us' has transferred to science. With the decline of philosophy, science has also inherited the faith in human reason which was the hallmark of the European Enlightenment. If the sciences were used by men of real wisdom, they would certainly provide benefit for humanity. But if we view 'human wisdom' as the ability to use our resources to realize the purposes for which we were originally created, it is clear that science has actually contributed very little. Indeed, as we have seen, we have come closer to this 'real wisdom' in historical periods which long preceded modern science.

Our instinctive faith in science is misplaced, because scientists – as a community – are no more or less virtuous than anyone else. Being a scientist is no more a guarantee of being a fully rounded human being than being an accountant, a bartender, or a professional athlete. Whatever legitimate human needs science can fulfill, and whatever ideals may guide it, in the context of free market democracy it is invariably used to stimulate the lower range of human needs and to secure economic and political advantage. While science has a great potential to serve the principle of the Cosmos of Man, it is not presently playing that role.

To return to the fate of the Cosmos of Man, one decisive result of democratic government in the context of a free-market economy is that *Mankind has increasingly become its own point of reference*. And to the extent that this occurs we seal ourselves off from those levels of the universe that transcend the human.

This tendency, which had its roots in the eighteenth-century Enlightenment, took a quantum leap at the time of the first Industrial Revolution, with the rise of the business classes to command positions, and a second quantum leap in the immediate wake of World War I. The first leap was inspired by the appearance of something new, the vision of a secular society where a rationalized business-like intelligence had free play. The second leap was the result of the destruction of something old: the inner cultural fabric of Old Europe. In a way the First World War was the war of the ascendant business classes, pushing the aristocratic regimes beyond the boundaries that had been established by the Congress of Vienna in 1814-15 and reinforced by the Metternich system that had grown out of it. The war was a signal of the failure of the *ancien regime* and, at the same time, an affirmation of the principle of power politics. In its wake Fascism and Communism immediately made their appearance. A certain kind of communication had failed; there was an end to enlightened patronage, to Mazzini's "good European,"[4] and to the intuitive sense of cosmos that had been part of the old regimes. While the worst excesses of Fascism and Communism have passed, what they destroyed in the course of the twentieth century has never been recovered.

World War I was the death knell of the Spirit of the Renaissance, which had – up to that point – been able to continuously regenerate itself in the fabric of European Civilization. It was as full of life at the end of the nineteenth century as it had been at the end of the sixteenth, for the spirit of the European Renaissance was extraordinarily flexible and creative. But after World War I the aristocratically managed superstructures of

---

4. Referring to a patriotism that goes beyond national feeling, to include the entire European cultural inheritance.

traditional European society gave way to the new pressures arising from its developing economic base. The rapid rise of the capitalist and communist world systems, and the rivalry that developed between them, created a global environment in which material values were determinant over culture.

In other words, by the mid-century, our culture ceased to be rooted in a vision of **the formation of Man** – the ideal that we had inherited from the ancient Greeks. The Greek *polis* had been based on the idea that its citizens would be formed, from childhood onward, by the *paideia* which produces *arête*. The goal of *arête* was immediately reflected in all of the different activities of life, and the result of pursuing this goal was inner transformation, or *morphosis*. This principle had resurfaced in post-classical Western Civilization in many different forms. It was explicit in the chivalric ideal of the perfect knight, which developed – in the Renaissance period – into the Spanish *caballero*, the French *chevalier*, and the English *gentleman* and *gentlewoman*. It was most succinctly expressed – in its final hour – in Johann Goethe's concept of culture as ***bildung*** or 'self-formation.'

THE FORMATION OF MAN:
GOETHE'S CONCEPT OF BILDUNG

Bildung is the developed ability to respond to every circumstance of life by acting from the highest part in oneself. In each act one affirms a higher energy over a lower energy, and at the same time receives the impressions of the outside world in their unstained actuality. In this way one is perpetually reformed by one's experience of life, and in this state one is capable of integrating real cultural ideals and making them central to one's existence.

The following quotations on *bildung* are from Johann Goethe.[5]

Moral Education is closely related to aesthetic education. They form one body, as it were, and neither one can be thought of as attaining perfection without a corresponding development on the part of the other. (GW&E, p. 152, from *Annals*)

Bildung begins along one specific line, to be sure, but it cannot end there. One-sided bildung is no bildung … the individual sciences are only the sense organs, as it were, which we train upon objects … the 'science of sciences' is [HJ: the development of] the *sensus communis* [HJ: the 'receiving plate' of consciousness that is behind every

---

5. See *Goethe: Wisdom and Experience*, compiled by Ludwig Curtius and translated by Hermann J. Weigand, Frederick Ungar Publishing Co., New York, 1964, pp. 152-154.

incoming datum and every sensory impression]. (GW&E, p. 152, from correspondence to Reimer)

> To expect of people that they should harmonize with our individuality is great folly. I have never done this. I have always regarded man as a self-contained individual whom it was up to me to explore and come to know in his peculiarity, without demanding any sympathetic response on his part … it is precisely in our contacts with individualities that do not appeal to us that we are put on our mettle. The need of somehow getting along with them stimulates a variety of facets in us and develops them. (GW&E, p. 154, from *Conversations with Goethe*, by Johann Peter Eckermann)

> To communicate one's personality is an impulse of nature. To accept what is communicated [HJ: from others] in the spirit in which it is offered is bildung. (GW&E, p. 153, from *Maxims and Reflections*)

> The highest point of kultur that a man can rise to is the conviction that he does not figure in the concerns of others. (GW&E, p. 155, from *Maxims and Reflections*)

> It is incredible how much a person of bildung can do for himself and others, when, without ambition to rule, he leads them to do at the right time what conforms to their own promptings, and helps them to the realization of ends which for the most part they clearly envisage while they stumble in their choice of the means. (GW&E, p. 151, from *Wilhelm Meister's Apprenticeship VIII*)

When a dinner guest proposed a toast to the remembrance of 'old times' Goethe replied:

> I do not subscribe to remembrance in your sense of the word. That is an inept way of putting things. Whatever great, beautiful, or significant experiences have come our way must not be recalled again from without and recaptured, as it were; they must rather become part of the tissue of our inner life from the outset, creating a new and better self within us, continuing forever as active agents of our bildung. I do not admit of anything past that we would be warranted in longing to recall; I admit only the existence of what is eternally new as it shapes itself out of the expanded elements of the past. True longing must always be productive and create something that is both new and better. (GW&E, p. 154, from the records of von Muller)

These 'internally formative' ideals – so beautifully summed by Goethe in the nineteenth century – were of ancient origin and once formed part of the fabric of our Civilization; they imply a sensitivity to different levels of energy, and a capacity to place a higher energy over a lower – both internally and externally. The self-referencing aspect of this discipline reaches back to the Greek ideal of *arête* and the ancient meaning of 'personal honor.' While this measure is internal it implies certain standards of external behavior

– and from this comes the responsibility to self-formation in every act, a self-formation that serves both the well-being of others and the life of the Civilizational Order. Thus, from the *arête* of ancient Greece, to the transparent heart of the Benedictine monk, to the vows of a twelfth-century squire entering knighthood, to the ideals of a nineteenth-century service aristocracy, there is continuity. There is a remembrance of things past, such that what is essential in the past enters into the 'tissue of our inner life' to shape what is 'eternally' new in the present.

These ideals were forgotten in the decades that followed World War I, and they were all the more forgotten because the words that described them remained in currency. As a result Europe was less alive in 1946 than it was in 1913, for the internal dimension of its existence had been reduced and flattened out. And thus, in the end, America failed to receive from European Civilization what it had to give, and by the mid-century – after two successive orgies of destruction – Europe no longer had these same cultural ideals to offer. By the early 1950s an emergent mass media could truly proclaim, for America and for the World, that 'the pops are tops.'

From the end of the Second World War the popular press, radio, television, and finally the Internet developed exponentially. All of this occurred in the context of a rapidly expanding consumer market, in which the creation of new human needs and the play on existing needs had become a science of its own. The result was the emergence of a kind of synthetic pseudo-reality, which has further reinforced the sense of Man being his own measure, and diminished the sense of the sacred to its vanishing point.

When we become our own point of reference in this way, we are less sensitive to our place in a living universe. We are less sensitive to the unity of nature that is below us, and less sensitive to the determining intelligence that is above our own. We then cease to feel any responsibility to form ourselves in relation to the order that is above our own. When we take ourselves, and our own subjective needs, as the exclusive point of reference we have lost the measure; we have forgotten the theme of the Story of Man.

The highest culture Man can aspire to is based on **1)** a true or objective understanding of what it means to realize human potential, **2)** an ability to recognize and to manage the different levels of energy that comprise the Cosmos of Man, and **3)** a full acknowledgment of the cosmos above the Cosmos of Man. Man was created to serve the level above the level he is on. He has, of course, the option not to do so, and for that very reason **he is defined by what he serves**. Whenever men and women serve the level one above, they become more like that level, and this affects not only themselves but the men and women on the level immediately below. When the level one below has working contact with the level that is serving something higher, it becomes more aware of the changes that are occurring in that level. It becomes aware that the people undergoing these changes do not become more alien and remote, but more inspiring and easier to work with. The level one below is then itself inspired to change, for the change that it desires is not abstract, but relates to something that is within its sphere of experience. And thus begins a vertical lift, level on level, that runs throughout the body of Mankind. To the extent we take **ourselves** as the sole reference point we become a population of self-preoccupied homonids, uncomfortably lodged in the outermost layers of Creation, unable to awaken from a fitful and unpleasant dream. To the extent that we work in the awareness of what is higher, we are alive – moving, growing, and fulfilling our destiny in every way.

The Relation of the Traditions to Humanity at Large

Having made these general points about Mankind's diminishing awareness of the vertical scale of Creation and of the changing place of the Spiritual Traditions in relation to that, it is appropriate to make a final remark concerning the relation of the Traditions to humanity as a whole. At those points in the line of time when the general Civilizational Order has been most imbued with their influence, the Traditions have often chosen to reveal themselves directly to the general population. These points of deliberate contact represent a significant part of their presence in the collective memory of Mankind. The Traditions have revealed themselves through sacred rituals, theater, dance, and pageants and performances of different kinds. In these moments of direct contact the Traditions represent the truth of Higher Worlds in the medium of everyday life and, in so doing, inseminate the body of Civilization with the energies of Worlds 6 and 12; they become, in the moment of their performance, a bridge between worlds.

Religion, too, attempts to represent the truth of a Higher Level to Mankind, but it does so in a formal or ritualistic manner. The Men of the Traditions, who know the states of consciousness behind the forms and symbols, can do this lightly and spontaneously, with the consummate artistry that allows them – in a chosen moment – to penetrate more deeply and leave indelible marks in the human mind and heart. In this respect no one can perform like the anonymous men and women of the Traditions; they have their own special genius – which grows out of their unique understanding of their personal nothingness. The effect of this understanding allows them to act as pure vessels, both for their art and for the higher influences they bring to humanity through that art. We think of the spellbinding intent of the old-kingdom priests at Saïs re-enacting the death of Osiris; of the cathartic power of the Orphic and Eleusinian mysteries of ancient Greece; of the sweet choiring music of the temple dances of Vedantic India; of the Miracle Plays that enthralled high-Medieval Europe; of the 'butter festival' ceremonies of Buddhist Lhasa, where a wave of presence breaks from a procession of monks winding through a pillared hall; of the magnificent Dervish dances of Turkey and the Levant, which fascinated Islam for a full six centuries.

In these moments of direct contact, an aura of enchantment is created; there may be a sudden stirring of deep emotion, flashes of unforgettable beauty, pathos, anxiety, joy, and then those sudden moments of transcendence where you feel that you have finally found what you were always looking for.

The captivated spectators see the anonymous companies of performers, who have relinquished their personal lives in service to the Gods, displaying an impossible lightness and plasticity. They are capable of complete self-abandonment: of states of possession, of joy, of passion, of celebration, of humor, and – above all – of presence sustained through time. The matchless sense of occasion that goes with these performances reaches back to the great rites of cyclical renewal known to the Original Religions in our shared prehistory. In light of this all the spectators are equal, all are children once again, all pretence is shed for the evening; the young, the old, the rich, the poor, the prince, and the mountebank are one before the enchanting art of the Traditions.

Now when these companies of players and performers finally pack their bags and fold up their tents and leave us to ourselves, it will be a sad hour for humanity. It will be the closing of a door through which light and love and magic of every kind has poured for so many centuries.

CHAPTER 42

Retrospect and Prospect

Looking at the Story of Man as it has unfolded over the full span of history, we see so much to excite our wonder and esteem – but do we see progress with relation to the unique set of spiritual potentials that Man was given in the beginning? Have we in truth moved further from the point that we reached at the time of the transition from tribal Shamanism to the Original Religions? It would appear that, over a period of nearly forty millennia, Man has failed to realize the potentials with which he was originally endowed. How are we to interpret this? What is its significance? When we consider the immense pains that have been taken – on a cosmic scale – to provide Man with the potentials that would place him on a level with the Gods and to create the situation in which those potentials could be realized, we must ask, 'What is the outcome of it all?' Let us take the time here to re-evaluate; let us sift the material we now have at hand.

Each stage and phase of the Story of Man has had its moment of perfection.

Firstly, there was the creation of Man: the initial revelation of the Gods to Mankind, and the ensuing Golden Age where Men and Gods worked openly together.

This was followed by the immeasurably long span of the ancient Shamanic Traditions: the original unity of Man in Nature. This original unity was realized in the great prehistoric cultures of the Russian Steppes, of Southern France, of Spain, and of Central Asia.

Then, in the immediate wake of the last Ice Age, came the age of the Original Religions. This had, as its foundation, the development of agriculture and of towns. In the dawn of our civilization the Gods gave Man the gift of developed language and, with each language type, a Religion relating it to the cosmic center. The first Great Religions became the means for Mankind to renew itself in relation to all that was most sacred to it.

In the Age of the Prophets, which followed from the descent of the Original Religions, we see the highest exemplars of the human race, giving their transcendent life to the communities that formed around them. The white heat of the prophetic community, with its transparent link to the Circle of the Gods, represents the highest level of human achievement.

We turn, then, to the Great Spiritual Traditions, as they are each in themselves – the Egyptian, the Vedic, the Toltec, the Buddhist, the Judaic, the Christian, the Sufi – each with its glorious works and its enduring legacies to Mankind.

Moving from the Traditions to the Civilizational Orders they engendered, we see – time and again – clear traces of the Pyramid of Man: the linked hierarchy that connects the different levels of man in a lift-on-lift upward movement. We remember, in the background of recorded history, the Civilization of the Vedas and the Pharaonic Civilization of ancient Egypt. Then came the paired Kings and Prophets of ancient Israel, the Mauryan Kings of India, and the Dharma Kings of Tibet. On an Imperial scale there was the magical blend of Taoism and Confucianism that helped to form Han, Tang, Song and Ming China, and the precious first generation of the Meiji Restoration in Japan. And in the New World there is the sacred city of Teotihuacan.

We consider again the vision of the completed Cosmos of Man: a Civilization governed and managed by a Spiritual Tradition. We have the echoes of this in Classical Greece and Augustan Rome, and – more than a millennium later – in the Italian city-states. We reflect on the incomparable art, literature, and philosophy that came from each of these. The Renaissance-Classical vision of a 'city' remains a high-water mark for the Civilizations of the West.

Finally, in the middle of the last century, we glimpse the faint semblance of an enlightened international community in Cordell Hull's draft for the Charter of the United Nations and in Dag Hammarskjöld's concept of the International Civil Servant.

When we reflect on these images we begin to have a sense of what they were, each in and for themselves. They shine like the "patines of bright gold" that line the floor of heaven.

And behind all of this there is the consummating vision of humanity transcending itself in the perfection of its common life: Zoroaster's prophecy of the passage of humanity into the Realm of Eternal Light; the coming of a New Heaven and a New

Earth spoken of in the Book of Revelation; the Vedic prophecy of the last Avatar; the Buddha's prophecy of the coming of the Maitreya; Muhammad's prophecy of the return of Christ at the end of time.

We have seen many traces of the archetypal community, where the relation between True Individuality and Collective Life has been momentarily achieved, and the link to the next highest cosmos momentarily secured. For a generation or two, here and there through history, there has been a healing of the wound that occurred in our prehistory, when the Gods withdrew from open contact with Mankind. Wherever the necessary balance of True Individuality and Collective Life has been achieved, there have been a number of enlightened men and women in contact with, and held accountable to, the Gods – and a much larger circle of men and women in contact with and held accountable to these enlightened individuals.

We see the promise, but not the potential realized. We see the patterns of the archetypes shining through the social fabric, but, at the same time, we see little evidence of their full realization. None of the enlightened societies that we know from history are more than the flowering of a generation or two, although there are often periodic movements of renewal. Whenever we do see the golden hour of a civilization, we see the tragedy of its decline. It is only the light of the Great Spiritual Traditions that we see perpetuated over centuries, and even here the path is sometimes difficult to follow.

Thus, it seems that human history is not a great theodicy of the kind envisaged by G. W. F. Hegel in *The Phenomenology of Spirit*, where a succession of civilizations is destined to culminate in the self-recognition of the Absolute; where all of the frustrations, agonies, and apparently meaningless sufferings of humanity issue finally – without miscarriage – into the enhanced lucidity of Absolute Spirit.

Messianic speculations such as these may have seemed tenable at the beginning of the nineteenth century, but they are much more difficult to entertain at the beginning of the twenty-first. Yet if we were to sit down with Hegel and point out to him all that has transpired in the last 200 years – the population explosion, the perversion of the ideals that originally informed both liberal democracy and socialism, the two world wars, the development of weapons of mass destruction, the damage to the planet's ecosystem, the disappearance of Living Religion, and the displacement of high art by popular culture – he might simply smile and remind us that the Absolute is not in hurry. And perhaps he is right. Perhaps a New Age is yet to dawn, a synthetic phase of civilization where humanity is effectively globalized, and national, ethnic, gender, and class rivalries are finally transcended. But, in the historical present, conflict in each of these areas continues unabated. And even should a global polity of peace, tolerance, and accountability be achieved in our time, it would not indicate – with certainty – a conscious connection to the level above our own. We have yet to see any sign of a Prophet, or of a circle of conscious beings active in public life, or – more generally – a re-emergence of the Pyramid of Man. These things usually come at the beginning of the new age.

Perhaps there are older Traditions secretly regenerating themselves, waiting for the moment to make themselves known? Perhaps there will be a sudden renewal of the Buddhist, the Taoist, or the Sufi Traditions? Perhaps, indeed, there are entirely new Traditions in the offing? But if Spiritual Traditions were suddenly to make their appearance, would an increasingly secular humanity accept their leadership? The greatest and the least acknowledged problem of the twenty-first century is that the ground has not been prepared for a re-emergence of the Pyramid of Man.

Even if all the stones for the pyramid's apex were cut and ready, stacked in the corner of some unknown quarry, we would still need the thousands of rougher-cut stones that form the base. While the stones of the apex may exist without our knowledge, the mountain of stones needed to form the base could never be concealed. The base does not exist. The experience of our past has not been assimilated into the historical present. There is not – on a general level – a sensitivity to Man's place in the vertical scale of the universe. And, with respect to the particular station that Man occupies in that scale, *the sense of cosmos* diminishes with each passing generation. Indeed, the apparent absence of a Spiritual Tradition in our own time is not nearly so alarming as our civilization's almost total loss of memory with respect to what the Traditions were and what they stood for. It appears that the memory of our true place in the cosmic order – a memory retained over most of the last forty millennia – is finally failing.

It may be, then, that we have entered a Dark Age: the *Kali Yuga* of the Hindus, the *al-Jahiliyyah* of Muhammad, or the final corruption of Mankind by *Angra Mainyu*. And there are aspects of our situation which do correspond to this. When we consider the potentials originally given: **1)** individual awakening, **2)** the formation of Living Traditions, and **3)** the formation of School Civilizations, it appears that we have only fully realized the first. The potential for individual development has been proven in almost every generation. The potential to form Traditions of the Great Work has been realized intermittently over most of Man's forty-thousand years. But the potential for a School

Civilization – a society directly governed by a Spiritual Tradition – has never been fully realized, and this lack of a direct connection to the level of the Gods precludes Man's ability to orchestrate the processes of organic life, and so to foster the harmonious development of the planet itself. Presently we have neither Living Tradition, Living Religion, nor true Civilizational Order – an indication that there are very few correctly crystallized conscious beings amongst the seven billion people who presently walk the earth. It appears that the ratio of conscious beings to the general population has reached a point where the former can have no significant influence over the latter. At the same time we have so overpopulated the planet that our consumption endangers the medium of organic life itself. In the language of the twenty-first century, we are not sustainable. Considering all of these things, it appears that we have lost direction with respect to the purposes given at the time of our creation.

But even if we have entered the *Kali Yuga*, it remains a challenge to understand what our situation is within it. All the myths of the Dark Age give it a duration of centuries, and some even of millennia. A closer examination of the Dark Ages of history shows an exponential factor – an acceleration of events towards the end of the age. Where do we stand within that span? What are the possibilities of our own time? Can we still sow seeds in the present that will bear fruit in the future? Can we use our lives to create a value that endures? The answers to these questions – apart from how they may apply on a personal basis – are not obvious. However, it can be said that, according to all the myths, a new phase of civilizational order is not initiated from within the civilization of the Dark Age. Significant technical, social, and artistic developments may occur within a decadent civilization, but they do not represent a fundamental renewal of values; they are the 'high notes' in a gradually accelerating descent. And, however long the *Kali Yuga* may continue, it ends in the destructive/transformative act of Shiva, which completely 'clears the slate' for the age to follow, while bringing through a small number of prepared survivors. These prepared survivors are the carriers of a new Spiritual Tradition, which had developed secretly, pursuing hidden lines of work within the old civilizational order. They are the seeds of a new civilization. Thus, rather than a renewed *synthetic* civilization developing out of the existing order, we have an erasure of the existing order and the renewal of Mankind on a new foundation – such as has actually occurred in the past. In this way, the destruction and subsequent rebirth of civilization allows the Spiritual Traditions' connection to a higher level to be formed anew, and to be formed in a right alignment with the archetype. The new civilization may itself be based on a select number of elements or essential aspects drawn from the preceding civilizations, combined with whatever new elements the Gods see fit to introduce.

In considering this rather ominous possibility, we are, of course, in no position to make a categorical statement. Zoroaster, Muhammad, and the Buddha all prophesied that Mankind's understanding would reach the lowest point in the years preceding the final prophet – Zoroaster's Saoshyant, the Buddha's Matreiya, or Muhammad's Second Coming of Christ. In this view, how can we ever know exactly when the lowest point is reached? Whatever the degeneracy of the Dark Age, any real efforts we make will help both ourselves and the coming of the next Prophet. And those of the Traditions that persist through the darkest hour perform the greatest transformative labor of them all. Thus, whatever variant of the future presents itself, Man's individual efforts to enable consciousness always have an objective value.

But there is a third possibility, or rather a third way of looking at things. Perhaps the archetypes that we glimpse in the succession of Traditions and Civilizations will not be realized in our own line of time, but each Tradition and each true Civilization will nevertheless continue to develop in a different dimension of time. In other words, perhaps our fate – both individual and collective – is not wholly defined by the dimension of time that we are in. There are many more dimensions than we are aware of, and they are all somehow co-present with the dimension that we are in. On first consideration this is a strange idea to suddenly factor in, but it is not as strange as it might seem. The modern sciences of mathematics and physics both accept that there are multiple dimensions existing outside of our normal awareness, and that these dimensions are somehow co-present with the dimension that we are in, forming a unified structure that is the overarching context of our existence.

In this view all of the different Schools, Civilizations, and emergent conscious beings may continue to evolve, despite the dreadful, and even apparently terminal, disasters that may befall them. Seen from the dimension in which all possibilities are realized – which, in the Hermetic terminology, is the sixth – the different Schools, Civilizations, and developing beings appear as so many carbon crystals, which, through tremendous heat and pressure, slowly evolve into translucent diamonds. Each one of these delicate crystalline structures will then realize its potential in a dimension that is presently invisible to us, and in some unknowable way we will participate in this transcendence.

Peter Ouspensky came to this conclusion in the late 1930s, while reflecting on the situation in his native Russia. His colleague Rodney Collin reported:

No one felt the tragedy of Russia more acutely than Ouspensky. But he knew or found something else. He knew and proved that while on one line of time – that to which the newspapers refer – everything decent, everything true is being and will be corrupted, both for our dying civilization and for individuals, on another invisible line all possibilities actually exist, all can be remade and redeemed, both the past and future, personal and historical.[1]

This same possibility is represented allegorically, with great beauty, by C.S. Lewis in the final chapter of his novel *The Last Battle*, where the Pevensie children discover the "all possibilities" of a dying world.

Whichever of these possibilities is true – Hegel's theodicy, the *Kali Yuga* of the Hindus, or Ouspensky's vision of development in multiple lines of time – our commitment, as beings descended from the Absolute, is to disengage from the limiting illusions of our own age and re-center ourselves in the timeless space of the Great Work. In order to become conscious of our true place in the Absolute's universe we must separate ourselves from the self-contained set of reference points, constantly reproduced by a proliferating mass media, that states – in a thousand different ways – 'Man is his own measure.' A measure that has no connection to a higher cosmos is a dead measure, and any civilization that accepts such a measure is a dying civilization. To the extent that we, as individuals, make such a measure our own, we will never serve what is highest in ourselves. The visions of Zoroaster, Muhammad, and Ouspensky are all more true than this, and, perhaps in some wonderful way they are all true at once.

In reflecting on the vista presented by the Great Spiritual Traditions, from the end of the last Ice Age to the beginning of the twenty-first century, we see much that is glorious and much that is tragic; we see the agony and the ecstasy. The work of the Spiritual Traditions has always been attended by the greatest uncertainty, yet it has persisted – in one form or another – from the time that the original unity of Men and Gods was sundered to the present day.

We can learn something more from this spectacle by relating it to the idea of tragedy with transcendence, which comes down to us from the School of Greek Drama. When we view the full span of history from this perspective, the tenuous relation between 'potential' and 'actual' that we see threaded through the storyline no longer appears as

1. Rodney Collin, *Theory of Conscious Harmony*, p. 95, Letter, December 12, 1952.

an indication of meaninglessness, but as the portent of 'tragedy with transcendence.' What, then, is the truth contained in this ancient dramatic form?

Tragedy with Transcendence

Approximately thirty examples of Greek tragic drama still survive, all of which are the work of three conscious dramatists: Aeschylus, Sophocles, and Euripides. Each of these men were members of an unknown Spiritual Tradition that was central to the working of the Greek city-state in the late Archaic/early Classical period. The tragedies that survive give rare glimpses into a social space that was directly continuous with the civic life of the *polis* itself and formative for that Civilizational Order. Together with the dramatic works of Shakespeare, these masterpieces stand outside of time, like translucent gems, illuminating from the inside out the essential aspects of human existence in its relation to the Sphere of Sentient Being.

The greatest of the Greek tragedies do not present us with the absolute destruction of the hero, but end by showing him rise, phoenix-like, from the ashes of a ruined life. This is a kind of tragedy, which, in its highest expression, reveals the self-transcendence of the hero. In such a tragedy a person of noble character fails in certain of the critical tests of life, and is made aware of his failure and of exactly how the flaws in his character brought this about. The suffering is such that the tragic hero loses the very justification for his existence. At the same time, and almost unbeknownst to him, something deep in his nature transcends the tragic moment and is renewed to continue on another plane. The tragic hero, in order to enable his own transcendence, must drop the very sense of 'I' that binds him to the 'tragic' level. For the man who is unaware of his connection to Higher Centers, this is tragedy without qualification. But, for the initiate, the way in which the protagonist bears the tragic moment reveals the nature of the payment that he makes – or fails to make – to enter into existence on a higher level. The measure of the dramatic artist is, then, the extent to which he can reveal the great uncertainty of the tragic moment – the infinite abyss of 'I' and 'Not-I' – and so allow the audience to participate in a transcendence which is not of the four lower centers. The tragedies of transcendence were the crowning achievement of Greek drama, and amongst the greatest of these were Sophocles' *Oedeipus at Colonus* and Euripides' *Iphigenia in Aulis*.

The tragedies that show the absolute destruction of the hero were also fundamental to Greek drama. Aeschylus' *Agamemnon* is a perfect example of this genre. These tragedies were necessary to create the environment in which the tragedies of transcendence could have their full effect. For example, in Aeschylus' *Oresteia* trilogy, the appalling destruction of the first play – *Agamemnon* – is necessary to fully realizing the transcendence represented in the third play, *The Eumenides*. In the example of the *Oresteia* we see clearly that the initial tragedy of destruction represents the destruction of the protagonist, for King Agamemnon is indeed unredeemed. But, at the same time, it is true that the whole dramatic structure of the play was engineered to produce a movement towards transcendence in the audience. The representation of the transcendence of the protagonist is then developed through *The Libation Bearer*s and finally realized in *The Eumenides*.[2]

Let us then examine the theme of our story from the standpoint of 'tragedy with transcendence.' To do so we must briefly re-create the cosmic context of Books II and III, which is – from this point of view – the 'theater' in which our drama takes place.

The Cosmic Theater

We began our story with the idea that the Absolute initiated Creation in response to a crisis. By willing his own negation – by taking the incredible risk of internalizing his own Not-Being – he transcended himself. This act generated the hierarchy of cosmoses that comprises the Created Universe. The one requirement that the Absolute placed on Creation was that consciousness be generated out of it – through the same act of transcendence by which he first created himself. It is this requirement, operative "as above so below" that defines the parameters of conscious life at every level of Creation. And this is particularly true for the theater of life on earth, where, according to the Absolute's plan, conscious beings were to be generated out of organic matter.

The Gods, in executing the Absolute's plan to make a Cosmic Theater of life on earth, devised the special formula that enables the individual human being to concentrate consciousness within himself, to penetrate the Sphere of Sentient Being, and to sustain himself therein. There is, then, a cosmic measure for Man, and our struggle to realize our potentials – both individual and collective – is a cosmic drama, relating to the will of the Absolute and to his initial act of creation. It is a drama that is infused, at every point, with great uncertainty.

Thus, in reviewing our general situation, we appear as a community of homonid life forms who have been asked to join the Gods in eternity. Because we have such

---

2. We note that the *Oresteia* is the only classical trilogy to survive intact, and we are fortunate to have it because the Greek Tradition did make extensive use of this form.

remarkable potential and because we face such formidable resistance, the theater of earthly life seems well prepared for tragedy with transcendence.

The Elements of Tragedy

We shall now analyze the elements of tragedy, as the Greeks defined them. On the scale of the individual these are **1)** the protagonist's 'original nature' or underlying nobility of character, **2)** his 'tragic flaw,' and **3)** his struggle with the tragic flaw and the resolution of that struggle. Let us see how these translate into the larger scale of the Story of Man.

1. ***The protagonist's original nature*** is found in the gift given Mankind at the beginning – the precious link to Worlds 6 and 12 that is contained in Man's latent Higher Centers. To fully realize this gift, Mankind must create the unity of Tradition and Civilization that enables a continuing communication with the Gods, and so enables us to serve under them. This and this alone turns a multitude of homonids into a real humanity.

2. ***The tragic flaw*** is revealed in the course of history. Here we see the repeated assertion of Man's animal nature. Whenever there is a moment of transcendence there is immediately a recreation of the domain of the Lower Self, often with remarkable speed and efficiency. René Guénon said that when he viewed contemporary society, it was as if "an organism with its head cut off were to go on living a life which was both intense and disordered."[3] More clinically: the forces under the control of the Black Queen always regroup quickly after a dispersal, with the aim of immediately disrupting the spiritually integrative effects of a moment of transcendence. Just as we can see this in ourselves on a moment-to-moment basis, we can see it in human society through history.

3. ***The protagonist's struggle with tragic uncertainty*** is The Great Work that threads the entire storyline. In the life of the Spiritual Traditions we see the vision, the sacrifice, the suffering, and the unremitting effort that has been sustained century after century, millennium after millennium. And it is here that we see the tragic moment in all its depth, the terrible tension that exists between Being and Void when the two stand in the balance. To bear this moment is the crucial test of the Spiritual Traditions. Whenever the Traditions do not fail

---

3. Guénon, René (trans. Martin Lings) *East and West*, Sophia Perennis, Hillsdale NY, 2004, p. 106.

– whenever this tension is accepted in its depth and the effects transformed – we see the periodic flashes of transcendence that illuminate all of history. But both the triumphs and the failures of the Traditions reveal shades and nuances of the greatest beauty. Here, in the midst of tragic uncertainty, we see most clearly the heroic aspect: the aspiration to True Individuality; the constant return to a higher state through struggle; the remembrance of the Self; the service to Mankind; and, ultimately, the imitation of the Absolute.

Thus we have outlined the Cosmic Theater that is the context of our story. This brings us to the final concept needed to draw together the loose strands that remain.

The Invisible Axis

In each one of the Golden Ages of man, when the Work of a Spiritual Tradition has linked a human society to the level one above, there has been an invisible axis connecting Civilization to Religion, Religion to Tradition, and Tradition to the Circle of Gods in Eternity. We can clarify this with a metaphor taken from the Great Work. Each of the Gothic Cathedrals was built around a central axis which is not there, which is not inscribed in the physical structure of the building, but which has nevertheless been the guiding principle in its construction. The line of connection through to the Gods is such an invisible axis; nothing is more important, and nothing more easily lost. While this connecting axis existed at the beginning of the Story of Man and has been intermittently in place over the last 40,000 years, it is not in place now. To recognize this axis in history, and to enable its realization in the present, is what we have called the Great Work.

When we view humanity from the standpoint of the invisible axis, we become aware of the unceasing struggle that is needed to simply maintain that axis, but we see – even more clearly – the intense disorder of the a-cosmic forces that are resistant to it. We see "a darkling plain swept with confused alarms of struggle and flight."[4] But beyond this chaos and confusion we see traces of a great and almost terrible beauty: the beauty of the Apostle Peter, who, having met the risen Christ, walks back into Rome to face his own crucifixion; the beauty of the Sufi Orders of Islam, coming into their own in the wake of a century of Umayyad persecution; the sudden beauty of the emergence of Orthodox Monasticism in fourth-century Byzantium; the tragic beauty of the thirteenth

---

4. From Matthew Arnold's poem, *Dover Beach*.

Dalai Lama's struggle to realize the vision of Eternal Tibet in the shadow of the Chinese invasion; the beauty of the rabbinic community that labored, in the wake of the genocidal destruction of Second-Temple Judaism, to create the *Talmud* as a blueprint for the new civilization-in-exile; the beauty of the unknown Toltecs who centered the ancient Mesoamerican family of Civilizations in the Sacred City of Teotihuacan; the awesome beauty we can still trace in the surviving remnants of Pharaonic Egypt.

These transcendent beauties are the creation of Mankind; they are the contribution of Mankind to the Life of the Absolute. In some way they make him more than what he was in the moment of his Self-Creation. This is a beauty such that anyone who knows it will be moved to his depths. It mirrors the extraordinary beauty of the Absolute's original act: real will, real sacrifice, real suffering, real love ... value incarnate.

If, at some point in the future, humanity should realize its full potential, this strange and searing beauty will merge with the transcendent truth of the archetype that is behind it, making Mankind more than what it was originally conceived to be. And even if we do not realize our full potential, the beauty of the struggle remains ... as do all of the conscious beings, and all of the conscious art, and all of the conscious life that we have generated through history.

Our story, then, does not sum in the liberal-democratic myth of the self-creating individual, or in the socialist myth of a society liberated from alienation and want, or in the New Age myth of a secular Shambhala. It sums in the passionate, flickering candle flame that is the life of all of those who have struggled to keep this invisible axis in place. It sums in the inner life of the Spiritual Traditions. It sums ultimately in presence sustained through time, to the point where the sustaining link breaks, and the inner circle of humanity enters into the timeless presence of the cosmos one above. This is what is essential to the Story of Man; this is our link to the Gods and to the Sphere of Sentient Being that they inhabit.

The End Of The Story

We noted in Book III that the Great Work of the Traditions has both an internal and an external aspect. The internal aspect relates to our deepening experience of the present, and to our awakening to the levels of Creation that are above our own. The external aspect is harder to describe; it is related to forming an objective view of Man's place in the Universe, and it is related to fulfilling the specific historical tasks given the Traditions from Higher School. As such, the external aspect includes the entire external work of the Traditions; it is their story as we have presented it in Books II through IV. The external aspect is the effect or resultant of the internal aspect. In other words the dramatic impact of the story of the Traditions, as we have traced that over forty-seven millennia, is a direct consequence of the vital inner work they have sustained. And thus we see that, from a higher vantage point, the internal and the external are one, and together they spring up to form the passionate flickering candle flame of life that keeps the invisible axis in its place.

When we are able to look at history from this point of view, we see clearly the magnificent achievements of the past, and we are able to possess those achievements as part of our inheritance. We can literally enter into the states of consciousness that produced the Pyramids, the Gothic Cathedrals, the Upanishads, the Gospels, or the great dramatic works of the Greeks – and in so doing realize the awe and the wonderment that is necessary to penetrating more deeply the theme of our Story. With the expanded sense of Self that this inheritance brings, we can connect more directly to the vertical lift-on-lift structure of the Macrocosm described in Book I. We realize that we can have the context of the Traditions as the context for our lives.

Having finally reached the historical present, this book must come to an end, but the Story of Man itself – of course – goes on. The aim in trying to document the story up to the present point in time has been to isolate its theme: the development of the potentials originally given Mankind. Our ability to recognize this theme, as it was understood by its Celestial Authors in the time before the embodiment of this particular humanity, gives us the focus to live moment by moment … to value and treasure each moment – for ourselves, for the generations that will follow us, and for the Living Whole of which we are a part.

In sum, a clear sense of the Story of Man connects us to the invisible vertical axis that alone makes sense of human history. It helps us to overcome the smaller sense of 'self' that hinders us from becoming true children of the Absolute: children able to recognize their own Father – whether in Himself or in His works. In letting go the smaller self, in dissolving our personal past and future, and in willing ourselves into the Eternal Now, we render the Absolute the very service he required of us in the beginning, and in so doing we become thematic elements in the story he devised.

We shall let Socrates have the final word. In the last lines of the *Republic*, Glaucon asks Socrates if the city that he has described can be found anywhere on earth. Socrates does not claim that it can. He replies only: "Perhaps there is a pattern of it laid up in heaven for him who wishes to contemplate it, and so beholding to constitute himself its citizen. But it makes no difference whether it exists now or whether it will ever come into being in the future. The politics of this city will be his, and no other."

Glossary

Words in capital letters denote other terms that can be found in the Glossary.

ABSOLUTE   All Spiritual Traditions acknowledge the unconditional, transcendent reality that we have called the Absolute. Equivalent terms have been used by the Brahmans, the Buddhists, the Jains, the Israelite Traditions, the Christian Traditions, and the Traditions of Islam.

Chapter 2 is a concentrated attempt to present a cosmological view of the Absolute that is common to all of the Traditions.

A minimum definition would be that the Absolute or Absolute Spirit is a view of the Whole – both material **CREATION** and what is uncreated – which acknowledges that the Creator infinitely transcends what He has created. While we can know the Absolute through His Works, He is incomprehensible in Himself.

In Chapters 1 and 2 we have presented the idea that the Spiritual Traditions are Mankind's living connection to the Absolute.

We have sometimes referred to the Absolute as the First Cause, or **FIRST PRINCIPLE**.

ALCHEMY   From a twenty-first century point of view alchemy is the proto-science of modern chemistry. It is a science of substances and their combination that in ancient times was the basis of medicine, metallurgy, glassmaking, and the production of inks, dyes, paints, and cosmetics. The word alchemy is the Greek word *chemia* with the prefix of the Arabic definite article *al*. The first rudimentary periodic tables came from the alchemical proto-chemistry of Islam.

The traditional or hermetic science of chemistry deals not only with matter in the solid, liquid, and gaseous states, but with the living range of **CELLULAR ENERGY, MOLECU-LAR ENERGY**, and **ELECTRONIC ENERGY**. Alchemy had its origins in Mesopotamia and

Egypt and was a major part of the Hermetical Schools of classical times. In the post-classical period it was further developed by both the Sufi Orders of Islam and the Renaissance Hermetic schools. While the traditional science of alchemy never developed the periodic table, it was advanced in its study of the invisible range of energies and in its knowledge of the relation between the invisible energies and matter in the solid, liquid, and gaseous states.

ARCHETYPE Comes from the Greek word ἀρχή (*arkh-ey*) meaning **FIRST PRINCIPLE**, first cause, origin, beginning. From this root come the words:

- ἀρχαῖος (*ark-he-aios*) from the beginning, ancient, primeval
- ἀρχαί (*ark-he-ai*) first causes or principles
- ἀρχιτεκτονική (*ark-hi-tekonikeh*) supreme directing faculty
- ἀρχηγενής (*ark-hai-genais*) what causes the beginning of a thing; first birth; first coming into being
- ἀρχέτυπο (*ark-he-tupo*) form, type, pattern, model, paradigm. The root of the English word archetype.

Archetype is somehow all of these. In Plato's usage a cosmic archetype is an essential form (or paradigm) existing outside of space and time, which is the cause of the forms that we see.

An example would be the archetypal form (or idea) of a horse. This form is realized in the vast range of variations that we see in all horses that have existed in space and time. **HIGHER CENTERS** are actually capable, under certain conditions, of seeing these archetypal forms. We have suggested that there are also archetypal forms for **CIVILIZATIONS** and **SPIRITUAL TRADITIONS**. These are the creations of the **GODS**, serving the **ABSOLUTE** in his management of **CREATION**.

BEING/NOT-BEING/BEYOND-BEING These three terms – in the use we have made of them here – come to us from the ancient Greeks. They were first used in this way by Heraclitus and Parmenides, re-cast and re-formed by Plato and Aristotle, and finally refined and nuanced by the Neoplatonist philosophers and the Graeco-Roman hermeticists. The original Greek terms are derived from variant forms of the verb to be (*eimi*/εἰμι) combined with a certain usage of (*the Nous*/ὁ νοῦς), referring to Higher Mind. (The transcendent dimension of Beyond-Being is sometimes referred to as ὑπερούσιος, which derives from the verb to transcend, ὑπεροχέω.) We have adjusted the English usage of these terms to fit with the original Greek usage. It is just as easy to find the same original terms in Sanskrit, Persian, Tibetan, or Arabic.

In Chapter 2 we used these three terms to define the **ABSOLUTE**. Our use of being – in this instance – conforms with Plato's. In his view, being does not refer to an entity but to a state of being: a presence, or a 'being there.' In this frame of reference being can exist on many different scales. It begins in any moment that we feel our 'being there' independently of whatever thoughts, feelings, and sensations may be circulating within us. It ends in a transcendent Being that contains the created universe. The former – the PRESENCE of the individual – can (through the application of the WORK OF THE STEWARD) be developed into a universal state of Being that is capable of a certain knowledge of the Absolute. While the qualities of being change with its expansion from one scale to another, its essence is continuous through the change of scales.

But on whatever scale you think of being, it must have some kind of substance that distinguishes it from what it is not. This introduces the dimension of Not-Being. For example, if you choose to think of Being in its purity – on the scale of God – you must think of it in relation to what is Not-God. The Absolute, however, is the Whole, and so, in some sense, the Being of the Absolute is both God and Not-God, Being and Not-Being. Because there is always a context, or larger container, for the opposition of two forces, the Being of the Absolute must somehow include that context. This, then, is the dimension of Beyond-Being.

We could say that the Absolute, as inclusive of Not-Being, is a Being without predicates of any kind. He cannot be opposed to something that is outside of Himself, for He always includes the context of the opposition. He is, quite literally, Beyond-Being. In Chapter 2, where we elaborate this principle, we show the way in which Beyond-Being transcends both Being and Not-Being and the way in which it is constitutive of them. We could say that Beyond-Being represents a higher and more intelligent dimension of existence. It is the dimension of the Absolute that is utterly unknowable to us.

BEYOND-BEING   See entry for BEING, NOT-BEING, BEYOND-BEING.

BLACK QUEEN   A term used in the teaching of Robert Earl Burton (see the biographical notes in the Subject Bibliography) to define a division of the four LOWER CENTERS.

Technically, according to George Gurdjieff's divisions of the lower functions described in Chapter 3, the Black Queen is the emotional division of the intellectual part of the instinctive center or, in the symbolism of the playing cards, the nine of clubs. It is an organismic intelligence that we share with the animals, which ultimately controls the working of the four Lower Centers. Its aim is self-preservation and self-maintenance.

The natural role of the Black Queen is to defend the life of the organism against external and internal threats. It is behind both the working of the immune system and the sudden access of energy and awareness that comes in times of danger. It is, at the same time, the foundation for the sense of unity on which our sense of 'I' is based. Both the sense of 'I' and the complicated self-image that develops out of it are directly threatened by the unlimited openness and dynamic energy of HIGHER CENTERS. For this reason the Black Queen – as the animal will to self-preservation and self-maintenance – will do everything in her power to resist and oppose the development of the Higher Centers. She is thus the natural foe of the WORK OF THE STEWARD and her counterpart within the Steward, the WHITE QUEEN.

Under normal conditions the Black Queen can exercise control over both intellect and emotion. For this reason she has been called the intelligence behind the LOWER SELF. Her sleepless vigilance makes her a very formidable adversary to the White Queen.

CELESTIAL CITY   In classical times this term was used by the Stoics to describe an emergent conscious order in the human race. Those men and women in whom the celestial fire (WORLD 12) was established would be able to survive the death of their physical bodies and enter into a conscious community. The Celestial City was thus the cumulation of humanity's 'graduates' who, in their disembodied form, would work to awaken the other members of the human race. This term appears again at the end of the classical period in the work of St. Augustine, who used it as an alternative for the City of God. The Celestial Hierarchy described by Dante and Dionysius the Areopagite has also been called the Celestial City. The term was later used by John Bunyan to describe the destination of the Pilgrim in *Pilgrim's Progress*. In the mythology of Tibetan Buddhism, the myth of the sacred city of Shambhala corresponds approximately to the Western idea of the Celestial City.

Robert Earl Burton (see the biographical notes in the Subject Bibliography) has used this term in relation to the term HIGHER SCHOOL, which refers to a school that regenerates beings who possess molecular and electronic (rather than cellular) bodies. The Celestial City, in his usage, refers to a city of Gods, some of whom are transcended human beings. It is the spiritual center of the MACROCOSM of creation, below the level of the Absolute.

We have, in these pages, spoken of the SPHERE OF SENTIENT BEING as being the abode of the Gods. This is meant in the general way that it is the natural medium of their existence. It is the state of existence (which is at the same time the state of consciousness) most conducive to their normal functioning. The Celestial City, by contrast, is a specific point of congregation.

CELLULAR ENERGY   Cellular energies are the energies of physical life. They constitute the matter of our body and its organs. A good quality of cellular energy ensures physical strength, good health, and the ability to efficiently process the different matters that pass through the body. We associate cellular bodies with defined surfaces, physical substance, and definite weight. Cellular energy is not in itself a sufficient condition for life. For any organism to have life, its field of cellular energies must be completed by at least some MOLECULAR ENERGY.

The cellular body disintegrates at the time of death. See also ENERGIES/FOUR ENERGIES.

CIVILIZATION (OR TRUE CIVILIZATION)   A human community that is integrally connected to a SPIRITUAL TRADITION. A true Civilization is founded by a Spiritual Tradition, which remains active within it through most of its longer life. The Tradition may or may not support a LIVING RELIGION, which helps to define the Civilization. From a different point of view, true Civilization (as opposed to simple society) is the human community given life by the thread of a connection to the Celestial Hierarchy. This connection may come through

- a Spiritual Tradition acting on a Living Religion, as the Orthodox Monastic Tradition influenced the Byzantine Civilization through the Christian Religion.
- a Spiritual Tradition acting directly on a society, as the School of Athens directly influenced the City-State of Athens in the fifth century BC.

The legacy of the Tradition to the Civilization is a coherent set of values, with a defining art and culture. A true Civilization shows at least some semblance of a COSMOS, as the process of regeneration – in the form of the GREAT WORK – is alive within it.

The highest possibility of a Civilization is to be actually governed by a Spiritual Tradition. This is the strongest possible link to the Gods, as the process of regeneration then permanently orchestrates the other five processes. (See entry for PROCESSES.) Under these circumstances a Civilization becomes a COSMOS OF MAN.

CONSCIOUS BEING   As defined by George Gurdjieff, a person who has reached the level of MAN NUMBER FIVE or beyond. The HIGHER EMOTIONAL CENTER is continuously active and the HIGHER INTELLECTUAL CENTER has become active, at least to a degree. This person will see his or her place in the universe significantly differently from a person in whom the Higher Centers are not active. While a conscious being may – under duress – display human failings, his or her essential values are fundamentally different from the values that normally govern human life.

COSMIC PROCESSES   See PROCESSES.

COSMOS   A term that comes to us from the Greeks. For Plato a cosmos (κόσμος) is a whole which is greater than just the sum of its parts. It is made on a universal pattern and contains within itself all possibilities. It has the potential to transcend itself. Pythagoras called a cosmos a "self-perfecting whole." Thus a cosmos is a system, with its own internal coherence, which is capable – at least potentially – of self-transcendence. In this sense each individual human being is a cosmos. The human cosmos is distinguished from a simple organism by the fact that it can coordinate its functions in relation to an aim, beyond the mere will to survival and the impulse of self-gratification. We could say that a cosmos is an organism with a spiritual dimension.

The Created Universe itself is a cosmos on a higher scale. We call it a macrocosm, which is a complete interlocking system of cosmoses. This system is a hierarchy. As we proceed downwards, each lower cosmos is contained within – and created out of – the cosmos immediately above it. From the point of view of a higher cosmos, the cosmos on the level immediately below it is a microcosm, and from the point of view of a lower cosmos, the higher cosmos that contains it is a macrocosm. But however far down the chain you go, the microcosm contains the signature of the whole. Because the universe was created from the top down – and not from the bottom up – the possibility always exists for a microcosm to transcend itself and enter into the life of the cosmos that contains it. Through successive acts of self-transcendence, it can enter consciously into the life of the whole. In so doing it remains true to its original creative principle.

We have accepted the idea – put forward by Peter Ouspensky and Rodney Collin (see the biographical notes in the Subject Bibliography) – that a cosmos is comprised of three substances and six processes. On every scale a cosmos is a being which takes in three substances (for man: food, air, and impressions), which are combined internally to support six processes (regeneration, growth, digestion, healing, destruction, and crime). See the respective entries for PROCESSES and SUBSTANCES.

We can look at the idea of a cosmos comparatively in relation to **1)** an individual man, **2)** a Spiritual Tradition, and **3)** a True Civilization.

- An individual man is a complete microcosmos, exhibiting all six processes. He can transcend himself by awakening his latent HIGHER CENTERS.
- A Spiritual Tradition is a kind of intermediary or artificial cosmos, created by the action of men and GODS according to a plan and supporting the six processes. It is designed to bridge the very considerable gap between mankind and the cosmos of HIGHER SCHOOL, comprised of molecular – rather than cellular – beings.
- A True Civilization is a civilization governed by a Spiritual Tradition, which, in its developed form, connects mankind both to the level one above and the level one below. It gives mankind the potential to serve HIGHER SCHOOL, and to actualize the purposes of Higher School on earth. It transcends itself by producing a continuing stream of conscious life.

COSMOS OF MAN   See the entry for COSMOS. We characterized a cosmos as a whole which is greater than the sum of its parts, made on a universal pattern, and containing within itself all possibilities. We also characterized a cosmos as a being with an intake of three substances (for man: food, air, and impressions), which are combined internally to support six PROCESSES (regeneration, growth, digestion, healing, destruction, and crime).

CIVILIZATION, in its highest phase, can take the form of the Cosmos of Man. It would then be a social order under conscious leadership, capable of developing itself in relation to the order of the GODS above and in relation to the fabric of ORGANIC LIFE from which it emerged.

More specifically the Cosmos of Man is a Civilization governed by a SPIRITUAL TRADITION. The Tradition, realizing the process of regeneration, orchestrates the other five processes. Each individual member of this civilization feels his or her relation to the Whole in a way that is not abstract but life enhancing. Each function or social institution (connected to one or another of the six processes) also has a dynamic connection to the Whole and to the other processes.

For further clarification of this idea, see the entry on the PYRAMID OF MAN.

CREATION   Creation is a term used in relation to the **ABSOLUTE**; it refers to what the Absolute created or, from another point of view, how the Absolute took manifest form in the physical universe. While the Absolute Himself is unknowable, Creation is a structured whole that can be known, although only a very small part of it can be known by beings like ourselves. Creation, viewed as an organization of **COSMOSES**, is a **MACROCOSM** (or cosmos of cosmoses). In other words it contains the complete system of cosmoses originally generated by the Absolute, and this includes the several realms of the **GODS**, which are antecedent to the particular realm that we inhabit. From the standpoint of the Gods, our knowledge of Creation will always be woefully inadequate.

Creation is a term that must be understood with some relativity, in the sense that the word itself generally relates to either **1)** an act that takes place in the line of time or **2)** a thing that exists in time and space. However, in these pages, the term refers to a context that transcends the human perception of time and space.

The term creation, referring to an act, has often been used in conjunction with a theistic view of God, for example, "God created the World" – just as a man would create or fashion a tool. This is not, however, the view taken by the Spiritual Traditions. From the standpoint of the dimensions existing outside of space and time (at least as we know them) the theistic view of creation (which in the post-Darwinian world has become known as creationism) has little meaning. Certain of the Traditions even found it necessary to avoid the use of this term. Yet every dimension has its correlate of space and time, and we have kept the usage of the term Creation here because it is relevant to the analogical perspective taken in our story.

Note on Creationism and Emanationism   In these pages we often speak of Creation, but the creator is not a creating subject. Creation is the result of a three-fold process existing outside of time and space. From this perspective the early parts of creation and the later parts of creation all exist at once. We could go a step further and say that, because our linear sense of time is completely irrelevant at this level, the act of Creation can be viewed as an eternal moment. It is, from one perspective, legitimate to view the universe as something that never begins and never ends: either a never-ending cycle of creations or a single ongoing act of Creation which represents a permanent connection to a dimension that is outside of time as we know it. But these views – valid in their own terms – downplay or de-emphasize the accountability of mankind to its source in a higher level.

Certain of the Spiritual Traditions did view the elaborate, articulated system of forms that comprises the visible universe as an ongoing emanation or manifestation of the Divinity. But they did not – at least the serious Teachers within these Traditions – view it as an endless dream-like proliferation of forms. In physical terms, the emanation outward from a point is a fact. The physical theory of Georges Lemaître (now known as the Big Bang theory) has been more or less proven. So the Creation that we see is not endless. But to think in a definitive way about the implications of this and of the first causes that bear on it, we would have to think from a place that is several dimensions outside of the human experience. Thus we must, with Omar Khayyam, "let Philosopher and Doctor preach," while relying on the indications of revealed truth (the recorded perceptions of HIGHER CENTERS) and at the same time realizing that even these are only indications of something that is utterly inexpressible on this level.

In sum, our use of Creation is not based on a theistic conception of God. The emphasis is rather on 1) the intention behind Creation and 2) the independent integrity of what has been created, meaning, that it is not simply a continuously emanating dream. Our use of Creation thus emphasizes the integrity of the Macrocosm, which stands over and against the BEING (and the BEYOND-BEING) of the Absolute. The Macrocosm has its own integrity, and it must sustain that integrity in order to serve as a vehicle for the generation of consciousness.

CULT   Cults are groups undertaking esoteric or occult work without a conscious teacher. The Cults make use of the materials and techniques left by GROUPS and by SPIRITUAL TRADITIONS, but they do so in an idiosyncratic or fragmented way. They are unpracticed in either the FIRST WORK or the WORK OF THE STEWARD; thus the anarchic nature of occult and pseudo-esoteric teachings. Cults may come into being when a conscious teacher dies and his teaching is carried on by students who are not themselves conscious. In the cults there is no contact with the Gods nor with the cosmos that they inhabit.

DEAD RELIGION   A religion which is not connected to a SPIRITUAL TRADITION and which does not otherwise acknowledge conscious influence. Its worship is based entirely on prescribed forms and procedures and previously recorded knowledge, rather than on the direct experience of HIGHER CENTERS. A dead religion can sometimes become the opposite of the LIVING RELIGION from which it originally derived, engaging directly in acts of violence and barbarism. History provides us many examples of dead religions attacking other religions (dead and living) and destroying Spiritual Traditions.

DEATH OF THE STEWARD   The intentional cessation of the activity of the STEWARD in the moment that HIGHER CENTERS appear. The Steward must learn to immediately and unconditionally yield to the Higher Centers in the moment they appear, or it will impede their coming. The Death of the Steward is a learned discipline, requiring great rigor. All Traditions highlight this moment in one way or another: in the Sanskrit of the Vedas it is the release of *ahamkara* ('I'-related activity); in the Pali canon of the Buddha's teachings it is *anatta* (not 'I-making'); in the Sufi teaching it is *fana* (the annihilation of self in God); in Christian monasticism it is the transition from active contemplation (πράξις) to infused contemplation (θεωρία). The Death of the Steward is the final moment of the transition through to the new level. If the Steward does not yield, the new level will not come.

DEITY   Used in these pages as a generic reference to the directing principle of the universe, with the universe viewed as a conscious or sentient whole. The term Deity is not as explicit as **ABSOLUTE** (which in these pages is seen as triadic) and it is without the theistic connotations which the term **GOD** can carry.

DEMIURGE/DEMIOURGOS   A term sometimes used by Plato to refer to the source of the Created Universe. The original meaning of the Greek term *demiourgos* (δεμιουργος) is craftsman, or creator, or maker. Plato sometimes uses this term to refer to the act of Creation, on the analogy of the making of a master-craftsman, but at other times he refers to an inscrutable demiurge which is beyond it all: beyond God, beyond Creation, beyond anything we can know. It is this demiurge that is the unknowable source of everything. Plato here refers to what we have called the **BEYOND-BEING** of the **ABSOLUTE**. In this sense, and in this sense only, Plato's demiurge is equivalent to what the ancient Vedantic teachers called the *Para-Brahma*.

ELECTRONIC ENERGY   An energy much finer than the **MOLECULAR ENERGY** which forms the basis for a normal human psychology (thoughts, feelings, motor impulses, and sensations). Electronic energy vibrates at a much higher frequency than molecular energy.

The electronic energies are not part of the pattern of a normal human life, for the cellular body is not normally able to register the electronic range. In other words the electronic energies are realized in states of consciousness so far removed from the experience of everyday that we would not normally be able to remember them. We may momentarily experience electronic energies in moments of crisis, or in near-death experiences. Each man and woman experiences electronic energy directly at the time of birth and at the time of death, and this is part of what draws the veil of memory between lifetimes.

Matter in the electronic state illuminates everything upon which it falls, just as X-rays illuminate the interior of solid objects or ultraviolet rays cause substances to glow or fluoresce. A body comprised of such matter would be its own illuminant, and a community of such bodies would live in a state of complete transparency to one another. A completed electronic body would give free access to **WORLD 6**, and, under certain conditions, to **WORLD 3**. See also **ENERGIES/FOUR ENERGIES**.

ENERGIES/FOUR ENERGIES   The classification of energies relevant to human development includes four general categories: **ELECTRONIC ENERGY, MOLECULAR ENERGY, CELLULAR ENERGY**, and **MINERAL ENERGY**. This classification originated in the ancient alchemical schools, and it was brought to its highest level of refinement in the work of Peter Ouspensky and Rodney Collin (see the biographical notes in the Subject Bibliography). We have used their terminology here. For an in-depth discussion of these energies, see Rodney Collin's *Theory of Celestial Influence* and *Theory of Eternal Life*.

The four energies – electronic, molecular, cellular, and mineral – represent a scale of vibrational frequencies. Electronic energies vibrate at the highest speed, molecular energies at a lesser speed, cellular energies at a lesser speed yet, and mineral energies at the slowest speed of all. These energies are combined in quite specific proportions in every human being, and – particularly in an evolving human being – they react on one another and affect one another. While each of these energies is part of the human experience, normal human life is centered in the cellular and the lower range of the molecular energies.

ESSENCE   Briefly stated essence is who we are at the level of the four LOWER CENTERS, without artifice of any kind. In the Hermetic classification used by George Gurdjieff (see the biographical notes in the Subject Bibliography), it corresponds to the level of World 24. It is the natural state of an infant. In certain moments we have all seen infants at one with whatever is around them, yet at the same time existent in themselves. They are who they are, in a very open and receptive frame of mind. This is essence. It is a state reflected in each of the four lower centers, but it is based in the emotional center. In other words, the emotional center is the seat of essence. Normally essence recedes as a child grows older and a mature personality develops, which occurs particularly from the time of adolescence. Indeed essence can become completely dormant in adults, but it does have its place in a normal adult life: in the deepest moments of love, in young parents playing with their children, and in the presence of great beauty. Having a healthy essence is a condition for succeeding in spiritual work, for the work must be based on what is most real in us.

Thus, it is the responsibility of the SPIRITUAL TRADITIONS to ensure the development of essence. Without a right development of essence the WORK OF THE STEWARD will not produce a proper connection to HIGHER CENTERS. Just as this difficult and demanding work must be based on what is most real in us, so what is most real in us is profoundly affected by that work. The deepest challenge that essence can face, beyond the experiences of love and art, is the experience of Higher Centers. In the process of awakening something within a fully-developed essence actually fuses with the emergent Higher Centers.

FIRST-BORN GODS   Beings created by the ABSOLUTE prior to or concurrent with the creation of the MACROCOSM. They were created as the highest level of conscious life under the Absolute. The First-born Gods have not transcended themselves, as the Absolute did, but in all of their activities they anticipate the act of transcendence. They are the Absolute's closest colleagues and confederates, and they come closer to understanding His intentions than any other beings in the universe. See also TWICE-BORN GODS.

FIRST WORK   A work preparatory to the WORK OF THE STEWARD. From one point of view it is the preparation of the four LOWER CENTERS for the direct work on the HIGHER CENTERS, as that occurs within the SPIRITUAL TRADITIONS. In the European Middle Ages it was called the Work on the Virtues.

Both the First Work and the Work of the Steward are focused on presence, but this focus takes different forms. The difference in focus between the First Work and the Work of the Steward is given by the different respective conditions of the four lower centers. The

First Work is for someone who is still striving to win a degree of freedom from **1)** certain personal problems and preoccupations and **2)** certain congential and recurrent negative emotions. The Work of the Steward is for someone whose lower centers are already in an open and receptive state, and who has – in some degree – transcended his personal desires. At this stage awakening is no longer something that 'I' want for 'myself.'

The First Work, then, has a primary focus on the lower functions, while the Second Work is direct work on consciousness or **PROLONGED PRESENCE**.

The First Work is a main point of focus for **LIVING RELIGIONS** and also for esoteric **GROUPS**. The First Work is also practiced by the Spiritual Traditions, but only as a means of enabling the Work of the Steward. If the First Work is incomplete, the Work of the Steward will very likely produce wrong results.

FIRST PRINCIPLE (THE) A more abstract reference to the **ABSOLUTE**, which, while emphasizing its centrality and control, emphasizes less its deeper sentience. Also sometimes referred to as First Cause.

FOURTH WAY Spiritual practice undertaken not in a monastery or a spiritual retreat but in the medium of everyday life. George Gurdjieff (see the biographical notes in the Subject Bibliography) originated this term and defined it in relation to the Way of the Monk (monastic), the Way of the Yogi (in retreat), and the Way of the Fakir (in a direct rejection of the life of everyday). Different forms of the Fourth Way are practiced in the Hindu, Sufi, and Tibetan Buddhist Traditions. In all three cases they are referred to in terms which translate approximately as the way of the good householder. The good householder is someone who evolves while fulfilling his full responsibilities in society. This way is, for that reason, particularly suited to the work of originating a new Civilization.

GOD The term God is used in the Religions of history to refer to the directing sentience of the universe. At the level of **RELIGION** the term is often used to refer to a supreme subjectivity, who can be placed over and against the created universe. He is the creator, and He can be petitioned directly for assistance and guidance. But this vision of a divine subjectivity is only an expanded form of human subjectivity. It is what we have called a theistic view of God, and it is a point of view rejected by the **SPIRITUAL TRADITIONS**.

Those Traditions working directly in close conjunction with **LIVING RELIGIONS** which endorse a theistic view avoid this anthropomorphism (in their internal usage) by acknowledging God to be utterly unknowable as He is, in and for Himself. For convenience we may speak of Him as a philosophical subject, as we speak of an individual man, and we can indeed know something of His attributes, but He remains in himself unknowable. In this book we have used the term the **ABSOLUTE** to represent the latter view, acknowledging that many Spiritual Traditions retain the term God – or its equivalent – in the higher usage we have just described.

Indeed, within the Spiritual Traditions the term God often has a double usage, referring to **1)** the ruling sentience of the universe and **2)** the connection to the latent higher sentience that exists within oneself. When the Hindu yogi states 'I am Atman,' he is referring not to the creator of the physical universe but to a state of unity that displaces the subjective feeling of 'I'.

GODS/THE GODS   The Gods are immortal beings to whom we are connected in both our origins and in our destiny. They exist in a state of direct, conscious service to the ABSOLUTE. Their existence is not based, like our own, in bodies comprised of cellular matter but in bodies comprised of MOLECULAR ENERGY and ELECTRONIC ENERGY, or in other words, in molecular and electronic energy fields.

For each SPIRITUAL TRADITION, LIVING RELIGION, and related Civilizational Order that existed prior to the modern era, the hierarchy of Gods was held to be real on some level. Man's connection to the Absolute was seen as a divine hierarchy comprised of many levels of Gods, at least one level of which could directly assist mankind. It was the Spiritual Traditions alone, however, that understood that the Gods are the incarnation – in molecular and electronic energy fields – of states of consciousness which man himself could experience in glimpses. They are not cosmic super-men but entirely different kinds of beings, unknowable to man except through the development of his own Higher Centers. Because the development of the Higher Centers was the condition for forming a direct relation to the Gods, this became a primary task of the Spiritual Traditions.

Each Spiritual Tradition recognizes several different levels of Gods, but, for the purposes of The Story of Man, we emphasize two major divisions: **1)** the FIRST-BORN GODS who were created by the Absolute prior to or concurrent with the creation of the physical universe and **2)** the TWICE-BORN GODS who were originally generated – after creation – out of the thin film of ORGANIC LIFE that forms on certain of the planets, that is, man or mankind.

The First-born Gods appear in the revealed truth of the Traditions as the angels and archangels of Judaism, Christianity, and Islam; the Buddha Manifestations, *tathagatas*, and *bodhissatvas* of India, China, and Tibet; and the *amesha spentas* and *yazatas* of Zoroastrian Persia.

The first birth of the Twice-born Gods was their birth as organic beings (with HIGHER CENTERS latent) and their second birth was the awakening of those Higher Centers, which signals their birth into the MOLECULAR and ELECTRONIC WORLDS. These Twice-born Gods have also been called CONSCIOUS BEINGS. Some of these conscious beings we know as the Great Prophets – Abraham, Zoroaster, Moses, Buddha, Jesus, Muhammad – while others, equally important to the Traditions, have names that are lost to history.

Both levels of Gods were part of the original plan of the Absolute with respect to the MACROCOSM of CREATION.

All Gods – First born and Twice-born – are participants in HIGHER SCHOOL, where the regeneration of beings higher than ordinary man is conducted. As students in Higher School they are attempting to

1) achieve the level of work that defines the next concentric ring of the Celestial Hierarchy;

2) help the most developed members of the human race enter the SPHERE OF SENTIENT BEING; and

3) maintain the MACROCOSM of creation so that it can fulfill its function of generating conscious life.

GREAT WORK   The work of HIGHER SCHOOL as it involves humanity. Higher School relates to humanity – taken as a whole – through the SPIRITUAL TRADITIONS. It has a clear understanding of the plan for each Tradition and of the plan for humanity itself, which is quite different from the plans that humanity invents for itself. The plan of the Great Work is much more along the lines of a gardener's plan for breeding new varieties of roses. The gardener makes tests and watches carefully for the result. He then takes new initiatives on the basis of these results. Where the gardener works for an ideal of beauty, Higher School works for an archetype representing the perfect balance of TRUE INDIVIDUALITY and collective life. Thus, while the plan for humanity allows for experiment, it is a plan designed to produce definite results. These results were implicit in the derivative archetypes that were created from the original archetype. Derivative archetypes were created for individual men and women, for Spiritual Traditions, and for Civilizational Orders.

The plan for humanity translates into the many particular plans implemented by the different Spiritual Traditions. Higher School executes its plans through these Traditions. The specific tasks that are produced from these plans may include the creation of new civilizations, the regeneration of existing civilizations, the development of new social institutions, or the creation of great art, monumental sculpture, and enduring architectural works. The necessary condition for fulfilling all of these tasks is that, for the members of the Traditions, awakening is the first priority, and thus the WORK OF THE STEWARD is always the first dimension of the Great Work.

GROUP   A Group is an esoteric teaching directed by a CONSCIOUS BEING, which works independently of any SPIRITUAL TRADITION. Groups usually – but not always – work independently from the LIVING RELIGIONS that are connected to the Spiritual Traditions. Groups practice the FIRST WORK, the aim of which is to bring the LOWER CENTERS into the present while igniting the HIGHER CENTERS as and when possible. In general Groups are able to exist in the medium of civil society and tend to work independently of one another. However, this independence sets them at a disadvantage in that they are unable to draw screened candidates from the work of the Living Religions.

Within a Group, there is not a well-defined hierarchy beginning from a TEACHER with both higher centers active, extending to a number of student-teachers with the HIGHER

EMOTIONAL CENTER fully active, carrying through to a majority of students working to open the Higher Emotional Center, and completing itself in the work of those trying to bring the Lower Centers into the present.

While the work of Groups lacks the universality of the GREAT WORK, the GODS do monitor the work of the Teacher, who is a fully conscious being and who must do his best under the circumstances. We should not fail to note that a Group can have a very high Teacher. This may relate to the contribution that a particular Teacher has to make in creating the ground for Spiritual Traditions in the generations to follow. Or it may be simply that the potential was there in the Teacher but not in the society of which he was a part.

HERMETICISM   Hermetic teachings originated in Egypt, probably in the third century AD as a composite of the teachings of certain Greek, Egyptian, and alchemical schools. The serious work done under the name of Hermeticism sought to preserve the triadic (non-theistic) conception of the Absolute that is found in the ancient Egyptian creation myths. It also preserved and elaborated the Greek concepts of COSMOS, MACROCOSM, and MICROCOSM, and in this regard, it seriously developed the work already done by Pythagoras and Plato. At the same time Hermeticism integrated the different forms of proto-chemistry that existed in Greece and Egypt and went under the general name of ALCHEMY. In the post-Classical period the efforts of the Hermetic Teachings to create a coherent all-embracing cosmology were guided and inspired by the integration of much earlier Sumerian/Chaldean material.

What unites the Teachings that come under the heading of Hermetic is a concern with the different levels of energy in the universe, and how the relation between these levels is the expression of universal cosmic laws. While the records of the Hermetic teachings appear syncretic – and often bizarre – the threads of something greater run through them. There were certainly great Hermetic teachers, now unknown to us, who produced formulations of great integrity.

HIGHER CENTERS   A term introduced by George Gurdjieff (see the biographical notes in the Subject Bibliography) to designate the higher faculties of Man. The lower functions of thought, emotion, sensation, and motor activity do not represent the full range of the human experience. There are two higher functions, latent in all human beings, which are capable of opening men and women to a much broader range of experience, and ultimately to a full experience of the SPHERE OF SENTIENT BEING. In Gurdjieff's terminology these two higher functions are the HIGHER EMOTIONAL CENTER and the HIGHER INTELLECTUAL CENTER. While the four LOWER CENTERS link Mankind to the cosmos one below (the earth and nature), the two Higher Centers link Mankind to the cosmos one above (the Sphere of Sentient Being).

HIGHER EMOTIONAL CENTER   A term introduced by George Gurdjieff (see the biographical notes in the Subject Bibliography) to refer to one of two higher faculties that potentially link Man to the SPHERE OF SENTIENT BEING. When the Higher Emotional Center becomes active in us, there is a different sense of self, no longer based on the feeling of 'I'. There is a sense of identity which is rooted, not in thought, feeling, sensation, or movement, but in presence itself, presence without reference point or qualification of any kind. From this place the world around us may appear quite differently from the way that it normally does. Equally, one could have a complete experience of the Higher Emotional Center without having an altered perception of one's surroundings. What is important is that the Higher Emotional Center recognize itself and learn to sustain this self-recognition through time. Mr. Gurdjieff referred to this sphere of experience as being a world under twelve orders of laws, or WORLD 12.

HIGHER INTELLECTUAL CENTER   A term introduced by George Gurdjieff (see the biographical notes in the Subject Bibliography) to refer to one of two higher faculties that potentially link Man to the SPHERE OF SENTIENT BEING. Where the HIGHER EMOTIONAL CENTER brings a profound change in our experience of both ourselves and the external world, the Higher Intellectual Center transcends experience itself. It transcends the duality of the one who has the experience and the external content of his or her experience. It is a state of unity that is impossible to describe in words. Here the very idea of 'I' loses its meaning. From this place we can begin to understand cosmic laws. We can begin to see, in the unfolding pattern of the world around us, the expression of the laws that govern a higher level. Indeed, it is as though the universal laws begin to know themselves through us. Words, concepts, and language are utterly inadequate to describe this level of perception. Gurdjieff referred to it as a world under six orders of laws, or WORLD 6. When a man is stationed or centered in World 6 he feels his vehicle – his body, heart, and mind – as something external. When an unprepared man experiences World 6, he feels himself near to the death of his body.

HIGHER SCHOOL   A term first used by Rodney Collin and refined and developed in the work of Robert Earl Burton (see the bibliographical notes in the Subject Bibliography). Higher School is a school in which the regeneration of beings higher than ordinary man is conducted. In the PYRAMID OF MAN it refers to the level of school that is one above the schools for the regeneration of men. But it is also sometimes used as a shorthand reference for all levels of school above the human. In this regard it is also – and at the same time – the community of the GODS as that exists in the SPHERE OF SENTIENT BEING.

The Gods who are students in Higher School are attempting to

1) help the most developed members of the human race enter the Sphere of Sentient Being and

2) achieve the level of work that defines the next concentric ring of the Celestial Hierarchy.

As the Gods need to put someone in their place in order to ascend, so they need to draw into their company those men and women in whom HIGHER CENTERS have begun to become active.

In relation to Mankind, Higher School created the ARCHETYPES that are behind both the SPIRITUAL TRADITIONS and the true CIVILIZATIONS.

HIGHER SELF   Or sometimes Self, as a less clinical way of referring to the HIGHER CENTERS. See also LOWER SELF.

IMAGINATION   When the four LOWER CENTERS function in relation to the illusion of a personal identity (the illusion of 'I'), they are, as it were, turned in on themselves. They do not take in impressions directly but process them in relation to an imagined 'self.' As a result they generate, on a continuous basis, internal discourse: speculations about the past and the future, waste images, desires and fears of different kinds. This panorama appears to have unity, as our so-called personal life — but in fact, it is simply an ongoing amalgam brought into alignment by the illusion of 'I'. Untimately, of course, the panorama is controlled by what is behind the illusion of 'I', the BLACK QUEEN. The unity of the Black Queen and the principal forms of imagination generated by the Lower Centers is the LOWER SELF. Imagination is referred to as *phantasia* in Orthodox monasticism, as the *nafs* in the Sufi Traditions, and as the *tamas* in the Hindu teachings. The primary tool the Traditions use in breaking the link between the illusion of 'I' and the ongoing (and in every adult already well-established) imagination is the use of a mantra, zikr, or sequence, as described in Chapter 3.

LIVING RELIGION   A Religion that acknowledges and receives life from a SPIRITUAL TRADITION (or Spiritual Traditions). An example of this would be a Religion that supports a conscious monastic order and acknowledges its authority in certain areas. Such a Religion is capable of recognizing consciousness in the senior members of the monastic Spiritual Tradition with which it is connected. In this environment a Living Religion is able to sustain the FIRST WORK and may even support conscious roles in relation to that work — for not all conscious beings are exclusively involved with the Spiritual Traditions.

Living Religion shows openness and compassion; it is the charity of the European Middle Ages or the spirit of the bodhissatva vow in ancient India. There is not judgment of the world outside of religion, but understanding and a genuine acceptance of the human condition.

Whenever a Religion receives life from a Tradition, it is in turn able to give life to humanity. Religion unconnected to Tradition, or DEAD RELIGION, is only a system of belief, without grounding in first-hand experience. The light of higher worlds cannot reach humanity through such an opaque medium.

LOWER CENTERS (FOUR LOWER CENTERS)   The theory of the four Lower Centers (and the two HIGHER CENTERS) came out of the work of certain Central Asian Spiritual Traditions. It was used to describe the normal functions of human psychology in relation to its supernormal functions. It was introduced in the West by George Gurdjieff (see the biographical notes in the Subject Bibliography). The point of departure for the theory of the four Lower Centers is that we do not possess one brain, but that our psychology is comprised of seven different brains or centers, which work independently of one another and which pre-empt one another along the line of time. It is the identity (or sense of self) created through the normal process of socialization that conceals this lack of unity from us. The Traditions divide the seven centers into five lower centers and two HIGHER CENTERS. The five lower centers are the intellectual center, the emotional center, the moving center, the instinctive center, and the sex center. As the sex center functions differently from the other four centers, and impacts their working in a different way, it is generally studied as it manifests through the other four. Indeed some teachings treat it as an energy, generated by the organism, which is not localized in a center but profoundly affects the workings of the other four centers. The teachings of ancient times refer to the four lower centers – intellect, emotion, movement, and instinct – by their characteristic energies: air, fire, water, and earth.

These four centers are integrally connected, and within each center there are many subdivisions. To complicate this still further, each center and each part of a center is divided into positive and negative halves, which communicate the positive and negative experiences of that center. For the emotional center this would be positive and negative emotional perceptions; for the instinctive center, physical sensations of pain and pleasure; for the moving center, the experience of motion and rest; and for the intellectual center, the experience of affirmative as opposed to critical thought.

LOWER SELF   The term Lower Self refers to the part of us that is resistant to awakening. It is more suitable than the term ego, because what resists awakening is not a thing, but a complicated process that happens all by itself. It is this process that sustains the illusion of 'I' through time.

The process of the Lower Self is an expression of the instinctive will to survive that we share with the animals. This will originates in the hidden control center that we call the BLACK QUEEN. As our sense of 'I' forms – in the normal process of our socialization – the Black Queen gets behind it, backs it, and, in so doing, determines much of how our personality is formed around it. Once this sense of 'I' is securely in place, the Black Queen has – through it – control over the vast majority of the 'I's generated from the four LOWER CENTERS. It does not exercise this control in an intentional or premediated way, but as an instinctive reflex. So from one point of view, it is blind and unknowing, but from another, it is extremely intelligent and relentlessly persistent.

Although the Lower Self is a completely mechanical system of reflexes, it operates all of the time, and it is based on the Black Queen's instinctive awareness of our entire inner landscape. Thus the STEWARD, under the direction of the WHITE QUEEN, has a very formidable opponent.

MACROCOSM   See COSMOS. The created universe is a Macrocosm, an interlocking system of cosmoses formed into a hierarchy, with each lower cosmos contained within a higher cosmos. Indeed, each lower cosmos is actually created out of the cosmos immediately above it.

From the standpoint of a higher cosmos the cosmos immediately below it is a microcosm, and from the standpoint of the lower cosmos, the higher cosmos that contains it is a Macrocosm.

MAN NUMBER FOUR, FIVE, SIX, SEVEN, EIGHT   The set of terms that follows was first introduced by George Gurdjieff (see the biographical notes in the Subject Bibliography) to describe the different levels of spiritual development possible for Man.

MAN NUMBER FOUR   When a man has subordinated the activity of his four LOWER CENTERS to the pursuit of the HIGHER CENTERS, we speak of him as a Man Number Four. He has reduced imagination to a point where the HIGHER EMOTIONAL CENTER can periodically emerge, and the more concentrated experiences of presence that then occur guide and center his work.

MAN NUMBER FIVE   When the HIGHER EMOTIONAL CENTER has become permanently active in a man, he has made the transition through to Man Number Five. He is a CONSCIOUS BEING. A complete Man Number Five is capable of functioning independently of his cellular body and of withstanding the shock of death. He has thus achieved a kind of immortality. Such a person would have more frequent glimpses of the HIGHER INTELLECTUAL CENTER and would be able to interpret and integrate these experiences in a way that a Man Number Four cannot. George Gurdjieff (see the biographical notes in the Subject Bibliography), who introduced this idea, emphasized that a Man Number Five can still lose everything he has gained, whereas a Man Number Six cannot. In other words, being a Man Number Five carries with it no guarantee of permanence, although it can be permanent and lead to higher things.

MAN NUMBER SIX   While a MAN NUMBER FIVE has the HIGHER EMOTIONAL CENTER open and awake and experiences glimpses of the HIGHER INTELLECTUAL CENTER, the working of the Higher Intellectual Center is not stable in him. In other words the two Higher Centers are not linked. When the two HIGHER CENTERS finally reach a point where they begin to work in unison, we speak of a Man Number Six. The two Higher Centers, at a certain point, recognize their profound kinship and lock. This union is irreversible and defines forever the course of evolution of the being who supports them.

We could say that while a Man Number Five is transparent to himself, a MAN NUMBER SIX actually becomes translucent, so that the light of a higher level shines through him.

While the appearance of a Man Number Five is rare and significant for humanity, it is the level of Man Number Six that is important for the Spiritual Traditions, for it is from this level that a working relation with the GODS can be established.

A Man Number Six creates a very dynamic teaching environment. He, and he alone, is competent to create the situation where a MAN NUMBER FOUR – who has made all the necessary preparations – can make the transition through to Man Number Five. And at the same time he is capable of stabilizing and correcting a mature Man Number Five in relation to WORLD 6.

MAN NUMBER SEVEN   We noted that a MAN NUMBER SIX has both HIGHER CENTERS open and awake. Not only are they active, but they are integrally linked. What, then, lies beyond this level? The range of development of the fused Higher Centers is so great that it makes little sense to speak of all men in this category as belonging to the same order. Indeed it has been said that the range of development from the level of six on is greater than the range that begins with a spiritual novice and ends in a Man Number Six. For this reason the SPIRITUAL TRADITIONS have spoken of levels beyond six. All Traditions speak of MAN NUMBER SEVEN in whatever terminology they may use. George Gurdjieff (see the biographical notes in the Subject Bibliography) actually spoke of Jesus, Buddha, and Moses as being MAN NUMBER EIGHT. Fortunately we do not need to understand the substance of these further divisions to tell the Story of Man. It is enough to know that there have been men with both Higher Centers open and connected.

MAN NUMBER EIGHT   Similar to a MAN NUMBER SEVEN in that the HIGHER EMOTIONAL CENTER (giving access to WORLD 12) and the HIGHER INTELLECTUAL CENTER (giving access to WORLD 6) are both open and have fused. In a MAN NUMBER EIGHT, however, they have fused in such a way that they give a certain access to WORLD 3. This kind of fusion can only be engineered by the GODS who control human destiny. A Man Number Eight is almost invariably a Prophet.

MANY 'I'S   A term used to characterize Man's normal psychological state. Chapter 3 presents the theory of the four LOWER CENTERS as elucidated by George Gurdjieff: intellect, emotion, motor-function, and instinct. Each center has many subdivisions, based on a combination of the energy of that center with the energies of the other three. Each of these parts is again divided into parts of parts. To complicate this still further, each center and each part of a center is divided into positive and negative halves, which communicate the positive and negative experiences of that center. The result is that each of these centers releases a series of impulses immediately communicating its state: its concerns, its fears, its desires, and its needs. These are the many 'I's.

In the process of socialization, we are taught that we possess a unified identity, and in this process a kind of artificial control center does actually develop in us. (See the entry for LOWER SELF). From the standpoint of this artificial control center, the many 'I's are the rational expressions of a unified identity. They are who we are. The identification of who we are with the many 'I's has the effect of blocking the HIGHER CENTERS. As spiritual aspirants work on themselves and become more conscious, they begin to see the endless stream of chaotic and unconnected impulses that exist under the illusion of a unified identity. This awareness helps the aspirant to sustain a presence that is independent of the many 'I's.

MEN OF THE TRADITION A generic reference to the men and women who work within, and so comprise, the Great SPIRITUAL TRADITIONS.

MERCILESS HEROPASS (LAW OF THE) A term coined by George Gudjieff (see the biographical notes in the Subject Bibliography) to describe a cosmic law that regulates the relation that exists between CREATION and the ABSOLUTE. Mr. Gurdjieff stated that the MACROCOSM of Creation was only able to come into being because of a universal law that registered the limiting effect of what he called the "unconditioned infinite." The unconditioned infinite was (amongst other things) a state of entropy that threatened the Absolute in the state in which He existed before He created the physical universe.

Prior to the act of Creation, the unconditioned infinite existed outside of the Absolute and exercised a debilitating effect on Him. As such it was a signal of His mortality, and acted as time in relation to Him. Perceiving this entropic effect, the Absolute, in a single act, internalized the unconditioned infinite and generated Creation, under the limiting condition of a single universal law. This was the Law of the Merciless Heropass.

The physical universe that resulted necessarily incorporated the Law of the Heropass. Under this law it took the form of a Macrocosm (a cosmos of cosmoses), which enabled the generation of consciousness out of matter. In other words, it enabled a consciousness which did not already exist in the BEING of the Absolute. The Macrocosm was thus potentially able to neutralize the entropic effect of the unconditioned infinite. The generation of consciousness out of the Macrocosm is an eternally on-going process. See Chapter 2 for a more complete description.

MICROCOSM See COSMOS. A microcosm is a cosmos within a cosmos. The created universe is a cosmos on the highest scale. We call it a Macrocosm, which is an interlocking hierarchy of cosmoses, each one contained within the next. As we proceed downwards in the hierarchy, each lower cosmos is contained within – and at the same time created out of – the cosmos immediately above it. From the point of view of the higher cosmos, the cosmos internal to it is a microcosm, and from the point of view of the lower cosmos, the higher cosmos that contains it is a Macrocosm.

But however far down you go in the chain, the microcosm contains the signature of the whole. Because the universe was created from the top down – and not from the bottom up – the possibility always exists for a microcosm to transcend itself and to enter into the life of the cosmos that contains it. Through successive acts of transcendence, it can enter consciously into the life of the whole. In so doing it remains true to its original creative principle.

MINERAL ENERGY   Simply put, crystalline mineral compounds viewed as energy or as matter having a certain vibrational frequency and so being – in some degree – animate. Mineral energy is an essential component of the human organism. Indeed it is the heaviest energy connected with human embodiment. It is certainly not what defines us as human, but mineral salts are essential to the composition of both our blood and our bones. It could be said that we are mineral by our bone structure. Because mineral energy is part of our composition, we can psychologically experience the extraordinary limitations of the mineral world. In the Hermetic classification, the average bandwidth of the mineral world is that corresponding to World 384, although it extends – through its metallic elements – down to World 768. Thus, as **ELECTRONIC ENERGY (WORLD 6** and **WORLD 3)** is at the top of the human range (opening into an experience of transparent luminosity, radiance, and cosmic love), Mineral Energy is at the bottom of that range (opening into a state of utter hoplessness and despair, bringing with it the sense of an ultimate evil from which there is no escape). See also **ENERGIES/FOUR ENERGIES.**

MOLECULAR ENERGY   Molecular energy is finer than the **CELLULAR ENERGY** of the physical body. It vibrates at a much higher frequency. It is the energy internal to each of the **FOUR LOWER CENTERS**, and, as such, it is the substance of our thoughts and feelings. It has much greater powers of penetration and diffusion than cellular energy. Our ability to focus attention at will is an example of molecular energy. Also, sometimes, for example, we can know the thoughts and feelings of others, although we are separate from them in space. What we call phantoms or spirits are formations of this energy, independent of a cellular body.

It is the molecular range of energies that defines our character or who we are. In the normal course of life, the energies of thought, feeling, and sensation combine into habitual states of anger, fear, envy, love, hope, and joy. As our personality takes form, these habitual molecular states combine in a particular way, in response to the external impacts and pressures of our lives, to form a kind of *ad hoc* energetic body.

This haphazardly formed molecular body (sometimes called the desire body) can survive the death of the host cellular body for a period of time, but not indefinitely. It needs the anchoring of the five senses to relate it to the external world, or it will eventually disperse. A molecular form that is permanently independent of the cellular body can be created by making an intentional use of the higher range of molecular energies, in other words, those that correspond to **WORLD 24** (see the entry for **ESSENCE**) and **WORLD 12.**

When the molecular body begins to exist independently of the cellular body, it can itself be centered by **ELECTRONIC ENERGY.** When this occurs, a man has acquired a conscious soul. See also **ENERGIES/FOUR ENERGIES.**

NINE OF CLUBS   See BLACK QUEEN.

NINE OF HEARTS   See WHITE QUEEN.

NOT-BEING   See BEING, NOT-BEING, BEYOND-BEING.

ORGANIC LIFE ON EARTH   The hierarchy of organic life forms that has developed on the planet earth and certain other planets. The medium of Organic Life appears to us as an aggregate of many different life forms – plants, animals, insects, and bacteria – with which we constantly interact. But Organic Life is fundamentally a unity, and we are part of that unity. All of our organs and tissues and cells are by-products of the process of Organic Life, and we occupy a carefully defined place within its order.

Organic Life is more than just the physical aggregate of organic life forms, it is the living unity of their experience. Just as an individual human body is a unity of cells, tissues, and organs, in which the whole has an intelligence independent of its parts, so the Unity of Organic Life has an intelligence independent of, while at the same time embracing, the many different species which comprise it. The Unity of Organic Life can thus develop and perfect its manifold functions through the complex hierarchy of life forms which are its extended body.

PRESENCE   The word presence is important to the telling of the Story of Man, but our usage differs from the standard English-language usage of the term. The conventional usage refers to the presence of the four LOWER CENTERS. In these pages the term is used to refer to the presence of the two HIGHER CENTERS.

The lower centers can be present to what is before them in the moment, but they cannot know presence itself, independently of thought, emotion, sensation, and movement. Indeed, a profound moment of wordless presence is a break in the life of the four lower centers. It is an entirely different quality of experience. It is a kind of presence that knows itself, moment after moment after moment. The life of the Higher Centers begins in these gaps and culminates in the transcendent, universal life of a God. The aim of the SPIRITUAL TRADITIONS is the permanent realization of a presence that is independent of the four Lower Centers.

PRESENCE AWARE OF ITSELF   A term used in the teaching of Robert Earl Burton (see the biographical notes in the Cosmology/Philosophy section of the Subject Bibliography), referring to a state of presence that knows itself as such. In this state there is not just presence, but presence self-aware. In the moment when presence is self-aware, it exists independently of the four LOWER CENTERS and so of the medium of ORGANIC LIFE ON EARTH. This presence is connected to the COSMOS above the COSMOS OF MAN. See also PRESENCE.

PROCESSES / SIX PROCESSES   The groups of Peter Ouspensky, George Gudjieff, and Rodney Collin (see the biographical notes in the Subject Bibliography) undertook specific research into the idea of cosmoses. They determined that, on every level of the universe, a **COSMOS** takes into itself three different kinds of sustenance. These three kinds of sustenance – or foods as they were called by the above-named – are transformed through six processes to generate all of the energy, consciousness, and insight that are possible for the cosmos in question. The process of transformation of the three foods via the six processes develops according to the law of musical octaves. Through the progressive transformation of the three incoming substances, a cosmos develops, or fails to develop, the potentials given in the moment of its creation.

- *The Three Substances* In an individual man the three substances are food, air, and the impressions of the senses. Each substance enters the body at a different point. The progressive transformation of these substances can, under very special conditions, be taken to the point where a man develops a conscious soul which functions independently of his physical body.

- *The Six Processes* These have been called by many names. On the scale of the human organism, we could call them growth, healing, regeneration, digestion, elimination (or destruction), and crime (or disease). Each of these processes leaves the incoming matter on which it works at either a higher level or a lower level than it was when the process began. The process that completes the development of a cosmos is regeneration. In a man this represents his spiritual life; it is everything that leads to and supports states of **PROLONGED PRESENCE**. If the process of regeneration is weak or undeveloped, the life of the cosmos will be driven in an arbitrary way by the other five processes. If the process of regeneration is strong enough to regulate the other five processes, the microcosmos will ultimately transcend itself. In the case of a man, he will make the transition through to the **SPHERE OF SENTIENT BEING**. In the case of a Civilization, it will produce a completed **COSMOS OF MAN**.

PROPHET   A world-historical **TEACHER** sent to humanity from **HIGHER SCHOOL**. The Prophet is tasked from Higher School with forming a **SPIRITUAL TRADITION** and – through that Tradition – a new **CIVILIZATION** which will support the Tradition through time. He is also usually (but not always) tasked with forming a world **RELIGION** that links the new Civilization to the Spiritual Traditions. The Prophet is the foremost vehicle of the **GREAT WORK**.

PROLONGED PRESENCE   A term used in the teaching of Robert Earl Burton (see the biographical notes in the Subject Bibliography). Prolonged Presence is a state of presence, independent of the **FOUR LOWER CENTERS**, that is sustained through time. When presence is able to sustain itself through time, we have the beginning of a new kind of identity. The completion of this identity (completely self-sustaining presence) is sometimes called the Self or Soul. See also **PRESENCE**.

PROPHETIC TRADITION This is a SPIRITUAL TRADITION that takes form under the influence of a PROPHET. It develops out of the life of the prophetic community which forms around the Prophet when he begins to teach. In the intensity of the first years of the Prophet's teaching, the distinctions between Spiritual Tradition, LIVING RELIGION, and CIVILIZATION are blurred. The external forms of these different lines of work usually crystallize after the death of the Prophet. Within the Prophet's community we could say that the Tradition is the inner form of this teaching and the Religion is the outer form. A minority of Spiritual Traditions are Prophetic Traditions, but most of the Traditions that we know of do refer themselves to one or another of the Prophets.

PYRAMID OF MAN The hierarchy of the different levels of man, linked in a lift-on-lift upward movement to HIGHER SCHOOL. The Pyramid of Man has as its base the level of unregenerate man and as its general context the medium of ORGANIC LIFE. Its five levels comprise a hierarchy of conscious influence:

1) The GODS or Higher School, existing above Mankind, who recruit from (and regenerate) …

2) SPIRITUAL TRADITION at the top of the human pyramid, which recruits from (and regenerates) …

3) LIVING RELIGION, which recruits from (and regenerates) …

4) CIVILIZATION, which recruits from (and regenerates) …

5) The general human community.

The Pyramid of Man links these different levels by enabling the phenomenon of replacement. That is, when one person moves up to a new level, he creates a space (or vacuum) on the level he was on, into which another person, on the level immediately below, may shift. This, then, is our connection through to the Gods. When the Gods themselves move up, they create a space for us to enter the SPHERE OF SENTIENT BEING which they inhabit.

The linked system of replacements – set in motion by upward movement – is not arbitrary but law-governed. It is partly determined by the limitations imposed by the LAW OF THE MERCILESS HEROPASS. In Hermetic terms the system of replacements is an alchemical process, involving subtle energies that are outside the scope of modern chemistry.

RELIGION We have sometimes used this term in a descriptive, generic sense to refer to the great religions, such as the Judaic, the Islamic, or the Christian. These Religions may be at one time LIVING RELIGIONS and at another time DEAD RELIGIONS.

SCHOOL An organization which teaches, and which generally encourages in its participants, the development of consciousness. Minimally, this is an organization in which MAN NUMBER FOUR is instructed in the awakening of his or her HIGHER CENTERS so that he or she may become a MAN NUMBER FIVE. The term has also been used to encompass the work of the SPIRITUAL TRADITIONS, which are more focused on instructing MAN NUMBER FIVE to become MAN NUMBER SIX. The term has also been used, particularly by the teachers of the FOURTH WAY, to refer to refer to celestial schools where molecular and electronic entities continue their evolution from one level to the next. (We consider here the description of the Celestial Hierarchy given by Dionysius the Areopagite in Chapter 1.) In this context the term HIGHER SCHOOL is often used.

SCHOOL CIVILIZATION This is a CIVILIZATION that has been prepared from its very inception – by the GODS and by the plans of HIGHER SCHOOL – to be governed by a SPIRITUAL TRADITION. A Civilization governed by a Tradition connects Mankind both to the level one above and the level one below. It enables Mankind to serve Higher School directly and to actualize the purposes of Higher School on earth. It completes Mankind in its relation to the medium of organic life and so (at least in theory) changes the relation of the earth to the other planets, enabling the earth and its inhabitants to participate in developments that occur at the level of the sun and the solar system.

While every true Civilization has a connection to a Spiritual Tradition, a School Civilization is directly governed by a Ruling Tradition, without the intermediary of LIVING RELIGION. Under these circumstances the Civilization in question may take the form of a COSMOS. It does not simply have the semblance of a cosmos, as some developed Civilizations do; it is a cosmos – where the process of regeneration governs the other self-constitutive processes. What we call a School Civilization is more potential than actual in humanity. We see only the traces of it in history. See also PROCESSES.

SIX PROCESSES See PROCESSES.

SPHERE OF SENTIENT BEING Each of the Traditions has its own terminology for the state of consciousness that this non-denominational term represents. The Sphere of Sentient Being refers to the world-containing, world-sustaining space that is the context of human existence: pure BEING without limit or boundary in any direction. The Sphere of Sentient Being both contains and transcends material CREATION. From within this sphere, Creation is seen as a unity.

The Sphere of Sentient Being is the abode of Beings whose identity is rooted, not in organs or cells but in consciousness itself. These Beings we have called the GODS. The Gods assist men to penetrate and to sustain themselves in the Sphere of Sentient Being. They do this by nurturing the seed-form of a conscious soul that exists within Man so that it may function independently of a cellular body.

From a Hermetic point of view the Sphere of Sentient Being is a deep WORLD 12 experience, viewed as the gateway to WORLDS 6 and 3.

SPIRITUAL TRADITION A Spiritual Tradition is the special community required to transmit the WORK OF THE STEWARD. This is the work that enables Man to enter the SPHERE

OF SENTIENT BEING and to sustain himself therein. The leaders of the Spiritual Traditions are directly answerable to the GODS, who inhabit the Sphere of Sentient Being. Within the confines of the Spiritual Tradition, the laws governing the development of human potential are understood objectively. To work within a Tradition is to work with its other members as though they were equivalent beings in the common presence of God. Internally the Tradition adopts the standards of the level one above. Each member is permanently committed to disengaging himself from his animal nature: his aggression, his territoriality, his greed, his fear, his selfishness, his vanity, his inertia, and his sloth.

To bring men and women through to the Sphere of Sentient Being, the Traditions must ensure that the the link between Mankind and the Sphere of Sentient Being is perpetuated from one generation to the next. This task has quite specific requirements; it involves men working on different levels, engaged in different tasks, whose roles interlock harmoniously. In the longer term it requires that the Civilizational Order supporting the Tradition be sustained at a certain level. For this reason the Spiritual Traditions may be tasked by the Gods – at different times – to raise the level of particular Civilizational Orders.

STEWARD   The Steward is a concentrated group of WORK 'I'S capable of pre-empting the LOWER SELF and so of creating a space in which the HIGHER CENTERS may emerge. It is the combination of a specially developed WHITE QUEEN with the small retinue of work 'I's which are at her immediate command. The WORK OF THE STEWARD is for someone whose lower centers are in an open and receptive state and who has – in some degree – transcended the preoccupation with both personal problems and personal desires – including even the desire to awaken. See WORK OF THE STEWARD.

SUBSTANCES/THREE SUBSTANCES   The groups of Peter Ouspensky, George Gudjieff, and Rodney Collin (see the biographical notes in the Subject Bibliography) undertook specific research into the idea of cosmoses. They determined that, on every level of the universe, a COSMOS takes into itself three different kinds of sustenance. These three kinds of sustenance – or foods, as they were called by the above-named – are transformed through six processes to generate all of the energy, consciousness, and insight that are possible for the cosmos in question. Through the progressive transformation of the three incoming substances, a cosmos develops, or fails to develop, the potentials given in the moment of its creation.

- *The Three Substances* In an individual man the three substances are food, air, and the impressions of the senses. Each substance enters the body at a different point. The progressive transformation of these substances can, under very special conditions, be taken to the point where a man develops a conscious soul which functions independently of his physical body.

- *The Six Processes* These have been called by many names. On the scale of the human organism we could call them growth, healing, regeneration, digestion, elimination (or destruction), and crime (or disease). Each of these processes leaves the incoming matter on which it works at either a higher level or a lower level than it was when the process began. The process that completes the development of a cosmos is regeneration. In a man this represents his spiritual life; it is everything that leads to and supports states of PROLONGED PRESENCE. If the process of regeneration is weak or undeveloped, the life of the cosmos will be driven in an arbitrary way by the other five processes. If the process of regeneration is strong enough to regulate the other five processes the micro-cosmos will ultimately transcend itself. In the case of a man, he will make the transition through to the SPHERE OF SENTIENT BEING. In the case of a Civilization it will produce a completed COSMOS OF MAN.

TEACHER   One who teaches others, on the basis of his own first-hand experience, how to activate the latent HIGHER CENTERS. With respect to activating the Higher Centers and penetrating the SPHERE OF SENTIENT BEING, men need to be taught. This is more like being taught how to swim than being taught philosophy or theology. The one who teaches swimming must know how to swim. It is a very practical matter. We have chosen the term Teacher over terms like guru, master, or saint because of the romantic and subjective overtones the latter have acquired.

TRADITION   See SPIRITUAL TRADITION.

THREE SUBSTANCES   See COSMOS, COSMOS OF MAN, SUBSTANCES.

TRUE INDIVIDUALITY   The degree of True Individuality attained is an objective measure for all beings created as MICROCOSMOSES under the ABSOLUTE. The Absolute is Himself the only completely self-existent individual in the universe. In all sentient beings below the level of the Absolute, True Individuality exists only in a degree.

The development of True Individuality in Man occurs in direct opposition to the animal self-assertion of the LOWER SELF, which sees its relation to others as a relation to entities external to itself. True Individuality requires an ever-deepening understanding of the equivalence of all created beings and a deepening awareness of the existence of the SPHERE OF SENTIENT BEING as the substrate of their being. Thus we can say that True Individuality has a universal quality. It is qualitatively different from the simple self-assertion of the Lower Self.

A man acquires True Individuality to the extent that

1) his feeling of identity extends outward to include the external context of his life-experience and the other beings who are part of that context;

2) he is able to see his own behavior and his own habitual responses as part of that context;

3) he has within himself a presence which exists independently of both the external context and his mechanical reactions to what occurs in that context;

4) he is able to act, in some degree, from the understanding resulting from the above three characteristics.

TWICE-BORN GODS Gods originally generated out of the medium of ORGANIC LIFE who have transcended their cellular bodies to produce completed molecular bodies. In their second birth, these Gods produced consciousness that did not originally exist in the MACROCOSM of CREATION, and for this reason – becoming conscious – they helped to neutralize the state of entropy that existed within the Macrocosm. It is the Twice-born Gods who, because of their experience of life on the cellular level, usually work with individual men and women to help to bring them through to the awakened state. See FIRST-BORN GODS.

UNIVERSE As we use the term in this book, the Universe is the Whole, viewed from the standpoint of one who studies it but cannot fully comprehend it. This is the natural standpoint of science. It implies nothing about the content of that Whole, except the commitment to accept it as a global context.

WHITE QUEEN A term used in the teaching of Robert Earl Burton (see the biographical notes in the Subject Bibliography). The White Queen is a division of the FOUR LOWER CENTERS which can be trained to recognize and to remember the experience of consciousness, as distinct from the range of experiences given from the other centers. This is an inner division of the emotional center, permeated with the energies of the intellect. (In the study of the divisions of centers, it is called the Nine of Hearts.) We could say that it is intelligent emotion. The intense and refined energies that are associated with the intellectual division of the emotional center allow a memory of peak emotional experiences, such as the crowning moment of a great concert, a pledge of love, a vow to change one's life, or a glimpse of the HIGHER CENTERS. It is the capacity to remember the experience of Higher Centers that gives us our chance at evolution, for when these experiences can be remembered, they can be assimilated and they can be made to give direction to our lives. It is the presence of this quality of energy in the cellular body of Man that makes him – at least potentially – a self-evolving being. This is the basis of our link to the SPHERE OF SENTIENT BEING.

When the White Queen has been developed in the FIRST WORK, and repeatedly exposed to the Higher Centers, it becomes able to make two different kinds of perceptions:

1) negative perceptions of what it means to live under the control of the LOWER SELF;

2) positive perceptions of PRESENCE aware of itself, or of Higher Centers.

These perceptions are, respectively, the perceptions of the negative and positive halves of the White Queen. The two halves can be trained to work together, in the constantly changing circumstances of external life, to produce a continuity of effort in service of the emergent Higher Centers.

WORK 'I'S The Work 'I's are a subset of the MANY 'I's. The Many 'I's are the thoughts, emotions, motor impulses, or sensations generated from the FOUR LOWER CENTERS. The Work 'I's are those 'I's which are capable of serving the emergent HIGHER CENTERS, specifically those 'I's which can promote PRESENCE at the behest of the WHITE QUEEN.

Through constant practice aspirants develop a core of Work 'I's that more or less cover the range of different situations that they encounter in the course of life. In each of these different areas, three aspects of their practice cumulate:

1) the understanding of what it means to be fully awake in this particular situation;

2) the desire to maintain the awakened state at any cost;

3) observations of failure and of the mis-application of Work 'I's.

The body of understanding that develops in each area can be condensed into a single Work 'I' or several Work 'I's, which sum it all up. Examples of Work 'I's would include: 'Be here now' or 'You are not your own negative emotions' or 'What you cannot accept in others is what you have not understood in yourself.' When there is enough experience behind a Work 'I', it can even be reduced to a point-syllable, which simplifies, and so heightens, its impact. In this way a whole world of understanding and observation can be concentrated into a single phrase, which can in turn be concentrated into a single syllable, such as Act, Now, or Aim.

WORK OF THE STEWARD The Work of the Steward is the defining line of inner work taught by the SPIRITUAL TRADITIONS. It is designed to bring the HIGHER CENTERS into being and to directly enable the transition through to the SPHERE OF SENTIENT BEING. For the practitioners of this work everything becomes irrelevant but the present or – put differently – everything becomes a means to presence.

The development of the Steward gives us the means of overcoming the insuperable difficulties of the FIRST WORK, which is focused on the opening and purification of the LOWER CENTERS. The First Work is the necessary preparation for the more advanced work that directly enables transference to the Sphere of Sentient Being.

In the First Work the medium of uninterrupted IMAGINATION (which is, at the same time, the life of the FOUR LOWER CENTERS) is replaced by a medium of active struggle in which the Higher Centers may intermittently appear. But, from the standpoint of the emergent Higher Centers, all of the efforts we can make to prepare the ground for their coming are just part of the chorus of 'I's that continuously arises from the lower centers. There is a struggle and that in itself creates extraneous noise. There is not enough inner stillness for the Higher Centers to come into being and sustain themselves.

The Work of the Steward takes us past the sticking point of the First Work by creating an internal space which is between the world of the four lower centers and the world of the Higher Centers. This is possible because there is a division within the Lower Centers that can recognize and respond to the Higher Centers. This is the NINE OF HEARTS, which, because of its special qualities is sometimes called the WHITE QUEEN. The White Queen gathers to herself a small and very concentrated group of WORK 'I's. We might say that the 'I's that are part of the entourage of the White Queen are precision-engineered in the sense that they are activated in silence in accordance with the Queen's changing perception of the needs of the moment; they are not the occasional spin-offs of an ongoing internal discourse about the work. The Steward is, then, the combination of a specially developed White Queen with a small retinue of Work 'I's which are at her immediate command. With this level of precision there is much less extraneous noise and at the same time the Steward itself can go into passive mode the moment the Higher Centers come into being. The Higher Centers can thus be specifically encouraged, and at the same time the White Queen (in passive mode) can be instructed by them in the moment they appear. She can thus learn to serve them ever more accurately.

WORLD   The World refers to everything within the scope of our experience, both the events of our personal lives and everything that is external to us. This takes into account the fact that our experience may include things not accessible to the senses. Thus, the World does not refer to the planet earth because we know it only through our general conception of it, not through our direct experience. What we take to be our World changes profoundly with our state of consciousness, and for this reason we can say that a man literally experiences different Worlds.

The term World, taken as a coherent whole of experience, is also used to define the Hermetic hierarchy of different worlds. Such a system of reference was developed comprehensively by George Gurdjieff and Peter Ouspensky (see the biographical notes in the Subject Bibliography). It was they who developed the terms, used so frequently in these pages, **WORLD 12**, **WORLD 6**, and **WORLD 3**.

WORLD 3   A world of experience that is close to the **ABSOLUTE**. While we are connected to **WORLD 12** and **WORLD 6** by the **HIGHER EMOTIONAL CENTER** and the **HIGHER INTELLECTUAL CENTER** respectively, World 3 does not correspond to a center connected with the human body. Mankind can only have a relationship to World 3 through those rare individuals in whom both the Higher Emotional Center and the Higher Intellectual Center are fully developed. But World 3 does have a relationship to this World! This relationship is secured principally through the work of the **PROPHETS**. While the relationship to World 3 is a distant relationship for our species, it is important to our common destiny.

WORLD 6   The world of experience that corresponds to the **HIGHER INTELLECTUAL CENTER**. When a man is stationed or centered in World 6, he feels such a degree of unity with higher sentience in the universe that his mortal vehicle – his body, heart, and mind – seem external to him. When an unprepared man experiences World 6, he feels himself near to the death of his body.

WORLD 12   The world of experience that corresponds to the HIGHER EMOTIONAL CENTER. In World 12 one is relieved of all of the restrictions on thought, feeling, and action that occur when the lower centers are subordinated to the false sense of 'I'. It is this sense of 'I' that ties us to the feelings of guilt, fear, recrimination, aggression, and general frustration that are the unspoken backdrop of human existence. Indeed, it is hard for us to imagine a world completely free of this all-too-human shadow. But so it is with World 12. Energies of the level of World 12 also exist in the world outside of us and are experienced by most people in the course of a normal life. In this context, these energies may not generate a complete experience of World 12, but they may enrich our normal experience of life in the most unusual ways. World 12 energies may be experienced through art, music, and the highest moments of human love. This is why many Traditions have used art to evoke and sustain the Higher Emotional Center or to produce timeless experiences of the Self.

WORLD 24   A world of experience comprised of the most refined energies connected with the life of our cellular body. This was described by George Gurdjieff (see the biographical notes in the Subject Bibliography) as the world of ESSENCE. The interaction of essence (World 24) with the HIGHER EMOTIONAL CENTER (World 12) is necessary for the right formation of our HIGHER SELF.

WORLD 96   A world of experience comprised of the coarser energies which we share with the animals. It is dominated by instinctive sensations: pain and pleasure, animal fear, greed, jealousy, competitiveness, and aggression. These strong vital energies are quite capable of overriding human emotion and subordinating it. Indeed, the negative emotions which have the strongest hold over us are those infused with these instinctive energies. Humanity is fundamentally connected to World 96. Below World 96 are worlds below the animal – 192 and 384 – which reach into the even more limited experiences characteristic respectively of the vegetable and mineral realms.

YOGA   By the term yoga we refer to a range of practices developed and perfected in the Shamanic schools of prehistoric times. These are specific techniques that utilize the instinctive and moving centers to enhance awareness in different ways. Technically, they can bring the energies of WORLD 12 into the human organism. These techniques may involve breath awareness and the development of the awareness of different energy channels that exist in relation to the physical or cellular body. They may include the use of stimulants or the sexual act. They may be quite dangerous, in which case they should not be attempted without guidance, or they may be very simple and directly conducive to health.

The usage we have adopted here is common in both the Vedantic and the Buddhist traditions. At the same time, we acknowledge that within the Vedantic Tradition the term was often used in a more universal way (by Patanjali, for example) to refer to all meditative practices. In these pages we are limiting ourselves to the more narrow usage.

Subject Bibliography

Cosmology/Philosophy – Philosophy of History – Prehistory – The Original Religions – Ancient Mesopotamia: Sumeria, Babylon, Chaldeans – Mongolia – Ancient/Shamanic Taoist – New World Civilizations – Vedic/Vedantic – Zoroaster – Judaic – Buddhist – China – Byzantium – Christianity: General – Christianity: Western – Christianity: Eastern – Islam – Greece – Hellenistic/Stoic – Rome – Middle Ages – Renaissance – Post-Renaissance West

Many sources have been consulted in the writing of *The Story of Man*, over a period of many years. There are undoubtedly instances where we have failed to credit certain of these sources within the text itself. We hope that the following extensive bibliography will convey the debt that we owe to these profound sources and to their authors.

The first three subjects of this subject bibliography (Cosmology, Philosophy, and the Philosophy of History) include comment, and the entries are ordered in terms of the comment. The remaining subjects will be ordered alphabetically, with any comments inserted parenthetically.

COSMOLOGY/PHILOSOPHY

The great Prophets of revealed truth – the Buddha, Jesus, and Muhammad – spoke little about what we have called the Absolute, for they were concerned to emphasize or draw attention to its existence, without reducing in any way its enigmatic and inscrutable quality. And they themselves, as beings testifying directly for the First Principle, were enough of an enigma that not a lot had to be said. Revealed truth of this kind, whether from a Prophet or from a Teacher with both Higher Centers developed, comes from a "face-to-face" contact with the Absolute. Such contact is far from knowing the Absolute as it is in and for itself. Thus, revealed truth is always the experience of a particular dimension of the Absolute, and it is always given in a particular context so that it will have optimal value for those receiving it. Under these circumstances it is only useful to say so much and no more. The Spiritual Traditions following from Teachers of this level may build upon or elaborate these foundational statements or they may not. But any genuine elaboration must be based on experience, and this implies that Teachers of a very high level must follow from the first.

The **Vedic/Vedantic** is rooted in the teachings of the great Vedic rishis.

Rig Veda, a metrically restored text (ed. and trans. B. van Nooten and G. Holland), Harvard University Press, Cambridge MA and London UK, 1994.

> While the *Rig Veda* is of the greatest interest to us, its interpretation requires a considerable depth of experience in several different areas. The Old Sanskrit in which it was originally written contains a wealth of inflections and a complexity of verbal forms, voices, and moods that had gone out of use by the time of the Upanishads.

The Thirteen Principal Upanishads (trans. Robert Ernest Hume and George C.O. Hass), Oxford University Press, Oxford, 1921.

The Ten Principal Upanishads (trans. Shree Purohit Swami and W.B. Yeats), Macmillan Publishing Co., Inc., New York, 1975.

Bhagavad-Gita: Song of God (trans. Swami Prabhavananda and Christopher Isherwood), Signet/Penguin, New York, 2002.

Hindu Scriptures (ed. Dominic Goodall and R.C. Zaehner, trans. Dominic Goodall), Phoenix Press, London, 2005.

> A good selection of the Vedic and revealed Vedantic texts, well translated. The selection is what constitutes the principal revealed teachings of Hinduism.

An invaluable overview of the Vedantic teaching by a late nineteenth-/early twentieth-century scholar who was in touch with several of the Vedantic teachers of his own time. He has a good grasp of the double use of Vedantic terms, many of which have different meanings in different contexts.

Deussen, Paul, *The System of the Vedanta* (trans. from the German by Charles Johnston), Dover Publications, New York, 1974.

Using the general frame of reference of the Vedantic Tradition (Advaita Vedanta), but based on first-hand experience and very beautifully expressed, are the following:

Merrell-Wolff, Franklin, *Pathways Through to Space, A Personal Record of Transformation in Consciousness,* Julian Press, New York, 1973.

Merrell-Wolff, Franklin, *The Philosophy of Consciousness Without an Object, Reflections in the Nature of Transcendental Consciousness*, Julian Press, New York, 1973.

Merrell-Wolff, Franklin, *Transformations in Consciousness, The Metaphysics and Epistemology*, State University of New York Press, Albany, 1995.

The greater part of the **Zoroastrian** corpus was destroyed firstly, by Alexander, and later during the Islamic conquest of Persia. Thus we know very little of what Zoroaster himself said about the Absolute. But this dimension of the teaching of Zoroastrianism was brought out in the struggle of fifth-century Zoroastrianism with its variant form Zurvanism. Under the Achaemenid kings Zoroastrianism had become a state religion, a development which always reinforces the popular doctrines at the expense of the esoteric. Zurvanism emerged as a reaction to the descent of the late-Achaemenid theology, perhaps around 300 BC. It presented Zurvan as the transcendent Beyond-Being of Angra Mainyu, thus giving a triadic diety (Zurvan/Ahura Mazda/Angra Mainyu). One could argue that Zurvanism was a restatement or clarification of the original doctrine. It was a recognized variant of Zoroastrianism which received royal sanction under the Persian Sassanid kings in the period 226-651 AD. The fact that it disappeared with the Muslim invasion points, perhaps, to the completeness of the Zurvanite embrace of Islam as being the teaching of the Prophet who Zoroaster had predicted would succeed him.

Boyce, Mary (ed. and trans.) *Textual Sources for the Study of Zoroastrianism*, The University of Chicago Press, Chicago, 1984.

Chapter 10, "Classical Zurvan," in Zaehner, R.C., *The Dawn and Twilight of Zoroastrianism*, G.P. Putnam's Sons, New York, 1961.

Zaehner, R.C., *Zurvan, A Zoroastrian Dilemma*, Clarendon Press, Oxford, 1955.

The **Buddhist** sense of the Absolute is that of a transcendent and utterly inconceivable Being, centered in itself, which is – at the same time – an interconnected, dynamic, high-energy process. This process has the nature of a Logos or ongoing authentic utterance. The destruction of the texts of the Indian Buddhist Tradition by the Mughals left us with three separate Buddhist canons: Pali, Chinese, and Tibetan. The variety that they present makes generalization difficult; nevertheless a few things can be said. The term that most closely corresponds to the Absolute in these pages is *dharmakaya*, which refers to the truth body of the Buddha. This is the Buddha's unmanifest dimension, his manifest dimension being the world of form and appearances that we know. The concept of *dharmakaya* emphasizes the Buddha's utter transcendence of the manifest universe, but the nature of this transcendence is not specified. Buddhism has sometimes been mistakenly viewed, particularly in the West, as a kind of non-transcendent pantheism. But while Buddhism rejects simple theism, the *dharmakaya* represents an explicit transcendence of the world of form. The Buddha's recorded teachings focus neither on the moment of transcendence nor on the relations of necessity deriving from it that determine the world of form. They emphasize rather the utterly transcendent nature of *dharmakaya* and, by contrast, the relative illusion of its manifest dimension. All Buddhist teachings have emphasized that, because the *dharmakaya* is infinite, it cannot be represented in concepts. Its particular qualities are revealed (at least in certain of the teaching lineages) in the Buddha manifestations. For example, the Absolute's dimension of love and compassion might be represented by *Avelokitesvara*, while the unfettered dynamism – which is the destruction of everything false – might be represented by *Vajrapani*. In this difficult area, the following texts have been helpful.

Conze, Edward (ed. and trans.), *Buddhist Scriptures*, Penguin Books, Baltimore MD, 1968.

Conze, Edward (ed. and trans.), *Buddhism, Its Essence and Development*, Oxford University Press, Oxford, 1963.

Conze, Edward (ed. and trans.), *Perfect Wisdom: The Short Prajanaparamita Texts*, Buddhist Publishing Group, Totnes, UK, 2003.

Conze, Edward (ed. and trans.), *The Large Sutra on Perfect Wisdom: With the Divisions of the Abhisamayalankara*, University of California Press, Berkeley, 1984.

Thornton, John (ed. with Susan Varenne) *Buddhist Wisdom: The Diamond Sutra and the Heart Sutra* (trans. Edward Conze), Vintage Books, New York, 2001.

Williams, Paul, *Buddhist Thought, A Complete Introduction to the Indian Tradition*, Routledge, London and New York, 2000.

Williams, Paul, *Mahayana Buddhism: The Doctrinal Foundations*, Routledge Taylor and Francis Group, London and New York, 2009.

Dionysius the Areopagite (now more commonly known as Pseudo-Dionysius) is a representative of the Christian Tradition in the fifth century AD. His God is similar to the Absolute as presented in these pages, in that it: **1)** entirely transcends the conception of a theistic deity, and **2)** is acknowledged as unknowable in itself. Dionysius' detailing of immaterial Creation, as that proceeds from the Absolute, is particularly impressive. This is presented in his essay called *Celestial Hierarchy*.

The Western Church, in Medieval Times, took the Celestial Hierarchy as revealed truth. There is a tendency amongst contemporary scholars, lacking in contemplative experience, to reduce these texts to a range of Neo-Platonist sources. But these texts are fundamentally a report on experience, making use of the language of Neo-Platonism.

Dionysius the Areopagite, *Pseudo-Dionysius, The Complete Works* (trans. Colm Luibheid), Paulist Press, Mahwah, NJ, 1987.

Dionysius the Areopagite, *Celestial Hierarchy and Mystical Theology* (anonymous early twentieth-century translation) Shrine of Wisdom (no publication date).

This is a less exact and more intuitively satisfying translation.

This **Islamic** cosmology builds from Muhammad's teachings as recorded in the *Koran* and in the *Hadith*. These are no more explicit than those of the Buddha or of Jesus Christ. There are a certain number of key statements, which must be understood in context. But the Sufi teachers who followed from Muhammad elaborated upon these statements, some on the basis of first-hand experience. Of the latter, Ibn Arabi's presentation is one of the best known. The two most relevant texts are these:

Arabi, Ibn, Muhyiddin (ed. Michel Chodkiewics) *The Meccan Revelations* (Al-Futūhāt al-Makkiyya) (trans. Cyrille Chodkiewics, Denis Gril, and David Streight), Pir Press, 2002.

Arabi, Ibn, *The Ringstones of Wisdom* (Fusūs al-Hikam) (trans. Caner K. Daqli), Kazi Publications Inc., Chicago, 2004.

The **Greek Tradition** of cosmological thought, sourced in Plato and Aristotle, profoundly influenced both Christianity and Islam.

Plato's presentation, which is both mythic and philosophic, is concentrated in the following texts.

Parmenides, in *The Collected Dialogues of Plato* (ed. Edith Hamilton and Huntington Cairns), Princeton University Press, Princeton NJ, 1980.

> This establishes the ground by destroying the popular conception of Being and so the possibility of a theistic deity.

Timaeus, in *The Collected Dialogues of Plato* (ed. Edith Hamilton and Huntington Cairns), Princeton University Press, Princeton NJ, 1980.

> Treats of Being and Becoming, the Demiurge, the Platonic forms as paradigms, and the kind of causation that this implies. Provides a significant mythic presentation of the Absolute and Creation.

Sophist, in *The Collected Dialogues of Plato* (ed. Edith Hamilton and Huntington Cairns), Princeton University Press, Princeton NJ, 1980.

> Contains Plato's account of Being and Not-Being and clarifies his understanding of the forms as paradigms.

For a complete collection of Plato's myths put into an appropriate style of English prose, see J.A. Stewart, *The Myths of Plato*, Barnes and Noble, Inc., New York, 1970.

Aristotle's presentation is purely philosophic.

Metaphysics, Books VII-X (trans. Montgomery Furth), Hackett Publishing Company, Indianapolis, Indiana, 1985.

> This is a literal translation, which leaves the text – originally a set of lecture notes – in its original terse and elliptical form.

Metaphysical {complete} (trans. W.D. Ross) in *The Basic Works of Aristotle* (ed. Richard McKeon) Random House, New York. 1941.

> An excellent translation that is intuitively satisfying.

Nichomachean Ethics (trans. Terence Irwin), Hackett Publishing Company, Indianapolis, Indiana, 1985.

> This is an attempt at an exact translation, which can be complemented by the richer and more intuitive translation of W.D. Ross in *The Basic Works of Aristotle* (ed. Richard McKeon). The *Nichomachean Ethics* presents Man in his relation to the Prime Mover Unmoved with both inspiration and philosophic genius. The implications of this work have not yet been thought out and actualized. It is the source of the idea of the *ergon anthropawn* (the Work of Man) which is one of the bases of the term the Great Work that is used in this book.

Plotinus' *Enneads* are based on an extraordinary vision of the *Logos*. His vision of the Absolute is less developed than Plato's enigmatic gestures – as sketched in the *Parmenides*, the *Timaeus*, and the *Sophist* – but his representation of the levels of immaterial Creation is inspired.

Plotinus, *The Enneads* (trans. Stephen MacKenna), Faber and Faber, London, 1962.

Proclus was a late fifth century Neo-Platonist. His work addresses the Aristotelian critique of the Platonic Idea, and – with several centuries of hindsight – relates the cosmology of Plato to the cosmology of Aristotle. Proclus understood Aristotle's achievement, and attempted to integrate the Aristotelian theory of cause into the Platonic cosmology. For Aristotle form acts as a final cause within the time/space manifold, and as a consequence the Absolute does not will Creation, but simply exists in a relation to it. For Plato the Absolute does will Creation. Proclus reconciles the two points of view by showing how, what Aristotle calls an efficient cause, can operate – not just in a linear sequence – from a higher level to a lower level. Proclus then demonstrates how Plato's Absolute can act as an efficient cause to determine (or to generate) the paradigmatic level of the Ideas, and – through the Ideas – to generate the structure of Creation as we know it. Proclus identifies Aristotle's four different types of cause in the text of Plato's *Timaeus*, and to these he adds two other types of cause, which he finds implicit in that text. These are the instrumental cause (from the level of the Absolute) and the paradigmatic cause (from the level of the Ideas). Together these six types of cause explain the relation between levels in a hierarchical universe which originates from a single source.

Proclus, *The Elements of Theology* (trans. E.R. Dodds) Oxford University Press, at the Clarendon, 1963.

Proclus, *The Commentaries of Proclus on the Timaeus of Plato* (trans. Thomas Taylor) Theophania Publishing, Calgary Alberta, 2012.

The **Judaic Tradition** excels in depicting the cosmic context of Man's existence, the levels of immaterial Creation, and the presence of Not-Being within Creation. The *Sefirot* – found in the *Kabbalah* – represents a full cosmological picture of Creation. There is, throughout the *Kabbalah*, the triadic tension which characterizes the teaching of the Traditions with respect to the Absolute.

Matt, Daniel C., *The Essential Kabbalah: The Heart of Jewish Wisdom*, HarperCollins, New York, 1996.

Berg, Rav P.S., *The Essential Zohar: The Source of Kabbalistic Wisdom*, Three Rivers Press, New York, 2002.

Sperling, Harry and Simon, Maurice, *The Zohar, An English Translation* (in five volumes), The Soncino Press, London and New York, 1984.

Modern Western philosophy, as the inheritance of the Renaissance and the Enlightenment, has made legitimate contributions to the understanding of Man's place in the universe.

Immanuel Kant and **George William Fredrick Hegel** were not Men of the Tradition, but they were men whose respective philosophies were grounded in the insight of Higher Centers, and who heavily impacted European intellectual life in the two or three generations to follow, although not, perhaps, in the way they would have expected. The effects of their writings include some of the most cogent formulations of the underlying principles of liberal democracy, the historical dialectic of Karl Marx, and the century of communist revolutions that followed from it. Their work, in its original conception, was a resonance of the "theater of enlightened civic life" which modern Western

Civilization inherited from the Classical World. Had the roles of Kant and Hegel been complemented by the presence of conscious or enlightened roles in public life, other kinds of results might have been possible. But that historical moment has passed.

At the beginning of the twenty-first century, we can say that the impulses of Kantianism and Hegelianism have finally exhausted themselves. The residue of their profound insight into Man's place in the universe has been overridden by the merely intellectual insights of modern philosophies (empiricist, logical-positivist, deconstructionist, or post-modernist).

The philosophy of **Immanuel Kant** begins from the individual and, from that point of departure, extends to the universal. In Kant's view we must begin from what we can know directly, yet this is not to deny the existence of universal truth. It simply qualifies our access to it. To achieve these ends Kant makes the distinction of *noumenal* and *phenomenal*. The phenomenal is what we can see and feel and touch; it is what is external to us and known through the senses. The noumenal is what we cannot see and feel and touch. It is the dimension of a thing existing outside of time and space, which is its completion. It cannot be known by the intellect, but would have to be known by "a non-sensible form of intuition." While Kant does not specify what this is, we can affirm, from the teachings of the Traditions, that we are possessed of such an intuition in the form of the two Higher Centers. Because the noumenal is a dimension of every created thing (its sixth dimension), we cannot know how a thing is "in and for itself" without reference to its noumenal dimension. This is an important limiting guideline for science. Our own noumenal side includes the awareness of being aware, culminating in the transcendental unity of apperception; self-awareness in its highest sense. Kant called our multiple interfaces with the external, phenomenal world the forms. He claimed, for example, that space and time are two pure forms of sensuous intuition. He stated that things-in-themselves – in their noumenal being – are neither spatial nor temporal. The limited view of the universe given us by the forms means that we are unable to see things as they are in themselves, their noumenal side. At the same time the forms are the universal and necessary conditions of the appearance of anything whatsoever to our human perception.

Kant elaborated his theory of the forms in *Critique of Judgment*. This teaching is entirely compatible with 1) the precepts of modern science and 2) a complete freedom of religious belief. Kantian ethics is based on the acknowledgment of the noumenal side of others, which is expressed in the injunction to "act only on maxims (HJ: of behavior) that can be willed as universal laws." In following this injunction you are serving your own noumenal side. A general acknowledgment of the noumenal dimension of things, and of the noumenal side of others, is what would make democracy work – for the principle behind it is non-partisan, non-religious, and unrelated to ethnicity or to any specific cultural content. Yet such a recognition would – at the same time – allow for the recognition of noumenal insight in art, in ethics, and in Man's view of the universe. Kant's individuality corresponds to the free individual described by Jean Jacques Rousseau a generation earlier in his seminal work *On the Social Contract*. We could say that Kant began from this point and then proceeded to deepen the understanding of the noumenal side of individuality. Indeed Kantian philosophy could be viewed as an expression of the truth of modern liberal democracy, anticipating the transparency that democracy enables. It was once seriously taught as one of the bases of Western law.

Kant, Immanuel, *Critique of Pure Reason* (trans. Norman Kemp Smith), Macmillan and Co., Ltd, Edinburgh, 1929.

> The limits of reason, determining the point from which reasoning must begin, while giving the context.

Kant, Immanuel, *Foundation of the Metaphysic of Morals* (trans. Lewis White Beck), The Bobbs-Merrill Company, Inc., Indianapolis, 1959.

> From one point of view, this describes the individual's connection to his own noumenal side.

Kant, Immanuel, *Critique of Judgment* (trans. J.H. Bernard), Hafner Press, Macmillan Publishing Co., Inc., New York, 1951.

> This text outlines Kant's forms, which are the different aspects of our psychology or the different interfaces that we have with the external phenomenal world. We achieve transcendental unity of apperception by accurately judging what we intuit through the forms.

George William Fredrick Hegel then reverses Kant, beginning not from the subjective individual but from the universal. For Hegel, the only real individual is the Absolute, with all other forms of individuality being derivative. Hegel's philosophy was called objective idealism, as opposed to the subjective idealism of Kant. Whereas, with Kant, the counter on the board is the free self-sustaining human individual, with Hegel you have **1**) a return to the universal/objective and **2**) a rediscovery of the classical idea of cosmos, albeit stated in different terms. In Hegel's work the principle of the Cosmos of Man – as we have outlined this in Chapter 4 – is present throughout as a background ordering principle. We might liken Kant's stance to that of the Buddha, who begins from the bottom up, and Hegel's stance to that of the Vedanta, which begins from the top down.

Whereas Kant's ideal social order is democracy, Hegel's ideal social order makes use of democratic forms, but is based on an initial differentiation of the basic social functions, which are each embodied in particular political structures. This social differentiation produces the concept of estates: the peasant, the landowner, the burgher, and the administrative class. (Hegel was writing at the beginning of the nineteenth century in what is now Germany, when the entire agricultural sector of the economy was still feudal.) Within each of Hegel's four estates there are forms of democratic representation, appropriate to the functions that the estate in question performs. There are also forms of representation that connect the estates to the national government itself. The national government, as the province of the administrative class, has its own forms of representation. Hegel's administrative class is a service aristocracy, and its members play roles comparable to the roles played by the guardians in Plato's *Republic*.

Hegel's social system, taken as a whole, is a civil-service aristocracy, making use of democratic forms of representation. The members of the administrative class, in fulfilling their governmental duties, are striving to achieve true individuality and to experience the life of the whole. This can only be achieved by truly serving that life, and in so doing serving both their invisible Self and the Absolute. As the measure for true individuality is inscribed in human nature, it is just as real (if rather more difficult to determine) than the measure of profitability is for the burgher class. In this way Hegel hoped that the free individuality enabled by democratic forms could be raised, in stages, to the universal. We remark that it would take very little to adjust Hegel's four estates to mirror the six processes outlined in Chapter 33.

> **NOTE:** This side of Hegel's thought has been significantly obscured by two historical developments which occurred after his death: **1)** the rise of the Prussian state, culminating in the German Fascist state seventy years later and **2)** the rise of state communism. The fact that individuals involved with these historical movements were influenced by a defective interpretation Hegel's thought has nothing to do with Hegel's motivations and understandings any more than the religious persecutions of the Reformation and Counter-Reformation have anything to do with the work of the apostles.

Hegel saw the fundamental weakness of the formula "democracy + unregulated free enterprise = good government." The economic life of a nation, as the resultant of the actions of a multitude of independent entrepreneurs, is both disorderly and accidental. The notion of the "hidden hand of the market," always working independently of externalities, is one of the myths of classical political economy that took form in Hegel's time. Hegel understood that the market is a necessary equilibrating factor, but he argued that it does not in itself bring optimal development to the national economy. If no one is responsible for the total outcome of all economic acts, this outcome may at certain points be disastrous for different social strata and even for the life of the nation itself. The administrative class, as the class responsible for harmonizing the different social functions, is responsible for considering and assessing the total outcome of all economic acts.

While Kant's democracy would be satisfying to any radical nineteenth-century liberal (and quite acceptable to Adam Smith), it is an order that could never be realized in fact because you would never have more than a small portion of a population functioning from their noumenal side. The Kantian democracy would have to see a steady development of the noumenal side, yet there is no means of managing this, and no democracy has achieved it. The Hegelian state, by contrast, embodies a fully developed civic life and acknowledges the requirements for what we have called the process of regeneration (see Glossary entry for PROCESSES). While this is, perhaps, no more likely to be realized, it is more of a mirror of the archetypal Cosmos of Man. Hegel's ideal of the state, presented in the *Philosophy of Right*, is thus very much in the spirit of Plato's *Republic*.

Hegel's philosophy is grounded in some direct insight into the nature of the Absolute. In the *Phenomenology of Spirit* and the *Science of Logic*, Hegel brings out all the fundamental tensions relating to a transcendent Being and to what is Beyond-Being. At least some of this is a conceptual representation of the experience of Higher Centers. While Hegel's very considerable philosophic acumen was in service to some original experience of Absolute Spirit, the translation of this into the various branches of philosophy is quite uneven. If you do not have a sense of what Hegel's underlying goals are, the study of his work can be frustrating.

From Hegel's *Philosophy of Right* we have taken the idea of a Triadic Absolute, the theory of true individuality, the theory of negation, and the reflections on what we have called the Cosmos of Man. What we do not take from Hegel is his particular form of teleology. (When, towards the end of his life, Hegel was able to read translations of the

Bhagavad-Gita, he himself saw that it eclipsed the place he had given it in the sequence of civilizations as consecutive moments in the self-realization of the Absolute.) Where we differ from Hegel with respect to history is with reference to the archetypes, which are not teleological in the sense that they are each their own truth and there is not a line of inner necessity uniting them.

Hegel, G. W. F. (ed. H.D. Lewis), *Hegel's Science of Logic* (trans. A.V. Miller), George and Allen Unwin Ltd., New York, 1969.

Hegel, G. W. F., *Phenomenology of Spirit* (trans. A.V. Miller), Oxford at the Clarendon Press, Oxford, 1977.

Hegel, G. W. F., *Hegel's Philosophy of Right* (trans. T.M. Knox), Oxford University Press, Oxford, 1969.

Bernard Bosanquet, working in the tradition of Hegel, brings out and develops the implications of Hegel's theory of true individuality on several different levels and in a way that shows him a worthy successor of his master.

Bosanquet, Bernard, *The Principal of Individuality and Value* (Gifford Lectures for 1911), Macmillan and Co., London, 1927.

Bosanquet, Bernard, *The Value and Destiny of the Individual* (Gifford Lectures for 1912), Macmillan and Co., London, 1913.

George Gurdjieff, a Cappadocian Greek born in Alexandropol in 1866, traveled extensively in Central Asia and the Near East seeking ancient wisdom. In the last half of the nineteenth century it was still possible to connect with many spiritual sources in this part of the world which have since ceased to exist, and Gurdjieff took full advantage of this opportunity. In 1913 he suddenly appeared in Russia (Moscow and Saint Petersburg) as an accomplished Teacher of a very high level. Beyond the immediate communication of an extraordinary depth of presence, he taught a revitalized Hermeticism. While many commentators have attempted to source Gurdjieff's hermetic/cosmological teachings in other known teachings or combinations thereof, the teachings that he presented are unique. They seamlessly fuse elements known to **1)** the Greek and Egyptian Hermeticists of Classical times, **2)** the Sufi Hermeticists, and **3)** Renaissance Hermeticism. At the same time they include formulations entirely unknown to these teachings, which are central to his presentation. While Gurdjieff left hints with regard to his sources, he never revealed them.

Gurdjieff, G.I., *All and Everything, Beelzebub's Tales to his Grandson*, E.P. Dutton and Co., Inc., New York, 1964.

> We have drawn heavily on Gurdjieff's mythic/hermetic presentation in the pages of this book.

Peter Damien Ouspensky, born in Moscow in 1879, was a writer and journalist who devoted his life to the search for ancient wisdom. He met George Gurdjieff in Moscow in 1915 and became his foremost student. Ouspensky has provided us with a record of Gurdjieff's verbal teachings on cosmology, which are much more direct and accessible than the cosmological material available in *Beelzebub's Tales*. Gurdjieff endorsed Ouspensky's record, saying – when the text was read aloud to him – that he could "hear himself speaking."

Ouspensky, Peter Damien, *In Search of the Miraculous: Fragments of an Unknown Teaching*, Routledge and Kegan Paul, London, 1977.

Ouspensky developed and elaborated on Gurdjieff's teachings, both practically and theoretically. He was himself a gifted hermeticist, both in the sense that the hermetic form of thinking was natural to him and that he applied the hermetic teachings with great rigor to produce the intended results.

Ouspensky, Peter Damien, *The Fourth Way, A Record of Talks and Answers to Questions based on the Teachings of G.I. Gurdjieff*, Routledge & Kegan Paul, London, 1972.

Ouspensky, Peter Damien, *The Psychology of Man's Possible Evolution and The Cosmology of Man's Possible Evolution*, Agora Books, Robertsbridge UK, 1989.

Some further value can be garnered by studying his repetition of these themes in different contexts.

Ouspensky, Peter Damien (ed./compiler not given), *A Further Record, Extracts from Meetings 1928-1945*, Arkana, London and New York, 1986.

Ouspensky, Peter Damien (ed./compiler not given), *A Record of Meetings*, Arkana/Penguin, London, 1992.

Ouspensky, Peter Damien (ed./compiler not given), *Conscience, The Search for Truth*, Routledge and Kegan Paul, London, 1979.

In the months preceding his death, as a result of his application of the methods that he taught, Ouspensky was able to re-establish a connection to the Gods and to Higher School. He placed his closest students under great pressure during this time and was able – in greater or lesser degree – to include them in this experience of the cosmos above the cosmos of man. In the wake of Ouspensky's death, his foremost student, Rodney Collin, was able to assemble a document which conveyed something of the insights of that time.

Rodney Collin wrote *The Theory of Celestial Influence,* which contains extensive reflections on the Great Work, civilization, and history. While it was composed in a very short period of time and contains many weaknesses of fact, the fundamental insights that are behind these writings are clear to anyone who is open to them. It is a book that bears reading many times.

Collin, Rodney, *The Theory of Celestial Influence, Man, The Universe and Cosmic Mystery,* Watkins Books, 1980.

Robert Earl Burton is a Teacher in the Fourth Way tradition, which descends from George Gurdjieff, through Peter Ouspensky, Rodney Collin, and Alexander Francis Horn. His book, *Self-Remembering*, published by Globe Press Books, New York, 1991, and reissued by Weiser Books in 1995, contains his teaching of what we have called in these pages the First Work. Since 2003 he has focused his teaching on the Second Work – The Work of the Steward – which is partially presented in Chapter 3 of this book. The principles of the Second Work are outlined in his more recent book *Awakening*, edited by Dianne Crosby and published by Fellowship of Friends Publishing, Oregon House, California, 2017. His introduction of the Second Work was based on an extensive exploration of the teaching of the Great Spiritual Traditions through history. Few have maintained, as consistently as he, that 'All Traditions are One Tradition,' or have given the same recognition to the place of the Gods in their relation to the Spiritual Traditions.

This is the one person that the author has heard speak directly about the Nature of the Absolute on the basis of experience. Burton's teaching is principally oral, and very practically oriented. While his comments about the Absolute are given in a context that generally conforms to the teachings of Gurdjieff and Ouspensky, they are in no way an intellectual elaboration of the previous teachings – as, for example, the Vedantic teachings are an elaboration of the Vedic. Rather, Burton's statements are a product of his own experience, given in a form that is suitable to his students in the moment that he speaks. The investigation of the Absolute is, for him, an ongoing area of study rather than a doctrine, and is constantly subject to revision.

The following presentation of his teachings is based on a number of short statements given at dinners or meetings in conjunction with other teaching topics.

The Absolute exists in an omnidirectional void; he never had a beginning and he will never have an end. At some point – prior to the creation of the universe – the Absolute was threatened by 'unconscious hostile forces.' At this time he existed in a less-developed or less-evolved state. In the struggle to address these unconscious forces the Absolute, in an act of "enormous suffering," transcended himself. With reference to this act Burton sometimes states, putting it very strongly, that the Absolute "created himself." He once put it that, "The Absolute struggled unspeakably to create himself." The result of this act was not only his own self-transcendence, but the creation of the universe as we know it.

The Absolute is qualitatively different from any other being that inhabits the created universe; he exists on an entirely different scale. "The Absolute is a transcendent genius" and "even the oldest angels are in awe of him." The Absolute is presented as being distant from mankind: we cannot pray to him nor is he actively ushering in a New Age. The Absolute communicates primarily to his own inner circle – the oldest of the Gods – and his direct influence reaches humanity at large only through the extended hierarchy of the Gods. The hierarchy under the Absolute is determined by the capacity to serve. While the Absolute is unknowable, as he is in himself, he may choose to make himself known to a conscious being. (**Note:** This would be one in whom both Higher Centers were active, and the connection between them had developed to the level of a Man Number Seven.) In sum, there can be direct contact with the Absolute in a context of conscious service: a context well known to the Great Traditions of history. The overall impression that Burton conveys is that the Absolute is a figure of immeasurable authority.

Burton relates our personal potentials to the Absolute's original act of self-transcendence. He emphasizes that "The Absolute went through certain barriers, which enabled all the rest of us to do the same." Man is thus a microcosmos of the Absolute. "We all have the same gift as the Absolute" (the capacity for self-transcendence) and "we must all do as he did." When asked to elaborate on these tantalizing fragments, Burton will say something like: "This kind of study is really for the next level of School."

Following from his parallel between an evolving human being and the Absolute, Burton has speculated that World 1 may act as the Absolute's Higher Intellectual Center while World 3 acts as his Higher Emotional Center.

PHILOSOPHY OF HISTORY

G. W. F. Hegel presents history as the realization of Absolute Spirit in time, culminating in the self-knowledge of Absolute Spirit. His writings are imbued with a kind of teleology that is foreign to the thinking of the present writer. The historical material itself is now somewhat dated, yet *The Philosophy of History* is filled with the most profound insights concerning the unity of the historical process and the workings of reason in history.

Hegel, G. W. F., *The Philosophy of History* (trans. J. Sibree), Dover Publications, New York, 1966.

His vision of the Cosmos of Man (not phrased in the hermetic terminology) is found in the following book:

Hegel, G. W. F., *Hegel's Philosophy of Right* (trans. T.M. Knox), Oxford University Press, Oxford, 1969.

His presentation of the transcendent dimensions of art is found in this book:

Hegel, G. W. F., *Aesthetics, Lectures on Fine Art* (in two volumes) (trans. T.M. Knox), Oxford at the Clarendon Press, Oxford, 1975.

Hegel notes that although art can teach, edify, provoke, and adorn, he was concerned with identifying its distinctive or primary function. This is, he claims, to give intuitive, sensuous expression to the freedom of spirit – what we have called the Self or the unity of Worlds 12 and 6. In representing human beings, the object of art is not to imitate nature but to show us what divine and human freedom look like. Such sensuous expression of spiritual freedom is what Hegel calls the "Ideal" or true beauty.

Hegel defines the Ideal in terms of Classical sculpture. He begins by specifying the realm of the sensuous as the realm of material objects, individualized in space and time. Ideality (freedom from these limitations) can find expression within space and time (can be given sensuous expression) when it is embodied in the image of an individual who is completely self-existent, who stands alone, and whose outward parts reflect an inward unity of presence. This was achieved in Classical Greek sculpture. In the Dionysos of the Parthenon's east pediment, for example, the Ideal is immanent. It shows us what freedom looks like. It is neither abstract and formal (as in archaic Greek sculpture) nor static and rigid (as in Egyptian sculpture) but animated by freedom and life, while retaining the stillness and inner repose of the Ideal.

Art, for Hegel, is the sensuous expression or manifestation of free spirit in a medium (such as metal, stone or color) that has been deliberately shaped or worked by human beings into the expression of freedom.

The different stages and forms of expression of art through history are, from one point of view, forms of the self-realization of the Absolute, as those become manifest in the succession of civilizations that unfolds within the time-space manifold. The forms of beauty which define a culture help it to realize itself. England would not be England without Shakespeare's sonnets; Germany would not be Germany without Bach's cantatas. Art gathers sensuous perception under what stands above and outside of it, and, by doing so, it realizes the truth of higher worlds in the medium of human existence.

Bernard Bosanquet was able to relate these themes more successfully to civilization and to history.

Bosanquet, Bernard, *A History of Aesthetic*, George Allen and Unwin, London, 1966. First published in 1892 by Swan Sonnenschein, London.

For Bosanquet art reveals the spiritual character of the world, and the study of art – aesthetics – is the attempt to understand how different artists and works of art have contributed to this process. Bosanquet divided the study of aesthetics into four principal areas: **1**) the nature and evolution of aesthetic consciousness, **2**) artistic production, **3**) aesthetic appreciation – the experience of beauty, ugliness, and the sublime, and **4**) the role of art in the development of character.

Art strives towards a synthesis of **1**) content (subject matter) and **2**) the means of expression of that content, which are imbued with the artist's feeling, perception, and sense of value. These elements synthesize in **3**) "the penetrative imagination" which reaches to the very life of the thing itself as an element of the living whole.

Seeing this synthesis expressed in the art of different civilizations through history gives insight into the core values of those civilizations: their ideality and the unique note they sound in the sequence of civilizations.

The creation of a work of art is an expression of spirit or feeling for life. Yet, at the same time, there is a content communicated so that it is representative. It is not representative in the sense that it copies a natural object but in the sense that it embodies the soul or essence of an object (or an ideal) in the medium of that art. While artists have some preconception of the effect they wish to produce, they also learn as they engage in the activity itself. A work of art, then, is the product of a process of expression, but this expression must normally be completed in an object in the physical world. Bosanquet calls a work of art a "concrete universal"; it possesses an organization and a unity that shows a relation of interdependence among its parts, and it presents certain general principles in a concrete form. To the extent it has the quality of universality, it can become a reference point within a civilizational order, helping to center and lift that order and define its values. It not only helps us to understand different aspects of the world; it also reveals the spiritual character of the world.

Bernard Berenson deserves mention at this point. While he was not a philosopher of history, he did more to open the author to the art of the European Renaissance (and, through that experience, to the art of other civilizations) than any other writer. By teaching the art of looking in quite a practical way, he made it possible to understand in what way art is a key to Civilizational Order. Berenson was not – like Hegel and Bosanquet – a specialist in aesthetics. He was an art critic who learned how to penetrate the visual arts by opening the doors of perception. Or perhaps we should say that he learned how – by a certain preparation and study – to allow great works of art to open the doors of perception for him. Berenson distinguished perceptual categories such as tactile value, form, movement, space composition, ideated sensations, significance, value, color composition, atmosphere, and visual imagination, and described each of these categories in relation to the individual painters who excelled in them. He did this in such a way that one can clearly recognize the exceptional achievement of each painter in each area. When Berenson taught his students how to look, he introduced them to a discipline, which, if taken seriously, is severe. He stated that one must "look and look and look, and look, until one is sick of looking – and then continue to look." This practice breaks certain internal barriers to seeing things the way they really are. By pursuing this discipline, one can actually be instructed by the great painters of the past and learn to see the world as they saw it. Ultimately, one can experience the combined effect of these perceptual enhancements. Having emphasized Berenson's grounded approach, we must note that he was not limited by his empirical point of departure and came to certain conclusions that echo the conclusions of Hegel and Bosanquet whose works he never studied. He once stated that a single work of art can embody and express an entire culture. Berenson's techniques have been almost entirely lost to the mainstream of modern art criticism.

Berenson, Bernard, *Aesthetics and History*, Constable Publishers, London, 1950.

Berenson, Bernard, *Seeing and Knowing*, The Macmillan Company, New York, 1953.

Berenson, Bernard, *Sketch for a Self-Portrait*, Pantheon Books, Inc., New York, 1949.

Berenson, Bernard, *The Italian Painters of the Renaissance*, Oxford at the Clarendon Press, 1930.

This is the core text in which Berenson presents his categories in relation to the painters most representative of them. It is the most useful one to study for learning his technique.

Ernst Cassirer, working from the 1910s to the 1940s attempted to fuse Kantian and Hegelian insights, to produce a science of man, and on that basis he produced writings on the civilizations of Western history which the author has found instructive. Cassirer was able to combine, in the study of human society, the specificity of Kantian science with elements of Hegelian universality.

Reflecting on the science of man in relation to the methods of the natural sciences, Cassirer decided that science would have to take human culture as a whole as its datum. He defined Man as a symbolic animal living and communicating meaning by signs, symbols, and language systems. These systems are strongly affectively and emotionally charged. They are not neutral but laden with meaning. They constitute the underpinning of a mythical level of consciousness. Man's sign and symbol systems are existent in the culture as a whole. They give the "fact of culture" in all its richness and diversity.

Cassirer pointed out that Kant's *Critique of Pure Reason* was written from the point of view of human temporality or finitude. The rest of the Kantian system, including the *Foundation of the Metaphysics of Morals*, grounds this finite experience in our link with the noumenal world. The *Critique of Judgment* and the *Foundation* point towards a much wider conception of what Cassirer called "the intelligible substrate of humanity." Here there is a movement towards the universal, and in this movement towards universality, we see the fundamental connectedness of art, activity, religion, social roles, and so on.

Although every "cultural object" (sacred text, work of art, monument) has its place in historical time and in cultural/geographical space, it has also a trans-historical and trans-local cultural meaning. Great or formative works of art (in our terms, near to the archetype of civilizational order) have a significance that grows in both time and space. This emerges as the "cultural object" that is continually and successively interpreted and reinterpreted at other such times and places. The truly universal cultural meaning of such an object emerges only as the never-to-be-fully-completed limit of such a sequence. (In the framework of the archetypes and the Gods presented in the first chapters of this book, this universal cultural meaning would have been given at the beginning in its ideal form.)

Cassirer, Ernst, *The Philosophy of Symbolic Forms* (in three volumes), (trans. Ralph Manheim)
- Volume I: *Language*, Yale University Press, New Haven and London, 1964.
- Volume II: *Mythical Thought*, Yale University Press, New Haven and London, 1966.
- Volume III: *The Phenomenology of Knowledge*, Yale University Press, New Haven and London, 1963.

Cassirer's balance of developed intuition with precise, scholarly attention to fact yielded remarkable studies on the Renaissance and Enlightenment periods. He was able to represent the positive face of the Italian Renaissance and the European Enlightenment with some genius.

Eric Voeglin produced a seminal work in the philosophy of history with his *Order and History* (in five volumes)

- Volume I: *Israel and Revelation*, Louisiana State University Press, Baton Rouge and London, 1991.
- Volume II: *The World of the Polis*, Louisiana State University Press, Baton Rouge and London, 1991.
- Volume III: *Plato and Aristotle*, Louisiana State University Press, Baton Rouge and London, 1990.
- Volume IV: *The Ecumenic Age*, Louisiana State University Press, Baton Rouge and London, 1990.
- Volume V: *In Search of Order*, Louisiana State University Press, Baton Rouge and London, 1987.

Voeglin was an Austrian, forced to flee his home country for the stand he took there against National Socialism. He knew the civilization of Old Europe well, and through the course of his life he saw – step by step – that way of life being destroyed. This gave an edge to his determination to find expression for what is real and essential in civilizational order. Voeglin is unique amongst the historians we have mentioned in that he accepts revealed truth as the core of true civilizational order. He retains the category of transcendence, and he affirms revealed truth as the measure of human social order. But he does not clearly understand the place of Higher Centers as a link between the Cosmos of Man and the cosmos one above. Consequently he does not understand the role of conscious beings in relation to the human race and so cannot understand the place and role of the Spiritual Traditions. Nevertheless his reflections on history are of the greatest value. The historians who have followed him have either been unable to develop his many fruitful leads, or, in the present deconstructionist environment, have been shy of taking up the themes he has elaborated.

Arnold Toynbee's *A Study of History* was originally issued in ten volumes but abridged to four by D.C. Somervall in the late 1930s. The 1003-page, four-volume set, which has been the source book used here, was published by Thames and Hudson/Oxford University Press, Oxford, 1946/47.

Toynbee had a vision of the civilizations of history as great living beings. In the terminology in Chapter 3, we would say that he saw something of their molecular fields and, through that, something of their inner nature and vision. He saw this in relation to the formative challenges that civilizations face in the line of time, and thus he attempted to study their lives as we would study the life of an individual man. He attempted to determine what was essential to each civilization, and having determined this he marked its finitude in the line of time.

Toynbee's list of civilizations includes Western, Orthodox, Iranic, Arabic, Hindu, Far Eastern, Hellenic, Syriac, Indic, Sinic, Minoan, Sumeric, Hittite, Babylonic, Egyptiac, Andean, Mexic, Yucatec, and Mayan.

Toynbee sees the history of each civilization in terms of challenge and response. He explained the decline of civilizational order as a failure of the creativity and moral power of a creative minority, which precedes a withdrawal of allegiance on the part of a less creative majority. There is a consequent loss of social unity, and a reduced capacity to respond to challenge. Decline is, in a sense, moral failure. Toynbee emphasizes myth and religion as the carriers of social ideals, and thus, to some extent, the creative minority can be seen as an embodiment of the formative civilizational myth. The failure of this creative minority is at the same time and over several generations the weakening of the formative myth and the gradual dimming of the social ideals. Here we must keep in mind – from our own point of view – that the core values of a civilization, which are put to the test in these formative trials, are never directly the work of a Tradition but of a Tradition working under the circumstances of history and in the cultural backdrop of its own time. The fate of a civilization in facing its great challenges is given, then, by the inevitable mix of its original cultural ideals with the baser motives that emerge from the popular religion and the popular culture. While, as a result of this mix, the general level of Civilizations varies greatly, the cultural ideals vary less for the Traditions which are behind those ideals and instill objective values, given from Higher Centers, which vary not at all.

Toynbee's sketches of challenge and response and his measure of response (affirmation or moral failure) are promising themes to develop in the study of the history of civilizations. They would complement a study of the work of the formative Spiritual Traditions.

PREHISTORY

Bennett, J.G., *The Masters of Wisdom*, Bennett Books, Santa Fe, New Mexico, 1995.

> We have used Bennett's presentation of the four Original Religions without accepting it as established fact. Our view is that something like this happened, and

Bennett's particular presentation serves to bridge the gap between prehistoric and historic man with a substantive hypothesis.

Bradshaw Foundation (website) http://www.bradshawfoundation.com.

The Bradshaw Foundation provides a continually updated reconstruction of the origin and the major migrations of homo sapiens and homo sapiens sapiens in prehistory.

Clottes, Jean and Lewis-Williams, David, *The Shamans of Prehistory: Trance and Magic in the Painted Caves*, Harry N. Abrams, New York, 1998.

Eliade, Mircea, *Shamanism: Archaic Techniques of Ecstasy*, Princeton University Press, Princeton, 2004.

Fagan, Brian, *World Prehistory: A Brief Introduction*, Prentice-Hall, New York, Seventh Edition, 2007.

THE ORIGINAL RELIGIONS

Castledon, Rodney, *Minoans, Life in Bronze Age Crete*, Routledge, London and New York, 1993.

Drews, Robert, *The End of the Bronze Age, Changes in Warfare and the Catastrophe ca. 1200 BC*, Princeton University Press, Princeton NJ, 1993.

Eliade, Mircea, *A History of Religious Ideas* Volume 1: *From the Stone Age to the Eleusinian Mysteries* (trans. Willard R. Trask), The University of Chicago Press, Chicago 1978.

Mircea Eliade did groundbreaking work on the religion of prehistory and actually practiced many of the techniques of which he speaks. His works on Shamanism and the Myth of the Eternal Return have been orientation points in our presentation of the Original Religions.

Eliade, Mircea, *Shamanism: Archaic Techniques of Ecstasy*, Princeton University Press, Princeton, 2004.

Eliade, Mircea, *The Myth of the Eternal Return: Cosmos and History* (trans. Willard R. Trask), Princeton University Press, Princeton, 1971.

Eliade, Mircea, *The Sacred and the Profane: The Nature of Religion* (trans. Willard R. Trask), Harper Torchbooks, New York, 1961.

James, E.C., *The Cult of the Mother-Goddess: An Archaeological and Documentary Study*, Barnes and Noble, New York, 1959.

ANCIENT MESOPOTAMIA: SUMERIA, BABYLON, CHALDEANS

Bottéro, Jean, *Religion in Ancient Mesopotamia*, University of Chicago Press, Chicago, 2001.

Finkel, I.L. and Seymour, M.J., *Babylon*, Oxford University Press, Oxford, 2009.

Oppenheim, F. Leo, *Ancient Mesopotamia: Portrait of a Dead Civilization*, University of Chicago Press, Chicago, 1977.

EGYPT

Abt, Theodor, and Hornung, Erik, *Knowledge for the Afterlife: The Egyptian Amduat – A Quest for Immortality*, Living Human Heritage Publications, Zurich, 2003.

    A very nice presentation, with excellent illustrations.

Aldred, Cyril, *Egypt to the End of the Old Kingdom*, McGraw-Hill, New York, 1965.

Allen, James P., *Genesis in Egypt: The Philosophy of Ancient Egyptian Creation Accounts* (Yale Egyptological Studies, 2) Yale University Department of Near Eastern Languages and Civilizations, New Haven, 1988.

Allen, Thomas George, *The Egyptian Book of the Dead or Going Forth by Day* (University of Chicago Oriental Institute Publications, Vol. 82), University of Chicago Press, Chicago, 1974.

Armour, Robert A., *Gods and Myths of Ancient Egypt*, The American University in Cairo Press, Cairo, 2001.

    A casual telling of the ancient myths, but with a lot of experience and study behind it.

Faulkner, R.C., *The Ancient Egyptian Coffin Texts*, Aris and Phillips, Warminster, UK, 1973.

Faulker, R.C., *The Ancient Egyptian Pyramid Texts*, Oxford: Clarendon, Oxford, 1969.

Hornung, Erik, *The Conceptions of God in Ancient Egypt: The One and the Many* (trans. John Baines), Cornell University Press, Ithaca, 1982.

Addresses well the myth of Egyptian polytheism.

Lichtheim, Miriam, *Ancient Egyptian Literature: A Book of Readings* (Volumes 1-3), University of California Press, Berkeley, 1980.

Prichard, James B., *The Ancient Near East: An Anthology of Texts and Pictures*, Princeton University Press, Princeton, NJ, 1958.

Pritchard, James B. (ed), *Ancient Near Eastern Texts Relating to the Old Testament*, Princeton University Press, Princeton, NJ, 1969.

What appears, by its title, to be a work of background Christian scholarship provides some of the best and most thorough research work on the Egyptian myths available, and this is still true nearly fifty years after its publication. The book provides a comprehensive range of ancient texts: Sumerian, Egyptian, Babylonian, Hittite, and Ugaritic. Given the fragmentary nature of the original records, the work done in sorting and ordering is exemplary.

Sauneron, Serge, *The Priests of Ancient Egypt* (trans. David Lorton), Cornell University Press, Ithaca, 2000.

Schafer, Byron E. (ed.) *Religion in Ancient Egypt: Gods, Myths, and Personal Practice*, Cornell University Press, Ithaca, 1991.

MONGOLIA

Bawden, Charles R., *The Modern History of Mongolia*, Kegan Paul, London, 2002.

Cleaves, Francis Woodman (trans.), *The Secret History of the Mongols; For the First Time Done into English out of the Original Tongue and Provided with an Exegetical Commentary*, Harvard University Press, Cambridge, 1982.

ANCIENT/SHAMANIC TAOIST

Bennett, J.G., *The Masters of Wisdom*, Bennett Books, Santa Fe, New Mexico, 1995.

Frye, Richard N., *The Heritage of Central Asia*, Marcus Weiner Publishers, Princeton, 1998.

Harmatta, Janos with A.H. Dani, V.M. Masson, B.A. Litvinsky, *History of Civilizations of Central Asia* (in six volumes), Motilal Barnasidass, Delhi, 1999.

- Volume 1, *History of Civilizations of Central Asia*, Motilal Barnasidass, Delhi, 1999.
- Volume 2, *The Development of Sedentary and Nomadic Civilizations: 700* BC *to* AD *250*, Motilal Barnasidass, Delhi, 1999.

Ross, Edward Denison, *Heart of Asia: A History of Russian Turkestan and the Central Asian Khanates from the Earliest Times*, Routledge Curzon, Oxford, 2004.

NEW WORLD CIVILIZATIONS

Davies, Nigel, *The Toltecs: Until the Fall of Tula*, Civilization of the American Indian series, Vol. 153, University of Oklahoma Press, Norman, 1977.

Davies, Nigel, *The Toltec Heritage: From the Fall of Tula to the Rise of Tenochtitlan*, Civilization of the American Indian series, Vol. 153. University of Oklahoma Press, Norman, 1980.

Diel, Richard A., *Tula: The Toltec Capital of Ancient Mexico*, Thames and Hudson, New York, 1983.

Florescano, Enrique, *The Myth of Quetzalcoatl* (trans. Lysa Hochroth), Johns Hopkins University Press, Baltimore, 1999.

Malpass, Michael Andrew, *Daily Life in the Inca Empire*, The Greenwood Press, Westport, CT and London, 1996.

Markham, Clements, *The Incas of Peru*, E.P. Dutton and Company, New York, 1910.

Miller, Mary and Taube, Karl, *The Gods and Symbols of Ancient Mexico and the Maya: An Illustrated Dictionary of Mesoamerican Religion*, Thames and Hudson, London, 1993.

Sejourne, Laurette, *Cosmogonia de Mesoamérica*, Siglo Veintiuno Editores, Mexico, 2004.

Sejourne, Laurette, *El Universo de Quetzalcóatl*, Fondo de Cultura Económica, Mexico, 2003.

Sejourne, Laurette, *Teotihuacan, capital de los Toltecas*, Siglo Veintiuno Editores, Mexico, 1994.

The New World Encyclopedia http://www.newworldencyclopedia.org

This website has proved a very useful resource.

VEDIC/VEDANTIC

Basham, A.L., *The Wonder that was India: A Survey of the History and Culture of the Indian Sub-Continent before the coming of the Muslims*, Grove Press, New York, 1959.

This book is a classic in its field, combining an excellent understanding of the history of pre-Mughal India with a comprehensive grasp of the variety of the religious teachings which existed in that time. The author has sorted out a daunting complexity of source material and fitted it together both coherently and meaningfully. His translations of Vedic and Vedantic material into English, which occur throughout the book, are superb.

Bhagavad-Gita: Song of God (trans. Swami Prabhavananda and Christopher Isherwood), Signet/Penguin, New York, 2002.

If this is not the most clinically accurate translation, it may be the best translation into English.

Chaudhuri, Nirad C., *Hinduism: A Religion to Live By*, Oxford University Press, New Delhi, 1979.

Coomaraswamy, Ananda K., *Perception of the Vedas*, Manohar Publishers and Distributors, 2000.

Deussen, Paul, *Outline of the Vedanta System of Philosophy According to Shankara* (trans. from the German by J.H. Woods and C.B. Runkle) Harvard University Press, Cambridge, MA, 1927.

Paul Deussen was a late nineteenth- to early twentieth-century scholar who mastered Sanskrit down to its slightest inflections and who was in touch with several of the Vedantic teachers of his own time.

Deussen, Paul, *The Philosophy of the Upanishads* (trans. from the German by A.S. Geden), Dover Publications, New York, 1966.

Deussen, Paul, *The System of the Vedanta* (trans. from the German by Charles Johnston), Dover Publications, New York, 1974.

Guénon, René, *Introduction to the Study of Hindu Doctrines* (trans. Marco Pallis), Sophia Perennis, Hillsdale NY, 2004.

> René Guénon is a significant commentator on the Vedic/Vedantic culture. While still in his twenties, he met a group of Hindus in Paris, working in the lineage of Shankara, who expounded to him the principles of Vedantism in exactly the same way we have expounded the principles of a Tradition in Book I, Chapters 2 and 3. This marked Guénon for life, yet he did not connect with a Vedantic teaching, but very shortly after joined the Egyptian Shadhiliyya Sufi Order and remained a practicing member until his death. Nonetheless, the majority of Guénon's publications relate to Vedantism because he believed that the Vedantic teachings, as expression of the eternal teachings of the Traditions, would be more accessible to a Western audience.

Guénon, René, *Man and His Becoming, according to the Vedanta* (trans. Richard C. Nicholson), the Noonday Press, New York, 1958.

Hopkins, Thomas J., *The Hindu Religious Tradition*, Wadsworth Publishing Company, Belmont CA, 1971

> An outstanding overview of the Vedic / Vedantic period. While it is only 150 pages long, and pretends to be an introduction, the author has succeeded in generalizing meaningfully on his subject matter – resolving, at least in some degree, the horrendous complexity of the source material. This book provides the best presentation of the relation between the Vedic and Vedantic teachings, and the best description of the relation between these teachings and the social structure, that the author has found.

Maharshi, Sri Ramana (ed. Arthur Osborne), *The Teachings of Bhagavan Sri Ramana Maharshi in his own words*, Samuel Weiser, Inc., New York, 1971.

> This is a book of Sri Ramana Maharshi's practical teaching, with reference to the theology, cosmology, and philosophy of Hinduism. It is of particular interest in that it probably comes close to the balance between the practical and the cosmological that was taught by the Vedic Rishis of ancient times.

Rig Veda, a metrically restored text (ed. and trans. B. van Nooten and G. Holland) Department of Sanskrit and Indian Studies, Harvard University, Harvard University Press, Cambridge, MA and London, England, 1994.

Rizvi, S.A.A., *The Wonder that was India, Part II: A Survey of the History and Culture of the Indian Sub-Continent from the Coming of the Muslims to the British Conquest 1200-1700*, Rupa and Co., Kolkatta, India, 1999.

> This is a companion volume to A.C. Basham's 1959 publication *The Wonder that was India* (which then became Part I). Rizvi has been able to achieve the same scholarly standards, and this is a useful source book.

Temple, Richard Carnac, *India: The Eternal Cycle*, Aryan Books International, 2004.

> Richard Carnac Temple (1850-1931) was a British orientalist, born in India and resident for most of his life in that country. He had the opportunity to talk to many people who understood things that are no longer in the common pool of understanding. Despite the sometimes peculiar titles of his works, all of his writings are worthy of close study.

Temple, Richard Carnac, *The World of Lalla the Prophetess*, Cambridge University Press, 1924.

The Thirteen Principal Upanishads (trans. Robert Ernest Hume and George C.O. Hass), Oxford University Press, Oxford, 1921.

Zaehner, R.C. (ed. with Dominic Goodall), *Hindu Scriptures*, Phoenix, London, 1996.

Zaehner, R.C., *Hinduism*, Oxford University Press, Oxford, 1966.

ZOROASTER

Boyce, Mary (ed. and trans.), *Textual Sources for the Study of Zoroastrianism*, University of Chicago Press, Chicago, 1984.

Boyce, Mary, *Zoroastrians: Their Religious Beliefs and Practices*, Routledge, London, 2001.

Frye, Richard N., *The Heritage of Persia*, The World Publishing Company, Cleveland, 1963.

Zaehner, R.C., *The Dawn and Twilight of Zoroastrianism*, G.P. Putnam's Sons, New York, 1961.

> While in his twenties Zaehner had a formative experience of Higher Centers, which he interpreted in terms of the Vedantic and Zoroastrian teachings that he

was studying at that time. What he knew of these teachings allowed him to place the experience in a context and so allow the experience itself to live within him. This gave him an insight into both the Zoroastrian and Vedantic cultures that is rare. Additionally, he spent much of his adult life in Iran and India. While the scholarly research is now a bit dated, Zaehner's instinct for Zoroastrian theology is unmatched.

Zaehner, R.C., *The Teachings of the Magi*, Oxford University Press, New York, 1956.

Zaehner, R.C., *Zurvan, A Zoroastrian Dilemma*, Clarendon Press, Oxford, 1955.

JUDAIC

Ben-Sasson, Haim Hillel (ed.), *A History of the Jewish People*, Harvard University Press, 1976.

Grabbe, Lester L., *An Introduction to Second Temple Judaism: History and Religion of the Jews in the Time of Nehemiah, the Maccabees, Hillel, and Jesus*, T&T Clark International, London, 2010.

Landman, Isaac (ed.), *The Universal Jewish Encyclopaedia* (in ten volumes), Universal Jewish Encyclopaedia Co. Inc., New York, 1948.

Matt, Daniel C., *The Essential Kabbalah: The Heart of Jewish Wisdom*, HarperCollins, New York, 1996.

Rainer, Albertz (trans. John Bowden), *A History of Israelite Religion, Volume I: From the Beginnings to the End of the Monarchy*, SCM Press Ltd., London, 1994.

Rainer, Albertz (trans. John Bowden), *A History of Israelite Religion, Volume II: From the Exile to the Maccabees*, SCM Press Ltd., London, 1994.

Sperling, Harry, and Simon, Maurice, *The Zohar, An English Translation* (in five volumes), The Soncino Press, London and New York, 1984.

Voeglin, Erik, *Order and History* (in five volumes), *Volume I: Israel and Revelation*, Louisiana State University Press, Baton Rouge and London, 1991.

BUDDHIST

Hirakawa, Akira, *A History of Indian Buddhism: From Sakyamuni to Early Mahayana*, University of Hawaii Press, Honolulu, 1990.

Beckwith, Christopher I., *The Tibetan Empire in Central Asia*, Princeton University Press, Princeton NJ, 1987.

Bell, Sir Charles, *Portrait of a Dalai Lama*, Collins, London, 1946.

Sir Charles Bell was the British diplomatic liaison to the thirteenth Dalai Lama, Thupten Gyatso. Bell's book provides a unique portrait of the man and of his period. He shows us the thirteenth Dalai Lama as a man of vision, striving to redefine Tibet's relation to the great powers which loom on its horizon: China, Russia, Britain, and India. What we can easily read between the lines is: **1)** the ability of the thirteenth Dalai Lama to bring a nineteenth-century Englishman into his own world and **2)** the Dalai Lama's fundamental work to reform the orders internally and his strategy to develop a unified Tibet "from the inside out." Thupten Gyatso clearly understands the relation between Tradition, Religion, and Civilization that is detailed in Chapters 3 and 4 of this book.

Chang, Garma C.C., *The Hundred Thousand Songs of Milarepa*, (in two volumes), Shambhala, Boulder, 1989.

A good translation of the single best-known classic of Tibetan Buddhism.

Chang, Garma C.C., *The Practice of Zen*, Harper and Row, New York, 1970.

Conze, Edward (ed. and trans.), *Buddhist Scriptures*, Penguin Books, Baltimore MD, 1968.

A pioneer translator of Buddhist texts, and still a reference point.

Conze, Edward (et al), *Buddhist Texts Through the Ages*, Harper Torchbooks, New York, 1964.

Conze, Edward (ed. and trans.), *Perfect Wisdom: The Short Prajanaparamita Texts*, Buddhist Publishing Group, Totnes, UK 2003.

Conze, Edward (ed. and trans.), *The Large Sutra on Perfect Wisdom: With the Divisions of the Abhisamayalankara*, University of California Press, Berkeley, 1984.

Govinda, Lama Anagarika, *The Way of the White Clouds*, The Overlook Press, Woodstock, 2005.

> The Lama Govinda (born Ernst Hoffman) entered Tibet in the 1930s and joined the Gelug Order. He is able to paint a unique picture of Tibet and of its teachings in the years before the Chinese invasion.

Guenther, Herbert V., *Matrix of Mystery*, Shambhala, Boulder and London, 1984.

> A presentation of the ancient line of Dzogchen teachings, initially brought from India to Tibet by Padmasambhava, and elaborated – principally by Nyingma teachers – until the present day. It is replete with translations from the original texts.

Guenther, Herbert V., *Treasures on the Tibetan Middle Way*, Shambhala, Berkeley, 1976.

Hanh, Thich Nhat, *Old Path White Clouds, Walking in the Footsteps of the Buddha*, Full Circle, New Delhi, 1991.

> Drawn from Pali, Sanskrit, and Chinese sources, this is a beautiful retelling of the life of the Buddha. Thich Nhat Hanh was nominated by Martin Luther King, Jr. for the Nobel Prize in 1967.

Laird, Thomas, *The Story of Tibet, Conversations with the Dalai Lama*, Grove Press, New York, 2006.

Lhalungpa, Lobsang P., *The Life of Milarepa: A New Translation from the Tibetan*, Shambhala, Boston, 1977.

Norbu, Thubten Jigme, *Tibet is My Country* (as told to Heinrich Harrer) (trans. from the German by Edward Fitzgerald), Wisdom Publications, London, 1986.

> A tantalizing taste of pre-China Tibet.

Powers, John, *Introduction to Tibetan Buddhism*, Snow Lion Publications, Ithaca, New York, 1995.

> A scholarly introduction to the history of the Tibetan Orders, based on extensive research and on conversation and cooperation with many lamas and Tibetan Buddhist practitioners.

Ray, Reginald, *Indestructible Truth, the Living Spirituality of Tibetan Buddhism*, Shambhala, Boston, 2000.

> Reginald Ray, a committed student of Chogyam Trungpa, provides us with an excellent history of the Tibetan Buddhist teachings.

Ray, Reginald, *Secret of the Vajra World, The Tantric Wisdom of Tibet*, Shambhala, Boston, 2001.

Trungpa, Chogyam, *Born in Tibet*, Penguin, Harmondsworth, 1971.

> One of the few first-hand pictures of pre-China Tibet left us by an enlightened lama, and the story of how – immediately following the Chinese invasion of Tibet – a nineteen-year-old tulku-lama led 200 expatriate Tibetans out of Tibet into India. Of the original 200 only thirteen ultimately entered India, under fire from Chinese soldiers. Chogyam Trungpa was perhaps the greatest of the Tibetan lamas to relocate and teach in the West, and he succeeded in translating the teachings of Tibetan Buddhism into a completely Western idiom. He was a unique and remarkable individual of the kind that occurs only a few times in a century.

Trungpa, Chogyam, *Cutting Through Spiritual Materialism* (ed. John Baker and Marvin Casper), Shambhala, Berkeley, 1973.

Trungpa, Chogyam, *Glimpses of Abhidharma*, Prajna Press, Boulder, 1978.

Trungpa, Chogyam, *Journey Without Goal, The Tantric Wisdom of the Buddha*, Prajna Press, Boulder, 1981.

Trungpa, Chogyam, *Meditation in Action*, Shambhala, Berkeley, 1969.

Trungpa, Chogyam, *The Mishap Lineage, Transforming Confusion into Wisdom* (ed. Carolyn Rose Gimian), Shambhala, Berkeley, 1973.

Trungpa, Chogyam, *The Myth of Freedom and the Way of Meditation* (ed. John Baker and Marvin Casper), Shambhala, Berkeley, 1976.

Trungpa, Chogyam and Fremantle, Francesca, *The Tibetan Book of the Dead, The Great Liberation Through Hearing the Bardo*, Shambhala, Berkeley, 1975.

Trungpa, Chogyam and Guenther, Herbert, *The Dawn of Tantra*, Shambhala, Boston, 1975.

Tulku, Tarthang, *Time, Space, and Knowledge*, Dharma Publishing, Emeryville CA, 1977.

> This presentation – in an entirely modern Western idiom – of very ancient Nyingma teachings is highly recommended.

Williams, Paul, *Buddhist Thought, A Complete Introduction to the Indian Tradition*, Routledge, London and New York, 2000.

> Paul Williams undertook to reconstruct a bottom line of what is known about the Buddha's original teachings. He cross-referenced Pali, Tibetan, and Chinese sources and studied the inscriptions and artifacts surviving in India. Having undertaken this formidable labor, he then attempts to understand how the Buddhist teachings developed in the centuries immediately following the Buddha's death. A work of great value.

Williams, Paul, *Mahayana Buddhism: The Doctrinal Foundations*, Routledge Taylor and Francis Group, London and New York, 2009.

CHINA

Ames, Roger T. and Hall, David L., *Daodejing: A Philosophical Translation and Commentary*, Ballantine Books, NewYork, 2002.

> A competent scholarly commentary, specifically intended to open the text to a Western audience.

Ames, Roger T. and Rosemont, Henry, *The Analects of Confucius: A Philosophical Translation and Introduction*, Ballantine Books, New York, 1999.

> A reliable sourcebook.

Cahill, James, *Chinese Painting*, Skira/Rizzoli, New York, 1985.

Cao, Xueqin, *The Story of the Stone or Dream of the Red Chamber* (trans. David Hawkes), Penguin, London, 1974.

> The greatest Chinese novel, written in about 1750, documents the rise and fall of an aristocratic Chinese family, as part of the rise and fall of the Qing dynasty. This book provides us with a brilliant and accurate insight into eighteenth-century court life.

De Bary, William Theodore, Chan, Wing-tsit, Watson, Burton eds., *Sources of Chinese Tradition*, Columbia University Press, New York, 1960.

Good extracts and excellent commentary. A useful overview.

Dorter, Kenneth, *The Concept of the Mean in Confucius and Plato*, in *Journal of Chinese Philosophy* 29:3 (September 2002), pp. 317-335.

Fairbank, John K. and Reischauer, Edwin O., *China*, Houghton-Mifflin, Boston, 1989.

A good general introduction and overview.

Hartzell, Richard W., *Harmony in Conflict*, Caves Books, Taipei, 1988.

The work of an American diplomat stationed in Taipei, it explores, beginning from Lao-tzu, the difference between Chinese and Western psychology.

Larre, Claude and Rochat de la Valle, Elizabeth, *Rooted in Spirit*, Station Hill Press, Barrytown NY, 1995.

Focusing on a certain chapter of the Yellow Emperor's medical classic line by line, this book examines its Daoist aspects and mind/body/spirit configurations.

Liao, Waysun, *T'ai Chi Classics*, Shambhala, Boston and London, 1990.

Ancient texts with commentary from ancient times.

Pine, Red, *Lao-tzu's Taoteching* (translation with selected ancient commentaries), Mercury House, San Francisco, 1996.

Ancient texts with commentary from ancient times.

Star, Jonathan (trans. and commentary), *Tao Te Ching: The Definitive Edition*, Penguin Putnam, New York, 2001.

Includes a deeper study of the Chinese characters. The commentary is excellent.

Sullivan, Michael, *The Arts of China*, SMC Publishing, Taipei, 1984.

Excellent single-volume coverage.

Wang, Gungwu, *The Chineseness of China*, Oxford University Press, New York, 1991.

Essays on Confucianism which provide a good general background.

Watson, William, *Art of Dynastic China*, Harry N. Abrams, New York, 1981.

Valuable articles and a very good selection of pictures.

BYZANTIUM

Graves, Robert, *Count Belisarius*, Random House, New York, 1938.

A novel, based on considerable historical research, providing a vivid picture of sixth-century Byzantium.

Haussig, H.W., *A History of Byzantine Civilization* (trans. J.M. Hussey), Thames and Hudson, London, 1971.

Haussig's magistral history is unique in its ability to show the place of the Eastern Orthodox Church in the development of the Byzantine Civilization.

Diehl, Charles, *Byzantium: Greatness and Decline* (trans. Naomi Walford), Rutgers University Press, New Brunswick, NJ, 1957.

Diehl, a scholar deeply imbued in the Byzantine source-material, has a genius for meaningful generalization and for recreating atmosphere.

Diehl, Charles, *Byzantine Portraits* (trans. Harold Bell), Alfred Knopf, New York, 1927.

Diehl, Charles, *Byzantine Empresses* (trans. Harold Bell and Theresa de Kerpely), Alfred Knopf, New York, 1963.

CHRISTIANITY: GENERAL

Balleine, R.R., *Christianity as St. Peter Saw It*, Home Words Printing and Publishing Co. Ltd., London, 1910.

An excellent work of reconstruction.

Dionysius the Areopagite, *Celestial Hierarchy and Mystical Theology* (anonymous early twentieth-century translation) Shrine of Wisdom

The Stanford Dictionary of Philosophy states that Dionysius the Areopagite was "writing around 500 AD," and we can accept this date. He is certainly familiar with the language of late Neo-Platonism, but in his works there is original insight, given expression in Neo-Platonist terminology. The body of work preserved under this name may be composite, with an original author writing from experience and secondary authors compiling and adding material of their own. It appears that behind these writings there runs a deeper current of understanding, which has been lost to history. Certain formulations of the *Celestial Hierarchy* are not found in the historical record of Neo-Platonism. For example, the principle of a "lift on lift" movement, running throughout the angelic hierarchy, up to a transcendent Absolute, is expressed much more succinctly in the *Celestial Hierarchy* than in any of the works of Proclus or Iamblichus. The great medieval theologians recognized this originality, but many of the modern commentators – who have no firm grounding in contemplative experience – tend to reduce the writings of Dionysius to sources that are known to history.

Dionysius the Areopagite, *Pseudo-Dionysius, The Complete Works* (trans. Colm Luibheid), Paulist Press, Mahwah, NJ, 1987.

Ehrman, Bart D., *The New Testament, A Historical Introduction to the Early Christian Writings*, Oxford University Press, Oxford, 1997.

Gospel According to Thomas, (Coptic text edited, translated, and commentated on by Antoine Guillaumont, Henri-Charles Puech, Gilles Quispel, Walter Till, and Yassah Abd Al-Masih), Harper & Row, New York, 1959.

Herbermann, Charles (ed.), *The Catholic Encyclopaedia* (in fifteen volumes), Robert Appleton Company, New York, 1912.

While its commentary on what is external to Catholicism (e.g., Orthodox Christianity or the internal history of the Christian monastic orders) is often quite limited, it provides a valuable and comprehensive view of what has been going on inside the Catholic Church. It has been an indispensable help to understanding the Catholic point of view through history.

Holy Bible, King James Version, Cambridge University Press, Cambridge, 1979.

Jaeger, Werner, *Early Christianity and Greek Paideia*, Oxford University Press, New York, 1961.

A brilliant study of the relation of Greek culture to early Christianity.

Kohlenberger III, John R. (ed.), *The Precise Parallel New Testament*, Oxford University Press, Oxford, 1977.

The Greek original of the New Testament plus seven of the most accredited translations into English The pages of the seven different texts are shown together, in exact parallel, on two facing pages. A tool of great value for the study of the New Testament.

McManners, John, (ed.), *The Oxford History of Christianity*, Oxford University Press, Oxford, 1993.

An invaluable reference work, with many good contributions.

Origen, *Contre Celsum* (trans. Henry Chadwick), Cambridge University Press, Cambridge, 1980.

Origen, *Origen on First Principles* (*De Principiis*, trans. G.W. Butterworth), S.P.C.K, London, 1936.

Oulton, John Ernest Leonard and Chadwick, Henry, (eds.), *Alexandrian Christianity*, SCM Press, London, 1954.

Robinson, James M., (ed.), *The Nag Hammadi Library*, Harper, San Francisco, 1990.

Sanders, E.P., *The Historical Figure of Jesus*, Penguin Books, London, 1995.

E.P. Sanders developed a good understanding of Judaism and Judaic society in the time of Christ and so provides us with a well-grounded context for the teachings of the New Testament. In bringing to light the unspoken, taken-for-granted general view of Judaism at that time, Sanders brings out many nuances of Jesus' teachings.

Sanders, E.P., *Paul and Palestinian Judaism*, SCM Press, London, 1977.

Paul was born and raised a Pharisee and, as such, was bound to the principle of a historical covenant. He was profoundly impacted by Jesus Christ, when – in his molecular body – Christ entered Paul's experience. Thus, the formative experience of Paul's life occurred outside of any historical covenant. Sanders shows how, after this experience, and in reaction to his own Pharisaical upbringing, Paul taught Christianity outside of any covenant or formal guarantee. Salvation can never be a given thing; rather it is the moment-by-moment product of one's works, both internal and external.

Sanders, E.P., *Jesus and Judaism*, SCM Press, London, 1985.

Sanders, E.P., *Paul: A Very Short Introduction*, Oxford University Press, Oxford, 1991.

Sanders, E.P. and Davies , Margaret, *Studying the Synoptic Gospels*, SCM Press, London, 1996.

CHRISTIANITY: WESTERN

Anonymous English Monk, *The Cloud of Unknowing and Other Works* (trans. A.C. Spearing), Penguin Books, London, 2001.

> More than any other book in this bibliography, this work is psychologically closest to the presentation of the Work of the Steward given in Chapter 3.

Boethius, *The Consolation of Philosophy* (trans. V.E. Watts), Penguin Books, London, 1969.

Chadwick, Henry, *Augustine*, Oxford University Press, Oxford, 1986.

Charpentier, Louis, *The Mysteries of Chartres Cathedral* (trans. Sir Ronald Fraser), Research into Lost Knowledge Organization, London, 1972.

Cochrane, Charles Norris, *Christianity and Classical Culture*, Oxford University Press, Oxford, 1940.

Drane, A.T., *Christian Schools and Scholars*, Benziger, New York, 1924.

Kenny, Anthony, *Aquinas*, Oxford University Press, Oxford, 1980.

Merton, Thomas, *The Ascent to Truth*, Harcourt, Brace and Company, New York, 1951.

St. Augustine, *The City of God*, The Modern Library/Random House, New York, 1950.

> The last comprehensive statement of classical Christianity and a formative text for Western Christianity in the centuries following.

St. John of the Cross, *The Dark Night of the Soul* (trans. E. Allison Peers), Image Books/Doubleday, 1959.

> One of the few great Christian writings authored after the fall of Rome.

St. John of the Cross, *Poems of St. John of the Cross* (trans. Roy Campbell), Collins Sons and Co. Ltd., Glasgow, 1979.

St. Teresa of Avila, *The Interior Castle* (ed. and trans. E. Allison Peers), Dover Publications, New York, 2007.

St. Thomas Aquinas (ed. Anton C. Pegis), *Saint Thomas Aquinas*, The Modern Library/Random House, New York, 1948.

Voeglin, Eric, *History of Political Ideas* (in eight volumes)
- Volume I (ed. Athanasios Moulakis) *Hellenism, Rome, and Early Christianity*, University of Missouri Press, Columbia, 1997.

Voeglin, Eric, *Order and History* (in five volumes)
- Volume IV: *The Ecumenic Age*, Louisiana State University Press, Baton Rouge and London, 1990.

CHRISTIANITY: EASTERN

Anonymous, *The Philokalia, The Complete Text* (in four volumes), compiled by St. Nikodimos of the Holy Mountain and St. Makarious of Corinth (ed. and trans. by G.E.H. Palmer, Philip Sherard, and Kallistos Ware)
- Volume I: Faber & Faber, London, 1983.
- Volume II: Faber & Faber, London, 1990.
- Volume III: Faber & Faber, London, 1995.
- Volume IV: Faber & Faber, London, 1998.

 > The *Philokalia* stands as one of the great religious texts of history. While St. Nikodimos claims completeness for his collection, there are many other Philokalia texts.

Anonymous, *The Way of the Pilgrim and The Pilgrim Continues His Way* (trans. Helen Bacovcin) Image Books/Doubleday, New York, 1978.

 > These two short booklets, first published in 1884, stand as a record of the sweeping impact of the Orthodox Prayer of the Heart in nineteenth-century Russia.

Anonymous, *Writings from the Philokalia on the Prayer of the Heart* (trans. into English from Russian by E. Kadloubovsky and G.E.H. Palmer), Faber & Faber, London, 1983.

 > This work was originally the translation of a selection of Greek Philokalia texts into Russian by the Russian starets (or spiritual guide) Theophan the Recluse. Kadloubovsky and Palmer then chose to translate this Russian work into English because of the privileged insights of its Russian translator. These texts reproduce with

meticulous accuracy, in a very different language and context, the principles of the Work of the Steward.

Chariton, Igumen (compiler) and Ware, Timothy (ed.), *The Art of Prayer, An Orthodox Anthology* (trans. E. Kadloubovsky and E.M. Palmer), Faber & Faber, London, 1985.

Largely selections from the teachings of Theophan the Recluse, a lucid and articulate nineteenth-century starets, who discourses on the Prayer of the Heart.

Chitty, Derwas J., *The Desert a City*, Oxford University Press, Oxford, 1966.

Sherrard, Phillip, *Athos: The Holy Mountain*, Overlook Press, New York, 1985.

Silouan the Athonite (ed. Archimandrite Sophrony), *Wisdom from Mount Athos, the Writings of Staretz Silouan 1866-1938*, St. Vladimir's Seminary Press, New York, 1975.

Perhaps the greatest and at the same time the most unpretentious saint of the Orthodox Church in modern times.

Sophrony, Archimandrite, *The Monk of Mount Athos* (trans. Rosemary Edmonds), Mowbrays, London and Oxford, 1973.

Ware, Timothy (Kallistos), *The Orthodox Church*, Penguin Books, London, 1997.

Timothy Ware has given us an outstanding history of the Orthodox Church.

Ware, Timothy (Kallistos), *A Study of the Greek Church under Turkish Rule*, Oxford at the Clarendon Press, Oxford, 1964.

Ware, Timothy (Kallistos), *The Orthodox Way*, Saint Vladimir's Seminary Press, New York, 1995.

ISLAM

Abdel-Krader, Dr. Ali Hassan (ed. and trans.), *The Life, Personality and Writings of Al-Junayd*, Gibb Memorial Trust, London, 1976.

A penetrating study of one of the most influential Sufi teachers. One of the few best books on Sufism.

Al-Hayat, Rashahat Ain, *Beads of Dew from the Source of Life, Histories of the Khwaja-gan Masters of Wisdom* (trans. Muktar Holland), Al-Baz Publishing, Inc., Fort Lauderdale, 2000.

A Sufi classic, first published in 909 AD, and as readable now as it was then.

Al-Kalabadhi, Abu Bakr, *The Doctrine of the Sufis* (trans. Arthur John Arberry), Sh. Muhammad Ashraf Publishers, Lahore, 1999.

First published before 1000 AD (perhaps 980?). A work of considerable historical importance.

Arabi, Ibn, *Journey to the Lord of Power* (trans. Terri Rabia Harris), Inner Traditions International, Vermont, 1989.

Baha' al-Din Valad (Bahauddin), *The Drowned Book: Ecstatic and Earthly Reflections of Bahauddin, the Father of Rumi* (trans. Coleman Barks and John Moyne), Harper, San Francisco, 2004.

Bakhtiar, Laleh, *Sufi: Expressions of the Mystic Quest*, Thames and Hudson, New York, 2004.

Bennett, J.G., *Journeys in Islamic Countries*, Bennett Books, Santa Fe, New Mexico, 2000.

Bennett, J.G., *The Masters of Wisdom*, Bennett Books, Santa Fe, New Mexico, 1995.

Hafiz of Shiraz, *Teachings of Hafiz* (trans. Gertrude Lowthian Bell), The Octagon Press, London, 1975.

Hodgson, Marshall G.S., *The Venture of Islam: Conscience and History in a World Civilization* (in three volumes)
- Volume I, *The Classical Age of Islam*, University of Chicago Press, Chicago and London, 1984.
- Volume II, *The Expansion of Islam in the Middle Periods*, University of Chicago Press, Chicago and London, 1977.
- Volume III, *The Gunpowder Empires and Modern Times*, University of Chicago Press, Chicago and London, 1974.

A seminal work on Islam and an excellent general background.

Lewisohn, Leonard (ed.), *The Heritage of Sufism* (in three volumes)

- Volume I, *Classical Persian Sufism from its Origins to Rumi (700-1300)*, Oneworld Publications, Oxford, 1999.
- Volume II, *The Legacy of Medieval Persian Sufism (1150-1500)*, Oneworld Publications, Oxford, 1999.
- Volume III, *Late Classical Persian Sufism (1501-1750)*, Oneworld Publications, Oxford, 1999.

> These are collections of essays by scholars of Sufism. While they are of uneven quality there are excellent essays interspersed throughout. In sum, *The Heritage of Sufism* is one of the best sources on the Sufi Orders.

Lings, Martin, *Muhammad: his life based on the earliest sources*, Inner Traditions International, Vermont, 1983.

> A highly recommended book, guided by genuine depth of feeling for the Prophet, and free of both ideological coloration and overly religious sentiment. Lings was a close associate of Réne Guénon (mentioned above for his works on the Vedic Tradition) and spent many years with Guénon in Cairo.

Muhammad, *The Glorious Quran* (trans. Muhammad Marmaduke Pickthall), Muslim World League, New York, 1977.

Pickthall, Muhammad Marmeduke, *The Cultural Side of Islam*, Kitab Bhavan, New Delhi, 1990.

> Comprised of lectures given in 1925, giving a picture of life in Ottoman Islam by one who lived and traveled extensively in Egypt, Syria, and Turkey. Pickthall writes, "But when I saw it (Islam) it was manifestly in decay. What struck me even in its decay and poverty was the joyousness of that life compared with anything that I had seen in Europe … They undoubtedly had something that was lacking in the life of Western Europe." Pickthall documents for us what is now a lost world.

Roolvink, R., *Historical Atlas of the Muslim Peoples*, Djambatan/George Allen and Unwin Ltd., London, 1957.

> If you are interested in the history of Islam, this beautifully presented book will provide hours of pleasure and great stimulus to thought.

Rumi, Jalal ad-Din, *Rumi: In the Arms of the Blessed* (trans. Jonathan Starr), Jeremy M. Tarcher/Putnam, New York, 2000.

Rumi, Jalal ad-Din, *The Essential Rumi* (trans. Coleman Barks), Harper Collins, New York, 1995.

Schuon, Frithjof (ed. Seyyed Hossein Nasr), *The Essential Frithjof Schuon*, World Wisdom, Bloomington, Indiana, 2005.

Shushud, Hasan Lutfi, *Masters of Wisdom of Central Asia*, Coombe Springs Press, Moorcote (Yorkshire), 1983.

> As of 2018 this work, first published in Turkish in 1958, still appears to be the principal source on the Sufi Khwajagan Masters. The writer himself was a practicing Sufi, trained in the environment that existed before the fall of the Ottoman Caliphate.

Shimmel, Annemarie, *Islam, An Introduction*, State University of New York Press, New York, 1992.

Schimmel, Annemarie, *Mystical Dimensions of Islam*, University of North Carolina Press, Chapel Hill, 1975.

Smith, Margaret, *Studies in Early Mysticism in the Near and Middle East*, Oneworld Publications, Oxford 1995.

> Margaret Smith writes confidently and competently on the basis of very wide study.

Smith, Margaret, *The Way of the Mystics: the Early Christian Mystics and the Rise of the Sufis*, Oxford University Press, New York, 1978.

Trimingham, John Spencer, *The Sufi Orders of Islam*, Oxford University Press, Oxford, 1998.

> John Spencer Trimingham lived and traveled extensively in North Africa and the Levant from about the year 1937, only twelve years after Kemal Attaturk's suppression of the Sufi orders in 1925. He was able to locate and speak to many practicing Sufis, who knew the Sufi Orders as they had been in the previous period and who were the recipients of verbal histories and transmissions that have not been preserved. This is the definitive history of the Sufi Orders. The histories that the orders have produced from themselves are invariably centered on the experience of a particular Order and have been given an ideological caste in relation to the caliphate in place at the time of writing. Trimingham's work is pervaded by a delicate sense of tragedy, and one senses in him the striving to preserve and record things of great value, which were fast fading into history.

GREECE

Aristotle, *Metaphysics Books VII-X* (trans. Montgomery Furth), Hackett Publishing Company, Indianapolis IN, 1986.

Aristotle, *Nichomachean Ethics* (trans. Terence Irwin), Hackett Publishing Company, Indianapolis IN, 1985.

Aristotle (ed. Richard McKeon), *The Basic Works of Aristotle*, Random House, Inc., New York, 1941.

Boardman, John (ed.), *The Oxford History of Classical Art*, Oxford University Press, Oxford, 1993.

> The essays that comprise this book are – for each phase of Greek art – standards in their field.

Berve, Helmut and Gruben, Gottfried, *Greek Temples, Theatres, and Shrines*, Thames and Hudson, London, 1963.

> An outstanding book on the subject of Greek architecture. The authors have penetrated the *symmetria* of the ancient Greek temples and have been able to communicate their discoveries to a modern audience.

Bury, J.B. and Meiggs, Russell, *A History of Greece*, Macmillan, London, 1994.

> First published in 1900, this remains one of the best general introductions to classical Greece.

Dorter, Kenneth, *Form and Good in Plato's Eleatic Dialogues: The Parmenides, Theaetetus, Sophist, and Statesman*, University of California Press, Berekley, Los Angeles, London, 1994.

> A trenchant study of Plato's four most challenging dialogues. We owe a debt to Dr. Dorter.

Dorter, Kenneth, *Plato's Phaedo: An Interpretation*, University of Toronto Press, Toronto and London, 1982.

Dorter, Kenneth, *The Transformation of Plato's Republic*, Lexington Books/Rowan and Littlefield Publishers Inc., London and New York, 2006.

> Perhaps the best study of the *Republic* available.

Drews, Robert, *The Coming of the Greeks, Indo-European Conquests in the Aegean and the Near East*, Princeton University Press, Princeton NJ, 1988.

Ehrenberg, Victor, *From Solon to Socrates*, Routledge, London and New York, 1993.

Ehrenberg, Victor, *Society and Civilization in Greece and Rome*, Harvard University Press, Cambridge MA, 1965.

> Ehrenberg is one of the best writers on the polity of the ancient city-state. German born, he was forced to emigrate in the 1930s with the rise of National Socialism. Having felt poignantly the decline of Western civilization in his own lifetime, his studies of classical civilization are an attempt to isolate what is most real and enduring in the Western order of civilizations.

Ehrenberg, Victor, *The Greek State*, W.W. Norton and Company, Inc., New York, 1964.

Fideler, David R. (ed.), *The Pythagorean Sourcebook* (trans. Kenneth Sylvan Guthrie), Phanes Press, Grand Rapids, MI, 1987.

Godolphin, Francis R.B. (ed.), *The Greek Historians, the Complete and Unabridged Historical Work of Herodotus, Thucydides, Xenophon, Arrian* (in two volumes), Random House, New York, 1942.

Heidegger, Martin, *Parmenides* (trans. Andre Schuwer and Richard Rojcewics), Indiana University Press, Bloomington and Indianapolis, 1992.

> The commentaries on Parmenides are invaluable in understanding the usage of ancient Greek terms in philosophy.

Heidegger, Martin and Fink, Eugen, *Heraclitus Seminar* (trans. Charles H. Seibert), Northwestern University Press, Evanston, Illinois, 1993.

> The commentaries on Heraclitus are invaluable in understanding the usage of ancient Greek terms in philosophy.

Heraclitus, *The Art and Thought of Heraclitus* (trans. Charles H. Kahn), Cambridge University Press, Cambridge, 1995.

Hesiod, *Hesiod: The Works and Days, Theogony, The Shield of Herakles* (trans. Richmond Lattimore), University of Michigan Press, Ann Arbor, 1988.

Homer, *The Odyssey* (trans. Robert Fitzgerald), The Franklin Library, Pennyslvania, 1976.

Homer, *The Illiad* (trans. Robert Fitzgerald), The Franklin Library, Pennyslvania, 1976.

Jaeger, Werner, *Aristotle, Fundamentals of the History of His Development* (trans. Richard Robinson), Oxford at the Clarendon Press, Oxford, 1950.

> Outlines the trajectory of Aristotle's work against the backdrop of his life story. This valuable work includes a representation of the relationship between Aristotle and Plato, which combines its personal and philosophical aspects. It takes into account the fact that these two philosophers were, in their mature works, the expression of two different historical epochs.

Jaeger, Werner, *Demosthenes, The Origin and Growth of His Policy* (trans. Edward S. Robinson), Octagon Books/Farrar, Strauss and Giroux, New York, 1977.

Jaeger, Werner, *Paidea: the Ideals of Greek Culture* (in three volumes, trans. Gilbert Highet)
· Volume I: *Archaic Greece, The Mind of Athens*, Oxford University Press, New York, 1945.
· Volume II: *In Search of the Divine Centre*, Oxford University Press, New York, 1943.
· Volume III: *The Conflict of Cultural Ideas in Plato*, Oxford University Press, New York, 1944.

> Werner Jaeger is one of the outstanding classical scholars of modern times. While other classical writers may possess valuable understandings that are not to be found in Jaeger's works, Jaeger has penetrated particular aspects of the Greek culture in a way no other scholar has done. The three volumes of *Paidea* were published in German in 1933-47 and in English – in the excellent translation of Gilbert Highet – in 1939-1944. Jaeger was German-born and emigrated to America in the 1930s as the National Socialist government began to persecute him for his writings. This background made him particularly sensitive to what is real and enduring in civilizational order, and what is not.

Jaeger, Werner, *The Theology of the Early Greek Philosophers, The Gifford Lectures 1936* (trans. Edward S. Robinson), Oxford at the Clarendon Press, Oxford, 1960.

James, Hugh, *The Life and Work of Plato*, Apollo University Press, Apollo CA, 2004.

Kerenyi, Carl, *Eleusis, Archetypal Image of Mother and Daughter* (trans. Ralph Mannheim), Princeton University Press, Princeton NJ, 1967.

Kerenyi, Carl, *The Gods of the Greeks* (trans. Norman Cameron), Thames and Hudson, New York, 1985.

> Carl Kerenyi has gathered and sifted all of the material on the Greek myths and assembled it, myth by myth, into a coherent whole. Thus Kerenyi attempts to provide the minimal context which allows the individual myths to be presented in a style most closely corresponding to the original oral presentation.

Kerenyi, Carl, *The Heroes of the Greeks* (trans. H.L. Rose), Thames and Hudson, New York, 1997.

Kitto, H.D.F., *Form and Meaning in Drama: A study of six Greek plays and of Hamlet*, Methuen and Company, London, 1964.

> H.D.F. Kitto is one of the most valuable sources on Greek drama.

Kitto, H.D.F., *Greek Tragedy, A Literary Study*, Methuen and Co. Ltd., London, 1961.

Kitto, H.D.F., *The Greeks*, Penguin Books, Harmondsworth UK, 1958.

Marx, Werner, *The Meaning of Aristotle's Ontology*, Martinus Nijhoff, The Hague, 1954.

> This book is excellent on its subject, and the attending discussions of Greek usage and Greek philosophical terms are of the greatest value.

Moon, W.G. (ed.), *Polykleitos, The Doryphoros, and Tradition* (trans. I. Mark), The University of Wisconsin Press, Madison WI, 1995.

> Shows an exceptional understanding of the canon (*kanon*/κανόν) informing Polykleitos' work and so of the archetype that found embodiment in it. More generally it provides important keys to understanding the relation of Greek art to the principle of archetype (*arkhetupon*/ἀρχέτυπον).

Mure, G.R.G., *Aristotle*, Greenwood Press, Westport CT, 1975.

> An exceptional little book, which provides the intellectual stimulation of a direct encounter with Aristotle's philosophy.

Mylonas, George E., *Eleusis and the Eleusinian Mysteries*, Princeton University Press, Princeton NJ, 1972.

Oates, Whitney J. and O'Neill Jr., Eugene, *The Complete Greek Drama, All the Extant Tragedies of Aeschylus, Sophocles and Euripides, and the Comedies of Aristophanes and Menander in a Variety of Translations* (in two volumes), Random House, New York, 1938.

Papaioannou, K., *The Art of Greece*, Harry N. Abrams, Inc., New York, 1989.

> Valuable for its comprehensiveness, Papaioannou's book aspires to be a complete listing of the surviving sculptures, temples, steles, etc. along with the Roman copies of Greek originals.

Parmenides of Elea, *Fragments* (trans. David Gallop), University of Toronto Press, Toronto, Buffalo and London, 1995.

Plato (ed. John M. Cooper), *Plato: Complete Works*, Hackett Publishing Company, Indianapolis/Cambridge, 1997.

Plato (ed. Edith Hamilton and Huntington Cairns), *The Collected Dialogues of Plato*, Princeton University Press, Princeton NJ, 1980.

Plutarch, *The Lives of the Noble Grecians and Romans* (trans. John Dryden and Arthur Hugh Clough), Random House/Modern Library, New York, publication date not given.

Pollitt, J.J., *The Ancient View of Greek Art*, Yale University Press, New Haven and London, 1974.

> Pollitt has assembled all the classical comments (in both Greek and Latin) on Greek art. This book is a must for any serious student of Greek art.

Pollitt, J.J., *Art and Experience in Classical Greece*, Cambridge University Press, London, 1972.

> The most valuable single book on Greek art the author has encountered.

Proclus, *The Elements of Theology* (trans. E.R. Dodds), Oxford University Press, at the Clarendon, 1963.

> The *Elements of Theology* is an introduction to the metaphysics of the Platonic Academy in the late fifth century. It incorporates both Aristotle's critique of the Platonic Idea, and the real achievements of the Aristotelian theory of cause. It preserves the Platonic notion of a determining Absolute, which Plato referred to – depending

on the context – as The Good or The Demiurge. To defend the Platonic Absolute in a fifth century environment, Proclus must show how Plato's theory of Ideas works in relation to the Absolute, and, at the same time, how Plato's theory works in relation to the level we are on. To this end, Proclus expands upon Plato's theory, by integrating the Aristotelian theory of cause. He shows how: **1)** the Absolute can act as an efficient cause in relation to Creation, **2)** there is a paradigmatic cause applicable to the level of the Ideas, and **3)** how, on the level we are on, form can act as a final cause. Proclus' writings suggest the presence of a Hermetic School, in that they represent, ultimately, a report on experience. To what extent this primary experience is that of Proclus himself, and to what extent that of his acknowledged master Syrianus, we cannot know. Whatever the case, Proclus is not attempting a meta-theory, but presenting an image of man's place in the universe, that can guide practical attempts to achieve presence. While Proclus, as a philosopher, does have a tendency towards system building, his philosophic expression is something that can – with effort over time – be compacted to the point of simplicity. This simplification would have to be done by the individual putting the theory into practice, as it would have to relate to that person's level of being, and to the peculiarities of their psychology. The process of compaction we are describing is the defining feature of Hermeticism: subordinating one's personal psychology to the understanding of the great cosmic laws, and the relation between levels that they describe, in such a way as to enable the infant Self. If, then, one has a glimpse of Higher Centers, and momentarily sees into the workings of the Whole, the essential matrix of Hermetic truths will clarify this experience in memory, make it easier to recall, and make it easier for it to provide ongoing orientation.

Sallis, John, *Being and Logos, The Way of the Platonic Dialogue*, Humanities Press International Inc., Atlantic Highlands NJ, 1986.

An excellent discussion of Being and *Logos* which is relevant to our chapter on Early Christianity.

Stewart, J.A., *The Myths of Plato*, Barnes and Noble, Inc., New York, 1970.

Voeglin, Eric, *Order and History* (in five volumes)
- Volume II: *The World of the Polis*, Louisiana State University Press, Baton Rouge and London, 1991.
- Volume III: *Plato and Aristotle*, Louisiana State University Press, Baton Rouge and London, 1990.

Voeglin's books on Greece are perhaps his best. His reflections on the origin of the polis are of great value.

HELLENISTIC/STOIC

Ferguson, John, *The Heritage of Hellenism*, Thames and Hudson, London, 1973.

Gruen, Erich S., *The Hellenistic World and the Coming of Rome*, University of California Press, Berkeley, Los Angeles, London, 1986.

   Gruen's massive study shows a comprehensive knowledge of the period.

Gruen, Erich S., *Studies in Greek Culture and Roman Policy*, University of California Press, Berkeley, Los Angeles, London, 1990.

Habicht, Christian, *Athens From Alexander to Anthony* (trans. Deborah Lucas Schneider), Harvard University Press, Cambridge MA and London UK, 1977.

   A magnificent picture of Hellenistic Athens.

Hadas, Moses, *Hellenistic Culture: Fusion and Diffusion*, W.W. Norton and Company, London, 1972.

Hammond, N.G.L., *The Genius of Alexander the Great*, The University of North Carolina Press, Chapel Hill NC, 1997.

   A valuable attempt to recreate the impact and effect of this world historical individual.

Iamblichus, *The Exhortation to Philosophy* (trans. Thomas R. Johnson), Phanes Press, Grand Rapids, MI, 1988.

   Iamblichus, a Neo-Platonist philosopher of the fifth century AD, is of interest to us for the connections he reveals between the late Platonic Academy, the still surviving Chaldean priest caste, the Zoroastrian Magi, and the Egyptian temple-priests. Of particular value is the record he has left of their shared interest in opening and sustaining contact with a hierarchy of celestial beings.

Iamblichus, *Theurgia, Or, The Egyptian Mysteries* (ed. and trans. Alexander Wilder), The Metaphysical Publishing Co., New York, 1911.

Inwood, Brad, *Ethics and Human Action in Early Stoicism*, Oxford University Press at the Clarendon, Oxford, 1987.

Pollitt, J.J., *Art in the Hellenistic Age*, Cambridge University Press, Cambridge, 1980.

> An outstanding book on Hellenistic art, which conveys a sense of the Hellenistic times and of the pattern of Hellenistic history which is unmatched.

Voeglin, Eric, *History of Political Ideas* (in eight volumes)
- Volume I (ed. Athanasios Moulakis), *Hellenism, Rome, and Early Christianity*, University of Missouri Press, Columbia, 1997.

Voeglin, Eric, *Order and History* (in five volumes)
- Volume IV: *The Ecumenic Age*, Louisiana State University Press, Baton Rouge and London, 1990.

ROME

Aurelius, Marcus, *Meditations* (trans. Maxwell Staniforth), Penguin Books, 1977.

> An excellent translation of the Greek text accompanied by a useful essay on Stoic philosophy.

Birly, Anthony, *Hadrian, the Restless Emperor*, Routledge, London and New York, 2000.

> A recommended biography. Birly is a student of Ronald Syme's (mentioned below) who is, perhaps, the greatest scholar of ancient Rome.

Birly, Anthony, *Marcus Aurelius, A Biography*, Barnes and Noble Books, N.Y., 1993.

> A recommended biography.

Burkhardt, Jacob, *The Age of Constantine the Great* (trans. Moses Hadas), Dorset Press, New York, 1989.

Dorey, T.A. (ed.), *Cicero*, Basic Books, Inc., New York, 1965.

Epictetus, *Moral Discourses, Enchiridion and Fragments* (trans. Elizabeth Carter), Everyman's Library/Dent, London 1966.

Grant, Michael, *The Climax of Rome, The Final Achievements of the Ancient World*, Weidenfeld, London, 1995.

Hadas, Moses (ed.), *A History of Rome, from its origins to 529 AD as told by Roman historians*, Doubleday and Company, Inc., New York, 1956.

Horace (Quintus Horatius Flaccus), *The Complete Works of Horace* (ed. and trans. Casper J. Kraemer Jr.), Modern Library/Random House, New York, 1936.

Plutarch, *The Lives of the Noble Grecians and Romans* (trans. John Dryden and Arthur Hugh Clough), Random House/Modern Library, New York, publication date not given.

Polybius, *Polybius on Roman Imperialism* (trans. Evelyn S. Shuckburgh), Regnery/Gateway, Inc., South Bend IN, 1980.

Syme, Ronald, *The Roman Revolution*, Oxford University Press, London, 1960.

> A scholar with an extraordinary insight into Roman history and particularly into the animating spirit of the Augustan Age. His work is unique.

Syme Ronald, *Ammianus and the Historia Augusta*, Oxford: The Clarendon Press, 1968.

Virgil (Publius Virgilius Maro), *The Aeneid* (trans. C. Day Lewis), Doubleday and Company, Inc., New York, 1953.

Virgil (Publius Virgilius Maro), *Virgil's Works: The Aeneid, Ecologues, Georgics* (trans. J.W. Mackail), Modern Library/Random House, New York, 1950.

Voeglin, Eric, *History of Political Ideas* (in eight volumes)
· Volume I (ed. Athanasios Moulakis), *Hellenism, Rome, and Early Christianity*, University of Missouri Press, Columbia, 1997.

Vogt, Joseph, *The Decline of Rome, the Metamorphosis of Ancient Civilization* (trans. Janet Sondheimer), Weidenfeld, London, 1993.

> A revealing account of the third, fourth, and fifth centuries AD, showing the birth of the Christian Civilization within the Classical integument. This valuable work shows us how the Classical and the Christian Civilizations coexisted before the modern period.

MIDDLE AGES

Anderson, Perry, *Passages from Antiquity to Feudalism*, New Left Books, London, 1974.

> Provides a cogent analysis of the Late Classical world, from the perspective of its socio-economic relations.

Barber, Malcolm, *The Two Cities: Medieval Europe 1050-1320*, Routledge, London, 1993.

Huizinga, Johan, *The Waning of the Middle Ages*, Dover Publications, New York, 1999.

Previté-Orton, C.W., *The Shorter Cambridge Medieval History* (in two volumes)
- Volume I: *The Later Roman Empire to the Twelfth Century*, Cambridge University Press, Cambridge, 1952.
- Volume II: *The Twelfth Century to the Renaissance*, Cambridge University Press, Cambridge, 1952.

  A well-researched and well-presented Medieval history. This work is a model of scholarship and a recommended source book.

Southern, R.W., *Western Society and the Church in the Middle Ages*, Penguin Books, London, 1970.

Southern, R.W., *The Making of the Middle Ages*, Yale University Press, New Haven, 1961.

  The principal work of a great scholar of the Middle Ages. Richard Southern reveals the unity of the Medieval worldview, in a way that shows us something that we have lost.

Voeglin, Erik, *History of Political Ideas* (in eight volumes)
- Volume II (ed. Peter von Sivers), *The Middle Ages to Aquinas*, University of Missouri Press, Columbia, 1997.
- Volume III (ed. David Walsh), *The Later Middle Ages*, University of Missouri Press, Columbia, 1998.

  Voeglin's analysis of the Germanic tribes, their mythologies, their peculiar psychological makeup, and their integration into what became modern Europe is of great value.

RENAISSANCE

Baron, Hans, *In Search of Florentine Civic Humanism, Essays on the Transition from Medieval to Modern Thought* (in two volumes), Princeton University Press, Princeton NJ, 1988.

  Hans Baron was one of the many brilliant German scholars driven to America by the Third Reich. His two volumes of essays on Florentine civic humanism are seminal.

Baron, Hans, *Petrarch's Secretum: Its Making and Its Meaning*, Medieval Academy of America, Cambridge MA, 1985.

Baron, Hans, *The Crisis of the Early Italian Renaissance*, Princeton University Press, Princeton NJ, 1966.

Berenson, Bernard, *Italian Painters of the Renaissance*, Oxford at the Clarendon Press, Oxford, 1930.

> Bernard Berenson was a very great art critic, who, by cultivating the art of looking, learned how to learn from painters how they actually saw the world. The study of painting became, for Berenson, a means of changing his perception of the world.

Burke, Peter (et. al.), *Renaissance Thinkers*, Oxford University Press, Oxford, 1993.

> This compendium combines four valuable short biographies: Peter Burke on Michel de Montaigne, Anthony Kenney on Thomas More, James McConica on Erasmus, and Anthony Quinton on Francis Bacon.

Burckhardt, Jacob, *The Civilization of the Renaissance in Italy* (trans. S.G.C. Middlemore), The Phaidon Press, no date given.

> This pathbreaking work, first published in 1860, opened what we now call the Renaissance to scholarly research. It places an emphasis on gifted – and often eccentric – individuality, which has been corrected by the more recent studies of civic context and humanistic culture by Hans Baron and Ernst Cassirer.

Cassirer, Ernst, *The Individual and the Cosmos in Renaissance Philosophy* (trans. Mario Domandi), University of Pennsylvania Press/Harper and Row, Philadelphia, 1972.

> The contribution of a gifted scholar, who is himself a Renaissance man.

Cassirer, Ernst, Kristeller, Paul Oskar, and Randall Jr., John Herman, *The Renaissance Philosophy of Man*, The University of Chicago Press, Chicago, 1948.

Cassirer, Ernst, *Platonic Renaissance in England* (trans. James P. Pettegrove), Gordian Press, New York, 1970.

Fergusson, Francis, *Dante's Drama of the Mind*, Princeton University Press, Princeton NJ, 1953.

Fergusson, Francis, *The Idea of a Theater*, Princeton University Press, Princeton NJ, 1972 (first published 1949).

> A study of the context of Western theater and a profound reflection on the Western mind. Francis Fergusson expounds the cosmic context of Greek and Elizabethan drama where "theater was itself a mirror which had been formed at the center of the culture of its time, and at the center of the life and awareness of the community." He shows how the theater of Shakespeare and Sophocles "focused … the complementary insights of the whole culture." In the post-classical world he explores Dante's *Divine Comedy* and the Medieval Miracle Plays as a representation of the unstated cosmic context of Elizabethan theater, not that the Elizabethans read Dante but that the context in which Dante and the writers of the Miracle Plays functioned still existed in Elizabethan England. Dante, the writers of the Miracle Plays, and Shakespeare all shared a background, which derives ultimately from the vertical scale of the earlier prophetic teachings.

Fergusson, Francis, *Trope and Allegory: Themes Common to Dante and Shakespeare*, University of Georgia Press, Athens GA, 1977.

French, Peter, *John Dee, the World of an Elizabethan Magus*, Ark Paperbacks, London, 1987.

Gombrich, Ernst, *Gombrich on the Renaissance* (in four volumes)
- Volume I: *Norm and Form*, Phaidon Press Ltd., London, 1966.
- Volume II: *Symbolic Images*, Phaidon Press Ltd., London, 1972.
- Volume III: *The Heritage of Apelles*, Phaidon Press Ltd., London, 1976.
- Volume IV: *New Light on Old Masters*, Phaidon Press Ltd., London, 1986.

Gombrich, Ernst, *The Story of Art*, Phaidon Press Ltd., Oxford, 1989.

> Ernst Gombrich stands with Bernard Berenson, Hans Baron, Erwin Panofsky, and Ernst Cassirer as one of the seminal figures in the study of the Italian Renaissance. All of his works merit serious study.

Hale, John, *The Civilization of Europe in the Renaissance*, Fontana Press/HarperCollins, London, 1993.

Panofsky, Erwin, *Meaning in the Visual Arts*, Penguin, London, 1993.

> An art critic with a profound understanding of symbol in Renaissance art. One of the seminal figures in the study of the Italian Renaissance.

Rowdon, Maurice, *Lorenzo the Magnificent*, Weidenfeld and Nicolson/Purnell Book Services Ltd., London, 1974.

Voeglin, Eric, *History of Political Ideas* (in eight volumes)
• Volume IV (ed. David Walsh and William Thompson), *Renaissance and Reformation*, University of Missouri Press, Columbia, 1998.

Wolfflin, Heinrich, *Classic Art, An Introduction to the Italian Renaissance*, Phaidon Press Ltd., London, 1994.

Young, G.F., *The Medicis*, Modern Library/Random House, New York, 1930.

Yates, Frances A., *Astraea, The Imperial Theme of the Sixteenth Century*, Pimlico, London, 1993.

Yates, Frances A., *Giordano Bruno and the Hermetic Tradition*, University of Chicago Press, Chicago, 1964.

Yates, Frances A., *Lull and Bruno*, Routledge and Kegan Paul, London, 1982.

> The premier writer on Renaissance hermeticism and occultism, Frances Yates taught at the Warburg Institute in London and was a member of the Courtauld Institute. She was a colleague of Ernst Gombrich.

Yates, Frances A., *The Art of Memory*, Pimlico, London, 1991.

Yates, Frances A., *The Occult Philosophy in the Elizabethan Age*, Routledge and Kegan Paul, London, 1979.

POST-RENAISSANCE WEST

Aaron, Raymond (ed. Franciszek Draus), *History, Truth, Liberty, Selected Writings of Raymond Aaron*, The University of Chicago Press, Chicago and London, 1985.

> Raymond Aaron achieved a rarely ecumenic appreciation of European civilization.

Anderson, Perry, *Lineages of the Absolutist State*, New Left Books, London 1974.

> An excellent outline of the Absolutist period from the standpoint of political economy.

Barea, Ilsa, *Vienna, Legend and Reality*, Pimlico, London, 1993.

Barzun, Jacques, *From Dawn to Decadence, 1500 to the Present, 500 Years of Western Cultural Life*, Harper/Collins, New York, 2000.

Barzun, Jacques (ed. Arthur Krystal), *The Culture We Deserve*, Wesleyen University Press, New England, 1989.

Behrens, C.B.A., *The Ancien Regime*, Thames and Hudson, London, 1967.

Bonney, Richard, *The European Dynastic States 1494-1660*, Oxford University Press, Oxford, 1991.

Burckhardt, Jacob, *Judgments on History and Historians* (trans. Harry Zohn), Beacon Press, Boston, 1958.

> While Burckhardt is known for his *Civilization of the Renaissance in Italy*, his two books on European history, *Judgments on History and Historians* and *Reflections on History*, written later in his life, are his masterpieces. These are actually lecture notes and show great spontaneity of expression, based on a comprehensive grasp of the material. While certain of the material is dated, perhaps no other modern history reveals so beautifully – and apparently effortlessly – a connected flow of events, one driving into the next. One feels that, in this history, nothing is held back; the darkest expressions of human nature are accommodated as easily as the highest achievements of art. The whole seems alive, active and reactive, resonating with life throughout.

Burckhardt, Jacob, *Reflections on History* (trans. M.D.H. Burckhardt), George Allen and Unwin Ltd., London, 1944.

Cassirer, Ernst, *Rousseau, Kant, Goethe* (trans. James Gutman, Paul Oskar Kristeller, John Herman Randall, Jr.), Princeton University Press, Princeton NJ, 1970.

Cassirer, Ernst, *The Philosophy of the Enlightenment* (trans. Fritz C.A. Koelln and James P. Pettegrove), Princeton University Press, Princeton NJ, 1979.

Cassirer, Ernst, *The Question of Jean Jacques Rousseau* (trans. Peter Gay), Indiana University Press, Bloomington, 1975.

Crankshaw, Edward, *The Fall of the House of Hapsburg*, Longmans, Green and Co, Ltd., 1963.

> Edward Crankshaw, a teacher, journalist, and – throughout the Second World War – an intelligence officer, was resident in Vienna for much of his professional life. He developed a remarkable feeling for the Hapsburg world, a world that was destroyed forever by the First World War.

Croce, Benedetto, *History of Europe in the Nineteenth Century* (trans. Henry Furst), George Allen and Unwin Ltd., London, 1953.

> This beautifully written history gives us the positive face of nineteenth-century liberalism in a way that no one but a nineteenth-century liberal could do.

Droz, Jacques, *Europe Between Revolutions 1815-1848* (trans. Robert Boldick), Collins/Fontana, London, 1967.

Doyle, William, *The Old European Order 1660-1880*, Oxford University Press, Oxford, 1978.

Goethe, Johann Wolfgang von, (compiled by Peter Eckermann) *Conversations with Eckermann* (trans. John Oxenford), North Point Press, San Francisco, 1984.

> Goethe is the complete and rounded Renaissance Man. His understanding of culture as *Bildung* sums up the spirit of the Renaissance in Europe and is directly continuous with the core understandings of the Classical world. One would have hoped that his cultural achievement represented a position taken once and for all. Yet the art of self-creation that he described has been more or less lost to the twenty-first century.

Goethe, Johann Wolfgang von, *Faust, Part One* (trans. Philip Wayne), Penguin Books, London 1949.

Goethe, Johann Wolfgang von, *Faust, Part Two* (trans. Philip Wayne), Penguin Books, London 1959.

Gombrich, Ernst, *The Story of Art*, Phaidon Press Ltd., Oxford, 1989.

Hazard, Paul, *The European Mind 1680-1715*, Meridian Books, Cleveland OH, 1968.

Hobsbawn, E.J., *The Age of Revolution, Europe 1789-1848*, Cardinal, London, 1991.

Hobsbawn, E.J., *The Age of Capital 1848-1875*, Cardinal, London, 1991.

Hobsbawn, E.J., *The Age of Empire 1875-1914*, Abacus, London, 1987.

Huyghe, René, *Art and the Spirit of Man*, Harry N. Abrams Inc., New York, 1962.

Lefebvre, George, *The Coming of the French Revolution* (trans. R.R. Palmer), Princeton University Press, Princeton NJ, 1969.

Lings, Martin, *The Eleventh Hour: The Spiritual Crisis of the Modern World in the Light of Tradition and Prophecy*, Archetype, Cambridge, 1977.

Mayer, Alfred, *The Annals of European Civilization, 1501-1900*, Barnes and Noble Books, New York, 1993.

Mayer, Arno J., *The Persistence of the Old Regime, Europe to the Great War*, Pantheon Books, New York, 1977.

> Shows the surprising extent to which old Europe was alive and well into the early twentieth century, and thus the extent to which it was destroyed by the First World War.

McManners, John, *Lectures on European History 1789-1914, Men, Machines and Freedom*, Basil Blackwell, Oxford, 1966.

> A brilliant and well-rounded history of the nineteenth century, showing a remarkable understanding of both economics and religion.

Mure, G.R.G., *Idealist Epilogue*, Oxford University Press, Oxford, 1978.

> Reflections on Western philosophy and on recent Western history, written in the last year of the author's life. One of the few thoughtful comments on the twentieth century that is based on a significant remembrance of what had gone before.

Mure, G.R.G., *Retreat from Truth*, Basil Blackwell, Oxford, 1958.

> Mure accurately defines certain tendencies in Western philosophy which have come to their full fruition in the years since the author's death.

Reed, T.J., *The Classical Centre, Goethe and Weimar 1775-1837*, Oxford University Press, 1986.

Schiller, Friedrich, *On the Aesthetic Education of Man* (trans. Reginald Snell), Routledge and Kegan Paul/Fredrick Ungar Publishing Co., New York, 1977.

Scruton, Roger, *An Intelligent Person's Guide to Modern Culture*, St. Augustine's Press, South Bend, Indiana, 2000.

Thompson, David, *Europe Since Napoleon*, Penguin, London, 1990.

> A wonderful overview of modern European history in one great sweep, as though a single human life had spanned the entire period; almost a recovery of memory.

Trevor-Roper, Hugh, *From Counter-Reformation to Glorious Revolution*, Pimlico, London, 1993.

Trevor-Roper, Hugh (ed.), *The Golden Age of Europe, from Elizabeth to the Sun King*, Thames and Hudson, London, 1987.

Voeglin, Eric (ed. John H. Hallowell), *From Enlightenment to Revolution*, Duke University Press, Durham, NC, 1975.

Voeglin, Eric, *History of Political Ideas* (in eight volumes)
- Volume IV (ed. David Walsh and William Thompson), *Renaissance and Reformation*, University of Missouri Press, Columbia, 1998.
- Volume V (ed. James L. Wiser), *Religion and the Rise of Modernity*, University of Missouri Press, Columbia, 1998.
- Volume VI (ed. Barry Cooper), *Revolution and the New Science*, University of Missouri Press, Columbia, 1998.
- Volume VII (ed. Jurgen Gebhardt and Thomas A. Hollwek), *The New Order and Last Orientation*, University of Missouri Press, Columbia, 1999.
- Volume VIII (ed. David Walsh), *Crisis and the Apocalypse of Man*, University of Missouri Press, Columbia, 1999.

HUGH JAMES was born in Vancouver, British Columbia in 1951. He completed a doctoral degree in Sociology at the University of British Columbia in 1983 and has, since that time, travelled extensively in Europe and Asia, living for longer periods in Denmark, France, and the UK. He has worked for different software houses and for the government in both the UK and the US. Hugh has presented courses for the Apollo University since its inception in 1998, and in 2004 published *Plato's Life and Work* through Apollo University Press. He lives with his wife, Tamara, in the foothills of Northern California.

PHOTO CREDITS

STATEMENT OF FAIR USE

CPSIA information can be obtained
at www.ICGtesting.com
Printed in the USA
FFHW010736060619
52840422-58399FF